Emerging Trends in Computational Biology, Bioinformatics, and Systems Biology

Emerging Trends in Computational Biology, Bioinformatics, and Systems Biology

Algorithms and Software Tools

Edited by

Quoc Nam Tran

Hamid Arabnia

AMSTERDAM • BOSTON • HEIDELBERG • LONDON
NEW YORK • OXFORD • PARIS • SAN DIEGO
SAN FRANCISCO • SINGAPORE • SYDNEY • TOKYO
Morgan Kaufmann is an imprint of Elsevier

Acquiring Editor: Steve Elliot
Editorial Project Manager: Amy Invernizzi
Project Manager: Priya Kumaraguruparan
Cover Designer: Maria Inês Cruz

Morgan Kaufmann is an imprint of Elsevier
225 Wyman Street, Waltham, MA 02451, USA

ISBN: 978-0-12-802508-6

Library of Congress Cataloging-in-Publication Data
A catalog record for this book is available from the Library of Congress

British Library Cataloguing in Publication Data
A catalogue record for this book is available from the British Library

For information on all MK publications visit
our website at http://store.elsevier.com/

Working together
to grow libraries in
developing countries

www.elsevier.com • www.bookaid.org

Contents

Contributors

Vida Abedi
The Center for Modeling Immunity to Enteric Pathogens, and Nutritional Immunology and Molecular Medicine Laboratory, Virginia Bioinformatics Institute, Virginia Tech, Blacksburg, VA, USA

Ruben Acuña
Scientific Data Management Laboratory, Arizona State University, Tempe, AZ, USA

Mohammad Ayache
Islamic University of Lebanon, Khaldeh, Lebanon

Mahmood Bahar
Department of Physics, Islamic Azad University, Tehran North Branch, Tehran, Iran

Azita A. Bahrami
IT Consultation, Savannah, GA, USA

Josep Bassaganya-Riera
The Center for Modeling Immunity to Enteric Pathogens, and Nutritional Immunology and Molecular Medicine Laboratory, Virginia Bioinformatics Institute, Virginia Tech, Blacksburg, VA, USA

Christian Baumgartner
Institute of Electrical and Biomedical Engineering, UMIT, Hall in Tirol, and Institute of Heath Care Engineering with European Notified Body of Medical Devices, Graz University of Technology, Graz, Austria

Paul Bejjani
Associate Professor of Neurology, Director of the Parkinson's Disease and Memory Center, Notre Dame de Secours Hospital, Byblos, Lebanon

Christian Berger-Vachon
INSERM U1028, Lyon Neuroscience Research Center, DYCOG Team/ PACS Group (Speech, Audiology, Communication Health); CNRS UMR5292, Lyon Neuroscience Research Center, DYCOG Team/ PACS Group (Speech, Audiology, Communication Health), and University Lyon 1, Lyon, France

Jonathan Berkhahn
Department of Computer Science, Virginia Tech, Blacksburg, VA, USA

Michael Berry
South African National Bioinformatics Institute, University of the Western Cape, Cape Town, South Africa

H.B. Çakmak
Yıldırım Beyazıt University, Atatürk Education and Research Hospital, Ankara, Turkey

E. Çalık
Karabük University, School of Health Sciences, Karabük, Turkey

A. Çavuşoğlu
Scientific and Technological Research Council of Turkey, Ankara, Turkey

Adria Carbo
BioTherapeutics Inc., Blacksburg, VA, USA

Steven M. Carr
Department of Biology, Memorial University of Newfoundland; Department of Computer Science, Memorial University of Newfoundland, and Terra Nova Genomics, Inc., St. John's NL, Canada

Gloria Castellano
Departamento de Ciencias Experimentales y Matemáticas, Facultad de Veterinaria y Ciencias Experimentales, Universidad Católica de Valencia San Vicente Mártir, València, Spain

QinQun Chen
School of Medical Information Engineering, Guangzhou University of Chinese Medicine, Guangzhou, China

Xiumin Chen
Department of Rheumatology, Guangdong Provincial Hospital of Chinese Medicine, Guangzhou, China, and Postdoctoral Mobile Research Station, Guangzhou University of Chinese Medicine, Guangzhou, China

Jacques Chomilier
IMPMC, Sorbonne Universités, Université Pierre et Marie Curie, CNRS, MNHN, IRD, Paris, France; RPBS, Université Paris Diderot, Paris, France

Donald Craig
eHealth Research Unit (Faculty of Medicine), Memorial University of Newfoundland, St. John's NL, Canada

Andreas Dander
Division for Bioinformatics, Biocenter, Innsbruck Medical University, Innsbruck, Austria

H. Dawn Marshall
Department of Biology, Memorial University of Newfoundland, St. John's NL, Canada

Leonidas Deligiannidis
ElderSafe Technologies, Inc., Harvard, MA, USA

J. Demongeot
Université J. Fourier Grenoble, Faculté de Médecine, AGIM CNRS/UJF FRE 3405, La Tronche, France

Luis R. Domingo
Departamento de Química Orgánica, Universidad de Valencia, Burjassot, Valencia, Spain

Andrei Doncescu
University Paul Sabatier – INSERM – CNRS, CRCT, France

Zhong-Hui Duan
Department of Computer Science, College of Arts and Sciences, University of Akron, Akron, USA

Abbass Zein Eddine
Laboratory of GREAH (Groupe de Recherche en Electrotechnique et Automatique), University of Le Havre, Le Havre, France

Behrouz H. Far
Department of Electrical and Computer Engineering, Schulich School of Engineering, University of Calgary, Calgary, AB, Canada

Joaquim Cezar Felipe
Department of Computing and Mathematics, Faculty of Philosophy, Sciences, and Languages of Ribeirão Preto, University of São Paulo at Ribeirão Preto, Brazil, Ribeirão Preto, SP, Brazil

C. Ferrer
Departament de Microelectrònica i Sistemes Electrònics, Universitat Autònoma de Barcelona, and Institut de Microelectrònica de Barcelona (CNM-CSIC), Bellaterra (Barcelona), Spain

Burtram Fielding
Department of Medical Biosciences, University of the Western Cape, Cape Town, South Africa

Junaid Gamieldien
South African National Bioinformatics Institute, University of the Western Cape, Cape Town, South Africa

Dan Gnansia
Neurelec, Vallauris, France

Thomas Goulding
Department of Mathematics and Computer Science, Lawrence Technological University, Southfield, MI, USA

D. Graveron-Demilly
Laboratoire CREATIS-LRMN, CNRS UMR 5220, Inserm U630, Université Claude Villeurbanne, France

François Guerin
Laboratory of GREAH (Groupe de Recherche en Electrotechnique et Automatique), University of Le Havre, Le Havre, France

Michael Handler
Institute of Electrical and Biomedical Engineering, UMIT, Hall in Tirol, Austria

Mohammad Shabbir Hasan
Department of Computer Science, College of Arts and Sciences, University of Akron, Akron, USA

Ray R. Hashemi
Department of Computer Science, Armstrong State University, Savannah, GA, USA

H. Hazgui
Université J. Fourier Grenoble, Faculté de Médecine, AGIM CNRS/UJF FRE 3405, La Tronche, France

Wei He
The First Affiliated Hospital, Guangzhou University of Chinese Medicine, Guangzhou, China

A. Henrion Caude
Université Paris Descartes, INSERM U 781, Hôpital Necker-Enfants Malades, Paris, France

Raquel Hontecillas
The Center for Modeling Immunity to Enteric Pathogens, and Nutritional Immunology and Molecular Medicine Laboratory, Virginia Bioinformatics Institute, Virginia Tech, Blacksburg, VA, USA

Stefan Hoops
The Center for Modeling Immunity to Enteric Pathogens, and Nutritional Immunology and Molecular Medicine Laboratory, Virginia Bioinformatics Institute, Virginia Tech, Blacksburg, VA, USA

Arnaud Jeanvoine
INSERM U1028, Lyon Neuroscience Research Center, DYCOG Team/ PACS Group (Speech, Audiology, Communication Health); CNRS UMR5292, Lyon Neuroscience Research Center, DYCOG Team/ PACS Group (Speech, Audiology, Communication Health), Lyon, and Neurelec, Vallauris, France

V. Kantabutra
Department of Electrical Engineering, Idaho State University, Pocatello, USA

Lina J. Karam
School of Electrical, Computer, and Energy Engineering, Arizona State University, Tempe, AZ, USA

D.A. Karras
Department of Automation, Sterea Hellas Institute of Technology, Evia, Greece

H. Kaya
Yıldırım Beyazıt University, Department of Computer Engineering, Ankara, Turkey

Bo Kim
Division of Computer Science, Daniel Webster College, Nashua, NH, USA

Zoé Lacroix
Scientific Data Management Laboratory, School of Electrical, Computer, and Energy Engineering, Arizona State University, Tempe, AZ ,USA

Dimitri Lefebvre
Laboratory of GREAH (Groupe de Recherche en Electrotechnique et Automatique), University of Le Havre, Le Havre, France

Andy Lin
Department of Molecular and Medical Pharmacology, David Geffen School of Medicine, University of California, LA, USA

Jian-Qin Liu
National Institute of Information and Communications Technology, Hyogo, Japan

Pinyi Lu
The Center for Modeling Immunity to Enteric Pathogens, and Nutritional Immunology and Molecular Medicine Laboratory, Virginia Bioinformatics Institute, Virginia Tech, Blacksburg, VA, USA

Yongguo Mei
The Center for Modeling Immunity to Enteric Pathogens, and Nutritional Immunology and Molecular Medicine Laboratory, Virginia Bioinformatics Institute, Virginia Tech, Blacksburg, VA, USA

B.G. Mertzios
Department of Electrical and Computer Engineering, Democritus University of Thrace (DUTH), Greece

Kato Mivule
Computer Science Department, Bowie State University, Bowie, MD, USA

Emad A. Mohammed
Department of Electrical and Computer Engineering, Schulich School of Engineering, University of Calgary, Calgary, AB, Canada

Vicente Molieri
School of Electrical, Computer, and Energy Engineering, Arizona State University, Tempe, AZ, USA

Asish Mukhopadhyay
University of Windsor, Windsor, Ontario, Canada

Christopher Naugler
Departments of Pathology and Laboratory Medicine and Family Medicine, University of Calgary and Calgary Laboratory Services, Diagnostic and Scientific Centre, Calgary, AB, Canada

Michael Netzer
Institute of Electrical and Biomedical Engineering, UMIT, Hall in Tirol, Austria

Haruhiko Nishimura
Graduate School of Applied Informatics, University of Hyogo, Hyogo, Japan

Sou Nobukawa
Department of Management Information Science, Fukui University of Technology, Fukui, Japan

J. Oliver
Departament de Microelectrònica i Sistemes Electrònics, Universitat Autònoma de Barcelona, Bellaterra (Barcelona), Spain

Zhihui Pang
Laboratory of National Key Discipline Orthopaedics and Traumatology of Chinese Medicine, Guangzhou University of Chinese Medicine, Guangzhou, China

Satish Ch. Panigrahi
University of Windsor, Windsor, Ontario, Canada

G.A. Papakostas
Department of Computer and Informatics Engineering, Eastern Macedonia and Thrace Institute of Technology, Kavala, Greece

Nikolaos Papandreou
Department of Biotechnology, Agricultural University of Athens, Athens, Greece

Vitor Manuel Dinis Pereira
LanCog (Language, Mind and Cognition Research Group), Philosophy Centre, University of Lisbon, Lisbon, Portugal

Bernhard Pfeifer
Institute of Electrical and Biomedical Engineering, UMIT, Hall in Tirol, Austria

Casandra Philipson
The Center for Modeling Immunity to Enteric Pathogens, and Nutritional Immunology and Molecular Medicine Laboratory, Virginia Bioinformatics Institute, Virginia Tech, Blacksburg, VA, USA

R. Ponalagusamy
Department of Mathematics, National Institute of Technology, Tiruchirappalli, Tamilnadu, India

Jacob Porter
Department of Computer Science, Virginia Tech, Blacksburg, VA, USA

Junfeng Qu
Department of Computer Science and Information Technology, Clayton State University, Morrow, GA, USA

Ponnadurai Ramasami
Computational Chemistry Group, Department of Chemistry, University of Mauritius, Réduit, Mauritius

Lydia Rhyman
Computational Chemistry Group, Department of Chemistry, University of Mauritius, Réduit, Mauritius

Branko Ristic
Defence Science and Technology Organisation, Melbourne, VIC, Australia

Ali Saad
Laboratory of GREAH (Groupe de Recherche en Electrotechnique et Automatique), University of Le Havre, Le Havre, France; Islamic University of Lebanon, Khaldeh, Lebanon

Mariana Yuri Sasazaki
Department of Computing and Mathematics, Faculty of Philosophy, Sciences, and Languages of Ribeirão Preto, University of São Paulo at Ribeirão Preto, Ribeirão Preto, SP, Brazil

Jose A. Sáez
Departamento de Química Orgánica, Universidad de Valencia, Burjassot, Valencia, Spain

B. Şen
Yıldırım Beyazıt University, Department of Computer Engineering, Ankara, Turkey

Md. Shafiul Alam
University of Windsor, Windsor, Ontario, Canada

Maad Shatnawi
Higher Colleges of Technology, Abu Dhabi, UAE

Pierre Siegel
Aix Marseille University, CNRS, LIF, Marseille, France

B.G. Sileshi
Departament de Microelectrònica i Sistemes Electrònics, Universitat Autònoma de Barcelona, Bellaterra (Barcelona), Spain

Alex Skvortsov
Defence Science and Technology Organisation, Melbourne, VIC, Australia

Desmond J. Smith
Department of Molecular and Medical Pharmacology, David Geffen School of Medicine, University of California, Los Angeles, USA

Yinglei Song
School of Electronics and Information Science, Jiangsu University of Science and Technology, Zhenjiang, Jiangsu, China

Liao Shaoyi Stephen
Department of Information Systems, City University of Hong Kong, Hong Kong, China

Daniel Swain
Department of Computer Science, Armstrong State University, Savannah, GA, USA

Peter Sylvester
ElderSafe Technologies, Inc., Harvard, MA, USA

Francisco Torrens
Institut Universitari de Ciència Molecular, Universitat de València, Edifici d'Instituts de Paterna, València, Spain

Eric Truy
Audiology and ORL Department, Edouard Herriot Hospital; INSERM U1028, Lyon Neuroscience Research Center, DYCOG Team/ PACS Group (Speech, Audiology, Communication Health); CNRS UMR5292, Lyon Neuroscience Research Center, DYCOG Team/ PACS Group (Speech, Audiology, Communication Health), Lyon, France

Nicholas R. Tyler
School of Pharmacy, University of Georgia, Athens, GA, USA

D. van Ormondt
Applied Physics, Delft University of Technology, Delft, Netherlands CN

Todd Wareham
Department of Computer Science, Memorial University of Newfoundland, St. John's NL, Canada

Yujing Xu
Department of Information Systems, City University of Hong Kong, Hong Kong, China

Teruya Yamanishi
Department of Management Information Science, Fukui University of Technology, Fukui, Japan

Iyad Zaarour
Doctoral School of Science and Technology, Lebanese University, Beirut, Lebanon

Liqing Zhang
Department of Computer Science, Virginia Tech, Blacksburg, VA, USA

Guangquan Zhou
The First Affiliated Hospital, Guangzhou University of Chinese Medicine; Laboratory of National Key Discipline Orthopaedics and Traumatology of Chinese Medicine, Guangzhou University of Chinese Medicine, Guangzhou, and Department of Information Systems, City University of Hong Kong, Hong Kong, China

Preface

It is a great pleasure to introduce this collection of chapters to the readers of the book series *Emerging Trends in Computer Science and Applied Computing* (Morgan Kaufmann/Elsevier). This book is entitled *Emerging Trends in Computational Biology, Bioinformatics, and Systems Biology—Algorithms and Software Tools*. We are indebted to Quoc-Nam Tran (professor and department chair) of the University of South Dakota for accepting our invitation to be the senior editor. His leadership and strategic plan made the implementation of this book project a wonderful experience.

Computational biology is the science of using biological data to develop algorithms and relations among various biological systems. It involves the development and application of data-analytical algorithms, mathematical modeling, and simulation techniques to the study of biological, behavioral, and social systems. The field is multidisciplinary, in that it includes topics that are traditionally covered in computer science, mathematics, imaging science, statistics, chemistry, biophysics, genetics, genomics, ecology, evolution, anatomy, neuroscience, and visualization, where computer science acts as the topical bridge between all such diverse areas (for a formal definition of computational biology, refer to http://www.bisti.nih.gov/docs/compubiodef.pdf). Many consider the area of bioinformatics to be a subfield of computational biology that includes methods for acquiring, storing, retrieving, organizing, analyzing, and visualizing biological data. The area of systems biology is an emerging methodology applied to biomedical and biological scientific research. It is an area that overlaps with computational biology and bioinformatics. This book attempts to cover the emerging trends in many important areas of computational biology, bioinformatics, and systems biology.

The book is composed of selected papers that were accepted for the 2013 and 2014 International Conference on Bioinformatics & Computational Biology (BIO-COMP'13 and BIOCOMP'14), July, Las Vegas, USA.

The BIOCOMP annual conferences are held as part of the World Congress in Computer Science, Computer Engineering, and Applied Computing (WORLD-COMP; http://www.world-academy-of-science.org/). An important mission of WORLDCOMP includes "Providing a unique platform for a diverse community of constituents composed of scholars, researchers, developers, educators, and practitioners. The congress makes concerted effort to reach out to participants affiliated with diverse entities (such as universities, institutions, corporations, government agencies, and research centers/labs) from all over the world. The congress also attempts to connect participants from institutions that have *teaching* as their main mission with those who are affiliated with institutions that have *research* as their main mission. The congress uses a quota system to achieve its institution and geography diversity objectives." Since this book is mainly composed of the extended versions of the accepted papers of BIOCOMP annual conferences, it is no surprise that the book has chapters from highly qualified and diverse group of authors.

We are very grateful to the many colleagues who offered their services in organizing the BIOCOMP conferences. Their help was instrumental in the formation of this book. The members of the editorial committee included:

- Ali Abedi
- Department of Electrical and Computer Engineering and Cooperating Associate Professor of CIS; Director, Center for Undergraduate Research (CUGR); Director, Wireless Sensor Networks (WiSe-Net) Lab; University of Maine, Orono, Maine, USA; Associate Editor: IEEE/KICS Journal of Communications and Networks and IET Wireless Sensors Systems; Vice President of Technology and Board Member, Beyran Corp, Maryland, USA; Co-Founder and CTO, Navindor Company, Maryland, USA
- Nizar Al-Holou (Congress Steering Committee)
- Professor and Chair, Electrical and Computer Engineering Department; Vice Chair, IEEE/SEM-Computer Chapter; University of Detroit Mercy, Detroit, Michigan, USA
- Hamid R. Arabnia (Congress Steering Committee)
- Professor of Computer Science; University of Georgia, Graduate Studies Research Center, Athens, Georgia, USA; Editor-in-Chief, *Journal of Supercomputing* (Springer); Editor-in-Chief, *Emerging Trends in CS and Applied Computing* (Elsevier); Editor-in-Chief, *Transactions of Computational Science and Computational Intelligence* (Springer); Elected Fellow, International Society of Intelligent Biological Medicine (ISIBM)
- Michael Panayiotis Bekakos (Congress Steering Committee)
- Professor of Computer Systems; Director, Laboratory of Digital Systems, Department of Electrical and Computer Engineering, Democritus University of Thrace, Greece; Head, Parallel Algorithms and Architectures Research Group (PAaRG)
- Dr. Sidahmed Benabderrahmane
- INRIA (French National Computer Science Institute), Rocquencourt, France
- Juan-Vicente Capella-Hernandez
- Executive and Quality Manager, Wireless Sensor Networks Valencia, Inc.; Member, Editorial Board: *IEEE RITA Journal*; Universitat Politecnica de Valencia, Valencia, Spain
- Juan Jose Martinez Castillo
- Director of the Acantelys Research Group and Coordinator of the Computer Engineering Department, Universidad Gran Mariscal de Ayacucho, Venezuela
- Dr. Daniel Bo-Wei Chen
- Department of Electrical Engineering, Princeton University, Princeton, New Jersey, USA
- Dr. Xin Chen

- Research Corporation of the University of Hawaii/Institute for Astronomy, Honolulu, Hawaii, USA
- Kevin Daimi (Congress Steering Committee)
- Director, Computer Science and Software Engineering Programs, Department of Mathematics, Computer Science, and Software Engineering, University of Detroit Mercy, Detroit, Michigan, USA
- Somdip Dey
- School of Computer Science, University of Manchester, Manchester, UK
- Mary Mehrnoosh Eshaghian-Wilner (Congress Steering Committee)
- Professor of Engineering Practice, University of Southern California, Los Angeles, California, USA; Adjunct Professor, Electrical Engineering, University of California, Los Angeles (UCLA), California, USA
- Oleg Finko (PDPTA)
- Krasnodar Higher Military Command Engineering School Rocket Forces, Russia; Institute of Information Technology and Security, Kuban State Technological University, Russia
- Mohammad Shahadat Hossain
- Department of Computer Science and Engineering, University of Chittagong, Chittagong, Bangladesh; Visiting Professor, Trisakti University, Indonesia; Visiting Academic Staff, University of Manchester, UK
- Dr. Guofeng Hou (ICOMP)
- Bell Laboratories and Microsoft Corporation, USA
- George Jandieri (Congress Steering Committee and Vice Chair of CSC and BIOCOMP Co-Editor)
- Georgian Technical University, Tbilisi, Georgia; Chief Scientist, Institute of Cybernetics, Georgian Academy of Science, Georgia
- Young-Sik Jeong (Congress Steering Committee)
- Department of Multimedia Engineering, Dongguk University, Seoul, South Korea
- Dr. Christos Kartsaklis (PDPTA)
- Oak Ridge National Laboratory, Oak Ridge, Tennessee, USA
- Dattatraya V. Kodavade (Congress Steering Committee)
- Head of Computer Science and Engineering, DKTE Society's Textile and Engineering Institute, Ichalkaranji, Maharashtra State, India
- Dr. Ying Liu
- Division of Computer Science, Mathematics and Science; College of Professional Studies, St. John's University, Queens, New York, USA; lifetime member, Association for Computing Machinery (ACM)
- George Markowsky (Congress Steering Committee)
- Professor and Associate Director, School of Computing and Information Science; Chair International Advisory Board of IEEE IDAACS; Director 2013 Northeast Collegiate Cyber Defense Competition; Chair, Bangor Foreign Policy Forum;

President, Phi Beta Kappa Delta Chapter of Maine; Cooperating Professor of Mathematics and Statistics Department, University of Maine, Orono, Maine, USA; Cooperating Professor of School of Policy and International Affairs, University of Maine, Orono, Maine, USA

- Dr. Andrew Marsh (Congress Steering Committee)
- CEO, HoIP Telecom Ltd, UK; Secretary General of World Academy of BioMedical Sciences and Technologies (WABT) a UNESCO nongovernmental organization, United Nations
- Dr. Kamal Mehta
- Department of Computer Engineering, Institute of Technology, Nirma University, Ahmedabad, India
- G. N. Pandey (Congress Steering Committee)
- Vice-Chancellor, Arunachal University of Studies, Arunachal Pradesh, India; Adjunct Professor, Indian Institute of Information Technology, Allahabad, India
- James J. (Jong Hyuk) Park (Congress Steering Committee)
- Department of Computer Science and Engineering (DCSE), SeoulTech, Korea
- R. Ponalagusamy
- Department of Mathematics, National Institute of Technology, Tiruchirappalli, India
- Dr. Xinyu Que (PDPTA)
- IBM T. J. Watson Research Center, Yorktown Heights, New York, USA
- Dr. Alberto Cano Rojas
- Department of Computer Science, University of Cordoba, Spain
- Pokkuluri Kiran Sree
- Department of Computer Science and Engineering (CSE), Jawaharlal Nehru Technological University, India
- Fernando G. Tinetti (Congress Steering Committee; BIOCOMP Co-Editor)
- School of Computer Science, Universidad Nacional de La Plata, La Plata, Argentina; Co-editor, *Journal of Computer Science and Technology (JCS&T)*
- Quoc-Nam Tran (BIOCOMP Co-Editor, Session Chair)
- Professor and Chair, Department of Computer Science, University of South Dakota, Vermilion, South Dakota, USA
- Patrick S. P. Wang (Congress Steering Committee)
- Fellow: IAPR, ISIBM, WASE; Professor of Computer and Information Science, Northeastern University, Boston, Massachusetts, USA and Zijiang Visiting Chair, ECNU, Shanghai, NTUST, Taipei; iCORE Visiting Professor, University of Calgary, Canada; Otto-von-Guericke Distinguished Guest Professor, University Magdeburg, Germany
- Shiuh-Jeng Wang (Congress Steering Committee)
- Department of Information Management, Central Police University, Taiwan; Program Chair, Security and Forensics, Taiwan; ROC; Director, Information Crypto and Construction Lab (ICCL) and ICCL-FROG
- Mary Q. Yang (Congress Steering Committee and Vice Chair of ABDA and BIOCOMP)

- Director, Mid-South Bioinformatics Center and Joint Bioinformatics Ph.D. Program, Medical Sciences and George W. Donaghey College of Engineering and Information Technology, University of Arkansas, Fayetteville, Arkansas, USA
- Dr. Hao Zheng; ThermoFisher Scientific, Sunnyvale, California, USA

We are grateful to all authors who submitted their contributions to us for evaluation. We express our gratitude to Steve Elliot (executive editor at Elsevier) and his staff. We hope that you enjoy reading this book as much as we enjoyed editing it.

On Behalf of Editorial Board:
Hamid R. Arabnia, PhD

Acknowledgments

We are very grateful to the many colleagues who offered their services in preparing and publishing this edited book. In particular, we would like to thank the members of the Program Committee of the BIOCOMP'14 and BIOCOMP'13 annual international conferences (their names appear at http://www.worldacademyofscience.org/worldcomp14/ws/conferences/biocomp14/committee and http://www.worldacademyofscience.org/worldcomp13/ws/conferences/biocomp13/committee, respectively). We would also like to thank the members of the Steering Committee of Federated Congress, WORLDCOMP 2014 (http://www.world-academy-of-science.org/) and the referees that were designated by them. The American Council on Science and Education (ACSE; http://www.americancse.org/about) provided a computer and a web server for managing the evaluations of the submitted chapters. We would like to extend our appreciation to Steve Elliot (executive editor at Elsevier) and Amy Invernizzi (editorial project manager at Elsevier) for the outstanding professional service that they provided to us.

Quoc-Nam Tran, PhD

Senior Editor, Emerging Trends in Computational Biology, Bioinformatics, and Systems Biology—Algorithms and Software Tools
Professor of Computer Science and Department Chair, University of South Dakota, Vermilion, SD, USA

Hamid R. Arabnia, PhD

Coeditor, Emerging Trends in Computational Biology, Bioinformatics, and Systems Biology—Algorithms and Software Tools
Editor-in-Chief, Emerging Trends in Computer Science and Applied Computing
Professor, Department of Computer Science, University of Georgia, Athens, GA, USA

Introduction

It gives us immense pleasure to present this edited book to the computational biology, bioinformatics, and systems biology research communities. As stated in the preface of this book, computational biology is the science of using biological data to develop algorithms and relations among various biological systems. It involves the development and application of data-analytical algorithms, mathematical modeling and simulation techniques to the study of biological, behavioral, and social systems. The field is multidisciplinary, in that it includes topics that are traditionally covered in computer science, mathematics, imaging science, statistics, chemistry, biophysics, genetics, genomics, ecology, evolution, anatomy, neuroscience, and visualization, and computer science acts as the topical bridge between these diverse areas. We consider the area of bioinformatics to be an important subfield of computational biology that includes methods for acquiring, storing, retrieving, organizing, analyzing, and visualizing biological data. The area of systems biology is an emerging methodology applied to biomedical and biological scientific research. It is an area that overlaps with computational biology and bioinformatics. This book is designed to cover the emerging trends in many important areas of computational biology, bioinformatics, and systems biology. The book is composed of 33 chapters, divided into four sections.

Section I, entitled "Computational Biology, Genetic Regulatory Networks, and Molecular Classification," is composed of 9 chapters. They utilize various technologies, software tools, and algorithms to solve and address important problems. More specifically, the methods include supervised learning, neural networks, artificial intelligence, modeling, simulation, high-performance computing methods, statistical methods, clustering algorithms, classification techniques, and visualization.

The collection of 11 chapters compiled in Section II, "Bioinformatics, Databases, Data Mining, Pattern Discovery, Assistive Technologies, Signal Processing, and AI," presents a number of important applications and describes novel uses of methodologies, including several in bioinformatics, databases, data mining, pattern discovery, assistive technologies, signal processing, and artificial intelligence (AI). More specifically, these chapters present clustering biological sequences, microRNA annotation, analysis of gene expressions, feature selection methods, DNA sequences and processing, health-care informatics and applications, toxicity prediction, biomedical methods, assistive tools and systems, neural models, and a philosophy of mind and cognition.

Section III, entitled "Systems Biology, Modeling and Simulation, Drug Design, and Discovery" is composed of 7 chapters. These chapters provide an insight and understanding of how different technologies are intertwined and used in concert to solve real and practical problems. More specifically, the topics presented in this section include combinatorial therapy of cancer, the DNA double-strand break (DSB) model, annotation of noncoding RNA, protein-folding methods, prediction techniques, the use of Bayesian belief networks for the diagnosis of main behavioral syndromes for Parkinson's disease, virtual screening, and molecular docking.

Finally, Section IV, "Big Data and Data Analytics, Data Science, Data Processing, Medical Diagnosis, Computational Biology and Bioinformatics," includes 6 chapters that describe algorithms and applications that are particularly data dependent. More specifically, they present methods for discovering knowledge in proteomic mass spectrometry data, next-generation sequencing data, quantification of *in vivo* magnetic resonance spectroscopy (MRS) metabolites, three-dimensional (3D) simulation of the cornea, business intelligence framework for a clinical laboratory, and methods for raw genomic data privacy.

The 33 chapters that appear in the four sections of this book are extended and edited versions of selected papers that were accepted for presentation at the 2013 and 2014 International Conference on Bioinformatics & Computational Biology (BIOCOMP'13 and BIOCOMP'14), which were held in July in Las Vegas, Nevada. Other authors (not affiliated with BIOCOMP) were also given the opportunity to contribute to this book by submitting their chapters for evaluation. We were fortunate to be coeditors of the proceedings of these annual conferences where the preliminary versions of most of these chapters first appeared. We are grateful to all authors who submitted papers for consideration. We thank the referees and members of the editorial board of BIOCOMP and the federated congress, WORLDCOMP. Without their help, this project would have neither been initiated nor finalized.

We hope that you learn from and enjoy reading the chapters of this book as much as we did.

Quoc-Nam Tran, PhD
Hamid R. Arabnia, PhD

Supervised Learning with the Artificial Neural Networks Algorithm for Modeling Immune Cell Differentiation

Pinyi Lu[1,2], Vida Abedi[1,2], Yongguo Mei[1,2], Raquel Hontecillas[1,2], Casandra Philipson[1,2], Stefan Hoops[1,2], Adria Carbo[3], and Josep Bassaganya-Riera[1,2]

The Center for Modeling Immunity to Enteric Pathogens, Virginia Bioinformatics Institute, Virginia Tech, Blacksburg, VA, USA[1]
Nutritional Immunology and Molecular Medicine Laboratory, Virginia Bioinformatics Institute, Virginia Tech, Blacksburg, VA, USA[2]
BioTherapeutics Inc., Blacksburg, VA, USA[3]

1 INTRODUCTION

1.A IMMUNE CELL DIFFERENTIATION AND MODELING

The process of immune cell differentiation plays a central role in orchestrating immune responses. It is based on the differentiation of naïve immune cells that, upon activation of their transcriptional machinery through a variety of signaling cascades, become phenotypically and functionally different entities capable of responding to a wide range of viruses, bacteria, parasites, or cancer cells. Functionally, immune cells have been classified into either regulatory or effector cell subsets. The cell differentiation process involves a series of sequential and complex biochemical reactions within the intracellular compartment of each cell. The Systems Biology Markup Language (SBML) is an Extensible Markup Language (XML)–based format widely used to represent as well as store models of biological processes. SBML allows the encoding of biological process including their dynamics. This information can be unambiguously converted into a system of ordinary differential equations (ODEs). Of note, ODE models are extensively used to model biological processes such as cell differentiation, immune responses toward specific pathogens, autoimmune processes, or intracellular activation of specific cellular pathways (Carbo et al., 2013, 2014a, b). Several equations are usually required to adequately represent these complex immunological processes, being either at the level of the whole organism, tissue, cells, or molecules.

Carbo et al. (2014b) published the first comprehensive ODE model of CD4+ T cell differentiation, which encompassed both effector T helper (Th1, Th2, Th17) and regulatory Treg cell phenotypes. CD4+ T cells play an important role in regulating adaptive immune functions as well as orchestrating other subsets to maintain homeostasis (Zhu and Paul, 2010). They interact with other immune cells by releasing cytokines that could further promote, suppress, or regulate immune responses. CD4+ T cells are essential in B-cell antibody class switching, in the activation and growth of CD8+ cytotoxic T cells, and in maximizing bactericidal activity of phagocytes such as macrophages. Mature T helper cells express the surface protein CD4, for which this subset is referred to as *CD4 + T cells*. Upon antigen presentation, naïve CD4+ T cells become activated and undergo a differentiation process controlled by the cytokine milieu in the tissue environment. The cytokine environmental composition, therefore, represents a critical factor in CD4+ T cell differentiation. As an example, a naïve CD4+ T cell in an environment rich in IFNγ or IL-12 will differentiate into Th1. In contrast, an environment rich in IL-4 will induce a Th2 phenotype. Some other phenoptypes are also balanced by each other: Th17 cells, induced by IL-6, IL-1β, and TGF-β, are closely balanced by regulatory T cells (induced by TGFβ only) (Eisenstein and Williams, 2009). Furthermore, competition for cytokines by competing clones of CD4+ T cells within an expanding cell population (proliferation), cell death, and expression of other selective activation factors such as the T cell receptor, OX40, CD28, ICOS, and PD1 are key steps that influence CD4+ T cell differentiation.

Computational approaches allow concurrent multiparametric analysis of biological processes and computational algorithms and models have become powerful and widely used tools to improve the efficiency and reduce the cost of the knowledge discovery process. Systems modeling approaches, combined with experimental immunology studies *in vivo*, can integrate existing knowledge and provide novel insights on rising trends and behaviors in biological processes such as CD4+ T cell differentiation and function. The CD4+ T cell differentiation model was built upon the current paradigms of molecular interactions that occur in CD4+ T cells, which consists of 60 ODEs, 53 reactions, and 94 species. The mathematical model ensures proper modulation of intracellular pathways and cell phenotypes via external cytokines representing the cytokine milieu. Two types of kinetic equations were employed to mathematically compute dynamic biological processes in the CD4+ T cell model: (i) mass action and (ii) Hill equation kinetics. Despite their simplicity, mass-action kinetics are widely accepted and extensively validated in biological systems due to their inherent ability to accurately represent elementary reactions and species degradation (Goldbeter, 1991). Mass-action rates are also extremely reliable for stochastic modeling simulations. In the CD4+ T cell model, the natural loss of model species due to messenger RNA (mRNA) and protein decay was fit using mass-action rate laws. On the other hand, sigmoidal Hill equations were used to model more complex molecular processes that behave via an on/off switch mechanism, including protein phosphorylation, cytokine-receptor binding, and transcription. Extensive studies have demonstrated the benefits of the Hill equation for studying combinatorial regulation, especially in sigmoidal Hill equations (Mangan and Alon, 2003); thus, this equation set captures complexities arising when a particular model species can be modified by more than one input. Results from modeling the pleotropic and highly dynamic regulation of CD4+ T cell differentiation has guided experimentation to elucidate underlying regulatory mechanisms, identify novel putative CD4+ T cell subsets or potential targets, and enrich our understanding of the dynamics of the process (Kidd *et al.*, 2014; Yosef *et al.*, 2013).

ODE-based modeling approaches require detailed knowledge of kinetic parameters, some of which can be estimated from the research literature and some from *in silico* experiments. However, models that are based on a large parameter set will be subject to more inaccuracies. Thus, the use of novel modeling approaches applicable to the immune system, and specifically to the CD4+ cell differentiation, has a high value for investigation.

1.B MSM AND MODEL REDUCTION

Current biomedical research involves performing experiments and developing hypotheses that link different scales of biological systems, such as intracellular signaling or transcriptional interactions, cellular behavior, and cell population behavior, tissue, and organism-level events. Computational modeling efforts exploring such multiscale systems quantitatively have to incorporate an array of techniques due to the different time and space scales involved. In a previous study, Mei et al. (2012) presented the Enteric Immunity Simulator (ENISI), an agent-based simulator for modeling mucosa immune responses to enteric pathogens. ENISI uses a rule-based approach and can simulate cells, cytokines, cell movement, and cell-cell interactions. To be able to model fine-grained intracellular behaviors, a multiscale modeling (MSM) approach that embeds intracellular models into the intercellular tissue level models is needed. Indeed, the MSM approach includes four scales: Intracellular, Chemokine/Cytokine Diffusion (Intercellular), Cellular, and Tissue. Our current version of ENISI incorporates the Cellular, Chemokine, and Tissue Scales. The cellular scale represents how the cells interact with nearby cells and incorporates the plasticity of a cell based on stochastic and temporal rules. The chemokine scale represents the chemokine concentration and diffusion process. Finally, the tissue scale represents the spatial and compartmental information (Figure 1.1).

FIGURE 1.1 Integration of four-order spatiotemporal scales.

Modeling fine-grained intracellular behaviors requires a MSM approach that embeds intracellular models into the intercellular tissue level models. The MSM approach includes intracellular, chemokine/cytokine diffusion (intercellular), cellular, and tissue scales.

Fine-grained ODE models of intracellular pathways controlling immune cell differentiation are adequate for studying the mechanisms of cell differentiation. However, they can be highly complex and expensive from a computational standpoint, especially when embedded within large-scale, agent-based simulations. ENISI Visual models a large number of cells and microbes in the gastrointestinal mucosa.

If each agent is represented by 60 ODEs, for example, the simulation will be hardly scalable. Therefore, to be able to develop efficient, agent-based, multiscale models, model reduction needs to be performed. In addition, multiscale models usually do not require all the internal details of intracellular scales to have predictive value. In essence, novel model reduction strategies could be used to address the multiscale scalability requirements to reduce molecular models before integrating them into large-scale, agent-based, tissue-level models.

1.C ANN ALGORITHM AND ITS APPLICATIONS

The artificial neural networks (ANN) algorithm, inspired by the biological neural systems, is powerful in modeling and data-mining tools based upon the theory of connectionism (Yegnanarayana, 2009). In biological systems, neurons are connected to each other through synapses. A neuron receives inputs from multiple neurons and outputs a value based upon the activation function. The perceptron is one of the easiest data structures for the study of neural networking. The perceptron models a neuron's behavior in the following way: First, the perceptron receives several input values. The connection for each input has a weight in the range of 0 to 1, these values are randomly picked and have an arbitrary unit (a.u.). The threshold unit then sums the inputs, and if the sum exceeds the threshold value, a signal is sent to the output node; otherwise, no signal is sent. The perceptron can "learn" by adjusting the weights to approach the desired output (Nielsen, 2001).

Building on the algorithm of the simple perceptron, the multilayer perceptron (MLP) model not only gives a perceptron structure for representing more than two classes, it also defines a learning rule for this kind of networks. The MLP is divided into three layers: the input layer, the hidden layer, and the output layer, where each layer in this order processes inputs and deliver outputs to the next layer (Nielsen, 2001). The extra layers give the structure needed to recognize nonlinearly

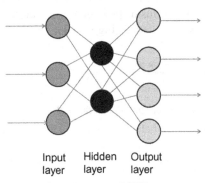

Input   Hidden   Output
layer   layer   layer

FIGURE 1.2 The multilayer perceptron structure of ANN.

The multilayer perceptron structure of artificial neural network is divided into three layers: the input layer, the hidden layer and the output layer, where each layer processes inputs and deliver outputs to next layer. The extra layers give the structure the ability to recognize nonlinearly separable classes.

separable classes (Figure 1.2). The network structures and the parameters of the activation function are important factors when developing neural network models. Feedforward neural networks are frequently used structures in modeling. There are effective learning algorithms for the parameters once the structures are set in the feedforward ANNs.

Neural network algorithms are widely used for data mining tasks such as classification and pattern recognition. Neural network algorithms are especially effective in modeling nonlinear relationships, which makes them ideal candidates for differentiation processes. Importantly, this process is scalable. However, there are also some practical challenges. It is not possible to know in advance the ideal network topology; therefore, ANN-based methods require testing several network settings or topologies in order to find the best solution. This technical challenge triggers an extended training period. Our initial pilot study was the first to apply neural network algorithms to studying immune cell differentiation (Mei *et al.*, 2013). Based on the initial success of this approach, the study was systematized and expanded. More specifically, the effect of artificial noise on the data is assessed. We use neural network algorithms to reduce the intracellular CD4+ T cell differentiation ODE model into a neural network model with four inputs, five outputs, and one hidden layer of seven nodes. The four input nodes represent the four external cytokines that regulate the cell differentiation; the five output nodes represent the five cytokines that are externalized and secreted by the T-cell subsets. After training, the model achieves high accuracy in predicting the concentrations of output cytokines. For instance, if the outputs are in the range of [0, 1], then the largest average prediction error is 0.0562 for IL17.

2 RELATED WORK

Modeling the CD4+ T cell differentiation is challenging because of the complexity of the immune system, plasticity between phenotypes, feedback loops involved in regulation, and combinatorial effects of cytokines. The immune system protects the human body from pathogens by recognizing, containing, and destroying nonself or foreign antigens (Boyd, 1946; O'Shea and Paul, 2010). At the highest level, the immune system can be divided into innate and adaptive branches. The innate immune system, involving cells such as macrophages, epithelial cells, neutrophils, and dendritic cells, responds quickly but nonspecifically to stimuli (Akira *et al.*, 2006). On the contrary, the adaptive immune system involving T cells and B cells responds more specifically to antigens (Alberts, 2002). Immune cells are activated and differentiated into ever-growing numbers of cell subsets such as CD4+ T cells and macrophages (Mosmann and Sad, 1996; Groux *et al.*, 1997, Murray and Wynn, 2011). These cells are regulated by different cytokines in their microenvironment. Using CD4+ T cells as an example, Th1 cells stably express IFNγ, whereas Th2 cells express IL-4. The discovery and investigation of two other CD4+ T cell subsets, induced regulatory T (iTreg) cells, and Th17 cells, has led to a rethinking of the notion that helper T-cell subsets represent irreversibly differentiated end points. Mounting evidence supports the tissue environment-dependent plasticity of CD4+ T-cell subsets and suggests the emergence of new phenotypes. When both transforming growth factor-b (TGFβ) and IL-6 are present in the environment, naïve CD4+ T cells differentiate into Th17 (Mangan *et al.*, 2006, Korn *et al.*, 2008). When TGFβ alone presents in the environment, CD4+ T cells differentiate into Treg [14]. When IFNγ and IL-12 are present, T cells differentiates into Th1 (Kohno *et al.*, 1997).

Systems biology has become an important paradigm in immunology research, using mathematical and computational models to synthesize and mine existing knowledge, and discover new knowledge from big data (Kitano, 2002a). Biological systems and processes can be modeled using a variety of methods (Kreeger and Lauffenburger, 2010; Noble, 2002; Kitano, 2002b). In some instances, biological processes can be mapped to networks where nodes and edges represent biological agents such as cells and their interactions (Kitano *et al.*, 2005). Furthermore, mathematical or computational dynamics can be applied to the network models so that *in silico* simulations can be performed (Foster and Kesselman, 2003; Carbo *et al.*, 2014a). SBML is used to represent computational models of biological processes (Hucka *et al.*, 2003). There are many types of models used for modeling biological processes, such as Bayesian networks, ODE, and agent-based models (Machado *et al.*, 2011). For metabolic and signaling networks, the biochemical reactions can be represented by first-order ODEs (Gillespie, 1992).

In line with our systems and translational immunology efforts under modeling immunity to enteric pathogens (www.modelingimmunity.org) of computational model building, calibration, refinement and validation, Carbo et al. (2013) published the first ODE model of CD4+ T cell differentiation, which comprises of 60 ODEs. The model shown in Figure 1.3 represents the intracellular pathways that are critical for CD4+ T cell differentiation. The hypotheses generated by this model were fully validated using *in vivo* animal models of inflammatory bowel disease (IBD). Computational modeling and mouse adoptive transfer studies were combined to gain a better mechanistic understanding of the modulation of CD4+ T cell differentiation and plasticity at the intestinal mucosa of mice. Sensitivity analyses highlighted the importance of PPARγ in the regulation of Th17 to iTreg plasticity. Indeed, validation experiments demonstrated that PPARγ is required for the plasticity of Th17, promoting a functional shift toward an iTreg phenotype. More specifically, PPARγ activation is associated with up-regulation of FOXP3 and suppression of IL-17A and RORγt expression in colonic lamina propria CD4+ T cells. Conversely, the loss of PPARγ in T cells results in colonic immunopathology driven by Th17 cells in adoptive transfer studies.

In another study, Mei et al. (2012) presented ENISI Visual, an agent-based simulator for modeling enteric immunity. ENISI Visual provides high-quality visualizations for simulating gut immunity to enteric pathogens and is capable of simulating gut immunity, including pathogen invasion, proinflammatory immune responses, pathogen elimination, regulatory immune responses, and restoring homeostasis. ENISI Visual can also help immunologists test novel hypotheses and design

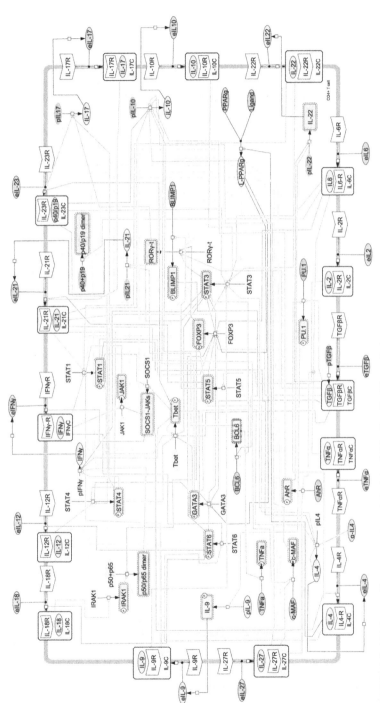

FIGURE 1.3 SBML-compliant network model of the CD4+ T-cell differentiation process.

This diagram illustrates network topologies associated with the naive T-cell differentiation toward T helper (Th)1, Th2, Th17, and induced regulatory T cells. The network is built in an SBML-compliant format.

biological experiments accordingly. Undoubtedly, a holistic model of the immune response could provide even more valuable insight; however, it needs to take into consideration complexities at the different layers: intracellular, cellular, intercellular, tissue, and whole organism. Modeling a complex system at four levels of magnitude—*i.e.*, MSM—poses a new set of challenges. MSM requires considering different spatial and temporal scales, ranging from nanometers to meters and nanoseconds to years. Therefore, different technologies have to be integrated to provide the most accurate predictions. MSM frameworks have been recently developed and attempted to address some of these challenges (Mancuso *et al.*, 2014; Buganza Tepole and Kuhl, 2014; Mei *et al.*, 2014). In our recent work, we have developed ENISI MSM, a MSM platform driven by high-performance computing and designed specifically for computational immunology, which integrates agent-based modeling (ABM), ODEs, and partial differential equations (PDEs) (Mei *et al.*, 2014). Our ENISI MSM platform is calibrated with experimental data and tested for the CD4 + T cell differentiation model, which is able to perform a variety of *in silico* experimentation for generating new hypotheses. However, running simulations on the MSM platform that requires COPASI (Hoops *et al.*, 2006) to solve complex ODEs is computationally expensive and time consuming. Replacing the ODE-based steps in the MSM by machine learning methods would significantly improve its computational performance and allow researchers to perform broad and comprehensive hypotheses generating *in silico* experimentation that uncovers emerging properties of the immune system and results in new, nonintuitive, computational hypotheses about immune responses.

Machine learning methods—supervised learning methods in particular—are key in building predictive models from observations, therefore facilitating knowledge discovery for complex systems. The neural network algorithm is a supervised learning approach that has been widely used in data mining (Craven and Shavlik, 1997; Lu *et al.*, 1996) as well as medical applications (Dayhoff and DeLeo, 2001; Ling *et al.*, 2013). Snow et al. (1994) developed neural networks for prostate cancer diagnosis and prognosis. Lek and Guégan (1999) introduced using neural networks in ecological modeling. Brusic et al. (1994) used neural networks for predicting major histocompatibility complex (MHC) binding peptides. Learning is an important research topic in neural networks. White (1989) presented neural network learning algorithms from the statistical perspective. Hagan and Menhaj (1994) presented an effective learning algorithm called *back-propagation* for training feedforward networks. In addition to modeling and predictions, the neural network algorithm has been used for solving ordinary and partial differential equations (Lagaris *et al.*, 1998).

Our initial work (Mei *et al.*, 2013) presented ANN as an alternative to solving ODEs using *in silico* data; in that study, ANN was compared with the linear regression (LR) model, and it was shown to outperform the latter. In the present work, we compare three different learning methods: ANN, LR, and support vector machine (SVM). We optimize the parameters of the models and apply them to *in silico* data with and without added noise.

3 MODELING IMMUNE CELL DIFFERENTIATION

To model cell differentiation, we first define the problem and make the following assumptions. There are m input cytokines that regulate immune cell differentiation: $C_{i1}, C_{i2}, ..., C_{im}$. There are also n output cytokines secreted by immune cells: $C_{o1}, C_{o2}, ..., C_{on}$. The cytokine concentrations are positive continuous values.

The problem of modeling immune cell differentiation is to develop one model for the following functional relationship:

$$\{C_{o1}, C_{o2}, ..., C_{on}\} = F_c(C_{i1}, C_{i2}, ..., C_{im}). \tag{1.1}$$

The model is designed to predict the output cytokine concentrations given the concentrations of input cytokines.

3.1 T CELL DIFFERENTIATION PROCESS AS A USE CASE

This study focuses on the T-cell differentiation. However, the techniques and algorithms developed herein can be applied to differentiations of other types of immune cells, such as macrophages, dendritic cells, B cells, etc. The input cytokines are internalized by the naïve T cells and regulate the T-cell differentiation process. The output cytokines are externalized and secreted.

3.2 DATA FOR TRAINING AND TESTING MODELS

The data for modeling the relationship from the input and output cytokines can be derived from the T-cell differentiation ODE model (Carbo et al., 2013), which was calibrated using data from biological experiments. By changing the concentrations of the input cytokines, the steady state of the ODE model is calculated. The steady-state results provide a measure of the output cytokines that can be used in the model. Creation of data sets was achieved by using the parameter scan task of COPASI tool (Hoops et al., 2006). COPASI is a software application designed for the simulation and analysis of biochemical networks and their dynamics, which supports models in the SBML standard and can simulate their behavior using ODEs. A five-dimensional scan was performed, where five output cytokines were independently measured. All the data is normalized to the range of [0, 1]. The method used to create data sets is equal-distance sampling. For each input cytokine, five values were chosen (0, 0.25, 0.5, 0.75, and 1). Since there are five input cytokines, 625 data points were created by the parameter scan process. A total of 100 of the data points were selected randomly for training, and the remaining 525 data points were used for testing. Additionally, uniformly distributed noise was added to the output for a quantitative analysis. Table 1.1 shows an example of data points used in the study.

3.3 ANN MODEL

The ANN model can be used to model nonlinear relationships. We developed the ANN model for T-cell differentiation using a package in R named neuralnet (Günther and Fritsch, 2010). The learning algorithm used is back-propagation.

Table 1.1 Sample Data Sets Used for Training and Testing the Models

	Input Data				Output Data					
	IFNγ	IL12	IL6	TGFβ	IL17	RORγt	IFNγ	Tbet	FOXP3
Sample Data without Noise	1	0	0.5	0	0.996	0.989	0.122	0.547	7.51E-06
	0.75	0.75	0	0.75	0.156	0.117	0.942	0.677	0.000103
	0.5	0.5	0.25	0.5	0.989	0.967	0.282	0.404	1.25E-05
	0.25	0	0	1	0.155	0.117	0.401	0.645	0.000105
Sample Data with Noise	1	0	0.5	0	0.974	0.913	0.118	0.545	7.12E-06
	0.75	0.75	0	0.75	0.148	0.106	0.900	0.644	9.91E-05
	0.5	0.5	0.25	0.5	0.950	0.922	0.264	0.391	1.28E-05
	0.25	0	0	1	0.144	0.115	0.390	0.640	0.000105

Table 1.2 Prediction Errors of the Neural Network Models with Different Numbers of Hidden Layers (The bolding indicates the neural network model with the best performance.)

Number of Hidden Neurons	IL17	RORγt	IFNγ	Tbet	FOXP3	Sum of Prediction Error
1	0.0551	0.0408	0.0831	0.114	0.0233	0.316
2	0.0559	0.0415	0.049	0.114	0.0369	0.297
4	0.0562	0.0411	0.0527	0.109	0.0362	0.295
5	0.0562	0.0415	0.0367	0.0396	0.0368	0.211
6	0.0562	0.0423	0.0482	0.0436	0.0357	0.226
7	**0.0561**	**0.0419**	**0.0407**	**0.0142**	**0.0368**	**0.190**
8	0.0561	0.0421	0.0426	0.0234	0.0368	0.201
10	0.0561	0.0415	0.0503	0.0453	0.0362	0.230
11	0.0561	0.0424	0.0423	0.0148	0.0360	0.192

The function neuralnet is used for training neural networks, which provides the opportunity to define the required number of hidden layers and hidden neurons. The most important arguments of the neuralnet function include formula, a symbolic description of the model to be fitted; data, a data frame containing the variables specified in formula; and a hidden vector, specifying the number of hidden layers and hidden neurons in each layer (Günther and Fritsch, 2010). To optimize the performance of the ANN model, we tested different sizes of hidden layers, including 1, 2, 4, 5, 6, 7, 8, 10, and 11 hidden neurons. By comparing the average absolute difference between the model predictions and real outputs from the test data, the neural network model with seven hidden neurons was identified to perform best (Table 1.2). The number of hidden layers is a critical model parameter. If the number of layers is too small, under-learning can occur, whereas too many layers can cause overlearning or overfitting. In this study, our results demonstrated that with the network of four inputs and five outputs, seven hidden neurons were necessary to best model the complex nonlinear system of cell differentiation using back-propagation (Figure 1.4).

3.4 COMPARATIVE ANALYSIS WITH THE LR MODEL AND SVM

The LR model was tested for its simplicity. R has a linear regression module lm, which was adapted and used in this study. The lm function is used to fit linear models, which can be used to carry out regression, single stratum analysis of variance, and analysis of covariance (Ihaka and Gentleman, 1996). The result of the linear regression model can be summarized as a linear transformation from the input cytokines to the output cytokines, as shown by Eq. (1.2). The transformation matrix, M_{Tran} [Eq. (1.3)], summarizes the relationship between input and output cytokine concentrations.

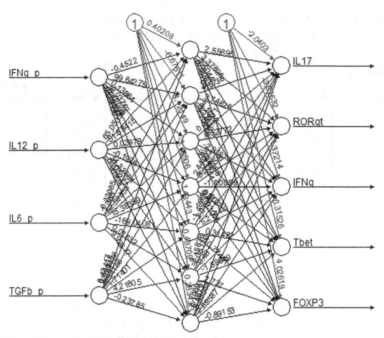

FIGURE 1.4 ANN model of CD4+ T cell differentiation.

The ANN model for T-cell differentiation was built using a package in R named neuralnet. The network of four inputs and five outputs needs seven hidden neurons to best model the complex cell differentiation system using back-propagation.

$$\begin{bmatrix} FOXP3 \\ IFN_{\gamma i} \\ IL17 \\ ROR_{\gamma t} \\ Tbet \end{bmatrix} = M_{Tran} \times \begin{bmatrix} 1 \\ IFN_{\gamma o} \\ IL12 \\ IL6 \\ TFG_{\beta} \end{bmatrix} \qquad (1.2)$$

$$M_{Tran} = \begin{bmatrix} 0.0386 & 0.531 & 0.408 & 0.387 & 0.663 \\ -0.0259 & -0.0536 & 0.155 & 0.146 & 0.0267 \\ -0.0303 & 0.297 & -0.0466 & -0.0592 & 0.129 \\ -0.0191 & -0.568 & 0.773 & 0.811 & -0.302 \\ 0.00558 & 0.0551 & -0.130 & -0.132 & -0.198 \end{bmatrix}, \qquad (1.3)$$

where the rows represent IFNγ, IL12, IL6, and TGFβ, respectively.

Furthermore, a model was created using the SVM algorithm, which is another widely used supervised learning algorithm for classification and regression problems. SVM contains all the main features that characterize a maximum margin algorithm (Smola and Schölkopf, 2004). The R package, e1071 (Dimitriadou *et al.*, 2008), was applied to build the SVM models using the same training data and test data as used by our previous modeling approaches. To optimize the performance of the SVM model, we tested different widths of radial kernel, including baseline (0.25), 1, 0.1, 0.01, and 0.001 (Table 1.3).

Table 1.3 Prediction Error of SVM Models with Different Widths of Radial Kernel

Width of Radial	IL17	RORγt	IFNγ	Tbet	FOXP3	Sum of Prediction Error
Baseline	0.181	0.179	0.146	0.122	0.0355	0.665
1	0.189	0.192	0.149	0.126	0.0349	0.691
0.1	0.193	0.192	0.160	0.130	0.0360	0.711
0.01	0.257	0.263	0.216	0.148	0.0366	0.920
0.001	0.343	0.351	0.259	0.174	0.0368	1.163

Note: The baseline width is the inverse of the dimension of the data (in this case, Baseline will be 0.25).

The prediction errors, average absolute difference between the model predictions, and real outputs from the test data of the different models are shown in Table 1.4. Considering that the data are normalized within [0, 1], the prediction error of linear regression model is obviously larger than that of neural network model. This corroborates that the T-cell differentiation process is highly nonlinear and linear regression will not be an appropriate method for this highly complex and nonlinear process. Additionally, the neural network model with seven hidden neurons was identified to perform best. By calculating the prediction error, it is concluded that the performance of the SVM model is better than the LR model, but worse than the ANN model (Table 1.4).

Table 1.4 Comparison of the Prediction Error of the ANN, LR, and SVM Models

Approach	IL17	RORγt	IFNγ	Tbet	FOXP3	Sum of Prediction Error
ANN	0.0561	0.0419	0.0407	0.0142	0.0368	0.190
LR	0.256	0.258	0.213	0.141	0.0362	0.904
SVM	0.181	0.179	0.146	0.122	0.0355	0.665

3.5 CAPABILITY OF ANN MODEL TO ANALYZE DATA WITH NOISE

Stochasticity is an inherent component of biological processes and an important aspect in modeling such systems (Kaern *et al.*, 2005; Munsky *et al.*, 2012; Frank, 2013; Hebenstreit *et al.*, 2012). Thus, we incorporated noise to the output data points.

A uniformly distributed noise in the range of $[-0.5\%, 0.5\%]$ was added to all five output data points independently in order to assess whether the ANN model could model the system with the same level of accuracy. The ANN model with seven hidden neurons was used to test the data set with noise. In a similar manner, 100 data points were selected randomly as the training data set. The remaining 525 data points were used for testing. Table 1.5 shows that the ANN model still outperforms the LR model and the SVM model when noise is added to the data. However, the performance of the ANN model deteriorates slightly when compared to data without added noise.

Table 1.5 Comparison of the Prediction Error of LR Model, ANN Model with Seven-Node Hidden Layer, and SVM Model

Approach	IL17	RORγt	IFNγ	Tbet	FOXP3	Sum of Prediction Error
ANN	0.0671	0.0698	0.042	0.0362	0.0354	0.250
LR	0.235	0.235	0.190	0.129	0.0355	0.824
SVM	0.0329	0.146	0.182	0.178	0.111	0.649

4 DISCUSSION

This study presented the ANN model of CD4+ T cell differentiation. Immune cell differentiation is an important immunological process that is not fully characterized at the systems level. Based upon our previous studies on the ODE model of CD4+ T cell differentiation and agent-based modeling for enteric mucosal immunity with ENISI, developing multiscale models requires significant reduction of the intracellular signaling and transcriptional ODE models before integrating them into the intercellular agent-based models.

Immune cell differentiation is a nonlinear process, and LR models are not capable of fitting the data well. To address this problem, a feedforward ANN model has been developed, focusing on modeling the relationship between the input external cytokines regulating the cell differentiation through interactions with receptors expressed on the surface of the cell, and the output cytokines secreted and externalized by the immune cell subsets. After training performed by using a back-propagation algorithm, this ANN model predicts the concentrations of the output cytokines with an average prediction error of 0.0379 for the five output cytokine concentrations. The ANN model significantly reduces the complexity of the ODE model by focusing on the needs of multiscale models and provides outstanding prediction accuracy. This approach is scalable and can be integrated into future MSM efforts such as ENISI MSM.

Comparative studies were performed to assess the ability of LR models for modeling T-cell differentiation. LR models provide a simplistic approach that is highly scalable and was shown to outperform ANN models in a recent comparison of the performances of an ANN model with three input variables and a regression model for glomerular filtration rate (GFR) estimation (Liu *et al.*, 2013). In our analysis, ANN models outperformed the LR models for the data with and without noise. This can be partly attributed to the fact that our models are competing to represent the complexity of CD4+ T cell differentiation; an immunological process that is highly nonlinear. Also, this can be partly determined by the variable (feature) selection.

A similar study was performed to evaluate SVM as an alternative to ANN, as they provide a number of advantages. The ANN algorithm is more prone to overfitting (Panchal *et al.*, 2011) than SVM. In addition, unlike ANN, computational complexities of SVM do not depend on the dimensionality of the input space (Patil *et al.*, 2012), and therefore, it could provide a more scalable framework. Finally, solution to SVM is global (Burges, 1998), where ANN could suffer from multiple local minima (Olson and Delen, 2008). However, in our analysis, ANN significantly outperformed SVM and therefore will be the method of choice.

Finally, analysis of noisy data is an important step toward appropriately comparing computational algorithms, since immunological systems are prone to variation and stochastic processes are present. When adding noise to the data, we observed that the performance of the ANN system deteriorates but only marginally. Therefore, the constructed modeling framework is stable and robust to slight variations.

5 CONCLUSION

This is the first study using ANN to model immune cell differentiation. We have shown that the proposed modeling framework is robust to noise and outperforms two other widely utilized machine learning algorithms, LR and SVM. Furthermore, ANN models represent ideal candidates for integration into the agent-based models that we have developed using ENISI MSM to study the intracellular signaling and transcriptional immunological processes comprehensively and systematically. Using machine learning as opposed to ODE-based methods will reduce the computational complexity of the system and facilitate a deeper mechanistic understanding of the complex interplay between the molecules, cells, and tissues of the immune system to advance the development of safer and more efficacious therapeutics for infectious and immune-mediated diseases.

ACKNOWLEDGMENTS

This work was supported in part by NIAID Contract No. HHSN272201000056C to JBR and funds from the Nutritional Immunology and Molecular Medicine Laboratory (URL: www. nimml.org).

REFERENCES

Akira, S., Uematsu, S., Takeuchi, O., 2006. Pathogen recognition and innate immunity. Cell 124, 783–801.

Alberts, B., 2002. Molecular Biology of the Cell. Garland Science, New York.

Boyd, W.C., 1946. Fundamentals of immunology. Interscience Publishers, New York.

Brusic, V., Rudy, G., Harrison, L.C., 1994. Prediction of MHC binding peptides using artificial neural networks. Complex Sys.: Mech. Adapt., 253–260.

Buganza Tepole, A., Kuhl, E., 2014. Computational modeling of chemo-bio-mechanical coupling: a systems-biology approach toward wound healing. Comput. Methods Biomech. Biomed. Engin., 1–18.

Burges, C.C., 1998. A tutorial on support vector machines for pattern recognition. Data Min. Knowl. Disc. 2, 121–167.

Carbo, A., Hontecillas, R., Kronsteiner, B., Viladomiu, M., Pedragosa, M., Lu, P., et al., 2013. Systems modeling of molecular mechanisms controlling cytokine-driven CD4 + T cell differentiation and phenotype plasticity. PLoS Comput. Biol. 9, E1003027.

Carbo, A., Hontecillas, R., Andrew, T., Eden, K., Mei, Y., Hoops, S., Bassaganya-Riera, J., 2014a. Computational modeling of heterogeneity and function of CD4 + T cells. Front. Cell Dev. Bio. 2, 31.

Carbo, A., Olivares-Villagomez, D., Hontecillas, R., Bassaganya-Riera, J., Chaturvedi, R., Piazuelo, M.B., et al., 2014b. Systems modeling of the role of interleukin-21 in the maintenance of effector CD4+ T cell responses during chronic Helicobacter pylori infection. mBio 5, E01243–14.

Craven, M.W., Shavlik, J.W., 1997. Using neural networks for data mining. Fut. Gen. Comput. Sys. 13, 211–229.

Dayhoff, J.E., Deleo, J.M., 2001. Artificial neural networks. Cancer 91, 1615–1635.

Dimitriadou, E., Hornik, K., Leisch, F., Meyer, D., Weingessel, A., 2008. Misc functions of the Department of Statistics (E1071), Tu Wien. R Package 1.5–24.

Eisenstein, E.M., Williams, C.B., 2009. The T(Reg)/Th17 cell balance: a new paradigm for autoimmunity. Pediatr. Res. 65, 26r–31r.

Foster, I., Kesselman, C., 2003. The Grid 2: Blueprint for a New Computing Infrastructure. Elsevier, Waltham, MA, USA.

Frank, S.A., 2013. Evolution of robustness and cellular stochasticity of gene expression. PLoS Biol. 11, E1001578.

Gillespie, D.T., 1992. A rigorous derivation of the chemical master equation. Physica A: Stat. Mech. Appl. 188, 404–425.

Goldbeter, A., 1991. A minimal cascade model for the mitotic oscillator involving cyclin and Cdc2 kinase. Proc. Natl. Acad. Sci. U. S. A. 88, 9107–9111.

Groux, H., O'Garra, A., Bigler, M., Rouleau, M., Antonenko, S., De Vries, J.E., Roncarolo, M.G., 1997. A CD4+ T-cell subset inhibits antigen-specific T-cell responses and prevents colitis. Nature 389, 737–742.

Günther, F., Fritsch, S., 2010. Neuralnet: training of neural networks. R Journal 2, 30–38.

Hagan, M.T., Menhaj, M.B., 1994. Training feedforward networks with the Marquardt algorithm. IEEE Trans. Neural Netw. 5, 989–993.

Hebenstreit, D., Deonarine, A., Babu, M.M., Teichmann, S.A., 2012. Duel of the fates: the role of transcriptional circuits and noise in CD4 + cells. Curr. Opin. Cell Biol. 24, 350–358.

Hoops, S., Sahle, S., Gauges, R., Lee, C., Pahle, J., Simus, N., et al., 2006. COPASI—a complex pathway simulator. Bioinform. 22, 3067–3074.

Hucka, M., Finney, A., Sauro, H.M., Bolouri, H., Doyle, J.C., Kitano, H., et al., 2003. The Systems Biology Markup Language (SBML): a medium for representation and exchange of biochemical network models. Bioinform. 19, 524–531.

Ihaka, R., Gentleman, R., 1996. R: a language for data analysis and graphics. J. Comp. Graph. Stat. 5, 299–314.

Kaern, M., Elston, T.C., Blake, W.J., Collins, J.J., 2005. Stochasticity in gene expression: from theories to phenotypes. Nat. Rev. Genet. 6, 451–464.

Kidd, B.A., Peters, L.A., Schadt, E.E., Dudley, J.T., 2014. Unifying immunology with informatics and multiscale biology. Nat. Immunol. 15, 118–127.

Kitano, H., 2002a. Computational systems biology. Nature 420, 206–210.

Kitano, H., 2002b. Systems biology: a brief overview. Science 295, 1662–1664.

Kitano, H., Funahashi, A., Matsuoka, Y., Oda, K., 2005. Using process diagrams for the graphical representation of biological networks. Nat. Biotech. 23, 961–966.

Kohno, K., Kataoka, J., Ohtsuki, T., Suemoto, Y., Okamoto, I., Usui, M., et al., 1997. IFN-gamma-inducing factor (IGIF) is a costimulatory factor on the activation of Th1 but not Th2 cells and exerts its effect independently of IL-12. J. Immunol. 158, 1541–1550.

Korn, T., Mitsdoerffer, M., Croxford, A.L., Awasthi, A., Dardalhon, V.A., Galileos, G., et al., 2008. IL-6 controls Th17 immunity in vivo by inhibiting the conversion of conventional T cells into FOXP3+ regulatory T cells. Proc. Natl. Acad. Sci. U. S. A. 105, 18460–18465.

Kreeger, P.K., Lauffenburger, D.A., 2010. Cancer systems biology: a network modeling perspective. Carcinogen. 31, 2–8.

Lagaris, I.E., Likas, A., Fotiadis, D.I., 1998. Artificial neural networks for solving ordinary and partial differential equations. IEEE Trans. Neural Netw. 9, 987–1000.

Lek, S., Guégan, J.-F., 1999. Artificial neural networks as a tool in ecological modelling, an introduction. Eco. Model. 120, 65–73.

Ling, H., Samarasinghe, S., Kulasiri, D., 2013. Novel recurrent neural network for modelling biological networks: oscillatory P53 interaction dynamics. Biosys. 114, 191–205.

Liu, X., Li, N.S., Lv, L.S., Huang, J.H., Tang, H., Chen, J.X., et al., 2013. A comparison of the performances of an artificial neural network and a regression model for GFR estimation. Am. J. Kidney Dis. 62, 1109–1115.

Lu, H., Setiono, R., Liu, H., 1996. Effective data mining using neural networks. IEEE Trans. Knowl. Data Eng. 8, 957–961.

Machado, D., Costa, R.S., Rocha, M., Ferreira, E.C., Tidor, B., Rocha, I., 2011. Modeling formalisms in systems biology. AMB Exp. 1, 1–14.

Mancuso, J.J., Cheng, J., Yin, Z., Gilliam, J.C., Xia, X., Li, X., Wong, S.T., 2014. Integration of multiscale dendritic spine structure and function data into systems biology models. Front. Neuroanat. 8, 130.

Mangan, S., Alon, U., 2003. Structure and function of the feed-forward loop network motif. Proc. Natl. Acad. Sci. U. S. A. 100, 11980–11985.

Mangan, P.R., Harrington, L.E., O'Quinn, D.B., Helms, W.S., Bullard, D.C., Elson, C.O., et al., 2006. Transforming growth factor-B induces development of the Th17 lineage. Nature 441, 231–234.

Mei, Y., Hontecillas, R., Zhang, X., Bisset, K., Eubank, S., Hoops, S., et al., 2012. ENISI visual: an agent-based simulator for modeling gut immunity. In: Bioinformatics and Biomedicine (BIBM), 2012 IEEE International Conference on, pp. 1–5. IEEE, 2012.

Mei, Y., Hontecillas, R., Zhang, X., Carbo, A., Bassaganya-Riera, J., 2013. Neural network models for classifying immune cell subsets. In: Bioinformatics and Biomedicine (BIBM), 2013 IEEE International Conference on, pp. 5–11. IEEE, 2013.

Mei, Y., Carbo, A., Hontecillas, R., Hoops, S., Liles, N., Lu, P., et al., 2014. ENISI MSM: a novel multiscale modeling platform for computational immunology. In: Bioinformatics and Biomedicine (BIBM), 2014 IEEE International Conference on, pp. 391–396. IEEE, 2014.

Mosmann, T.R., Sad, S., 1996. The expanding universe of T-cell subsets: Th1, Th2, and more. Immunol. Today 17, 138–146.

Munsky, B., Van Neuert, G., Oudenaarden, A., 2012. Using gene expression noise to understand gene regulation. Science 336, 183–187.

Murray, P.J., Wynn, T.A., 2011. Protective and pathogenic functions of macrophage subsets. Nat. Rev. Immunol. 11, 723–737.

Nielsen, F., 2001. Neural Networks Algorithms and Applications. Neil S Brock Business College, Dec. Available from: URL: http://www.glyn.dk/download/Synopsis.pdf.

Noble, D., 2002. Modeling the heart—from genes to cells to the whole organ. Science 295, 1678–1682.

O'Shea, J.J., Paul, W.E., 2010. Mechanisms underlying lineage commitment and plasticity of helper CD4+ T cells. Science 327, 1098–1102.

Olson, D.L., Delen, D., 2008. Advanced Data Mining Techniques. Springer, Berlin-Heidelberg, Germany.

Panchal, G., Ganatra, A., Shah, P., Panchal, D., 2011. Determination of over-learning and over-fitting problem in back propagation neural network. Intl. J. Soft Comput. 2, 40–51.

Patil, R.A., Gupta, G., Sahula, V., Mandal, A., 2012. Power aware hardware prototyping of multiclass SVM classifier through reconfiguration. In: 25th IEEE International Conference on VLSI Design (VLSID).pp. 62–67.

Smola, A.J., Schölkopf, B., 2004. A tutorial on support vector regression. Stat. Comput. 14, 199–222.

Snow, P.B., Smith, D.S., Catalona, W.J., 1994. Artificial neural networks in the diagnosis and prognosis of prostate cancer: a pilot study. J. Urol. 152, 1923–1926.

White, H., 1989. Learning in artificial neural networks: a statistical perspective. Neural Comp. 1, 425–464.

Yegnanarayana, B., 2009. Artificial Neural Networks. Phi Learning Pvt. Ltd, New Delhi, India.

Yosef, N., Shalek, A.K., Gaublomme, J.T., Jin, H., Lee, Y., Awasthi, A., et al., 2013. Dynamic regulatory network controlling Th17 cell differentiation. Nature 496, 461–468.

Zhu, J., Paul, W.E., 2010. Peripheral CD4 T cell differentiation regulated by networks of cytokines and transcription factors. Immunol. Rev. 238, 247–262.

Accelerating Techniques for Particle Filter Implementations on FPGA

2

B.G. Sileshi[1], C. Ferrer[1,2], and J. Oliver[1]

Departament de Microelectrònica i Sistemes Electrònics, Universitat Autònoma de Barcelona,
Bellaterra (Barcelona), Spain[1]
Institut de Microelectrònica de Barcelona (CNM-CSIC), Bellaterra (Barcelona), Spain[2]

1 INTRODUCTION

Estimating the state of a dynamic system from a set of observations that arrive sequentially in time and are corrupted by noise has different applications. For systems where the amount of nonlinearity is limited, the parametric Kalman filters (extended or unscented versions) can be applied. However, for systems with nonlinear or non-Gaussian dynamics, the Kalman filters were found to perform poorly (Meinhold and Singpurwalla, 1989; Ristic *et al.*, 2004). On the other hand, a nonparametric sequential Bayesian estimation technique called *particle filters (PFs)* present accurate estimates under such circumstances (Gordon *et al.*, 1993; Arulampalam *et al.*, 2002) and have been used in applications such as navigation and positioning (Gustafsson, 2010; Nordlund and Gustafsson, 2001; Atia *et al.*, 2010, 2012; Georgy *et al.*, 2012), tracking (Happe *et al.*, 2011; Medeiros *et al.*, 2008), and robotics (Grisetti *et al.*, 2007). There has been also extensive research in recent years for the application PFs to estimate the states and parameters in biological systems. For example, several studies (Nakamura *et al.*, 2009; Yang *et al.*, 2007; Gokdemir and Vikalo, 2009; Liu and Niranjan, 2012) demonstrate the applicability of PFs in the state estimation of biological models by considering biological systems as dynamical, nonlinear, and generally partially observed processes.

PFs have the flexibility of efficiently representing a wide range of probability densities using sets of points called *particles*. Such representational power of PFs, however, comes at the cost of a great computational complexity that has so far limited their application in different types of real-life problems. It is in this sense that hardware- or hardware/software-based implementations of PFs are essential to accelerate the computational time and achieve the objective of real-time computation. With regard to this, the research literature tackles the real-time constraint of the PFs through hardware implementation platforms such as field-programmable gate arrays (FPGAs). Interesting features of FPGAs, such as their ability to introduce massive parallelization and their low power consumption, which is critical for many applications such as navigation, make them the primary choice for the implementation of PFs in real-life applications.

The hardware implementation of PFs based on FPGA platforms has been proposed by several researchers. For example, Chau *et al.* (2012) studied the implementation of PFs on an FPGA in a mobile robot localization problem, where the size of the particle set is adapted to reduce the run-time computational complexity of the algorithm. In Fross *et al.*, (2010), the FPGA hardware implementation of PF for location estimation is presented and compared with the software solution running on an ARM7-based microcontroller. A recent study (Chau *et al.*, 2013) presents a heterogeneous reconfigurable system consisting of an FPGA and a central processing unit (CPU) for a simultaneous mobile robot localization and people-tracking application. In this study, they adapt the number of particles dynamically and utilize the run-time reconfigurability of the FPGA to reduce power and energy consumption. According to their results, a speed increase of up to 7.39 times is achieved compared to the Intel Xeon X5650 CPU software implementation. Li et al. (2011) presented a hardware/software codesign approach based on a system on a chip technique that uses a NIOS II processor to calculate the weight for each particle and a hardware implementation to update the particles. They claim that their proposed method significantly improves the efficiency and provides flexibility in the design step for various applications due to the software implementation of the importance weight step. Ye and Zhang (2009) presented hardware architecture for an FPGA implementation of the sampling importance resampling (SIR) PF. The hardware architecture is simulated with ModelSim and the real-time performance of the hardware architecture is evaluated using a universal asynchronous receiver/transmitter (UART) for the input sensor data. Saha et al. (2010) presented a System-on-Chip architecture involving both hardware and software components for a class of PFs. In this chapter, a parameterized framework is used to enable the reuse of the architecture with minimal redesign for a wide range of particle filtering applications. In El-Halym et al. (2012), three different hardware architectures are proposed, and this suggests the use of a piecewise linear function instead of the classical exponential function in order to decrease the complexity of the hardware architecture in the weighting step.

With the objective to reduce the high computational requirements of the PF, this chapter presents PF acceleration techniques based on a hardware/software codesign approach with the following specific contributions:

- As the underlying computations in particle filtering vary from one application to the next, a generic approach is presented for the analysis, design, and speed-up of the PF computational steps. The same approach can be used in the development of other application-specific PF implementations.
- The embedded hardware/software implementation of the PF focuses on a grid-based fast simultaneous localization and mapping (SLAM) algorithm. In order to increase the throughput of the algorithm, two main mechanisms are introduced in the algorithm acceleration:

- Fast hardware Gaussian random number generator design and its application to PF for grid-based Fast SLAM algorithm is presented.
- The design and implementation of the custom COordinate Rotation DIgital Computer (CORDIC) hardware module for the evaluation of the complex mathematical operations involved in several steps of the PF algorithm is presented.

This chapter is an extended version of the work presented by Sileshi et al. (2014), and it is organized as follows: Section 2 first introduces the theory behind the PF algorithm, followed by a discussion on its application with the SLAM algorithm called Grid-based Fast SLAM. Section 3 provides a discussion on the identification of the computational bottlenecks of the PF algorithm and the partitioning of the different steps for hardware and software implementations. Section 4 explains the PF acceleration techniques, and section 5 is dedicated to the hardware architecture design of the proposed acceleration techniques. Section 6 discusses the proposed hardware/software architecture of the PF and Section 7 presents the implementation results. Finally, Section 8 provides a conclusion of these topics.

2 PF AND SLAM ALGORITHMS
2.1 PARTICLE FILTERING

The problem of nonlinear filtering is defined by a state space representation of dynamic system given by a discrete-time stochastic model of the state $x_t \in R^{d_x}$ and measurement $z_t \in R^{d_z}$ vectors with dimensions d_x and d_z, respectively:

$$x_t = f_t(x_{t-1}, v_{t-1}) \tag{2.1}$$

$$z_t = h_t(x_t, w_t) \tag{2.2}$$

where f_t and h_t are possibly nonlinear function of the state x_{t-1} and the measurement z_t, respectively; v_{t-1} and w_t are the process and measurement noise sequences, respectively; and t is the time index. The process and measurement noise sequences are assumed to be white, with known probability density functions and mutually independent.

In Bayesian estimation framework, the estimation to the state vector x_t at time t is obtained from a noisy measurement z_t, where the initial target state is assumed to have a known probability density function (pdf) $p(x_0)$ and is also independent of the noise sequences. The estimate of the unknown state x_t is performed based on the sequence of all available measurements $Z_{1:t} = \{z_i, i = 1, ..., t\}$ up to time t. The posterior distribution $p(x_t|Z_t)$ is calculated recursively based on the following two prediction [Eq. (2.3)] and update [Eq. (2.4)] equations (Arulampalam et al., 2002):

$$p(x_t|Z_{t-1}) = \int p(x_t|x_{t-1})p(x_{t-1}|Z_{t-1})dx_{t-1} \tag{2.3}$$

$$p(x_t|Z_t) = \frac{p(z_t|x_t)p(x_t|Z_{t-1})}{p(z_t|Z_{t-1})} \tag{2.4}$$

where the probabilistic model of the state evolution $p(x_t|x_{t-1})$, is defined by the system equation [Eq. (2.1)], $p(z_t|x_t)$ is defined by the measurement equation [Eq. (2.2)], and $p(z_t|Z_{t-1})$ is a normalizing constant given by

$$p(z_t|Z_{t-1}) = \int p(z_t|x_t)p(x_t|Z_{t-1})dx_t. \tag{2.5}$$

While the assumption of the linear and Gaussian conditions is satisfied, the optimal analytic solution to the integrals given by Eqs. (2.3) and (2.4) is obtained by using the Kalman filtering method. However, it is often difficult to find an analytical solution to these integrals in most nonlinear/non-Gaussian estimation problems, and Sequential Monte Carlo (SMC) approximation method is used in the approximation of these integrals.

PF is an SMC-based approach that approximates a pdf by a discrete set of particles with their associated weights $\left\{x_t^i, w_t^i\right\}_{i=1}^N$, where i and N denote the index of the particles and the total number of particles, respectively; $x_t^i \in R^{d_x}$ and w_t^i denotes the state of the particles and their weights, respectively; and d_x is the dimension of the state. The posterior pdf $p(x_t|Z_t)$ of the state vector is approximated by (Ristic *et al.*, 2004)

$$p(x_t|Z_t) \approx \sum_{i=1}^N w_t^i \delta(x_t - x_t^i), \tag{2.6}$$

where $\delta(.)$ is a Dirac Delta function and w_t^i is the importance weight, given by

$$w_t^i \propto w_{t-1}^i \frac{p(z_t|x_t^i)p(x_t^i|x_{t-1}^i)}{q(x_t^i|x_{t-1}^i, z_t)}. \tag{2.7}$$

In particle filtering, the particle set $S_t = \left\{x_t^i, w_t^i\right\}_{i=1}^N$ at time t is recursively propagated from the set S_{t-1} at the previous time $t-1$ in such a way that they provide an approximation of the posterior distribution at each iteration. The initial particle set S_0 is obtained from samples drawn from the prior density $p(x_0)$. In this approach, a major problem called *particle degeneracy phenomenon* arises. That is, after a certain number of iterations, a small number of normalized importance weights tend to value of one, while the remaining weights are negligible. This is not a desirable phenomenon, as only a few particles contribute to the approximation of the posterior density and much computation is wasted on the particles with negligible weight. A common measure of the degeneracy of the algorithm is the effective sample size N_{eff}, given by (Arulampalam *et al.*, 2002)

$$N_{eff} = \frac{1}{\sum_{i=1}^N \left(w_t^i\right)^2}. \tag{2.8}$$

The degeneracy problem can be reduced by using a very large value of samples N but, since that approach is impractical, other alternative techniques are commonly used. These includes the use of an optimal importance density and resampling

(Arulampalam *et al.*, 2002). The optimal choice of the importance density is commonly considered the prior density. In resampling, particles are resampled N times with replacement from the discrete approximation of the posterior density. In this process, particles with low importance weight are eliminated and particles with high importance weight are replicated. This step is performed while N_{eff} falls below a certain predefined threshold, N_T. The resampling step is intended to reduce the degeneracy problem, but it leads to the limitation that it parallelizes the algorithms and loses diversity among the particles. The loss of diversity among the particles may lead to the occupancy of the same point in the state space by all N particles, giving poor representation of the posterior density.

The basic steps of the PF discussed so far, which correspond to an SIR PF, is given as follows:

```
Input: [{xᵢₜ₋₁, wᵢₜ₋₁}ᴺᵢ₌₁, zₜ]
```

```
Output: [{xᵢₜ, wᵢₜ}ᴺᵢ₌₁]
```

```
FOR i = 1:N
Draw xᵢₜ ~ q(xₜ|xₜ₋₁, zₜ)
Calculate the nonnormalized importance weights w̃ᵢₜ
```

$$\tilde{w}_t^i = w_{t-1}^i \frac{p(z_t|x_t^i)p(x_t^i|x_{t-1}^i)}{q(x_t^i|x_{t-1}^i, z_t)}$$

```
END FOR
Calculate sum of the weights: W = ∑ᴺᵢ₌₁ w̃ᵢₜ
FOR i = 1:N
Normalize: wᵢₜ = W⁻¹ w̃ᵢₜ
END FOR
Calculate Nₑff using Eq. (2.8)
If Nₑff ≤ Nₜ
RESAMPLE
END IF
```

SIR is one of the most commonly used variants of the basic particle filtering known as sequential importance sampling (SIS) PF, where the prior density $p(x_t^i|x_{t-1}^i)$ is used as the importance density $q(x_t^i|x_{t-1}^i, z_t)$ and the weights of the particles is given by $w_t^i \propto p(z_t|x_t^i)$.

2.2 APPLICATION OF PF TO SLAM

SLAM involves the problem of localizing and building a map of a given environment simultaneously (Chen *et al.*, 2007). It is usually described with a joint posterior probability density distribution [Eq. (2.9)] of the map (m) and the robot states (x_t) at time t, given the observations ($z_{0:t}$) and control inputs ($u_{0:t}$) up to and including time t, together with the initial state of the robot (x_0):

$$p(x_t, m | z_{0:t}, u_{0:t}, x_0).$$

(2.9)

For the computation of the conditional probability given by Eq. (2.9) for all times t, a recursive solution based on the Bayes theorem is used in SLAM by starting with an estimate for the distribution $p(x_{t-1}, m | z_{0:t-1}, u_{0:t-1})$ at time $t-1$ and following a control u_t and observation z_t. Therefore, the SLAM algorithm is implemented with the two standard steps of the recursive prediction and measurement update process. The recursion is a function of the robot motion model $p(x_t | x_{t-1}, u_t)$ and an observation model $p(z_t | x_t, m)$.

The prediction is obtained from the following equation:

$$p(x_t, m | z_{0:t-1}, u_{0:t-1}, x_0) = \int p(x_t | x_{t-1}, u_t) p(x_{t-1}, m | z_{0:t-1}, u_{0:t-1}, x_0) dx_{t-1}$$

(2.10)

and the measurement update is calculated using

$$p(x_t, m | z_{0:t}, u_{0:t}, x_0) = \frac{p(z_t | x_t, m) p(x_t, m | z_{0:t-1}, u_{0:t-1}, x_0)}{p(z_k | z_{t-1}, U_{0:t})}.$$

(2.11)

The solution to a probabilistic SLAM problem involves an efficient and consistent computation of the prediction and update equations. Based on different estimation frameworks for performing these computations, there are different variants of the SLAM algorithm (Thrun, 2002; Chen et al., 2007; Aulinas et al., 2008). The Grid-based Fast SLAM algorithm is a variant that applies particle filtering methods to solve the SLAM problem (Thrun et al., 2005). Grid-based Fast SLAM incrementally processes the observations and odometry readings as they are available and updates the set of samples representing the posterior about the map and trajectory of the robot. The steps of the Fast SLAM based on PF are summarized as follows:

Initialization: At time $t = 0$, sample $\{x_0^i\}_{i=1}^N$ from the initial density function $p(x_0)$.

Sampling: Based of the state of the system at time $t-1$ represented by $\{x_{t-1}^i, w_{t-1}^i\}_{i=1}^N$ and the observation at z_t, propose a set of new particles $\{x_t^i\}_{i=1}^N$ from the proposal function $q(x_t | x_{t-1}, z_t)$. The motion model of the robot is often used as the proposal.

Importance weight: An individual weight w_t^i is assigned for each proposed particle $\{x_t^i\}_{i=1}^N$. The weight of each particle is proportional to the likelihood $p(z_t | x_t, m)$ of the most recent observation given the map m associated with the particle and the corresponding pose x_t.

Resampling: This step involves sampling new set of particles from the set $\{x_t^i, w_t^i\}_{i=1}^N$ according to the weights of the particles; i.e., particles with larger weights are replicated, while lighter particles are discarded. The resulting particle set is then used in the next time step to predict the posterior probability. Resampling helps to improve the quality of the estimation by reducing the variance of the particles. In this step, different resampling algorithms (Douc and Cappe, 2005) can be used, as they are not application-specific algorithms. The specific resampling method adopted in this study is the Independent Metropolis

Hasting (IMHA) resampling algorithm. This algorithm has the lowest computational complexity of most conventional resampling schemes like systematic resampling (Sileshi *et al.*, 2013). As a result of these interesting characteristics, it is preferred for this work.

Map estimation: For each particle, the corresponding map estimate is updated based on the observation and the pose represented by that particle.

3 COMPUTATIONAL BOTTLENECK IDENTIFICATION AND HARDWARE/SOFTWARE PARTITIONING

In tackling the speed-up of the overall computation in PFs, a preliminary study of the identification of the critical bottlenecks of the algorithm is crucial for the design of hardware modules in order to accelerate the computational bottleneck steps. The study is based on the Grid-based Fast SLAM algorithm discussed in section 2. For an embedded implementation of the Grid-based Fast SLAM algorithm on the FPGA platform, an accurate analysis of the timing required in each step of the PF is obtained in order to identify the computational bottlenecks in each step of the PF.

Figure 2.1 summarizes the critical computational bottlenecks obtained from such preliminary study. In the sampling step, the computation of sine and cosine functions and Gaussian random number generator (GRNG) accounts to 45.91% and 53.62% of its execution time. In the importance weight step, the computation of sine and cosine, and exponential functions contribute 75.34% and 7.65% of the execution time,

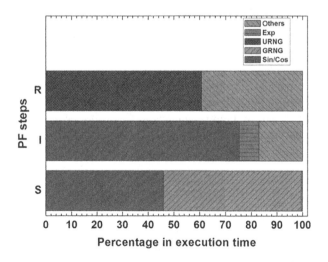

FIGURE 2.1

Computational bottlenecks identifications in the sampling (s), importance weight (I), and resampling (R) steps of the PF in the Grid-based Fast SLAM application.

respectively. For the resampling step, the generation of uniform random numbers accounts for most of the execution time (i.e., 60.71%). For each step of the PF computations shown in Figure 2.1, "others" corresponds to other related computations involved in each step.

The profiling information of the PF given in Figure 2.1 can used in the hardware/software partitioning; i.e., which parts of the algorithm should be implemented in hardware and which ones can be kept in software (running on the FPGA's embedded processor). It is clear from Figure 2.1 that the sine and cosine functions and random number generation are the critical bottlenecks of the Grid-based Fast SLAM algorithm, thus requiring acceleration with a hardware implementation.

The techniques used in the speed-up of the computational bottleneck steps of the PF in the Grid-based Fast SLAM application are based on the use of the CORDIC algorithm (Volder, 1959) for the evaluations of the sine, cosine, and exponential functions, and the Ziggurat (Marsaglia and Tsang, 2000) and Tausworthe (Ecuyer, 1996) algorithms for generation of Gaussian and uniform random numbers, respectively. The details of these techniques are provided in section 4, and the respective hardware designs are given in section 5.

4 PF ACCELERATION TECHNIQUES
4.1 CORDIC ACCELERATION TECHNIQUE

CORDIC is an iterative algorithm capable of evaluating many basic arithmetic operations and mathematical functions (Aulinas *et al.*, 2008). It involves the rotation of a vector $v = (x, y)$ with an angle z in circular, linear, and hyperbolic coordinate systems depending on the functions to be evaluated. Using shift and add operations, it performs a rotation iteratively using a series of specific incremental rotation angles. It can operate in one of three configurations (circular, linear, or hyperbolic) and two different modes (rotation or vectoring). In rotation mode, it performs a general rotation by a given angle z, and in vectoring mode, it computes the unknown angle z of a vector by performing a finite number of microrotations.

The unified CORDIC iteration equations for evaluation of a wide range of functions are given by Eq. (2.12) (Walther, 1971; Lakshmi and Dhar, 2010):

$$x_{i+1} = x_i - \mu d_i y_i 2^{-i}$$
$$y_{i+1} = y_i + d_i x_i 2^{-i} \qquad (2.12)$$
$$z_{i+1} = z_i - d_i e_{i,}$$

where (x, y) defines a vector with angle z; μ defines a circular ($\mu = 1$), linear ($\mu = 0$), or hyperbolic ($\mu = -1$) coordinate system; d_i represents either a clockwise or counterclockwise direction of rotation in rotation mode $d_i = sing(z_i)$ and vectoring mode $d_i = -sing(y_i)$; and e_i defines a table of constant values in circular ($e_i = \tan^{-1} 2^{-i}$), linear ($e_i = 2^{-i}$), and hyperbolic ($e_i = \tanh^{-1} 2^{-i}$) configurations. With the unified

CORDIC iteration equations, a wide range of functions can be evaluated. However, the discussion is focused to the evaluation of the different functions involved in the PF steps for Grid-based Fast SLAM application and the Ziggurat Gaussian random-number generator algorithm. These include the sine, cosine, exponential, and natural logarithm functions. The configurations to the variables x, y, and z, and the set of equations that the unified CORDIC iteration equations converges after i iterations in rotation and vectoring modes is given in Table 2.1, where, in circular-rotation mode of configuration, the functions f_1 and f_2 correspond to the sine () and cosine () functions, respectively; and for hyperbolic-rotation configuration, f_1 and f_2 correspond to the sinh () and cosh () functions. In vectoring-hyperbolic configuration, the function f_3 corresponds to $tanh^{-1}$.

Table 2.1 Configuration to CORDIC for Evaluation of Different Functions

	Circular	Hyperbolic
Rotation $x = K(xf_1z - yf_2z)$ $y = K(yf_1z - xf_2z)$ $z = 0$	Sine/Cosine $x = 1/K, y = 0$ and z as input, $K = 1.646$	Exponential $x = 1/K, y = 0$ and z as input $K = 0.828159$
Vectoring $x = K\sqrt{x^2 - y^2}$ $y = 0$ $z = z + f_3\left(\frac{y}{x}\right)$	-	Logarithmic $x = 1, z = 0$ and y as input

The evaluation of the sine and cosine functions is obtained directly by applying the properties given in Table 2.1; however, for the evaluation of exponential and natural logarithm functions, indirect properties are used. The evaluation of the exponential function is obtained indirectly by applying the following property:

$$exp(z) = sinh(z) + cosh(z). \tag{2.13}$$

Similarly, in the case of the natural logarithm function, the property given by the following equation is used for its indirect evaluation:

$$lnw = 2tanh^{-1}\left(\frac{y}{x}\right), \tag{2.14}$$

where, $x = w + 1$ and $y = w - 1$.

As the CORDIC algorithm works for a limited range of the input arguments for the evaluation of the elementary functions, it is required to extend the range of the inputs for each mode of operation by applying proper prescaling identities. This is achieved by dividing the original input arguments to the CORDIC algorithm by a constant to obtain a quotient Q and remainder D (Boudabous *et al.*, 2004). In the case of the sine and cosine functions, the constant value corresponds to $\frac{\pi}{2}$, and log_e2 for the exponential and logarithmic functions. The prescaling identities for all the required functions are given in Table 2.2.

Table 2.2 Prescaling Identities for Function Evaluations

Identity	Domain
$\sin\left(Q\frac{\pi}{2}+D\right)=\begin{cases}\sin D \text{ if } Q \bmod 4=0\\\cos D \text{ if } Q \bmod 4=1\\-\sin D \text{ if } Q \bmod 4=2\\-\cos D \text{ if } Q \bmod 4=3\end{cases}$	$\lvert D\rvert<\frac{\pi}{2}$
$\cos\left(Q\frac{\pi}{2}+D\right)=\begin{cases}\cos D \text{ if } Q \bmod 4=0\\-\sin D \text{ if } Q \bmod 4=1\\-\cos D \text{ if } Q \bmod 4=2\\\sin D \text{ if } Q \bmod 4=3\end{cases}$	$\lvert D\rvert<\frac{\pi}{2}$
$\exp(Q\log_e 2+D)=2^Q(\cosh D+\sinh D)$	$\lvert D\rvert<\log_e 2$
$\log_e(M2^M)=\log_e(M)+E\log_e 2$	$0.5\le M<1.0$

Source: Walther (1971); Lakshmi and Dhar, 2010; Boudabous et al. (2004).

4.2 ZIGGURAT ACCELERATION TECHNIQUE

The sampling step of the PF for the Grid-based Fast SLAM application requires the generation of normal random numbers. For fast generation of such random numbers in this study, a Ziggurat algorithm was used. The Ziggurat algorithm is an efficient method for generating normally distributed random variates from an arbitrary decreasing probability density function $y=f(x)$ by applying the acceptance-rejection method. This method involves conditionality in accepting correct random values that are part of the target distribution and rejecting incorrect ones.

The Ziggurat technique partitions the standard normal density function $(x)=\exp(-0.5x^2)$, $x>0$, into n horizontal rectangular blocks R_i, where $i=0,1,2,\ldots,(n-1)$, extending horizontally from $x=0$ to x_i and vertically from $f(x_i)$ to $f(x_{i-1})$. The bottom of the block consists of a rectangular area joined with the remainder of the density starting from a point r (Figure 2.2). All the rectangular blocks have equal area v, given by

$$v=x_i[f(x_{i-1})-f(x_i)]=rf(r)+\int_r^\infty f(x)dx. \tag{2.15}$$

The description of the Ziggurat algorithm based on Doornik (2005) for generating normally distributed random variates by partitioning of the normal density distribution, and with the application of the acceptance-rejection method, is given by

```
Input: {xᵢ}ⁿ⁻¹₁₌₀
Output: normal random number x.
Draw an index i of a rectangle (0 ≤ i ≤ n−1) at random with probability 1/n.
Draw a random number x from the rectangle i as x = U₀xᵢ, where U₀ is a uniform
random number drawn from a uniform distribution U(0, 1).
Rectangular:
```

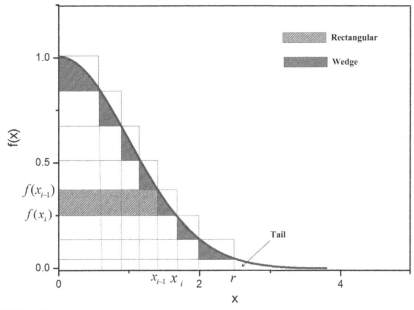

FIGURE 2.2

Partitioning of a Gaussian distribution with the Ziggurat method.

```
IF i≥1 and x<xᵢ₋₁ accept x.
Tail:
IF i=0, accept x from the tail.
Wedge:
ELSE IF i>0 and U₁|f(xᵢ₋₁)−f(xᵢ)|< f(x)−f(xᵢ) accept x, where U₁ is a uniform
random number.
RETURN to step 1
```

where, in line 4, the method to generate the normal random numbers from the tail of the distribution is obtained as follows:

```
DO
Generate i.i.d. uniform (0, 1) variates u₀ and u₁
x←− ln(u₀)/r, y←− ln(u₁)
WHILE (y+y)< x²
RETURN x>0?(r+x):−(r+x)
```

The Ziggurat algorithm requires a table of x_i points and their corresponding function values f_i. The number of rectangular blocks n is normally considered as a power of 2 (64, 128, 256, ...), and for n = 128, a value of $r = 3.442619855899$ is used to determine the x_i points that are required in the hardware realization of the algorithm

(Marsaglia and Tsang, 2000). The uniform random numbers U_0 and U_1 required in the Ziggurat algorithm are generated with a Tausworthe Uniform Random Number Generator (URNG). For evaluating the exponential and natural logarithmic functions in the wedge (line 5) and tail regions (line 4), respectively, a CORDIC algorithm was used.

5 HARDWARE IMPLEMENTATION

This section describes the hardware designs for the PF acceleration techniques listed in section 4 for Grid-based Fast SLAM applications. The hardware design for the CORDIC acceleration technique is based on a CORDIC hardware module (shown in Figure 2.3) composed of three hardware computational submodules: CORDIC core, prescaling, and postscaling. The implementation of these submodules is based on the unified CORDIC iteration equations given in section 4 for the CORDIC-core submodule, and the identity equations given in Table 2.2 for the prescaling and post-scaling submodules. The identity equations are used by the prescaling and postscaling modules to extend the range of input arguments while evaluating the different functions. The evaluation of the different functions by a single CORDIC module is required to avoid the use of multiple instances of the CORDIC module and consequently save the additional resource requirements. This is achieved by providing a runtime configuration to the CORDIC module through its *Config* port to configure the module to a specific function evaluation.

A serial CORDIC algorithm with 24-bit accuracy is implemented in the CORDIC core shown in Figure 2.3. In the input/output interfaces for the CORDIC module shown in Figure 2.3, one of the two possible inputs U_0 and U_1 is evaluated for a specific function, one at a time. The configuration to a specific function evaluations is provided by the configuration bits at the *Config* input port, where, depending on these

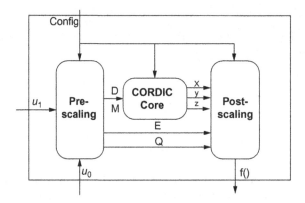

FIGURE 2.3

Architecture of the CORDIC module.

bits, a specific function is evaluated and the result is provided to the output interface $f()$. The functions $f()$ that can be obtained at the output are the sin (), cos (), exp () and ln () functions.

The hardware architecture for the generation of both uniform and Gaussian random numbers is given in Figure 2.4. The three hardware submodules involved in Figure 2.4 are the Ziggurat NRNG submodule for generation of normally distributed random numbers; the Tausworthe submodule for the generation of two uniform random numbers (U_0 and U_1) that are used in the Ziggurat NRNG submodule and resampling step of the PF; and the CORDIC submodule for evaluating the complex functions required by the Ziggurat NRNG submodule. The CORDIC submodule implements the architecture presented in Figure 2.3. In the hardware architecture of the Ziggurat NRNG submodule, independently working individual hardware blocks for the generation of normal random variates from the rectangular, tail, and wedge regions are implemented. The computation of the exponential and natural logarithmic functions while normal variates are generated from the wedge and tail regions of the distribution, respectively, is achieved with the CORDIC algorithm.

To further speed up the normal random number generation process in the Ziggurat NRNG submodule, an effective mechanism for the simultaneous access to the coefficients x_i and f_i is required. This is achieved by dividing the random index i in to even and odd values, and storing the respective x_i and f_i in separate memories (Figure 2.5). While the generated index i is an odd value, x_i and x_{i-1} are read from the odd and even memories at the same memory index positions simultaneously. However, if the generated index is with an even value, then x_i is read from the even memory and x_{i-1} is read from the odd memory at the next memory position in parallel. As a result, parallel access of the coefficients is achieved.

6 HARDWARE/SOFTWARE ARCHITECTURE

The global architecture of the proposed system for the PF in a grid based Fast SLAM algorithm is given in Figure 2.6. It comprises of an embedded Microblaze processor responsible for the execution of software functions, the PF hardware accelerator (PF HW accelerator) and, timer and UART cores with the purpose to help the analysis and verification of the system. The PF HW accelerator contains the CORDIC and the random number generator cores explained in section V, and they are connected to the Microblaze soft-core processor through a dedicated one-to- one communication bus (Fast simplex Link) for fast streaming of data.

To test the Grid-based Fast SLAM algorithm, real-time odometry and laser data collected from a mobile robot platform interfaces with random access memory (RAM) in order to synchronize data for processing. The odometry data are used in the sampling step to generate new particle instances, and the laser data are used in the importance weight step for the evaluation of particle weights. The particles and their associated weights are buffered to Block RAM for fast accessing. Individual

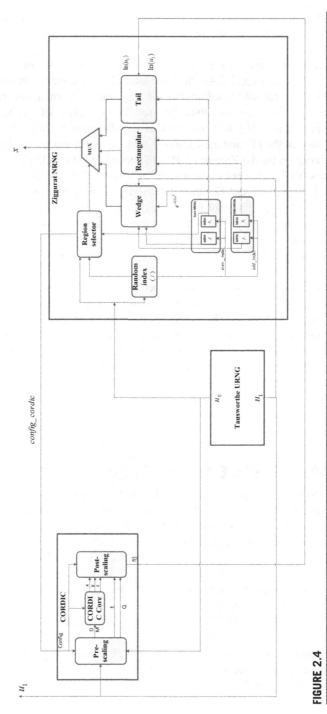

FIGURE 2.4

Hardware architecture for Gaussian and uniform random number generators

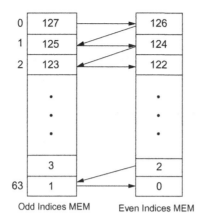

FIGURE 2.5

Illustration of the storage of the x_i and f_i coefficients in memory (MEM) and the parallel access of the x_i, x_{i-1}, f_i and f_{i-1} for $n=128$.

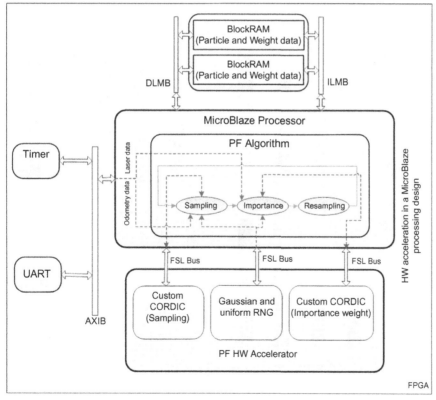

FIGURE 2.6

Global architecture of the hardware/software co-design system for PF.

CORDIC hardware modules are assigned to evaluate the functions in the sampling and importance weight steps. Uniform and Gaussian random numbers are provided to the resampling and sampling steps of the PF, respectively, by the random number generator module.

7 RESULTS AND DISCUSSION

The implementation of the architecture shown in Figure 2.6 is performed on a Xilinx Kintex-7 KC705 FPGA device running at 100 MHz. The design of the hardware modules is written in VHSIC Hardware Description Language (VHDL). For the implementation of the Ziggurat NRNG module, a value of $n = 128$ is used and, the x_i and f_i coefficients are represented as fixed-point numbers with $Q_{8:24}$ format (i.e., 8 bits for the integer part and 24 bits for the fractional part). The same fixed-point format is used for the representation of the data in the CORDIC module design. For the different variables in the software part of the algorithm, a 32-bit floating-point representation is used by enabling the floating-point unit (FPU) of the MicroBlaze processor.

Figure 2.7 summarizes the execution time given by the number of clock cycles for each step of the PF in the Grid-based Fast SLAM algorithm. The results show that the

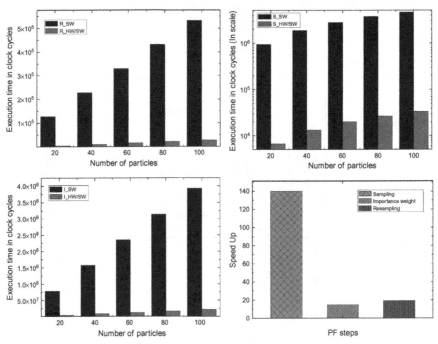

FIGURE 2.7

Comparison on execution times for the sampling (S), importance weight (I), and resampling (R) steps for embedded software implementation (SW) versus hardware/software (HW/SW)–embedded implementation and the corresponding increase in execution time.

hardware acceleration leads to greater speed in the execution time of the PF in all three steps of the algorithm. In particular, a significant speed-up is achieved in the sampling step, which can be attributed to the fast generation of Gaussian random numbers by the random number generator hardware module. Compared to the other steps, the importance weight step shows a relatively higher clock cycle, as shown in Figure 2.7. This is because for the evaluation of the weight of each particle in the importance weight step, first it is required to transform every laser scan measurement point of data (range and bearing angle) from a robot frame of reference to a global frame of reference, where normally more than hundreds of laser scan points have to be evaluated from the sensor. This requires the evaluation of the sine and cosine functions for every scan point. After this step comes a search for the closest point between every laser scan end point and occupied points in a map (which is a computationally intensive step). Though at this stage, this step is implemented in software in the embedded MicroBlaze processor, it is intended to speed up this process in hardware. Furthermore, the computation of an exponential function is required in the calculation of the weight of each particle for every laser scan points. These are the main reasons for the relatively large clock cycles obtained in the importance weight step.

8 CONCLUSIONS

This chapter presented techniques aimed to minimize the huge computational demand in PFs applied to a Grid-based Fast SLAM application. With initial identification of the computational bottlenecks in each step of the algorithm, techniques are proposed in order to tackle the computational bottlenecks of the algorithm. Based on the proposed techniques, and with a hardware/software codesign approach, hardware acceleration blocks are designed and implemented to speed up the computational time. The presented approach leads to an improvement in the speedup of $140\times$, $14.87\times$, and $19.36\times$ in the sampling, importance weight and resampling steps, respectively (Figure 2.7). Due to the flexibility in the hardware/software codesign and the presented approach, the acceleration in the computational time of other real-time particle filtering applications can be easily adopted following the approach presented here.

REFERENCES

Arulampalam, M.S., Maskell, S., Gordon, N., Clapp, T., 2002. A tutorial on particle filters for online nonlinear/non-Gaussian Bayesian tracking. IEEE Trans. Signal Process. 50 (2), 174–188.

Atia, M.M., Georgy, J., Korenberg, M.J., Noureldin, A., 2010. Real-time implementation of mixture particle filter for 3D RISS/GPS integrated navigation solution. Electron. Lett. 46 (15), 1083–1084.

Atia, M.M., Korenberg, M.J., Noureldin, A., 2012. Particle-Filter-Based WiFi-Aided Reduced Inertial Sensors Navigation System for Indoor and GPS-Denied Environments. International Journal of Navigation and Observation. 2012, Article ID 753206, 12 pages, http://dx.doi.org/10.1155/2012/753206.

Aulinas, J., Petillot, Y., Salvi, J., Lladò, X., 2008. The slam problem: a survey. In: Proceedings of the 2008 conference on Artificial Intelligence Research and Development, pp. 363–371.

Boudabous, A., Ghozzi, F., Kharrat, M.W., Masmoudi, N., 6–8 Dec. 2004. Implementation of hyperbolic functions using CORDIC algorithm. In: Microelectronics, 2004. ICM 2004 Proceedings. The 16th International Conference, pp. 738–741.

Chau, T.C.P., Niu, X., Eele, A., Luk, W., Cheung, P.Y.K., Maciejowski, J.M., Mar. 2013. Heterogeneous reconfigurable system for adaptive particle filters in real-time applications. In: Proc. Int. Conf. on Reconfigurable Computing: Architectures, Tools and Applications (ARC). Springer, pp. 1–12.

Chau, T.C.P., Luk, W., Cheung, P.Y.K., Eele, A., Maciejowski, J., 29–31 Aug. 2012. Adaptive Sequential Monte Carlo approach for real-time applications. In: Field Programmable Logic and Applications (FPL), 2012 22nd International Conference, pp. 527–530.

Chen, Z., Samarabandu, J., Rodrigo, R., 2007. Recent advances in simultaneous localization and map-building using computer vision. Adv. Robot. 21 (3–4), 233–265.

Doornik, J.A., 2005. An Improved Ziggurat Method to Generate Normal Random Samples. University of Oxford.

Douc, R., Cappe, O., 15–17 Sept. 2005. Comparison of resampling schemes for particle filtering. In: Image and Signal Processing and Analysis, 2005. ISPA 2005. Proceedings of the 4th International Symposium, pp. 64–69.

Ecuyer, P.L., 1996. Maximally equidistributed combined Tausworthe generators. Math. Comput. 65 (213), 203–213.

El-Halym, H.A.A., Mahmoud, I., Habib, S., 2012. Proposed hardware architectures of particle filter for object tracking. EURASIP J. Adv. Signal Process. 2012(17).

Fross, D., Langer, J., Fross, A., Rössler, M., Heinkel, U., 15–17 Sept. 2010. Hardware implementation of a Particle Filter for location estimation. In: Indoor Positioning and Indoor Navigation (IPIN), 2010 International Conference, pp. 1–6.

Georgy, J., Noureldin, A., Goodall, C., 2012. Vehicle navigator using a mixture particle filter for inertial sensors/odometer/map data/GPS integration. EEE Trans. Consum. Electron. 58 (2), 544–552.

Gokdemir, M., Vikalo, H., 17–21 May 2009. A particle filtering algorithm for parameter estimation in real-time biosensor arrays. In: Genomic Signal Processing and Statistics, 2009. GENSIPS 2009. IEEE International Workshop on, pp. 1–4.

Gordon, N.J., Salmond, D.J., Smith, A.F.M., 1993. Novel approach to nonlinear/non-Gaussian Bayesian state estimation. IEE proc. 140 (2), 107–113.

Grisetti, G., Stachniss, C., Burgard, W., 2007. Improved techniques for grid mapping with Rao-Blackwellized particle filters. IEEE Trans. Robot. 23 (1), 34–46.

Gustafsson, F., 2010. Particle filter theory and practice with positioning applications. IEEE Aero. Electron. Syst. Mag. 25 (7), 53–82.

Happe, M., et al., 2011. A self-adaptive heterogeneous multi-core architecture for embedded real-time video object tracking. J. Real Time Image Process.

Lakshmi, B., Dhar, A.S., 2010. CORDIC architectures: a survey. VLSI Des. 2010, Article ID 794891, 19 pages.

Li, S.-A., Hsu, C.-C., Lin, W.-L., Wang, J.-P., 8–10 June 2011. Hardware/software co-design of particle filter and its application in object tracking. In: System Science and Engineering (ICSSE), 2011 International Conference, pp. 87–91.

Liu, X., Niranjan, M., 2012. State and parameter estimation of the heat shock response system using Kalman and particle filters,. Bioinformatics 28, 1501–1507.

Marsaglia, G., Tsang, W.W., 2000. The ziggurat method for generating random variables. J. Stat. Soft. 5, 1–7.

Medeiros, H., Park, J., Kak, A., 23–28 June 2008. A parallel color-based particle filter for object tracking. In: Computer Vision and Pattern Recognition Workshops, 2008. CVPRW '08. IEEE Computer Society Conference on, pp. 1–8.

Meinhold, R.J., Singpurwalla, N.D., 1989. Robustification of Kalman filter models. J. Am. Stat. Assoc. 84, 479–486.

Nakamura, K., Yoshida, R., Nagasaki, M., Miyano, S., Higuchi, T., 2009. Parameter estimation of in silico biological pathways with particle filtering towards a petascale computing. Pac. Symp. Biocomput. 14, 227–238.

Nordlund, P.-J., Gustafsson, F., 2001. Sequential Monte Carlo filtering techniques applied to integrated navigation systems. In: American Control Conference, 2001. Proceedings of the 2001, vol. 6, pp. 4375–4380.

Ristic, B., Arulampalam, S., Gordon, N.J., 2004. Beyond the Kalman Filter: Particle Filters for Tracking Applications. Artech House Publishers, Norwood, MA.

Saha, S., Bambha, N.K., Bhattacharyya, S.S., 2010. Design and implementation of embedded computer vision system based on particle filters. Comput. Vis. Image Understand. 114 (11), 1203–1214.

Sileshi, B.G., Ferrer, C., Oliver, J., 24–27 Jul. 2014. Hardware/software co-design of particle filter in grid based Fast-SLAM algorithm. In: International Conference on Embedded Systems and Applications (ESA), 2014 Conference.

Sileshi, B.G., Ferrer, C., Oliver, J., 8–10 Oct. 2013. Particle filters and resampling techniques: Importance in computational complexity analysis. In: Design and Architectures for Signal and Image Processing (DASIP), 2013 Conference, pp. 319–325.

Thrun, S., 2002. Robotic mapping: a survey. In: Lakemeyer, G., Nebel, B. (Eds.), Exploring Artificial Intelligence in the New Millenium. Morgan Kaufmann, San Mateo, CA, pp. 1–35.

Thrun, S., Burgard, W., Fox, D., August 2005. Probabilistic Robotics (Intelligent Robotics and Autonomous Agents series). Intelligent Robotics and Autonomous Agents. The MIT Press.

Volder, J.E., Sept 1959. The CORDIC trigonometric computing technique. IRE Trans. Electron. Comput. 330–334.

Walther, J.S., 1971. A unified algorithm for elementary functions. In: Proceedings of the Spring Joint Computer Conference, pp. 379–385.

Yang, J., Kadirkamanathan, V., Billings, S.A., 2007. In vivo intracellular metabolite dynamics estimation by sequential Monte Carlo filter. In: IEEE Symposium on Computational Intelligence, Bioinformatics and Computational Biology, pp. 387–394.

Ye, B., Zhang, Y., 26–30 Oct. 2009. Improved FPGA implementation of particle filter for radar tracking applications. In: Synthetic Aperture Radar, 2009. APSAR 2009. 2nd Asian-Pacific Conference, pp. 943–946.

Biological Study on Pulsatile Flow of Herschel-Bulkley Fluid in Tapered Blood Vessels

3

R. Ponalagusamy

Department of Mathematics, National Institute of Technology, Tiruchirappalli, Tamilnadu, India

1 INTRODUCTION

The presence of constriction (medically called *stenosis*) in the lumen of an artery disturbs the normal blood flow and causes arterial diseases (myocardial infarction, hypertension, and cerebral strokes). It is believed that hydrodynamic factors (e.g., wall shear stress) play a pivotal role in the development and progression of arterial stenosis. It is further evident that the investigation of blood flow in tapered arteries could play an important role in the fundamental understanding, diagnosis, and treatment of many cardiovascular diseases (Chaturani and Ponnalagarsamy, 1983; Dwivedi *et al.*, 1982; Ponnalagarsamy and Kawahara, 1989). Looking at the immense importance of the fundamental understanding of blood flow, the objective of this analysis is motivated to provide a generalized model of blood and obtain some information about the flow.

Chakravarthy and Mandal (2000), How and Black (1987), Mandal (2005), Oka (1973), and Oka and Murata (1969) studied the flow of blood through tapered arteries by treating blood as a Newtonian fluid, Bingham plastic fluid, Power-law fluid, and Casson fluid, and they found the relationship between the flow rate and pressure drop. Scott Blair and Spanner (1974) suggested that blood obeys Casson's model only for moderate shear rate flows, and that there is no difference between Casson's and Herschel-Bulkley plots over the range where Casson's plot is valid (for blood). Furthermore, Sacks *et al.* (1963) have experimentally pointed out that blood shows behavior characteristic of a combination of Bingham plastic and pseudoplastic fluid–Herschel-Bulkley fluid with the fluid behavior index greater than unity. In view of the experimental observation (Sacks *et al.*, 1963) and a suggestion made in Scott Blair and Spanner (1974), it is pertinent to consider the behavior of blood as a Herschel-Bulkley fluid. Based on the foregoing views, it is worthwhile to describe a model taking the factors of pulsatility, nonuniform cross-section of a tube, and non-Newtonian character into the present analysis and study the flow characteristics.

The studies performed by Chaturani and Ponnalagarsamy (1986), Aroesty and Gross (1972a,b), Sankar and Hemalatha (2006, 2007) and Dash et al. (1999) reveal that they adopted a standard perturbation technique and obtained an approximate solution in which the flow characteristics are expressed as asymptotic natures in powers of the Womersley number α (Womersley, 1955). Rohlf and Tenti (2001) argued that the use of the Womersley number as a perturbation parameter to produce approximate solutions of the pulsatile flow of non-Newtonian fluid is not suitable; and considering the Reynolds number (ε) as a perturbation parameter, they made an attempt to validate their results through their perturbation theory in comparison with a numerical integration of the full mathematical model for blood flow.

It is further observed that the Womersley number α is not dependent on the flow velocity, and consequently, the same value of α can represent massively different flow conditions; hence, the Womersley number α is not an appropriate perturbation parameter. Sankar and Hemalatha (2006, 2007) and Sankar (2011) analyzed the pulsatile flow of Herschel-Bulkley fluid through the arteries. It is pertinent to point out here that the analytic expressions for flow variables such as velocity, wall shear stress, and flow rate obtained by Sankar and Hemalatha (2006, 2007), Sankar (2011), and by the present investigation, respectively, are entirely different. The reason is that they neglected the higher-order terms in the binomial expansion of the relationship between the velocity gradient and the shear stress involved the constitutive equation of Herschel-Bulkley fluid. Hence, the results obtained by Sankar and Hemalatha (2006, 2007) and Sankar (2011) do not represent the actual behavior of biorheological flow characteristics. Also, they have not derived the analytic expression for flow resistance. In view of this circumstance, we sought approximate solutions to the nonlinearity of the equation of motion (involved in this analysis) in terms of the Reynolds number (ε) as the perturbation parameter and derived the analytic expressions for velocity profile, wall shear stress, flow rate, and mean flow resistance. Further, an effort has been made to investigate the influence of the tapered angle on the flow-resistance and stream-line patterns.

The combined effects of the non-Newtonian behavior of the blood, taper angle, and the axial distance have been discussed. Section 2 of this chapter deals with the general mathematical formulation of the problem, in which the equation of motion using Herschel– Bulkley's constitutive equation and the nondimensionalization procedure are given. In section 3, the analytic expressions for flow quantities such as velocity, flow rate, wall shear stress, and flow resistance are obtained. Comparison between the velocities obtained by the present mathematical model and the experimental observation is made, and the effects of parameters of the present study on wall shear stress and flow resistance are discussed and analyzed in section 4. Finally, in section 5, the main conclusions of the work are drawn and the future research works have been indicated.

2 FORMULATION OF THE PROBLEM

Consider a laminar, pulsatile, and fully developed flow of blood (i.e., Herschel-Bulkley fluid) in the z^* -direction through a slightly tapered artery, as shown in Figure 3.1. The wall profile of the flow geometry may mathematically be described as

$$R^*(z^*) = R_0^* - z^* \tan\phi, \tag{3.1}$$

where $R^*(z^*)$ is the radius of the tube in the tapered section, R_0^* is the radius of the tube in the normal region, z^* is the axial direction, and ϕ is the angle of taper. Further, L_1^* represents the axial distance of the cross section between $z^* = 0$ and the cone apex, and L_2^* indicates the axial distance of any cross section at z^* from the apex. We shall take cylindrical coordinate system (r^*, ϕ^*, z^*), whose origin is located on the tube axis.

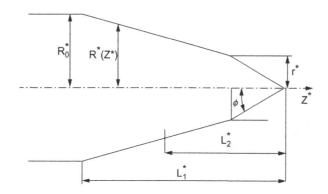

FIGURE 3.1

Geometry of tapered tube.

Let us introduce the following nondimensional variables:

$$r = \frac{r^*}{R_0^*}, z = \frac{z^*}{R_0^*}, t = \frac{t^*}{T^*}, u = \frac{u^*}{U_0^*}, \theta = \frac{\tau_y^*}{\left(\mu^* \frac{U_0^*}{R_0^*}\right)}, \tau = \frac{\tau^*}{\left(\mu^* \frac{U_0^*}{R_0^*}\right)}, p = \frac{p^*}{\left(\mu^* \frac{U_0^*}{R_0^*}\right)}, \tag{3.2}$$

where T^* is the characteristic time; μ^* the Newtonian viscosity; U_0^* the characteristic velocity, which is expressed by the relation $R_0^* = U_0^* T^*$; u^* the axial component of the velocity; t^* the time; r^* the radial direction; τ_y^* the yield stress; p^* the fluid pressure; and τ^* the shear stress. (* over a letter denotes the dimensional form of the corresponding quantity.) Further, θ is the dimensionless yield stress.

Based on the discussions made by Oka (1973), Oka and Murata (1969) and Ponalagusamy (1986), the radial velocity is negligibly small and can be neglected for a low Reynolds number flow through a tapered tube with an angle of taper up to 2^0. Since the lumen radius is very small in comparison with the wavelength of the pressure wave, equation of motion in the radial direction reduced to $-\frac{\partial p}{\partial r} = 0$, and hence the fluid pressure becomes a function of the axial distance (z) and time (t).

Keeping these in mind, and using nondimensional variables, the momentum equations governing the flow are given as

$$\varepsilon \frac{\partial u}{\partial t} = \beta q(z) f(t) + \frac{1}{r} \frac{\partial}{\partial r}[r\tau], \tag{3.3}$$

$$\frac{\partial u}{\partial r} = \frac{1}{k}\left[1 - \frac{\theta}{|\tau|}\right]^n |\tau|^{n-1}\tau, \quad if\, |\tau| \geq \theta \tag{3.4}$$

$$= 0, \quad if\, |\tau| \leq \theta, \tag{3.5}$$

where

$$k = \left(\frac{k^*}{\mu^*}\right)\left(\frac{R_0^*}{U_0^*\mu^*}\right)^{n-1}, \quad \varepsilon = U_0^* R_0^* \frac{\rho^*}{\mu^*}, \quad \beta = \frac{q_0^* R_0^{*2}}{\mu^* U_0^*}, \quad q(z) = -\frac{\partial p}{\partial z} = \frac{q^*(z^*)}{q_0^*}.$$

In that expression, $f(t) = 1 + A\sin(\Omega t)$, k^* is the consistency index of blood, n is the Power-law index, $q^*(z^*)$ is the pressure gradient in the tapered arterial region, and q_0^* is the constant pressure gradient in the normal tube region. Eqs. (3.4) and (3.5) are reduced to that for a Bingham fluid, when $n = 1.0$, to that for a Power-law fluid when $\theta = 0.0$, and to that for a Newtonian fluid when $n = 1.0$ and $\theta = 0.0$. Here, $\Omega = \frac{\omega^* R_0^*}{U_0^*}$ is the Strouhal number, where ω^* is the frequency of the oscillations of the flow. The dimensionless parameter ε is the Reynolds number of the flow. Taking $\beta = 1$, characteristic velocity U_0^* is expressed as

$$U_0^* = \frac{q_0^* R_0^{*2}}{\mu^*} \tag{3.6}$$

Consistency then requires that the time scale be derived as

$$T^* = \frac{\mu^*}{q_0^* R_0^*} \tag{3.7}$$

The geometry of the tapered tube in dimensionless form is given by

$$R(z) = 1 - z\tan\phi \tag{3.8}$$

The boundary conditions in dimensionless form are

$$\text{(i)}\ \tau \text{ is finite at } r = 0 \text{ and (ii)}\ u = 0 \text{ at } r = R(z) \tag{3.9}$$

The volumetric flow rate $Q(t)$ is given by

$$Q(t) = 2 \int_0^{R(z)} ru(r, z, t)dr \tag{3.10}$$

As mentioned elsewhere (Ponnalagarsamy and Kawahara, 1989), we take

$$R(z) = 1 - z\phi \text{ and } z = L_1 - L_2 \tag{3.11}$$

3 SOLUTION

The flow variable G is assumed to have the following form:

$$G(r,z,t) = G_0(r,z,t) + \varepsilon G_1(r,z,t) + O(\varepsilon^2), \tag{3.12}$$

where $G(r,z,t)$ refers to the velocity and shear stress. In what follows, for convenience, we write only function notation deleting its variables. Substituting Eqs. (3.4)–(3.5) into Eq. (3.3) and integrating twice with the help of the boundary conditions [Eq. (3.9)], the analytic expression for velocity distribution may be obtained as follows:

$$u = \frac{(qf)^n(1-z\phi)^{n+1}}{k(n+1)2^n}\left[(1-S)^{n+1} - (r/(1-z\phi)-S)^{n+1} + \left\{n\varepsilon A\Omega\cos(\Omega t)(1-z\phi)^{n+1}/2kf\right\}(qf)^{n-1}.\right.$$

$$\left[(1-S)^n(n+S)\left\{\frac{(1-S)^{n+1} - \left(\frac{r}{(1-z\phi)}-S\right)^{n+1}}{n+1} + \left((1-S)^n - \left(\frac{r}{(1-z\phi)}-S\right)^n\right)/n\right.\right.$$

$$\left.-\frac{n}{(n+1)(n+3)}\left(1-\left(\frac{r}{(1-z\phi)}\right)^{2n+2}\right)\right\} + \frac{S(4n^3+8n^2-6n-6)}{(n+2)(n+3)(2n+1)}\left(1-\left(\frac{r}{(1-z\phi)}\right)^{2n+1}\right)$$

$$-2S^2\sum_{j=0}^{2n-1}\frac{(-1)^j(2n)c_jS^j}{(2n-j)}\left(1-\left(\frac{r}{(1-z\phi)}\right)^{2n-j}\right)\left\{\frac{(2n+1)(2n+2)}{(j+1)(j+2)(n+3)}-\frac{(2n+1)^2}{(j+1)(n+2)}+1\right\}$$

$$\left.\left.+\frac{6(-1)^{2n}}{(n+2)(n+3)}S^{2n+2}\log\left(\frac{r}{(1-z\phi)}\right)\right]\right]$$

$$\tag{3.13}$$

Multiplying Eq. (3.13) by r and integrating with respect to r, the analytic expression for a stream function $\psi(r,z)$ may be obtained. Invoking Eq. (3.10) into Eq. (3.13), after tedious manipulation, the analytic expression for flow rate is obtained as

$$Q(t) = \frac{(qf)^n[(1-z\phi)]^{3+n}}{2^{n-1}k(n+1)(n+2)(n+3)}\left[(1-S)^{n+1}\{(n+2)(n+1)+2S(n+1+S)\}\right.$$

$$+\frac{n\varepsilon A\Omega\cos(\Omega t)k\{1-z\phi\}^2}{2^{2n-2}f}[qf_1(1-z\phi)]^{n-1}\left[(1-S)^{2n}(n+S)\right.$$

$$\left\{(n+2)+3S+\frac{6S^2}{n(n+1)}(1+S)\right\}-n(1-S^{2n+4})+\frac{S(4n^3+8n^2-6n-6)}{(2n+3)}$$

$$(1-S^{2n+3})-3S^{2n+2}(1-S^2)-2S^2\sum_{j=0}^{2n-1}\frac{(-1)^j(2n)c_jS^j}{(2n+2-j)}\left\{\frac{(2n+1)(2n+2)(n+2)}{(j+1)(j+2)}\right.$$

$$\left.\left.\left.-\frac{(n+3)(2n+1)^2}{(j+1)}+(n+2)(n+3)(1-S^{2n+2-j})\right\}\right]\right],$$

$$\tag{3.14}$$

where $S = 2\theta/\{qf_1(1-z\phi)\}$.

It is of interest to note that the Womersley number α is obtained as

$\alpha = (\varepsilon\Omega)^{\frac{1}{2}} = R_0^* \left(\frac{w^*}{\gamma^*}\right)^{\frac{1}{2}}$, where γ^* is the kinematic viscosity.

The steady flow rate Q_s is expressed as

$$Q_s = \frac{q^n\{(1-z\phi)\}^{3+n}}{2^{n-1}k(n+1)(n+2)(n+3)} \left[\left\{1 - \frac{2\theta}{q(1-z\phi)}\right\}^{n+1}\right. $$
$$\left. \left\{(n+2)(n+1) + \left\{\frac{4\theta}{q(1-z\phi)}\right\}\left\{n+1+\frac{2\theta}{q(1-z\phi)}\right\}\right\}\right]. \tag{3.15}$$

The shear stress on the wall τ_w is a physiologically important quantity, given by

$$\tau_w = \frac{qf(1-z\phi)}{2}\left[1 + \frac{\varepsilon A\Omega\cos(\Omega t)\{1-z\phi\}^{n+1}\left\{\frac{qf}{2}\right\}^{n-1}}{2^{n+1}(n+1)(n+2)(n+3)f}\cdot\{1-S^n\}\left\{\begin{array}{l}n(n+1)(n+2)+\\3n(n+1)S+6nS^2+6S^3\end{array}\right\}\right]. \tag{3.16}$$

It is pertinent to mention here that Chaturani and Ponnalagarsamy (1986) explained the method of calculating the value of the steady pressure gradient $q(z)$ for any value of θ using Eq. (3.14).

The flow resistance λ is defined as

$$\lambda = \frac{f(t)\Delta p}{Q(t)}, \tag{3.17}$$

where Δp is the pressure drop.

The mean flow resistance over the period of the flow cycle is defined as

$$\bar{\lambda} = \frac{1}{2\pi}\int_0^{2\pi}\left(\frac{p_0-p_1}{Q(t)}\right)f(t)dt. \tag{3.18}$$

For any value of S, one can numerically compute the values of the flow resistance λ and the mean flow resistance $\bar{\lambda}$, respectively, from Eqs. (3.17) and (3.18) for different values of the parameters involved in this investigation. It is mathematically and physiologically important to obtain an analytic expression for the mean flow resistance. Eqs. (3.14) and (3.18) reveal that it is not possible to obtain the analytic expression for the mean flow resistance for any value of S. For small values of S [with fluid having low yield stress value (θ), such as blood (Sacks et al., 1963)], the analytic expression for the mean flow resistance from Eqs. (3.14) and (3.18) may be obtained as

$$\bar{\lambda} = \left(\frac{n}{3\phi}\right)(2^n k(n+3))^{\frac{1}{n}}\bar{Q}\left\{\left(\frac{1}{1-z\phi}\right)^{3/n} - 1\right\} + \left\{\frac{2(n+3)\theta Q^*}{\phi(n+2)}\right\}\log\left(\frac{1}{1-z\phi}\right), \tag{3.19}$$

where

$$\bar{Q} = \frac{1}{2\pi}\int_0^{2\pi}\frac{dt}{[Q(t)]^{1-\frac{1}{n}}} \text{ and } Q^* = \frac{1}{2\pi}\int_0^{2\pi}\frac{dt}{Q(t)}.$$

The values of $\bar{Q}$ and Q^* are to be numerically computed after computing the value of steady pressure gradient $q(z)$ using Eq. (3.15) for different values of the parameter involved in the present paper.

4 DISCUSSION

The results of a comparison between the velocity profiles for Newtonian, Power-law, Bingham plastic, and Herschel-Bulkley fluids obtained from the present study and the experimental data (Ponalagusamy, 1986) is shown in Figure 3.2. The graph reveals that blood behaves more like a Herschel-Bulkley fluid than like Bingham plastic, Power-law, and Newtonian fluids.

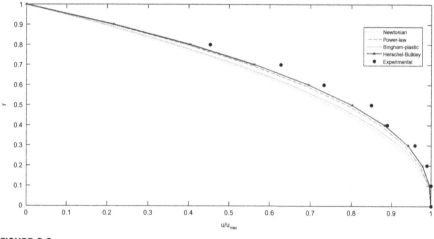

FIGURE 3.2

Comparison of velocity profiles for various fluids with experimental results.

It is of interest to note from Figure 3.3 that the flow rate decreases with the increase in the axial distance (Z) and taper angle. The percentage of decrease in the flow rate as the value of Z increases is found to be higher for higher values of the taper angle.

The analytic expression for wall shear stress is derived and its variation with the axial distance and the taper angle has been studied (see Figure 3.4). This graph shows that as the taper angle increases, the rate of increase in the wall shear stress with respect to an increase in the axial distance Z is found to be very significant. Another pivotal result is concerning the variation of mean flow resistance $(\bar{\lambda})$ with respect to the taper for different values as the axial distance (Z) and it is shown in Figure 3.5. The mean flow resistance increases as the value of the taper angle increases. The main effect of pulsatility on the flow is the phase lag between the pressure gradient

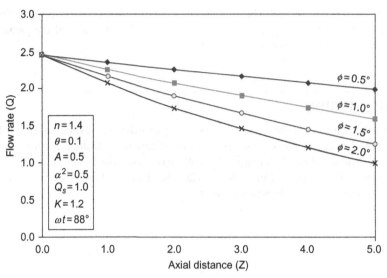

FIGURE 3.3

Variation of flow rate with axial distance for different values of the taper angle.

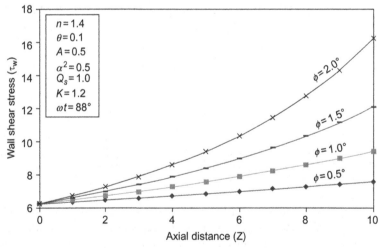

FIGURE 3.4

Variation of wall shear stress with axial distance for different values of the taper angle.

and flow rate and wall shear stress. It can be seen from the present analysis that the phase lag between pressure gradient and flow rate (or wall shear stress) has been found to be 2.03 deg, and its value is unaltered as the values of axial distance and taper angle increase or decrease. It may be important to note that many standard results regarding steady and uniform tube flow of Power-law, Bingham, and Newtonian fluids can be obtained as special cases in the present investigation.

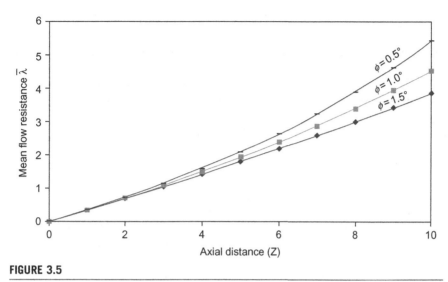

FIGURE 3.5

Variation of mean flow resistance with axial distance for different values of the taper angle.

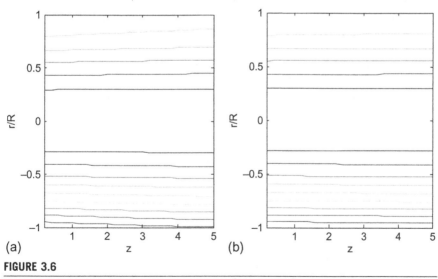

FIGURE 3.6

Stream lines for different values of ϕ (a) $\phi= 0.5^0$, (b) $\phi = 2^0$.

The influence of the taper angle (ϕ) on the stream-line pattern has been analyzed for a given value of $n=1.4, K=1.2, \theta=0.1, A=0.5, \alpha^2 =0.5, Q_s =1.0$ and $\Omega t = 88°$, and shown in Figure 3.6. It is observed that the value of stream function decreases as the taper angle (ϕ) increases.

5 CONCLUSION

The main objective of this investigation was studying the problem of pulsatile flow of blood (Herschel-Bulkley fluid) through a tapered arterial stenosis. A perturbation technique was adopted to study the flow. The analytical expressions for velocity, flow rate, wall shear stress, and mean flow resistance were obtained, and the results depicted in graphs. Using the finite volume technique, the quasi-steady, nonlinear, coupled, implicit system of differential equations has been solved numerically and the axial velocity computed. It is verified that the error between the axial velocities obtained by the present perturbation method and the numerical technique becomes less than 1.052% for the values of α^2 between 0.0 and 1.0. Furthermore, the error becomes more than 9.0% when α^2 is greater than 2.10.

When the flow characteristics are expressed in terms of α^2, the present perturbation results coincide with the results found in other papers (Sankar and Hemalatha, 2006, 2007). Hence, our predictions coincide with theirs and further comparison is unnecessary, so long as $\alpha^2 < 1.0$. Further, their predictions are valid when the Reynolds number is small (<10) since the Strouhal number Ω is unity in their analyses. But our approach is applicable even to larger blood vessel and moderate Reynolds numbers. One of the most remarkable merits of the present perturbation scheme is that it is very suitable to any mathematical models of blood flow in tubes with uniform and nonuniform cross sections compared to the models developed by others (Chaturani and Ponnalagarsamy, 1986; Aroesty and Gross, 1972a, 1972b; Sankar and Hemalatha, 2006, 2007; Sankar, 2011).

The theoretically computed velocity profiles were compared with the experimental data, and it was observed that blood behaves like a Herschel-Bulkley fluid rather than Power-law or Bingham fluid. The increase in the taper angle (ϕ) leads to a decrease in the flow rate, wall shear stress, and resistance to flow. It is evident that for abnormal hearts, an increase in shear stress on the blood vessel could be very dangerous, as it can result in paralysis or ultimate death. The resistance to flow is one of the physiologically important flow variables to be investigated because it indicates whether the required amount of blood supply to vital organs is ensured (Ponalagusamy, 2007, 2012; Chaturani and Ponnalagarsamy, 1984).

It is well established that hemodynamic factors (such as wall shear stress, flow resistance) play a key role in the development and progression of arterial diseases (Fry, 1973). Caro *et al.* (1971) experimentally demonstrated that during the initial stage of arterial disease, there may be an important intercorrelation between atherogenesis and detailed characteristics of blood flow through the damaged, diseased, or otherwise affected artery. Keeping in view the importance of hemodynamic and rheologic factors in the understanding of blood flow and arteriosclerostic diseases, it may be said that the important results obtained in this analysis could be helpful to acquire knowledge regarding the characteristics of blood flow. Hence, the present investigation could be useful for analyzing the blood flow through a tube of nonuniform cross section, which in turn could lead to the development of new diagnostic tools for the effective treatment of patients suffering from cancer, hypertension, myocardial infarction, stroke, and paralysis.

Zamir (2000) pointed out that the oscillatory nature of pulsatile flow of blood prompts other forces, apart from driving and retarding forces in the case of steady flow, and other variables and the heat and mass transport through endothelial cells lying in the inner layer of the vessel wall is very much altered when viscoelastic properties of blood and its vessel wall have been taken into account. When artery walls are viscoelastic, a 10% variation in the artery radius over a cardiac cycle is typically observed and the shear stress at the wall is primarily affected by the radial wall motion in comparison with that of rigid arteries. Bugliarello and Sevilla (1970) and Bugliarello and Hayden (1963) have experimentally observed that there exists a cell-free plasma layer near the wall when blood flows through arteries. It is well understood that blood consists of a suspension of a variety of cells. Hookes *et al.* (1972) pointed out that the microrotation and spinning velocity of blood cells increase flow resistance and wall shear stress. In view of their experiments and the aforementioned arguments, it is preferable to represent the flow of blood through arteries with their viscoelastic nature by a two-layered model instead of one layer and the rheology of blood as a micropolar viscoelastic fluid while investigating the realistic mathematical model on investigating blood flow. Hence, a modest effort will be made to investigate the problem of blood flow by incorporating the factors mentioned in this chapter (two or three factors at a time, since it is impossible to consider all the factors simultaneously) and the numerical findings will be published in the future.

REFERENCES

Aroesty, J., Gross, J.F., 1972a. The mechanics of pulsatile flow in small vessel-I, Casson Theory. Microvasc. Res. 4, 1–12.

Aroesty, J., Gross, J.F., 1972b. Pulsatile flow in small blood vessels-I, Casson Theory. Biorheology 9, 33–43.

Bugliarello, G., Hayden, J.W., 1963. Detailed characteristics of the flow of blood in vitro. J. Rheol. 7, 209–230.

Bugliarello, G., Sevilla, J., 1970. Velocity distribution and other characteristics of steady and pulsatile blood flow in fine glass tubes. Biorheology 17, 85–107.

Caro, C.G., Fitzgerald, J.M., Schroter, R.C., 1971. Atheroma and arterial wall: observation, correlation and proposal of a shear dependent mass transfer mechanism of atherogenesis. Proc. Roy. Soc. Lond. B 177, 109–159.

Chakravarthy, S., Mandal, P.K., 2000. Two dimensional blood flow through tapered arteries under stenotic conditions. Int. J. Non Linear Mech. 35, 779–793.

Chaturani, P., Ponnalagarsamy, R., 1983. Dilatency effects of blood on flow through arterial stenosis. In: Proceedings of the Twenty Eighth Congress of the Indian Society of Theoretical and Applied Mechanics. IIT Kharagpur, India, pp. 87–96.

Chaturani, P., Ponnalagarsamy, R., 1984. Analysis of pulsatile blood flow through stenosed arteries and its applications to cardiovascular diseases. In: Proceedings of 13th National Conference on Fluid Mechanics and Fluid Power (FMFP-1984). REC, Tiruchirappalli, India, pp. 463–468.

Chaturani, P., Ponnalagarsamy, R., 1986. Pulsatile flow of Casson's fluid through stenosed arteries with applications to blood flow. Biorheology 23, 499–511.

Dash, R.K., Jayaraman, G., Mehta, K.N., 1999. Flow in a catheterized curved artery with stenosis. J. Biomech. 32, 49–61.

Dwivedi, A.P., Pal, T.S., Rakesh, L., 1982. Micropolar fluid model for blood flow through a small tapered Tube. Indian J. Techn. 20, 295–299.

Fry, D.L., 1973. Responses of the arterial wall to certain physical factors: in atherogenesis: initiating factors. Ciba Found. Symp. 12, 93–125.

Hookes, L.E., Nerem, R.M., Benson, T.J., 1972. A momentum integral solution for pulsatile flow in a rigid tube with and without longitudinal vibration. Int. J. Eng. Sci. 10, 989–1007.

How, T.V., Black, R.A., 1987. Pressure losses in non-Newtonian flow through rigid wall tapered tubes. Biorheology 24, 337–351.

Mandal, P.K., 2005. An unsteady analysis of non-Newtonian blood flow through tapered arteries with stenosis. Int. J. Non Linear Mech. 40, 151–164.

Oka, S., 1973. Pressure development in a non-Newtonian flow through a tapered tube. Biorheology 10, 207–212.

Oka, S., Murata, T., 1969. Theory of the steady slow motion of non-Newtonian fluids through a tapered tube. Jpn. J. Appl. Phys. 8, 5–8.

Ponalagusamy, R., 1986. Blood Flow Through Stenosed Tube. PhD thesis, IIT, Bombay, India.

Ponalagusamy, R., 2007. Blood flow through an artery with mild stenosis: a two-layered model, different shapes of stenoses and slip velocity at the wall. J. Appl. Sci. 7, 1071–1077.

Ponalagusamy, R., 2012. Mathematical analysis on effect of non-Newtonian behavior of blood on optimal geometry of microvascular bifurcation system. J. Franklin Inst. 349, 2861–2874.

Ponnalagarsamy, R., Kawahara, M., 1989. A finite element analysis of unsteady flows of viscoelastic fluids through channels with non-uniform cross-sections. Int. J. Numer. Meth. Fluid. 9, 1487–1501.

Rohlf, K., Tenti, G., 2001. The role of the Womersley number in pulsatile blood flow: a theoretical study of the Casson model. J. Biomech. 34, 141–148.

Sacks, A.H., Raman, K.R., Burnell, J.A., Tickner, E.G., 1963. Auscultatory Versus Direct Pressure Measurements for Newtonian Fluids and for Blood in Simulated Arteries, VIDYA Report #119, Dec. 30.

Sankar, D.S., 2011. Two-phase non-linear model for blood flow in asymmetric and axisymmetric stenosed arteries. Int. J. Non Linear Mech. 46, 296–305.

Sankar, D.S., Hemalatha, K., 2006. Pulsatile flow of Herschel-Bulkley fluid through stenosed arteries – a mathematical model. Int. J. Non Linear Mech. 41, 979–990.

Sankar, D.S., Hemalatha, K., 2007. Pulsatile flow of Herschel-Bulkley fluid through catheterized arteries-a mathematical model. Appl. Math. Model. 31, 1497–1517.

Scott Blair, G.W., Spanner, D.C., 1974. An Introduction to Biorheology. Elsevier Scientific Publishing Company, Amsterdam, Oxford, pp. 1–163.

Womersley, J.R., 1955. Method for the calculation of velocity, rate of flow and viscous drag in the arteries when the pressure gradient is known. J. Physiol. 127, 553–562.

Zamir, A., 2000. The Physics of Pulsatile Flow. Springer-Verlag, New York.

Hierarchical *k*-Means: A Hybrid Clustering Algorithm and Its Application to Study Gene Expression in Lung Adenocarcinoma

Mohammad Shabbir Hasan and Zhong-Hui Duan

*Department of Computer Science, College of Arts and Sciences, University of Akron,
Akron, USA*

1 INTRODUCTION

Gene products such as proteins or RNA are created from the inheritable information contained in a gene (Hunter and Holm, 1992). Traditional molecular biology focuses on studying individual genes in isolation for determining gene functions. However, it is not suitable for determining complex gene interactions or for explaining the nature of complex biological processes due to the large number of genes. For this purpose, examining the expression pattern of a large number of genes in parallel is required (Michaels *et al.*, 1998). With the advancement of large-scale transcription profiling technology, DNA microarrays have become a useful tool that allows the analysis of the gene expression pattern at the genome level (Gresham *et al.*, 2008). In genetic-mapping studies, DNA microarrays have been widely used on polymorphisms between parental genotypes and have facilitated the discovery of gene expression markers (Gresham *et al.*, 2008; Wang *et al.*, 2009). Due to its importance, efficient algorithms are necessary to analyze the DNA microarray data set accurately (Hasan, 2013). Studies have showed that a group of genes with similar gene expressions are likely to have related gene functions (Mount, 2004). Therefore, how to find the genes that share similar expression patterns across samples is an important question that is frequently asked in the DNA microarray studies (Qin *et al.*, 2014).

Clustering, which is a useful technique to constitute unknown groupings of objects (Kaufman and Rousseeuw, 2009), has become an important part of gene expression data analysis (Qin *et al.*, 2014; Eisen *et al.*, 1998). By investigating the clusters of genes having similar expression patterns across samples, researchers can elucidate gene functions, genetic pathways, and regulatory circuits. Clustering helps to find a distinct pattern for each cluster, as well as more information about functional similarities and gene interactions within the cluster (Hasan and Duan, 2014). For clustering DNA microarray data, a good number of algorithms have been developed that include *k*-means (Tavazoie *et al.*, 1999), hierarchical clustering (Eisen *et al.*, 1998; Luo *et al.*, 2003; Wen *et al.*, 1998), self-organizing maps (Tamayo *et al.*, 1999; Törönen *et al.*, 1999; He *et al.*, 2003), support vector machines (Brown *et al.*, 2000), Bayesian networks (Friedman *et al.*, 2000), and fuzzy logic approach (Woolf and Wang, 2000). In addition to these algorithms, there are others that use genomic information, along with gene expression data, to improve clustering efficiency. Algorithms that fall into this category include an ontology-driven clustering algorithm (Wang *et al.*, 2005) and the ones that use information about TS2 upstream regions of the coding sequences and gene expression profiles to get more biologically relevant clusters (Holmes and Bruno, 2000; Barash and Friedman, 2002; Kasturi *et al.*, 2003).

Among the existing clustering algorithms, *k*-means and hierarchical clustering algorithms are the most commonly used. *k*-means is computationally faster than hierarchical clustering and produces tighter clusters than the hierarchical clustering algorithm. On the other hand, the hierarchical clustering algorithm computes a complete hierarchy of clusters and hence is more informative than *k*-means. Despite these advantages, both of these algorithms suffer from some limitations. The performance of *k*-means clustering depends on how effectively the initial number of clusters (i.e., the value of *k*) is determined, and the advantage of hierarchical clustering comes at the cost of low efficiency. Moreover, being computationally expensive, both of these algorithms impede the wide use of these algorithms in gene expression data analysis (Garai and Chaudhuri, 2004; Ushizawa *et al.*, 2004; Bolshakova *et al.*, 2005). As a solution to this problem, a combined approach was proposed by Chen *et al.* (2005), who first applied the *k*-means algorithm to determine the *k* clusters and then fed these clusters into the hierarchical clustering technique to shorten the merging cluster time and generate a treelike dendrogram. However, this solution still suffers from the limitation of determining the initial value for *k* (Hasan, 2013; Hasan and Duan, 2014).

In this chapter, we propose a new algorithm, hierarchical *k*-means, that combines the advantages of both *k*-means and the hierarchical clustering algorithm to overcome their limitations. Combining different algorithms to overcome their own limitations and produce better results is a popular approach in research (Che *et al.*, 2011, 2012; Hasan *et al.*, 2012). In this proposed algorithm, initially we applied the hierarchical clustering algorithm and then used the result to decide the initial number of clusters and fed this information into *k*-means clustering to obtain the final clusters. Since similar gene expression profiles indicate similarity in their gene functionalities (Azuaje and Dopazo, 2005), after applying the proposed algorithm to the microarray data set of lung adenocarcinoma using gene ontology (GO) annotations, we explored the change in the enrichment of molecular functionalities of the genes of each cluster for normal tissue and *KRAS*-positive tissues. Our results showed that in each cluster, genes were grouped together based on their expression pattern and molecular functions, which indicate the correctness of this proposed algorithm.

2 METHODS

***k*-means clustering algorithm:** For clustering genes, *k*-means clustering, a well-known method for cluster analysis partition expression levels of *n* genes into *k* clusters, so that the total distance between the cluster's genes and its corresponding centroid, representative of the cluster, is minimized. In short, the goal is to partition the *n* genes into *k* sets S_i, $i = 1, 2..., k$ in order to minimize the within-cluster sum of squares (WCSS), defined as

$$WCSS = \sum_{j=1}^{k} \sum_{i=1}^{n} ||x_i^j - c_j||^2, \tag{4.1}$$

where $||x_i^j - c_j||^2$ provides the distance between a gene and the cluster's centroid.

In this clustering algorithm, the initial cluster centroids are selected randomly. After that, each gene is assigned to the closest cluster centroid. Then each cluster centroid is moved to the mean of the points assigned to it. This algorithm converges when the assignments no longer change. Algorithm 4.1 shows the pseudocode of the *k*-means clustering algorithm.

Hierarchical clustering algorithm: In gene clustering, hierarchical clustering is a method of cluster analysis that builds a hierarchy of clusters (as its name indicates). This clustering method organizes genes into tree structures based on their relation. The basic idea is to assemble a set of genes into a tree, where genes are joined by very short branches if they have very great similarity to each other, and by increasingly long branches as their similarity decreases.

The approaches for hierarchical clustering can be classified into two groups: agglomerative and divisive. The agglomerative approach is a "bottom-up" approach, where each gene starts in its own cluster and pairs of clusters are merged as one moves up the hierarchy. On the other hand, divisive approach is a "top-down" approach, where all genes starts in one cluster and splits are performed recursively as one moves down the hierarchy. In this chapter, we mainly focus on the agglomerative approach for hierarchical clustering.

The first step in hierarchical clustering is to calculate the distance matrix between the genes in the data set. The clustering starts once this matrix of distances is computed. The agglomerative hierarchical clustering technique consists of repeated cycles where the two closest genes having the smallest distance are joined by a node known as a *pseudonode*. The two joined genes are removed from the list of genes being processed and replaced by the pseudonode that represents the new branch. The distances between this pseudonode and all other remaining genes are computed,

ALGORITHM 4.1

k-means

Input: $X = \{x_1, x_2, \ldots, x_n\}$ // set of genes to be clustered.
k // number of clusters.
Output: $C = \{c_1, c_2, \ldots, c_k\}$ // set of cluster centroids.
$L = \{l(x) | x = 1, 2, \ldots, n\}$ // set of cluster labels of X.

foreach $c_i \in C$ **do**

   $c_i \leftarrow x_j \in E$ // random selection

end

foreach $x_i \in X$ **do**

   $l(x_i) \leftarrow calculateMinDistance(x_i, c_j)\, j \in \{1, 2, \ldots, k\}$

end

changed $\leftarrow$*false*

iter $\leftarrow 0$

repeat

   foreach $c_i \in C$ **do**

     updateCluster(c_i)

   end

   foreach $x_i \in X$ **do**

     minDist $\leftarrow calculateMinDistance(x_i, c_j)\, j \in \{1, 2, \ldots, k\}$

     if (*minDist* $\neq l(x_i)$) **then**

       $l(x_i) \leftarrow minDist$

       changed $\leftarrow$*true*

     end

   end

   iter++

until (*changed* = *true*) // no more change in the cluster takes place after the assignment and the process is repeated until only one node remains. Note that there are a variety of ways to compute distances while dealing with a pseudonode: centroid linkage, single linkage, complete linkage, and average linkage. In this chapter, we use average linkage, which defines the distance between two clusters as the average pairwise distance between genes in cluster C_i and C_j calculated using Eq. (4.2):

$$\delta(C_i, C_j) = \frac{\sum_{x \in C_i} \sum_{y \in C_j} \delta(x, y)}{n_i.n_j}, \tag{4.2}$$

where $\delta(x, y)$ is typically given by the Euclidean distance calculated using Eq. (4.3):

$$\delta(x, y) = \sqrt{\sum_{i=1}^{d} (x_i - y_i)^2}. \tag{4.3}$$

The pseudocode of agglomerative hierarchical clustering using average linkage is illustrated in Algorithm 4.2.

ALGORITHM 4.2

Hierarchical Clustering

Input: $G = \{V,E,d\}$ // Weighted graph, V is the set of all genes, E is the set of edge, d is the weight meaning the distance between two genes.

Output: $T = \{V_T, E_T\}$ // Cluster hierarchy or dendrogram.

$C \leftarrow \{\{v\} \mid v \in V\}$ // Initial clustering. Each gene is placed in separate clusters where each cluster //contains one gene.

$V_T \leftarrow \{\{v_c\} \mid c \in C\}, E_T \leftarrow \emptyset$ // Initial dendrogram

repeat

   $updateDistanceMatrix(C, G, d)$ //updates the distance matrix such that distance between the //new cluster and all remaining clusters are computed.

   $\{C, C'\} \leftarrow$ calculateMinDistance d(C_i, C_j) where $\{C_i, C_j\} \in : C_i \neq C_j$ //calculates the minimum //distance between cluster Ci and Cj

   $C \leftarrow (C \setminus \{C, C'\}) \cup \{C \cup C'\}$ // Merging of clusters to form a new cluster.

   $V_T \leftarrow V_T \cup \{v_{C, C'}\}, E_T \leftarrow E_T \cup \{\{v_{C, C'}, v_C\}, \{v_{C, C'}, v_{C'}\}\}$ //building up the dendrogram

until $(|C| > 1)$ // keep doing until only one cluster remains

---

Hierarchical *k*-means: In this proposed algorithm, we selected the value of *k* (i.e., the number of clusters) in a systematic way. Initially, we used the agglomerative hierarchical clustering algorithm for clustering the data set using average linkage and then checked at what level the distance between two consecutive nodes of the hierarchy was the maximum. Using this information, the value of *k* is determined, which is then fed into the *k*-means clustering algorithm to produce the final clusters. In both algorithms, the Pearson correlation coefficient (r) was used as the similarity metric between two samples and $1 - r$ was used as the distance metric. Algorithm 4.3 shows the pseudocode of the proposed algorithm.

ALGORITHM 4.3

Hierarchical *k*-means Clustering

Input: $G = \{V,E,d\}$ // Weighted graph, V is the set of all genes, E is the set of edge, d is the weight meaning the distance between two genes.

Output: $C = \{c_1,c_2,....,c_k\}$ // set of cluster centroids.

$R = \{r(v)|v = 1,2,...,n\}$ // set of cluster labels of V.

$T \leftarrow hierarchicalClustering(V, E, d)$ // Initial hierarchical clustering that returns a dendrogram T

maxDistance $\leftarrow \emptyset$

$l \leftarrow 0$ // at which level the maximum distance with the previous level found in T.

$N[] \leftarrow$ nodes in T

for $i \leftarrow 2$ to $N.length$

    distance $\leftarrow$ getDistance(N_i, N_{i-1}) //calculating the distance between two consecutive nodes

    if (distance > maxDistance) then

       distance $\leftarrow$ maxDistance

        $l \leftarrow$ level of node i in T

end

$k \leftarrow 1 + l$

$(C, R) \leftarrow kMeansClustering(V, k)$

3 DATA SET

Lung adenocarcinoma, the most frequent type of non-small-cell lung cancer (NSCLC) accounts for more than 50% of NSCLC, and the percentage is increasing (Okayama *et al.*, 2012). Recent studies revealed that activation of the *EGFR, KRAS,* and *ALK* genes defines three different pathways that are responsible for a considerable fraction (30%–60%) of lung adenocarcinomas (Pao and Girard, 2011; Ihle *et al.*, 2012; Janku *et al.*, 2010; Bronte *et al.*, 2010; Gerber and Minna, 2010). The data set used in this research contains expression profiles for 246 samples, of which 20 samples belonged to normal lung tissue. Out of the remaining 226 lung adenocarcinoma samples, 127 were with *EGFR* mutation, 20 with *KRAS* mutation, 11 with *EML4-ALK* fusion, and 68 with triple negative cases. The platform used for this data set was GPL570 [HG-U133_Plus_2] Affymetrix Human Genome U133 Plus 2.0 Array. This data set was collected from the GEO database (accession number GSE31210). The data set contained 54,675 genes. In this study, we considered 40 samples consisting of 20 samples from normal tissues and 20 samples from *KRAS*-positive tissues.

To determine the differentially expressed genes, we performed paired student *t*-test (Hsu and Lachenbruch, 2008) and Bonferroni corrections (Bonferroni, 1936), followed by the calculation of the value of fold change of the genes. In this study, after performing Bonferroni correction, we selected the genes as the most differentially expressed ones, which have adjusted p-values ≤ 0.05. In addition, we considered only those genes where the value of fold change (increase or decrease) is significant; i.e., the average fold change between cancer and normal is ≥ 2. Besides this preprocessing, we considered only those genes that are associated with molecular functions according to Gene Ontology (GO).

After performing the t-test, we obtained 21,880 genes having significant p-values (≤ 0.05). We performed Bonferroni correction on these genes and found 1988 genes that had a significantly adjusted p-value (≤ 0.05). Adding the fold change criterion, we reduced the set of differentially expressed genes to 1005. We then performed another step of filtering to keep only those genes that have GO terms and responsible for molecular functions. Finally, we came up with 464 genes in the final data set. The final data set is given partially in Table 4.1, and the complete data set is available in http://www.ncbi.nlm.nih.gov/geo/query/acc.cgi?acc=GSE31210 (Accessed 06/18/2013).

4 RESULTS AND DISCUSSION

The result of hierarchical clustering for normal tissue data set is shown in Figure 4.1. There are 463 interior nodes in the tree where each node is labeled based on the increasing order of its height. Therefore, the ID for the root is 463. To determine the number of clusters from the output of hierarchical clustering, we used a bar graph to show the difference of height between two consecutive interior nodes (see Figure 4.2).

Table 4.1 A Brief Overview of the Final data set

Affymatrix ID	Gene Symbol	Samples		
		GSM 773551	...	GSM 773784
1555579_s_at	PTPRM	3441.22	...	3569.13
211986_at	AHNAK	4395.68	...	7080.40
222392_x_at	PERP	21707.73	...	11350.53
236715_x_at	UACA	1303.01	...	1867.76
244704_at	NFYB	124.08	...	277.49
...	...	...	...	...
211237_s_at	FGFR4	22.41	...	11.07
203980_at	FABP4	257.25	...	920.44
207302_at	SGCG	47.09	...	9.61
210081_at	AGER	241.63	...	2001.28
217046_s_at	AGER	132.42	...	1016.05

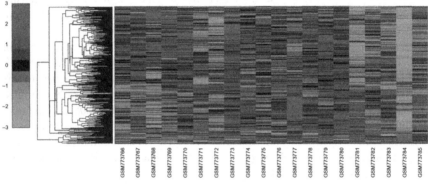

FIGURE 4.1

Hierarchical clustering of the normal tissue data set.

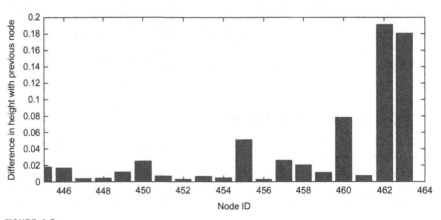

FIGURE 4.2

Height difference between two consecutive interior nodes in the hierarchical tree generated from the normal tissue. Since Pearson distance is used, the maximum height of the tree is 1.

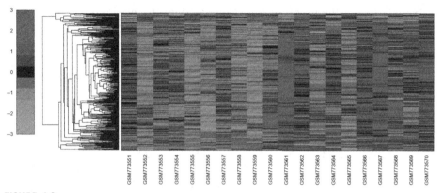

FIGURE 4.3

Hierarchical clustering of the KRAS positive data set.

From Figure 4.2, we can see that the difference is the maximum for nodes 461 and 462. As there is a total of 463 nodes in the tree, node 461 is on level 3 from the top. So, according to the proposed algorithm, the total number of clusters for k-means clustering should be 4.

Similarly, the number of clusters for the *KRAS*-positive data set can also be determined. Figure 4.3 shows the hierarchical clustering of *KRAS*-positive data set, and Figure 4.4 shows the height difference between two consecutive nodes. The results indicate that the number of clusters for *KRAS*-positive data set should be 4.

After determining the value for the initial number of clusters (k), we passed the value to k-means algorithms, and k numbers of clusters were formed for both normal and *KRAS*-positive tissues. We explored their common features (genes) and explained the change of molecular function of the genes captured in the clusters

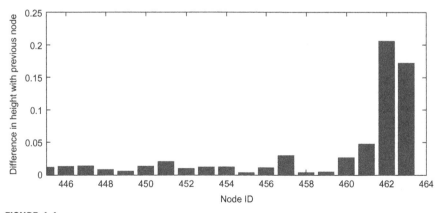

FIGURE 4.4

Height difference between two consecutive nodes in the hierarchical tree generated from a *KRAS*-positive data set.

Table 4.2 List of the Clusters to Be Compared for the Alteration in Molecular Function

Clusters to Compare		Number of Genes in Common
Normal Tissue	**KRAS-Positive**	
Cluster 1	Cluster 1	20
Cluster 2	Cluster 3	52
Cluster 3	Cluster 4	46
Cluster 4	Cluster 2	69

of both normal tissue and *KRAS*-positive tissue using GO annotations. For comparing the molecular function of the clusters of normal tissue and *KRAS*-positive tissues, we took one cluster from the normal tissue data set and one from the *KRAS*-positive data set that have the maximum number of common genes. Table 4.2 shows the clusters that we selected for comparing their molecular functions with the number of genes they have in common.

We explored the molecular functions of the genes in each cluster using GO annotations. Relationships among the genes were represented using a directed acyclic graph (DAG), termed the *GO graph*. We used a web-based tool called the *Gene Ontology Enrichment Analysis Software Toolkit (GOEAST)* (Zheng and Wang, 2008) to generate these graphs. This graph displays enriched Gene Ontology IDs (GOIDs) and their hierarchical relationships in molecular function GO categories. Figures 4.5 and 4.6 show the GO graph for cluster 1 for normal tissue and *KRAS*-positive tissue data set, respectively.

In Figures 4.5 and 4.6, boxes represent GO terms, each labeled by its GOID and term definition. Note that significantly enriched GO terms are shaded yellow. The degree of color saturation of each node is positively correlated with the significance of enrichment of the corresponding GO term. Nonsignificant GO terms within the hierarchical tree are shown as white boxes. In both of these graphs, edges stand for connections between different GO terms. Edges colored in red stand for the relationship between two enriched GO terms, black solid edges stand for the relationship between enriched and unenriched terms, and black dashed edges stand for the relationship between two unenriched GO terms.

In brief, these two figures show that the significant GO terms GO: 0005488 (binding) and GO: 0005515 (protein binding) remain the same in both clusters. GO terms such as GO: 0030234 (Enzyme Regulator Activity), GO: 0019207 (Kinase Regulator Activity), GO: 0019210 (Kinase Inhibitor Activity), GO: 0019887 (Protein Kinase Regulator Activity), and GO: 0004860 (Protein Kinase Inhibitor Activity), which are unenriched in normal tissue, become highly enriched in the *KRAS*-positive tissues, indicating that our proposed algorithm can cluster representative genes of both data sets correctly.

To compare the enrichment status of the two clusters better, we used Multi-GOEAST, which is an advanced version of GOEAST, and it is helpful to identify

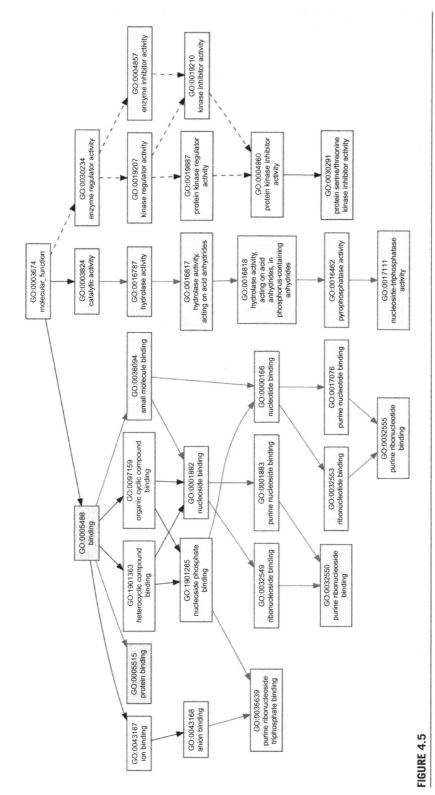

FIGURE 4.5

GO graph for cluster 1 of the normal tissue data set.

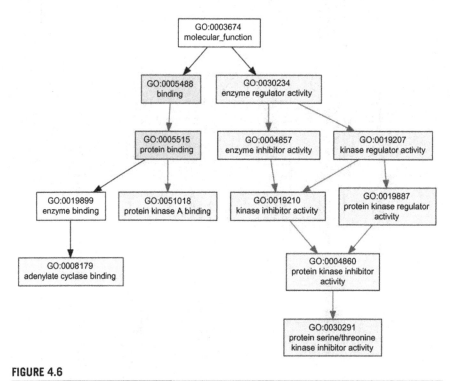

FIGURE 4.6

GO graph for cluster 1 of the *KRAS*-positive tissue data set.

the hidden correlation between the two clusters (Zheng and Wang, 2008). Figure 4.7 shows the comparative GO graph for cluster 1 of both data sets.

In the comparative GO graph, significantly enriched GO terms in both clusters are marked yellow, and light yellow color indicates the GO terms that are enriched in both clusters. Nodes marked with coral pink indicate the GO terms that are enriched in the normal tissue data set but not in the *KRAS*-positive data set. In addition, green nodes represent the GO terms that are unenriched in normal tissue but enriched in *KRAS*-positive tissue. Note that the degree of color saturation of each node is positively correlated with the significance of enrichment of the corresponding GO term.

Table 4.3 lists the genes associated with the GO terms that are enriched in cluster 1 of the *KRAS*-positive tissue data set, but not in cluster 1 of the normal tissue data set. These GO terms are marked green in the comparative GO graph shown in Figure 4.7. We believe that these are responsible for the alteration of the molecular activity in the cell and are linked to the development of KRAS lung cancer. Similarly, we can generate and compare the GO enrichment graph for the rest of the clusters (see supplementary materials).

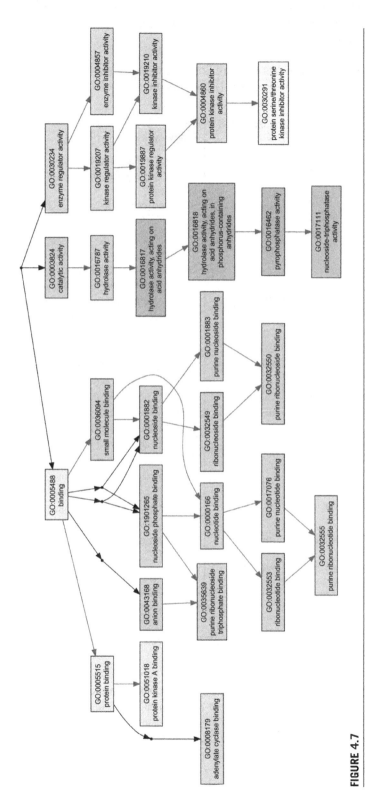

FIGURE 4.7

Comparative GO graph for comparing GO enrichment status for cluster 1 of both the normal tissue and *KRAS*-positive data sets.

Table 4.3 GO Terms and Pathways That Are Enriched in Molecular Functions of the Genes of Cluster 1 of *KRAS*-Positive Tissue but Unenriched in the Genes of Cluster 1 of Normal Tissue Data Set

GO ID	GO Term	Associated Genes	Pathway
GO:0030234	Enzyme regulator activity	TIMP3	1 Matrix_metalloproteinases
		CDKN1C	G1_to_S_cell_cycle_reactome
		PAK1	Integrin mediated_cell_adhesion_KEGG
		ECT2	N/A
		RALGPS2	N/A
		SFN	Calcium_regulation_in_cardiac_cells Smooth_muscle_contraction
GO:0019207	Kinase regulator activity	CDKN1C	G1_to_S_cell_cycle_reactome
		SFN	Calcium_regulation_in_cardiac_cells Smooth_muscle_contraction
GO:0004857	Enzyme inhibitor activity	TIMP3	Matrix_metalloproteinases
		CDKN1C	G1_to_S_cell_cycle_reactome
		SFN	Calcium_regulation_in_cardiac_cells Smooth_muscle_contraction
GO:0019887	Protein kinase regulator activity	CDKN1C	G1_to_S_cell_cycle_reactome
		SFN	Calcium_regulation_in_cardiac_cells Smooth_muscle_contraction
GO:0019210	Kinase inhibitor activity	CDKN1C	G1_to_S_cell_cycle_reactome
		SFN	Calcium_regulation_in_cardiac_cells Smooth_muscle_contraction
GO:0004860	Protein kinase inhibitor activity	CDKN1C	G1_to_S_cell_cycle_reactome
		SFN	Calcium_regulation_in_cardiac_cells Smooth_muscle_contraction
GO:0051018	Protein kinase A binding	AKAP12	G_protein_signaling
GO:0008179	Adenylate Cyclase binding	AKAP12	G_protein_signaling

5 CONCLUSIONS

In this chapter, we propose hierarchical *k*-means, a new combined clustering algorithm designed to cluster genes in a microarray data set based on their expression levels. In this algorithm, using the output from hierarchical clustering, we systematically determined the value of *k* required for *k*-means clustering. This way, the proposed algorithm overcomes the limitation of *k*-means clustering. This proposed algorithm takes advantage of the ability of hierarchical clustering to get a complete hierarchy of clusters and uses this information in k-means clustering to produce tighter clusters.

In this study, we examined 40 samples and 464 genes from the data set of lung adenocarcinoma, which is one of the most frequent types of NSCLC. Out of the 40 samples, 20 were from normal tissue and 20 were from *KRAS*-positive tissue. We applied t-test, Bonferroni correction, and fold change cutoff techniques to find the significantly differentially expressed genes, and among them, only the genes having GO terms and responsible for molecular functions were included in the final data set.

After applying the proposed clustering algorithms, we obtained four clusters for both the normal tissue data set and *KRAS*-positive data set. Hereafter, we examined the genes contained in each cluster with respect to their molecular functions based on GO annotation to see what changes in the enrichment of the molecular functions of genes took place from normal tissues to *KRAS*-positive tissues. This way, after checking the change in enrichment of the GO terms, we verified that the proposed algorithm can cluster representative genes of both data sets based on their expression patterns. The coherent approach presented in this chapter shows its correctness to cluster genes, and we believe that it can be generalized for clustering other types of large data sets as well.

REFERENCES

Azuaje, F., Dopazo, J., 2005. Data Analysis and Visualization in Genomics and Proteomics: Wiley Online Library.

Barash, Y., Friedman, N., 2002. Context-specific Bayesian clustering for gene expression data. J. Comput. Biol. 9, 169–191.

Bolshakova, N., Azuaje, F., Cunningham, P., 2005. An integrated tool for microarray data clustering and cluster validity assessment. Bioinformatics 21, 451–455.

Bonferroni, C.E., 1936. Teoria statistica delle classi e calcolo delle probabilita. Libreria internazionale Seeber.

Bronte, G., Rizzo, S., La Paglia, L., Adamo, V., Siragusa, S., Ficorella, C., et al., 2010. Driver mutations and differential sensitivity to targeted therapies: a new approach to the treatment of lung adenocarcinoma. Cancer Treat. Rev. 36, S21–S29.

Brown, M.P., Grundy, W.N., Lin, D., Cristianini, N., Sugnet, C.W., Furey, T.S., et al., 2000. Knowledge-based analysis of microarray gene expression data by using support vector machines. Proc. Natl. Acad. Sci. 97, 262–267.

Che, D., Hasan, M.S., Wang, H., Fazekas, J., Huang, J., Liu, Q., 2011. EGID: an ensemble algorithm for improved genomic island detection in genomic sequences. Bioinformation 7, 311.

Che, D., Hasan, M.S., Wang, H., Fazekas, J., Chen, B., Tao, X., 2012. M are better than one: an ensemble method for genomic island prediction. In: International Conference on Bioinformatics and Biomedical Engineering, pp. 426–429.

Chen, T.-S., Tsai, T.-H., Chen, Y.-T., Lin, C.-C., Chen, R.-C., Li, S.-Y., et al., 2005. A combined K-means and hierarchical clustering method for improving the clustering efficiency of microarray. In: Intelligent Signal Processing and Communication Systems, 2005. ISPACS 2005. Proceedings of 2005 International Symposium on, pp. 405–408.

Eisen, M.B., Spellman, P.T., Brown, P.O., Botstein, D., 1998. Cluster analysis and display of genome-wide expression patterns. Proc. Natl. Acad. Sci. 95, 14863–14868.

Friedman, N., Linial, M., Nachman, I., Pe'er, D., 2000. Using Bayesian networks to analyze expression data. J. Comput. Biol. 7, 601–620.

Garai, G., Chaudhuri, B., 2004. A novel genetic algorithm for automatic clustering. Pattern Recogn. Lett. 25, 173–187.

Gerber, D.E., Minna, J.D., 2010. ALK inhibition for non-small cell lung cancer: from discovery to therapy in record time. Canc. cell 18, 548–551.

Gresham, D., Dunham, M.J., Botstein, D., 2008. Comparing whole genomes using DNA microarrays. Nat. Rev. Genet. 9, 291–302.

Hasan, M.S., 2013. Investigating Gene Relationships in Microarray Expressions: Approaches Using Clustering Algorithms. The University of Akron.

Hasan, M.S., Duan, Z.-H., 2014. A hybrid clustering algorithms and functional study of gene expression in lung adenocarcinoma. In: Proceedings of the World Comp: International Conference on Bioinformatics and Computational Biology, pp. 23–29.

Hasan, M.S., Liu, Q., Wang, H., Fazekas, J., Chen, B., Che, D., 2012. GIST: Genomic island suite of tools for predicting genomic islands in genomic sequences. Bioinformation 8, 203–205.

He, J., Tan, A.-H., Tan, C.-L., 2003. Self-organizing neural networks for efficient clustering of gene expression data. In: Neural Networks, 2003. Proceedings of the International Joint Conference on.pp. 1684–1689.

Holmes, I., Bruno, W.J., 2000. Finding regulatory elements using joint likelihoods for sequence and expression profile data. In: Ismb, pp. 202–210.

Hsu, H., Lachenbruch, P.A., 2008. Paired t test. In: Wiley Encyclopedia of Clinical Trials.

Hunter, L., Holm, L., 1992. Artificial Intelligence and Molecular Biology. AAAI, pp. 866–868.

Ihle, N.T., Byers, L.A., Kim, E.S., Saintigny, P., Lee, J.J., Blumenschein, G.R., et al., 2012. Effect of KRAS oncogene substitutions on protein behavior: implications for signaling and clinical outcome. J. Natl. Canc. Inst. 104, 228–239.

Janku, F., Stewart, D.J., Kurzrock, R., 2010. Targeted therapy in non-small-cell lung cancer—is it becoming a reality? Nat. Rev. Clin. Oncol. 7, 401–414.

Kasturi, J., Acharya, R., Ramanathan, M., 2003. An information theoretic approach for analyzing temporal patterns of gene expression. Bioinformatics 19, 449–458.

Kaufman, L., Rousseeuw, P.J., 2009. Finding Groups in Data: An Introduction to Cluster Analysis, vol. 344 John Wiley & Sons.

Luo, F., Tang, K., Khan, L., 2003. Hierarchical clustering of gene expression data. In: Bioinformatics and Bioengineering, 2003. Proceedings. Third IEEE Symposium on, pp. 328–335.

Michaels, G.S., Carr, D.B., Askenazi, M., Fuhrman, S., Wen, X., Somogyi, R., 1998. Cluster analysis and data visualization of large-scale gene expression data. In: Pacific Symposium on Biocomputing, pp. 42–53.

Mount, D.W., 2004. Sequence and genome analysis. Bioinformatics: Cold Spring Harbour Laboratory Press: Cold Spring Harbour, 2.

Okayama, H., Kohno, T., Ishii, Y., Shimada, Y., Shiraishi, K., Iwakawa, R., et al., 2012. Identification of genes upregulated in ALK-positive and EGFR/KRAS/ALK-negative lung adenocarcinomas. Canc. Res. 72, 100–111.

Pao, W., Girard, N., 2011. New driver mutations in non-small-cell lung cancer. Lancet Oncol. 12, 175–180.

Qin, L.-X., Breeden, L., Self, S.G., 2014. Finding gene clusters for a replicated time course study. BMC Res. Notes 7, 60.

Tamayo, P., Slonim, D., Mesirov, J., Zhu, Q., Kitareewan, S., Dmitrovsky, E., et al., 1999. Interpreting patterns of gene expression with self-organizing maps: methods and application to hematopoietic differentiation. Proc. Natl. Acad. Sci. 96, 2907–2912.

Tavazoie, S., Hughes, J.D., Campbell, M.J., Cho, R.J., Church, G.M., 1999. Systematic determination of genetic network architecture. Nat. Genet. 22, 281–285.

Törönen, P., Kolehmainen, M., Wong, G., Castrén, E., 1999. Analysis of gene expression data using self-organizing maps. FEBS Lett. 451, 142–146.

Ushizawa, K., Herath, C.B., Kaneyama, K., Shiojima, S., Hirasawa, A., Takahashi, T., et al., 2004. cDNA microarray analysis of bovine embryo gene expression profiles during the pre-implantation period. Reprod. Biol. Endocrinol. 2, 77.

Wang, H., Azuaje, F., Bodenreider, O., 2005. An ontology-driven clustering method for supporting gene expression analysis. In: Computer-Based Medical Systems, 2005. Proceedings. 18th IEEE Symposium on, pp. 389–394.

Wang, Z., Gerstein, M., Snyder, M., 2009. RNA-Seq: a revolutionary tool for transcriptomics. Nat. Rev. Genet. 10, 57–63.

Wen, X., Fuhrman, S., Michaels, G.S., Carr, D.B., Smith, S., Barker, J.L., et al., 1998. Large-scale temporal gene expression mapping of central nervous system development. Proc. Natl. Acad. Sci. 95, 334–339.

Woolf, P.J., Wang, Y., 2000. A fuzzy logic approach to analyzing gene expression data. Physiol. Genom. 3, 9–15.

Zheng, Q., Wang, X.-J., 2008. GOEAST: a web-based software toolkit for Gene Ontology enrichment analysis. Nucleic Acids Res. 36, W358–W363.

SUPPLEMENTARY MATERIALS

List of genes of the clusters and detailed results from GO enrichment analysis are presented in the supplementary figures which can be found at http://www.cs.uakron.edu/~duan/Chapter04/SupplementaryMaterials.pdf.

Molecular Classification of *N*-Aryloxazolidinone-5-carboxamides as Human Immunodeficiency Virus Protease Inhibitors

Francisco Torrens[1] and Gloria Castellano[2]

Institut Universitari de Ciència Molecular, Universitat de València, Edifici d'Instituts de Paterna, València, Spain[1]

Departamento de Ciencias Experimentales y Matemáticas, Facultad de Veterinaria y Ciencias Experimentales, Universidad Católica de Valencia San Vicente Mártir, València, Spain[2]

1 INTRODUCTION

Acquired immunodeficiency syndrome (AIDS) is an end-stage disease that is manifested by the gradual deterioration of the immune competence of infected patients (Alberts *et al.*, 2002). Human immunodeficiency virus type 1 (HIV-1) is the causative organism for AIDS (Volberding and Deeks, 2010); it belongs to the family *lentiviridae* of pathogenic retroviruses, which depends on RNA to encode the genetic message (Chakravarty, 2006). The protease (PR) of HIV-1 is a homodimeric aspartyl PR; it cleaves a 55-kDa polyprotein precursor: by that process, it produces smaller functional protein fragments (*e.g.*, p17, p24, p9, p7), which are responsible for packing and infectivity for budding virions. The inhibition of PR inhibits the processing steps; it causes noninfectious and immature progeny virions. Some HIV-1 PR inhibitors (such as indinavir, ritonavir, and nelfinavir) are marketed as anti-HIV-1 drugs, none of which is devoid of adverse effects (Katzung, 2004). Phenotypic cross/resistance restricted the use of these drugs (Tripathi, 2003). The search for HIV-1 PR inhibitors with better therapeutic efficacy and lesser toxicity is in progress.

Ali *et al.* (2006) described the design, synthesis, and bioevaluation of HIV-1 PR inhibitors, incorporating *N*-phenyloxazolidinone-5-carboxamides into (hydroxyethylamino)sulphonamide scaffold as P2 ligands. Series of inhibitors were synthesized with changes at P2 phenyloxazolidinone and P2' phenylsulphonamide moieties. The compounds with the (*S*)-enantiomer of substituted phenyloxazolidinones at P2 showed potent inhibitory activities versus HIV-1 PR. Inhibitors possessing 3/4-acetyl and

3-trifluoromethyl groups at oxazolidinone phenyl ring were the most potent, with K_i values in the low pM range. The electron-donating groups 4-methoxy and 1,3-dioxolane were preferred at P2' phenyl, as compounds with other substitutions showed less binding affinity. Attempts to replace the isobutyl at P1' with small cyclic moieties caused a loss of affinity. Crystal structure analysis of both most potent inhibitors, in a complex with HIV-1 PR, provided information on the inhibitor–PR interactions. In inhibitor and enzyme complexes, oxazolidinone carbonyl H-bonded with conserved PR Asp[29]. Potent inhibitors were selected from each series by incorporating various phenyloxazolidinone-based P2 ligands, and their activities versus a panel of multidrug-resistant (MDR) PR variants were determined. The most potent PR inhibitor started with tight affinity for the wild-type enzyme ($K_i = 0.8$ pM) and, even versus MDR variants, it retained pM to low nM K_i, which is comparable to the best PR inhibitors approved by the US Food and Drug Administration (FDA). Halder and Jha (2010) applied quantitative structure–activity relationships (QSARs) to some N-aryloxazolidi-none-5-carboxamides (NCAs, *cf.* Figure 5.1) to find structural requirements for more active anti-HIV-1 PR agents. Wang *et al.* (2011) reported mangiferin as anti-HIV-1 tar-geting PR and effective versus resistant strains. Zhang *et al.* (2012) investigated inter-actions for HIV drug cross-resistance among PR inhibitors. Liu *et al.* (2013) informed 4862 F, an inhibitor of HIV-1 PR, from a *Streptomyces* culture.

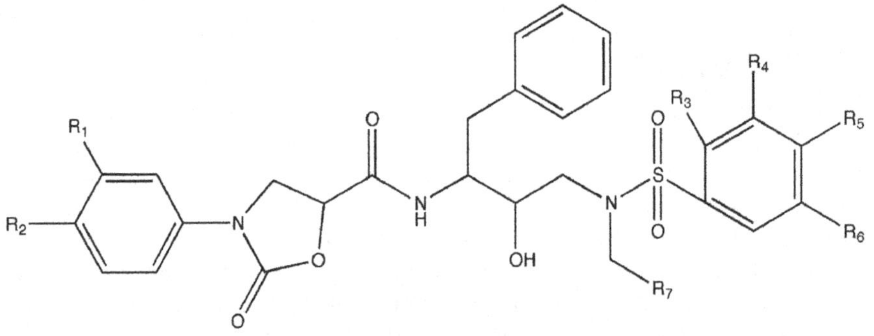

FIGURE 5.1

General molecular structure of N-aryloxazolidinone-5-carboxamide.

A simple code is proposed that could be useful for establishing a chemical structure–biosignificance relationship (Benzecri, 1984; Varmuza, 1980). The starting point is to use information entropy (IE) for pattern recognition. The IE is formulated based on the *similarity matrix* between two biochemical species. As IE is weakly dis-criminating for classification, the more powerful concepts of *IE production* and its *equipartition conjecture* (EC) are introduced (Tondeur and Kvaalen, 1987). In earlier publications, it was analyzed the PTs of local anesthetics (Castellano-Estornell and Torrens-Zaragozá, 2009; Torrens and Castellano, 2006, 2011a), HIV inhibitors (Torrens and Castellano, 2009a, 2010, 2011b, 2012a–d, 2014), anti-cancers (Torrens and Castellano, 2009b, 2013a, 2013b), phenolics (Castellano *et al.*, 2012), flavomoids (Castellano *et al.*, 2013), stilbenoids (Castellano *et al.*, 2014) in *Ganoderma* (Castellano and Torrens, 2015). The main aim of this chapter is to develop the code-learning potentialities and, since molecules are more naturally described by structured representation of varying sizes, study general approaches to structured information processing. A second goal is to present NCA PT. A third objective is to validate PT with an external property, anti-HIV-1 PR activity, which is not used in the development of PT.

2 COMPUTATIONAL METHOD

The key problem in classification studies is to define *similarity indices* with several criteria. The first step in quantifying the similarity concept for NCAs is to list the most important moieties. A *vector of properties* $\bar{i}=<i_1,i_2,...i_k,...>$ should be associated with every NCA i, whose components correspond to characteristic groups in a hierarchical order according to the importance of their pharmacological potency. If the mth portion of a molecule is more significant for the inhibitory effect than the kth portion, then $m<k$. The components i_k are either 1 or 0, depending on whether an identical portion of rank k is either present or absent in NCA i, compared to a reference. The analysis includes seven regions of structural variation in NCAs: R_{1-7} positions showing diverse substitution patterns. The structural elements of an NCA are ranked according to their contribution to inhibitory potency as $R_3>R_6>R_7>R_4>R_5>R_2>R_1$. Index $i_1=1$ denotes $R_3=H$ (0 otherwise), $i_2=1$, $R_6=H$, $i_3=1$, $R_7=i$Pr, $i_4=1$, $R_4=H$, $i_5=1$, $R_5=OCH_3$, $i_6=1$, $R_2=H$ and $i_7=1$, and $R_1=Ac$. In NCA 5, $R_3=R_6=R_4=R_2=H$, $R_7=i$Pr, $R_5=OCH_3$, and $R_1=Ac$; its vector is $<1111111>$, which was selected as a reference because of its greatest inhibitory activity versus HIV-1. Table 5.1 contains the vectors associated with 38 NCAs. Vector $<1111110>$ is associated with NCA 1 since $R_3=R_6=R_4=R_2=R_1=H$, $R_7=i$Pr and $R_5=OCH_3$.

Denote by r_{ij} $(0\leq r_{ij}\leq 1)$ the similarity index of two NCAs associated with vectors $\bar{i}$ and $\bar{j}$, respectively. The similitude is characterized by the *similarity matrix* $\mathbf{R}=[r_{ij}]$. The similarity index between two NCAs $\bar{i}=<i_1,i_2,...i_k...>$ and $\bar{j}=<j_1,j_2,...j_k...>$ is

$$r_{ij} = \sum_k t_k(a_k)^k \quad (k=1,2,...), \qquad (5.1)$$

where $0\leq a_k\leq 1$, and $t_k=1$ if $i_k=j_k$, but $t_k=0$ if $i_k\neq j_k$. The definition assigns a weight $(a_k)^k$ to any property involved in the description of molecule i or j.

3 CLASSIFICATION ALGORITHM

The *grouping algorithm* uses the *stabilized* similarity matrix obtained by applying the *max–min composition rule o,* defined by

$$(\mathbf{R}o\mathbf{S})_{ij} = \max_k \left[\min_k \left(r_{ik}, s_{kj} \right) \right], \qquad (5.2)$$

Table 5.1 Vector of Properties of NCAs for Molecular Substitutions (R_3, R_6, R_7, R_4, R_5, R_2, R_1)

1. –H –H –iPr –H –OCH$_3$ –H –H <1111110>
2. –H –H –iPr –H –OCH$_3$ –H –F <1111110>
3. –H –H –iPr –H –OCH$_3$ –F –F <1111100>
4. –H –H –iPr –H –OCH$_3$ –H –CF$_3$ <1111110>
5. –H –H –iPr –H –OCH$_3$ –H –Ac <1111111>
6. –H –H –iPr –H –OCH$_3$ –Ac –H <1111100>
7. –H –H –iPr –H –OCH$_3$ –H –OCH$_3$ <1111110>
8. –H –H –iPr –H –NH$_2$ –H –H <1111010>
9. –H –H –iPr –H –NH$_2$ –H –F <1111010>
10. –H –H –iPr –H –NH$_2$ –F –F <1111000>
11. –H –H –iPr –H –NH$_2$ –H –CF$_3$ <1111010>
12. –H –H –iPr –H –NH$_2$ –H –Ac <1111011>
13. –H –H –iPr –H –NH$_2$ –Ac –H <1111000>
14. –H –H –iPr –O–CH$_2$–O– –H –F <1110010>
15. –H –H –iPr –O–CH$_2$–O– –F –F <1110000>
16. –H –H –iPr –O–CH$_2$–O– –H –CF$_3$ <1110010>
17. –H –H –iPr –O–CH$_2$–O– –H –Ac <1110011>
18. –H –H –iPr –O–CH$_2$–O– –Ac –H <1110000>
19. –H –H –iPr –F –OCH$_3$ –H –F <1110110>
20. –H –H –iPr –F –OCH$_3$ –F –F <1110100>
21. –H –H –iPr –F –OCH$_3$ –H –CF$_3$ <1110110>
22. –H –H –iPr –F –OCH$_3$ –H –Ac <1110111>
23. –H –H –iPr –F –OCH$_3$ –Ac –H <1110100>
24. –H –H –iPr –H –OCF$_3$ –H –CF$_3$ <1111010>
25. –H –H –iPr –H –OCF$_3$ –H –Ac <1111011>
26. –H –H –iPr –OCH$_3$ –H –H –H <1110010>
27. –H –H –iPr –OCH$_3$ –H –Ac –H <1110000>
28. –H –H –cPr –H –H –H –F <1101010>
29. –H –H –cPr –H –OCH$_3$ –F –F <1101100>
30. –H –H –cPr –H –OCH$_3$ –Ac –H <1101100>
31. –H –H –2-TP^a –OCH$_3$ –H –H –H <1100010>
32. –H –H –2-TP^a –OCH$_3$ –H –H –F <1100010>
33. –H –H –2-TP^a –OCH$_3$ –H –Ac –H <1100000>
34. –F –F –2-TP^a –H –F –H –H <0001010>
35. –F –F –2-TP^a –H –F –H –F <0001010>
36. –F –F –2-TP^a –H –F –Ac –H <0001000>
37. –H –H –2THF^b –OCH$_3$ –H –H –H <1100010>
38. –H –H –2THF^b –OCH$_3$ –H –H –F <1100010>

^{a}2-TP = thiophene
^{b}2THF = 2-tetrahydrofuran

where $\mathbf{R}=[r_{ij}]$ and $\mathbf{S}=[s_{ij}]$ are matrices of the same type, and $(\mathbf{R}o\mathbf{S})_{ij}$ is the (i,j)th element of the $\mathbf{R}o\mathbf{S}$ matrix (Cox, 1994; Kaufmann, 1975; Kundu, 1998; Lambert-Torres *et al.*, 1999). When applying the composition rule max–min iteratively so that $\mathbf{R}(n+1)=\mathbf{R}(n)\,o\,\mathbf{R}$, an integer n exists such that $\mathbf{R}(n)=\mathbf{R}(n+1)=\ldots$ Matrix $\mathbf{R}(n)$ is called the *stabilized similarity matrix*. The importance of stabilization lies in the fact that in classification, it generates a partition into disjoint classes. The stabilized matrix is designated by $\mathbf{R}(n)=[r_{ij}(n)]$. The *grouping rule* follows, to wit: i and j are assigned to the same class if $r_{ij}(n)\geq b$. The class of i noted that $\widehat{i}$ is the set of species j that satisfies the rule: $r_{ij}(n)\geq b$. The matrix of classes is

$$\widehat{\mathbf{R}}(n)=\left[\widehat{r_{\widetilde{ij}}}\right]=\max_{s,t}(r_{st})\ \left(s\in\widehat{i},t\in\widehat{j}\right), \tag{5.3}$$

where s stands for any index of the species belonging to class $\widehat{i}$ (similarly for t and $\widehat{j}$). Eq. (5.3) means finding the largest similarity index between species of two different classes.

4 INFORMATION ENTROPY

In information theory, the IE h measures the surprise that a source emitting sequences can give (Shannon, 1948a, 1948b). Consider the use of a qualitative spot test to determine the presence of Fe in a sample of water. Without any history of testing, an analyst must begin by assuming that the two outcomes 0/1 (Fe absent or present) are equiprobable with probabilities 1/2. When up to two metals may be present in the sample (*e.g.*, Fe and Ni), four possible outcomes exist, ranging from neither being present (0,0) to both (1,1), with probabilities $1/2^2$. Which of the four possibilities turns up is determined by using two tests, each with two observable states. With three elements, eight possibilities exist with probabilities $1/2^3$; three tests are needed. The following pattern relates the uncertainty and information needed to resolve it. The number of possibilities is expressed to a power of 2. The power to which 2 must be raised to give the number of possibilities N is defined as the logarithm to base 2 of that number. Information and uncertainty are defined by the logarithm to base 2 of the number of possible analytical outcomes: $\log_2 N$.

The initial uncertainty is defined in terms of the probability of the occurrence of every outcome; *e.g.*, for the above-mentioned probabilities, the following definition results: $I=H=\log_2 N=\log_2 1/p=-\log_2 p$, where I is the information contained in an answer given that there were N possibilities, with H as the initial uncertainty resulting from the need to consider N possibilities and p, the probability of every outcome if all N possibilities are equally likely to occur. The expression is generalized to a situation in which the probability of every outcome is not the same. If one knows that some elements are more likely to be present than others, the equation is adjusted so that the logarithms of individual probabilities suitably weighted are summed: $H=-\Sigma\,p_i\log_2 p_i$, where $\Sigma\,p_i=1$. Consider the original example, except that in this case, past experience showed that 90% of the samples contained no Fe. The degree of uncertainty is calculated by: $H=-(0.9\ \log_2\ 0.9+0.1\ \log_2\ 0.1)=0.469$ bits. For a single event occurring with probability p, the degree of surprise is proportional to $-\ln p$. By generalizing the result to a random variable X (which can take N possible values $x_1, \ldots, x_N$ with probabilities $p_1, \ldots, p_N$), the average surprise received on learning the X value is $-\Sigma\, p_i \ln p_i$. The IE associated with $\mathbf{R}$ similarity matrix is

$$h(\mathbf{R}) = -\sum_{i,j} r_{ij} \ln r_{ij} - \sum_{i,j} \left(1 - r_{ij}\right) \ln \left(1 - r_{ij}\right). \tag{5.4}$$

Denote by C_b the set of classes and by $\widehat{\mathbf{R}}_b$, the similarity matrix at grouping level b. The IE satisfies several properties: (i) $h(\mathbf{R}) = 0$ if either $r_{ij} = 0$ or $r_{ij} = 1$; (ii) $h(\mathbf{R})$ is at its maximum if $r_{ij} = 0.5$ (*i.e.*, when the imprecision is at its maximum); (iii) $h\left(\widehat{\mathbf{R}}_b\right) \leq h(\mathbf{R})$ for any b (*i.e.*, classification leads to IE loss); (iv) $h\left(\widehat{\mathbf{R}}_{b_1}\right) \leq h\left(\widehat{\mathbf{R}}_{b_2}\right)$ if $b_1 < b_2$ (*i.e.*, IE is a monotone function of the grouping level b).

5 THE EC OF ENTROPY PRODUCTION

In the classification algorithm, every *hierarchical tree* corresponds to IE dependence on the grouping level, and an h–b diagram is obtained. Tondeur and Kvaalen (1987) proposed the *EC of IE production* is proposed as the selection criterion among different variants, resulting from classification among hierarchical trees. According to EC, for a given charge, the binary tree (BT) with the best configuration is one in which IE production is the most uniformly distributed. One proceeds by analogy by using IE instead of thermodynamic entropy. The EC implies linear dependence (*i.e.*, constant IE production) along scale b so that the *EC line* is

$$h_{\text{eqp}} = h_{\max} b. \tag{5.5}$$

Since the classification is discrete, the way of expressing EC would be a regular staircase function. The best variant is chosen to be one that minimizes the sum of the squares of the deviations:

$$SS = \sum_{b_i} \left(h - h_{\text{eqp}}\right)^2. \tag{5.6}$$

6 LEARNING PROCEDURE

Learning procedures (LPs), similar to those encountered in *stochastic methods,* are implemented (White, 1989). Consider a partition into classes as *good* from observations, which corresponds to a *reference* similarity matrix $\mathbf{S} = [s_{ij}]$, obtained for equal weights $a_1 = a_2 = \ldots = a$ and for an arbitrary number of fictious properties. Consider also the same set of species as in the good classification and actual properties. The degree of similarity r_{ij} is computed by Eq. (5.1), giving matrix $\mathbf{R}$. The number of properties for $\mathbf{R}$ and $\mathbf{S}$ differs. The LP consists in finding classification results for $\mathbf{R}$, as close as possible to the *good* classification. The a_1 weight is taken to be constant and the following weights $a_2, a_3, \ldots$ are subjected to random variations.

A new similarity matrix is obtained via Eq. (5.1) and new weights. The distance between the partitions into classes, characterized by **R** and **S**, is

$$D = -\sum_{ij}\left(1 - r_{ij}\right)\ln\frac{1 - r_{ij}}{1 - s_{ij}} - \sum_{ij} r_{ij}\ln\frac{r_{ij}}{s_{ij}} \qquad \forall 0 \leq r_{ij}, s_{ij} \leq 1. \qquad (5.7)$$

The definition was suggested by that introduced in information theory by Kullback (1959), in order to measure the distance between two probability distributions. It is a measure of the distance between the **R** and **S** matrices. Since a corresponding classification exists for every matrix, two classifications will be compared by the distance, which is a nonnegative quantity that approaches zero as the resemblance between **R** and **S** rises. The result of the algorithm is a set of weights allowing classification. The procedure was applied to the synthesis of complex BTs using IE (Baez and Dolan, 1995; Crans, 2000; Iordache, 2011, 2012; Iordache *et al.*, 1993; Leinster, 2004).

Our code MolClas is a simple, reliable, efficient, and fast procedure for molecular classification, based on IE-production EC, according to Eqs. (5.1)–(5.7). With IE, but without EC, an excessive number of results appear compatible with the data and suffer a combinatorial explosion; however, after EC, the best configuration is that in which IE production is most uniformly distributed. The MolClas reads the number of properties and molecular properties; it allows the optimization of the coefficients; it optionally reads the starting coefficients and the number of iteration cycles. The correlation matrix can be either calculated by MolClas or read from the input file. The MolClas allows correlation-matrix transformation in the range [−1,1] to [0,1]; it calculates the similarity matrix of the property in symmetric storage mode; it applies the graphical correlation model to obtain the partial correlation diagram (PCD); it computes the classifications, tests if the groupings are different, calculates the distances between classifications, computes the similarity matrices of groupings, works out classifications of IE, optimizes the coefficients, performs single/complete-linkage hierarchical cluster analyses, and plots cluster diagrams; it was written not only to analyze IE-production EC, but also to explore the world of molecular classification.

7 CALCULATION RESULTS AND DISCUSSION

Structural data of anti-HIV-1 NCAs reported by Halder and Jha (2010) were used as the model data set. The matrix of Pearson correlation coefficients (PCCs) was calculated between the pairs of vectors $<i_1,i_2,i_3,i_4,i_5,i_6,i_7>$ of 38 NCAs. The PCCs are illustrated in a PCD, which could contain high ($r \geq 0.75$), medium ($0.50 \leq r < 0.75$), low ($0.25 \leq r < 0.50$), and no ($r < 0.25$) partial correlation. Pairs of inhibitors with high partial correlations show similar vectors; however, the results should be taken with care because NCA with constant vector $<1111111>$(Entry 5) shows null standard deviation, causing the greatest partial correlations $r = 1$ with any NCA, which is an artifact. With EC, correlations are illustrated in PCD, which contains 598 high

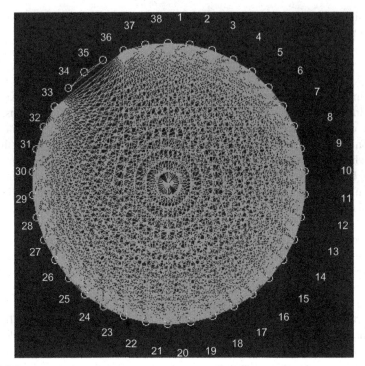

FIGURE 5.2

Partial correlation diagram: High (red) intercorrelations of NCAs.

(*cf.* Figure 5.2, red lines) and 105 zero (black) partial correlation. Notice that 3 out of 37 high partial correlations of Entry 5 were corrected: its correlations with Entries 34–36 are zero partial correlations.

The grouping rule in the case of equal weights $a_k = 0.5$ for $b_1 = 0.97$ allows the following classes:

$C-b_1 = (1-7)(8-13,24,25)(14-18,26,27)(19-23)(28)(29,30)(31-33,37,38)$ $(34-36)$.

Eight classes are obtained with associated IE $h-\mathbf{R}-b_1 = 21.18$. The BT matching to $<i_1,i_2,i_3,i_4,i_5,i_6,i_7>/C-b_1$ (*cf.* Figure 5.3) is calculated (IMSL, 1989; Jarvis and Patrick, 1973; Tryon, 1939); it provides a BT of Table 5.1 that separates the same classes: the data bifurcate into classes 5, 1–4, and 6–8 with 1, 7, 8, 7, 5, 2, 5, and 3 NCAs, respectively (Page, 2000). NCAs 1–7 with the greatest inhibitory activity are grouped into the same class. The NCAs in the same cluster appear highly correlated in PCD (Figure 5.2).

At level b_2 with $0.93 \le b_2 \le 0.94$, the set of classes turns out to be:

$C-b_2 = (1-13,24,25)(14-23,26,27)(28-30)(31-33,37,38)(34-36)$

Five classes result, and IE decays to $h-\mathbf{R}-b_2 = 7.98$. The BT matching to $<i_1,i_2,i_3, i_4,i_5,i_6,i_7>$ and $C-b_2$ (*cf.* Figure 5.4) divides the same five classes: 1–5 with 15, 12, 3,

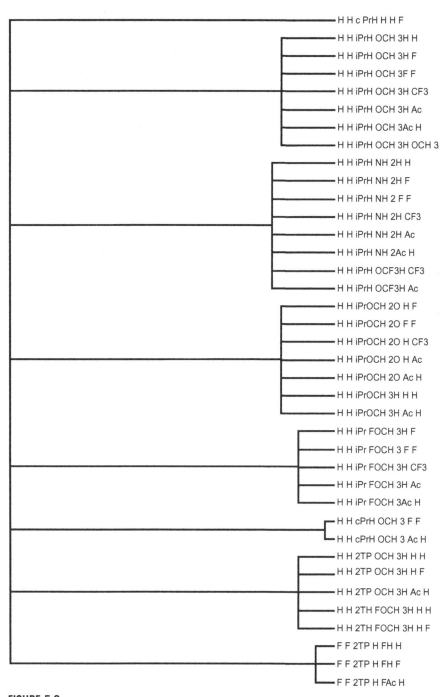

FIGURE 5.3

N-aryloxazolidinone-5-carboxamides dendrogram with anti-HIV activity: level b_1.

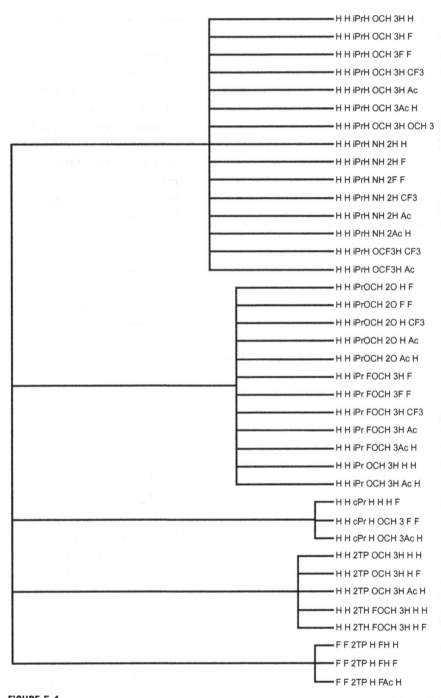

FIGURE 5.4

N-aryloxazolidinone-5-carboxamides dendrogram with anti-HIV activity: level b_2.

Table 5.2 Classification Level, Number of Classes and Entropy for the Vector of Properties of NCAs

Classification Level *b*	Number of Classes	Entropy *h*
1.00	38	444.62
0.99	18	100.94
0.98	14	63.35
0.97	8	21.18
0.94	5	7.98
0.91	4	4.33
0.88	3	2.75
0.75	2	1.20
0.07	1	0.05

5, and 3 NCAs, respectively. Again, NCAs with the greatest inhibitory activity are grouped into the same class. The NCAs belonging to the same cluster appear highly correlated in a PCD, in qualitative agreement with BT (Figures 5.2 and 5.3).

Table 5.2 shows an analysis of the set containing 1–38 classes, agreeing with PCD and BTs (Figures 5.2–5.4).

In view of PCD and BTs (Figures 5.2–5.4), the data are split into the same classes above. Figure 5.5 displays the BT. Again, NCAs with the greatest inhibitory activity are grouped into the same class.

The illustration of the classification in a radial tree (RT; *cf.* Figure 5.6) shows the same groupings as already discussed, in qualitative agreement with the PCD and BTs (Figures 5.2–5.5). Again, NCAs with the greatest inhibitory activity (1–13, *etc.*) are grouped into the same cluster.

The SplitsTree program allows analyzing the cluster analysis (CA) data (Huson, 1998). Based on the method of *split decomposition,* it takes as input the *distance matrix* and produces a graph that represents the relationships between the taxa. For ideal data, the graph is an RT, whereas less ideal data will give rise to an RT-like net, which is interpreted as possible evidence for conflicting data. Furthermore, as split decomposition does not attempt to force the data onto an RT, it can provide a good indication of how *RT*-like are given data. The splits graph (SG) for 38 NCAs in Table 5.1 (*cf.* Figure 5.7) shows that 1–27 collapse, as well as 28–33-37-38 and 34–36. It reveals no conflicting relationship between classes. It is in qualitative agreement with PCD, BTs, and RT (Figures 2–6).

Usually, in structure–property relationships (SPRs), the data file contains less than 100 objects and more than1000 *X*-variables. So many *X*-variables exist that no one can discover by *inspection* the patterns in objects. The *principal components analysis (PCA)* is useful to *summarize* the information contained in an **X**-matrix and put it in an understandable form (Hotelling, 1933; Jolliffe, 2002; Kramer, 1998; Patra *et al.*, 1999; Shaw, 2003; Xu and Hagler, 2002). The PCA works by decomposing **X**-matrix as the product of two smaller matrices **P** and **T**. The loading matrix (**P**)

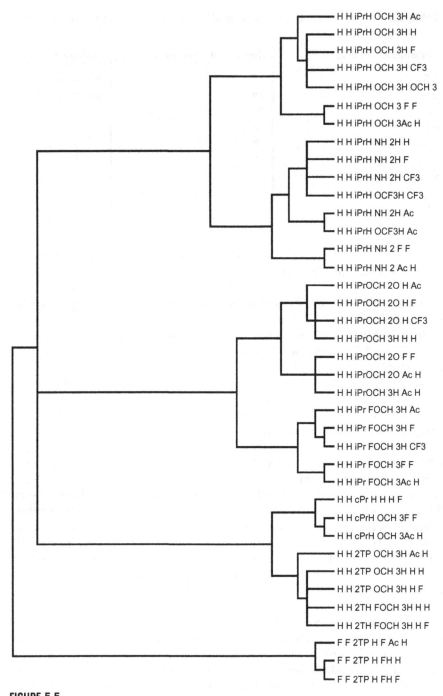

FIGURE 5.5

Dendrogram of N-aryloxazolidinone-5-carboxamides with anti-HIV inhibitory activity.

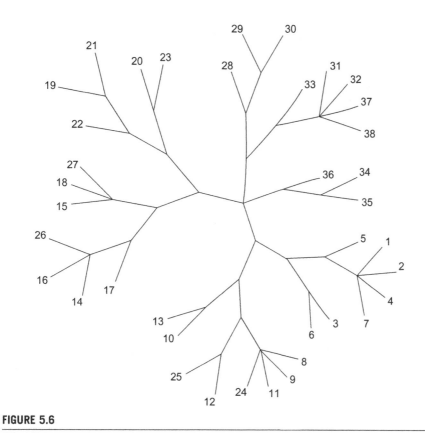

FIGURE 5.6

RT of N-aryloxazolidinone-5-carboxamides with anti-HIV inhibitory activity.

with information about variables contains a few vectors, the principal components (PCs), which are obtained as the linear combinations (LCs) of the original X-variables. The score matrix ($\mathbf{T}$), with information about the objects, is such that every object is described in terms of the projections onto PCs instead of the original variables: $\mathbf{X} = \mathbf{TP'} + \mathbf{E}$, where ' denotes the transpose matrix.

The information not contained in the matrices remains as the *unexplained X-variance* in the residual matrix ($\mathbf{E}$). Every PC_i is a new coordinate expressed as LC of the old features x_j: $PC_i = \Sigma_j b_{ij} x_j$. The new coordinates PC_i are called *scores* or *factors*, while the coefficients b_{ij}, loadings. Scores are ordered according to their information content with regard to the total variance among all objects. *Score–score plots (SPs)* show the positions of compounds in the new coordinate system, while *loading–loading plots (LPs)* show the locations of features that represent compounds in the new coordinates. The PCs show two properties: (i) They are extracted in decaying order of importance. The first PC F_1 always contains more information than F_2, F_2 more than F_3, etc.; and (ii) every PC is orthogonal to one another. No correlation exists between information contained in the different PCs. A PCA was performed for

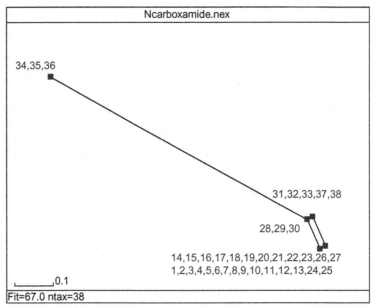

FIGURE 5.7

SG of N-aryloxazolidinone-5-carboxamides with anti-HIV inhibitory activity.

Table 5.3 Importance of PCA Factors for the Vectors of Properties of NCAs

Factor	Eigenvalue	Percentage of Variance	Cumulative Percentage of Variance
F_1	2.52038704	36.01	36.01
F_2	1.32473387	18.92	54.93
F_3	1.22151048	17.45	72.38
F_4	0.70630076	10.09	82.47
F_5	0.67263324	9.61	92.08
F_6	0.55443462	7.92	100.00
F_7	0.00000000	0.00	100.00

NCAs. The importance of PCA factors F_1–F_7 for $\{i_1, i_2, i_3, i_4, i_5, i_6, i_7\}$ is collected in Table 5.3. Factors are LCs of the vectors. Factor F_1 explains 36% of variance (64% error); $F_{1/2}$, 55% of variance (45% error); F_{1-3}, 72% of variance (28% error); etc.

The PCA factor loadings are shown in Table 5.4.

Table 5.4 PCA Loadings for the Vectors of Properties of NCAs[a]

PCA Factor Loadings[a]

Prprt.	F_1	F_2	F_3	F_4	F_5	F_6	F_7
i_1	0.59637237	−0.10094594	−0.11589113	0.19084837	0.10208832	0.27179778	**0.70710678**
i_2	0.59637237	−0.10094594	−0.11589113	0.19084837	0.10208832	0.27179778	**−0.70710678**
i_3	0.42229981	0.18796773	0.25838970	−0.21712853	0.36848370	**−0.73255766**	0.00000000
i_4	−0.17914678	0.23137929	0.66442571	0.34714693	0.49054502	0.33430991	0.00000000
i_5	0.22944642	−0.12897077	0.63241885	0.07483329	**−0.72193407**	−0.06307494	0.00000000
i_6	0.00985543	0.66131843	−0.25251206	0.62028918	−0.25230381	−0.22446065	0.00000000
i_7	0.15970753	0.66089036	0.03458013	−0.60756837	−0.13377322	0.38663556	0.00000000

[a]Loadings greater than 0.7 are in bold.

Table 5.5 Profile of the PCA Factors for the Vectors of the Properties of NCAs

Factor	% of i_1	% of i_2	% of i_3	% of i_4	% of i_5	% of i_6	% of i_7
F_1	35.57	35.57	17.83	3.21	5.26	0.01	2.55
F_2	1.02	1.02	3.53	5.35	1.66	43.73	43.68
F_3	1.34	1.34	6.68	44.15	40.00	6.38	0.12
F_4	3.64	3.64	4.71	12.05	0.56	38.48	36.91
F_5	1.04	1.04	13.58	24.06	**52.12**	6.37	1.79
F_6	7.39	7.39	**53.66**	11.18	0.40	5.04	14.95
F_7	50.00	50.00	0.00	0.00	0.00	0.00	0.00

Note: *Percentages greater than 50% are in bold.*

The PCA F_{1-7} profile for the vectors is listed in Table 5.5. For factors F_1 and F_7, variables $\{i_1,i_2\}$ show the greatest weight in profile; however, F_1 cannot be reduced to both variables without a 29% error, although F_7 is reduced to both variables with a 0% error. For F_2, the variable i_6 presents the greatest weight; notwithstanding, F_2 cannot be reduced to two variables $\{i_6,i_7\}$ without a 13% error. For F_3, the variable i_4 assigns greatest weight; nevertheless, F_3 cannot be reduced to two variables $\{i_4,i_5\}$ without a 16% error. For F_4, the variable i_6 consigns the greatest weight; however, F_4 cannot be reduced to two variables $\{i_6,i_7\}$ without a 25% error. For F_5, the variable i_5 represents the greatest weight; however, F_5 cannot be reduced to two variables $\{i_4,i_5\}$ without a 24% error. For F_6, the variable i_3 shows the greatest weight; nevertheless, F_6 cannot be reduced to two variables $\{i_3,i_7\}$ without a 31% error.

In PCA F_2–F_1 SP, NCAs with the same vector collapse. Five NCA classes are distinguished: (i) class 1, with 15 compounds ($0<F_1<F_2$, cf. Figure 5.8, *top*); (ii) grouping 2, with 12 substances ($F_1>F_2\approx0$, *right*); cluster 3, with 3 molecules ($F_1<F_2\approx0$, *center*); class 4, with 5 organics ($0>F_1>F_2$, *bottom*); and cluster 5 (3 units, $F_1<<F_2$, *left*). Classification agrees with PCD, BTs, RT, and SG (Figures 5.2–5.7).

From the PCA factor loadings of NCAs (Table 5.4), F_2–F_1 LP (cf. Figure 5.9) depicts seven vectors, and properties $R_{3/6}$ collapse. As a complement to SP (Figure 5.8) for loadings (Figure 5.9), NCAs in class 1, located at the top, present a contribution of $R_1=$ Ac situated on the same position in Figure 5.8. The NCAs in grouping 2 on the right have greater contributions of $R_7=i$Pr. The NCAs in classes 3 and 4 in the middle-bottom present a contribution of $R_3=R_6=$ H. The NCAs in class 5 on the left present a contribution of $R_4=$ H. Two classes of properties are distinguished in LP: class 1 $\{R_3,R_6,R_7,R_4,R_5,R_2\}$ ($F_1>F_2$, Figure 5.9 *bottom*); and grouping 2 $\{R_1\}$ ($F_1<F_2$, *top*).

Instead of 38 NCAs in the space $\mathfrak{R}^7$ of seven vectors, consider seven properties in the space $\mathfrak{R}^{38}$ of 38 NCAs. The BT of the vectors (cf. Figure 5.10) separates the first property R_1 (class 2), then R_2, R_5, R_4, R_7, R_3, and R_6 (class 1), agreeing with PCA LP (Figure 5.9).

The RT for the vectors (cf. Figure 5.11) separates the same classes as given previously, agreeing with PCA LP and BT (Figures 5.9 and 5.10).

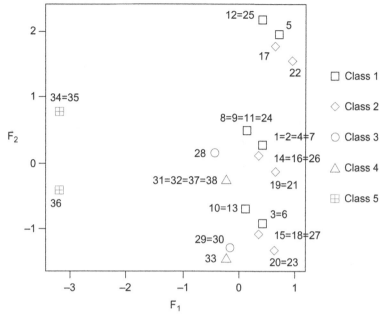

FIGURE 5.8

PCA F_2 versus F_1 scores plot for anti-HIV NCAs.

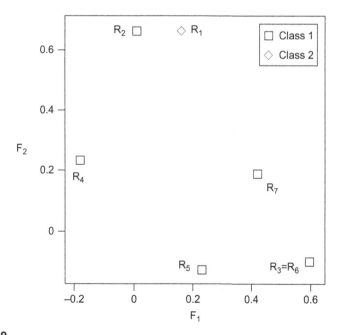

FIGURE 5.9

PCA F_2 versus F_1 loadings plot for anti-HIV NCAs.

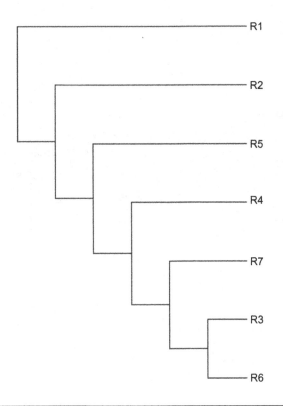

FIGURE 5.10

Dendrogram for the vectors of properties corresponding to anti-HIV NCAs.

The SG for the vectors (*cf.* Figure 5.12) shows that R_{3-7} collapse. No conflicting relationship appears between the classes. The SG agrees with PCA LP, BT, and RT (Figures 5.9–5.11).

Another PCA was performed for the vectors, which are described by their occurrence in molecules, and new factors are LCs of the compounds. The use of factor F_1 explains 41% of the variance (59% error), $F_{1/2}$, 58% of variance (42% error), F_{1-3}, 74% of variance (26% error), etc. In PCA F_2–F_1 SP, R_{3-6} collapse. Two classes of properties are distinguished: class 1 $\{R_3, R_6, R_7, R_4, R_5, R_2\}$ ($F_1 > F_2$, *cf.* Figure 5.13, *right*); and grouping 2 $\{R_1\}$ ($F_1 < F_2$, *left*), agreeing with PCA LP, BT, RT, and SG (Figures 5.9–5.12).

The recommended format for the NCA PT (*cf.* Table 5.6) shows that they are classified first by i_1, then by i_2, i_3, i_4, i_5, i_6, and, finally, by i_7. Periods of eight units are assumed; *e.g.*, group g00010 stands for $<i_1, i_2, i_3, i_4, i_5> = <00010>: <0001000>$ (–F –F –2-TP –H –F –Ac –H), etc. The NCAs in the same column appear close in PCD, BTs, RT, SG, and PCA SP (Figures 5.2–5.8).

The variation of property P (HIV-1 PR inhibitory activity) of vector $<i_1, i_2, i_3, i_4, i_5, i_6, i_7>$ (*cf.* Figure 5.14) is expressed in the decimal system

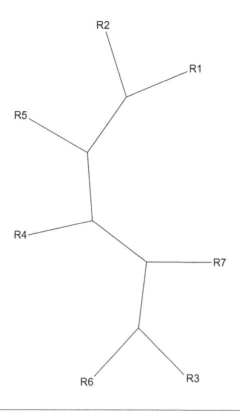

FIGURE 5.11

RT for the vectors of properties corresponding to anti-HIV NCAs.

$P = 10^6 i_1 + 10^5 i_2 + 10^4 i_3 + 10^3 i_4 + 10^2 i_5 + 10 i_6 + i_7$ versus structural parameters $\{i_1, i_2, i_3, i_4, i_5, i_6, i_7\}$ for NCAs. Most data collapse. Parameter i_1 shows greater variation i_2, i_3, i_4, i_5 and i_6. The property P was not used in the development of the PT and serves to validate it. The results agree with PT of properties with vertical groups defined by $\{i_1, i_2, i_3, i_4, i_5\}$ and horizontal periods, by $\{i_6, i_7\}$.

The change of property P of vector $<i_1, i_2, i_3, i_4, i_5, i_6, i_7>$ in base 10 versus the number of the group in the NCA PT (*cf.* Figure 5.15) reveals minima and maxima corresponding to compounds with $<i_1, i_2, i_3, i_4, i_5> ca.$ $<00010>$ (group g00010) and $<11111>$ (g11111), respectively. Most points collapse, especially in groups 5–8. Periods p00, p10, and p11 represent rows 1–3 in Table 5.6. The function $P(i_1, i_2, i_3, i_4, i_5, i_6, i_7)$ denotes series of periodic waves (PWs) limited by minima and maxima, which suggest a PW behavior that recalls the form of a trigonometric function. For $<i_1, i_2, i_3, i_4, i_5, i_6, i_7>$, a minimum is shown. The distance in $<i_1, i_2, i_3, i_4, i_5, i_6, i_7>$ units between each pair of consecutive minima is eight, which coincides with NCA sets in successive PWs. The minima occupy analogous positions in the curve and are in phase. The representative points in phase should correspond to elements in the same group in PT. For $<i_1, i_2, i_3, i_4, i_5, i_6, i_7>$ minima, coherence exists between the two representations;

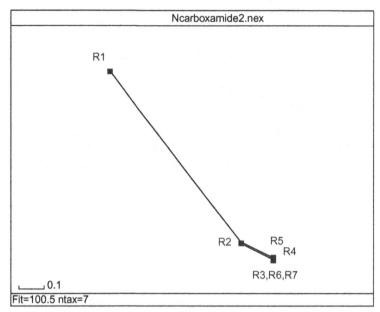

FIGURE 5.12

SG for the vectors of properties corresponding to anti-HIV NCAs.

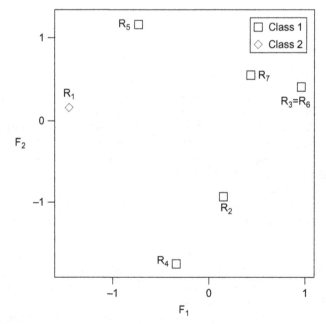

FIGURE 5.13

PCA F_2 versus F_1 scores plot for vectors of properties of NCAs.

Table 5.6 Periodic Properties for N-aryloxazolidinone-5-carboxamide Derivatives

Property	g00010	g11000	g11010	g11011	g11100	g11101	g11110	g11111
p00	F F 2-TP H F Ac H	H H 2-TP OCH$_3$ H Ac H		H H cPr H OCH$_3$ F F H H cPr H OCH$_3$ Ac H	H H iPr –O– F F H H iPr –O– CH$_2$–O– Ac H H H iPr OCH$_3$ H Ac H	H H iPr F OCH$_3$ F F H H iPr F OCH$_3$ Ac H	H H iPr H NH$_2$ F F H H iPr H NH$_2$ Ac H	H H iPr H OCH$_3$ F F H H iPr H OCH$_3$ Ac H
p10	F F 2-TP H F H H H H F F 2-TP H F H F	H H 2-TP OCH$_3$ H H H H H 2-TP OCH$_3$ H H F H H 2THF OCH$_3$ H H H H 2THF OCH$_3$ H H F	H H cPr H H H F		H H iPr –O– CH$_2$–O– H F H H iPr –O– CH$_2$–O– H CF$_3$ H H iPr OCH$_3$ H H H	H H iPr F OCH$_3$ H F H H iPr F OCH$_3$ H CF$_3$	H H iPr H NH$_2$ H F H H iPr H NH$_2$ H H H H iPr H NH$_2$ H F H H iPr H NH$_2$ H CF$_3$ H H iPr H OCF$_3$ H CF$_3$	H H iPr H OCH$_3$ H H H H iPr H OCH$_3$ H H H H iPr H OCH$_3$ H F H H iPr H OCH$_3$ H CF$_3$ H H iPr H OCH$_3$ H OCH$_3$
p11					H H iPr –O– CH$_2$–O– H Ac	H H iPr F OCH$_3$ H Ac	H H iPr H NH$_2$ H Ac H H iPr H OCF$_3$ H Ac	H H iPr H OCH$_3$ H Ac

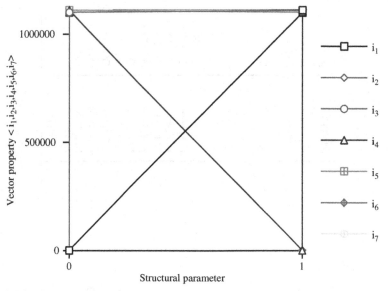

FIGURE 5.14

Variation of property P(p) of NCAs versus counts $\{i_1, i_2, i_3, i_4, i_5, i_6, i_7\}$.

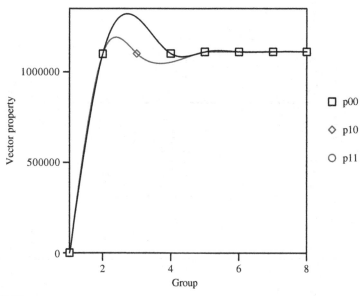

FIGURE 5.15

Variation of property P(p) of N-aryloxazolidinone-5-carboxamides versus group number.

however, the consistency is not general. Wave comparison shows two differences: (i) all PWs are incomplete, and (ii) PWs p00 and p10 are staircaselike. Most characteristic points of the plot are minima that lie about group g00010. Values of $<i_1,i_2,i_3,i_4,i_5,i_6,i_7>$ are repeated, as the periodic law (PL) states.

An empirical function $P(p)$ reproduces different $<i_1,i_2,i_3,i_4,i_5,i_6,i_7>$ values. A minimum of $P(p)$ has meaning only if it is compared with the former $P(p-1)$ and later $P(p+1)$ points, needing to fulfill:

$$P_{min}(p) < P(p-1)$$

$$P_{min}(p) < P(p+1). \tag{5.8}$$

Order relations [Eq. (5.8)] should repeat at determined intervals equal to PW size and are equivalent to

$$P_{min}(p) - P(p-1) < 0$$

$$P(p+1) - P_{min}(p) > 0. \tag{5.9}$$

As Eq. (5.9) is valid only for minima, other more general expressions are desired for all values of p. The differences $D(p) = P(p+1) - P(p)$ are calculated by assigning every value to NCA p:

$$D(p) = P(p+1) - P(p). \tag{5.10}$$

Instead of $D(p)$, $R(p) = P(p+1)/P(p)$ is taken by assigning them to NCA p. If PL were general, elements in the same group in analogous positions in different PWs would satisfy

$$\text{either } D(p) > 0 \text{ or } D(p) < 0 \tag{5.11}$$

$$\text{either } R(p) > 1 \text{ or } R(p) < 1 \tag{5.12}$$

However, the results show that this is not the case, so that PL is not general, existing some anomalies. Change of $D(p)$ versus group number (*cf.* Figure 5.16) presents a lack of coherence between $<i_1,i_2,i_3,i_4,i_5,i_6,i_7>$ Cartesian and PT representations. Most results collapse, mainly in groups 5–7. The datum for group 8, PW p00, should be taken with care because it was calculated with the first point in the following PW. If consistency were rigorous, all points in every PW would have the same sign. Trend exists in points to give $D(p) > 0$ for lower groups, but not for greater ones. However, irregularities exist in which NCAs for successive PWs are not always in phase.

The change of $R(p)$ versus group number (*cf.* Figure 5.17) confirms the lack of constancy between Cartesian and PT charts. Most data collapse, especially in groups 5–7. If steadiness were exact, all points in every PW would show $R(p)$ as either lesser or greater than 1. A trend in the points exists to give $R(p) > 1$ for lower groups, but not for greater ones. Notwithstanding, confirmed incongruities exist in which NCAs for the successive PWs are not always in phase.

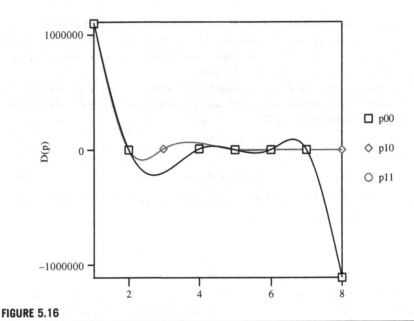

FIGURE 5.16

Variation of property $D(p) = P(p+1) - P(p)$ versus group number. P is the vector property.

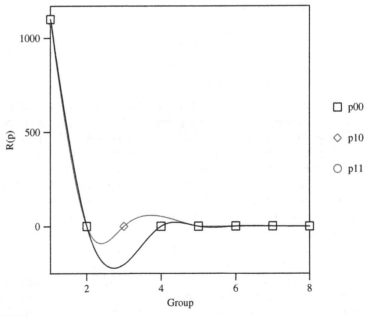

FIGURE 5.17

Variation of property $R(p) = P(p+1)/P(p)$ versus group number. P is the vector property.

The IE approach identifies cliffs. The method was applied to 74 flavonoids and is being used for 177 phenolic compounds. The technique is not sensitive to the number of compounds; otherwise, it could result in one-case classes that could be outliers. The impact of noisy experimental data on the method performance is expected to be small. Matched molecular pair analysis (MMPA) focuses on the effects of specific structural changes on properties of interest; its assumption is that differences in a property are predicted more accurately than the property itself; it is applied to structural diverse data sets, which rises confidence that observed effects of structural changes are globally relevant; it is related to bioisosterism in its focus on specific substructural transformations (Birch *et al.*, 2009; Griffen *et al.*, 2011; Kenny and Sadowski, 2005; Leach *et al.*, 2006; Papadatos *et al.*, 2010; Schultes *et al.*, 2012; Warner *et al.*, 2012). However, consider the following: (i) it goes further in providing quantitative estimates of the changes that result from the application of particular transformations and provides an inverse QSAR; (ii) it models not only bioactivity, but also any chemical, physicochemical, or pharmacokinetic property.

It is an inverse QSAR, which is gaining popularity in the retrospective analysis of large experimental data sets. While much focus was on the differences in properties between structurally related groups of existing compounds, attempts to extend it to the *de novo* design of structures were limited. Using IE, one looks for trends and central tendencies for novel drugs, mixtures, or properties; however, when one uses MMPA to look at activities that involve some kind of interaction with a binding site, one is looking for exceptions.

8 CONCLUSIONS

From these results and discussion, the following conclusions can be drawn:

1. Several criteria, selected to reduce the analysis to a manageable quantity of N-aryloxazolidinone-5-carboxamides, refer to substitutions at positions $R_{1/2}$, R_{3-6} on different phenyls and R_7. Many classification algorithms are based on IE. For sets of moderate size, an excessive number of results appear compatible with the data and suffer a combinatorial explosion. However, after the EC, the best configuration is that in which the entropy production is most uniformly distributed. Molecular structural elements are ranked according to inhibitory activity: $R_3 > R_6 > R_7 > R_4 > R_5 > R_2 > R_1$. In compound 5, $R_3 = R_6 = R_4 = R_2 = H$, $R_7 = i\text{Pr}$, $R_5 = OCH_3$, and $R_1 = Ac$ <1111111>, which was selected as reference. Substances are grouped into five classes. This method avoids the problem of others of continuum variables because for <1111111>, null standard deviation causes a Pearson correlation coefficient of 1. The results agree with the principal component analyses.

2. The periodic law does not satisfy the laws of physics: (i) the inhibitory activity of N-aryloxazolidinone-5-carboxamides is not repeated, as the periodic law states, which is perhaps due to their chemical character; (ii) the order relationships are

repeated with exceptions. The analysis forces the statement: The relationships that any compound p has with its neighbor $p+1$ are approximately repeated for every period. The periodicity is not general; however, if a natural order of substances is accepted, the periodic law must be phenomenological. The inhibitory activity was not used in the generation of the PT and serves to validate it. Work to be done is the periodic analysis of any other molecular properties (*e.g.*, cytotoxicity) that are not used in the construction of the PT. It would give insight into the possible generality of the PL. The authors are happy with the PT, although it should be tested for all properties: adverse effects, etc. The method is thought for medicinal, nutritional and phylogenetic chemists. However, the obtained PT deserves a broader spectra (*e.g.*, for doctors to mix carboxamides of different classes with dissimilar types of properties: high anti-viral activity, low cytotoxicity, etc.)

3. Code MolClas is a simple, reliable, efficient and fast procedure for molecular classification, based on EC of entropy production. It was written not only to analyze EC, but also to explore the world of molecular classification.

ACKNOWLEDGMENTS

One of the authors, F. T., acknowledges support from the Spanish Ministerio de Economía y Competitividad (Project No. BFU2013-41648-P) and EU ERDF.

REFERENCES

Alberts, B., Johnson, A., Lewis, J., Raff, M., Roberts, K., Walter, P., 2002. Molecular Biology of the Cell. Garland, New York, NY.

Ali, A., Reddy, G.S.K.K., Cao, H., Anjum, S.G., Nalam, M.N.L., Schiffer, C.A., Rana, T.M., 2006. Discovery of HIV-1 protease inhibitors with picomolar affinities incorporating *N*–aryl–oxazolidinone–5–carboxamides as novel P2 ligands. J. Med. Chem. 49, 7342–7356.

Baez, J., Dolan, J., 1995. Higher dimensional algebra and topological quantum field theory. J. Math. Phys. 36, 6073–6105.

Benzecri, J.P., 1984. L'analyse des données, vol. 1. Dunod, Paris, France.

Birch, A.M., Kenny, P.W., Simpson, I., Whittamore, P.R.O., 2009. Matched molecular pair analysis of activity and properties of glycogen phosphorylase inhibitors. Bioorg. Med. Chem. Lett. 19, 850–853.

Castellano, G., Torrens, F., 2014. AIDS destroys immune defences: hypothesis. New Front. Chem. 23, 11–20. Classification by information entropy of triterpenoids and steroids of Ganoderma. Phytochemistry

Castellano, G., Tena, J., Torrens, F., 2012. Classification of polyphenolic compounds by chemical structural indicators and its relation to antioxidant properties of *Posidonia oceanica* (L.) Delile. MATCH Commun. Math. Comput. Chem. 67, 231–250.

Castellano, G., González-Santander, J.L., Lara, A., Torrens, F., 2013. Classification of flavonoid compounds by using entropy of information theory. Phytochemistry 93, 182–191.

Castellano, G., Lara, A., Torrens, F., 2014. Classification of stilbenoid compounds by entropy of artificial intelligence. Phytochemistry 97, 62–69.

Castellano-Estornell, G., Torrens-Zaragozá, F., 2009. Local anaesthetics classified using chemical structural indicators. Nereis 2, 7–17.

Chakravarty, A.K., 2006. Immunology and immunotechnology. Oxford University, New Delhi, India.

Cox, E., 1994. The fuzzy systems handbook. Academic, New York, NY.

Crans, S., 2000. On braidings, syllepses and symmetries. Cahiers Topologie Géom. Différentielle Catég. 41 (1), 2–74.

Griffen, E., Leach, A.G., Robb, G.R., Warner, D.J., 2011. Matched molecular pairs as a medicinal chemistry tool. J. Med. Chem. 54, 7739–7750.

Halder, A.K., Jha, T., 2010. Validated predictive QSAR modeling of N-aryl-oxazolidinone-5-carboxamides for anti-HIV protease activity. Bioorg. Med. Chem. Lett. 20, 6082–6087.

Hotelling, H., 1933. Analysis of a complex of statistical variables into principal components. J. Educ. Psychol. 24, 417–441.

Huson, D.H., 1998. SplitsTree: analizing and visualizing evolutionary data. Bioinformatics 14, 68–73.

IMSL, 1989. Integrated Mathematical Statistical Library (IMSL). IMSL, Houston, TX.

Iordache, O., 2011. Modeling Multi-Level Systems. Springer, Berlin, Ger.

Iordache, O., 2012. Self-Evolvable Systems: Machine Learning in Social Media. Springer, Berlin, Ger.

Iordache, O., Corriou, J.P., Garrido-Sánchez, L., Fonteix, C., Tondeur, D., 1993. Neural network frames. Application to biochemical kinetic diagnosis. Comput. Chem. Eng. 17, 1101–1113.

Jarvis, R.A., Patrick, E.A., 1973. Clustering using a similarity measure based on shared nearest neighbors. IEEE Trans. Comput. C22, 1025–1034.

Jolliffe, I.T., 2002. Principal Component Analysis. Springer, New York, NY.

Katzung, B.G. (Ed.), 2004. Basic and Clinical Pharmacology. McGraw-Hill, New Delhi, India.

Kaufmann, A., 1975. Introduction à la théorie des sous-ensembles flous, vol. 3. Masson, Paris, France.

Kenny, P.W., Sadowski, J., 2005. Structure modification in chemical databases. In: Oprea, T.I. (Ed.), Chemoinformatics in Drug Discovery. Wiley-VCH, Weinheim, Ger, pp. 271–285.

Kramer, R., 1998. Chemometric Techniques for Quantitative Analysis. Marcel Dekker, New York, NY.

Kullback, S., 1959. Information Theory and Statistics. Wiley, New York, NY.

Kundu, S., 1998. The min–max composition rule and its superiority over the usual max–min composition rule. Fuzzy Set. Syst. 93, 319–329.

Lambert-Torres, G., Pereira Pinto, J.O., Borges da Silva, L.E., 1999. Minmax techniques. In: Wiley Encyclopedia of Electrical and Electronics Engineering. Wiley, New York, NY.

Leach, A.G., Jones, H.D., Cosgrove, D.A., Kenny, P.W., Ruston, L., MacFaul, P., Wood, J.M., Colclough, N., Law, B., 2006. Matched molecular pairs as a guide in the optimization of pharmaceutical properties; a study of aqueous solubility, plasma protein binding and oral exposure. J. Med. Chem. 49, 6672–6682.

Leinster, T., 2004. Higher Operands, Higher Categories. Cambridge University Press, Cambridge, UK.

Liu, X., Gan, M., Dong, B., Zhang, T., Li, Y., Zhang, Y., Fan, X., Wu, Y., Bai, S., Chen, M., Yu, L., Tao, P., Jiang, W., Si, S., 2013. 4862 F, a new inhibitor of HIV-1 protease, from the culture of *Streptomyces* I03A-04862. Molecules 18, 236–243.

Page, R.D.M., 2000. Program TreeView. Universiy of Glasgow, Glasgow, UK.

Papadatos, G., Alkarouri, M., Gillet, V.J., Willett, P., Kadirkamanathan, V., Luscombe, C.N., Bravi, G., Richmond, N.J., Pickett, S.D., Hussain, J., Pritchard, J.M., Cooper, A.W.J., Macdonald, S.J.F., 2010. Lead optimizatioin using matched molecular pairs: inclusion of contextual information for enhanced prediction of hERG inhibition, solubility, and lipophilicity. J. Chem. Inf. Model. 50, 1872–1886.

Patra, S.K., Mandal, A.K., Pal, M.K., 1999. State of aggregation of bilirubin in aqueous solution: principal component analysis approach. J. Photochem. Photobiol. A 122, 23–31.

Schultes, S., de Graaf, C., Berger, H., Mayer, M., Steffen, A., Haaksma, E.E.J., de Esch, I.J.P., Leurs, R., Krämer, O., 2012. A medicinal chemistry perspective on melting point: matched molecular pair analysis of the effects of simple descriptors on the melting point of druglike compounds. Med. Chem. Comm. 3, 584–591.

Shannon, C.E., 1948a. A mathematical theory of communication: part I, discrete noiseless systems. Bell Syst. Tech. J. 27, 379–423.

Shannon, C.E., 1948b. A mathematical theory of communication: part II, the discrete channel with noise. Bell Syst. Tech. J. 27, 623–656.

Shaw, P.J.A., 2003. Multivariate Statistics for the Environmental Sciences. Hodder-Arnold, New York, NY.

Tondeur, D., Kvaalen, E., 1987. Equipartition of entropy production. An optimality criterion for transfer and separation processes. Ind. Eng. Chem. Fundam. 26, 50–56.

Torrens, F., Castellano, G., 2006. Periodic classification of local anaesthetics (procaine analogues). Int. J. Mol. Sci. 7, 12–34.

Torrens, F., Castellano, G., 2009a. Classification of complex molecules. In: Hassanien, A.-E., Abraham, A. (Eds.), In: Foundations of Computational Intelligence, vol. 5. Springer, Berlin, Ger, pp. 243–315.

Torrens, F., Castellano, G., 2009b. Modelling of complex multicellular systems: tumour–immune cells competition. Chem. Cent. J.. 3 (Suppl. I), 75–1-1.

Torrens, F., Castellano, G., 2010. Table of periodic properties of human immunodeficiency virus inhibitors. Int. J. Comput. Intell. Bioinformatics Syst. Biol. 1, 246–273.

Torrens, F., Castellano, G., 2011a. Information entropy and the table of periodic properties of local anaesthetics. Int. J. Chemoinform. Chem. Eng. 1 (2), 15–35.

Torrens, F., Castellano, G., 2011b. Molecular classification of thiocarbamates with cytoprotection activity against human immunodeficiency virus. Int. J. Chem. Model. 3, 269–296.

Torrens, F., Castellano, G., 2012a. Structural classification of complex molecules by artificial intelligence techniques. In: Castro, E.D., Haghi, A.K. (Eds.), Advanced Methods and Applications in Chemoinformatics: Research Progress and New Applications. IGI Global, Hershey, PA, pp. 25–91.

Torrens, F., Castellano, G., 2012b. Complexity, emergence and molecular diversity via information theory. In: Orsucci, F., Sala, N. (Eds.), Complexity Science, Living Systems, and Reflexing Interfaces: New Models and Perspectives. IGI Global, Hershey, PA, pp. 196–208.

Torrens, F., Castellano, G., 2012c. Molecular diversity classification via information theory: a review. ICST Tran. Compl. Syst. 12 (10-12), e41–e48.

Torrens, F., Castellano, G., 2012d. Structural classification of complex molecules by information entropy and equipartition conjecture. In: Putz, M.V. (Ed.), Chemical Information and Computational Challenges in 21st Century. Nova, New York, NY, pp. 101–139.

Torrens, F., Castellano, G., 2013a. Molecular classification by information theoretic entropy: oxadiazolamines as potential therapeutic agents. Curr. Comput. Aided Drug Des. 9, 241–253.

Torrens, F., Castellano, G., 2013b. Molecular classification of 5-amino-2-aroylquinolines and 4-aroyl-6,7,8-trimethoxyquinolines as highly potent tubulin polymerization inhibitors. Int. J. Chemoinform. Chem. Eng. 3 (2), 1–26.

Torrens, F., Castellano, G., in press-a. Molecular classification, diversity and complexity via information entropy. In: Stavrinides, S.G., Banerjee, S., Caglar, H., Ozer, M. (Eds.), Chaos and Complex Systems, vol. 4. Springer, Berlin, Ger.

Torrens, F., Castellano, G., in press-b. AIDS destroys immune defences: hypothesis. In: New Frontiers in Chemistry.

Tripathi, K.D., 2003. Essentials of Medical Pharmacology. Jaypee Brothers, New Delhi, India.

Tryon, R.C., 1939. A multivariate analysis of the risk of coronary heart disease in Framingham. J. Chronic Dis. 20, 511–524.

Varmuza, K., 1980. Pattern Recognition in Chemistry. Springer, New York, NY.

Volberding, P.A., Deeks, S.G., 2010. Antiretroviral therapy and management of HIV infection. Lancet 376, 49–62.

Wang, R.R., Gao, Y.D., Ma, C.H., Zhang, X.J., Huang, C.G., Huang, J.F., Zheng, Y.T., 2011. Mangiferin, an anti-HIV-1 agent targeting protease and effective against resistant strains. Molecules 16, 4264–4277.

Warner, D.J., Bridgland-Taylor, M.H., Sefton, C.E., Wood, D.J., 2012. Prospective prediction of antitarget activity by matched molecular pairs analysis. Mol. Inform. 31, 365–368.

White, H., 1989. Neural network learning and statistics. AI expert 4 (12), 48–52.

Xu, J., Hagler, A., 2002. Chemoinformatics and drug discovery. Molecules 7, 566–600.

Zhang, J., Hou, T., Liu, Y., Chen, G., Yang, X., Liu, J.S., Wang, W., 2012. Systematic investigation on interactions for HIV drug resistance and cross-resistance among protease inhibitors. J. Proteome Sci. Comput. Biol. 1 (2), 1-1-8.

Review of Recent Protein-Protein Interaction Techniques

6

Maad Shatnawi

Higher Colleges of Technology, Abu Dhabi, UAE

1 INTRODUCTION

Proteins are the building blocks of all living organisms. The primary structure of a protein is the linear sequence of its amino acid (AA) units, starting from the amino-terminal residue (N-terminal) to the carboxyl-terminal residue (C-terminal). Amino acids consist of carbon, hydrogen, oxygen, and nitrogen atoms that are clustered into functional groups. All amino acids have the same general structure, but each has a different R group. The carbon atom to which the R group is connected is called the *alpha carbon*. There are 20 amino acids in proteins and are connected by a chemical reaction in which a molecule of water is removed, leaving two amino acids residues connected by a peptide bond. These 20 amino acids are alanine, arginine, asparagine, aspartic acid, cysteine, glutamic acid, glutamine, glycine, histidine, isoleucine, leucine, lysine, methionine, phenylalanine, proline, serine, threonine, tryptophan, tyrosine, and valine. These amino acids are represented by one-letter abbreviations: A, R, N, D, C, Q, E, G, H, I, L, K, M, F, P, S, T, W, Y, and V, respectively (Berg *et al.*, 2002).

The secondary structure of a protein is the general three-dimensional form of its local parts. The most common secondary structures are alpha (α) helices and beta (β) sheets. The α-helix is a right-handed spiral array, while the β-sheet is made of beta strands connected crosswise by two or more hydrogen bonds, forming a twisted, pleated sheet. These secondary structures are linked by tight turns and loose, flexible loops (Berg *et al.*, 2002). Protein domains are the basic functional units of protein tertiary structures. A protein domain is a conserved part of a protein sequence that can evolve, function, and exist independently. Each domain forms a three-dimensional structure and can be stable and folded independently. Several domains are joined in different combinations to form multidomain protein sequences (Chothia, 1992; Yoo *et al.*, 2008).

A protein interacts with other proteins to perform certain tasks. Protein-protein interaction (PPI) occurs at almost every level of cell function. The identification of interactions among proteins provides a global picture of cellular functions and biological processes. Since most biological processes involve one or more protein-protein interactions, the accurate identification of the set of interacting proteins in an organism is very useful for deciphering the molecular mechanisms underlying given biological functions, as well as for assigning functions to unknown proteins based on their interacting partners (Zaki *et al.*, 2009; Xenarios and Eisenberg, 2001; Kim *et al.*, 2002). Protein interaction prediction is also a fundamental step in the construction of PPI networks for humans and other organisms. The identification of possible viral-host protein interactions can lead to a better understanding of infection mechanisms and, in turn, to the development of several medication drugs and treatment optimization. Abnormal PPIs are implicated in several neurological disorders, including Creutzfeld-Jakob and Alzheimer's diseases (Bader and Hogue, 2002; Von Mering *et al.*, 2002; Qi *et al.*, 2006). Therefore, the development of accurate and reliable methods for identifying PPIs has very important impacts in several protein research areas.

This chapter, as an extension of a previous paper (Shatnawi, 2014), provides a comprehensive and comparative study and categorization of the existing computational approaches in PPI prediction. It also discusses the technical challenges and open issues in this field. The rest of this chapter is organized as follows: The next section addresses the key technical challenges that face PPI prediction and the open issues in this field. Section 3 discusses the performance measures that are typically used in PPI prediction. Section 4 provides a comprehensive description and comparison of the most current computational PPI predictors. Concluding remarks are presented in Section 5.

2 TECHNICAL CHALLENGES AND OPEN ISSUES

There are several technical challenges that face computational analysis of protein sequences in general and PPI prediction in particular. First, there have been a huge amount of newly discovered protein sequences in the past genomic era. Second, protein chains are typically long, which makes them difficult, time consuming, and expensive to characterize by experimental methods. Third, the availability of large, comprehensive, and accurate benchmark data sets is required for the training and evaluation of prediction methods. Fourth, appropriate performance measures to evaluate the significance of the predictors should be developed to minimize the number of false positives and false negatives. Fifth, it is difficult to distinguish between novel interactions and false positives. Sixth, computational PPI methods are based on experimentally collected data, and therefore, any error in the experimental data will affect the computational PPI predictions.

One of the challenges of protein prediction methods is protein representation. Protein prediction methods vary in protein representation and feature extraction in order to build their classification models. There are two kinds of models that were generally used to represent protein samples; the sequential model and the discrete model. The most and simplest sequential model for a protein is its entire AA sequence. However, this representation does not work well when the query protein does not have high sequence similarity to any attribute-known proteins. Several non-sequential models, or discrete models, have been proposed. The simplest discrete model is AA composition, which is the normalized occurrence frequencies of the 20 native amino acids in a protein. However, all the sequence-order knowledge will be lost using this representation, which in turn will negatively affect the prediction quality (Chou, 2011). Some approaches use AA physiochemical properties, while others use pairwise similarity. Some approaches are template-based, while others are statistical-based or machine learning (ML)–based.

There are various challenges that face ML protein interaction prediction methods. Selecting the best ML approach is a great challenge. There are many techniques that vary in accuracy, robustness, complexity, computational cost, data diversity, over-fitting, and ability to deal with missing attributes and different features. Most ML approaches of protein sequences are computationally expensive and often suffer from low prediction accuracy. They are also susceptible to overfitting (Melo *et al.*, 2003).

Most PPI prediction approaches have achieved a reasonable performance on balanced data sets containing an equal number of interacting and noninteracting protein pairs. However, this ratio is highly imbalanced in nature, and these approaches have not been comprehensively assessed with respect to the effect of the large number of noninteracting pairs in realistic data sets. In addition, since highly imbalanced distributions usually lead to large data sets, more efficient prediction methods, algorithmic optimizations, and continued improvements in hardware performance are required to handle such challenging tasks.

3 PERFORMANCE MEASURES

There are several performance measures that are used to evaluate a PPI predictor and compare it with other approaches. The most frequently used evaluation measures in this field are accuracy, sensitivity, specificity, precision, F-measure (F1), Matthews correlation coefficient (MCC), receiver operating characteristic (ROC), and AUC (Area Under the ROC Curve).

Accuracy (Ac) is the proportion of correctly predicted interacting and noninter-acting protein pairs to all of the protein pairs listed in the data set. Sensitivity, or recall (R), is the proportion of correctly predicted interacting protein pairs to all of the interacting protein pairs listed in the data set. Precision (P) is the proportion of correctly predicted interacting protein pairs to all of the predicted interacting protein pairs. *Specificity (Sp)* is the proportion of correctly predicted noninteracting protein pairs to all the noninteracting protein pairs listed in the data set. These metrics can be represented mathematically as follows:

$$Ac = \frac{TP + TN}{TP + TN + FN + FP} \qquad (6.1)$$

$$R = \frac{TP}{TP + FN} \qquad (6.2)$$

$$P = \frac{TP}{TP + FP} \tag{6.3}$$

$$Sp = \frac{TN}{TN + FP}, \tag{6.4}$$

where TP, TN, FP, and FN represent true positive, true negative, false positive, and false negative, respectively.

F1 is an evaluation metric that combines precision and recall into a single value. It is defined as the harmonic mean of precision and recall (Sasaki, 2007; Powers, 2011):

$$F1 = \frac{2PR}{P + R}. \tag{6.5}$$

Matthews correlation coefficient (MCC) is a measure that balances prediction sensitivity and specificity. MCC ranges from -1, indicating an inverse prediction, through 0, which corresponds to a random classifier, to 1 for perfect prediction, and is calculated as follows:

$$MCC = \frac{TP \cdot TN - FP \cdot FN}{\sqrt{(TP + FN)(TP + FP)(TN + FP)(TN + FN)}}. \tag{6.6}$$

The receiver operating characteristic (ROC) curve is created by plotting the true positive rate (Recall) against the false positive rate (1 − Specificity) at various threshold settings. AUC is the area under the ROC curve, and it represents the probability that a classifier will rank a randomly chosen positive instance higher than a randomly chosen negative one. The AUC can also be interpreted as the average recall over the entire range of possible specificity, or the average specificity over the entire range of possible recalls (Fawcett, 2006; Hanley and McNeil, 1982; Metz, 1978).

4 COMPUTATIONAL APPROACHES

PPI prediction has been studied extensively by several researchers and a large number of approaches have been proposed. These approaches can be classified into physiochemical experimental and computational approaches. Physiochemical experimental techniques identify the physiochemical interactions between proteins which, in turn, are used to predict the functional relationships between them. These techniques include yeast two-hybrid based methods (Bartel and Fields, 1997), mass spectrometry (Gavin *et al.*, 2002), tandem affinity purification (Rigaut *et al.*, 1999), protein chips (Zhu *et al.*, 2001), and hybrid approaches (Tong *et al.*, 2002). Although these techniques have succeeded in identifying several important interacting proteins in several species such as *Saccharomyces cerevisiae* (Yeast), *Drosophila,* and *Helicobacter pylori* (Shen *et al.*, 2007), they are computationally expensive and significantly time consuming, and so far the predicted PPIs have covered only a small portion of the complete PPI network. As a result, the need for computational tools has been increased in order to validate physiochemical experimental results and to predict nondiscovered PPIs (Zaki *et al.*, 2009; Szilágyi *et al.*, 2005).

Several computational methods have been proposed for PPI prediction and can be classified into sequence-based and structure-based methods according to the used protein features. Sequence-based methods utilize AA features and can be further categorized into statistical and ML-based methods. The structure-based methods use three-dimensional structural features (Porollo and Meller, 2012) and can be categorized into template-based, statistical, and ML-based methods. This section provides an overview and discussion of some of the current computational sequence-based and structure-based PPI prediction approaches.

4.1 SEQUENCE-BASED APPROACHES

Sequence-based PPI prediction methods utilize AA features such as hydrophobicity, physiochemical properties, evolutionary profiles, AA composition, AA mean, or weighted average over a sliding window (Porollo and Meller, 2012). Sequence-based methods can be categorized into statistical and ML-based methods. This section presents and evaluates some of the existing sequence-based approaches.

4.1.1 Statistical sequence-based approaches

This section presents and describes several existing statistical sequence-based PPI prediction approaches.

4.1.1.1 Mirror tree method

Pazos and Valencia (2001) introduced the mirror tree method based on the comparison of the evolutionary distances between the sequences of the associated protein families and using the topological similarity of phylogenetic trees to predict PPIs. These distances were calculated as the average value of the residue similarities taken from the McLachlan amino acid homology matrix (McLachlan, 1971). The similarity between trees was calculated as the correlation between the distance matrices used to build the trees.

The mirror tree method does not require the creation of the phylogenetic trees; only the underlying distance matrices are analyzed, and therefore, this approach is independent of any given tree-construction method. Although the mirror tree method does not require the presence of fully sequenced genomes, it requires orthologous proteins in all the species under consideration. As a result, when more species' genomes become available, fewer proteins could be applied. In addition to that, the method is restricted to cases where at least 11 sequences were collected from the same species for both proteins. This minimum limit was set empirically as a compromise between being small enough to provide enough cases and large enough for the matrices to contain sufficient information. The approach can be improved by increasing the number of possible interactions by collecting sequences from a larger number of genomes. Further, since the distance matrices are not a perfect representation of the corresponding phylogenetic trees, it is possible that some inaccuracies are introduced by comparing distance matrices instead of the real phylogenetic trees.

4.1.1.2 PIPE

Pitre *et al.* (2006) introduced the Protein-protein Interaction Prediction Engine (PIPE) to estimate the likelihood of interactions between pairs of *Saccharomyces cerevisiae* proteins using protein primary structure information. PIPE is based on the assumption that interactions between proteins occur by a finite number of short polypeptide sequences observed in a database of known interacting protein pairs. These sequences are typically shorter than the classical domains and reoccur in different proteins within the cell. PIPE estimates the likelihood of a PPI by measuring the reoccurrence of these short polypeptides within known interacting protein pairs. To determine whether two proteins, A and B, interact, the two proteins are scanned for similarity to a database of known interacting protein pairs. For each known interacting pair (X; Y), PIPE uses sliding windows to compare the AA residues in protein A against that in X and protein B against Y, and then measures how many times a window of protein A finds a match in X and at the same time a window in protein B matches a window in Y. These matches are counted and added up in a two-dimensional matrix. A positive protein interaction is predicted when the reoccurrence count in certain cells of the matrix exceeds a predefined threshold value. PIPE was evaluated on a randomly selected set of 100 interacting yeast protein pairs and 100 noninteracting proteins from the database of interacting proteins (DIP; http://dip.doe-mbi.ucla.edu; also see Salwinski *et al.*, 2004) and Munich Information Center for Protein Sequences (MIPS; Mewes *et al.*, 2002) databases. PIPE showed a prediction sensitivity of 0.61 and specificity of 0.89.

Since PIPE is based on protein primary structure information without any previous knowledge about the higher structure, domain composition, evolutionary conservation, or function of the target proteins. It can identify interactions of protein pairs for which limited structural information is available. The limitations of PIPE are as follows. PIPE is computationally intensive and requires hours of computation per protein pair, as it scans the interaction library repeatedly every time. Second, PIPE shows a weakness in detecting novel interactions among genomewide, large-scale data sets as it reported a large number of false positives. Third, PIPE was evaluated on uncertain data of interactions that were determined using several methods, each with limited accuracy.

Pitre *et al.* (2008) then developed PIPE2 as an improved and more efficient version of PIPE, which showed a specificity of 0.999. PIPE2 represents AA sequences in a binary code, which speeds up searching the similarity matrix. Unlike the original PIPE that scans the interaction database repeatedly every time, PIPE2 precomputes all window comparisons in advance and stores them on a local disk.

Although PIPE2 achieves high specificity, it has a large number of false positives with a sensitivity of 0.146 only. The rate of false positives can be reduced by incorporating other information about the target protein pairs, including subcellular localization or functional annotation. A major limitation of PIPE2 is that it relies exclusively on a database of preexisting interaction pairs for the identification of reoccurring short polypeptide sequences; so in the absence of sufficient data, PIPE2 will be ineffective. PIPE2 is also less effective for motifs that span discontinuous primary sequence, as it does not account for gaps within the short polypeptide sequences.

4.1.1.3 CD

Liu *et al.* (2013) introduced a sequence-based coevolution PPI prediction method in human proteins. The authors defined *coevolutionary divergence (CD)* based on two assumptions. First, PPI pairs may have similar substitution rates. Second, protein interaction is more likely to conserve across related species. *CD* is defined as the absolute value of the substitution rate difference between two proteins. It can be used to predict PPIs, as the CD values of interacting protein pairs are expected to be smaller than those of noninteracting pairs. The method was evaluated using 172,338 protein sequences obtained from the Evola database (Matsuya *et al.*, 2008) for *Homo sapiens* and their orthologous protein sequences in 13 different vertebrates. The PPI data set was downloaded from the Human Protein Reference Database (Prasad *et al.*, 2009). Pairwise alignment of the orthologous proteins was made with ClustalW2 software. The absolute value of substitution rate difference between two proteins was used to measure the CDs of protein pairs, which were then used to construct the likelihood ratio table of interacting protein pairs.

The CD method combines coevolutionary information of interacting protein pairs from many species. The method does not use multiple alignments, thus taking less time than other alignment methods such as the mirror tree method. The method is not limited to proteins with orthologous across all species under consideration. However, increasing the number of species will provide more information to improve the accuracy of the CD method. Although this method could rank the likelihood of interaction for a given pair of proteins, it did not infer specific features of interaction, such as the interacting residues in the interfaces.

Table 6.1 summarizes these statistical sequence-based approaches including the features that are used, the technique and/or the tools applied, and the validation data sets used.

Table 6.1 Statistical Sequence-based PPI Prediction Approaches

Approach	Extracted Features	Technique/Tool	Data Sets
Mirror tree (Pazos and Valencia, 2001)	Similarity of phylogenetic trees	Evolutionary distance, McLachlan AA homology matrix	*Escherichia coli* protein (Dandekar *et al.*, 1998)
PIPE (Pitre *et al.*, 2006) PIPE2 (Pitre *et al.*, 2008)	Short AA polypeptides	Similarity measure	Yeast protein (DIP and MIPS)
CD (Liu *et al.*, 2013)	Coevolutionary information,	Pairwise alignment, ClustalW2	Human protein (Matsuya *et al.*, 2008, Prasad *et al.*, 2009)

4.1.2 ML sequence-based approaches

This section describes several existing ML sequence-based PPI prediction approaches.

4.1.2.1 Auto covariance

Guo *et al.* (2008) proposed a sequence-based method using auto covariance (AC) and support vector machines (SVMs). AA residues were represented by seven physicochemical properties: hydrophobicity, hydrophilicity, volumes of side chains, polarity, polarizability, solvent-accessible surface area, and net charge index of AA side chains. AC counts for the interactions between residues that are a certain distance apart in the sequence. AA physicochemical properties were analyzed by AC based on the calculation of covariance. A protein sequence was characterized by a series of ACs that covered the information of interactions between each AA residue and its 30 vicinal residues in the sequence. Finally, a SVM model with a radial basis function (RBF) kernel was constructed using the vectors of AC variables as input. The optimization experiment demonstrated that the interactions of 1 AA residue and its 30 vicinal AAs would contribute to characterizing the PPI information. The software and data sets are available at http://www.scucic.cn/Predict_PPI/index.htm. A data set of 11,474 yeast PPIs extracted from DIP (Xenarios *et al.*, 2002) was used to evaluate the model, and the average prediction accuracy, sensitivity, and precision achieved are 0.86, 0.85, and 0.87, respectively.

One of the advantages of this approach is that AC includes long-range-interaction information of AA residues, which are important in PPI identification. The use of SVM as a predictor is another advantage. SVM is a state-of-the-art ML technique with many benefits; it overcomes many limitations of other techniques. SVM has strong foundations in statistical learning theory (Cristianini and Shawe-Taylor, 2000) and has been successfully applied in various classification problems (Zaki *et al.*, 2011). SVM offers several related computational advantages, such as the lack of local minima in the optimization (Vapnik, 1998).

4.1.2.2 Pairwise similarity

Zaki *et al.* (2009) proposed a PPI predictor based on pairwise similarity of protein primary structure. Each protein sequence was represented by a vector of pairwise similarities against large AA subsequences created by a sliding window that passes over concatenated protein training sequences. Each coordinate of this vector is the E-value of the Smith-Waterman (SW) score (Smith and Waterman, 1981). These vectors were then used to compute the kernel matrix, which was exploited in conjunction with an RBF-kernel SVM. Two proteins may interact by the means of the score similarities they produce (Zaki *et al.*, 2006; Zaki, 2007). Each sequence in the testing set was aligned against each sequence in the training set, counted the number of positions that have identical residues, and then the number of positions was divided by the total length of the alignment.

The method was evaluated on a data set of yeast *S. cerevisiae* proteins created by Chen and Liu (2005) and contains 4917 interacting protein pairs and 4000 noninteracting pairs. The method achieved an accuracy of 0.78, a sensitivity of 0.81, a specificity of 0.744, and a ROC of 0.85.

SW alignment score provides a relevant measure of similarity between proteins. Therefore, protein sequence similarity typically implies homology, which in turn may imply structural and functional similarity (Liao and Noble, 2003). SW score parameters have been optimized over the past two decades to provide relevant measures of similarity between sequences and they now represent core tools in computational biology (Saigo *et al.*, 2004). The use of SVM as a predictor is another advantage. This work can be improved by combining knowledge about gene ontology, interdomain linker regions, and interacting sites to achieve more accurate prediction.

4.1.2.3 AA composition

Roy *et al.* (2009) examined the role of amino acid composition (AAC) in PPI prediction and its performance against well-known features such as domains, the tuple feature, and the signature product feature. Every protein pair was represented by AAC and domain features. AAC was represented by monomer and dimer features. Monomer features capture composition of individual amino acids, whereas dimer features capture composition of pairs of consecutive AAs. To generate the monomer features, a 20-dimensional vector representing the normalized proportion of the 20 AAs in a protein was created. The real-valued composition was then discretized into 25 bits, producing a set of 500 binary features. To generate the dimer features, a 400-dimensional vector of all possible AA pairs was extracted from the protein sequence and discretized into 10 bits, producing a set of 4000 binary features. The domains were represented as binary features with each feature identified by a domain name. To compare AAC against other nondomain sequence-based features, tuple features (Gomez *et al.*, 2003) and signature products (Martin *et al.*, 2005) were obtained. The tuple features were created by grouping AAs into six categories based on their biochemical properties, and then all possible strings of length 4 were created using these categories. The signature products were obtained by first extracting signatures of length 3 from the individual protein sequences. Each signature consists of a middle letter and two flanking AAs represented in alphabetical order. Thus, two 3-tuples with the first and third amino acid letter permuted have the same signature. The signatures were used to construct a signature kernel specifying the inner product between two proteins.

The proposed approach was examined using three ML classifiers (logistic regression, SVM, and the naive Bayes classifier) on PPI data sets from yeast, worm, and fly. Three data sets for *S. cerevisiae* were extracted from the General Repository for Interaction Datasets (GRID) database (Stark *et al.*, 2006), Yeast Two-hybrid (TWOHYB), Affinity pull down with Mass Spectrometry (AFFMS), and protein complementation assay. In addition to that, a data set each for worm, *Caenorhabditis elegans* (Biogrid data set; see Li *et al.*, 2004) and fly, *Drosophila melanogaster* (Stark *et al.*, 2006) were used. The authors reported that AAC features made almost equivalent contributions as domain knowledge across different data sets and classifiers, which indicated that AAC captures significant information for identifying PPIs. AAC is simple, computationally cheap, and applicable to any protein sequence, and it can be used when there is a lack of domain information. AAC can be combined with other features to enhance PPI prediction.

4.1.2.4 AA Triad

Yu *et al.* (2010) proposed a probability-based approach of estimating triad significance to alleviate the effect of AA distribution in nature. The relaxed variable kernel density estimator (RVKDE; see Oyang *et al.*, 2005) was employed to predict PPIs based on AA triad information. The method is summarized as follows. Each protein sequence was represented as AA triads by considering every three continuous residues in the protein sequence as a unit. To reduce the feature dimensionality vector, the 20 AA types were categorized into seven groups based on their dipole strength and side chain volumes (Shen *et al.*, 2007). The triads were then scanned one by one along the sequence, and each scanned triad was counted in an occurrence vector, O. Subsequently, a significance vector, S, was proposed to represent a protein sequence by estimating the probability of observing fewer occurrences of each triad than the one that is actually observed in O. Each PPI pair was then encoded as a feature vector by concatenating the two significance vectors of the two individual proteins. Finally, the feature vector was used to train a RVKDE PPI predictor. The method was evaluated on 37,044 interacting pairs within 9,441 proteins from the Human Protein Reference Database (HPRD) (Peri *et al.*, 2003; Mishra *et al.*, 2006). Data sets with different positive-to-negative ratios (from 1:1 to 1:15) were generated with the same positive instances and distinct negative sets, which were obtained by randomly sampling from the negative instances. The authors concluded that the degree of data set imbalance is important to PPI predictor behavior. With a 1:1 positive-to-negative ratio, the proposed method achieves 0.81 sensitivity, 0.79 specificity, 0.79 precision, and 0.8 F1. These evaluation measures drop as the data gets more imbalanced to reach 0.39 sensitivity, 0.97 specificity, 0.495 precision, and 0.44 F1, with a 1:15 positive-to-negative ratio.

RVKDE is an ML algorithm that constructs an RBF neural network to approximate the probability density function of each class of objects in the training data set. One main distinct feature of RVKDE is that it takes an average time complexity of $O(nlogn)$ for the model training process, where n is the number of instances in the training set. In order to improve the prediction efficiency, RVKDE considers only a limited number of nearest instances within the training data set to compute the kernel density estimator of each class. One important advantage of RVKDE, in comparison with SVM, is that the learning algorithm generally takes far less training time with an optimized parameter setting. In addition, the number of training samples remaining after a data reduction mechanism is applied is very close to the number of support vectors of SVM algorithm. Unlike SVM, RVKDE is capable of classifying data with more than two classes in one single run (Oyang *et al.*, 2005).

4.1.2.5 UNISPPI

Valente *et al.* (2013) introduced Universal In Silico Predictor of Protein-Protein Interactions (UNISPPI). The authors examined both the frequency and composition of the physicochemical properties of the 20 protein AAs to train a decision tree PPI classifier. The frequency feature set included the percentages of each of the 20 AAs in the protein sequence. The composition feature set was obtained by grouping each AA of a protein into one of three different groups related to seven physicochemical properties and calculating the percentage of each group for each feature, ending up with a total of 21 composition features. The seven physicochemical properties are hydrophobicity, normalized van der Waals volume, polarity, polarizability, charge, secondary structure, and solvent accessibility. When tested on a data set of PPI pairs of 20 different eukaryotic species (including eukaryotes, prokaryotes, viruses, and parasite-host associations), UNISPPI correctly classified 0.79 of known PPIs and 0.73 of non-PPIs. The authors concluded that using only the AA frequencies was sufficient to predict PPIs. They further concluded that the AA frequencies of asparagine (N), cysteine (C), and isoleucine (I) are important features for distinguishing between interacting and noninteracting protein pairs.

The main advantages of UNISPPI are its simplicity and low computational cost as small amount of features were used to train the decision tree classifier, which is fast to build and has few parameters to tune. Decision trees can be easily analyzed, and their features can be ranked according to their capabilities of distinguishing PPIs from non-PPIs. However, decision tree classifiers normally suffer from overfitting.

4.1.2.6 ETB-Viterbi

Kern *et al.* (2013) proposed the Early Traceback Viterbi (ETB-Viterbi) as a decoding algorithm with an early traceback mechanism in Interaction Profile Hidden Markov Models (ipHMMs) (Friedrich *et al.*, 2006), which was designed to optimally incorporate long-distance correlations between interacting AA residues in input sequences. The method was evaluated with real data from the 3did database (Stein *et al.*, 2005), along with simulated data generated from 3did data containing different degrees of correlation and reversed sequence orientation. ETB-Viterbi was able to capture the long-distance correlations for improved prediction accuracy and was not much affected by sequence orientation. The hidden Markov model (HMM) is a powerful probabilistic modeling tool for analyzing and simulating sequences of symbols that are emitted from underlying states and not directly observable (Rabiner and Juang, 1986). The Viterbi algorithm is a dynamic programming algorithm for finding the most likely sequence of hidden states. However, this algorithm is expensive in terms of memory and computing time. HMM training involves repeated iterations of the Viterbi algorithm, which makes it quite slow. HMM may not converge on a truly optimal parameter set for a given training set, as it can be trapped in local maxima, and can suffer from overfitting (Krogh *et al.*, 1994; 1998; Eddy, 1998; Yoon, 2009).

Table 6.2 summarizes these ML sequence-based approaches and compared them in terms of features, techniques, tools, and validation data sets.

Table 6.2 ML Sequence-based PPI Prediction Approaches

Approach	Extracted Features	Technique/ Tool	Data Sets
AC (Guo *et al.*, 2008)	AA physicochemical properties	Auto covariance, SVM	Yeast protein (DIP and MIPS)
Pairwise similarity (Zaki *et al.*, 2009)	Pairwise similarity	SVM	Yeast protein
AA composition (Roy *et al.*, 2009)	AAC	Logistic regression, SVM, Naive Bayes	Yeast protein (GRID), worm protein (Li *et al.*, 2004), fly protein (Biogrid)
AA triad (Yu *et al.*, 2010)	AA triad information	RVKDE	Human protein (HPRD)
UNISPPI (Valente *et al.*, 2013)	Frequency and composition of AA physiochemical properties	Decision tree	20 different eukaryotic species
ETB-Viterbi (Kern *et al.*, 2013)	AA residues	HMMs, ETB-Viterbi	3did database

4.2 STRUCTURE-BASED APPROACHES

Structure-based PPI prediction methods use three-dimensional structural features such as domain information, solvent accessibility, secondary structure states, and hydrophobic and polar surface locations (Porollo and Meller, 2012). Structure-based PPI prediction methods can be categorized into template-based, statistical, and ML-based methods. This section presents and evaluates some of the state-of-the-art structure-based approaches.

4.2.1 Template structure-based approaches
4.2.1.1 PRISM

Tuncbag *et al.* (2011) developed PRISM (Protein Interactions by Structural Matching) as a template-based PPI prediction method based on information regarding the interaction surface of crystalline complex structures. The two sides of a template interface are compared with the surfaces of two target monomers by structural alignment. If regions of the target surfaces are similar to the complementary sides of the template interface, then these two targets are predicted to interact with each other through the template interface architecture. The method can be summarized as follows. First, interacting surface residues of target chains are extracted using the Naccess software program (Hubbard and Thornton, 1993). Second, complementary chains of template interfaces are separated and structurally compared with each of the target surfaces by using MultiProt (Shatsky *et al.*, 2004). Third, the structural alignment results are filtered according to threshold values, and the resulting set of target surfaces is transformed into the corresponding template interfaces to form a complex. Finally, the Fiber-Dock (Mashiach *et al.*, 2010) algorithm is used to refine the interactions to introduce flexibility, compute the global energy of the complex, and rank the solutions according to their energies. When the computed energy of a protein pair is less than a threshold of -10 kcal/mol, the pair is determined to interact.

PRISM has been applied for predicting PPIs in a human apoptosis pathway (Acuner Ozbabacan *et al.*, 2012) and a p53 protein-related pathway (Tuncbag *et al.*, 2009), and has contributed to the understanding of the structural mechanisms underlying some types of signal transduction. PRISM obtained a precision of 0.231 when applied to a human apoptosis pathway that consisted of 57 proteins.

4.2.1.2 PrePPI

Zhang *et al.* (2012) proposed Predicting Protein-Protein Interaction (PrePPI) as a structural alignment PPI predictor based on geometric relationships between secondary structure information. Given a pair of query proteins, A and B, representative structures for the individual subunits (MA; MB) are taken from the Protein Data Bank (PDB) (Berman *et al.*, 2000) or from the ModBase (Pieper *et al.*, 2006) and SkyBase (Mirkovic *et al.*, 2007) homology model databases. Close and remote structural neighbors are found for each subunit. A template for the interaction exists if a PDB or PQS (Protein Quaternary Structure) (Henrick and Thornton, 1998) contains interacting pairs that are structural neighbors of MA and MB. A model is constructed by superposing the individual subunits, MA and MB, on their corresponding structural neighbors. The likelihood for each model to represent a true interaction is then calculated using a Bayesian network trained on 11,851 yeast interactions and 7409 human interactions data sets. Finally, the structure-derived score is combined with nonstructural information, including coexpression and functional similarity, into a naive Bayes classifier.

Although template-based methods can achieve high prediction accuracy when close templates are retrieved, the accuracy significantly decreases when the sequence identity of target and template is low.

4.2.2 Statistical structure-based approaches
4.2.2.1 PID matrix score

Kim *et al.* (2002) presented the potentially interacting domain (PID) pair matrix as a domain-based PPI prediction algorithm. The PID matrix score was constructed as a measure of interactability (interaction probability) between domains. The algorithm analysis was based on the DIP, which contains more than 10,000 mostly experimentally verified interacting protein pairs. Domain information was extracted from InterPro (Apweiler *et al.*, 2001), an integrated database of protein families, domains, and functional sites. Cross-validation was performed with subsets of DIP data (positive data sets) and randomly generated protein pairs from the TrEMBL/SwissProt database (negative data sets). The method achieved 0.50 sensitivity and 0.98 specificity. The authors reported that the PID matrix can also be used in the mapping of the genome-wide interaction networks.

4.2.2.2 PreSPI

Han *et al.* (2003, 2004) proposed a domain combination-based method that considers all possible domain combinations as the basic units of protein interactions. The domain combination interaction probability is based on the number of interacting protein pairs containing the domain combination pair and the number of domain combinations in each protein. The method considers the possibility of domain combinations appearing in both interacting and noninteracting sets of protein pairs. The ranking of multiple protein pairs were decided by the interacting probabilities computed through the interacting probability equation.

The method was evaluated using an interacting set of protein pairs in yeast acquired from the DIP (Salwinski *et al.*, 2004) and a randomly generated, noninteracting set of protein pairs. The domain information for the proteins was extracted from the PDB (http://www.ebi.ac.uk/proteome/; see Berman *et al.*, 2000; Apweiler *et al.*, 2001). PreSPI achieved a sensitivity of 0.77 and a specificity of 0.95.

PreSPI suffers from several limitations, though. First, this method ignores other domain-domain interaction information between the protein pairs. Second, it assumes that one domain combination is independent of another. Third, the method is computationally expensive, as all possible domain combinations are considered.

4.2.2.3 DCC

Jang *et al.* (2012) proposed a domain cohesion and coupling (DCC)–based PPI prediction method using the information of intraprotein domain interactions and interprotein domain interactions. The method aims to identify which domains are involved in a PPI by determining the probability that the domains cause the proteins to interact regardless of the number of participating domains. The coupling powers of all domain interaction pairs are stored in an interaction significance (IS) matrix, which is used to predict PPIs. The method was evaluated on *S. cerevisiae* proteins and achieved 0.82 sensitivity and 0.83 specificity. The domain information for the proteins was extracted from Pfam (http://pfam.sanger.ac.uk) (Punta *et al.*, 2011), a protein domain family database that contains multiple sequence alignments of common domain families.

4.2.2.4 MEGADOCK

Ohue *et al.* (2013a) developed MEGADOCK as a protein-protein docking software package using the real Pairwise Shape Complementarity (rPSC) score. First, they conducted rigid-body docking calculations based on a simplified energy function considering shape complementarities, electrostatics, and hydrophobic interactions for all possible binary combinations of proteins in the target set. Using this process, a group of high-scoring docking complexes for each pair of proteins were obtained. Then ZRANK (Pierce and Weng, 2007) was applied for more advanced binding energy calculation and the docking results were reranked based on ZRANK energy scores. The deviation of the selected docking scores from the score distribution of high-ranked complexes was determined as a standardized score (Z-score) and was used to assess possible interactions. Potential complexes that had no other high-scoring interactions nearby were rejected using structural differences. Thus, binding pairs that had at least one populated area of high-scoring structures were considered. MEGADOCK was applied for PPI prediction for 13 proteins of a bacterial chemotaxis pathway (Ohue *et al.* 2012; Matsuzaki *et al.*, 2013), and a precision of 0.4 was obtained. MEGADOCK is available at http://www.bi.cs.titech.ac.jp/megadock.

One of the limitations of this approach is the generation of false positives in cases in which no similar structures are seen in known complex structure databases.

4.2.2.5 Meta approach

Ohue *et al.* (2013b) proposed a PPI prediction approach based on combining the template-based and docking methods. The approach applies PRISM (Tuncbag *et al.*, 2011) as a template-matching method and MEGADOCK (Ohue *et al.* 2013a) as a docking method. A protein pair is considered to be interacting if both PRISM and MEGADOCK predict that this protein pair interacts. When applied to the human apoptosis signaling pathway, the method obtained a precision of 0.333, which is higher than that achieved using individual methods (0.231 for PRISM and 0.145 for MEGADOCK), while maintaining an F1 of 0.285 comparable to that obtained using individual methods (0.296 for PRISM and 0.220 for MEGADOCK).

Meta approaches have already been used in the field of protein tertiary structure prediction (Zhou *et al.*, 2009), and critical experiments have demonstrated improved performance of Meta predictors when compared with individual methods. The Meta approach has also provided favorable results in protein domain prediction (Saini and Fischer, 2005) and the prediction of disordered regions in proteins (Ishida and Kinoshita, 2008). Although some true positives may be dropped by this method, the remaining predicted pairs are expected to have higher reliability because of the consensus between two prediction methods that have different characteristics.

4.2.3 ML structure-based approaches

4.2.3.1 Random Forest

Chen and Liu (2005) introduced a domain-based Random Forest PPI predictor. Protein pairs were characterized by the domains existing in each protein. The protein domain information was collected from the Pfam database (Bateman *et al.*, 2004). Each protein pair was represented by a vector of features where each feature corresponded to a Pfam domain. If a domain existed in both proteins, then the associated feature value was 2. If the domain existed in one of the two proteins, then its associated feature value was 1. If a domain did not exist in both proteins, then the feature value was 0. These domain features were used to train a Random Forest classifier. The Random Forest constructs many decision trees, and each is grown from a different subset of training samples and random subset of features; the final classification of a given protein pair is determined by majority votes among the classes decided by the forest of trees.

When evaluated on a data set containing 9834 yeast protein interaction pairs among 3713 proteins, and 8000 negative randomly generated samples, the method achieved a sensitivity of 0.8 and a specificity of 0.64. Yeast PPI data was collected from the DIP (Salwinski et al., 2004; Deng et al., 2002; Schwikowski et al., 2000). The data set of Deng et al. (2002) is a combined interaction data experimentally obtained through two hybrid assays on *S. cerevisiae* by Uetz et al. (2000) and Ito et al. (2000). Schwikowski et al. (2000) gathered their data from yeast two-hybrid, biochemical, and genetic data.

The Random Forest classifier has several advantages. It is relatively fast, simple, robust to outliers and noise, and easily parallelized; avoids over-fitting; and performs well in many classification problems (Breiman, 2001; Caruana et al., 2008). Random Forest shows a significant performance improvement over the single tree classifiers. It interprets the importance of the features using measures such as decrease mean accuracy or Gini importance (Chang and Yang, 2013). Random Forest benefits from the randomization of decision trees, as they have low bias and high variance. Random Forest has few parameters to tune and is less dependent on tuning parameters (Izmirlian, 2004; Qi, 2012). However, the computational cost of Random Forest increases as the number of generated trees increases. One of the limitations of this approach is that PPI prediction depends on domain knowledge so proteins without domain information cannot provide any useful information for prediction. Therefore, the method excluded the pairs where at least one of the proteins has no domain information.

4.2.3.2 Struct2Net

Singh et al. (2006) introduced Struct2Net as a structure-based PPI predictor. The method predicts interactions by threading each pair of protein sequences into potential structures in the PDB (Berman et al., 2000). Given two protein sequences (or one sequence against all sequences of a species), Struct2Net threads the sequence to all the protein complexes in the PDB and then chooses the best potential match. Based on this match, it uses the logistic regression technique to predict whether the two proteins interact.

Later, Singh et al. (2010) introduced Struct2Net as a web server with multiple querying options; it is available at http://struct2net.csail.mit.edu. Users can retrieve yeast, fly, and human PPI predictions by gene name or identifier, while they can query for proteins of other organisms by AA sequence in FASTA format. Struct2Net returns a list of interacting proteins if one protein sequence is provided and an interaction prediction if two sequences are provided. When evaluated on yeast and fly protein pairs, Struct2Net achieves a recall of 0.80, with a precision of 0.30.

A common limitation of all structure-based PPI prediction approaches is the low coverage as the number of known protein structures is much smaller than the number of known protein sequences. Therefore, such approaches fail when there is no structural template available for the queried protein pair. Table 6.3 summarizes these structure-based approaches and compares them in terms of features, techniques, tools, and validation data sets.

Table 6.3 Structure-based PPI Prediction Approaches

Approach	Extracted Features	Technique/ Tool	Data Sets
PRISM (Tuncbag et al., 2011)	Interaction surface of crystalline complex structures	Naccess, MultiProt, Fiber-Dock	Human protein (Acuner Ozbabacan et al., 2012; Tuncbag et al., 2009)
PrePPI (Zhang et al., 2012)	Secondary structure	Bayesian networks, naive Bayes	Yeast protein, human protein
PID matrix score (Kim et al., 2002)	Potentially interacting domain pairs	PID matrix	DIP, InterPro, TrEMBL/SwissProt
PreSPI (Han et al., 2003, 2004)	Domain combination interaction probability	Interacting probability equation	Yeast protein (DIP), PDB
DCC (Jang et al., 2012)	Intraprotein and interprotein domain interactions	Interaction significance matrix	S. cerevisiae protein, Pfam
MEGADOCK (Ohue et al., 2013a)	Shape complementarities, electrostatics, and hydrophobic interactions	rPSC, ZRANK	Bacterial protein (Ohue et al., 2012; Matsuzaki et al., 2013)
Meta approach (Ohue et al., 2013b)	Interaction surface of crystalline complex structures, shape complementarities, electrostatics, and hydrophobic interactions	PRISM, MEGADOCK	Human protein
Random Forest (Chen and Liu, 2005)	Existence of similar domains	Random Forest	DIP, Deng et al., 2002; Schwikowski et al., 2000; Pfam
Struct2Net (Singh et al., 2006, 2010)	Homology with known protein complexes in PDB	Logistic regression	Yeast, fly, and human protein

5 CONCLUSION

This chapter provided a review of the computational techniques for PPI prediction, including the open issues and main challenges in this domain. We investigated several relevant existing approaches and provided a categorization and comparison of them. It is clearly noticed that PPI prediction still needs much more research to achieve reasonable prediction accuracy. One of the issues of the PPI prediction methods is that they do not use a uniform data set and evaluation measure. We recommend creating a freely available standard benchmark data set, taking into consideration the biological properties of proteins and examining the performance of all these methods on this benchmark data set using well-defined evaluation measures.

This will allow researchers to compare the performance of these prediction methods in a fair and uniform fashion. This work can be extended by investigating more recently published PPI prediction techniques, analyze them in depth, and compare their performance on a uniform data set according to a uniform evaluation metric. More focus should be given to the techniques that incorporate biological knowledge into the prediction process.

REFERENCES

Acuner Ozbabacan, S.E., Keskin, O., Nussinov, R., Gursoy, A., 2012. Enriching the human apoptosis pathway by predicting the structures of protein–protein complexes. J. Struct. Biol. 179 (3), 338–346.

Apweiler, R., Attwood, T.K., Bairoch, A., Bateman, A., Birney, E., Biswas, M., Bucher, P., Cerutti, L., Corpet, F., Croning, M.D.R., et al., 2001. The interpro database, an integrated documentation resource for protein families, domains and functional sites. Nucleic Acids Res. 29 (1), 37–40.

Bader, G.D., Hogue, C.W., 2002. Analyzing yeast protein–protein interaction data obtained from different sources. Nat. Biotechnol. 20 (10), 991–997.

Bartel, P.L., Fields, S., 1997. The Yeast Two-Hybrid System. Oxford University Press.

Bateman, A., Coin, L., Durbin, R., Finn, R.D., Hollich, V., Griffiths-Jones, S., Khanna, A., Marshall, M., Moxon, S., Sonnhammer, E.L., et al., 2004. The pfam protein families database. Nucleic Acids Res. 32 (Suppl. 1), D138–D141.

Berg, J.M., Tymoczko, J.L., Stryer, L., 2002. Protein Structure and Function. .

Berman, H.M., Westbrook, J., Feng, Z., Gilliland, G., Bhat, T., Weissig, H., Shindyalov, I.N., Bourne, P.E., 2000. The protein data bank. Nucleic Acids Res. 28 (1), 235–242.

Breiman, L., 2001. Random forests. Mach. Learn. 45 (1), 5–32.

Caruana, R., Karampatziakis, N., Yessenalina, A., 2008. An empirical evaluation of supervised learning in high dimensions. In: Proceedings of the 25th International Conference on Machine Learning. ACM, pp. 96–103.

Chang, K.Y., Yang, J.R., 2013. Analysis and prediction of highly effective antiviral peptides based on random forests. PLoS One 8 (8), e70166.

Chen, X.W., Liu, M., 2005. Prediction of protein–protein interactions using random decision forest framework. Bioinformatics 21 (24), 4394–4400.

Chothia, C., 1992. Proteins. One thousand families for the molecular biologist. Nature 357 (6379), 543.

Chou, K.C., 2011. Some remarks on protein attribute prediction and pseudo amino acid composition. J. Theor. Biol. 273 (1), 236–247.

Cristianini, N., Shawe-Taylor, J., 2000. An Introduction to Support Vector Machines and Other Kernel-Based Learning Methods. Cambridge university press.

Dandekar, T., Snel, B., Huynen, M., Bork, P., 1998. Conservation of gene order: a fingerprint of proteins that physically interact. Trends Biochem. Sci. 23 (9), 324–328.

Deng, M., Mehta, S., Sun, F., Chen, T., 2002. Inferring domain–domain interactions from protein–protein interactions. Genome Res. 12 (10), 1540–1548.

Eddy, S.R., 1998. Profile hidden markov models. Bioinformatics 14 (9), 755–763.

Fawcett, T., 2006. An introduction to roc analysis. Pattern Recogn. Lett. 27 (8), 861–874.

Friedrich, T., Pils, B., Dandekar, T., Schultz, J., Müller, T., 2006. Modelling interaction sites in protein domains with interaction profile hidden markov models. Bioinformatics 22 (23), 2851–2857.

Gavin, A.C., Bösche, M., Krause, R., Grandi, P., Marzioch, M., Bauer, Schultz, J., Rick, J.M., Michon, A.M., Cruciat, C.M., et al., 2002. Functional organization of the yeast proteome by systematic analysis of protein complexes. Nature 415 (6868), 141–147.

Gomez, S.M., Noble, W.S., Rzhetsky, A., 2003. Learning to predict protein–protein interactions from protein sequences. Bioinformatics 19 (15), 1875–1881.

Guo, Y., Yu, L., Wen, Z., Li, M., 2008. Using support vector machine combined with auto covariance to predict protein–protein interactions from protein sequences. Nucleic Acids Res. 36 (9), 3025–3030.

Han, D., Kim, H.S., Seo, J., Jang, W., 2003. A domain combination based probabilistic framework for protein-protein interaction prediction. Genome Inform, 250–260.

Han, D.S., Kim, H.S., Jang, W.H., Lee, S.D., Suh, J.K., 2004. Prespi: a domain combination based prediction system for protein–protein interaction. Nucleic Acids Res. 32 (21), 6312–6320.

Hanley, J.A., McNeil, B.J., 1982. The meaning and use of the area under a receiver operating characteristic (roc) curve. Radiology 143 (1), 29–36.

Henrick, K., Thornton, J.M., 1998. Pqs: a protein quaternary structure file server. Trends Biochem. Sci. 23 (9), 358–361.

Hubbard, S.J., Thornton, J.M., 1993. "Naccess," Computer Program, vol. 2. Department of Biochemistry and Molecular Biology, University College London, no. 1.

Ishida, T., Kinoshita, K., 2008. Prediction of disordered regions in proteins based on the meta approach. Bioinformatics 24 (11), 1344–1348.

Ito, T., Tashiro, K., Muta, S., Ozawa, R., Chiba, T., Nishizawa, M., Yamamoto, K., Kuhara, S., Sakaki, Y., 2000. Toward a protein–protein interaction map of the budding yeast: a comprehensive system to examine two-hybrid interactions in all possible combinations between the yeast proteins. Proc. Natl. Acad. Sci. 97 (3), 1143–1147.

Izmirlian, G., 2004. Application of the random forest classification algorithm to a seldi-tof proteomics study in the setting of a cancer prevention trial. Ann. N. Y. Acad. Sci. 1020 (1), 154–174.

Jang, W.H., Jung, S.H., Han, D.S., 2012. A computational model for predicting protein interactions based on multidomain collaboration. IEEE/ACM Trans. Comput. Biol. Bioinform. 9 (4), 1081–1090.

Kern, C., Gonzalez, A.J., Liao, L., Vijay-Shanker, K., 2013. Predicting interacting residues using long-distance information and novel decoding in hidden markov models. IEEE Trans. Nanosci. 12 (13), 158–164.

Kim, W.K., Park, J., Suh, J.K., et al., 2002. Large scale statistical prediction of protein-protein interaction by potentially interacting domain (pid) pair. Genome Informa, 42–50.

Krogh, A., Brown, M., Mian, I.S., Sjölander, K., Haussler, D., 1994. Hidden markov models in computational biology: applications to protein modeling. J. Mol. Biol. 235 (5), 1501–1531.

Krogh, A., et al., 1998. An introduction to hidden markov models for biological sequences. New Compr. Biochem. 32, 45–63.

Li, S., Armstrong, C.M., Bertin, N., Ge, H., Milstein, S., Boxem, M., Vidalain, P.O., Han, J.D.J., Chesneau, A., Hao, T., et al., 2004. A map of the interactome network of the metazoan c. elegans. Science 303 (5657), 540–543.

Liao, L., Noble, W.S., 2003. Combining pairwise sequence similarity and support vector machines for detecting remote protein evolutionary and structural relationships. J. Comput. Biol. 10 (6), 857–868.

Liu, C.H., Li, K.C., Yuan, S., 2013. Human protein–protein interaction prediction by a novel sequence-based co-evolution method: co-evolutionary divergence. Bioinformatics 29 (1), 92–98.

Martin, S., Roe, D., Faulon, J.L., 2005. Predicting protein–protein interactions using signature products. Bioinformatics 21 (2), 218–226.

Mashiach, E., Nussinov, R., Wolfson, H.J., 2010. Fiberdock: flexible induced-fit backbone refinement in molecular docking. Protein. Struct. Funct. Bioinforma. 78 (6), 1503–1519.

Matsuya, A., Sakate, R., Kawahara, Y., Koyanagi, K.O., Sato, Y., Fujii, Yamasaki, C., Habara, T., Nakaoka, H., Todokoro, F., et al., 2008. Evola: ortholog database of all human genes in h-invdb with manual curation of phylogenetic trees. Nucleic Acids Res. 36 (Suppl. 1), D787–D792.

Matsuzaki, Y., Ohue, M., Uchikoga, N., Akiyama, Y., 2013. Protein-protein interaction network prediction by using rigid-body docking tools: application to bacterial chemotaxis. Protein Pept. Lett.

McLachlan, A.D., 1971. Tests for comparing related amino-acid sequences. Cytochrome c and cytochrome c551. J. Mol. Biol. 61 (2), 409–424.

Melo, J.C., Cavalcanti, G., Guimaraes, K., 2003. Pca feature extraction for protein structure prediction. In: Neural Networks, 2003. Proceedings of the International Joint Conference on, vol. 4. IEEE, pp. 2952–2957.

Metz, C.E., 1978. Basic principles of roc analysis. In: Seminars in Nuclear Medicine, vol. 8. Elsevier, pp. 283–298, no. 4.

Mewes, H.W., Frishman, D., Güldener, U., Mannhaupt, G., Mayer, K., Mokrejs, Morgenstern, B., Münsterkötter, M., Rudd, S., Weil, 2002. Mips: a database for genomes and protein sequences. Nucleic Acids Res. 30 (1), 31–34.

Mirkovic, N., Li, Z., Parnassa, A., Murray, D., 2007. Strategies for high-throughput comparative modeling: Applications to leverage analysis in structural genomics and protein family organization. Protein. Struct. Funct. Bioinforma. 66 (4), 766–777.

Mishra, G.R., Suresh, M., Kumaran, K., Kannabiran, N., Suresh, S., Bala, P., Shivakumar, K., Anuradha, N., Reddy, R., Raghavan, T.M., et al., 2006. Human protein reference databaseâAT2006 update. Nucleic Acids Res. 34 (Suppl. 1), D411–D414.

Ohue, M., Matsuzaki, Y., Ishida, T., Akiyama, Y., 2012. Improvement of the protein–protein docking prediction by introducing a simple hydrophobic interaction model: an application to interaction pathway analysis. In: Pattern Recognition in Bioinformatics. Springer, pp. 178–187.

Ohue, M., Matsuzaki, Y., Uchikoga, N., Ishida, T., Akiyama, Y., 2013a. Megadock: an all-to-all protein-protein interaction prediction system using tertiary structure data. Protein Pept. Lett.. .

Ohue, M., Matsuzaki, Y., Shimoda, T., Ishida, T., Akiyama, Y., 2013b. Highly precise protein-protein interaction prediction based on consensus between template-based and de novo docking methods. In: BMC Proceedings, vol. 7. BioMed Central Ltd, no. Suppl. 7.

Oyang, Y.J., Hwang, S.C., Ou, Y.Y., Chen, C.Y., Chen, Z.W., 2005. Data classification with radial basis function networks based on a novel kernel density estimation algorithm. IEEE Trans. Neural Netw. 16 (1), 225–236.

Pazos, F., Valencia, A., 2001. Similarity of phylogenetic trees as indicator of protein–protein interaction. Protein Eng. 14 (9), 609–614.

Peri, S., Navarro, J.D., Amanchy, R., Kristiansen, T.Z., Jonnalagadda, C.K., Surendranath, V., Niranjan, V., Muthusamy, B., Gandhi, T., Gronborg, M., et al., 2003. Development of human protein reference database as an initial platform for approaching systems biology in humans. Genome Res. 13 (10), 2363–2371.

Pieper, U., Eswar, N., Davis, F.P., Braberg, H., Madhusudhan, M.S., Rossi, A., Marti-Renom, M., Karchin, R., Webb, B.M., Eramian, D., et al., 2006. Modbase: a database of annotated comparative protein structure models and associated resources. Nucleic Acids Res. 34 (Suppl. 1), D291–D295.

Pierce, B., Weng, Z., 2007. Zrank: reranking protein docking predictions with an optimized energy function. Protein. Struct. Funct. Bioinform. 67 (4), 1078–1086.

Pitre, S., Dehne, F., Chan, A., Cheetham, J., Duong, A., Emili, A., Gebbia, M., Greenblatt, J., Jessulat, M., Krogan, N., et al., 2006. Pipe: a protein-protein interaction prediction engine based on the reoccurring short polypeptide sequences between known interacting protein pairs. BMC Bioinformatics 7 (1), 365.

Pitre, S., North, C., Alamgir, M., Jessulat, M., Chan, A., Luo, X., Green, Dumontier, M., Dehne, F., Golshani, A., 2008. Global investigation of protein–protein interactions in yeast saccharomyces cerevisiae using reoccurring short polypeptide sequences. Nucleic Acids Res. 36 (13), 4286–4294.

Porollo, A., Meller, J., 2012. Computational methods for prediction of protein-protein interaction sites. In: Cai, W., Hong, H. (Eds.), In: Protein-Protein Interactions - Computational and Experimental Tools, vol. 472. InTech, pp. 3–26.

Powers, D., 2011. Evaluation: From precision, recall and f-measure to roc., informedness, markedness & correlation. J. Mach. Learn. Techn. 2 (1), 37–63.

Prasad, T.K., Goel, R., Kandasamy, K., Keerthikumar, S., Kumar, S., Mathivanan, Telikicherla, D., Raju, R., Shafreen, B., Venugopal, A., et al., 2009. Human protein reference database - 2009 update. Nucleic Acids Res. 37 (Suppl. 1), D767–D772.

Punta, M., Coggill, P.C., Eberhardt, R.Y., Mistry, J., Tate, J., Boursnell, C., Pang, N., Forslund, K., Ceric, G., Clements, J., et al., 2011. The pfam protein families database. Nucleic Acids Res., gkr1065.

Qi, Y., 2012. Random forest for bioinformatics. In: Ensemble Machine Learning. Springer, pp. 307–323.

Qi, Y., Bar-Joseph, Z., Klein-Seetharaman, J., 2006. Evaluation of different biological data and computational classification methods for use in protein interaction prediction. Protein. Struct. Funct. Bioinforma. 63 (3), 490–500.

Rabiner, L., Juang, B.H., 1986. An introduction to hidden markov models. IEEE ASSP Mag. 3 (1), 4–16.

Rigaut, G., Shevchenko, A., Rutz, B., Wilm, M., Mann, M., Séraphin, 1999. A generic protein purification method for protein complex characterization and proteome exploration. Nat. Biotechnol. 17 (10), 1030–1032.

Roy, S., Martinez, D., Platero, H., Lane, T., Werner-Washburne, M., 2009. Exploiting amino acid composition for predicting protein-protein interactions. PLoS One 4 (11), e7813.

Saigo, H., Vert, J.P., Ueda, N., Akutsu, T., 2004. Protein homology detection using string alignment kernels. Bioinformatics 20 (11), 1682–1689.

Saini, H.K., Fischer, D., 2005. Meta-dp: domain prediction meta-server. Bioinformatics 21 (12), 2917–2920.

Salwinski, L., Miller, C.S., Smith, A.J., Pettit, F.K., Bowie, J.U., Eisenberg, 2004. The database of interacting proteins: 2004 update. Nucleic Acids Res. 32 (suppl 1), D449–D451.

Sasaki, Y., 2007. The truth of the f-measure. Teach Tutor Mater, 1–5.

Schwikowski, B., Uetz, P., Fields, S., 2000. A network of protein– protein interactions in yeast. Nat. Biotechnol. 18 (12), 1257–1261.

Shatnawi, M., 2014. Computational methods for protein-protein interaction prediction. In: BIOCOMP'14..

Shatsky, M., Nussinov, R., Wolfson, H.J., 2004. A method for simultaneous alignment of multiple protein structures. Protein. Struct. Funct. Bioinform. 56 (1), 143–156.

Shen, J., Zhang, J., Luo, X., Zhu, W., Yu, K., Chen, K., Li, Y., Jiang, 2007. Predicting protein–protein interactions based only on sequences information. Proc. Natl. Acad. Sci. 104 (11), 4337–4341.

Singh, R., Xu, J., Berger, B., 2006. Struct2net: integrating structure into protein-protein interaction prediction. In: Pacific Symposium on Biocomputing, vol. 11. Citeseer, pp. 403–414.

Singh, R., Park, D., Xu, J., Hosur, R., Berger, B., 2010. Struct2net: a web service to predict protein–protein interactions using a structure-based approach. Nucleic Acids Res. 38 (Suppl. 2), W508–W515.

Smith, T.F., Waterman, M.S., 1981. Identification of common molecular subsequences. J. Mol. Biol. 147 (1), 195–197.

Stark, C., Breitkreutz, B.J., Reguly, T., Boucher, L., Breitkreutz, A., Tyers, M., 2006. Biogrid: a general repository for interaction datasets. Nucleic Acids Res. 34 (Suppl. 1), D535–D539.

Stein, A., Russell, R.B., Aloy, P., 2005. 3did: interacting protein domains of known three-dimensional structure. Nucleic Acids Res. 33 (Suppl. 1), D413–D417.

Szilágyi, A., Grimm, V., Arakaki, A.K., Skolnick, J., 2005. Prediction of physical protein–protein interactions. Phys. Biol. 2 (2), S1.

Tong, A.H.Y., Drees, B., Nardelli, G., Bader, G.D., Brannetti, B., Castagnoli, Evangelista, M., Ferracuti, S., Nelson, B., Paoluzi, S., et al., 2002. A combined experimental and computational strategy to define protein interaction networks for peptide recognition modules. Science 295 (5553), 321–324.

Tuncbag, N., Kar, G., Gursoy, A., Keskin, O., Nussinov, R., 2009. Towards inferring time dimensionality in protein–protein interaction networks by integrating structures: the p53 example. Mol. Biosyst. 5 (12), 1770–1778.

Tuncbag, N., Gursoy, A., Nussinov, R., Keskin, O., 2011. Predicting protein-protein interactions on a proteome scale by matching evolutionary and structural similarities at interfaces using prism. Nat. Protoc. 6 (9), 1341–1354.

Uetz, P., Giot, L., Cagney, G., Mansfield, T.A., Judson, R.S., Knight, J.R., Lockshon, D., Narayan, V., Srinivasan, M., Pochart, P., et al., 2000. A comprehensive analysis of protein–protein interactions in saccharomyces cerevisiae. Nature 403 (6770), 623–627.

Valente, G.T., Acencio, M.L., Martins, C., Lemke, N., 2013. The development of a universal in silico predictor of protein-protein interactions. PLoS One 8 (5), e65587.

Vapnik, V.N. 1998. Statistical learning theory (adaptive and learning systems for signal processing, communications and control series).

Von Mering, C., Krause, R., Snel, B., Cornell, M., Oliver, S.G., Fields, S., Bork, P., 2002. Comparative assessment of large-scale data sets of protein–protein interactions. Nature 417 (6887), 399–403.

Xenarios, I., Eisenberg, D., 2001. Protein interaction databases. Curr. Opin. Biotechnol. 12 (4), 334–339.

Xenarios, I., Salwinski, L., Duan, X.J., Higney, P., Kim, S.M., Eisenberg, 2002. Dip, the database of interacting proteins: a research tool for studying cellular networks of protein interactions. Nucleic Acids Res. 30 (1), 303–305.

Yoo, P.D., Sikder, A.R., Taheri, J., Zhou, B.B., Zomaya, A.Y., 2008. Domnet: protein domain boundary prediction using enhanced general regression network and new profiles. IEEE Trans. Nanobiosci. 7 (2), 172–181.

Yoon, B.J., 2009. Hidden markov models and their applications in biological sequence analysis. Curr. Genomics 10 (6), 402.

Yu, C.Y., Chou, L.C., Chang, D.T., 2010. Predicting protein-protein interactions in unbalanced data using the primary structure of proteins. BMC Bioinformatics 11 (1), 167.

Zaki, N., 2007. Protein-protein interaction prediction using homology and inter-domain linker region information. Adv. Electr. Eng. Comput. Sci. 67 (4), 635–645.

Zaki, N., Deris, S., Alashwal, H., 2006. Protein-protein interaction detection based on substring sensitivity measure. Int. J. Biomed. Sci. 2 (1), 148–154.

Zaki, N., Lazarova-Molnar, S., El-Hajj, W., Campbell, P., 2009. Protein-protein interaction based on pairwise similarity. BMC Bioinformatics 10 (1), 150.

Zaki, N., Wolfsheimer, S., Nuel, G., Khuri, S., 2011. Conotoxin protein classification using free scores of words and support vector machines. BMC Bioinformatics 12 (1), 217.

Zhang, Q.C., Petrey, D., Deng, L., Qiang, L., Shi, Y., Thu, C.A., Bisikirska, B., Lefebvre, C., Accili, D., Hunter, T., et al., 2012. Structure-based prediction of protein-protein interactions on a genome-wide scale. Nature 490 (7421), 556–560.

Zhou, H., Pandit, S.B., Skolnick, J., 2009. Performance of the pro-sp3-tasser server in casp8. Protein. Struct. Funct. Bioinform. 77 (S9), 123–127.

Zhu, H., Bilgin, M., Bangham, R., Hall, D., Casamayor, A., Bertone, P., Lan, Jansen, R., Bidlingmaier, S., Houfek, T., et al., 2001. Global analysis of protein activities using proteome chips. Science 293 (5537), 2101–2105.

Genetic Regulatory Networks: Focus on Attractors of Their Dynamics

J. Demongeot[1], H. Hazgui[1], and A. Henrion Caude[2]

Université J. Fourier Grenoble, Faculté de Médecine, AGIM CNRS/UJF FRE 3405,
La Tronche, France[1]
Université Paris Descartes, INSERM U 781, Hôpital Necker-Enfants Malades,
Paris, France[2]

1 INTRODUCTION

The present genomes are the result of a long evolution from the start of the life on the earth until the appearance of mammals and human. We will try in this chapter to show that the control of important genetic networks involved both on defense and energy processes of cells in numerous living systems is under the dependence of different regulators, among them microRNAs and circular RNAs. We show that these genetic networks have only a small number of asymptotic dynamical behaviors, called *attractors*. This small number is directly linked with the possibilities of differentiation of the concerned cells and is controlled inside the interaction graphs of the genetic networks, whose nodes are genes and signs of arrows between genes indicate the presence of interactions between these genes, + (resp. −) in the case of activation (resp. inhibition), by the circuits (closed paths between genes) of the strong connected components (*i.e.*, subgraphs containing a path between any couple of their genes), giving the network the possibility to have more than one attractor (and due to positive circuits, it is made of an even number of inhibitions) and the possibility for an attractor to be stable and possibly oscillating (due to negative circuits, made of an odd number of inhibitions); *i.e.*, having a large number of initial configurations of gene states giving birth, after a dynamical evolution, to its asymptotic behavior. Section 2 describes the circuits involved in adaptive and innate immunologic systems, giving a way to calculate the reduction of the attractor numbers due to the presence of intersecting circuits and to the inhibitory regulation by microRNAs often responsible of periodic protein signals (Bandiera et al., 2011, 2013; Bulet et al., 1999; Demongeot and Besson, 1983, 1996; Demongeot et al., 2003, 2009a, 2009b, 2010, 2011, 2012, 2013a, 2013b, 2014a, b; Weil et al., 2004). Section 3 presents the Ferritin control network, regulating the iron metabolism in mammals, section 4 is devoted to the study of the engrailed morphogenetic network, and section 5 concerns the network controlling a disease called biliary atresia.

2 IMMUNETWORKS

2.1 THE IMMUNETWORK RESPONSIBLE OF THE TOLL-LIKE RECEPTOR (TLR) EXPRESSION

The activation of natural killer (NK) cells, involved in innate immune response, is controlled by the ligands of the Toll-like receptors (TLRs) (see Figure 7.1 and Bulet et al., 1999; Elkon et al., 2007; Miyake et al., 2000). The gene *GATA-3* is activating the gene *BCL10,* which is crucial for NFκB activation by T- and B-cell receptors (Zhou et al., 2004), and the protein ICAM1 is a type of intercellular adhesion molecule continuously present in low concentrations in the membranes of leucocytes involved in the blood adaptive immune response. The network controlling TLR and ICAM1 expression contains a couple of circuits, one positive five-circuit tangent to a negative five circuits, giving only one attractor (see Figure 7.1 and Table 7.1, circle), which corresponds to the activation of the gene TLR.

2.2 THE LINKS WITH THE microRNAs

Most of the genes introduced here have links with microRNAs exerting a negative control on them and then, susceptible to deciding if the unique physiologic attractor will occur, by cancelling their target gene activity. Here are two examples of such micro-RNAs, negatively regulated by the circular RNA ciRs7 (Hansen et al., 2011, 2013):

1. for the subsequence pUNO-hRP105 of the TLR 2 gene (4937 bp) (http://mirdb. org/miRDB/; http://mirnamap.mbc.nctu.edu.tw/; Miyake et al., 2000), close to the reference sequence AL (*cf.* Annex A6 and Demongeot, 1978; Demongeot and Besson, 1983, 1996; Demongeot et al., 2003, 2009a, 2009b; Demongeot and Moreira, 2007), the hybridization is made by the microRNA miR 200a:
    5'-CCAUUCAAGAUGA**AUGGU**ACUG-3' AL 14 anti-matches
    5'-UCAUUGUUAUGCUACAGGUAUU-3' ciRs7 14 anti-matches
    3'-UGUAGCAAUGGUCUGUCACAAU-5' hsa miR 200a 12 anti-matches
    5'-UUGUGCUCAUUGAGAUGAAUGG-3' pUNO-hRP105 mRNA starting in position 531
    5'-UACUGCCAUUCAAGAUGAAUGG-3' AL 15 matches
    5'-CUGCCAUUCCUGAAGAAUAGCA-3' ciRs7 17 matches
    5'-AGGGAGCUACAAUUCAAGAUGA-3' ciRs7 17 matches (significance of 2x17 matches: 2.5‰)
2. For the GATA 3 gene, hybridization is made by miR 200c (http://mirdb.org/miRDB/; http://mirnamap.mbc.nctu.edu.tw/):
    5'-GCCAUUCAAGAUGA–**AUGGU**ACU-3' AL 13 anti-matches

5'-ACCAUCAUUAUCCCUAUUUUACA-3' ciRs7 15 anti-matches
3'-AGGUAGUAAUGGGC–CGUCAUAA-5' has miR 200c 15 anti-matches
5'-UCUGCAUUUUUGCAGGAGCAGUA-3' GATA 3 mRNA starting in
position 57

The gene expressing TLR contains the AGAUGAAUGG subsequence, belonging both to the D-loop of many tRNAs, to the reference sequence AL (Demongeot, 1978; Demongeot and Besson, 1983, 1996; Demongeot et al., 2003, 2009a, 2009b; Demongeot and Moreira, 2007) and to the circular RNA ciRs7, which signifies its affiliation to an ancestral genome, confirming the old origin of the innate immunologic system (Bulet et al., 1999; Elkon et al., 2007; Miyake et al., 2000) (see Annex A5 for the significance of the matches). In case of parallel updating (with $T=0$), the network controlling the TLR production has 4 (resp. 1) attractor, if miR200c is (resp. not) expressed (see Tables 7.1 and 7.6 left bottom, circles).

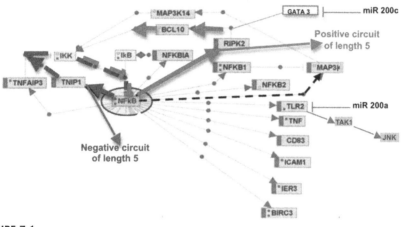

FIGURE 7.1

The network controlling the production of the TLR and the gene ICAM1 (adapted after Elkon et al., 2007).

2.3 THE ADAPTIVE IMMUNETWORKS

The adaptive immunetworks are essentially made of three couples of tangent circuits (Figure 7.2) concerning the key genes GATA 3, transcriptional activator binding to DNA sites with the consensus sequence [AT]GATA[AG]), which controls negatively T cell receptors β (TCRβ), PU.1 (PUrine-rich box-1 gene), controlling negatively the recombination-activating gene (RAG) responsible of the V(D)J rearrangements giving birth to the TCRα receptors, and Zap70 (Zeta-chain-associated protein kinase 70 gene), controlling negatively TCRβ synthesis (Demongeot et al., 2012; Georgescu et al., 2008). These circuits are inserted into a global immunetwork (Figure 7.3), whose

Table 7.1 Total number of attractors in parallel dynamics (with $T=0$), with 2 tangent circuits, left-circuit being negative of length l and right-circuit positive of length r (cf. Demongeot et al., 2012, and Annex A6).

l \ r	1	2	3	4	5	6	7	8	9	10	11	12	13	14
1	1	2	2	3	3	5	5	8	10	15	19	31	41	64
2	1	1	2	3	3	4	5	8	10	14	19	31	41	63
3	1	2	1	3	3	6	5	8	8	15	19	33	41	64
4	1	1	2	1	3	4	5	11	10	14	19	24	41	63
5	1	2	2	3	(1)	5	5	8	10	26	19	31	41	64
6	1	1	1	3	3	1	5	8	8	14	19	63	41	63
7	1	2	2	3	3	5	1	8	10	15	19	31	41	158
8	1	1	2	1	3	4	5	1	10	14	19	24	41	63
9	1	2	1	3	3	6	5	8	1	15	19	33	41	64

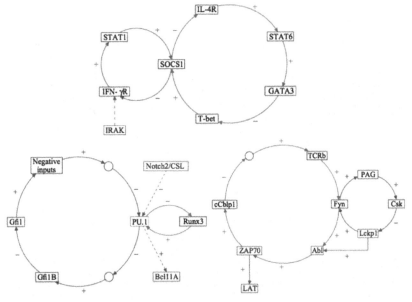

FIGURE 7.2

Left: Negative six-circuit tangent to a negative two-circuit controlling PU.1. Middle: negative three-circuit tangent to a positive five-circuit controlling GATA 3. *Right:* Tangent negative six-circuit and four-circuit controlling ZAP70 (adapted after Demongeot et al., 2012).

attractors are those of the three couples of circuits, the rest of the network being reducible to up- and down-trees connected to the circuits.

In the case of parallel updating (with $T=0$; cf. Annex A1), Table 7.7 shows that a negative six-circuit tangent to a negative two-circuit has only one attractor (Table 7.7, circle at the bottom right), less than an isolated negative six-circuit that

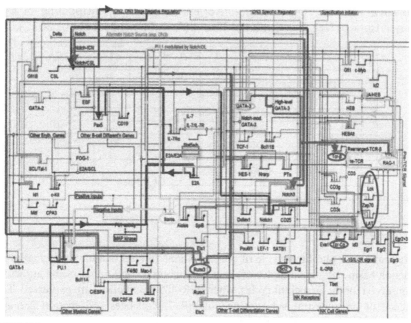

FIGURE 7.3

The global immunetwork controlling genes GATA 3, RAG, and ZAP70, with a negative circuit of length 6 controlling PU.1, which activates the NK cells through Ets1, and with circuits from the strong connected component controlling genes TCR-α, TCR-β and Bcl2 (adapted after Georgescu et al., 2008).

has six attractors (Table 7.2 circle), showing that for controlling RAG, Bcl1, and NK cells (*i.e.*, in the case of both adaptive and innate mechanisms), if Notch2/CSL is silent, PU.1 is on and hence can activate both RAG and Bcl1, as well as promote NK cells. On the contrary, if Notch2/CSL inhibits PU.1, the immunologic system is paralyzed. In the same way, we can show that GATA 3 and ZAP70 networks each have three attractors (Table 7.7, circles on the right).

3 THE IRON CONTROL NETWORK

The regulatory network controlling iron metabolism contains 10 elements, with one positive circuit of length 6 and one negative of length 4 (Figure 7.4, bottom): the number of attractors is 4 (Table 7.3), following the rules of Table 7.2 (circle). Depending on the inhibition by miR-485 or miRNA sponge ciRs7 (Hansen et al., 2011, 2013; Hentze et al., 1987; Sangokoya et al., 2013), we get either of two fixed

Table 7.2 Total Number of Attractors of Period p in Parallel Updating for a Unique Isolated Negative Circuit of Size n (After Demongeot et al., 2012).

p \ n	1	2	3	4	5	6	7	8
2	1	-	1	-	1	-	1	-
4	-	1	-	-	-	1	-	-
6	-	-	1	-	-	-	-	-
8	-	-	-	2	-	-	-	-
10	-	-	-	-	3	-	-	-
12	-	-	-	-	-	5	-	-
14	-	-	-	-	-	-	9	-
16	-	-	-	-	-	-	-	16
Total	1	1	2	2	4	6	10	16

configurations or one limit-cycle of configurations (the second having a negligible attraction basin size, equal to 4% of the possible initial conditions). Same attractors are observed for the first eight nodes, when miR-485 or anticiRs7 are expressed. The presence of an ancestral subsequence in ciRs7 sequences (*cf.* section 2.2 and Figure 7.4, top) is in favor of the seniority of the iron control system:

> 5'-AUGGGGCAACAUAUUGUAUGAA-3' FPN1a 14 anti-matches
> 3'-UCUCUCCUCUCGGCACAUACUG-5' miR-485 15 anti-matches
> 5'-UCUUUAUGUCCUCUACUGGCAGAGAGGAUGGGGGAGU
> UGUGUAUUCUUCCAGGUUC-3' ciRs7
> 5'-UCAAGAUGAAUGGUACUGCCAU-3' AL 12 matches
> 14 matches 5'-CCUGUUGGUCUCUUCCAGGUAC-3' IRP
> 10/17 anti-matches 3'-CUGGAUCAGUGGAUCUA-5' IRE-FPN1a

We can calculate a robustness parameter for the iron control network based on evolutionary entropy, defined by

$$E = \log 2^{10} - E_{attractor} = 10 \log 2 - \Sigma_{k=1,m} \mu(C_k) \log \mu(C_k),$$

where m is the attractor number and $C_k = B(A_k) \cup A_k$ is the union of the attractor A_k and of its attraction basin $B(A_k)$ (*cf.* Annex A2). Hence, $E_{attractor} = -\Sigma_{k=1,4} \mu(C_k) \log \mu(C_k) = 1/2\log 2 + 1/4\log 4 + 0.21\log(0.21) + 0.039\log(0.039)$. When $E_{attractor}$ decreases (*e.g.*, if c-Myc is cancelled, provoking the disappearance of one attractor), then the robustness of the network increases. In the stochastic parallel updating case with $T > 0$, we can calculate the derivative of E with respect to the randomness parameter T, the interaction weights being supposedly the same for each interaction (Demongeot et al., 2013a). This derivative gives an indication about the sensitivity to noise of the network.

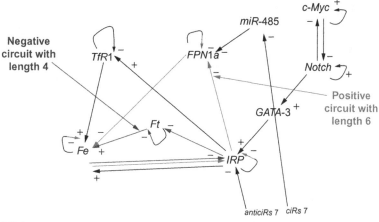

FIGURE 7.4

Top: matches between miR-485-3p and its target FPN1a (FerroPortiNe), and between the microRNAs sponge ciRs7 and its target miR-485-3p in the iron control network. Bottom: Iron control genetic network with coexistence of numerous circuits between FPN1a, Ft (Ferritin), iron regulatory protein (IRP) and transferrin receptor (TfR1), with a positive circuit of length 6 and a negative one of length 4.

Table 7.3 Recapitulation of the four attractors of the iron metabolic system, with miR-485 and anticiRs7 not expressed (state 0) and other genes expressed (state 1) or not (state 0) and (bottom) the attraction basin sizes for parallel updating (with $T=0$).

Position	Gene	Fixed Point 1	Fixed Point 2	Limit Cycle 1			Limit Cycle 2	
1	TfR1	0	0	0	0	1	1	0
2	FPN1a	0	0	0	0	0	0	0
3	c-Myc	0	1	0	0	0	0	0
4	Notch	0	0	1	1	1	1	1
5	GATA-3	0	0	1	1	1	1	1
6	IRP	0	0	0	1	0	0	1
7	Ft	0	0	0	0	0	0	0
8	Fe	0	0	0	0	1	0	1
9	miR-485	0	0	0	0	0	0	0
10	anticiRs7	0	0	0	0	0	0	0
	Attraction basin size	512	256	216			40	

4 MORPHOGENETIC NETWORKS

The morphogenetic network centered on the engrailed gene (*En* on Figure 7.5) controls in vertebrates the segmentation phase, as well as the morphogenesis of feathers and hairs in birds and mammals (Demongeot and Waku, 2012; Michon et al., 2008).

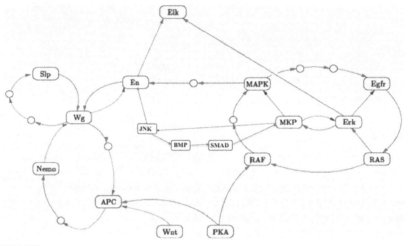

FIGURE 7.5

Engrailed centered network in *Drosophila*, with positive arcs and negative arcs.

Engrailed is not only required for the segmentation phase in vertebrates, but it efficiently represses the activity of numerous transcriptional factors like Elk (Saenz-Robles et al., 1995; Vickers and Sharrocks, 2002). Note that the engrailed centered network shown in Figure 7.5 was built by bringing together information about repressions and inductions from various sources:

- Inhibition of Engrailed by Wg and its activation by JNK is given in Gettings et al. (2010).
- Action of MPK through JNK inhibition is studied by Mantrova and Hsu (1998).
- Egrf positive feedback circuit is explained by McEwen and Peifer (2005).
- The whole Wnt pathway can be found in http://www.kegg.jp/kegg/pathway/dme/dme04310.
- Inhibition of ERK by MKP is described in Weil et al. (2004).
- Activation of Nemo by ARM, inhibited by APC, inhibited itself by Wg through Dsh (http://dev.biologists.org/content/131/12/2911/ F8.large.jpg).
- Inhibition of Wg by Nemo is described by Zeng and Verheyen (2004).

The genetic regulatory network of Figure 7.4 possesses six negative circuits of respective sizes 7, 5, 4, 3, and 2, and two positive circuits of respective sizes 7 and 4. Following Demongeot et al. (2012), we know that each of these circuits bring the following total number of attractors when isolated with parallel deterministic updating ($T = 0$):

- Negative circuit of size 7: 10 attractors (*cf.* Mathematical Annex Table 7.7, left bottom circle)
- Negative circuit of size 5: 4 attractors (*cf.* Mathematical Annex Table 7.7, left bottom circle)
- Negative circuit of size 4: 2 attractors (*cf.* Mathematical Annex Table 7.7, left bottom circle)
- Negative circuit of size 3: 2 attractors (*cf.* Mathematical Annex Table 7.7, left bottom circle)
- Negative circuit of size 2: 2 attractors (*cf.* Mathematical Annex Table 7.7, left bottom circle)
- Positive circuit of size 7: 20 attractors (*cf.* Mathematical Annex Table 7.7, left top circle)
- Positive circuit of size 4: 6 attractors (*cf.* Mathematical Annex Table 7.7, left top circle).

Table 7.4 Attractors in Parallel Mode (with $T=0$) for the MPK/ERK Centered Subnetwork, with Negative 7- and 3-Circuit Tangent

Gene	PF	Cycle Limit 1				Cycle Limit 2			
En	0	1	0	0	0	0	1	0	1
Elk	0	0	0	0	1	0	0	0	0
MAPK	0	0	0	0	1	1	0	1	0
Egfr	0	1	0	0	0	0	1	0	1
RAS	0	0	1	0	0	1	0	1	0
Erk	0	0	0	1	0	0	1	0	0
MKP	0	0	0	0	1	0	0	1	0
RAF	0	0	0	1	0	0	1	0	1
SMAD	0	0	0	0	0	0	0	0	0
BMP	0	0	0	0	0	0	0	0	0
JNK	0	0	0	0	0	0	0	0	0
TBA=2048	1320			648				80	
ABRS = 1	0,6445			0,31640625				0,0390625	

The results obtained recently on tangent and intersecting circuits [*cf.* Melliti et al. (2014); Richard, 2011) and Table 7.7 in Annex A3) show a drastic reduction of the attractor number to 3 or 1 (depending on source nodes PKA and Wnt), because the engrailed centered network has the following:

- One positive circuit of size 7 intersecting a negative circuit of size 7: 1 attractor, instead of 200 if the circuits are disjoint (*cf.* Mathematical Annex Table 7.7, right top, circle)
- One positive circuit of size 7 intersecting a negative circuit of size 3: 5 attractors, instead of 20 if the circuits are disjoint (*cf.* Mathematical Annex Table 7.7, right top, circle)

- One negative circuit of size 7 tangent to a negative circuit of size 4 : 2 attractors (*cf.* Mathematical Annex Table 7.7, right bottom circle)
- One negative circuit of size 7 intersecting a negative circuit of size 3: 3 attractors, instead of 20 if the circuits are disjoint (*cf.* Mathematical Annex Table 7.7, right bottom, circle)
- One negative circuit of size 4 tangent to a negative circuit of size 2: 2 attractors (*cf.* Mathematical Annex Table 7.7, right bottom circle)
- One negative circuit of size 3 tangent to a negative circuit of size 2: 2 attractors (*cf.* Mathematical Annex Table 7.7, right bottom circle)
- Three co-tangent circuits, one positive circuit of size 4, one negative circuit of size 5, and one negative circuit of size 2: 1 attractor, instead of 24 if the circuits are disjoint (*cf.* Mathematical Annex Table 7.7, right circles)

The corresponding attractors are given in Table 7.4, depending on the expression of the gene sources of the up-trees controlling the circuits; *i.e.*, *Wnt* and *PKA*. If both genes *Wnt* and *PKA* are expressed, there are three attractors with only one limit-cycle of period 6 as asymptotic dynamical behavior of the engrailed centered network, for which the gene *En* is not expressed and *Elk* is expressed one-third of the time, inhibiting both the dorsal closure and allowing the excitable cells differentiation. If *PKA* is silent and *Wnt* is either expressed or silent, there are also three attractors: two fixed points, where neither *En* nor *Elk* are expressed, and a limit cycle of period 4, where *En* is expressed half the time and *Elk* is expressed a quarter of the time. If the gene *Wnt* is silent and *PKA* expressed, there exists only a limit cycle of period 6, where *En* is expressed half the time and *Elk* is expressed 1/6 of the time. Other examples of genetic regulatory networks involving *Wnt* are given in Michon et al., (2008). All these examples show that more generally, the architecture of a genetic regulatory network consists of the strong connected components of its interaction graph, to which are attached three kinds of substructures:

- a set of up-trees, issued from the sources of the interaction graph of the network, made either of small RNAs (like microRNAs, translational inhibitors), or of genes repressors or inductors, self-expressed without any other genes controlling them, like the genes *Wnt* and *PKA*
- a set of circuits in the core (in a graphical sense) of the strong connected components of the interaction graph. These circuits are unique or multiple, reduced to one gene (if there is an auto-control loop) or made of several ones, negative or positive, and disjoint or not, like the circuits involving *Erk*
- a set of down-trees going to the sinks of the interaction graph; *i.e.*, to genes controlled by but not controlling any other genes, like the gene *Elk*

In *Drosophila* embryo, using the interaction graph of the engrailed centered network, a simple model based on the knowledge about the asymptotic dynamics of the network (*i.e.*, its attractors) shows that *Wg* is expressed and inhibits *Dsh* during the Mixer cell formation at the para-segment boundaries, during the polarization of epidermal cells during dorsal closure in *Drosophila,* where *Wnt* and *PKA* are expressed (Gettings et al., 2010).

5 BILIARY ATRESIA CONTROL NETWORK

The genetic network controlling the morphogenesis of the biliary canal can be summarized as in Figures 7.6 and 7.7 (Bessho et al., 2013; Choe et al., 2003; Girard et al., 2011, 2012; Kohsaka et al., 2002; Luedde et al., 2008; Matte et al., 2010; Nouws and Shadel, 2014; Ranganathan et al., 2011; Xiao et al., 2014). By using the gene expression data comparing normal individuals and patients suffering from biliary atresia (*cf.* Figure 7.6, left, and Melliti et al., 2014; Meyer and Nelson, 2011), we can locate and study three key genes inside or around the network, *Bcl-w, TGF-ß, and elf-2α* kinase (Figure 7.7 and Choe et al., 2003), and study the attractors of the network (Table 7.5).

Transcript identity	Intensity Normal	Intensity BA	Ratio (BA/Normal)
Bcl-w	16.7	28.8	1.7
Laminin BP (binding protein)	0.7	7.7	11
HRS (HGF-regulated tyrosine kinase substrate)	0.5	3.5	6.9
Thymosin β-4	0.6	4.1	6.5
Thymosin β-10	0.5	2.5	5.4
TGF-β	0.6	2.1	3.3
TIMP (tissue inhibitor of metalloproteinase)-1	1.8	3.9	2.2
SRP (signal recognition particle) 4	2	7.1	3.6
SRP9	1.7	5.6	3.3
SNAP (soluble NSF attachment proteins) 45	1.2	5.6	4.5
Alu RNA BP	0.8	6.9	8.5
supt5h (human homologue of the yeast transcription factor, SPT5)	1.9	4.5	2.3
eIF-2α kinase	4.5	12.1	2.7

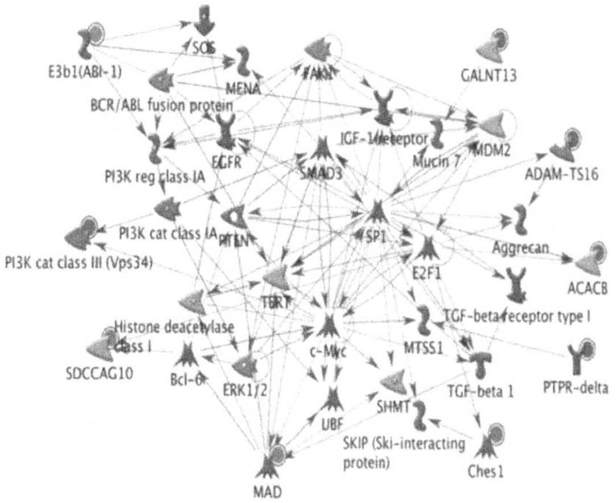

FIGURE 7.6

Left: biliary atresia gene expression (Choe et al., 2003), with three markers: *Bcl-w, TGF-ß,* and *elf-2α* kinase, whose level of expression is measured in a control group (Normal) and in patients suffering from biliary atresia (noted here as BA). *Right:* Genetic network controlling biliary atresia.

We can add to the network shown in Figure 7.6, provided initially by MetaCore™ and checked after in the literature. The following information has been added in Figure 7.7 to the network in Figure 7.6:

- The gene *JAG1* (mutated in case of biliary atresia (Kohsaka et al., 2002; Matte et al., 2010) activates Notch, necessary for the activation of EGFR (Franco et al., 2006; Ranganathan et al., 2011).
- Human microRNAs *miR 29* and *miR 39b* inhibits *IGF 1* and *PI3K*, respectively (Bessho et al., 2013; Gottwein et al., 2011; Hand et al., 2012).
- The gene *Bcl-w*/*Bcl-2* is inhibited by *SMAD 3,* and activated by *ERK ½* and *MAPK* (Kang and Pervaiz, 2013). Its protein is phosphorylated (hence inhibited) by *JNK* (Singh et al., 2009).
- The gene eIF-2α kinase phosphorylates (hence, inhibits) eIF-2α (Gurzov and Eizirik, 2011; Lee et al., 2000) and activates IRP and MAPK.

The strong connected component of the interaction graph of the biliary atresia network (Figure 7.7) shows the existence of a negative circuit of length 11 (by counting the auto-loops) tangent on the gene *FAK1* to a negative circuit of length 5 (Figure 7.8). The theoretical results of Demongeot et al. (2012) shows that we can expect seven attractors, which can be simulated (Table 7.5), whose only two limit-cycles (their attraction basins representing about half of all possible expression patterns) show the presence of the same gene expression than that detected in patients suffering from biliary atresia; *i.e.*, an increased expression of the three genes *Bcl-w*, *TGF-β*, and *elf-2α* kinase (Choe et al., 2003), an overexpression of IGF1 and a down-expression of JAG1, mutated in biliary atresia (Kohsaka et al., 2002), provoking a weak expression of EGFR (Matte et al., 2010). That partially validates the control network proposed for biliary atresia syndrome.

We can break the negative circuit of length 5 by using the microRNA *hsa miR 39b*, where one of the targets is the gene *PI3K* (Xiao et al., 2014; Kohsaka et al., 2002):

- 3'-uguaaacauccuacacucagcu-5' *hsa miR 30b*
- 5'-AUGGUACUGCCAUUCAAGAUGA-3' AL 13 anti-matches

The main result of the disappearance of the negative circuit of length 5 is an increase of the attractor number, passing from 7 to 10 (*cf.* Table 7.2, circle). Two other negative circuits do not increase the attractor number:

- The negative circuit of length 3 *FAK1-MDM2-IGF-1* is tangent at *FAK1* to the two previous circuits of lengths 7 and 4, but this coupling brings only one attractor (Figure 7.9, circle). It can be broken by the microRNA *hsa miR 29* (Matte et al., 2010) and can only change the configuration of expressed genes; for example, in the presence of *miR 29*, the *IGF-1* state becomes 0 in the attractor states of Table 7.5:
  - 3'-acugauuucuuuugguguucag-5' *hsa miR 29*
  - 5'-CCAUUCAAGAUGAAUGGUACUG-3' AL 13 anti-matches
- The negative circuit of length 3 FAK1-PI3K-PTEN also brings only one attractor and its break by miR 39b (Figure 7.7) changes only the attractor states by fixing at 0 the state of PI3K (*cf.* Table 7.5).

From the mathematical analysis of the attractors of the biliary atresia network, we can infer the existence of seven possible stationary behaviors; among them, only four have an attraction basin that is sufficiently stable (*i.e.*, containing a sufficient number of initial conditions to resist to large perturbations in the state space of the expression configurations). These four attractors represent the final evolution of 96% of the possible initial configurations; two of them being fixed configurations (called *fixed points* and denoted as PF in Table 7.5), and the other two being periodic configurations (called *limit cycles* and denoted as CL in Table 7.5). Among these attractors, notice that only one corresponds to all the characteristics observed in the pathologic case of the biliary atresia: *E2F1, TGF-β,* and *Bcl-w* are always expressed, *EGFR* is weakly expressed, as is *ERK ½,* due to its absence of inhibition of *Bcl-w*. The unique attractor satisfying these constraints is the fixed configuration PF 4 on Table 7.5. It has a small attraction basin (ABRS = 2%), but it can represent a nonphysiologic

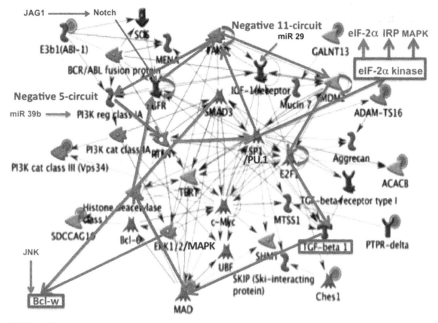

FIGURE 7.7

Biliary atresia control network, with three important genes: two on its frontier (up-tree), *Bcl-w* and *elf-2α* kinase; and one inside the strong connected component, *TGF-β 1*. The strong connected component (scc) contains two tangent (in FAK1) negative circuits: one of length 11 passing through *TGF-β 1*, and the other of length 5, passing through *PI3K*. Both can be broken by the microRNA *miR 39b*. The scc is on the control of *JAG1* by Notch, activates (through SP1/ PU.1 and *elF-2α* kinase) the genes *IRP* and *MAPK*, and inhibits the gene *elF-2α*.

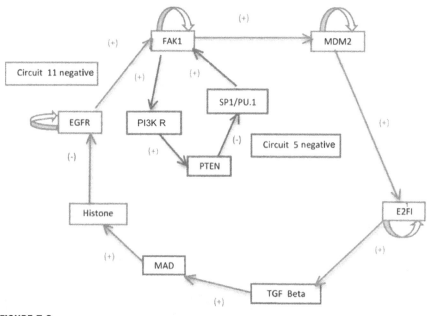

FIGURE 7.8

The two main negative circuits of the biliary atresia control network: one of length 11 and the other of length 5 (taking into account the auto-catalytic loops).

Table 7.5 Description of the Seven Attractors of the Biliary Atresia Control Network (with Parallel Updating and $T=0$)

	PF1	PF2	PF3	PF4	PF5	CL 1		CL 2	
FAK1	0	1	1	1	1	1	1	1	1
IGF-1	0	1	1	1	1	1	1	1	1
PI3K REG	0	1	1	1	1	1	1	1	1
EGFR	0	0	0	0	0	0	0	0	0
SMAD3	0	0	0	0	0	0	0	0	0
MDM2	0	1	1	1	1	1	1	1	1
SP1	0	0	0	0	0	0	0	0	0
PTEN	0	0	0	0	0	0	0	0	0
PI3K CAT CLASS	0	1	1	1	1	1	1	1	1
Histone	0	1	1	1	1	1	1	1	1
TERT	0	0	0	0	0	0	0	0	0
E2F1	0	1	1	1	1	1	1	1	1
TGF-β	0	1	1	1	1	1	1	1	1
MAD	0	1	1	1	1	1	1	1	1
C_myc	0	1	1	1	1	1	1	1	0
ERK 1/2	0	1	1	1	1	1	1	1	1
Bcl_6	0	1	1	1	1	1	1	1	0
TGF RECEPTOR	0	1	1	1	1	1	1	1	1
Bcl-w	0	0	0	0	0	1	0	1	0
PI3K CLASS III	0	1	1	1	1	0	0	1	0
E3B1	0	0	0	0	0	0	0	0	0
UBF	0	0	0	0	0	0	0	0	0
TBA	336	949200	1020024	82616	37600	1997032		107496	
ABRS	8,01086E-05	0,22630692	0,24319267	0,01969719	0,00896454	0,476129532		0,025629044	
TTBA	4194304								

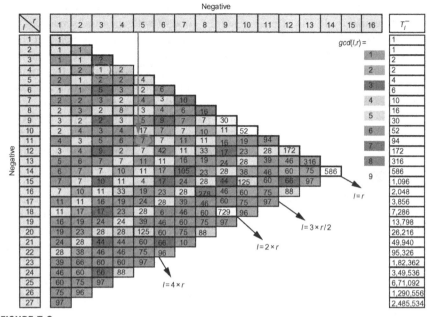

FIGURE 7.9

Calculation of the number of attractors of the biliary atresia control network (Demongeot et al., 2012). At the intersection of the column 5 and the line 11, one can find the attractor number, 7, due to a couple of tangent negative circuits, one of length 5 and the other of length 11.

possibility of differentiation in a few cases depending on initial conditions fixed by the genomic expression It could be interesting to observe in patients the expression activity of the gene *c-Myc,* which is absent in PF4 on Table 7.5, in order to confirm it as a candidate for explaining the pathologic behavior, due to the role of *EGFR* and *ERK ½* in the morphogenesis (see the network described in section 4, earlier in this chapter) that is necessary to activate Nemo.

6 CONCLUSION AND PERSPECTIVES

The genetic networks regulated by small RNAs fitting with ancestral sequences are showing interesting properties with a small number of attractors, allowing to control less than four main attractors in general, some inhibiting the function (the brakes), and the others activating it (the accelerators). The role of the microRNAs is to provide an unspecific inhibitory noise leaving active in the dynamics only the circuits with sufficiently strong interactions to be able to express these attractors. The circular RNAs are inhibiting in an unspecific way the microRNAs in order to have, as in neural networks, the possibility of obtaining a double reciprocal influence (inhibitory and anti-inhibitory) on mRNAs (*i.e.*, on gene expression). Because the sequences of the small regulatory RNAs offer in general a good fit with ancestral sequences, we can infer that the control of important domains involved in key metabolism or defense processes have been fixed early in the evolution to optimize systems like the immunologic, energetic and morphogenetic ones, which are crucial for survival. This resemblance with ancient genomes can come from two different mechanisms: (i) there are relics, having not mutated, that are still present in the genomes today (*e.g.*, in the most conserved and universal parts of RNA molecules like the tRNA loops); and (ii) there exists still a mimicking of the start of life, such as circular RNA.

In order to survive, it has to solve the following variational problem: (i) to be sufficiently small to remain not denatured in the cell cytoplasm and (ii) hybridize a sufficient number of microRNAs in order to serve as a brake to their inhibitory activity. Because these microRNAs have to be sufficiently nonspecific to target a great number of messenger RNAs, they have to contain in their 22 bases the maximum of codons from different classes of synonymy of the amino-acid. This variational problem is very close to that of the beginning of life, in which primitive RNAs [like the AL sequence (Demongeot, 1978; Demongeot and Besson, 1983, 1996; Demongeot et al., 2003, 2009a, 2009b; Demongeot and Moreira, 2007)] could have occurred and persisted due to the selective advantage to fix a great number of amino acids realizing a protein proto-membrane, an ancestor of the plasmic membrane that exists today. That could suffice to explain the similarity observed between the primitive and present circular RNA. Future studies could perform an exhaustive examination of small RNAs in order to reinforce the hypotheses of both (i) the existence of RNA relics still present in the evolved genomes and (ii) the biosynthesis of RNA molecules similar to those existing at the beginning of life, because the same variational problem is being solved. Further studies on the genetic regulatory networks could show that the role of all their inhibitors is crucial for getting a very limited number of attractors focusing only on the cell functions necessary to survive, eliminating all the nonfunctional attractors.

MATHEMATICAL ANNEX
A1 DEFINITIONS

The mathematical object modeling a real genetic regulatory network is called a *genetic threshold Boolean regulatory network* (denoted in the following as *getBren*). A getBren N can be considered as a set of random automata, defined by the following criteria (Robert, 1980):

1. Any random automaton i of the getBren N owns at time t a state $x_i(t)$ valued in $\{0,1\}$, 0 (resp. 1) meaning that gene i is inactivated or in silence (Respectively activated or in expression). The global state of the getBren at time t, called *configuration* in the sequel, is then defined by $x(t) = (x_i(t))_{i \in \{1,n\}} \in \Omega = \{0,1\}^n$

2. A getBren N of size n is a triplet (W, Θ, P), where
- W is a matrix of order n, where the coefficient $w_{ij} \in$ IR represents the interaction weight gene j has on gene i. Sign$(W) = (\alpha_{ij} = \text{sign}(w_{ij}))$ is the adjacency (or incidence) matrix of a graph G, called the *interaction graph*.
- Θ is a threshold of dimension n, its component θ_i being the activation threshold attributed to automaton i.
- $M: \mathbf{P}(\Omega) \to [0,1]^{m \times m}$, where $\mathbf{P}(\Omega)$ is the set of all subsets of Ω and $m = 2^n$ is a Markov transition matrix, built from local probability transitions P_i giving the new state of the gene i at time $t+1$ according to W, Θ, and configuration $x(t)$ of N at time t such that

$$\forall g \in \{0,1\}, \beta \in \Omega, P_{i,g}{}^{\beta}(\{x_i(t+1) = g \,|\, x(t) = \beta\}) = \exp\left[g\left(\Sigma_{j \in Ni} w_{ij}\beta_j - \theta_i\right)/T\right]/Z_i,$$

where $Z_i = [1 + \exp[(\Sigma_{j \in Ni} w_{ij}\beta_j - \theta_i)/T]$, N_i is the neighborhood of the gene i in the getBren N; i.e., the set of genes j (including possibly i) such that $w_{ij} \neq 0$, and $P_{i,g}{}^{\beta}$ is the probability for the gene i of passing to the state g at time $t+1$, from the configuration β at time t on N_i. M denotes the transition matrix built from the $P_{i,g}{}^{\beta}$'s. M depends on the update mode chosen for changing the states of the getBren automata. In this chapter, we use the parallel or synchronous mode of updating.

For the extreme values of the randomness parameter T, we have the following:

1. If $T = 0$, getBren becomes a deterministic threshold automata network and the transition can be written as

$$x_i(t+1) = h\left(\Sigma_{j \in Ni} w_{ij}x_j(t) - \theta_i\right),$$

where h is the Heaviside function: $h(y) = 1$, if $y > 0$;

$$h(y) = 0, \text{ if } y < 0,$$

except for the case $\Sigma_{j \in Ni} w_{ij}x_j(t) - \theta_I = 0$, for which, if necessary, 1 and 0 are both chosen with probability $\frac{1}{2}$. In this chapter, we chose $T = 0$.

2. When T tends to infinity, then $P_{i,g}{}^{\beta} = \frac{1}{2}$ and each line M_i of M becomes the uniform distribution on the basin of the final class of the Markov matrix M to which i belongs (corresponding to an attraction basin when $T = 0$).

We define (Demongeot et al., 2003) the energy U and frustration F of a getBren N by

$$\forall x \in \Omega, U(x) = \Sigma_{i,j \in \{1,n\}} \alpha_{ij}x_ix_j = Q_+(N) - F(x),$$

where $Q_+(N)$ is the number of positive edges in the interaction graph G of the network N and $F(x)$ the global frustration of x; i.e., the number of pairs (i,j) where the values of x_i and x_j are contradictory with the sign α_{ij} of the interaction between genes i and j: $F(x) = \Sigma_{i,j \in \{1,n\}} F_{ij}(x)$, where F_{ij} is the local frustration of the pair (i,j) defined by

$F_{ij}(x) = 1$, if $\alpha_{ij} = 1$, $x_j = 1$ and $x_i = 0$, or $x_j = 0$ and $x_i = 1$, and if $\alpha_{ij} = -1$, $x_j = 1$ and $x_i = 1$, or $x_j = 0$ and $x_i = 0$,
$F_{ij}(x) = 0$, elsewhere.

Eventually, we define the random global dynamic frustration D by

$$D(x(t)) = \Sigma_{i,j \in \{1,n\}} D_{ij}(x(t)),$$

where D_{ij} is the local dynamic frustration of the pair (i,j) defined by

$$D_{ij}(x(t)) = 1, \text{ if } \alpha_{ij} = 1, x_i(t) \neq h\left(\Sigma_{j \in Ni} w_{ij} x_j(t) - \theta_i\right) \text{ or } \alpha_{ij} = -1, x_i(t) = h\left(\Sigma_{j \in Ni} w_{ij} x_j(t) - \theta_i\right),$$
$$D_{ij}(x(t)) = 0, \text{ elsewhere.}$$

A2 FIRST PROPOSITIONS

Based on these definitions, we can prove the following propositions [*cf.* Demongeot and Waku (2012) and Demongeot et al. (2013b) for complete results]:

Proposition 1 Let us consider the random energy U and the random frustration F of getBren N having a constant absolute value w for its interaction weights, null threshold Θ, temperature T equal to 1, and being sequentially updated. Then:

1. $U(x) = \Sigma_{i,j \in \{1,n\}} \alpha_{ij} x_i x_j = Q_+(N) - F(x)$, where $Q_+(N)$ is the number of positive edges in the interaction graph G of the network.
2. $E_\mu(U) = \partial \log Z / \partial w$, where the free energy $\log Z$ is equal to the quantity $\log(\Sigma_{y \in \Omega} \exp(\Sigma_{j \in y, k \in y} w_{ij} y_j y_k))$, and μ is the invariant Gibbs measure defined by $\forall x \in \Omega$, $\mu(\{x\}) = \exp(\Sigma_{i \in x, j \in x} w_{ij} x_i x_j)/Z$.
3. $\text{Var}_\mu U = \text{Var}_\mu F = -\partial E_\mu / \partial \log w$, where $E_\mu = -\Sigma_{x \in \Omega} \mu(\{x\}) \log(\mu(\{x\})) = \log Z - w E_\mu(U)$ is the entropy of μ, maximal among entropies corresponding to all probability distributions ν for U having the same given expectation $E_\nu(U) = E_\mu(U)$.

Proof: (1) It is easy to check that $U(x) = Q_+(N) - F(x)$ and (2) the expectation of U, denoted $E_\mu(U)$, is given by

$$E_\mu(U) = \Sigma_{x \in \Omega} \Sigma_{i \in x, j \in x} \alpha_{ij} x_i x_j \exp\left(\Sigma_{i \in x, j \in x} w x_i x_j\right)/Z = \partial \log Z / \partial w$$

(3) Following Demongeot and Waku (2012), we have $\text{Var}_\mu U = \text{Var}_\mu F = -\partial E_\mu / \partial \log w$, and E_μ is maximal among the proposed entropies

Proposition 2 Let us consider getBren N with T=0, sequentially or synchronously updated, defined from a potential P defined by

$$\forall x \in \Omega, P(x) = \Sigma_k ({}^t x A_k x) x_k + {}^t x W x + \Theta x,$$

where A, W, and Θ are integer tensor, matrix, and line vector, respectively. Also suppose that

$$\forall i = 1, \ldots, n, \Delta x_i \in \{-1, 0, 1\}.$$

If h denotes the Heaviside function, consider now the potential automaton i defined by

$$x_i(t+1) = h(-\Delta P/\Delta x_i + x_i(t)),$$

and by the condition $x_i(t+1) \geq 0$, if $x_i(t) = 0$, such that the flow remains in Ω. Then, if the tensor A is symmetrical with vanishing diagonal (*i.e.*, if we have the equalities: $\forall$ i, j, $k = 1,...,n$, $a_{ijk} = a_{ikj} = a_{kij} = a_{jki} = a_{jik} = a_{kji}$ and $a_{iik} = 0$), and if each submatrix (on any subset J of indices in $\{1,...,n\}$) of A_k and W are nonpositive with vanishing diagonal, P decreases on the trajectories of the potential automaton, for any mode of implementation of the dynamics (sequential, block sequential, and parallel). Hence, the stable fixed configurations of the automaton correspond to the minima of its potential P.

Proof: We have, for a discrete function P on Ω:

$$\Delta P(x)/\Delta x_i = [P(x_1,...,x_i + \Delta x_i,...,x_n) - P(x_1, ..., x_i, ..., x_n)]/\Delta x_i$$

and the proof is based on the existence of a Lyapunov function proved in Demongeot et al. (2014).

Proposition 3 Let us consider the Hamiltonian getBren, which is a circuit with constant absolute value w for its interaction weights, null threshold Θ, and temperature T equal to 0, sequentially or synchronously updated, whose Hamiltonian H is defined by

$$H(x(t)) = \sum_{i=1,...,n}(x_i(t) - x_i(t-1))^2/2 = \sum_{i=1,...,n}\left(h\left(w_{i(i-1)}x_{i-1}(t-1) - x_i(t-1)\right)^2/2\right),$$

which equals the total discrete kinetic energy and the half of the global dynamic frustration $D(x(t))$. The result remains available if automata network is a circuit in which transition functions are Boolean identity or negation.

Proof: It is easy to check that $H(x(t)) = D(x(t))/2$.

Proposition 1 is used to estimate the evolution of the robustness of a network because from Demongeot et al. (2014a, 2014b), it results that the quantity $E = E_\mu - E_{attractor}$ ($= \log 2^n - E_{attractor}$, if μ is uniform), called *evolutionary entropy*, serves as a robustness parameter, being related to the capacity that a getBren has to return to μ, the equilibrium measure, after endogenous or exogenous perturbation. $E_{attractor}$ can be evaluated by the quantity

$$E_{attractor} = -\Sigma_{k=1, m \leq 2} n\mu(C_k)\log\mu(C_k),$$

where *m* is the number of attractors and $C_k = B(A_k) \cup A_k$ is the union of the attractor A_k and of its attraction basin $B(A_k)$. A systematic calculation of $E_{attractor}$ allows quantifying the complexification of a network ensuring a dedicated regulatory function in different species. For example, the increase of the inhibitory sources in up-trees converging on a conserved subgraph of a genetic network causes a decrease of its attractor number by cutting some inhibited circuits, hence a decrease of $E_{attractor}$ and an increase of the evolutionary entropy E, showing that the robustness of a network is positively correlated with its connectivity (*i.e.*, the ratio between the numbers of interactions and genes in the network). Propositions 2 and 3 give examples of extreme cases where the networks are either discrete potential (or gradient) systems, generalizing previous works on continuous dynamics in which authors attempt to explicit Waddington and Thom chreode's energy functions, conserved or dissipated. In Demongeot et al. (2012), a method was proposed for calculating the number of attractors in the case of circuits with Boolean transitions reduced to identity or negation. These results about attractors counting constitute a partial response to the discrete version of the 16th Hilbert's problem and can be approached by using Hamiltonian energy levels. For example, for a positive circuit of order 8, it is easy to prove that, in case of parallel updating, we have only even values for the global frustration D (they are odd for a negative circuit), corresponding to different values of the period of the attractors (Table 7.6).

Table 7.6 Values of the Global Frustration D, Attractor Numbers and Periods for Positive Circuits of Order 8 with Boolean Transition Identity or Negation

D (Frustration)	Attractor Number	Attractor Period
0	2	1
2	7	8
4	3	4
4	16	8
6	7	8
8	1	2

A3 TANGENT AND INTERSECTING CIRCUITS

The study of tangent and intersecting circuits in strong connected components of a genetic network is possible when interactions are either identity or negation (Demongeot et al., 2012; http://dev.biologists.org/content/131/12/2911/ F8.large. jpg), with a mixing rule monotonic when different arcs come on the same node. For example, such circuits with one or two genes in common are shown in Figure 7.10.

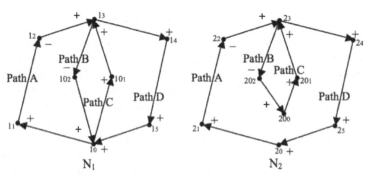

FIGURE 7.10

The two coupled networks N_i ($i=1,2$) are each made of the subnetworks N_i and N_{i0}, whose vertices (or nodes) are denoted as ij ($j=0,...,5$) and $i0k$ ($k=0,...,2$), respectively.

By looking on the networks of Figure 7.10, we see that each is made of four main paths of opposite senses: two are up (A and C), and two down (B and D), with the respective lengths of ℓ_A, ℓ_B, ℓ_C, and ℓ_D, and parities of s_A, s_B, s_C, and s_D, equal to 1 (resp. -1) if they have an even (resp. odd) number of negative arcs, with $s_A = \Pi_{a \in A} s_a$, where the sign s_a of the arc a of A is equal to -1 if a is negative (inhibition) and 1 if a is positive (activation).

For example, in Figure 7.10, the path A of N_1 is such as $\ell_A = 3$ and $s_A = -1$. The main paths have in N_1 two common nodes, 10 and 13, and in N_2, only one common node 23. Finally, with N_1, having four paths and two common nodes, there are four combinations giving four possible circuits (A,B), (B,C), (A,D), and (D,C), with a circuit like (A,C) having the parity $s_{A,C} = s_A s_C$. In the following discussion, to facilitate the reasoning, we will suppose that the state 0 of a gene is replaced by the state -1.

Let us denote as ((J,L),(L,M)) the general couple of circuits inside the set of the six possible couples created from these four circuits. If N((J,K),(L,M)) denotes the number of possible attractors of ((J,K),(L,M)), then the attractor number of N_1 is the minimum of the values of N((J,K),(L,M)) for the six couples of circuits. We conjectured (Demongeot and Moreira, 2007) that this number was less than the attractor number of N_2, the attractors of N_1 being those that allow the two common nodes to have the same state for each couple of circuits.

The minimum can be made more precise: suppose that two circuits (K,L) and (M,) have two common nodes with the same state. Any attractor of these intersected circuits has the same configurations as one of those of the tangent circuits that we can build by decoupling one on their two common nodes. Indeed, if not, there is at least one node different from the common nodes having an asymptotic sequence of states different for N_1 and N_2. Starting from this node and following the path going from this node to the common node of N_2, we would find for this node a sequence of states different that those observed in N_2 attractors, which is impossible. This reduces considerably the possible attractors for intersecting circuits, since they must always have the same state on their two intersected nodes. Then, counting attractors corresponds to a known combinatorial problem generalizing the necklace problem (*cf.* Demongeot et al., 2012; and Table 7.7). Then two new questions remain open:

Q1: Is a given attractor of the network N_2 respecting the constraint $x_{20_0}(t) = x_{2_0}(t)$), identical to an attractor of N_2?

Q2: If the answer to Q1 is yes, what are the constraints of its period?

The following propositions partially address Q1 and Q2.

Proposition 4 The attractors of the network N_2 respecting the constraint $x_{20_0}(t) = x_{2_0}(t)$), are the precise attractors of N_1.

Proof. From an initial condition identical for N_2 and N_1, where $x_{20_0}(0) = x_{2_0}(0) = x_{1_0}(0)$, the trajectories are the same for all the nodes, if $x_{20_0}(t) = x_{2_0}(t)$, for any $t \geq 1$. For the node 1_0 of the network N_1, we have, if the mixing rule is monotonic (*e.g.*, $\vee$ in N_1 and N_2):

$$x_{1_0}(t) = [s_B \times x_{1_3}(t - \ell_B)] \vee [s_D \times x_{1_3}(t - \ell_D)]$$
$$x_{20_0}(t) = s_B \times x_{2_3}(t - \ell_B) \, and \, x_{2_0}(t) = s_D \times x_{2_3}(t - \ell_D).$$

Note that the reasoning would be the same with rule $\wedge$ or any composition of $\vee$ and $\wedge$.

By imposing $x_{20_0}(t) = x_{2_0}(t)$, for any $t \geq 1$, then $s_B \times x_{2_3}(t - \ell_B) = s_D \times x_{2_3}(t - \ell_D)$, and we have in the network N_1:

$$x_{1_0}(t) = [s_B \times x_{1_3}(t - \ell_B)] \vee [s_D \times x_{1_3}(t - \ell_D)] = x_{20_0}(t) = x_{2_0}(t).$$

By recurrence on t, this common value for $x_{1_0}(t)$, $x_{20_0}(t)$ and $x_{2_0}(t)$ is equal to

$$s_B \times x_{1_3}(0) = s_B \times x_{2_3}(0), \, for \, any \, t = k\ell_B, \, with \, k \geq 0.$$

The same reasoning can apply to $t \equiv 1, \ldots, \ell_B\text{-}1 \pmod{\ell_B}$. Then, the trajectories being the same, the attractors of N_2 with the constraint $x_{20_0}(t) = x_{20}(t)$, are attractors of N_1.

Let us consider now an attractor of N_1, for which $x_{1_0}(t) = [s_B \times x_{1_3}(t\text{-} \ell_B)] \vee [s_D \times x_{1_3}(t\text{-} \ell_D)]$. If we identify $x_{1_0}(t)$ and $x_{2_0}(t)$, then, if $x_{1_3}(0) = x_{2_3}(0)$, this attractor is an attractor of N_2, where the two circuits (tangent in 2_3) have the signs $sup(s_A, s_B)s_C$ and $sup(s_A, s_B)s_D$, respectively, and where $x_{20_0}(t) = x_{2_0}(t)$

Remark If $\ell_D = \ell_B$, the constraint $s_D = s_B$ is necessary for observing in N_2 the coupling $x_{20_0}(t) = x_{2_0}(t)$. If not, the attractors of N_2 are not necessarily attractors of N_1.

Proposition 5 The attractors of N_2, with the coupling $x_{20_0}(t) = x_{2_0}(t)$, are characterized by the following property on their period p:

- If $s_B \times s_D = 1$ (resp. $s_A \times s_C = 1$), we have
  - p divides $(sup(\ell_B, \ell_D) - inf(\ell_B, \ell_D)) \Leftrightarrow p|(sup(\ell_B, \ell_D) - inf(\ell_B, \ell_D))$ (resp. p divides $(sup(\ell_A, \ell_C) - inf(\ell_A,\ell_C)) \Leftrightarrow p|(sup(\ell_A,\ell_C) - inf(\ell_A,\ell_C))$
  - if $s_B \times s_D = -1$ (resp. $s_A \times s_C = -1$), p does not divide $(sup(\ell_B,\ell_D) - inf(\ell_B,\ell_D))$ and p divides $2(sup(\ell_B,\ell_D) - inf(\ell_B,\ell_D)) \Leftrightarrow \neg[p|(sup(\ell_B,\ell_D) - inf(\ell_B,\ell_D))] \wedge p|2 (sup(\ell_B,\ell_D) - inf(\ell_B,\ell_D))$ (resp. p does not divide $(sup(\ell_A,\ell_C) - inf(\ell_A,\ell_C))$ and p divides $2(sup(\ell_A,\ell_C) - inf(\ell_A,\ell_C)) \Leftrightarrow \neg[p|(sup(\ell_A,\ell_C) - inf(\ell_A,\ell_C))] \wedge p|2(sup(\ell_A,\ell_C) - inf(\ell_A,\ell_C))$.

Proof. If p denotes the length (or period) of an attractor of N_2, with the coupling $x_{20_0}(t) = x_{2_0}(t)$, then we have

$$\forall t \geq 1, x_{20_0}(t) = x_{2_0}(t) \Leftrightarrow \forall t \geq 1, s_B \times x_{2_3}(t - \ell_B) = s_D \times x_{2_3}(t - \ell_D) \Leftrightarrow$$
$$\forall t \geq 1, x_{2_3}(t) = s_B \times s_D \times x_{2_3}(t + \ell_B - \ell_D)$$

and

$$\forall t \geq 1, x_{20_0}(t) = x_{2_0}(t) \Leftrightarrow \forall t \geq 1, s_A \times x_{2_3}(t - \ell_A) = s_C \times x_{2_3}(t - \ell_C) \Leftrightarrow$$
$$\forall t \geq 1, x_{2_3}(t) = s_A \times s_C \times x_{2_3}(t + \ell_A - \ell_C).$$

Hence, we have, if $s_B \times s_D = 1$: $x_{20_0}(t) = x_{2_0}(t) \Leftrightarrow \forall \, t \geq 1, \, x_{2_3}(t) = x_{2_3}(t + sup(\ell_B, \ell_D) - inf(\ell_B,\ell_D)) \Leftrightarrow$

$$\forall t \geq 1, p|(sup(\ell_B, \ell_D) - inf(\ell_B, \ell_D)).$$

The proof in the case of $s_B \times s_D = -1$ is similar

Table 7.7 *Left:* Total number of attractors of period p for positive (top) and negative (bottom) circuits of order n. *Right:* Total number of attractors in case of tangent circuits, where (a) the left circuit is negative and the right circuit positive and (b) both side circuits are negative with parallel updating and $T=0$ (after Demongeot et al., 2012]).

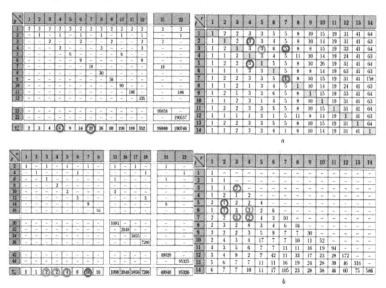

A4 STATE-DEPENDENT UPDATING SCHEDULE

A last important feature of the getBren dynamics is the existence of genes influencing directly the opening of the DNA inside the chromatine, hence allowing or disallowing the gene expression. If these genes are controlled by microRNA, it is necessary to generalize the getBren structure by considering that the possibility to update a block of genes at iteration t depends on the state of r clock genes (*i.e.*, involved in the chromatine updating clock) $k_1,...k_r$ (like histone acetyltransferase, endonucleases, exonucleases, helicase, replicase, and polymerases) depending on s microRNAs, $l_1,...,l_s$. Then the transition for a gene i, such as i, does not belong to $\{k_1,...k_r\}$, could be written as

$$\forall g \in \{0,1\}, \beta \in \{0,1\}^n, \text{ if } \forall j=1,...,r, x_{k_j}(t)=1,$$

then

(i) $P_{i,g}^{\beta}(\{x_i(t+1)=g|x(t)=\beta\})=\exp[g(\Sigma_{j\in Ni}\, w_{ij}\beta_j-\theta_i)/T]/[1+\exp[(\Sigma_{j\in Ni}\, w_{ij}\beta_j-\theta_i)/T]$, if microRNAs $l_1,...,l_s$ are dominant;

(ii) $P_{i,g}^{\beta}(\{x_i(t+1)=\beta_i|x(t)=\beta\})=1$, if not.

The case (i) implies that $\forall j = 1,\ldots, s, x_{lj}(t-1) = 0$. To make the transition rule more precise, we can, for the sake of simplicity, decide that the indices $k_1,\ldots k_r$ of the r clock genes are $1,\ldots, r$ and then we have the three possible following behaviors:

- If $y(t) = \Pi_{i=1,\ldots,r}\, x_i(t) = 1$, then rule (ii) is available.
- If $y(t) = 0$ and $\Sigma_{s=t,\ldots,t\text{-}c}\, y(s) > 0$, then $x(t+1) = x(t\text{-}s^*)$, where s^* is the last time before t, where $y(s^*) = 1$.
- If $y(t) = 0$ and $\Sigma_{s=t,\ldots,t\text{-}c}\, y(s) = 0$, then $x(t+1) = 0$ (by exhaustion of the pool of genes still in expression).

The dynamical system remains autonomous with respect to the time t [*i.e.*, it depends on t only through the set of state variables $\{x(t\text{-}c),\ldots, x(t\text{-}1)\}$], but a theoretical study of its attractors (as in Demongeot et al., 2012), with a state-dependent updating schedule is difficult to perform and will be investigated further in the future.

A5 THE CIRCULAR HAMMING DISTANCE

The most usual way to compare vectors with values in a finite alphabet is through the Hamming distance. Given two vectors x, y $\in A^n$, the Hamming distance between them is

$$d_H(x, y) = \#\{i \in \{0, \ldots, n-1\}: x_i \neq y_i\}.$$

In other words, it is the number of positions in which the values of the vectors differ. The function d_H is a metric: it is nonnegative and symmetric, it satisfies the triangle inequality, and a null distance implies identity of the vectors. It is also easy to see that

$$\forall i \in \{0, \ldots, n-1\}, d_H(x, y) = d_H\left(\sigma^i(x), \sigma^i(y)\right), \text{ and hence } d_H\left(x, \sigma^i(y)\right) = d_H\left(\sigma^{-i}(x), y\right).$$

Using this last property, we define the circular Hamming distance between two rings [x] and [y] as

$$d^c{}_H([x], [y]) = \min_{0 \leq k \leq n-1} d_H\left(x, \sigma^k(y)\right)$$

In general, the minimum between two metrics is not necessarily a metric, but here it holds.

Lemma 1. d^c_H is a metric on $A^n/\equiv$.

Proof. 1. If $d^c_H([x], [y]) = 0$, this implies that there exists k such that $d_H(x, \sigma^k(y)) = 0$; hence:

$$x = \sigma^k(y) \text{ and } [x] = [y].$$

2. Let us now prove the symmetry:

$$d^c{}_H([x], [y]) = \min_k d_H\left(x, \sigma^k(y)\right) = \min_k d_H\left(\sigma^{-k}(x), y\right) = \min_k d_H\left(y, \sigma^{-k}(x)\right) = d^c{}_H([y], [x]).$$

3. Let [x], [y], [z] $\in A^n/\equiv$. We must show that the triangular inequality is satisfied; i.e., that:

$$d^c{}_H([x], [y]) \leq d^c{}_H([x], [z]) + d^c{}_H([z], [y]).$$

Let i, j be such that: $d^c_H([z], [x]) = d_H(z, \sigma^i(x))$, $d^c_H([z], [y]) = d_H(z, \sigma^j(y))$
  In addition, we define

$$(y)) \leq d_H(\sigma^i(x), z) + d_H(z, \sigma^j(y)) = d^c_H([x], [z]) + d^c_H([z], [y])$$

The cumulative distribution function $F_{n,k}$ of the circular Hamming proximity $p^c_H = n - d^c_H$, defined by k permutations of a ring of length n can be calculated from the cumulative function $G_{n,p}$ of the binomial law $B(n,p)$ of order n, by the formula:

$$\forall i \in N, F_{n,k}(i) = P(\{p^c_H \leq i\}) = P\left(\left\{\sup_{j=1,k} p_{H,j} \leq i\right\}\right) = P\left(\bigcap_{j=1,k}\left\{p_{H,j} \leq i\right\}\right) = G_{n,p}(i)^k$$

For example, if n = 22, k = 22, and p = 4/16 = 1/4 (*i.e.,* the case of the circular Hamming distance between a small RNA of length 22 and the sequence AL):

$$F_{22,22}(12) = G_{22,1/4}(12)^{22} \approx (0.9993)^{22} \approx 0.985$$
$$F_{22,22}(13) = G_{22,1/4}(13)^{22} \approx (0.99998)^{22} \approx 0.9996$$

Note the following: the probability that the number of matches of a ring of length 22 with a linear sequence of length 22 is k or more is equal to $P_k = 1 - F_{22,22}(k-1) = 1 - G_{22,1/4}(k-1)^{22}$; *i.e.,* the probability that the circular Hamming distance is strictly less than k. For k = 14, $P_{13} = 1 - G_{22,1/4}(12)^{22}$; is about 1.5%. In the same way, the probability $P_{14} = 1 - G_{22,1/4}(13)^{22}$ is about 0.4‰, and $P_{17} = 1 - G_{22,1/4}(16)^{22}$ is about $8.8 \cdot 10^{-6}$. If the linear sequence is of length 129126 (like ciRs7), then the probability to observe at least 17 matches once is about 5%.
  In addition, if n = 22 and p = 6/16 = 3/8 = 0.375 (*i.e.,* the case of Hamming proximity with the constraint to match a substring of length 5 like AUGGU or UGGUA and authorize A–U, C–G and U–G coupling, between a small RNA of length 22 containing the substring and the sequence AL):

$$F_{22}(13) = G_{22,3/8}(13) \approx 0.9885$$

Hence, the probability $P_{14} = 1 - F_{22}(13)$ that Hamming proximity is 14 or more, is about 1.5‰.

A6 THE ARCHETYPAL SEQUENCE AL

In Demongeot and Moreira (2007), a sequence of bases called AL (for ArchetypaL) is described as follows: 5'-UGCCAUUCAAGAUGAAUGGUAC-3' corresponding to a putative circular RNA with a possible hairpin form (*cf.* Figure 7.6, and Demongeot and Moreira, 2007; Meyer and Nelson, 2011; Turk-Mcleod et al., 2012; de Vladar, 2012; Yarus, 1988, 2010, 2013). AL can serve as a primitive ribosome in the sense that its circular form can bind any amino acid [with the weak electromagnetic or van der Waals interactions described in the Direct RNA Templating (DRT) hypothesis on the origin of the genetic code, which is still under debate (Demongeot and Moreira, 2007; Meyer and Nelson, 2011; Turk-Mcleod et al., 2012; de Vladar, 2012; Yarus, 1988, 2010, 2013) to one of the triplets of its synonymy class in the genetic code, allowing the formation of small peptides (Yarus, 2013).

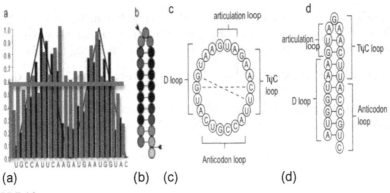

FIGURE 7.11

Relative frequencies of AL quintuplets in word matches, with Rfam sequences (Griffiths-Jones et al., 2005) in gray and ciRs7 sequence in red. For better comparison, the values have been normalized into the [0,1] interval by dividing by the maximal frequency (250/129126 for ciRs7). (a) The line is the (also normalized) distance of each base of AL with respect to the two interbase positions marked in (b); (c) shows the circular sequence of AL, with the correspondence with the tRNA loops; (d) shows the values graphed in (a) as shades of gray on the hairpin form of AL (Demongeot, 1978), with white and black representing the minimum and maximum values, respectively.

The sequence AL share many subsequences, like quintuplets, with small RNAs coming from Rfam (Griffiths-Jones et al., 2005), a database containing information about noncoding RNA families and structured RNA molecules, like transfer RNA (tRNA).

If we compare AL to the sequence of the circular RNA ciRs7, we find qualitative similarities, with 17/22 quintuplets passing the 5% upper threshold of significance (the 5%-threshold number of occurrences of a quintuplet in ciRs being equal to $129126/1024 + 1.6 \times 11 = 144$) of an unrandom frequency of common triplets (Figure 7.11). The occurrence numbers of the 22 successive quintuplets of AL inside the sequence ciRs7 of length 129126 have the following values, with the local maxima in red:

uucaa (Tψ-loop) 250 ucaag 154 caaga 146 aagau 163 agaug 163 gauga 122 augaa 211 ugaau 238 (articulation loop) gaaug 152 aaugg 145 auggu 156 (D-loop) uggua 120 gguac 62 guacu 90 uacug 143 acugc 129 cugcc 160 (anticodon-loop) ugcca 155 gccau 121 ccauu 198 cauuc 155 auuca 206.

The similarity between the function of circular RNAs, tRNAs and the sequence AL could come from the fact that they are all concerned by the protein synthesis, directly for the tRNAs and its ancestor AL, and indirectly, by inhibiting translational inhibitors as the microRNAs. This functional proximity could explain the frequent presence as relics of subsequences of AL inside the ciRs and tRNAs.

In the case of the tRNAs, the similitude concerns the conserved (inside and between species) bases of their loops (*cf.* Figure 7.12 and Alexander et al., 2010; Brown et al., 1986; Demongeot and Moreira, 2007; Shigi et al., 2002; Ueda et al., 1992; Yu et al., 2011), as well as of some particular tRNAs, such as where the ordered sequences of the loops is identical to AL except for two bases (Demongeot and Moreira, 2007).

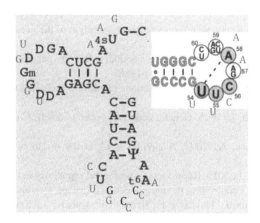

FIGURE 7.12

Matching of AL bases to the conserved bases of the tRNA loops (after Alexander et al., 2010; Brown et al., 1986; Demongeot and Moreira, 2007; Shigi et al., 2002; Yu et al., 2011).

ACKNOWLEDGMENTS

We acknowledge the financial support of the projects ANR-11-BSV5-0021, REGENR, EC Project VPH (Virtual Physiological Human), and Investissements d'Avenir VHP.

REFERENCES

Alexander, R.W., Eargle, J., Luthey-Schulten, Z., 2010. Experimental and computational determination of tRNA dynamics. FEBS Lett. 584, 376–386.

Bandiera, S., Rüberg, S., Girard, M., Cagnard, N., Hanein, S., Chrétien, D., Munnich, A., Lyonnet, S., Henrion-Caude, A., 2011. A nuclear outsourcing of RNA interference components to human mitochondria. PLoS One 6, e20746.

Bandiera, S., Mategot, R., Demongeot, J., Henrion-Caude, A., 2013. MitomiRs: delineating the intracellular localization of microRNAs at mitochondria. Free Radic. Biol. Med. 64, 12–19.

Bessho, K., Shanmukhappa, K., Sheridan, R., Shivakumar, P., Mourya, R., Walters, S., Kaimal, V., Dilbone, E., Jegga, A.G., Bezerra, J.A., 2013. Integrative genomics identifies candidate microRNAs for pathogenesis of experimental biliary atresia. BMC Syst. Biol. 7, 104.

Brown, G.G., Gadaleta, G., Pepe, G., Saccone, C., Sbisà, E., 1986. Structural conservation and variation in the D-loop-containing region of vertebrate mitochondrial DNA. J. Mol. Biol. 192, 503–511.

Bulet, P., Hetru, C., Dimarcq, J.L., Hoffmann, D., 1999. Antimicrobial peptides in insects; structure and function. Dev. Comp. Immunol. 23, 329–344.

Choe, B.H., Kim, K.M., Kwon, S., Lee, K.S., Koo, J.H., Lee, H.M., Kim, M.K., Kim, J.C., 2003. The pattern of differentially expressed genes in biliary atresia. J. Korean Med. Sci. 18, 392–396.

de Vladar, H.P., 2012. Amino acid fermentation at the origin of the genetic code. Biol. Direct 7, 6.

Demongeot, J., 1978. Sur la possibilité de considérer le code génétique comme un code à enchaînement. Revue de Biomaths 62, 61–66.

Demongeot, J., Besson, J., 1983. Code génétique et codes à enchaînement I. C.R. Acad. Sc. Série III 296, 807–810.

Demongeot, J., Besson, J., 1996. Genetic code and cyclic codes II. C.R. Acad. Sc. Série III 319, 520–528.

Demongeot, J., Moreira, A., 2007. A circular RNA at the origin of life. J. Theor. Biol. 249, 314–324.

Demongeot, J., Waku, J., 2012. Robustness in biological regulatory networks. III application to genetic networks controlling the morphogenesis. Compt. Rendus Math. 350, 289–292.

Demongeot, J., Aracena, J., Thuderoz, F., Baum, T.P., Cohen, O., 2003. Genetic regulation networks: circuits, regulons and attractors. C. R. Biol. 326, 171–188.

Demongeot, J., Drouet, E., Moreira, A., Rechoum, Y., Sené, S., 2009a. MicroRNAs: viral genome and robustness of the genes expression in host. Phil. Trans. Royal Soc. A 367, 4941–4965.

Demongeot, J., Glade, N., Moreira, A., Vial, L., 2009b. RNA relics and origin of life. Int. J. Mol Sci. 10, 3420–3441.

Demongeot, J., Hazgui, H., Escoffie, J., Arnoult, C., 2010. Inhibitory regulation by microRNAs and circular RNAs. In: Medicon'13 IFBME Proceedings. Springer Verlag, New-York, pp. 722–725.

Demongeot, J., Elena, A., Noual, M., Sené, S., Thuderoz, F., 2011. "Immunetworks", attractors and intersecting circuits. J. Theor. Biol. 280, 19–33.

Demongeot, J., Noual, M., Sené, S., 2012. Combinatorics of Boolean automata circuits dynamics. Discr. Appl. Math. 160, 398–415.

Demongeot, J., Hazgui, H., Bandiera, S., Cohen, O., Henrion-Caude, A., 2013a. MitomiRs, ChloromiRs and general modelling of the microRNA inhibition. Acta Biotheor. 61, 367–383.

Demongeot, J., Cohen, O., Henrion-Caude, A., 2013b. MicroRNAs and robustness in biological regulatory networks. A generic approach with applications at different levels: physiologic, metabolic, and genetic. In: Aon, M.A., Saks, V., Schlattner, U. (Eds.), Systems Biology of Metabolic and Signaling Networks.In: Springer Series in Biophysics, vol. 16, pp. 63–114.

Demongeot, J., Hamie, A., Hansen, O., Franco, C., Sutton, B., Cohen, E.P., 2014a. Dynalets: a new method of modelling and compressing biological signals. Applications to physiological and molecular signals. C. R. Biol. 337, 609–624.

Demongeot, J., Ben Amor, H., Hazgui, H., Waku, J., 2014b. Robustness in neural and genetic regulatory networks: mathematical approach and biological applications. Acta Biotheor. 62, 243–284.

Elkon, R., Linhart, C., Halperin, Y., Shiloh, Y., Shamir, R., 2007. Functional genomic delineation of TLR-induced transcriptional networks. BMC Genomics 8, 394.

Franco, C.B., Scripture-Adams, D.D., Proekt, I., Taghon, T., Weiss, A.H., Yui, M.A., Adams, S.L., Diamond, R.A., Rothenberg, E.V., 2006. Notch/Delta signaling constrains reengineering of pro-T cells by PU.1. Proc. Natl. Acad. Sci. U. S. A. 103, 11993–11998.

Georgescu, C., Longabaugh, W.J.R., Scripture-Adams, D.D., David-Fung, E.S., Yui, M.A., Zarnegar, M.A., Bolouri, H., Rothenberg, E.V., 2008. A gene regulatory network armature for T lymphocyte specification. Proc. Natl. Acad. Sci. U. S. A. 105, 20100–20105.

Gettings, M., Serman, F., Rousset, F.R., Bagnerini, P., Almeida, L., Noselli, S., 2010. JNK signalling controls remodelling of the segment boundary through cell reprogramming during drosophila morphogenesis. PLoS Biol. 8, e1000390.

Girard, M., Jannot, A.S., Besnard, M., Leutenegger, A.L., Jacquemin, E., Lyonnet, S., Henrion-Caude, A., 2011. Polynesian ecology determines seasonality of biliary atresia. Hepatology 54, 1893–1894.

Girard, M., Besnard, M., Jacquemin, E., Henrion-Caude, A., 2012. Biliary atresia: does ethnicity matter? J. Hepatol. 57, 700–701.

Gottwein, E., Corcoran, D.L., Mukherjee, N., Skalsky, R.L., Hafner, M., Nusbaum, J.D., Shamulailatpam, P., Love, C.L., Dave, S.S., Tushi, T., Ohler, U., Cullen, B.R., 2011. Viral microRNA targetome of KSHV-infected primary effusion lymphoma cell lines. Cell Host Microbe 10, 515–526.

Griffiths-Jones, S., Marshall, M., Khanna, A., Eddy, S.R., Bateman, A., 2005. Rfam: annotating non-coding RNAs in complete genomes. Nucleic Acids Res. 33, 121–124.

Gurzov, E.N., Eizirik, D.L., 2011. Bcl-2 proteins in diabetes: mitochondrial pathways of β-cell death and dysfunction. Trends Cell Biol. 21, 424–431.

Hand, N.J., Horner, A.M., Master, Z.R., Boateng, L.A., LeGuen, C., Uvaydova, M., Friedman, J.R., 2012. MicroRNA profiling identifies miR-29 as a regulator of disease-associated pathways in experimental biliary atresia. J. Pediatr. Gastroenterol. Nutr. 54, 186–192.

Hansen, T.B., Wiklund, E.D., Bramsen, J.B., Villadsen, S.B., Statham, A.L., Clark, S.J., Kjems, J., 2011. miRNA-dependent gene silencing involving Ago2-mediated cleavage of a circular antisense RNA. EMBO J. 30, 4414–4422.

Hansen, T.B., Jensen, T.I., Clausen, B.H., Bramsen, J.B., Finsen, B., Damgaard, C.K., Kjems, J., 2013. Natural RNA circles function as efficient microRNA sponges. Nature 495, 384–388.

Hentze, M.W., Rouault, T.A., Caughman, S.W., Dancis, A., Harford, J.B., Klausner, R.D., 1987. A cis-acting element is necessary and sufficient for translational regulation of human ferritin expression in response to iron. Proc. Natl. Acad. Sci. U. S. A. 84, 6730–6734.

http://dev.biologists.org/content/131/12/2911/F8.large.jpg.

http://mirdb.org/miRDB/.

http://mirnamap.mbc.nctu.edu.tw/.

http://www.kegg.jp/kegg/pathway/dme/dme04310.

Kang, J., Pervaiz, S., 2013. Crosstalk between Bcl-2 family and Ras family small GTPases: potential cell fate regulation? Front. Oncol. 2, 206.

Kohsaka, T., Yuan, Z.R., Guo, S.X., Tagawa, M., Nakamura, A., Nakano, M., Kawasasaki, H., Inomata, Y., Tanaka, K., Miyauchi, J., 2002. The significance of human jagged 1 mutations detected in severe cases of extrahepatic biliary atresia. Hepatology 36, 904–912.

Lee, W.J., Kim, S.H., Kim, Y.S., Han, S.J., Park, K.S., Ryu, J.H., Hur, M.W., Choi, K.Y., 2000. Inhibition of Mitogen-Activated Protein Kinase (MAPK) by a Drosophila dual-specific phosphatase. Biochem. J. 349, 821–828.

Luedde, T., Heinrichsdorff, J., de Lorenzi, R., De Vos, R., Roskams, T., Pasparakis, M., 2008. IKK1 and IKK2 cooperate to maintain bile duct integrity in the liver. Proc. Natl. Acad. Sci. U. S. A. 105, 9733–9738.

Mantrova, E.Y., Hsu, T., 1998. Down-regulation of transcription factor CF2 by *Drosophila* Ras/MAPK signaling in oogenesis: cytoplasmic retention and degradation. Genes Dev. 12, 1166–1175.

Matte, U., Mourya, R., Miethke, A., Liu, C., Kauffmann, G., Moyer, K., Zhang, K., Bezerra, J. A., 2010. Analysis of gene mutations in children with cholestasis of undefined etiology. J. Pediatr. Gastroenterol. Nutr. 51, 488–493.

McEwen, D.G., Peifer, M., 2005. Puckered, a *Drosophila* MAPK phosphatase, ensures cell viability by antagonizing JNK-induced apoptosis. Development 132, 3935–3946.

Melliti, T., Noual, M., Regnault, D., Sené, S., Sobieraj, J., 2014. Full characterisation of attractors of two intersected asynchronous Boolean automata cycles. eprint arXiv, 1310.5747v2.

Meyer, S.C., Nelson, P.A., 2011. Can the origin of the genetic code be explained by direct RNA templating? BIO-Complexity 2011, 1–10.

Michon, F., Forest, L., Collomb, E., Demongeot, J., Dhouailly, D., 2008. BMP-2 and BMP-7 play antagonistic roles in feather induction. Development 135, 2797–2805.

Miyake, K., Ogata, H., Nagai, Y., Akashi, S., Kimoto, M., 2000. Innate recognition of lipopolysaccharide by Toll-like receptor 4/MD-2 and RP105/MD-1. J. Endotoxin Res. 6, 389–912.

Nouws, J., Shadel, G.S., 2014. MicroManaging mitochondrial translation. Cell 158, 477–478.

Ranganathan, P., Weaver, K.L., Capobianco, A.J., 2011. Notch signalling in solid tumours: a little bit of everything but not all the time. Nat. Rev. Cancer 11, 338–351.

Richard, A., 2011. Local negative circuits and fixed points in non-expansive Boolean networks. Discr. Appl. Math. 59, 1085–1093.

Robert, F., 1980. Itérations sur des ensembles finis et automates cellulaires contractants. Lin. Algebra Appl. 29, 393–412.

Saenz-Robles, M.T., Maschat, F., Tabata, T., Scott, M.P., Kornberg, T.B., 1995. Selection and characterization of sequences with high affinity for Engrailed proteins of *Drosophila*. Mech. Dev. 53, 185–195.

Sangokoya, C., Doss, J.F., Chi, J.T., 2013. Iron-responsive miR-485-3p regulates cellular iron homeostasis by targeting ferroportin. PLoS Genet. 9, e1003408.

Shigi, N., Suzuki, T., Tamakoshi, M., Oshima, T., Watanabe, K., 2002. Conserved bases in the TΨC loop of tRNA are determinants for thermophile-specific 2-thiouridylation at position 54. J. Biol. Chem. 277, 39128–39135.

Singh, V.B., Pavithra, L., Chattopadhyay, S., Pal, J.K., 2009. Stress-induced overexpression of the heme-regulated eIF-2a kinase is regulated by Elk-1 activated through ERK pathway. Biochem. Biophys. Res. Commun. 379, 710–715.

Turk-Mcleod, R.M., Puthenvedu, D., Majerfeld, I., Yarus, M., 2012. The plausibility of RNA-templated peptides: simultaneous RNA affinity for adjacent peptide side chains. J. Mol. Evol. 74, 217–225.

Ueda, T., Yotsumoto, Y., Ikeda, K., Watanabe, K., 1992. The T-loop region of animal mitochondrial tRNA^{Ser} (AGY) is a main recognition site for homologous seryl-tRNA synthetase. Nucleic Acids Res. 20, 2217–2222.

Vickers, E.R., Sharrocks, A.D., 2002. The use of inducible Engrailed fusion proteins to study the cellular functions of eukaryotic transcription factors. Methods 26, 270–280.

Weil, G., Heus, K., Faraut, T., Demongeot, J., 2004. An archetypal basic code for the primitive genome. Theoret. Comp. Sc. 322, 313–334.

Xiao, J., Xia, S., Xia, Y., Xia, Q., Wang, X., 2014. Transcriptome profiling of biliary atresia from new born infants by deep sequencing. Mol. Biol. Rep. 41, 8063–8069.

Yarus, M., 1988. A specific amino acid binding site composed of RNA. Science 240, 1751–1758.

Yarus, M., 2010. Life from an RNA World: The Ancestor Within. Harvard University Press, Cambridge US.

Yarus, M., 2013. A ribonucleotide origin for life–fluctuation and near-ideal reactions. Orig. Life Evol. Biosph. 43, 19–30.

Yu, F., Tanaka, Y., Yamashita, K., Suzuki, T., Nakamura, A., Hirano, N., Suzuki, T., Yao, M., Tanaka, I., 2011. Molecular basis of dihydrouridine formation on tRNA. Proc. Natl. Acad. Sci. U. S. A. 108, 19593–19598.

Zeng, Y.A., Verheyen, E.M., 2004. Nemo is an inducible antagonist of Wingless signaling during Drosophila wing development. Development 131, 2911–2920.

Zhou, H., Wertz, I., O'Rourke, K., Ultsch, M., Seshagiri, S., Eby, M., Xiao, W., Dixit, V.M., 2004. Bcl10 activates the NF-kB pathway through ubiquitination of NEMO. Nature 427, 167–171.

Biomechanical Evaluation for Bone Allograft in Treating the Femoral Head Necrosis: Thorough Debridement or not?

8

Guangquan Zhou[1,2,4], **Wei He**[1], **Zhihui Pang**[2], **Xiumin Chen**[3], **Yujing Xu**[4], **Liao Shaoyi Stephen**[4], and **QinQun Chen**[5]

The First Affiliated Hospital, Guangzhou University of Chinese Medicine, Guangzhou, China[1]
Laboratory of National Key Discipline Orthopaedics and Traumatology of Chinese Medicine, Guangzhou University of Chinese Medicine, Guangzhou, China[2]
Department of Rheumatology, Guangdong Provincial Hospital of Chinese Medicine, Guangzhou, China, and Postdoctoral Mobile Research Station, Guangzhou University of Chinese Medicine, Guangzhou, China[3]
Department of Information Systems, City University of Hong Kong, Hong Kong, China[4]
School of Medical Information Engineering, Guangzhou University of Chinese Medicine, Guangzhou, China[5]

1 INTRODUCTION

There has been a rapid increase in the incidence of femoral head necrosis (FHN) all over the world which is caused by the widespread use of steroids (Chan and Mok, 2012; Weinstein, 2012) and alcohol (Matuso *et al.*, 1988; Hirota *et al.*, 1993; Wang *et al.*, 2003; Shigemura *et al.*, 2012). FHN is associated with high morbidity and disability. Patients with FHN often have a high risk of collapse of the femoral head, arthritis, or dearticulation, finally resulting in hip replacement (HR). The medium- and long-term effects of hip implants are obviously unsatisfactory; thus, the young patient will require several surgical treatments (Ditri *et al.*, 2006). Hence, various head-preserving procedures have been developed to protect the femoral head of patients and avoid HR, particularly in the early stage of FHN.

Fibular allograft with impaction bone grafting (FAIBG) is an effective head-preserving method for avoiding total hip replacement (THR) in the early stage of FHN. FAIBG provides both repaired materials and biomechanical structural support during the healing of the necrosis region (Brannon, 2007; Katz and Urbaniak, 2001; Malizos *et al.*, 1995; Urbaniak *et al.*, 1995). However, the question of whether thorough debridement should be used with FAIBG is controversial. "With thorough debridement" means that the necrotic bone should be cleaned up completely, while "without thorough debridement" means that the necrotic bone should undergo partial debridement. Theoretically, thorough debridement can better protect the anterolateral column and reduces the necrosis area of the stress concentration phenomenon compared to partial debridement, but it will cause a larger trauma region and higher incidence of complications and require more recovery time after surgery. In most cases, the choice is based on the experience and preference of different surgeons. At the same time, studies about comparing the risk of collapse of postoperative femoral head accompanied with thorough debridement and without thorough debridement are relatively rare.

To provide a scientific biomechanical basis for FAIBG, this study presents two subject-specific FHN cases without collapse of the femoral head to compare the mechanical performance between FAIBG with and without thorough debridement.

---

2 MATERIALS AND METHODS

2.1 JIC CLASSIFICATION

In 2001, the Japanese Investigation Committee (JIC) (Sugano *et al.*, 2002) revised the diagnostic criteria to clarify the definition of osteonecrosis of the femoral head (ONFH). According to the JIC classification criteria, FHN is classified into subtypes A, B, C1, and C2 based on the location of the lesion in the weight-bearing area. Type A lesions occupy the medial one-third or less of the weight-bearing portion. Type B lesions occupy the medial two-thirds or less of the weight-bearing portion. Type C1 lesions occupy more than the medial two thirds of the weight-bearing portion but do not extend laterally to the acetabular edge. Type C2 lesions occupy more than the medial two-thirds of the weight-bearing portion and extend laterally to the acetabular edge.

Recent studies showed that patients who conform to the JIC C criteria are suitable for FAIBG. However, these conclusions are mainly based on clinical observation experience and must be proved in both theory and practice. We postulated that the FAIBG procedure with different debridement regions has different biomechanical performances, which could affect the choice of treatment procedure for FHN. Hence, we reconstructed two subject-specific models (JIC C1 and C2; Figure 8.1) to provide a biomechanical basis for FAIBG to explore the performance of different debridement regions in treating FHN.

2.2 GENERATION OF INTACT FINITE ELEMENT MODELS

A JIC C1 FHN-diagnosed patient (P1) with a weight of 70 kg and a JIC C2 FHN-diagnosed patient (P2) with a weight of 60 kg were selected for the biomechanical evaluation of the proximal femur. Computed tomography data sets (0.5 mm

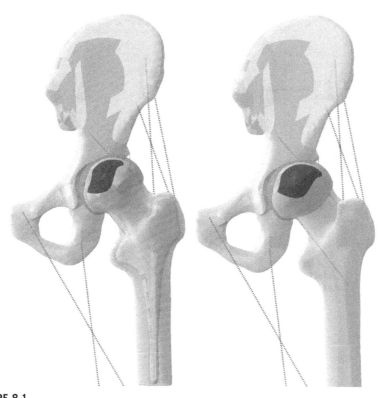

FIGURE 8.1

Three-dimensional subtype models of FHN.

thickness; Toshiba Aquilion 64, Toshiba, US) of each case were used to reconstruct solid models with gray-level processing of the software MIMICS 15.1 based on the function of Thresholding, Edit Masks, and Calculate 3D. The solid models in the STereo Lithography (STL) format were entered into the Rapidform preprocessor, and surface fitting was performed. Based on the Mesh and Autosurfacing functions, we found the fit hip to generate the Non-Uniform Rational B-Splines (NURBS) models. The interface between the ilium and femoral head was used to identify thecartilage geometry. All NURBS models in the format of igs were entered into ABAQUS V6.13 (Simulia, Dassault Systemes, France) to generate nonlinear elastic finite element models. Based on the initial hip geometry, we simulated the physiological and pathological models using different materials.

Then, all models were input into ABAQUS V6.13 to generate isotropic 10-node tetrahedral elements. The mesh size was 4 mm. The initial models consisted of elements (146,879 of P1; 156,471 of P2) and nodes (213,970 of P1; 230,541 of P2). In these models, the single-legged stance was considered as a representative body position, and a ground reaction force equivalent to the body weight was performed on a rigid plate, which was tied to the distal part of the femur in Figure 8.2. Constraints

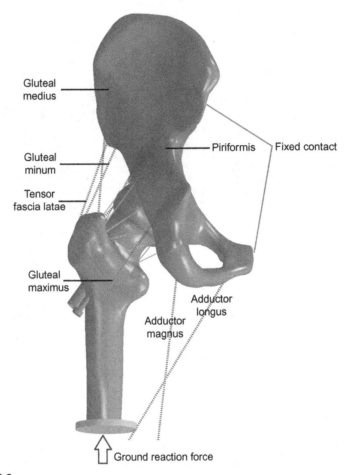

Gluteal
medius

Piriformis   Fixed contact

Gluteal
minum

Tensor
fascia latae

Gluteal
maximus

Adductor
longus

Adductor
magnus

Ground reaction force

FIGURE 8.2

Load and constraint conditions.

were applied to the pubic symphysis and sacroiliac joint. All six degrees of freedom were constrained to zero. Seven muscles were modeled as axial connectors, and the muscle forces were set according to the literature (Sverdlova and Witzel, 2010): adductor longus = 560 N; adductor magnus = 600 N; gluteal maximus = 550 N; gluteal medius = 700 N; gluteal minimus = 300 N; piriformis = 500 N; tensor fascia latae = 300 N. The models consist of cortical, trabeculae, cartilage, and lesion bone. The material properties used in the biomechanical experiment were obtained from the literature (Brown and Hild, 1983; Brown *et al.*, 1981; Grecu *et al.*, 2010): Ecortical = 15,100 MPa, Etrabeculae = 445 MPa, Ecartilage = 10.5 MPa, Elesion = 124.6 MPa, $v$cortical = 0.3, $v$trabeculae = 0.22, $v$cartilage = 0.45, and $v$lesion = 0.152.

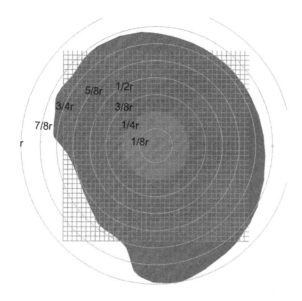

FIGURE 8.3

Debridement size of necrotic lesion.

The parametric analysis was designed to explore the effects of the debridement extent of necrotic bone for cases that require surgery. The maximum debridement radius was defined as r, and the debridement extent variants are schematically shown in Figure 8.3. We assumed that the anterolateral cortical stress corresponding to the debridement extent of necrotic lesions had an increased radius R (R = 1/4 r, 3/8 r, 1/2 r, 5/8 r, 3/4 r, 7/8 r and r), where R = 1/4r refers to the least debridement, and R = r denotes thorough debridement. To simulate the allogeneic fibular implant, the dimensions (80 mm in length and 6 mm in radius) were obtained from the manufacturer. The axial direction of fibula was defined by the entry point and lesion centroid. The entry point was located in the trochanteric lateral cortex of the femur. The distance of the cortical bone from the apex of the fibula was 5 mm. The remaining voids were occupied by impaction cancellous bone after the debridement.

3 RESULTS

3.1 STRESS TRANSFER PATH

The principal stress transfer characteristics are the most important biomechanical index in the process of evaluating the performance of FHN. In all femoral heads, the principal stress transfer patterns are computed when a midstance gait occurs. The principal stress transfer efficiency reduces markedly (see Figure 8.4).

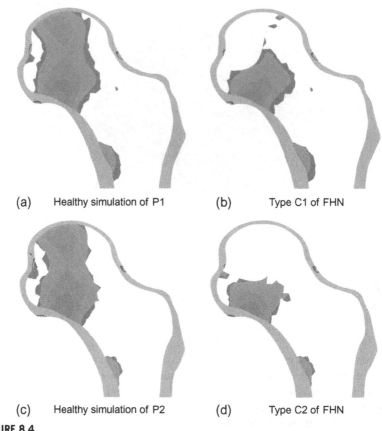

(a) Healthy simulation of P1 (b) Type C1 of FHN

(c) Healthy simulation of P2 (d) Type C2 of FHN

FIGURE 8.4

The principal stress distributions in the femoral head. a and c show that the principal stress distributions in the healthy conditions run from the top of the femoral head to the femoral calcar. In b and d, the stress transfer paths are broken off and the areas bearing principal stress are less than approximately 50% of the healthy simulations.

3.2 STRESS OF THE ANTEROLATERAL COLUMN

FAIBG has a considerably small risk of structure collapse compared with the untreated situation. Figures 8.5a and 8.6a show the healthy stress distribution of anterolateral cortical bone and the maximum stress values are 23.95 MPa of P1 and 25.99 MPa of P2. Figure 8.5b shows that JIC C1 stress of 30.31 MPa increases about 26.56%, which is more than the healthy condition (P1). Figure 8.6b shows that the JIC C2 stress of 34.58 MPa increases about 33.05%, which is higher than the healthy condition (P2). Figure 8.5c and 6C show that the postoperative stress is 23.52 MPa in P1 and 25.31 MPa in P2, which is approximately 22.4% less than the JIC C1 condition (P1) and 26.81% lower than the JIC C2 condition (P2) after the FAIBG procedure. The peak stresses of the two postoperative cases return to

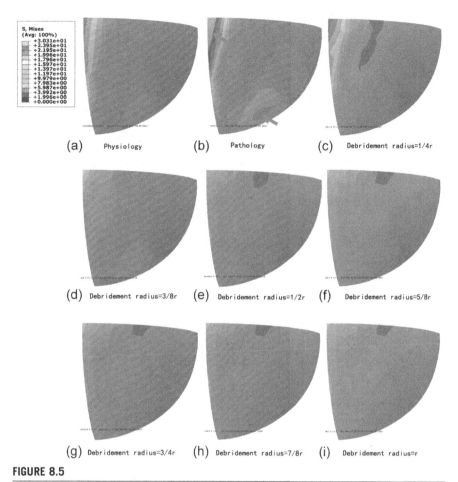

FIGURE 8.5

Anteroalteral stress distribution of P1.

near-healthy levels. It is obviously that the stress concentration regions in JIC C1 and C2 are the areas that the red arrows point to. After the FAIBG procedure, the stress concentration regions disappeared. Figure 8.5d–i and 8.6d–i show that stress has no significant changes as the debridement radius increasing.

3.3 PEAK STRESS OF THE RESIDUAL NECROTIC BONE

Figure 8.7 displays that the debridement size will affect the stress gradient in the residual necrotic bone. Seven different necrotic debridement sizes, ranging from $1/4r$ to r, are chosen to study the effect of the debridement radius on the residual necrotic bone. The relation between debridement size and the stress of the residual

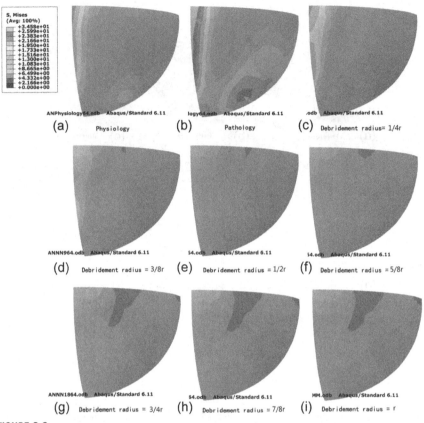

FIGURE 8.6

Anteroalteral stress distribution of P2.

necrotic bone is shown in Figure 8.7. When the debridement radius is $1/4r$, there is a 3762% increase in the peak stress compared to JIC C1 condition and a 1217% increase in the peak stress compared to the JIC C2 condition. When the debridement is not less than $3/8r$, the peak stress in the residual lesion is rapidly falling and returns to the physiological level.

3.4 MODEL VALIDATION

The principal compressive trabecula loads the principal compressive stress of the femoral head (Figures 8.8c–d), which correlates well with the bone density distribution (Figure 8.8b) (Jang and Kim, 2008). The shape and location of the biomechanical transfer path for both load cases are consistent with the trabecular features in the cross-sections of the cadaver bone (Figure 8.8a) (Boyle and Kim, 2011; Jang and Kim, 2009). It is clearly the case that trabeculae in the corresponding areas are thinner.

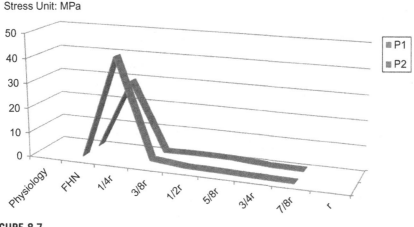

FIGURE 8.7

The peak stress of the residual necrotic bone.

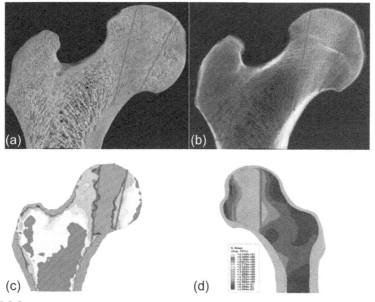

FIGURE 8.8

Photograph (a), radiograph (b), the previous simulation results (c), and the computational results (d) of human proximal femur in our study.

In the same time, there are strong similarities of stress patterns between the simulation results of our study and the previous results in the literature (Sverdlova and Witzel, 2010). Hence, we think that the FE results could mirror the physical phenomenon of the hip and evaluate the results.

4 DISCUSSION

FAIBG represents a proven technique for maintaining the shape of the femoral head and reducing the risk of collapse of FHN in its early stages. Rosenwasser *et al.*, (1994) first described thorough debridement and bone grafting for treating FHN. This technique is an effective method for young patients with FHN in early stages, which will delay the progression of osteoarthrosis and subsequent Total Hip Arthroplasty (THA). Tao *et al.* (2014) reported an 80% clinical success rate with a mean follow-up time of 24 months among 15 patients who had surgical therapy by thorough debridement with bone grafting. However, these procedures may cause serious artificial damage and complication by capsulotomies or the destruction of the cortical bone of the femur neck fundus, and also require relatively high surgical devices and technique. Shi *et al.* (2008) reported a study of 67 hips, with the treatment of internal bracket implanting with partial debridement for FHN. They came up with a 64.2% (43/67) success rate, with an average follow-up of 23 months. In 2013, Shi *et al.* commented on their results by treating 25 of 40 patients using the allograft fibula with partial debridement for FHN. They reported satisfactory results in 18/25 (72%) patients with 24 months follow-up. These minimally invasive procedures could reduce the artificial damage and complication but got a poorer clinical outcome, since they couldn't provide both repaired materials and biomechanical structural support during the healing of the necrosis region. FAIBG with proper debridement is an effective head-preserving method, and we achieved an average clinical success rate of 90.3%, with a mean follow up time of 37.5 months (He *et al.*, 2009). All these views are based on the clinical observation experience and lack of biomechanical basis. Hence, both thorough debridement and partial debridement are not accepted universally because these is no compelling evidence of which method could be better at reducing the collapse risk of the femoral head. It encourages us to describe our experiences of the computational biomechanical analysis of debridement extent to reduce the collapse risk of FHN.

In our study, we adopted a subject-specific computational approach to consider changes in stress distribution of anterolateral cortical bone and the residual necrotic bone. Figure 8.4 shows that the stress transfer path in both JIC C1 and C2 are completely broken off, which indicate that surgical intervention should be involved. The effect of debridement size with FAIBG on collapse risk is clearly demonstrated in Figure 8.5–8.6. After FAIBG, the stress of anterolateral cortical bone in all conditions could return to the physiological level and the decrement/increment of stress is less than 0.1% as the debridement radius increases in two cases; hence, the collapse risk of femoral head can be reduced effectively using allo-fibula support to bear the load. When debridement size is not less than $3/8r$, the von Mises stress of the residual bone also returns to the pathological level, which denotes that the progression of necrosis wouldn't deteriorate after surgical intervention. Our results provide specific biomechanical evidence to support the viewpoint that FAIBG can resist the collapse of FHN, and FAIBG with thorough debridement has a lower risk of collapse risk than with partial debridement.

Thorough debridement has been reported by previous studies (Rosenwasser *et al.*, 1994; Tao *et al.*, 2014; Meyers *et al.*, 1983; Ko *et al.*, 1995; Meyers and Convery, 1991; Gardeniers *et al.*, 1999). However, this procedure is difficult and time consuming, which is associated with serious artificial damage. FAIBG with partial debridement can not only reduce the anterolateral cortical stress, but also ensure that the stress of the residual bone will not increase. This technique has a distinct biomechanical basis, and it is time saving and requires relatively fewer surgical devices. It also brings a low risk of damage. Hence, FAIBG without thorough debridement seems to be superior to FAIBG with thorough debridement.

5 CONCLUSION

In this chapter, we propose employing computational biomechanical technology to explore the different mechanical performances of FAIBG with or without thorough debridement, which provides a biomechanical basis for choosing the proper treatment in clinic. A total of 18 computational models were constructed and used to simulate two subtypes of FHN with seven debridement radii of FAIBG. The simulation results provide specific biomechanical evidence that the use of FAIBG can resist the collapse of FHN. Furthermore, FAIBG without thorough debridement, which not only requires relatively low surgical devices but also reduces damage, seems to be a better method of resisting the collapse of JIC C1 and JIC C2 FHN. This chapter is a preliminary approach to investigate FAIBG with thorough debridement; more detailed analysis will be reported in the near future.

6 DISCLAIMER

The authors declared no potential conflicts of interest with respect to the research, authorship, and publication of this article.

6.1 FUNDING

This study was supported by the Natural Science Foundation of Guangdong Province (2014A030310214). There are no financial and personal relationships with other people or organizations that could inappropriately influence our work.

REFERENCES

Boyle, C., Kim, I.Y., 2011. Three-dimensional micro-level computational study of Wolff's law via trabecular bone remodeling in the human proximal femur using design space topology optimization. J. Biomech. 44 (Mar), 935–942.

Brannon, J.K., 2007. Influence of acetabular coverage on hip survival after free vascularized fibular grafting for femoral head osteonecrosis. J. Bone Joint Surg. Am. 89 (Feb), 448–449.

Brown, T.D., Hild, G.L., 1983. Pre-collapse stress redistributions in femoral head osteonecrosis–a three-dimensional finite element analysis. J. Biomech. Eng. 105 (May), 171–176.

Brown, T.D., Way, M.E., Ferguson Jr., A.B., 1981. Mechanical characteristics of bone in femoral capital aseptic necrosis. Clin. Orthop. Relat. Res. 156 (May), 240–247.

Chan, K.L., Mok, C.C., 2012. Glucocorticoid-induced avascular bone necrosis: diagnosis and management. Open Orthop. J. 6 (Oct), 449–457.

Ditri, L., Montanari, M., Melamed, Y., et al., 2006. Femoral head necrosis. In: Mathieu, D. (Ed.), Handbook on Hyperbaric Medicine. Springer, Netherlands, pp. 547–552.

Gardeniers, J., Yanmano, K., Buma, P., Sloff, 1999. Impaction grafting in the femoral head. In: Proceedings of the second afor symposium on osteonecrosis of the femoral head and hip around fracture, pp. 28–30.

Grecu, D., Pucalev, I., Negru, M., Tarnita, D.N., Ionovici, N., Dita, R., 2010. Numerical simulations of the 3D virtual model of the human hip joint, using finite element method. Rom. J. Morphol. Embryol. 51, 151–155.

He, W., Li, Y., Zhang, Q.W., et al., 2009. Primary outcome of impacting bone graft and fibular autograft or allograft in treating osteonecrosis of femoral head. Chin. J. Reparat. Reconstr. Surg. 23 (5), 530–533.

Hirota, Y., Hirohata, T., Fukuda, K., et al., 1993. Association of alcohol intake, cigarette smoking and occupational status with the risk of idiopathie osteonecrosis of the femoral head. Am. J. Epidemiol. 137 (5), 530–538.

Jang, I.G., Kim, I.Y., 2008. Computational study of Wolff's law with trabecular architecture in the human proximal femur using topology optimization. J. Biomech. 41 (Aug), 2353–2361.

Jang, I.G., Kim, I.Y., 2009. Computation simulation of trabecular adaptation progress in human proximal femur during growth. J. Biomech. 42 (Mar), 573–580.

Katz, M.A., Urbaniak, J.R., 2001. Free vascularized fibular grafting of the femoral head for the treatment of osteonecrosis. Tech. Orthop. 16 (Mar), 44–60.

Ko, J.Y., Meyers, M.H., Wanger, D.R., 1995. "Trapdoors" Procedure for osteonecrosis with segmental collapse of the femoral head in teenagers. J. Padiatt. Orthop. 15 (Jan-Feb), 7–15.

Malizos, K.N., Soucacos, P.N., Beris, A.E., 1995. Osteonecrosis of the femoral head. Hip salvaging with implantation of a vascularized fibular graft. Clin. Orthop. Relat. Res. 314 (May), 67–75.

Matuso, K., Hirohata, T., Sugioka, Y., et al., 1988. Influence of alcohol intake, cigarette smoking, and occupational status on idiopathie osteonecrosis of the femoral head. Clin. Orthopm. 234 (Sep), 115–123.

Meyers, M.H., Convery, F.R., 1991. Grafting procedure in osteonecrosis of the hip. Semin. Arthroplasty 2, 189–197.

Meyers, M.H., Jones, R.E., Bucholz, R.W., et al., 1983. Fresh autogenous grafts and ostaochondral altografts for the treatment of segmental collapse in osteonecrosis of the hip. Clin. Orthop. 174 (Apr), 10–12.

Rosenwasser, M.P., Garino, J.P., Kiernan, H.A., Michelsen, C.B., 1994. Long-term follow up of thorough debridement and cancellous bone grafting for osteonecrosis of the femoral head. Clin. Orthop. 306 (Sep), 17–27.

Shi, F.L., Lu, F.X., Li, X.H., et al., 2008. Clinical observation on internal bracket implanting for treatment of adult necrosis of femoral head and finite element analysis. Chin. J. Bone Joint Inj. 23 (3), 186–188.

Shi, F.L., Chen, J., Li, X.H., et al., 2013. Fan-shaped decompression and allograft fibula supporting internal fixation for treatment of early femoral head necrosis in adults. Chin. J. Tissue Eng. Res. 17 (44), 7758–7763.

Shigemura, T., Nakamura, J., Kishida, S., et al., 2012. The incidence of alcohol-associated osteonecrosis of the knee is lower than the incidence of steroid-associated osteonecrosis of the knee: an MRI study. Rheumatology 51 (4), 701–706.

Sugano, N., Atsumi, T., Ohzono, K., et al., 2002. The 2001 revised criteria for diagnosis, classification, and stagine of idiopathic osteonecrosis of the femoral head. J. Orthop. Sci. 7, 601–605.

Sverdlova, S.N., Witzel, U., 2010. Principles of determination and verification of muscle forces in the human musculoskeletal system: muscle force to minimise bending stress. J. Biomech. 43 (Feb), 387–396.

Tao, W., Wei, W., Zong, S.Y., 2014. Treatment of osteonecrosis of the femoral head with thorough debridement, bone grafting and bone-marrow mononuclear cells implantation. Eur. J. Orthop. Surg. Traumatol. 24 (Feb), 197–202.

Urbaniak, J.R., Coogan, P.G., Gunneson, E.B., Nunley, J.A., 1995. Treatment of osteonecrosis of the femoral head with free vascularized fibular grafting. A long-term follow-up study of one hundred and three hips. J. Bone Joint Surg. Am. 77, 681–694.

Wang, Y., Li, Y., Mao, K., et al., 2003. Alcohol-induced adipogenesis in bone and marrow: a possible mechanism for osteonecrosis. Clin. Orthop. Relat. Res. 410 (May), 213–224.

Weinstein, R.S., 2012. Glucocorticoid-induced osteonecrosis. Endocrine 41 (2), 183–190.

Diels-Alderase Catalyzing the Cyclization Step in the Biosynthesis of *Spinosyn A*: Reality or Fantasy?

Luis R. Domingo[1], Jose A. Sáez[1], Lydia Rhyman[2], and Ponnadurai Ramasami[2]

Departamento de Química Orgánica, Universidad de Valencia, Burjassot, Valencia, Spain[1]
Computational Chemistry Group, Department of Chemistry, University of Mauritius, Réduit, Mauritius[2]

Graphical Abstract

1 INTRODUCTION

The Diels-Alder (DA) reaction has been proposed as a key transformation in the biosynthesis of many cyclohexene-containing secondary metabolites. So far, only four purified enzymes have been implicated in these biotransformations: namely, solanapyrone synthase (Oikawa *et al.*, 1995), LovB (Auclair *et al.*, 2000; Ma *et al.*, 2009), macrophomate synthase (Watanabe *et al.*, 2000; Ose *et al.*, 2003), and riboflavin synthase (Eberhardt *et al.*, 2001; Kim *et al.*, 2010). Although the stereochemical outcomes of these reactions indicate that the product formation could be enzyme-guided in each case, enzymes typically demonstrate more than one catalytic activity, leaving their specific influence on the cycloaddition step undefined.

Spinosyn A (**1**) has attracted much attention as it possesses potent insecticidal activity, with low toxicity to beneficial insects and rapid degradation in the environment (Kirst *et al.*, 1991; Kirst, 2010). Very recently, Kim *et al.* (2011) published the first example of an *in vivo* enzyme-catalyzed [4+2] cycloaddition, and thus fully established the biosynthesis of *spinosyn A* (**1**) (see Scheme 9.1).

Four genes in the *spinosyn A* biosynthetic gene cluster of *Saccharopolyspora spinosa*—*spnF*, *spnJ*, *spnL,* and *spnM*—were proposed to convert the product (**2**) of the polyketide synthase (PKS) to the tetracyclic aglycone (**6**) (Waldron *et al.*, 2001). Kim *et al.* (2011) carried out experiments with the separated genes in order to establish which one was responsible for the conversion of intermediate (**3**) into the formal [4+2] cycloadduct (**5**), an intermediate in the formation of the tetracyclic compound (**6**) (see Scheme 9.1). These authors established that *SpnF* is a cyclase

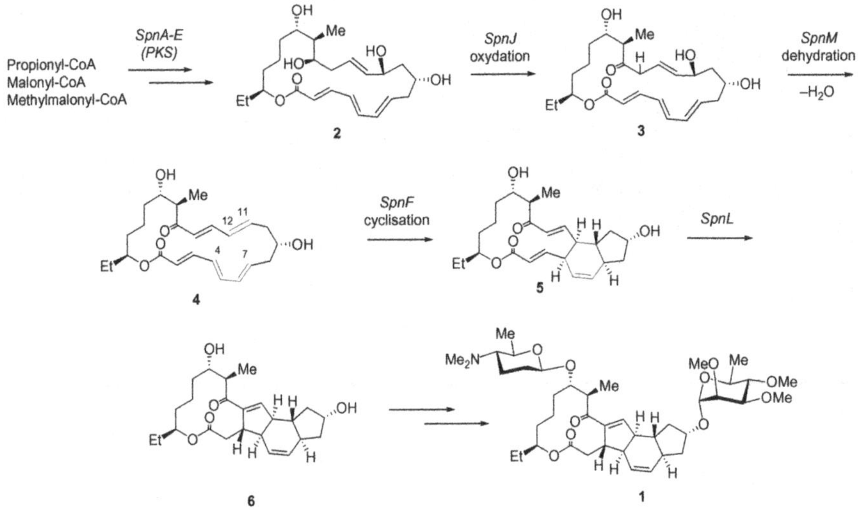

SCHEME 9.1

Biosynthesis of *spinosyn A* **1**.

catalyzing the conversion of (**4**) into (**5**) with an apparent k_{cat} of 14 ± 1.6 min^{-1}, presenting an estimated rate enhancement ($k_{cat,spnF}$ versus k_{non}) of approximately 500-fold (Kim *et al.*, 2011). In addition, Kim *et al.* (2011) suggested that in order to confirm the hypothesis that *SpnF* could catalyze the DA reaction, it is required to demonstrate that the reaction progresses through a single *pericyclic* transition state (TS). Therefore, a stepwise [4+2] cycloaddition mechanism was not ruled out.

The complete characterization of the mechanism of a DA reaction, which is difficult to predict experimentally, can be addressed *in silico* due to the availability of computational resources. Thus, very recently, Hess and Smentek (2012) performed a density functional theory (DFT) computational investigation on the enzyme-catalyzed cyclization reaction in the biosynthesis of *spinosyn A* (**1**). For this study, two computational models were selected (see **TS-M1** and **TS-M2** in Figure 9.1).

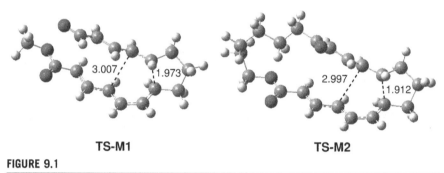

TS-M1   **TS-M2**

FIGURE 9.1

B3LYP/6-31G* transition state models for the cyclization involved in the biosynthesis of *spinosyn A* **1**. Lengths are given in angstroms.

In spite of the high asynchronicity found in the C—C single bond formation in both TSs, these authors suggested that the reaction takes place via a concerted mechanism since no zwitterionic intermediate was located (Hess and Smentek, 2012). The B3LYP activation energy associated with **TS-M2** was estimated to be 20 kcal/mol, while that obtained for this model at the MP2 level was 10 kcal/mol. They found an activation energy of 15 kcal/mol for the **TS-M1**-reduced model. Since some global electron density transfer (GEDT) (Domingo, 2014) was found at the B3LYP level, 0.10e, they also suggested that the possibility of additional stabilization of the polar TS by the enzyme might lower the activation energy to a value for which the reaction could easily be catalyzed enzymatically (Kim *et al.*, 2011). However, it is interesting to note that the GEDT at **TS-M2** is too low to cause an efficient stabilization by the enzyme. It should be highlighted that favorable polar Diels-Alder (P-DA) reactions present GEDT values in the range of 0.30e–0.40e (Domingo and Sáez, 2009).

Paraherquamide A (**9**) (Yamazaki *et al.*, 1981; Blanchflower *et al.*, 1991) and VM55599 (**11**) (Blanchflower *et al.*, 1993) (see Scheme 9.2) are indolic secondary metabolites isolated from various fungi. These alkaloids share an unusual

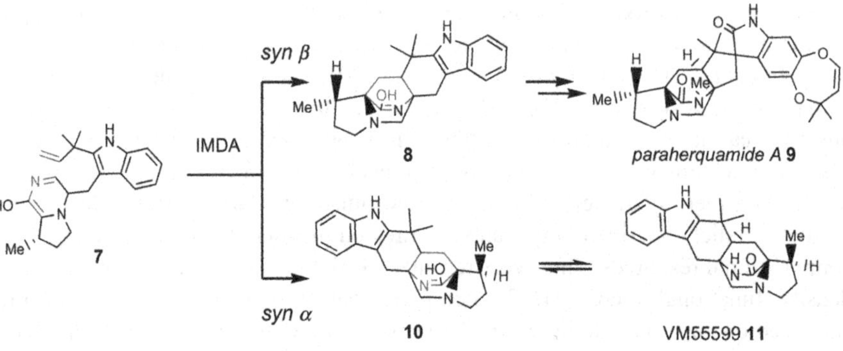

SCHEME 9.2

Proposed IMDA reactions in the biogenesis of the *paraherquamide A* (**9**) and VM55599 (**11**).

bicyclo[2.2.2]diazaoctane ring system that has been proposed to arise via an intra-molecular Diels-Alder (IMDA) reaction of the isoprene double bond across the α-carbons of the amino acid subunits (see Scheme 9.2) (Williams *et al.*, 1998; Stocking *et al.*, 2000, 2001; Sanz-Cervera and Williams, 2002; Williams and Cox, 2003).

A B3LYP/6-31G* study on the reaction model established that when the folded conformation of azadiene **7** is taken as an energy reference for the IMDA reaction, the activation free energy is *ca.* 24 kcal/mol, an energy that furnishes a rationalization for a spontaneous (*i.e.,* nonenzymatically catalyzed) cyclization process in the biosynthesis of *paraherquamide A* (**9**) and VM55599 (**11**) (Domingo *et al.*, 2003). Consequently, both the folding of the precursor at the active site of the putative oxidase that forms the azadiene system from the diketopiperazine precursor and the low negative activation entropy associated with the intramolecular process can thus be invoked to account for the feasibility of these biosynthetic cyclizations.

Recently, Houk *et al.* reported a theoretical prediction of an enzyme-catalyzed transannular 1,3-dipolar cycloaddition (13DC) reaction in the biosynthesis of *lycojaponicumins A and B* (Krenske *et al.*, 2013). DFT calculations using the M06-2X functional predict that the uncatalyzed 13DC reaction of the putative lyco-japonicumin precursor in water is moderately facile ($\Delta G_{act} = 21.5$ kcal/mol, $k = 10^{-3}$ s^{-1}) and that an enzyme could accelerate the cycloaddition by the formation of two hydrogen bonds (HBs) of two explicit water molecules to the enone oxygen while maintaining an otherwise nonpolar active site (see Scheme 9.3). The theoretical enzyme-catalyzed process presents ΔG_{act} *ca.* 17 kcal/mol, corresponding to a 2000-fold rate enhancement, and the predicted k_{cat} (2 s^{-1}) was found to be similar to those of known enzymes involved in secondary metabolic pathways.

Considering that the preliminary computational work carried out by Hess and Smentek (2012) does not allow to definitively establish if *SpnF* is a cyclase catalyzing the conversion of macrocyclic lactone (**4**) into tricyclic compound (**5**), we decided to perform a further DFT study using the actual molecular system **4** proposed

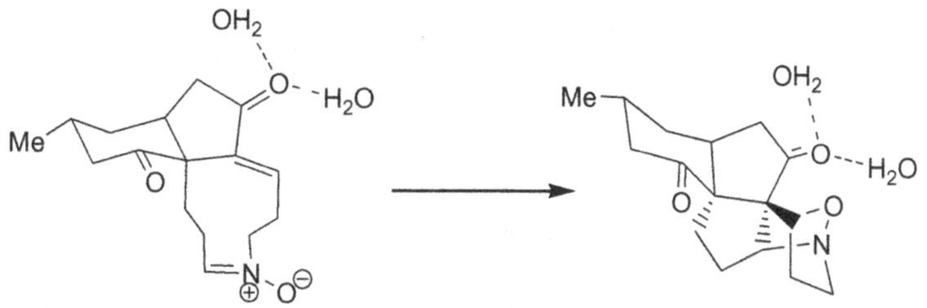

SCHEME 9.3

Houk's theozyme.

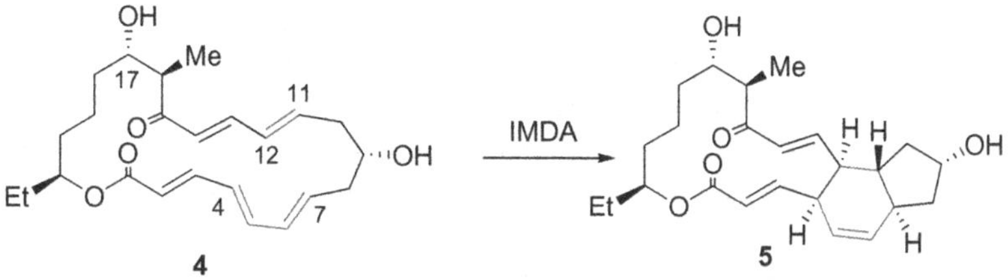

SCHEME 9.4

Cyclization reaction in this study.

by Kim *et al.* (2011) as intermediate in the biosynthesis of *spinosyn A* (**1**; see Schemes 9.1 and 9.4).

In addition, Kim *et al.* (2011), Hess and Smentek (2012), and Townsend (2011) proposed that the cyclization step in *SpnF* takes place via a concerted mechanism. Hess and Smentek also proposed that "the hallmark of Diels-Alder [4+2] cycloadditions is that they are concerted." Establishing whether the one-step mechanism of the *SpnF*-catalyzed cyclization has a concerted nature is important as pericyclic reactions, defined in 1965 (Woodward and Hoffmann, 1969), are commonly assumed to take place through a concerted mechanism. Although Hess and Smentek (2012) performed a complete geometrical analysis of the asynchronicity in the C—C single bond formation, this analysis offers no information about the evolution of the C—C double bonds. A rigorous study of the concerted nature of a reaction requires an exhaustive topological analysis of all changes in bonding along the reaction, which cannot be performed by experimental procedures.

The bonding evolution theory (BET) (Krokidis *et al.*, 1997; Gilmore, 1981), consisting of the joint use of electron localization functions (ELF) (Savin *et al.*, 1991, 1996, 1997; Silvi and Savin, 1994) and Thom's catastrophe theory (Thom, 1976; Woodcock and Poston, 1974), has been proposed as a tool for the understanding of electronic changes in chemical processes (Polo *et al.*, 2008). BET studies have shown that even the synchronous DA reactions between butadiene/ethylene (Berski *et al.*, 2003), cyclopentadiene/ethylene (Domingo *et al.*, 2010), and cyclopentadiene/tetracyoanoethylene (Domingo *et al.*, 2012) are nonconcerted processes.

Consequently, a topological ELF bonding analysis along the cyclization of macrocyclic lactone (**4**) is also performed in order to establish the nonconcerted nature of the reaction.

2 COMPUTATIONAL METHODS

DFT computations were carried out using the MPWB1K functional (Zhao and Truhlar, 2004), together with the 6-31G* and 6-311G** basis sets (Hehre *et al.*, 1986). Optimizations were carried out at the MPWB1K/6-31G* level using the Berny analytical gradient optimization method (Schlegel, 1982, 1994). Stationary points were characterized by frequency computations in order to verify that TSs have only one imaginary frequency. Intrinsic reaction coordinates (IRC) paths (Fukui, 1970) were traced in order to check the energy profiles connecting each TS to the two associated minima of the proposed mechanism using the second-order González-Schlegel integration method (González and Schlegel, 1990, 1991). Values of enthalpies, entropies, and free energies within a dielectric environment of an active site (Krenske *et al.*, 2013), modeled in implicit diethyl ether ($\varepsilon = 4.24$), were calculated at the MPWB1K/6-311G** level with standard statistical thermodynamics at reaction conditions (Hehre *et al.*, 1986). Thermodynamic calculations were corrected by a factor of 0.96 (Scott and Radom, 1996). Solvent effects of diethyl ether on the thermodynamic calculations were considered by using a self-consistent reaction field (SCRF) (Tomasi and Persico, 1994; Simkin and Sheikhet, 1995) based on the polarizable continuum model (PCM) of Tomasi's group (Cances *et al.*, 1997; Cossi *et al.*, 1996; Barone *et al.*, 1998). The electronic structures of stationary points were analyzed by the natural bond orbital (NBO) method (Reed *et al.*, 1985, 1988) and by ELF topological analysis, $\eta(\mathbf{r})$ (Savin *et al.*, 1991, 1996, 1997; Silvi and Savin, 1994). The ELF study was performed with the TopMod program (Noury *et al.*, 1999) using the corresponding monodeterminantal wavefunctions of the selected structures of the IRC. All computations were carried out with the Gaussian 09 suite of programs (Frisch *et al.*, 2009).

A conformational analysis for the precursor macrocyclic lactone **4** was performed to search the minimum energy structure using the Merck molecular force field (MMFF) in the MacroModel (MacroModel, 2009); see the "Supplementary Material" section for further details on these calculations). However, the MMFF global minimum geometry, once reoptimized at the MPWB1K/6-31G* level, was 2.3 kcal/mol above the macrocyclic lactone (**4**) conformation used as a reference in this study.

3 RESULTS AND DISCUSSION

An exploration of the potential energy surface for the conversion of macrocyclic lactone (**4**) into the tricyclic compound (**5**) allows establishing that this cyclization reaction takes place through a one-step mechanism. Consequently, the precursor

Table 9.1 MPWB1K/6-311G** total enthalpies (H, in au), entropies (S, in cal/mol K) and free energies (G, in au) and relative[a] enthalpies (ΔH, in kcal/mol), entropies (ΔS, in cal/mol K) and free energies (ΔG, in kcal/mol)[b], for the stationary points involved in the cyclisation reaction of lactone (4)

	H	ΔH	S	ΔS	G	ΔG
4	−1310.188420		189.5		−1310.278465	
4-S	−1310.183314	3.2	187.4	−2.1	−1310.272363	3.8
TS	−1310.156461	20.1	186.2	−3.4	−1310.244910	21.1
5	−1310.216944	−17.9	182.9	−6.6	−1310.303859	−15.9

[a]Relative to (4).
[b]Computed at 298.15 K and 1 atm in diethyl ether.

macrocyclic lactone (4), the only TS, and the tricyclic compound (5) were located and characterized. The energy results are summarized in Table 9.1.

The activation enthalpy associated with the cyclization of macrocyclic lactone (4) via TS is 20.1 kcal/mol. This value, which is close to the activation energy computed by Hess and Smentek (2012) for TS-M2 using the B3LYP functional (20 kcal/mol), indicates that the activation enthalpy for the conversion of macrocyclic lactone (4) into tricyclic compound (5) might be around 20 kcal/mol. Formation of tricyclic compound (5) is exothermic by −17.9 kcal/mol.

Interestingly, the activation free energy associated with TS is only 21.1 kcal/mol. Inclusion of the activation entropy increases the activation enthalpy by only 1.0 kcal/mol. This behavior is a consequence of the intramolecular nature of the cyclization process, which increases the entropy of TS by only −3.4 cal/mol K. Formation of tricyclic compound (5) is exergonic by −15.9 kcal/mol; thus, the cyclization can be considered irreversible. The computed activation free energy associated with TS, which is similar to that found by Houk et al. for the uncatalyzed 13DC reaction of the putative lycojaponicumin precursor in water (Krenske et al., 2013), predicts that the uncatalyzed cyclization of the putative spinosyn A precursor is moderately facile in a low-polar medium, in clear agreement with the fact that the cyclization takes place easily at room temperature (Kim et al., 2011).

The activation free energy associated with TS is less than that for the IMDA reaction of folded azadiene (7), $\Delta G_{act} = 24$ kcal/mol. Considering that this IMDA reaction takes place spontaneously at room temperature (Sanz-Cervera et al., 2000), we can conclude that cyclization of lactone (4) via TS can be easily performed at room temperature (Kim et al., 2011) without the participation of any Diels-Alderase.

One possibility to accelerate cyclization is to raise the polar character of the reaction by increasing the electrophilicity of the unsaturated ketone framework present in macrocyclic lactone (4). This electrophilic activation can be reached via the formation of HBs between the carbonyl oxygen and hydrogen-bond donor molecules; however, it is to be noted that the carbonyl oxygen is already intramolecularly hydrogen-bonded to the hydroxyl group present at C17. In spite of this behavior, we considered a theozyme in which one water molecule was also hydrogen-bonded to the carbonyl oxygen. Thermodynamic calculations for the theozyme and the geometry of the corresponding **TSw** are given in the "Supplementary Material" section. Although formation of the second hydrogen-bond decreased the activation enthalpy by 0.4 kcal/mol, it increased the free activation energy by 0.8 kcal/mol as a consequence of the unfavorable entropy decrease; −4.0 cal/mol K. Consequently, thermodynamic calculations for the proposed theozyme suggest that HBs are not involved in the observed acceleration in the *SpnF* gene. These energy results allow one to rule out Hess and Smentek's proposal that a stabilization of the highly polarized transition structure could also accelerate the reaction.

The geometries of macrocyclic lactone (**4**), **TS**, and the formal [4+2] cycloadduct (**5**) are given in Figure 9.2. In macrocyclic lactone (**4**), the distance between the C4 and C12, and C7 and C11 carbons are 4.659 and 2.927 Å, respectively. The length of this HB in lactone (**4**) is 2.024 Å. At **TS**, the distance between the C4 and C12, and C7 and C11 carbons are 2.772 and 1.918 Å, respectively. These values, which are close to those found by Hess and Smentek (2012) at **TS-M1** and **TS-M2**, clearly indicate that at this highly asynchronous **TS**, while the C7—C11 is being formed, no bonding interactions between the C4 and C12 carbons take place (as discussed later in this chapter). It is worth to note that at **TS**, the HB length is 1.988 Å. The shortening of this HB length with respect to that of the macrocyclic lactone (**4**) clearly indicates a stronger HB interaction at the polar **TS**, which in turn can increase the electrophilic character of the unsaturated ketone residue. In the tricyclic compound (**5**), the lengths of the C4—C12, and C7—C11 single bonds are 1.577 and 1.528 Å, respectively. Compound (**5**) remains hydrogen-bonded with an HB length of 2.069 Å.

Natural population analysis (NPA) allows evaluating GEDT along the cyclization process. The natural atomic charges at **TS** were shared between the two fragments resulting from the disconnection of the C8—C9 and C18—C19 bonds of the macrocyclic lactone ring. As some GEDT can take place in macrocyclic lactone (**4**) following this disconnection scheme, the natural atomic charges in lactone (**4**) were also computed. The net charges in the conjugated ketone frameworks in (**4**) and **TS** are 0.04e and −0.06e, respectively. Consequently, upon going from macrocyclic lactone (**4**) to **TS**, the GEDT that takes place from the unsaturated ester framework to the unsaturated ketone one is 0.10e; a value identical with that computed at **TS-M2** using the B3LYP functional (Hess and Smentek, 2012). This low GEDT, which points to a low-polar process, accounts for the high activation energy found at this cyclization reaction (Domingo and Sáez, 2009).

Macrocyclic lactone (**4**) has an ellipsoid structure that presents two main axes: (i) an *x*-axis along the two conjugated diene systems involved in the cyclization reaction, and (ii) a *y*-axis along the C—C single bond formation [see (**4**) in Figure 9.2]. While macrocyclic lactone (**4**) is relatively rigid along the *x*-axis, it may experience some flexibility along the *y*-axis. Therefore, when macrocyclic lactone (**4**) enters the active site of the enzyme, it may experience some strain, which may increase its internal energy. However, this energy penalty can be compensated by favorable HB interactions between the enzyme and the oxygenated functional groups, two alcohols and two carbonyl groups, that are present in macrocyclic lactone (**4**).

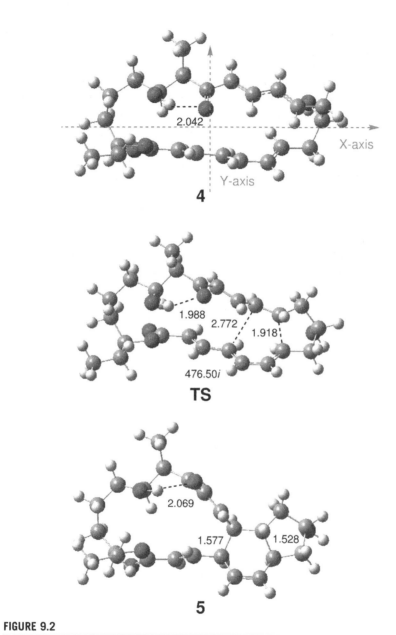

FIGURE 9.2

MPWB1K/6-31G* optimized geometries of (**4**), **TS**, and (**5**). Lengths are given in angstroms.

Thus, when macrocyclic lactone (**4**) is strained along the *y*-axis, reducing the C3—C15 distance by 0.4 Å, the stressed lactone **4-S** is found to be only 3.8 kcal/mol higher in free energy (3.2 kcal/mol in enthalpy) than the free lactone (**4**; see Table 9.1), a value that could easily be reached by lactone (**4**) as it enters the active site of the enzyme. Thus, when the strained lactone **4-S** is considered as the complex precursor of the cyclization process, the corresponding activation free energy to reach **TS** is found to be *ca.* 17.0 kcal/mol. This decrease of the activation free energy, which is similar to that found by Houk in the hydrogen-bonding activation and represents a 2000-fold rate enhancement (Krenske *et al.*, 2013), might account for the low acceleration of the cyclization reaction of (**4**) in the presence of the *SpnF* gene: 500-fold (Kim *et al.*, 2011). Note that this very low rate enhancement indicates that the strain inside the *SpnF* gene should be lower than the computed 3.8 kcal/mol, a very accessible value.

The IRC from **TS** connects it directly with macrocyclic lactone (**4**) and tricyclic compound (**5**), indicating the one-step nature of this cyclization reaction (see Figure 9.3). A geometrical analysis of the evolution of the C4—C12 and

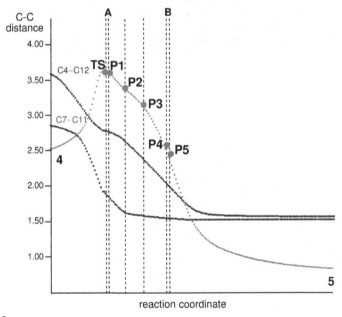

FIGURE 9.3

IRC plot of the cyclization reaction of macrocyclic lactone (**4**) showing the progress of the formation of the two C-C single bonds along the cyclization reaction of macrocyclic lactone (**4**). Point **P2** of the IRC shares the two-stage mechanism. **P1**, **P4**, and **P5** represent the most relevant points associated with the formation of the C7—C11 and C4—C12 single bonds. The C5—C6 double bond is formed at **P3**. A and B represent the short region of the IRC where the C7—C11 and C4—C12 single bond formation begins. Distances are given in angstroms.

C7—C11 single bond formation along the IRC, which is similar to that for **TS-M2** (Hess and Smentek, 2012), suggests that this one-step cyclization reaction takes place through a two-stage mechanism (Domingo *et al.*, 2008). While at the first stage of the reaction only the C7—C11 single bond is formed, the C4—C12 single bond is formed at the second stage of the reaction (as discussed later). Point **P2** of the IRC, which presents a minimum value in the energy gradient, shares the IRC in the two stages (see Figure 9.3). Interestingly, at this point, while the C7—C11 single bond is practically formed [d(C7—C11) = 1.624 Å], the formation of the C4—C12 single bond has not started yet [d(C4—C12) = 2.603 Å]. In addition, the high asynchronicity found at the TS in the C—C single bond formation, $\Delta l = d$(C4—C12)-d(C7—C11) = 0.95, slightly increases at point **P2**, where $\Delta l = 0.98$. Considering that ELF bonding analysis shows that the C—C single bond formation takes place in the short range of 1.9 – 2.0 Å (Domingo, 2014), this geometrical analysis clearly shows that the formation of the two new C—C single bonds is nonconcerted.

Finally, in order to establish the concerted or nonconcerted nature of this cyclization process, an ELF bonding analysis was performed. Details of the ELF bonding analysis are given in the "Supplementary Material" section. The topological ELF bonding analysis along the cyclization clearly supports the nonconcerted nature of the bond-breaking/bond-formation processes, which take place in the following order (see Table 9.2): (i) breaking of the C4—C5, C6—C7 and C11—C12 double bonds before reaching the TS geometry; (ii) creation of the *pseudoradical* centers at the C7 and C11 carbons present at TS; (iii) formation of the first C7—C11 single bond at **P1** by coupling of the aforementioned *pseudoradical* centers at a distance of 1.895 Å; (iv) formation of the C5—C6 double bond at **P3**; (v) creation of the *pseudoradical* centers at the C4 and C12 carbons; and finally, (vi) formation of the second C4—C12 single bond at **P5** by coupling of the aforementioned *pseudoradical* centers at a distance of 2.052 Å.

While the analysis of the geometrical parameters along the IRC accounts for the asynchronicity in the formation of the two new C—C single bonds (see Figure 9.3), the concerted or nonconcerted nature of the reaction demands an exhaustive topological ELF analysis of the changes of electron density along the cyclization path in order to establish when the bonding changes take place. Consequently, with a single geometrical analysis, Hess and Smentek were not able to establish the concerted or nonconcerted nature of the cyclization, although the high asynchronicity found in the formation of the two C—C single bonds along the IRC anticipates the nonconcerted nature of the cyclization.

4 CONCLUSIONS

The conversion of macrocyclic lactone (**4**) into tricyclic compound (**5**), as a key step in the biosynthesis of *spinosyn A* **1**, experimentally studied by Kim *et al.* (2011), has been theoretically investigated using DFT methods at the MPWB1K/6-31G* and the MPWB1K/6-311G** computational levels. The cyclization process takes place

Table 9.2 Sequential Bonding Changes Along the Nonconcerted One-Step Conversion of Macrocyclic Lactone (**4**) into Tricyclic Compound (**5**).

	IRC	d1	d2	Chemical Process	Topological Characterization [a]
a		<1.918	<2.772	Breaking of the Cx—Cy double bonds present in (**5**)	Formation of one single disynaptic basin V(Cx,Cy) in the Cx—Cy region
b	**TS**	1.918	2.772	Formation of the C7 and C11 pseudoradical centers	Formation of the two monosynaptic basins V(C7) and V(C11)
c	**P1**	1.895	2.766	Formation of the first C7—C11 single bond	Formation of the disynaptic basin V(C7,C11)
d	**P3**	1.590	2.406	Formation of the C5—C6 double bond	Formation of the two disynaptic basins V(C5,C6) and V('C5,C6)
e	**P4**	1.556	2.075	Formation of the C4 and C12 *pseudoradical* centers	Formation of the two monosynaptic basins V(C4) and V(C12)
f	**P5**	1.555	2.052	Formation of the second C4—C12 single bond	Formation of the disynaptic basin V(C4,C12)

*Note: The positions of **TS** and selected points **P1-P5** in the IRC are given in Figure 9.3.*
[a] The full topological ELF bonding analysis is given in the "Supplementary Material" section.

along a one-step mechanism characterized by a nonconcerted breaking/forming bond process. In spite of the high activation enthalpy computed for this cyclization process, 20.1 kcal/mol, the very low activation entropy associated with the cyclization of lactone (**4**), −3.4 cal/mol K, makes it feasible for the reaction to take place at room temperature due to the computed activation free energy of 21.1 kcal/mol. The large exergonic character of the cyclization, −15.9 kcal/mol, makes the cyclization process irreversible. The relatively low activation free energy found for this cyclization furnishes a rationalization of the spontaneous (*i.e.* nonenzymatically catalyzed) cyclization process in the biosynthesis of *spinosyn A* (**1**).

Modeling of a feasible theozyme, in which the carbonyl oxygen present at C17 is hydrogen bonded to an additional water molecule, suggests that although the hydrogen bonding slightly favors the cyclization enthalpically, the corresponding activation free energy is slightly disfavored due to the decrease of activation entropy associated with the HB formation.

A geometrical analysis of macrocyclic lactone (**4**) suggests that it has some flexibility along the Y-axis parallel to the C—C single bond formation. Consequently, a slight strain suffered by macrocyclic lactone (**4**) inside the active site of the *SpnF* gene may slightly increase its energy, thus decreasing the corresponding free activation energy. This behavior, which is similar to that found in the biosynthesis of *paraherquamide A* **9** and VM55599 **11** (Domingo *et al.*, 2003; Williams, 2011) accounts for the relatively low 500-fold acceleration found by Kim *et al.* (2011) in the *SpnF* gene.

A geometrical analysis for the C—C single bond formation along the IRC of the one-step mechanism indicates that formation of the two C—C single bonds takes place along a two-stage mechanism. While at the first stage only the C7—C11 single bond is formed at the terminal carbons of the two conjugated carbonyl frameworks of macrocyclic lactone (**4**), the second C4—C12 single bond is formed at the second stage.

Finally, an ELF bonding analysis of the breaking/forming bond processes along the one-step cyclization unambiguously allows the establishment of the nonconcerted nature of this process and thus clears up the hypothetical doubt for DA. While the three double bonds of unsaturated lactone (**4**) participating in the DA reaction are topologically broken before reaching the TS geometry, formation of the new bonds takes place after passing the TS in the sequence: (i) formation of the first C7—C11 single bond; (ii) formation of the C5—C6 double bond; and finally (iii) formation of the second C4—C12 single bond. These significant chemical changes, which take place in differentiated regions of the IRC, account for the nonconcerted nature of the bond-breaking and bond-formation processes as demanded in pericyclic reactions.

Supplementary Material: Conformational analysis of macrocyclic lactone (**4**). Modeling of a theozyme for the conversion of macrocyclic lactone (**4**) into tricyclic compound (**5**). ELF bonding analysis of the conversion of macrocyclic lactone (**4**) into tricyclic compound (**5**). Cartesian coordinates of the stationary points involved in the cyclization reaction of lactone (**4**).

ACKNOWLEDGMENTS

This work was supported by research funds provided by the University of Valencia (project UV-INV-AE13-139082). LR and PR acknowledge the facilities at the University of Mauritius.

REFERENCES

Auclair, K., Sutherland, A., Kennedy, K., Witter, D.J., van der Heever, J.P., Hutchinson, R., Vederas, J.C., 2000. J. Am. Chem. Soc. 122, 11519.

Barone, V., Cossi, M., Tomasi, J., 1998. J. Comput. Chem. 19, 404.

Berski, S., Andrés, J., Silvi, B., Domingo, L.R., 2003. J. Phys. Chem. A 107, 6014.

Blanchflower, S.E., Banks, R.M., Everett, J.R., Manger, B.R., Reading, C., 1991. J. Antibiot. 44, 492.

Blanchflower, S.E., Banks, R.M., Everett, J.R., Reading, C., 1993. J. Antibiot. 46, 1355.

Cances, E., Mennucci, B., Tomasi, J., 1997. J. Chem. Phys. 107, 3032.

Cossi, M., Barone, V., Cammi, R., Tomasi, J., 1996. Chem. Phys. Lett. 255, 327.

Domingo, L.R., Sáez, J.A., 2009. Org. Biomol. Chem. 7, 3576.

Domingo, L.R., Zaragozá, R.J., Williams, R.M., 2003. J. Org. Chem. 68, 2895.

Domingo, L.R., Sáez, J.A., Zaragozá, R.J., Arnó, M., 2008. J. Org. Chem. 73, 8791.

Domingo, L.R., Chamorro, E., Pérez, P., 2010. Org. Biomol. Chem. 8, 5495.

Domingo, L.R., Pérez, P., Sáez, J.A., 2012. Org. Biomol. Chem. 10, 3841.

Eberhardt, S., Zingler, N., Kemter, K., Richter, G., Cushman, M., Bacher, A., 2001. Eur. J. Biochem. 268, 4315.

Frisch, M.J., Trucks, G.W., Schlegel, H.B., Scuseria, G.E., Robb, M.A., Cheeseman, J.R., Scalmani, G., Barone, V., Mennucci, B., Petersson, G.A., Nakatsuji, H., Caricato, M., Li, X., Hratchian, H.P., Izmaylov, A.F., Bloino, J., Zheng, G., Sonnenberg, J.L., Hada, M., Ehara, M., Toyota, K., Fukuda, R., Hasegawa, J., Ishida, M., Nakajima, T., Honda, Y., Kitao, O., Nakai, H., Vreven, T., Montgomery Jr., J.A., Peralta, J.E., Ogliaro, F., Bearpark, M., Heyd, J.J., Brothers, E., Kudin, K.N., Staroverov, V.N., Kobayashi, R., Normand, J., Raghavachari, K., Rendell, A., Burant, J.C., Iyengar, S.S., Tomasi, J., Cossi, M., Rega, N., Millam, J.M., Klene, M., Knox, J.E., Cross, J.B., Bakken, V., Adamo, C., Jaramillo, J., Gomperts, R., Stratmann, R.E., Yazyev, O., Austin, A.J., Cammi, R., Pomelli, C., Ochterski, J.W., Martin, R.L., Morokuma, K., Zakrzewski, V.G., Voth, G.A., Salvador, P., Dannenberg, J.J., Dapprich, S., Daniels, A.D., Farkas, O., Foresman, J.B., Ortiz, J.V., Cioslowski, J., Fox, D.J., 2009. Gaussian 09, Revision A.01. Gaussian,Inc., Wallingford CT.

Fukui, K., 1970. J. Phys. Chem. 74, 4161.

Gilmore, R., 1981. Catastrophe Theory for Scientists and Engineers New York. .

González, C., Schlegel, H.B., 1990. J. Phys. Chem. 94, 5523.

González, C., Schlegel, H.B., 1991. J. Chem. Phys. 95, 5853.

Hehre, W.J., Radom, L., Schleyer, P.v.R., Pople, J.A., 1986. Ab initio Molecular Orbital Theory. Wiley,New York.

Hess Jr., B.A., Smentek, L., 2012. Org. Biomol. Chem. 10, 7503.

Kim, R.-R., Illarionov, B., Joshi, M., Cushman, M., Lee, C.Y., Eisenreich, W., Fischer, M., Bacher, A., 2010. J. Am. Chem. Soc. 132, 2983.

Kim, H.J., Ruszczycky, M.W., Choi, S., Liu, Y., Liu, H., 2011. Nature 473, 109.

Kirst, H.A., 2010. J. Antibiot. 63, 101.

Kirst, H.A., Michel, K.H., Martin, J.W., Creemer, L.C., Chio, E.H., Yao, R.C., Nakatsukasa, W.M., Boeck, L.D., Occolowitz, J.L., Paschal, J.W., Deeter, J.B., Jones, N.D., Thompson, G.D., 1991. Tetrahedron Lett. 32, 4839.

Krenske, E.H., Patel, A., Houk, K.N., 2013. J. Am. Chem. Soc. 135, 17638.

Krokidis, X., Noury, S., Silvi, B., 1997. J. Phys. Chem. A 101, 7277.

Ma, S.M., Li, J.W.-H., Choi, J.W., Zhou, H., Lee, K.K.L., Moorthie, V.A., Xie, X., Kealey, J.T., Da Silva, N.A., Vederas, J.C., Tang, L., 2009. Science 326, 589.

MacroModel, version 9.7, 2009. Schrödinger, LLC, New York, NY.

Noury, S., Krokidis, X., Fuster, F., Silvi, B., 1999. Comput. Chem. 23, 597.

Oikawa, H., Katayama, K., Suzuki, Y., Ichihara, A., 1995. J. Chem. Soc. Chem. Comm. 1321.

Ose, T., Watanabe, K., Mie, T., Honma, M., Watanabe, H., Yao, M., Oikawa, H., Tanaka, I., 2003. Nature 422, 185.

Polo, V., Andrés, J., Berski, S., Domingo, L.R., Silvi, B., 2008. J. Phys. Chem. A 112, 7128.

Reed, A.E., Weinstock, R.B., Weinhold, F., 1985. J. Chem. Phys. 83, 735.

Reed, A.E., Curtiss, L.A., Weinhold, F., 1988. Chem. Rev. 88, 899.

Sanz-Cervera, J.F., Williams, R.M., 2002. J. Am. Chem. Soc. 124, 2556.

Sanz-Cervera, J.F., Williams, R.M., Marco, J.A., López-Sánchez, J.M., González, F., Martínez, M.E., Sancenón, F., 2000. Tetrahedron Lett. 56, 6345.

Savin, A., Becke, A.D., Flad, J., Nesper, R., Preuss, H., Vonschnering, H.G., 1991. Angew. Chem. Int. Ed. 30, 409.

Savin, A., Silvi, B., Colonna, F., 1996. Can. J. Chem. 74, 1088.

Savin, A., Nesper, R., Wengert, S., Fassler, T.F., 1997. Angew. Chem., Int. Ed. Engl. 36, 1809.

Schlegel, H.B., 1982. J. Comput. Chem. 3, 214.

Schlegel, H.B., 1994. Modern Electronic Structure Theory. (Yarkony, D.R., Ed.)WorldScientific Publishing, Singapore.

Scott, A.P., Radom, L., 1996. J. Phys. Chem. 100, 16502.

Silvi, B., Savin, A., 1994. Nature 371, 683.

Simkin, B.Y., Sheikhet, I., 1995. Quantum Chemical and Statistical Theory of Solutions-A Computational Approach. EllisHorwood, London.

Stocking, E.M., Sanz-Cervera, J.F., Williams, R.M., 2000. J. Am. Chem. Soc. 122, 1675.

Stocking, E.M., Sanz-Cervera, J.F., Williams, R.M., 2001. Angew. Chem., Int. Ed. 40, 1296.

Thom, R., 1976. Structural Stability and Morphogenesis: An Outline of a General Theory of Models. Reading,MA.

Tomasi, J., Persico, M., 1994. Chem. Rev. 94, 2027.

Townsend, C.A., 2011. ChemBioChem. 12, 2267.

Waldron, C., Matsushima, P., Rosteck Jr., P.R., Broughton, M.C., Turner, J., Madduri, K., Crawford, K.P., Merlo, D.J., Baltz, R.H., 2001. Chem. Biol. 8, 487.

Watanabe, K., Mie, T., Ichihara, A., Oikawa, H., Honma, M., 2000. J. Biol. Chem. 275, 38393.

Williams, R.M., 2011. J. Org. Chem. 76, 4221.

Williams, R.M., Cox, R.J., 2003. Acc. Chem. Res. 36, 127.

Williams, R.M., Sanz-Cervera, J.F., Sancenón, F., Marco, J.A., Halligan, K., 1998. J. Am. Chem. Soc. 120, 1090.

Woodcock, A.E.R., Poston, T., 1974. Spinger-Verlag, Berlin.

Woodward, R.B., Hoffmann, R., 1969. Angew. Chem., Int. Ed. Engl. 8, 781.

Yamazaki, M., Okuyama, E., Kobayashi, M., Inoue, H., 1981. Tetrahedron Lett. 22, 135.

Zhao, Y., Truhlar, D.G., 2004. J. Phys. Chem. A 108, 6908.

SUBCHAPTER

Supplementary Material: Diels-Alderase Catalyzing the Cyclization Step in the Biosynthesis of *Spinosyn A*: Reality or Fantasy?

Luis R. Domingo[1], José A. Sáez[1], Lydia Rhyman[2], and Ponnadurai Ramasami[2]

Departamento de Química Orgánica, Universidad de Valencia, Valencia, Spain[1]

Computational Chemistry Group, Department of Chemistry, University of Mauritius, Réduit, Mauritius[2]

1 CONFORMATIONAL ANALYSIS OF MACROCYCLIC LACTONE (4)

Macrocyclic lactone (**4**), obtained from the retro-cyclization of compound (**5**), was first submitted to a preliminary minimization in the Macromodel [1] using the Merck molecular force field (MMFF)[2] and water as solvent. Taking the MMFF optimized structure, a conformational analysis was performed using a mixed torsional/large-scale low-mode sampling (LLMOD) analysis [3], with False Non-Match Rate (FNMR) as a minimizer with the recommended 1.0 gradient convergence threshold and 100,000 steps. The energy window to select structures was of 50 kJ/mol. The chirality of all the carbon atoms was the only variable fixed in this analysis. From the 12,777 structures found in this conformational analysis, only 7483 of them converged with the imposed criteria. Taking the structure with the lowest energy of this conformational analysis (see Figure S1), we can see that the C4=5-C6=C7 *s-cis* conformation of the unsaturated ester framework, and the *s-trans* conformation of the unsaturated ketone framework present in macrocyclic lactone (**4**) is preserved.

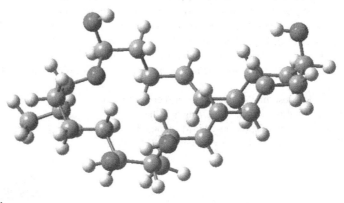

FIGURE S1

MMFF minimum conformation of macrocyclic lactone (**4**).

However, when the MMFF minimum conformation was reoptimized at the MPWB1K/6-31G* computational level, this MMFF minimum was found to be 2.3 kcal/mol more energetic than macrocyclic lactone (**4**).

2 MODELLING OF A THEOZYME FOR THE CONVERSION OF MACROCYCLIC LACTONE (4) INTO TRICYCLIC COMPOUND (5)

In principle, an enzyme may accelerate the cyclization of macrocyclic lactone (**4**) through selective hydrogen bonding to the oxygen of the unsaturated ketone framework. This HB would increase the electrophilicity of the unsaturated ketone framework, thus accelerating the cyclization through a more polar process [4]. Lactone (**4**) already presents an intramolecular HB between the carbonyl oxygen atom at C-15 and the hydroxyl group present at C—17. Apart from this HB, an additional rate enhancement coming from the hydrogen bonding of a water molecule to the unsaturated ketone oxygen at C—15 within a typical dielectric environment of an enzyme

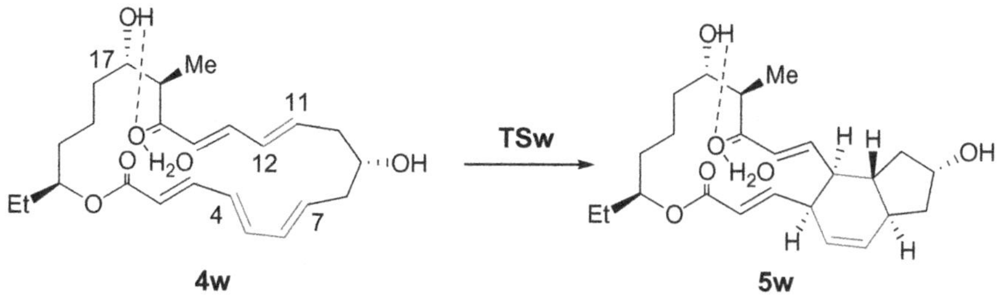

SCHEME S1

Proposed theozyme for the conversion of macrocyclic lactone (4) into tricyclic compound (5).

Table S1 MPWB1K/6-311G** Total enthalpies (H, in au), entropies (S, in cal/mol K) and free energies (G, in au) and relative[a] enthalpies (ΔH, in kcal/mol), entropies (ΔS, in cal/mol K) and free energies (ΔG, in kcal/mol),[b] for the stationary points involved in the cyclization reaction of lactone (4) in the presence of one water molecule.

	H	ΔH	S	ΔS	G	ΔG
4w	−1386.587654		204.2		−1386.684659	
TSw	−1386.556324	19.7	196.8	−7.4	−1386.649832	21.9
5w	−1386.614961	−17.1	194.6	−9.6	−1386.707416	−14.3

[a]relative to **4w**.
[b]computed at 298.15 K and 1 atm in diethyl ether.

active site was studied by optimizing **4w**, **TSw**, and **5w** at the MPWB1K/6-311G** computational level in implicit diethyl ether [5] (see Scheme S1). Thermodynamic data associated with the proposed theozyme are given in Table S1.

Although formation of the second HB decreases the activation enthalpy of **TSw** by 0.4 kcal/mol relative to that of **TS**, it increases the activation free energy of **TSw** by 0.8 kcal/mol relative to that of **TS** as a consequence of the unfavourable entropy decrease associated with the cyclization; $\Delta\Delta S^{\neq}$ −4.0 cal/mol K. Consequently, thermodynamic data suggest that hydrogen bonds are not involved in the acceleration observed in the *SpnF* gene. Note that formation of an additional HB at the lactone oxygen would disfavor the cyclization since it may decrease the nucleophilic character of the unsaturated ester framework.

The geometry of **TSw** is given in Figure S2. At **TSw**, the distance between the C4 and C12, and C7 and C11 carbons are 2.814 and 1.909 Å, respectively. Consequently, formation of the second HB with a water molecule makes the process slightly more advanced and more asynchronous. At this TS, while the intramolecular HB length is 1.917 Å, the intermolecular HB length involving the water molecule is 1.988 Å.

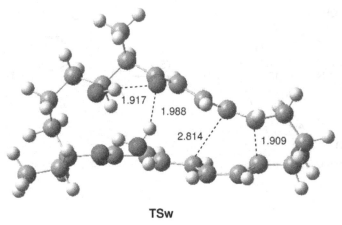

TSw

FIGURE S2

MPWB1K/6-311G** optimized geometry of TSw in diethyl ether. Lengths are given in angstroms.

3 ELF BONDING ANALYSIS OF THE CONVERSION OF MACROCYCLIC LACTONE (4) INTO THE TRICYCLIC COMPOUND (5)

Several theoretical studies have shown that topological ELF analysis along an organic reaction path can be used as a valuable tool to understand the bonding changes along a reaction [6,7]. After an analysis of the electron density, the ELF provides basins, which are the domains in which the probability of finding an electron pair is maximal. The basins are classified as core basins and valence basins. The latter are characterized by the synaptic order; *i.e.,* the number of atomic valence shells in which they participate. Thus, there are monosynaptic, disynaptic, and trisynaptic basins, and so on [8]. Monosynaptic basins, labeled *V(A)*, correspond to the lone pairs or nonbonding regions, while disynaptic basins connect the core of two nuclei A and B and, thus, correspond to a bonding region between A and B and are labeled *V(A,B)*. This description recovers the Lewis bonding model, providing a very suggestive graphical representation of the molecular system.

Recently, Domingo has shown that the C—C single-bond formation in organic reactions begins in the short C—C distance range of 1.9–2.0 Å by merging two monosynaptic basins, V(Cx) and V(Cy), into a new disynaptic basin V(Cx,Cy) associated with the formation of the new Cx—Cy single bond [9,10]. The Cx and Cy carbons characterized by the presence of the monosynaptic basins, V(Cx) and V(Cy), have been called *pseudoradical* centers [10,11].

In order to establish the nonconcerted nature of the one-step cyclization involved in conversion of the macrocyclic latone (**4**) into the tricyclic compound (**5**), an ELF bonding analysis along the IRC associated with the reaction path was performed. After an exhaustive ELF analysis of 150 points of the IRC from **(4)** to **(5)**, the most relevant points involved in the C4—C12 and C7—C11 single-bond formation, **TS**, **P1**, **P4**, and **P5**, were selected. Point **P2**, which shares the two-stage mechanism, and point **P3**, associated with the formation of the C5—C6 double bond present in the formal [4+2] cycloadduct **(5)**, were also analyzed. The most relevant ELF valence basins and their corresponding N populations of the selected points along the reaction paths are displayed in Table S2, while the attractor positions and atom numbering for **TS**, **P1**, **P4**, and **P5** are shown in Figure S3. For simplicity, only the monosynaptic V (A) and the disynaptic V(A,B) basins involved in the forming and breaking bonds along the cyclization will be discussed here.

At the highly asynchronous **TS**, d1(C7—C11)=1.918 Å and d2 (C4—C12)= 2.772 Å, the most relevant feature is the presence of two monosynaptic basins V(C7) and V(C11), integrating 0.37e and 0.45e, respectively. These monosynaptic basins, which are located at the end of the two conjugated carbonyl frameworks, are responsible for the subsequent C7—C11 single-bond formation. At **TS**, the two conjugated systems involved in the cyclization are characterized by the disynaptic basins V(C4,C5), 2.98e, V(C5,C6), 2.78e, V(C6,C7), 2.70e, and V(C11,C12), 2.74e, V(C12,C13), 2.53e, and V(C13,C14) 3.26e. No monosynaptic basin at the C4 or C12 carbons is found, indicating that the C4—C12 single-bond formation has not started yet.

At point **P1**, d1 = 1.895 Å and d2 = 2.766 Å, the two monosynaptic basins V(C7) and V(C11) present at **TS** have merged into the new disynaptic basin V(C7,C11), integrating 0.89e. This behavior indicates that the formation of the C7—C11 single bond has already started by coupling of the *pseudoradical* centers located at the C7 and C11 carbons with a high electron density. As in the case of **TS**, no monosynaptic basins at the C4 and C12 carbons were found at **P1**, indicating that the C4—C12 single-bond formation has not started yet.

At point **P2**, d1 = 1.628 Å and d2 = 2.613 Å, which divides the two stages of the one-step mechanism (see Figure 9.2 in the main chapter), no relevant topological change is observed with respect to **P1**. From **P1** to **P2**, the electron density of the new C7—C11 single bond has increased to reach 1.54e. The C7—C11 length at **P2**, 1.628 Å, indicates that the first C—C single bond is already formed. Note that in a stepwise DA reaction, the length of the first C—C single bond formed at the corresponding intermediates is in the range of 1.60–1.65 Å. No topological changes at the C4 or C12 carbons is observed at this point.

At point **P3**, d1 = 1.590 Å and d2 = 2.406 Å, the disynaptic basin V(C7,C11) has reached an electron density of 1.63e. At this point, a new monosynaptic basin V(C4) appears at C4, integrating 0.23e. No monosynaptic basin appears at C12. The disynaptic basin V(C5,C6) present at **P2** has been split into two disynaptic basins V(C5,C6) and V'(C5,C6), integrating 1.82, and 1.52e, indicating the formation of the C5—C6 double bond present in the tricyclic compound **(5)**. In this cyclization reaction, the C5—C6 double bond is formed before the second C4—C12 single bond. Note that in most DA reactions, the creation of the C—C double bond present

Table S2 Valence Basin Populations *N* Calculated from the ELF of Selected Points of the Conversion of Macrocyclic Latone **(4)** into the Tricyclic Compound **(5)**

	TS	P1	P2	P3	P4	P5
d(C7,C11)	1.918	1.895	1.628	1.590	1.556	1.555
d(C4,C12)	2.772	2.766	2.613	2.406	2.075	2.052
V(C4,C5)	2.98	2.96	2.70	2.45	2.18	2.17
V(C5,C6)	2.78	2.82	3.23	1.82	1.82	1.67
V'(C5,C6)				1.52	1.66	1.81
V(C6,C7)	2.70	2.65	2.23	2.17	2.11	2.10
V(C13,C14)	3.26	3.25	3.19	3.24	3.33	1.68
V'(C13,C14)						1.67
V(C12,C13)	2.53	2.56	2.77	2.78	2.27	2.24
V(C11,C12)	2.74	2.70	2.27	2.22	2.13	2.12
V(C7)	0.37					
V(C11)	0.45					
V(C7,C11)		0.89	1.54	1.63	1.72	1.73
V(C4)				0.23	0.59	
V(C12)					0.53	
V(C4,C12)						1.16

Note: d(Cx,Cy) distances are given in angstroms.

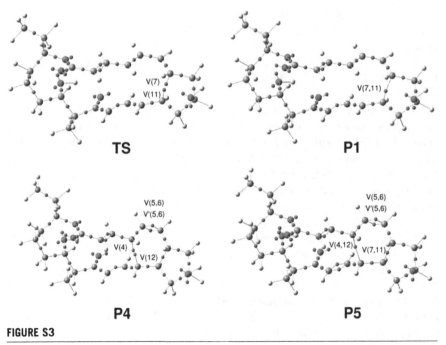

FIGURE S3

Attractor positions and atom numbering of some selected points of the IRC of the one-step mechanism associated with the conversion of macrocyclic lactone (4) into the tricyclic compound (5).

in the [4+2] cycloadduct takes place after formation of the second C—C single bond at the end of the IRC [6,9].

At point **P4**, d1 = 1.556 Å and d2 = 2.075 Å, while the monosynaptic basin V(C4) increases its electron density to reach 0.54e, and a new monosynaptic basin V(C12) appears at C12, integrating 0.23e. The monosynaptic basins V(C4) and C(12) are responsible for the subsequent C4—C12 single-bond formation.

Finally, at point **P5**, d1 = 1.555 Å and d2 = 2.052 Å, the two monosynaptic basins V(C4) and V(C12) present at **P4** have merged into the new disynaptic basin V(C4, C12), integrating 1.16e. This behavior indicates that the formation of second C4—C12 single bond has already started. At this point of the IRC, the disynaptic basin V(C13,C14) present at **P5** has been split into the two disynaptic basins, V(C13,C14) and V'(C13,C14), integrating 1.68e, and 1.67e, respectively, indicating the formation of the C13—C14 double bond present in the tricyclic compound (**5**).

Some interesting conclusions can be drawn from this ELF bonding analysis: (i) at **TS**, d1 = 1.918 Å, the presence of two monosynaptic basins, V(C7) and V(C11), indicates that the C7—C11 single-bond formation has not started. On the other hand, the two disynaptic basins, V(Cx,Cy) and V'(Cx,Cy), which topologically characterize the Cx—Cy double bonds present in macrocyclic lactone (**4**), have merged into one disynaptic basin, V(Cx,Cy), at **TS**. (ii) formation of the monosynaptic basins, V(C7) and V(C11), takes place at the end of the two conjugated carbonyl frameworks. (iii) formation of the first C7—C11 single bond takes place at the C7—C11 distance of 1.895 Å by coupling of the two *pseudoradical* centers located at the C7 and C11 carbons. (iv) from d1 = 1.90 to 1.63 Å, while the electron density of the V(C7,C11) disynaptic basin reaches 1.54e, the formation of the second C4—C12 single bond has not started. (v) at point **P2**, which divides the IRC into two stages, the C7—C11 length, 1.628 Å, indicates that this bond is practically formed. (vi) at point **P3**, the C5—C6 double bond present in the tricyclic compound (**5**) has been topologically formed with the creation of the two disynaptic basins, V(C5,C6) and V'(C5,C6). Interestingly, in this cyclization process, the C5—C6 double bond is created before the C4—C12 single bond. (vii) the C4—C12 single bond is created at the end of the IRC at the C4—C12 distance of 2.08 Å.

MPWB1K/6-31G* computed total energies, unique imaginary frequency, and Cartesian coordinates of the stationary points involved in the cyclization reaction of lactone (**4**).

4

$E(RmPW + HF - B95) = -1310.41143768$ a.u.

C	−1.12966600	3.61647900	−0.74493600
C	−1.10940100	2.09942600	−0.59726200
C	0.06645200	1.69405500	0.25591000

O	−0.08391500	1.30839500	1.40329800
C	−2.40075000	1.54058100	−0.00240700
C	−3.58394300	1.75711800	−0.91732600
C	−4.87561300	1.07861500	−0.48410000
C	−5.02624800	−0.39151000	−0.85889700
C	−4.34253500	−1.43522800	0.00651400
O	−2.91885600	−1.41172600	−0.12671500
C	−2.37069200	−1.89460000	−1.24053900
C	−0.90591100	−1.85466800	−1.20371100
C	−0.19614800	−1.62030100	−0.09238300
C	1.23590800	−1.69460300	−0.02079000
C	1.90510500	−1.66280500	1.14038900
C	3.34420500	−1.77468900	1.29583100
C	4.22403000	−1.51742800	0.32797200
C	5.70553900	−1.63391800	0.42157300
C	6.42219200	−0.51815200	−0.33562300
C	6.23515500	0.85525900	0.29838900
C	4.82180000	1.08948900	0.69763500
C	3.84707400	1.53460900	−0.09743700
C	2.48868100	1.54409600	0.37146100
C	1.39370700	1.78576400	−0.35567200
O	−2.69636000	2.15320200	1.23056900
C	−4.58605200	−1.27965600	1.49209600
C	−6.05516000	−1.29094300	1.86041300
O	−3.00648700	−2.32223200	−2.16978500
O	5.92448600	−0.40790700	−1.64655600
H	3.85875800	−1.21208200	−0.64321700
H	1.76901500	−1.86159100	−0.94773500
H	3.70428000	−2.03268800	2.28428600
H	1.32895200	−1.54705000	2.05007800
H	4.55626300	0.82550900	1.71265500
H	4.05354000	1.79352700	−1.12761100
H	6.88805700	0.93318900	1.16567100
H	6.56469300	1.59020800	−0.43349500
H	7.49301600	−0.73801600	−0.36049600
H	6.03723200	−1.66353800	1.45965400
H	6.01447900	−2.58613900	−0.02277000

```
H      2.33068800    1.27912200    1.41030300
H      1.45719200    2.05840200   -1.40006800
H     -0.42843600   -2.11301800   -2.13687900
H     -0.72171600   -1.38825300    0.82435500
H     -4.67832600   -2.41466600   -0.33355600
H     -2.24150300    0.48136000    0.15590800
H     -3.32118000    1.43368300   -1.92714400
H     -3.76003800    2.83185500   -0.96661100
H     -5.69997100    1.60772700   -0.96175300
H     -5.00857700    1.22899300    0.58717400
H     -4.71081100   -0.55268500   -1.88850200
H     -6.08720800   -0.64435400   -0.83393300
H     -0.95547600    1.64708900   -1.58095200
H      6.04397100   -1.24916200   -2.09160400
H     -1.84133000    3.91975000   -1.50841900
H     -1.42834600    4.06782600    0.19737400
H     -0.15417200    4.00919400   -1.02602300
H     -1.96593600    1.90168400    1.80768900
H     -4.06609100   -2.09010900    2.00143900
H     -4.11823400   -0.35195100    1.82437400
H     -6.55449900   -2.17877500    1.47378600
H     -6.18091300   -1.28541900    2.94031400
H     -6.57470100   -0.41943300    1.46662700
```

TS
E(RmPW + HF − B95) = −1310.37699308 a.u.
1 imaginary frequency: −476.4976 cm^{-1}

```
C     -2.27299900    4.04115800   -0.12121600
C     -1.76635400    2.66719500   -0.51468700
C     -0.47472700    2.34404400    0.19301700
O     -0.41991200    2.47546200    1.41072800
C     -2.73168500    1.53730900   -0.11200900
C     -4.00278200    1.52742200   -0.92648000
C     -4.96947900    0.41160000   -0.56249900
C     -4.60029100   -1.00041100   -1.01660800
C     -3.77321700   -1.90239400   -0.10874300
```

O	−2.37074100	−1.60315200	−0.11811500
C	−1.66596800	−1.95865900	−1.18740000
C	−0.22319400	−1.75067000	−1.01534000
C	0.36492000	−1.54489700	0.17213100
C	1.77718700	−1.47232000	0.35842000
C	2.34369100	−1.34699400	1.60504800
C	3.69687300	−1.11849500	1.81573000
C	4.57039700	−0.90903200	0.75220900
C	6.03560600	−0.65661800	0.92694300
C	6.48769200	−0.06224300	−0.39304800
C	5.42516300	0.95700400	−0.79612900
C	4.16703800	0.82710200	0.04349700
C	2.91263400	0.87925000	−0.57262200
C	1.77559900	1.45402400	0.03938600
C	0.62133000	1.79412100	−0.57832400
O	−3.08947400	1.64253900	1.23980000
C	−4.16243500	−1.86721300	1.35150300
C	−5.61378800	−2.23443100	1.58520600
O	−2.14466600	−2.42795500	−2.18817600
O	6.48328400	−1.04671900	−1.40152300
H	4.36586300	−1.44836000	−0.16421900
H	2.39687700	−1.64959800	−0.50714200
H	4.03192300	−0.89116600	2.81876700
H	1.67886700	−1.31683100	2.45789300
H	4.21958000	1.36849600	0.98073900
H	2.84124200	0.59723200	−1.61617800
H	5.80267200	1.97252600	−0.69450700
H	5.20209400	0.80156500	−1.84875800
H	7.47616500	0.39390400	−0.31747400
H	6.21236500	0.03847100	1.74837300
H	6.58237100	−1.57356800	1.15160900
H	1.83218700	1.66763500	1.10075100
H	0.49292600	1.65756600	−1.64204500
H	0.35629900	−1.89325400	−1.91509900
H	−0.26456000	−1.42720300	1.04393400
H	−3.87102700	−2.91502900	−0.49971900
H	−2.20456400	0.59738100	−0.28101800

```
H    −3.74390300    1.46171200   −1.98493600
H    −4.51012800    2.48032800   −0.77743400
H    −5.92378900    0.65188400   −1.03108500
H    −5.14883400    0.44770500    0.51073900
H    −4.11984100   −0.97579900   −1.99312100
H    −5.52963400   −1.55042300   −1.17076900
H    −1.61520600    2.60891300   −1.59274600
H     7.15408200   −1.69954200   −1.19278800
H    −3.21991700    4.26412100   −0.60606900
H    −2.41786700    4.08682400    0.95342000
H    −1.56073600    4.81348500   −0.40344700
H    −2.27933400    1.84784400    1.72570000
H    −3.51511800   −2.56386000    1.88316500
H    −3.94312500   −0.87415800    1.74333100
H    −5.85103400   −3.20481100    1.15008800
H    −5.83013000   −2.28821100    2.64935000
H    −6.29194800   −1.50228800    1.15107200
```

5

$E(RmPW + HF − B95) = −1310.44564187$ a.u.

```
C    −2.29525700    4.12630000   −0.32261700
C    −1.73680200    2.74062900   −0.57747300
C    −0.48749200    2.48471600    0.22095200
O    −0.46258700    2.74305800    1.40947600
C    −2.69571300    1.61567200   −0.12468800
C    −3.88326000    1.46446000   −1.04617600
C    −4.87944900    0.39238200   −0.63121400
C    −4.52257500   −1.06365800   −0.92370100
C    −3.63610900   −1.83778800    0.04396200
O    −2.23674800   −1.58721200   −0.15681900
C    −1.63790200   −2.25013300   −1.14483200
C    −0.17524900   −2.08691600   −1.14780000
C     0.50768700   −1.53031500   −0.15594200
C     1.99281500   −1.40361300   −0.11116100
C     2.58447200   −2.05198800    1.10980900
```

C	3.88149900	−1.91190400	1.35126200
C	4.63705500	−0.99606400	0.45630000
C	5.99218200	−0.45899400	0.86552100
C	6.19737400	0.68401400	−0.12669600
C	4.79756300	1.26496600	−0.36574300
C	3.83730500	0.29961700	0.32365100
C	2.46229200	0.09028900	−0.29718100
C	1.46073900	1.02984000	0.27051300
C	0.59914900	1.74797200	−0.44234000
O	−3.17490700	1.87729800	1.16698300
C	−3.89508100	−1.56289200	1.50743300
C	−5.31058800	−1.91497400	1.91931400
O	−2.22323500	−2.92885700	−1.94746100
O	6.63565900	0.18888300	−1.37215100
H	4.74250200	−1.43668500	−0.54129100
H	2.40015200	−1.92968900	−0.97807300
H	4.36198200	−2.39626800	2.18982600
H	1.94963100	−2.67024000	1.72845300
H	3.68676400	0.64136600	1.35048300
H	2.51522300	0.25312600	−1.37349900
H	4.70107900	2.27953500	0.01137400
H	4.63708100	1.29685700	−1.44145900
H	6.89808400	1.43280200	0.24683800
H	5.94693800	−0.07131200	1.88474700
H	6.79901100	−1.18953000	0.82153500
H	1.38276600	1.08414500	1.35129200
H	0.60159000	1.70527500	−1.52269700
H	0.31476700	−2.51011600	−2.01229500
H	−0.04387300	−1.14651500	0.69258000
H	−3.78563100	−2.89553000	−0.16726300
H	−2.13442700	0.67760200	−0.12982000
H	−3.51931100	1.26335600	−2.05522500
H	−4.40713100	2.41949400	−1.07921600
H	−5.80436700	0.59498600	−1.17105800
H	−5.11619700	0.53100500	0.42269200
H	−4.09680700	−1.16196700	−1.92153200

```
H    −5.45829800   −1.62292400   −0.95755900
H    −1.52851600    2.59723600   −1.63745600
H     7.50799400   −0.19074300   −1.25358700
H    −3.24143200    4.26789600   −0.83790000
H    −2.45984600    4.27334500    0.73973600
H    −1.60479100    4.89131600   −0.67060900
H    −2.41470100    2.12603300    1.70760200
H    −3.18553700   −2.15274500    2.08670000
H    −3.68375500   −0.51446100    1.71823100
H    −5.54135500   −2.95512000    1.69151300
H    −5.44692400   −1.77246400    2.98844000
H    −6.04607000   −1.29413300    1.41134700
```

MPWB1K/6-31G** computed total energies, unique imaginary frequency, and Cartesian coordinates of the stationary points involved in the cyclization reaction of lactone **(4)** in the presence of one water molecule and in implicit diethyl ether.

4w

$E(RmPW + HF - B95) = -1386.88023042$ a.u.

```
C    −1.17814700    3.89708800   −0.74863400
C    −1.01643300    2.38060300   −0.70917100
C     0.13137900    2.04832100    0.20813700
O    −0.06951700    1.69286000    1.36053100
C    −2.28681300    1.65283800   −0.26099100
C    −3.38479600    1.74543800   −1.29744200
C    −4.69746600    1.07043300   −0.92376100
C    −4.80731500   −0.43609800   −1.13806100
C    −4.24249600   −1.38790700   −0.09473400
O    −2.81022000   −1.49871700   −0.16367200
C    −2.30747500   −2.20455500   −1.18536000
C    −0.84854100   −2.31402300   −1.16477000
C    −0.08361500   −2.05920100   −0.09804600
C     1.34700200   −2.19966000   −0.08703800
C     2.07965000   −2.00313700    1.01753200
```

C	3.52979300	−2.03586500	1.07892200
C	4.32186000	−1.67899100	0.06876100
C	5.80978200	−1.66203300	0.08986600
C	6.41605300	−0.37757000	−0.47643900
C	6.23094100	0.86331900	0.39303200
C	4.81630800	1.12704800	0.77454800
C	3.89785200	1.69985300	−0.00693700
C	2.52732200	1.76886300	0.41396000
C	1.48470500	2.16431900	−0.32762500
O	−2.78973700	2.18868300	0.93544400
C	−4.55452800	−1.01367200	1.33622500
C	−6.04329800	−0.97143000	1.61628300
O	−2.99323500	−2.69558000	−2.04427300
O	5.86091500	−0.06392600	−1.72909000
H	3.86818300	−1.33658200	−0.85237500
H	1.83228400	−2.48156700	−1.01295300
H	3.97258700	−2.30637200	2.03019700
H	1.55495400	−1.79585300	1.94273900
H	4.49694400	0.77134200	1.74550900
H	4.16140500	2.04752200	−0.99663200
H	6.84567700	0.75268900	1.28420500
H	6.63123800	1.69862400	−0.17947100
H	7.49473300	−0.53149800	−0.57657300
H	6.18987700	−1.84182800	1.09554600
H	6.18107200	−2.48901400	−0.52508900
H	2.30287100	1.42431800	1.41622900
H	1.60829700	2.50798800	−1.34473500
H	−0.42636800	−2.68749500	−2.08578800
H	−0.54208000	−1.72968100	0.82480400
H	−4.63603600	−2.37875700	−0.31580900
H	−2.02426700	0.60377700	−0.11617900
H	−3.01445300	1.34527500	−2.24332300
H	−3.59167700	2.80292200	−1.46214400
H	−5.47127000	1.52097200	−1.54504800
H	−4.94754100	1.34300500	0.10085100
H	−4.39388800	−0.71408600	−2.10569400

```
H    −5.86853900   −0.68138800   −1.19856500
H    −0.74825200    2.02835700   −1.70782900
H     6.01427200   −0.79951200   −2.32493100
H    −1.87746000    4.19093200   −1.52656300
H    −1.56213300    4.24730200    0.20535400
H    −0.23029100    4.39317300   −0.94914000
H    −2.12558600    2.01339000    1.60850100
H    −4.07637400   −1.74298900    1.98966400
H    −4.10613600   −0.04515900    1.56239400
H    −6.52294400   −1.91133900    1.34576300
H    −6.22842100   −0.79635600    2.67285700
H    −6.53533800   −0.17511800    1.06118900
H    −0.89385500    0.19561700    2.26442000
O    −1.46664400   −0.52334400    2.54815700
H    −2.03433700   −0.68629700    1.79230900
```

TSw

$E(RmPW + HF − B95) = −1386.84870338$ a.u.

1 imaginary frequency: $−452.5880$ cm^{-1}

```
C    −2.16465800    4.06136700   −0.32175600
C    −1.67336400    2.66750900   −0.66610400
C    −0.37822200    2.35582300    0.03800500
O    −0.33759300    2.51145800    1.26398200
C    −2.64118700    1.55483400   −0.22859300
C    −3.94279100    1.57008600   −0.99414200
C    −4.91075700    0.45903400   −0.61663800
C    −4.58566400   −0.94157000   −1.13596500
C    −3.77821300   −1.89819300   −0.26951900
O    −2.37659400   −1.59923200   −0.25012700
C    −1.66389400   −1.94320300   −1.32201000
C    −0.21995200   −1.75184600   −1.14406500
C     0.35654700   −1.51328400    0.04251600
C     1.76951700   −1.45550300    0.23814800
C     2.30845200   −1.30036200    1.49312900
C     3.66515900   −1.10156000    1.72344800
C     4.57153600   −0.94062500    0.67969000
```

C	6.04035200	−0.73492700	0.88663200
C	6.54045400	−0.15692600	−0.42389600
C	5.52368000	0.89812200	−0.84865200
C	4.23990600	0.80454800	−0.04519400
C	3.00331000	0.88778100	−0.69575400
C	1.86669000	1.46297600	−0.09747300
C	0.70878600	1.80841700	−0.71957200
O	−2.93990000	1.65189100	1.14557200
C	−4.19057200	−1.95154300	1.18379400
C	−5.64863100	−2.31906000	1.37003300
O	−2.14470600	−2.39245700	−2.33110500
O	6.52201600	−1.14093900	−1.43249900
H	4.36824400	−1.47957000	−0.23706400
H	2.40261400	−1.65967400	−0.61256900
H	3.98496100	−0.86257800	2.72914200
H	1.61745100	−1.22329100	2.32212500
H	4.28181600	1.34691100	0.89187700
H	2.94926900	0.60621000	−1.74011100
H	5.93113100	1.90005500	−0.72887300
H	5.32447400	0.75657500	−1.90792900
H	7.54254800	0.26426400	−0.32764200
H	6.22108100	−0.04424100	1.71093300
H	6.55282400	−1.66817600	1.12437300
H	1.92359300	1.68215900	0.96276700
H	0.58186900	1.66807700	−1.78246500
H	0.36080100	−1.92658700	−2.03772900
H	−0.26021500	−1.33980600	0.91404700
H	−3.87529400	−2.88617900	−0.71837700
H	−2.13248700	0.60872800	−0.41524600
H	−3.72542700	1.52140200	−2.06292400
H	−4.43201100	2.52561500	−0.80738900
H	−5.88214600	0.73294000	−1.02751900
H	−5.03790100	0.46339900	0.46483800
H	−4.10233300	−0.88638000	−2.11008800
H	−5.52833500	−1.45979500	−1.31508800
H	−1.53307000	2.57324400	−1.74247200

H	7.16153700	−1.81942700	−1.20795400
H	−3.10194200	4.28147800	−0.82573400
H	−2.32081200	4.15565000	0.74900000
H	−1.43729300	4.81204000	−0.62233700
H	−2.17954400	2.07695300	1.56771000
H	−3.55473200	−2.68087800	1.68344300
H	−3.98169800	−0.98749600	1.64680800
H	−5.88779700	−3.25557500	0.86727900
H	−5.88206800	−2.44158800	2.42467300
H	−6.31205400	−1.55175700	0.97500100
H	−0.41014500	0.82922000	2.33239400
O	−0.81309400	−0.00625100	2.59326800
H	−1.68686000	0.04093600	2.19399200

5w

$E(RmPW + HF − B95) = −1386.91163283$ a.u.

C	−2.22822500	4.12560800	−0.43713100
C	−1.64667700	2.74863000	−0.69083300
C	−0.42394500	2.48984000	0.14635200
O	−0.46421400	2.72234400	1.34574900
C	−2.59632400	1.59778800	−0.28744900
C	−3.74682300	1.43692600	−1.25472800
C	−4.79603000	0.40546600	−0.86335400
C	−4.47448300	−1.06837400	−1.09472800
C	−3.62803600	−1.82479900	−0.08079500
O	−2.22449900	−1.57179100	−0.23663800
C	−1.60416400	−2.24255500	−1.21224800
C	−0.14489100	−2.07517000	−1.21052400
C	0.53719700	−1.51014400	−0.22185200
C	2.02548800	−1.40166700	−0.19033400
C	2.61456100	−2.06052800	1.02648500
C	3.91340300	−1.93398600	1.26522500
C	4.67497400	−1.01988900	0.37355300
C	6.03697300	−0.49855300	0.78033400
C	6.24904800	0.65043900	−0.20333300

C	4.85355300	1.24555400	−0.43328200
C	3.88737800	0.28462600	0.25407700
C	2.50986600	0.08773300	−0.36646000
C	1.51322800	1.02018400	0.21682300
C	0.68675000	1.78594100	−0.49186800
O	−3.11961500	1.82878100	0.99872500
C	−3.94741300	−1.52707700	1.36595300
C	−5.36495600	−1.91482300	1.73736700
O	−2.18350700	−2.93128600	−2.01139800
O	6.67914700	0.16265900	−1.45453700
H	4.77132100	−1.45228200	−0.62857600
H	2.42530200	−1.92592200	−1.06210400
H	4.39065000	−2.42250400	2.10317600
H	1.97151400	−2.66529800	1.64911800
H	3.74272200	0.61988200	1.28375400
H	2.56163500	0.26384300	−1.44075400
H	4.76841800	2.25904700	−0.05031100
H	4.68941100	1.28474300	−1.50826900
H	6.95733700	1.39031600	0.17394200
H	6.00012100	−0.11849200	1.80277000
H	6.83665400	−1.23638600	0.72739100
H	1.40127400	1.00532000	1.29417000
H	0.72595700	1.78478200	−1.57211200
H	0.34420900	−2.51154000	−2.06938600
H	0.00239300	−1.11031000	0.63244400
H	−3.76964300	−2.88622800	−0.27709200
H	−2.00980500	0.67401200	−0.28002100
H	−3.33847000	1.19484900	−2.23737700
H	−4.24616000	2.40123000	−1.34614400
H	−5.68025800	0.62122300	−1.46292800
H	−5.09354200	0.58394000	0.16936700
H	−4.02739800	−1.21343300	−2.07722000
H	−5.42435400	−1.60302000	−1.13156900
H	−1.40335000	2.62368800	−1.74499900
H	7.54460000	−0.23361100	−1.34002700
H	−3.17236400	4.25596500	−0.95834400

```
H   −2.40137200    4.27865000    0.62358900
H   −1.54515500    4.89892400   −0.78068100
H   −2.42574300    2.25589800    1.51652300
H   −3.23700400   −2.07366400    1.98532900
H   −3.79401900   −0.46496400    1.55875000
H   −5.55579900   −2.96532200    1.52195300
H   −5.54158300   −1.75669500    2.79821300
H   −6.09994700   −1.32542400    1.19192400
H   −0.66891400    0.95767800    2.39894300
O   −0.85935500    0.01773000    2.33886300
H   −1.72498500   −0.02341600    1.92696700
```

REFERENCES

[1] MacroModel, version 9.7, 2009. Schrödinger, LLC, New York, NY.

[2] Halgren, T.A., 1996. J. Comp. Chem. 17, 490–519.

[3] **a)** Kolossváry, I., Guida, W.C., 2001. J. Comp. Chem. 22, 21; **b)** Keseru, G.M., Kolossváry, I., 2001. J. Am. Chem. Soc. 123, 12708.

[4] Domingo, L.R., Sáez, J.A., 2009. Org. Biomol. Chem. 7, 3576.

[5] Krenske, E.H., Patel, A., Houk, K.N., 2013. J. Am. Chem. Soc. 135, 17638.

[6] Domingo, L.R., Chamorro, E., Pérez, P., 2010. Org. Biomol. Chem. 8, 5495.

[7] Domingo, L.R., Pérez, P., Sáez, J.A., 2012. Org. Biomol. Chem. 10, 3841.

[8] Silvi, B., 2002. J. Mol. Struct. 614, 3.

[9] Berski, S., Andrés, J., Silvi, B., Domingo, L.R., 2003. J. Phys. Chem. A 107, 6014.

[10] Domingo, L.R., Chamorro, E., Pérez, P., 2010. Lett. Org. Chem. 432.

[11] Domingo, L.R., Sáez, J.A., 2011. J. Org. Chem. 76, 373.

[12] Domingo, L.R., 2014. RSC adv. 4, 25268.

CLAST: Clustering Biological Sequences

10

Vicente Molieri, Lina J. Karam, and Zoé Lacroix

School of Electrical, Computer, and Energy Engineering, Arizona State University, Tempe, AZ, USA

1 INTRODUCTION

Sequence clustering is an important method in the bioinformatics world. Applications of clustering include development of nonredundant databases (Holm and Sander, 1998; Holm et al., 2000; Li and Godzik, 2006), discovery of motifs (Kim and Lee, 2006), identifying patterns of gene expression (Quackenbush, 2001), function prediction and automatic annotation (Fleischmann et al., 2001), and genome assembly (Pertea et al., 2003). Clustering methods typically deal with sequences relating to either messenger RNA (mRNA), complementary DNA (cDNA), proteins, or other special types of sequences such as expressed sequence tags (ESTs) or genome survey sequences (GSSs). In existing bioinformatics clustering methods, alignment is typically used, either as a preprocessing step or as a refinement technique in filtered sets of data. For species where a reference genome is unavailable, a similar species may be used as a guide for clustering. A reference genome is necessary for most clustering methods because sequences are first aligned to the genome to determine the approximate location of that sequence. This global alignment is used to determine which sets of sequences are close to one another on the genome so that they can then be clustered. Clustering can also be used as part of a workflow for alternative splicing analysis (Lacroix et al., 2007). When clustering is used in conjunction with alignment, the robustness of assembly calculations can be improved as well.

Sequence clustering typically follows one of two approaches: (i) partial-order-based graph models or (ii) equivalence-based graph models. Partial-order graphs are those that can be viewed as a hierarchical model, wherein one of the nodes should always precede another in the graph, although the relationship may not apply to all pairs of nodes in the graph. Equivalence-based graphs differ from partial-order graphs by creating symmetric, bidirectional relationships between nodes.

This paper presents a new algorithm, which we refer to as CLustering Any Sequence Tool (CLAST) and which does not require any reference to generate clusters. The proposed CLAST algorithm does not use precomputed alignment information or any other information beyond the sequence data to guide the computation of the clusters.

1.1 RELATED WORK

The use of clustering sequences is not a new concept in bioinformatics. Some existing tools require an alignment, either with or without a reference genome. Several tools have been created to cluster sequences for the purposes of eliminating redundancy in data sets. These types of tools typically work in a partial-order graph-based manner (Holm and Sander, 1998; Holm et al., 2000; Li and Godzik, 2006). Other approaches are equivalence-order graph-based and consist of an all-against-all comparison approach. Equivalence-order methods generally have applications different from the partial-order methods. Equivalence-order methods can have applications in discovery of motifs (Kim and Lee, 2006), function prediction, automatic annotation, and phylogenetics (Fleischmann et al., 2001). In equivalence-order methods, thresholds are developed to "cut" the data sets into clusters based on the weight of the links using a variety of methods. In partial-order-based methods, a set of tests is used to generate subgroups consisting of similar sequences, and then the resultant subgroups are aligned and clustered. In Holm and Sander (1998), a tool is proposed that iteratively filters an input data set of sequences by first grouping all sequences that share a decapeptide, then creating subgroups that share at least 50% pentapeptide composition. Finally, a local alignment using the Smith-Waterman algorithm is computed and a relatively small number of representative sequences is chosen for which all other sequences are at least 90% shared in common with the set of representative sequences. In (Holm et al., 2000), E-values (which correspond to the probability that a given sequence would have a greater alignment score in an alternate alignment due purely to chance) from aligned sequences are used to determine familial relationships. In CD-hit (Li and Godzik, 2006), a filtering hierarchy similar to that used in Holm and Sander (1998) is used. But, in CD-hit, instead of generating a representative sequence in the cluster, the longest existing sequence is used. Metrics in these algorithms can vary, although the use of Z-scores (which correspond to a normalized matching score, measured from the mean) is popular. In Kim and Lee (2006), Z-scores from Monte Carlo simulations based on Smith-Waterman scores are used, while in Fleischmann et al. (2001), Z-scores from pairwise match scoring are used. In Blastclust (Dondoshanky, 2002), a method based on E-values is used to create single-linkage clusters using BLAST and MegaBLAST with default parameters.

In Mounsef et al. (2008), a method of hashing is introduced for use in an assembly tool. The hashing method is used to reduce computational complexity of the assembly process. The method proposed in Mounsef et al. (2008) generates hashes by first padding sequences of variable lengths so that all are the length of the longest sequence in the data set, and then a random number vector is used to generate a single number per sequence in the data set.

In Tarjanb et al. (2004), a method of clustering using graph cuts is proposed for use in clustering of topics on Internet websites. The approach presented in that paper is unique in that it introduces the concept of a sink node in contrast to the source node (representing the data set) which is linked to all sequences in the data set with a certain weight. Minimum cuts are then calculated, and all cuts that are under a certain threshold (which is related to the weight of the introduced links to the sink node) are cut (taken to be zero). This edge-weight-based approach is used to generate a set of clusters that are more related to one another than they are to the sink node (which represents random chance; i.e., the resultant clusters are linked by more than just chance). In Quackenbush (2001), an overview of clustering approaches for analyzing gene expression data is presented. In addition, a hierarchical clustering scheme is presented which uses pairwise distance matrices to cluster the two "closest" clusters together (initially, all sequences in the data set belong to their own single-sequence cluster) based on a distance metric, and this process is repeated until clusters can no longer be merged. Furthermore, a k-means clustering algorithm is presented. But because the final number of clusters is not usually known beforehand, a principal component analysis (PCA) is used as preinformation to estimate the number of clusters to be generated. The final algorithm presented in Quackenbush (2001) is a self-organizing map, which is an iterative approach is similar to k-means clustering, which converges based on the intercluster and intracluster distance metrics. In Diaz-Uriarte and de Andres (2006), random forests are used on gene expression data to identify sets of genes that can be useful in clinical diagnostics.

2 METHODS

The methodology presented in this chapter aims to provide the ability to work independent of any data besides the sequence itself. The ability to work independent of precomputed or supplemental information (such as annotations, alignment, or a reference genome) beyond the actual sequence itself is important because, although this information is often useful, it may be incomplete or incorrect. Because the proposed algorithm has been designed not to use any supplemental information, the algorithm does not use it. The algorithm presented in this paper works in three steps: (i) hashing, (ii) matching and (iii) clustering. Details about each of these three steps are provided next.

2.1 HASHING

The hashing step of the algorithm generates a set of hash IDs for all sequences in the data set. The number of hash IDs generated for a given sequence will be equal to the length of the sequence less the size of the hashing window. Methods using a similar concept of hashing exist in computer science–based applications (Mounsef et al., 2008). Hashing in this work is meant to encompass the idea of representing multiple data points (in this case, nucleobases) with a single point (a hash ID). In this work, a block is used to denote a subsequence of nucleobases to be put into a single hash ID. Hashing is then done in the algorithm by generating a vector of random numbers equal to the length of the block, performing a pointwise multiplication, and then summing all the results to generate a single hash ID as follows:

$$ID[j] = \sum_{i=0}^{\ell-1} X[i+j]*h[i] \tag{10.1}$$

where j is the start position of the rectangular window within a sequence, ℓ is the length of the window and of the hashing vector, X is the sequence, and h is the hashing vector of random numbers. This operation is akin to a common signal processing operation known as *multiplication and accumulation*. Once the hash ID is computed, the window is slid forward by one nucleobase and the process is repeated until all possible hash IDs have been computed (when the end of the sequence X is reached). This operation is equivalent to an operation referred to in signal processing as *convolution*. Consolidating information into a single point enables faster searches for matching than pairwise nucleobase matching as is done in typical biological sequence alignment algorithms.

Given the sparse nature of the data (with only four unique characters in nucleotide sequences: A, C, G, T), it is essential to evaluate the data across multiple points in order to reduce the number of biologically meaningless matches. Additionally, false positives in the system (instances where a matching hash ID exists when a matching sequence does not) are reduced with longer hash windows. In our implementation, 32-bit floating point numbers are used in the hashing vector. Using a window of size 31 with four unique nucleobases and 32-bit floating point numbers yields a probability of false positives of approximately 1e-9. It should also be noted that the generation of a false positive hash ID will not necessarily yield an error in the final clustering result. Conversely, sequenced data have numerous atypical points, such as single-nucleotide polymorphisms (SNPs), deletions, insertions or gaps, which make it essential to choose a length of hash that is sufficiently small so that these atypical data points do not mask biologically significant matches between sequences. With a properly chosen hash size, this algorithm design is robust to SNPs, insertions, deletions, gaps, and other such atypical data points (that is, points other than A, C, G, and T) in low quantities. A sequence with a high proportion of atypical data points, SNPs or indels may not be clustered correctly by this algorithm. The choice of a proper hash size is empirical and can depend on the data set; the choice of the default length in the algorithm is discussed in section 3 of this chapter. The length is the only adaptable parameter of the hashing portion of the algorithm. The hashing vector must be the same for all data analyzed in a data set for the hash IDs to be comparable. The pseudocode for the algorithmic creation of hash IDs is shown in Algorithm 10.1.

2.2 MATCHING

Matching is done by comparing all hash IDs from a given sequence with all hash IDs from all other sequences. Comparing all elements of an unsorted vector to all other elements is an $O(N^2)$ problem, with N equal to the number of hash IDs generated, which approaches the number of nucleobases in the data set as the size of the data set increases. The concept of matching hash IDs at the sequence level is demonstrated in Figure 10.1. In this figure, the black boxes correspond to matching hash IDs, while the thinner lines correspond to mismatches. In the example shown in Figure 10.1, the second nucleobase of Sequence B represents a SNP (relative to Sequence A) and the seventh and eighth nucleobases in Sequence A have been deleted when

Input: hashsize : size of hash vector
hasharray : vector of random numbers ∈ [0, 1] with length=hashsize
S : class with elements sequence (string)
Output: X : vector of hashid class which has elements hash,
sequenceID, startPosition
count=0
for *i=0 to |S|* **do**
    for *j=0 to |S[i].sequence|* **do**
        sum=0
        for *k=0 to hashsize* **do**
            sum+=S[i].sequence[j+k]*hasharray[k]
        end
        X[count].hash=sum
        X[count].sequenceID=i
        X[count].startingPosition=j
        count++
    end
end

ALGORITHM 10.1

Hashing.

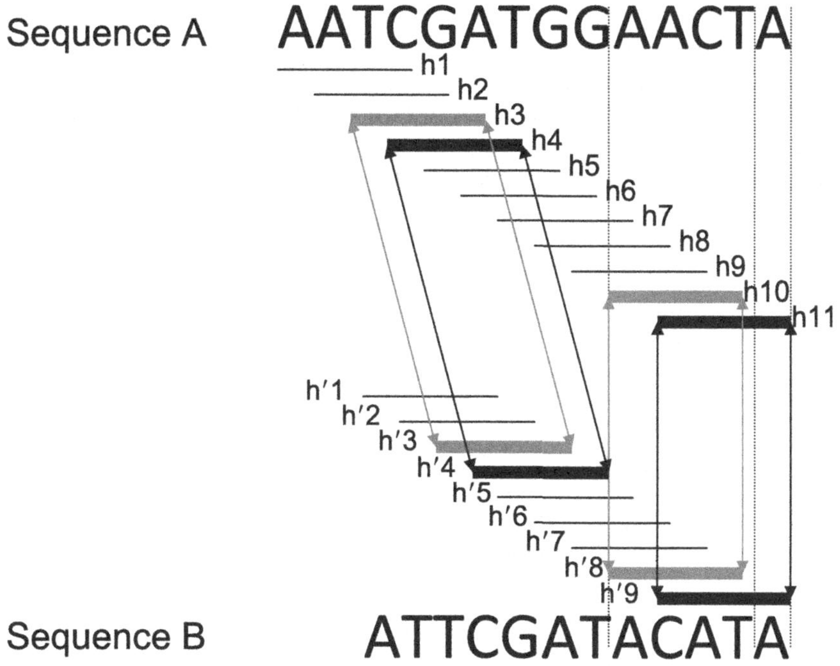

FIGURE 10.1

Example of a matching process. Hash IDs represented by a black box denote cases where a match was found between the two sequences. Hash IDs represented by a thin line find no match between the two sequences. Arrows are used to show the two linked hash IDs.

forming Sequence B. While the deletion has been shown explicitly for illustration purposes, this algorithm does not require prealignment; instead, two fewer hash IDs would
be generated for the second sequence than for the first sequence. As shown in
Figure 10.1, the matching hash IDs can be used to develop a concept of alignment
in the algorithm, as matching hash IDs correspond to 100% matching of the
corresponding sequence blocks, but this process is different than the pairwise distance
measurements typically used in alignment algorithms. This algorithm has been
designed to be much faster than $O(N^2)$, approximating more closely $O(N \log_2 N)$
operations. This has been done by first sorting the hash IDs by value, and then finding
ranges of positions for which the hash IDs are identical. For ranges of data that have the
same hash ID, information about the sequences is stored, creating equivalent symmetric links between the two sequences (i.e., A↔B rather than A→B and B→A). The C++
standard library sort function is used to sort the hash IDs by value. On average, the sort
has been determined to be $O(N \log_2 N)$, while the determination of ranges of consecutive matches requires a single exhaustive search of the sorted array, which is $O(N)$,
ignoring operations that take place once the ranges of indices are determined. Thus, the
final algorithm is $O(N (1+\log_2 N))$, which, as N becomes very large, is approximately
$O(N \log_2 N)$.

The matching algorithm is shown in Algorithm 10.2. This process is used to identify sets of matches between two sequences. Matching yields a two-dimensional (2D)
matrix of relationships between all sequences in the data set, and that matrix is
diagonally symmetric due to the creation of symmetric links. The resulting matrix
represents a graph of nodes and edges. In such a graph, nodes represent sequences
and edges represent a metric of relatedness, which, at this step of the algorithm, is the
number of matching hash IDs between the two considered sequences. Figure 10.2

Input: X : vector of hashid class which has elements hash, sequenceID,
          startPosition
Output: Y : vector of class with element vectors netmatches, locations
```
count=0
count2=0
repeat
    count=count2
    repeat
        count2++
    until X[count2].hash!=X[count2+1].hash
    for i=count to count2 do
        for j=count to count2 do
            Y[X[i].sequenceID].netmatches[j]++
            Y[X[j].sequenceID].netmatches[i]++
            push X[i].startPosition onto
            Y[X[i].sequenceID].locations[j]
            push X[j].startPosition onto
            Y[X[j].sequenceID].locations[i]
        end
    end
until count2>= |X|
```

ALGORITHM 10.2

Matching.

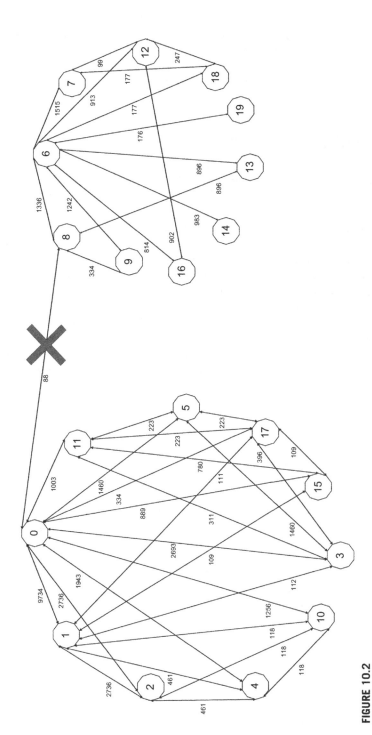

FIGURE 10.2

Graph representation. Nodes represent sequences and edges represent relations. The weight on an edge corresponds to the number of matching nucleotides between the sequences that are linked by that edge. The red cross (X) denotes the link to be cut.

specifically shows two groups of 10 sequences each, synthesized from data that originated from two separate genes (i.e., the two groups). The link between the two groups likely represents some sort of structural information shared between two mRNA sequences and serves as the basis for the need of the third clustering step to establish meaningful clusters.

2.3 CLUSTERING

We adopt the concept of a sink node based on the ideas presented in Tarjanb *et al.* (2004). Due to the computational complexity of minimum graph-based cuts algorithms, our algorithm was simplified to increase efficiency (which is necessary when dealing with large data sets as in bioinformatics applications) by removing the notion of paths and instead focusing exclusively on intersequence linkages. A relationship metric has been introduced with the goal of discerning biologically significant links from biologically insignificant links. In this case, biologically insignificant links are taken to be links that relate to random chance, structural information, repeats, and other similar phenomena that do not necessarily imply that sequences belong to the same gene, while biologically significant links are defined as links that indicate two sequences belonging to the same cluster (gene). The proposed relation metric (RM) is set to be the number of matching nucleobases divided by the minimum of the total number of nucleobases in the two sequences. This metric is a matching percentage that denotes how related any two sequences are and it can be expressed as:

$$RM(i,j) = \frac{\text{\# matching nucleobases}}{\min\left(\ell_{S_i}, \ell_{S_j}\right)} \tag{10.2}$$

where i and j are indices relating to the two considered sequences S_i and S_j, and ℓ_{S_i} and ℓ_{S_j} are the length of the sequences S_i and S_j, respectively. Given the result of the matching algorithm, this metric can be calculated for all links between any two sequences. The calculation of these matching percentages will again yield a diagonally symmetric matrix that represents a graph of nodes and edges, though edges have now been weighted according to the new metric of relatedness. The practical utility of this metric is illustrated in example where Sequence A consists of 120 nucleobases, Sequence B consists of 900 sequences, and Sequence C and Sequence D consist of 10,000 nucleobases each. Sequence A shares 100 of its 120 nucleobases with Sequence B, while Sequence C shares 200 nucleobases with Sequence D. In this case, a metric using only the number of matching nucleobases is problematic, and true meaning is seen only in how much of a sequence is shared between two sequences (i.e., a proportion). Between any two sequences of differing lengths, however, there are two proportions that exist in terms of the number of shared nucleobases, one for the proportion of the first sequence and one for the proportion of the second sequence. In this example, the important information is that 100 of the 120 nucleobases in Sequence A are shared with Sequence B, rather than the fact that 100 of the 900 nucleobases of Sequence B are shared with Sequence A because this likely indicates that Sequence A is a subsequence of Sequence B.

To develop clusters from the matrix, the first sequence in the data set is used as a seed cluster, and then sequences are added to a cluster if they have a match (weighted edge) above a specified threshold to any of the other sequences in the cluster. If the computed metric is below that threshold, it is seen as zero and will not be added to the cluster. If no matches exist for a given sequence, a new cluster is created for that sequence. Since some matches will not be found until later in the algorithm, clusters are also merged as necessary. The algorithm for clustering is shown in Algorithms 10.3 and 10.4. These algorithms prepare a matrix containing values for weighted edges between all nodes in the data set (with weighted edges below the specified clustering threshold being set to zero). This matrix can be used to generate the final graph. It is worth noting that if Sequence A belongs to a cluster and Sequence B shares a biologically significant link with Sequences A and C, even if Sequences A and C do not share a biologically significant link, all three sequences will be clustered together since B shares significant links with both (this is a reasonable solution given the intended application of alternative splicing). Thus, it is possible that any set of two sequences may have a low amount of shared nucleobases, but within the cluster, there must be a path between the two wherein all edge weights are above the specified clustering threshold of the clustering algorithm.

3 EVALUATION AND DISCUSSION

Transcript sequences have been retrieved from BIPASS (Lacroix *et al.*, 2007). While the method in BIPASS relies on the use of a published genome to perform the mapping and clustering of transcripts, the no-reference clustering approach proposed in this chapter clusters transcripts without the need for any additional genomic information. CLAST was implemented in C++ and compiled into an executable code

```
Input: X : vector of class with element vectors netmatches, 2-D
          connectivity matrix (graph) and element sequence (sequence)
       threshold : metric used to cut graph for clustering
Output: X: input with modified graph element
for i=0 to |X| do
    for j=0 to |X| do
        RM=X[i].netmatches[j]/min(|X[i].sequence|,|X[j].sequence|)
        if RM>threshold then
            | X[i].graph[j]=RM
        else
            | X[i].graph[j] = 0
        
    end
end
count=0
flag=false
```

ALGORITHM 10.3

Clustering, Part 1.

```
for i=0 to |X| do
    clear tocluster
    clear clusterlocations
    for j=i to |X| do
        if X[i].graph!=0 then
        |    push j onto tocluster

    end
    for j=0 to |Y| do
        for k=0 to |tocluster| do
            search=binarysearch for tocluster[k] in Y[j]
            if search!=false and flag!=false then
            |    push j onto clusterlocations
            |    flag=true

        end
        flag=false
    end
    if |clusterlocations|==0 then
        add new cluster
        for j=0 to |tocluster| do
        |    push tocluster[j] onto Y[count]sequenceIDs
        end
        count++
    else if |clusterlocations|==1 then
        for j=0 to |tocluster| do
            search=binarysearch for tocluster[j] in
            Y[clusterlocations[0]].sequenceIds
            if search==false then
                push tocluster[j] onto
                Y[clusterlocations[0]].sequenceIDs
                sort Y[clusterlocations[0]].sequenceIDs

        end
    else
        for j=0 to |tocluster| do
            if search==false then
                push tocluster[j] onto
                Y[clusterlocations[0]].sequenceIDs
                sort Y[clusterlocations[0]].sequenceIDs

        end
        for j=1 to |clusterlocations| do
            for k=0 to |Y[clusterlocations[j]].sequenceIDs| do
                search=binarysearch for
                Y[clusterlocations[j]].sequenceIDs[k] in
                Y[clusterlocations[0]].sequenceIDs
                if search==false then
                    push tocluster[j] onto
                    Y[clusterlocations[0]].sequenceIDs
                    sort Y[clusterlocations[0]].sequenceIDs

            end
        end
        for j=|clusterlocations|-1 to 0 do
        |    erase clusters[j]
        |    count–
        end

end
```

ALGORITHM 10.4

Clustering, Part 2.

for testing on a standard desktop PC running Linux. The threshold value used was 0.41000, and the hash size value (hash window value) was 31 in all tested cases (the choice of these values will be discussed in detail later in this chapter). For all tested data sets, the clustering execution time ranged from less than one second to 50 seconds.

The transcript sequences of 44 genes of the human organism or *Homo sapiens* (Hs) were retrieved from BIPASS with the queries *kinase, collegenase,* and *transcription factor,* as shown in Table 10.1. These data sets of single genes are referred to as *single-gene sets (SGS).* From those transcript sequences, we generated 25 data sets for testing containing a subset of the 44 SGS, denoted as *multigene sets (MGS).* Table 10.2 presents the SGS composition of the MGS data sets. As shown in Table 10.2, each MGS contains transcripts from more than one gene. Data sets MGS_1 to MGS_{17} were formed by selecting genes from Table 10.1. In order to test the overlapping gene case, we created the data sets MGS_{18} to MGS_{25} which were formed by merging transcripts from clusters corresponding to overlapping genes. For example, MGS_{18} is composed of genes *DLG4* and *ACADVL* which overlap head-to-head (Zhou and Blumberg, 2003). Similarly, gene *TOE1* has overlapping exons with *MUTYH* at the $5'$-end and with *TESK2* at the $3'$-end (Veeramachaneni *et al.,* 2004). This was done to evaluate the robustness of the proposed CLAST algorithm when there is an overlap between genes. In Table 10.2, SGS data sets that CLAST was unable to cluster into a single cluster are highlighted in pink, and the SGS data sets that were added to address the overlapping genes question are highlighted in blue. Some of the genes added to address the overlapping genes question were unable to be grouped into a single cluster by CLAST and are thus highlighted in both applicable colors.

To evaluate the proper default values for the variable parameters in the algorithm (hash size and threshold) during development, training data sets were evaluated by the algorithm over a range of values for both hash size and threshold until the algorithm returned the expected clusters (both in terms of the number of clusters and the content of the clusters). To develop the data sets used in this evaluation, sets of clusters were extracted from BIPASS and, using the exonic information, sequences were randomly constructed by splicing together exons in a biologically realistic fashion. These data sets represent a set of genes, each with a set of sequences that have undergone simple alternative splicing events. Although the values were determined empirically during development using a different training data set, testing was done during evaluation of the algorithm to assess the validity of the previously chosen values. It should be noted that in determining the expected number of clusters for any complex data set, it was necessary to account for the presence of the simpler data sets that the algorithm was unable to cluster correctly individually, so that sometimes the expected number of clusters in this evaluation was greater than the number of genes in the data set. Figure 10.3 shows the variation of the number of clusters found by the algorithm using MGS_{25}, which contains all genes used in the evaluation of this algorithm. In Figure 10.3, the impact of both the hash size and the threshold is clearly demonstrated. It is important to note the situation where the number of clusters remained steadily at the number of expected clusters over a short range of hash sizes at a given threshold (57 clusters, in this case). This condition is what we refer to as a

Table 10.1 MGS Formed by Combining Transcripts from Two or More BIPASS Clusters

Gene	Chromosome	# of Transcripts	Min length (bp)	Max length (bp)	Avg length (bp)
SRY (SOX15)	17	11	361	1788	1116
CD53	1	5	186	1572	864
AURKAIP1	1	29	107	3078	981
PLOD1	1	25	413	3004	715
SERPINH1	11	121	266	3390	641
CKB	14	155	66	1431	408
PKM2	15	55	110	2674	820
Chromosome 15 Genomic contig	15	17	533	4515	1640
HMOX2	16	22	101	1644	571
CDK3	17	8	487	3287	968
CAMK2N1	1	14	97	2371	375
CALM3	19	19	412	2537	799
COL7A1	3	2	600	9272	4936
CCNG1 variant 1	5	9	412	2484	997
CSNK2B	6	16	99	1128	515
PCOLCE	7	19	328	1510	583
IKBKB	8	20	510	3916	1050
PALM2-AKAP2	9	18	501	7522	1938
PGK1	X	14	536	2338	908
DLG4	17	2	214	3995	2104
ACADVL	17	59	92	2320	609
MUTYH	1	6	1710	1936	1830
TOE1	1	6	518	2173	1272
TESK2	1	2	3050	3093	3071
FCRL3	1	4	2229	3019	2597
PTPRF	11	17	1612	5227	2597
ITGA5	12	97	369	4267	623
EGRFP8	12	23	528	3887	703
CLEC1A	12	6	342	2701	1520
TNFRSF1A	12	67	269	2236	596
NR4A1	12	32	290	3513	843
NARG2	15	15	490	7209	2122
TRAP1	16	40	81	2309	794
RPSA	3	83	83	2058	509
GPR78	4	13	554	5390	1933
TRC8	5	3	1940	3362	2621
PDGFRB	5	5	564	5718	1632
IGF2R	6	9	91	9090	1301
OPRD1	1	2	1177	1774	1475
EPB41	1	7	2486	6369	4194
RPL34	4	99	79	2628	232
H4SN	4	2	450	579	514
LIXIL	1	4	579	3834	2281
TXNIP	1	45	302	2704	679

Note: Each of the 44 genes represents one SGS. Genes highlighted in pink (light gray in print version) were not clustered by CLAST into a single cluster.

Table 10.2 Gene Sequences Retrieved from BIPASS with Associated Statistics

Gene	MGS01	MGS02	MGS03	MGS04	MGS05	MGS06	MGS07	MGS08	MGS09	MGS10	MGS11	MGS12	MGS13	MGS14	MGS15	MGS16	MGS17	MGS18	MGS19	MGS20	MGS21	MGS22	MGS23	MGS24	MGS25
SRY (SOX15)	X				X												X							X	X
CD53	X				X											X	X								X
AURKAIP1							X								X	X	X								X
PLOD1						X									X	X									X
SERPINH1					X	X							X												X
CKB					X	X								X		X									X
PKM2												X	X	X		X									X
Chromosome 15 genomic contig						X					X	X	X	X		X									X
HMOX2						X					X		X	X		X									X
CDK3						X		X								X									X
CAMK2N1						X										X	X								X
CALM3						X																			X
COL7A1						X		X								X									X
CCNG1 variant 1						X		X								X									X
CSNK2B			X	X	X		X	X	X		X	X	X	X		X									X
PCOLCE			X	X	X		X	X		X	X	X	X	X		X									X
IKBKB			X	X	X		X			X	X	X	X	X	X	X									X
PALM2-AKAP2	X			X	X		X				X	X	X	X	X	X									X
PGK1	X			X	X		X				X	X	X	X		X		X							X
DLG4																		X	X						
ACADVL																		X	X						
MUTYH																				X		X			
TOE1																					X	X	X		X
TESK2																				X		X	X		
FCRL3																									X
PTPRF																									X
TGA5																									X
EGRFP8																									X
CLEC1A																									X
TNFRSF1A																									X
NR4A1																									X
NARG2																									X
TRAP1																									X
RPSA																									X
GPR78																									X
TRC8																									X
PDGFRB																									X
IGF2R																									X
OPRD1																								X	X
EPB41																								X	X
RPL34																								X	X
H4SN																								X	X
LIXIL																								X	X
TXNIP																								X	X

Note: The 44 genes listed on the top row each represents one SGS. Genes highlighted in pink (light gray in print version) were not cluster by CLAST into a single cluster. The gene composition of each MGS listed in the first column is shown in each corresponding row. MGS highlighted in blue (dark gray in print version) contain genes which are overlapping.

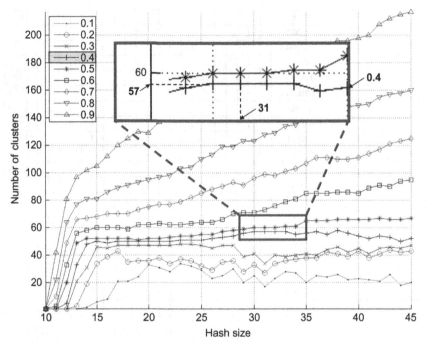

FIGURE 10.3

Number of clusters found by the algorithm for a given hash size and threshold. The boxed area is the point at which the expected number of clusters is found. When examined in greater detail, the data within the box computes the expected number of clusters (57) at a threshold of .4 and a hash size of 30–33.

steady-state solution, and this solution shows empirically that in the data sets evaluated, the default sizes chosen during development were optimal and provided a margin in both hash size and threshold choice. The values chosen during development and which were used in testing were a default hash size of 31 and a default threshold of .41000 when performing nucleotide clustering.

We first ran CLAST against each of the data sets described in Table 10.1. CLAST resulted in one cluster for each data set in 35 of the 44 SGS data sets from Table 10.1, while the other 10 genes produced more than the single expected cluster. One such scenario is presented in Figure 10.4. This is an interesting scenario where two distinct clusters of several sequences of high similarity exist, with two additional sequences (indicated by arrows) that would optimally link the two clusters together. The two sequences that have been clustered into a separate cluster contain a high proportion of DNA characters other than A, C, G, and T, which the algorithm treats as SNPs and thus treats the sequences as dissimilar. In all of the nine cases in which more than one cluster was found per gene, the failure to create one cluster stems from a high degree of sequence mismatch relative to the threshold being used. This can be introduced due to too few large sequences being shared or due to a large number of SNPs or

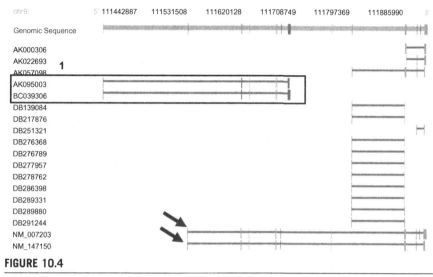

FIGURE 10.4

The *PALM2-AKAP2* gene cluster as visualized in BIPASS (Lacroix *et al.*, 2007). Only the vertical bars are part of the actual sequence, and the gaps exist as a result of alignment to the genome. The boxed sequences form a separate cluster from the rest of the data set due to the high proportion of SNPs in the two sequences.

DNA characters other than A, C, G, and T that are present in the transcript. Though CLAST is robust to some SNPs in a transcript, the proportions in these test sequences were too numerous for CLAST (a conservative approach) to still cluster the sequences correctly. Using postprocessing, it is likely that these clusters could be corrected by either using a lower threshold on small clusters, or using consensus voting to combine smaller clusters with a high degree of matching that did not meet the inital threshold.

The second testing phase was conducted against data sets MGS_1 to MGS_{25} and resulted in the expected clusters that match the original BIPASS clusters in number and in clustered sequences, except for those data sets that include transcripts from the genes highlighted in pink in Table 10.1 (SGS 6, 11, 18, 21, 25, 27, 34, 35 and 41), for which CLAST gives extra clusters as previously discussed. In this latter case, except for the extra clusters produced by these last nine gene clusters, the remaining resulting clusters match according to the annotations as well as the clustering as expected by BIPASS. Note that CLAST produced the expected results for MGS_{21} to MGS_2, which contain the transcripts of 11 overlapping genes.

The third testing phase included comparisons of CLAST to Blastclust (Dondoshanky, 2002) and CD-hit (Li and Godzik, 2006). Blastclust (version 2.2.21) and CD-hit-EST (a version of the algorithm presented in Li and Godzik, 2006) are standard algorithms used in the field to cluster nucleotide sequences and/or amino acid sequences. Like CLAST, these algorithms do not use a reference genome to perform clustering. Blastclust and CD-hit often provided poor results at the default values, and testing was done for these algorithms across a range of values that were seen as most analogous to those used in CLAST as well, though that did not seem to improve the results of these tools significantly (results not shown). The default values used for each tool during the evaluation are given in Table 10.3. The results of the computations using each tool's default values are given in Tables 10.4 and 10.5. As shown in Table 10.4, CLAST is much more effective at clustering the SGS data sets into fewer clusters (in all SGS data sets, ideally only one cluster will be discovered). In the complex MGS data sets, CLAST continues to cluster sequences correctly, accounting for the inaccuracies of the SGS clustering results. Blastclust does perform some clustering, but does not link many sequences from the same gene, and while CD-hit seems more successful in linking sequences from the gene, it is still not as successful as CLAST. For MGS_{25}, Blastclust and CD-hit generated hundreds of clusters when only 44 were expected (with sequences per cluster ranging from 2 to 155). CLAST generated the expected 57 clusters (44 plus the 13 excess clusters known from the SGS data-set tests). Results for the sequences for Fugu were more approximately equal. Since Fugu contains fewer sequences per cluster than do the MGS data sets, this suggests that Blastclust and CD-hit decrease in

Table 10.3 Default Values for Tools Used in Evaluation

Data sets \ Tool names	Evaluation Tool's Default Parameters			
	CLAST	**Blastclust**	**CD-hit-est**	**Uicluster2**
Default word size/ window size	H=31	W=32	n=8	H=8
Default matching-like threshold	T=0.41	L=0.9	c=0.9	M=40

Table 10.4 Cluster Results

Data sets \ Tool names	# of Experimental Clusters Obtained				Expected # of clusters in reference BIPASS
	CLAST	**Blastclust**	**CD-hit-est**	**uicluster2**	
44 independent datasets=44 clusters	1<#<4	1<#<37	1<#<16	0	1
MGS25	57 (44+13)	402	179	0	44
Fugu CoreNucleotide (1094 sequences)	471	518	568	440	N.A.
Fugu Core +dbEST (27163 sequences)	N.A.	15254	13742	10728	2094

Table 10.5 Execution Time Results

Data sets \ Tool names	Running Time in Seconds			
	CLAST	**Blastclust**	**CD-hit-est**	**uicluster2**
44 independent datasets = 44 clusters	$0.5 < T < 10$	$0.1 < t < 1.02$	$0.0005 < t < 0.317$	<1
MGS25	50	1.82	3.34	<1
Fugu CoreNucleotide (1094 sequences)	27.89	1.17	3.06	11
Fugu Core + dbEST (27163 sequences)	N.A.	62.52	50	219

accuracy as data is added, while CLAST increases in accuracy as data sets become more populated. As shown in Table 10.5, CLAST is computationally more expensive when running these tests, requiring 27.89 s to run the Fugu sequences, as opposed to the 1.17 s of blastClust or the 3.06 s of CD-hit-EST. However, it is important to note that the CLAST algorithm evaluated in this paper is an unoptimized developmental version.

4 CONCLUSIONS

This paper presents a no-reference hash-based clustering algorithm that outperforms existing no-reference techniques. The proposed CLAST algorithm incorporates a novel relation metric in order to assess the degree of matching between pairs of sequences. For this purpose, CLAST represents the input sequences as nodes on a graph with the weighted edges on the graph corresponding to links between sequences with matching nucleotides. Relatively low values of the weighted graph edges are removed (cut) from the graph, resulting in the final clusters. CLAST has been tested on real sequences and demonstrated its ability to produce biologically significant clusters. CLAST also generates information in a manner that makes it extremely easy to update clusters with minimal processing time (clusters do not need to be recomputed), including merging clusters, adding to existing clusters, and creating new clusters. Future work includes optimizing CLAST to improve time and memory usage, adopting CLAST in building efficient genomic applications including querying and updating genomic databases, as well as an expansion into alternative splicing applications. Indeed, the population of sequence databases such as BIPASS (Lacroix *et al.*, 2007) relies on generating clusters, and any update requires executing the clustering workflow (Lacroix and Legendre, 2008), recomputing all the clusters, and populating a new database. A method such as CLAST could be used to populate the database and update it without having to generating the whole database from scratch as is currently done. Moreover, it could support online submission of new transcripts and identifying which cluster they belong to.

ACKNOWLEDGMENTS

Funding: This research was partially supported by the National Science Foundation[1] (Grants IIS 0431174, IIS 0551444, IIS 0612273, IIS 0738906, IIS 0832551, and CNS 0849980, and several REU grants). We thank Naji Mounsef for sharing his hash-based approach for sequence assembly and prototype implemented in MatLab (Mounsef *et al.*, 2008). We thank Christophe Legendre and Ruben Acuña for helping to supervise the undergraduate students Matthew Land, Ben J. Piorkowski, and Christopfer Watson, who put the tool to the test. We also acknowledge Louiqa Raschid and Ben Snyder for their contribution to BIPASS.

REFERENCES

Diaz-Uriarte, R., de Andres, S.A., 2006. Gene selection and classification of microarray data using random forest. BMC Bioinformatics. 7(3).

Dondoshanky, I., 2002. Blastclust (NCBI Software Development Toolkit), Bethesda MD.

Fleischmann, W., Zdobnov, E.M., Kriventseva, E.V., Apweiler, R., 2001. CluSTr: a database of clusters of SWISS-PROT+TrEMBL proteins. Nucleic Acids Res. 29 (1), 33–36.

Holm, L., Sander, C., 1998. Removing near-neighbor redundancy from large protein sequence collections. Bioinformatics 14 (5), 423–429.

Holm, L., Heger, A., Park, J., Chothia, C., 2000. RSDB: representative protein sequence databases have high information content. Bioinformatics 16 (5), 458–464.

Kim, S., Lee, J., 2006. BAG: a fast program for clustering and sequencing large sets of protein or nucleotide sequences. Int. J. Data Min. Bioinformatics 1 (2), 178–200.

Lacroix, Z., Legendre, C., 2008. BIPASS: Design of Alternative Splicing Services. Int. J. Comput. Biol. Drug Des. 1 (2), 200–217.

Lacroix, Z., Legendre, C., Raschid, L., Snyder, B., 2007. BIPASS: Bioinformatics Pipelines Alternative Splicing Services. Nucleic Acids Res. 35, (Suppl. 2), W292–W296 (Web Server issue).

Li, W., Godzik, A., 2006. Cd-hit: a fast program for clustering and comparing large sets of protein or nucleotide sequences. Bioinformatics 22 (13), 1658–1659.

Mounsef, N., Karam, L.J., Lacroix, Z., Legendre, C., 2008. A low-complexity probabilistic genome assembly based on hashing. In: IEEE International Workshop on Genomic Signal Processing and Statistics (GENSiPS), pp. 1–4.

Pertea, G., et al., 2003. TIGR gene indices clustering tools (TGICL): a software system for fast clustering of large EST dataset. Bioinformatics 19 (5), 651–652.

Quackenbush, J., 2001. Computational analysis of microarray data. Nat. Rev. Genomics 2 (6), 385–408.

Tarjanb, R.E., Flake, G.W., Tsioutsiouliklis, K., 2004. Graph clustering and minimum cut trees. Internet Math. 1 (4), 385–408.

Veeramachaneni, V., Makalowski, W., Galdzicki, M., Sood, R., Makalowska, I., 2004. Mammalian Overlapping Genes: The Comparative Perspective. Genome Research 14 (2), 280–286.

Zhou, C., Blumberg, B., 2003. Overlapping gene structure of human VLCAD and DLG4. Gene 305 (2), 161–166.

---

[1] Any opinion, finding, and conclusion or recommendation expressed in this material are those of the authors and do not necessarily reflect the views of the National Science Foundation.

Computational Platform for Integration and Analysis of MicroRNA Annotation

11

Mariana Yuri Sasazaki and Joaquim Cezar Felipe

Department of Computing and Mathematics, Faculty of Philosophy, Sciences, and Languages of Ribeirão Preto, University of São Paulo at Ribeirão Preto, Ribeirão Preto, SP, Brazil

1 INTRODUCTION

MicroRNA (miRNA) consists of small, noncoding RNA genes that are about 25 nt long and are found in several organisms, which regulate the expression of target genes by binding to complementary regions of messenger transcripts to repress their translation or to regulate degradation. MiRNAs are highly conserved across species and have crucial functions in the regulation of important processes, such as development, proliferation, differentiation, apoptosis, and metabolism. An aberrant expression of miRNAs has been associated with the pathogenesis of several diseases, such as cancer (Ambros, 2004; Ferracin and Negrini, 2012; Esquela-Kerscher and Slack, 2006).

It is usual to explore meaningful molecular targets and infer new functions of genes through gene functional similarity measuring, specially using gene ontology (GO) (Gene Ontology Consortium, 2015). However, few studies are available in this field for miRNA genes due to limited miRNA functional annotations. On the other hand, it is known that two genes (including miRNA genes) that present similar functions are often associated with similar diseases, and the relationship of different diseases can also be represented by a structure of a directed acyclic graph (DAG), such as Medical Subject Headings (MeSH; U.S. National Library of Medicine, 2015).

A well-known database of miRNA annotation utilized by researchers from the biomedical area is miRBase (miRBase, 2015). It contains published information about miRNAs, such as sequences and annotations, as well as the species and the family to which they belong. In addition, this database allows the registration of names and new miRNAs considering standardization. The information in miRBase is frequently updated, and its current version contains more than 24,000 precursors of miRNAs and more than 30,000 mature miRNAs of 206 different species.

Other relevant miRNA databases that can be cited are as follows:

- *MicroRNA.org*: A comprehensive resource of microRNA target predictions and expression profiles. Target predictions are based on a development of the miRanda algorithm that incorporates current biological knowledge on target rules and on the use of an up-to-date compendium of mammalian miRNAs. MiRNA expression profiles are derived from a comprehensive sequencing project of a large set of mammalian tissues and cell lines of normal and disease origin (Betel *et al.*, 2008).
- *MiRNA—Target Gene Prediction at EMBL:* Contains a file with all miRNA—Target Gene Predictions for *Drosophila* miRNA. The file is structured as registers of predicted miRNA/gene pairs with the following categories: miRNA, CG-ID, gene name, Flybase-ID, validated or predicted untranslated region (UTR), score of best site, total score of all sites, number of sites (Brennecke *et al.*, 2005).
- *MicroCosm Targets (formerly miRBase Targets):* A web resource developed by the Enright Lab at the EMBL-EBI containing computationally predicted targets for miRNA across many species. The miRNA sequences are obtained from the miRBase Sequence database and most genomic sequence from EnsEMBL. It uses the miRanda algorithm to identify potential binding sites for a given miRNA in genomic sequences (Griffiths-Jones *et al.*, 2008).
- *MiRNAMap:* Contains experimental verified miRNAs and experimental verified miRNA target genes in human, mouse, rat, and other metazoan genomes. In addition to known miRNA targets, computational tools previously developed were applied for the purpose of identifying miRNA targets in 3'-UTR of genes (Hsu *et al.*, 2008).
- *miR2Disease:* A manually curated database aimed at providing a comprehensive resource of miRNA deregulation in several human diseases. Each entry in the miR2Disease contains detailed information on a miRNA-disease relationship, including miRNA ID, disease name, a brief description of the miRNA-disease relationship, miRNA expression pattern in the disease state, detection method for miRNA expression, experimentally verified miRNA target genes, and bibliographic references (Jiang *et al.*, 2009).
- *TargetScan Dataset:* A data set composed of all predicted biological targets of miRNA by searching for the presence of conserved 8-mer and 7-mer sites that match the seed region of each miRNA. As an option, nonconserved sites are also predicted. Sites with mismatches in the seed region that are compensated for by conserved 3' pairing are also identified (Lewis *et al.*, 2003).

The amount of records stored in these databases is increasing considerably. An example can be seen in Figure 11.1, which shows the number of associations between miRNA and diseases included in the Human MicroRNA Disease Database (HMDD).

Concerning standardization, Huang *et al.* (2010) created the first ontology about a miRNA domain called Ontology for MicroRNA Target (OMIT). With this formal representation of knowledge, it is possible to make easier knowledge acquisition

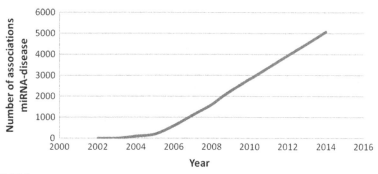

FIGURE 11.1

Increasing numbers of miRNA-disease associations in HMDD.

and data sharing from existing data sources, getting standardization of heterogeneous information that come from different miRNA databases. OMIT includes several concepts that cover different information contained in general miRNA annotation.

Furthermore, if we consider the structure of OMIT, one miRNA can be annotated with target genes, related diseases, its action as an oncogenic miRNA or as a tumor suppressor one, the organism to which it belongs, the experiment used to validate it, its associations with proteins and pathological events. Thus, the functional similarity between miRNAs can be inferred based on the similarity of target genes or associated diseases, supplemented with other information contained in their annotations. If all these annotations were integrated, we could infer the functional similarity of miRNAs based on a combination of all this information simultaneously, so that we could obtain a similarity value that is more effective and accurate, characterizing the calculation of a "composed" functional similarity.

In this chapter, we describe the creation and instantiation of the miRNA Integration and Analysis (MIRIA) platform. MIRIA consists of an integrative database for global miRNA information based on ontologies, together with a web tool for maintaining and querying this database and a method to calculate the functional similarity between miRNAs. The integrative database encompasses the information from a set of existing miRNA databases and was designed to cover the OMIT concepts. It also includes the deployment of related ontologies. The web tool allows the researchers to update and access miRNA annotation based on published articles and to use our composed functional similarity method.

2 MATERIAL

After searching and studying several different databases in the context of miRNAs, we chose those that best compose a robust integrative information set. The following describes the miRNA databases that we used to create our own database based on the OMIT structure, as well as some ontologies that we also integrated to MIRIA:

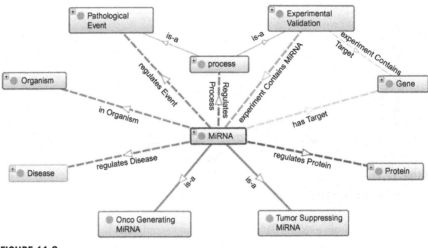

FIGURE 11.2

MiRNA concepts and their relations in OMIT.

- *Ontology for MicroRNA Target (OMIT):* The first ontology on the miRNA domain created to facilitate knowledge acquisition from existing sources. The miRNA concept and its relations with other concepts are represented in Figure 11.2. With this structure, we can retain a set of information related to a specific miRNA: organisms where it occurs, diseases regulated by it, its target genes, proteins regulated by it, related processes, and its nature as oncogenic or as a tumor suppressor.
- *GO:* The most famous and widely used ontology on genome domain, which provides a controlled vocabulary of terms used to describe gene product characteristics and annotation data. The aim of this project is standardizing the representation of gene and gene product attributes across species and databases. With this ontology, we can represent and compare the target genes of given miRNAs.
- *MeSH:* The National Library of Medicine's controlled vocabulary thesaurus. It consists of sets of terms naming descriptors in a hierarchical structure that allows searching at various levels of specificity. It is also used as a disease classification system. Using this "ontology," we can represent and compare the diseases regulated by given miRNAs.
- *miRBase:* A database of published miRNA sequences and annotation, including the species to which miRNAs belong. This database contains the basic information related to miRNAs.
- *HMDD:* A database with human microRNA-disease association data, which is manually collected from publications. Using this database, we can obtain the set of diseases related to a given miRNA (Lu *et al.*, 2008).

- *TarBase:* The largest available manually curated target database, indexing more than 65,000 miRNA-gene interactions experimentally tested. From this database, we can obtain the set of target genes of a given miRNA (Sethupathy *et al.*, 2006).
- *Genetic Association Database (GAD):* A public repository containing non-Mendelian, common complex disorders (diseases) associated with human genes that aim to standardize and archive genetic association study data. We used this database to verify redundancies concerning diseases and target genes, in order to calculate the similarity (Zhang *et al.*, 2010).
- *Human MicroRNA oncogenic and tumor suppressors:* Contains human miRNAs that have been identified as oncogenic or tumor suppressors by manually reviewing publications (Wang *et al.*, 2010).

All of these information sources were integrated in our MIRIA database so that we could collect a useful set of information about miRNAs. In addition, the direct information about miRNAs associated with related gene and disease information gathered in their specific ontologies allow the computation of the functional similarity measure that we proposed.

3 MIRIA DATABASE

The MIRIA database was developed using the Java language at NetBeans IDE and the database management system PostgreSQL. As we used the OMIT structure to develop our relational database, each concept from the ontology was represented as a table, and the associations between the concepts were represented by relationships. We chose the data sources cited in section 2 to populate our database because all of them use miRNA nomenclature as defined at miRBase; TarBase and GAD use the gene nomenclature Human Genome Organization (HUGO); and HMDD and GAD use disease nomenclature as defined in MeSH. All of the selected databases were obtained from their most recent published version, and some of them had their data preprocessed. For example, GAD has repeated instances of some diseases caused by insignificant differences such as changes in plurality or the appearance or omission of the letter *s* after an apostrophe; and other databases have similar typos.

Information about miRNAs, such as name, type, and sequence were taken from miRBase. Initially, we considered only human miRNAs, representing the inOrganism relationship. Information about miRNAs acting as oncogenic or tumor suppressors to populate isOncogenic and isTumorSuppressor relationships was extracted from the database of Human MicroRNAs Oncogenic and Tumor Suppressors. From HMDD, we obtained associations between miRNAs and human diseases, represented by the regulateDisease relationship, and we took from GAD direct associations between genes and human diseases to check for the existence of redundancies. Finally, from TarBase, it was possible to collect information about most relationships involving miRNAs in our database (*e.g.,* hasTarget, regulateProtein, regulatePathologicalEvent, and experimentContains.

Despite the fact that OMIT ontology does not have in its structure the concept of the family to which a given miRNA belongs, and given the importance of this information, we implemented in MIRIA a table to store information about the families, as well as the relationship between records of miRNAs and their families. This information was derived from miRBase.

Furthermore, GO and MeSH ontologies were downloaded from their respective websites and integrated to MIRIA. Moreover, as the miRBase website has a tree of all the species from which records of miRNAs have been discovered, we implemented an ontology of organisms and integrated it into our database.

In order to make easy the recovery of the sources of each record pertaining to relationships in our database (*e.g.,* records of associations between miRNAs and diseases, miRNAs and target genes, or a direct association between genes and diseases) and to guarantee MIRIA data reliability, we created a table containing information of their respective publications, such as PubMed ID, title, authors, year of publication, and a field for notes.

4 MiRNA CFSim

After the creation and instantiation of the MIRIA database, we decided to implement a method to evaluate the degree of similarity between two miRNAs. Our proposal was to make this calculation indirectly, using the similarity between the target genes and between associated diseases to each miRNA. For this, we studied various semantic similarity methods based on ontologies existing in the literature to calculate the similarity between two genes using GO or between two diseases using MeSH. We selected the Wang method (Wang *et al.*, 2007) to achieve this because it is a hybrid method, based in edges and nodes. In other words, the Wang method considers not only the position of the terms being compared within an ontology, but also their semantic relations with their ancestors.

The proposed method, composed functional similarity (CFSim), considers the existence of a set of information about the two miRNAs that are being compared, so that all this information is considered in the calculation of similarity. This may involve different similarity values obtained for different categories of information. For example, if both miRNAs have annotations in the category of target genes, we calculate the similarity between the target genes based on GO; in addition, if they have annotations in the disease category, we calculate the similarity between the diseases. Thus, the functional similarity is characterized here as "composed." Then, to calculate the CFSim between two miRNAs, we used the Wang method to the categories of information that have related ontologies, calculated the similarity for these categories, and then combined their values based on weights and redundancies.

As miRNAs belonging to the same family have very similar sequences and identical seed regions, regulating a common set of target genes and therefore having high functional similarity, we used miRNA families to validate our method. All implementations of CFSim and evaluation of this method was made in the C# language at Microsoft Visual Studio, accessing the database through PostgreSQL.

5 WEB FRAMEWORK

In order to make feasible the access of researchers to our integrated database, we developed a web framework with the following functional requirements:

- Search/insert/update/delete annotations about an miRNA, such as name, sequence, organism, family, functions, and its action as oncogenic or tumor suppressor
- Search/insert/update/delete annotations about associations between a miRNA and target genes
- Search/insert/update/delete annotations about miRNA-disease associations

On the other hand, the MIRIA environment also has the following nonfunctional requirements:

- *User-friendly interface:* The web framework interface should present its features in an intuitive way to the user.
- *Response time:* The environment must submit a short response time while executing its functions.
- *Usability:* The environment should be as simple as possible to enable the user to perform its tasks without any training and with the greatest possible satisfaction.
- *Portability:* The environment must allow access from any machine wherever the user is, so long as it is connected to a network and no installation is required.

Thus, the implementation of this web framework began with its integration with MIRIA in order to permit access to and update of the miRNA annotations. To search for annotations, we implemented methods that look for miRNA information and their relations with target genes and diseases in MIRIA. On the other hand, for the insert, update, and delete functionalities of miRNA annotations, we developed methods that execute these functions in our integrated database. Finally, to calculate functional similarity, the CFSim method described in section 4 was implemented.

This web framework was developed using C# at Visual Studio and the access to the annotations contained in the MIRIA database, as well as the insertions, updates, and deletions of information defined in PostgreSQL.

6 RESULTS

In order to achieve the objectives of the MIRIA platform proposal in an efficient and user-friendly way, we designed the framework interface by organizing its functions into two sections in the interface of the web framework: Home and Insert/Delete.

The Home section can be accessed through the first tab in the interface, which is the home page of the framework. On this tab, the user can search for information about an miRNA of interest (using the Search button) and calculate the functional similarity between two miRNAs through CFSim (using the Calculate button), as shown in Figure 11.3.

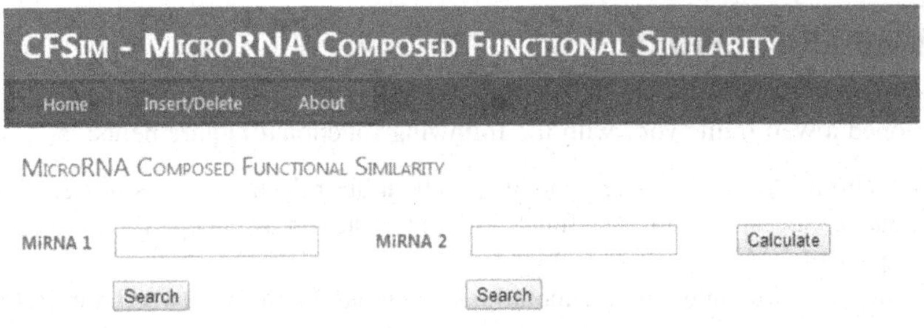

FIGURE 11.3

The Home tab of the web framework.

When conducting a search for a specific miRNA annotation, the framework returns all data about the miRNA of interest contained in the unified MIRIA database, organized in frames. Then, basic information about the miRNA of interest, such as name, family, sequence, organization, action (oncogenic or tumor suppressor), and its functions, are shown in the first frame. The second frame shows information about the associations of the miRNA with its target genes, such as name and symbol of the target gene, Ensembl code, type of experiment used on its validation, related pathological events, and the PubMedID from which this information was taken. Finally, the third frame presents the user with associations between the miRNA and various human diseases, with information such as the name of each disease, the pubmedID of the publication from where this data was taken, and some notes. An example of a search result (showing only part of the data due to space limitations) is presented in Figure 11.4.

When a user performs the calculation of similarity between two miRNAs, the system returns a numeric value consisting of the composed functional similarity. Also, some more detailed descriptions of both miRNAs are shown, such as names, families, related target genes, associated diseases, and if they act as oncogenic or tumor suppressors. Figure 11.5 presents an example of functional similarity calculated using CFSim for miRNAs belonging to distinct families.

The second tab, Insert/Delete, shown in Figure 11.6, allows the user to update the records in the MIRIA database through the insertion or modification of new information through clicking the Save button and delete existing information through clicking the Delete button. If the user wants to clear all fields to perform a new search or insert or update, he or she must click the Clear button.

When inserting a new miRNA, initially the user must search for information about the miRNA of interest, ensuring that it does not already exist in the database. If it is not present in MIRIA, the user can add new annotations about the new miRNA by clicking the blue plus sign buttons. In the insertion of each new association of a

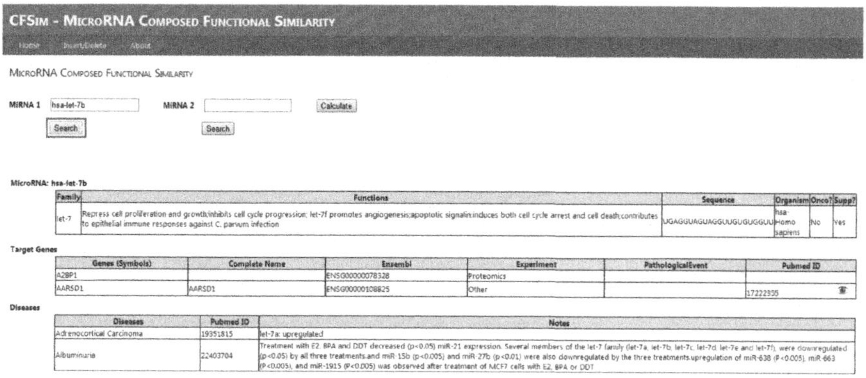

FIGURE 11.4

An example of the results of a search for information about an miRNA of interest.

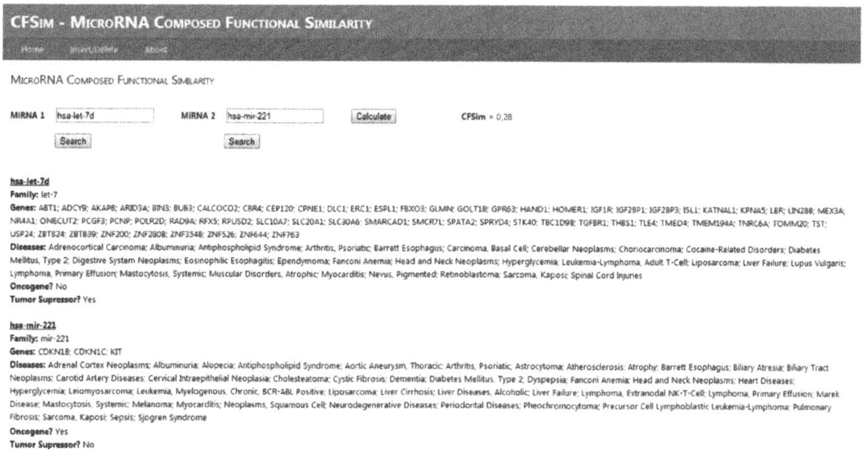

FIGURE 11.5

An example of CFSim applied on the miRNAs hsa-let-7d and hsa-mir-221.

disease with an miRNA, the framework allows the user to type and add a new disease (Figure 11.7) or to choose an already existing disease from the database (Figure 11.8). The same is true for associations between the miRNAs of interest and target genes.

On the other hand, if there is already information about this miRNA in the MIRIA database, the user can change or remove it by clicking the red X buttons in Figure 11.6. Whenever a user chooses to remove some information, a dialog box pops up for the user to click to actively confirm the deletion.

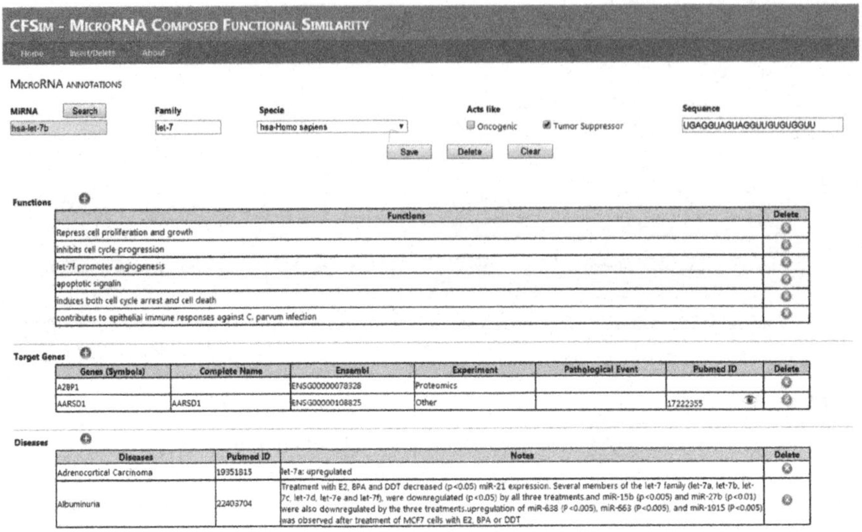

FIGURE 11.6

The Insert/Delete tab of the web framework.

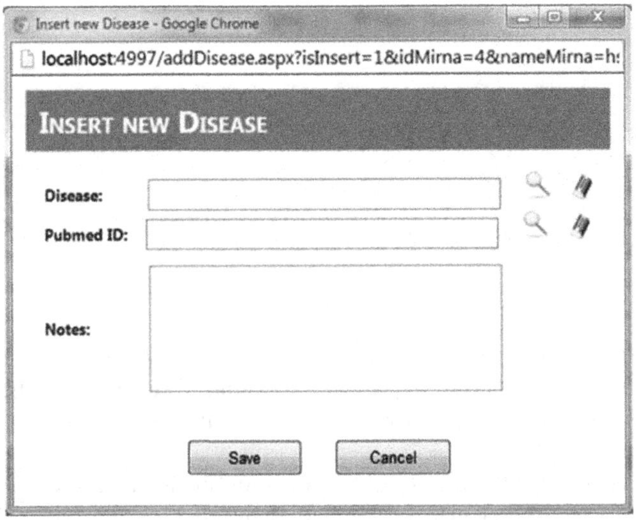

FIGURE 11.7

The user can insert a new disease in MIRIA to associate it to an miRNA.

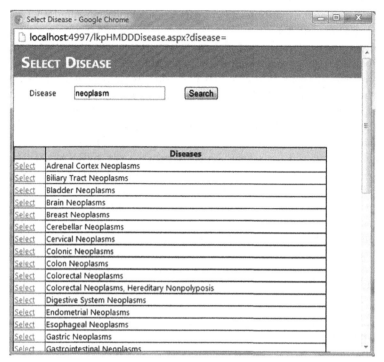

FIGURE 11.8

The user can choose an already-existing disease in MIRIA to associate it with a miRNA.

It is important to emphasize that the specification of pubmedID of the publication from which the information was taken is required to ensure data integrity in the MIRIA database. Along with the pubmedID, the user can add the name of the lead author and the year of publication (in citation form) and some notes. Consequently, there is also a feature where the user can view more detailed information about a publication by clicking on the magnifier icon represented by an eye in Figure 11.6.

Finally, there is a third tab, About, which contains the description of the framework and CFSim methodm as well as the contact of the project leaders and developers. The MIRIA web framework can be accessed at http://143.107.137.43/?pg=cfsim.

7 CONCLUSIONS

Currently, there are several different databases containing information related to miRNAs. However, the lack of standardization and integration of many of them makes it difficult for researchers to study, analyze, and compare miRNAs. Therefore, after studying different existing databases and environments described in the literature, we created a platform called MIRIA that includes an integrative database plus a method for miRNA comparison and a web framework for data maintenance and analysis. The MIRIA database is composed by annotations of miRNAs from data taken from heterogeneous existing sources, respecting the standardization of miR-Base, gene nomenclature defined by HUGO, and disease nomenclature defined by MeSH. In addition, the MIRIA database is organized with respect to the structure of OMIT ontology.

Furthermore, the web framework enables the user to search, insert, update, and delete information in the MIRIA database, and the CFSim method can be used to calculate the composed functional similarity between two miRNAs. MIRIA integrates several information about miRNAs originated from different databases and presents it in a standardized and structurally well organized way. The web framework presents a user-friendly interface that allows and facilitates miRNA data search, acquisition, and update from the existing literature by experts in this field.

In conclusion, the use of MIRIA has the potential to help researchers in biomedicine to better understand the important roles that miRNAs play in biological processes, their functions, and their associations with several human diseases, especially considering the functional similarity between them.

REFERENCES

Ambros, V., 2004. The functions of animal microRNAs. Nature 431, 350–355.

Betel, D., et al., 2008. The microRNA.org resource: targets and expression. Nucleic Acids Res. 36, 149–153.

Brennecke, J., et al., 2005. Principles of microRNA–target recognition. PLoS Biol. 3 (3), e85.

Esquela-Kerscher, A., Slack, F.J., 2006. Oncomirs - microRNAs with a role in cancer. Nat. Rev. Cancer 6, 259–269.

Ferracin, M., Negrini, M., 2012. MicroRNAs and Their Role in Cancer. *eLS*. John Wiley & Sons, Ltd.

Gene Ontology Consortium, 2015. Gene Ontology. [Online] Available from: http://www.geneontology.org/ (accessed 02.03.15.).

Griffiths-Jones, S., et al., 2008. miRBase: tools for microRNA genomics. Nucleic Acids Res. 36, 154–158.

Hsu, S.D., et al., 2008. miRNAMap 2.0: genomic maps of microRNAs in metazoan genomes. Nucleic Acids Res. 36 (Database issue), 165–169.

Huang, J., et al., 2010. Ontology for MiRNA target prediction in human cancer. In: First ACM International Conference on Bioinformatics and Computational Biology. Niagara Falls, NY. ACM, New York, NY, USA, pp. 472–474.

Jiang, Q., et al., 2009. miR2Disease: a manually curated database for microRNA deregulation in human disease. Nucleic Acids Res. 37, 98–104.

Lewis, B.P., et al., 2003. Prediction of mammalian microRNA targets. Cell 115, 787–798.

Lu, M., et al., 2008. An analysis of human microRNA and disease associations. PLoS One 3 (10), e3420. http://dx.doi.org/10.1371/journal.pone.0003420.

miRBase, 2015. miRBase: the microRNA database. [Online] Available from: http://www.mirbase.org/ (accessed 02.03.15.).

Sethupathy, P., Corda, B., Hatzigeorgiou, A.G., 2006. TarBase: a comprehensive database of experimentally supported animal microRNA targets. RNA 12, 192–197.

U. S. National Library of Medicine, 2015. Medical Subject Headings. [Online] Available from: http://www.nlm.nih.gov/mesh (accessed 02.03.15.).

Wang, J.Z., et al., 2007. A new method to measure the semantic similarity of GO terms. Bioinformatics (Oxford, England) 23, 1274–1281.

Wang, D., et al., 2010. Human MicroRNA oncogenes and tumor suppressors show significantly different biological patterns: from functions to targets. PLoS One 5 (9), e13067. http://dx.doi.org/10.1371/journal.pone.0013067.

Zhang, et al., 2010. Systematic analysis, comparison, and integration of disease based human genetic association data and mouse genetic phenotypic information. BMC Med. Genom. 3, 1.

Feature Selection and Analysis of Gene Expression Data Using Low-Dimensional Linear Programming

Satish Ch. Panigrahi, Md. Shafiul Alam, and Asish Mukhopadhyay

University of Windsor, Windsor, Ontario, Canada

1 INTRODUCTION

The availability of large volumes of gene expression data from microarray analysis [complementary DNA (cDNA) and oligonucleotide] has opened a new door to the diagnoses and treatments of various diseases based on gene expression profiling.

In a pioneering study, Golub *et al.* (1999) identified a set of 50 genes that can distinguish an unknown sample with respect to two kinds of leukemia with a low classification error rate. Following this work, other researchers attempted to replicate this effort in the diagnoses of other diseases. There were several notable successes. van't Veer *et al.* (2002) found that 231 genes were significantly related to breast cancer. Their MammaPrint test [approved by the U.S. Food and Drug Administration (FDA)] uses 70 genes as biomarkers to predict the relapse of breast cancer in patients whose condition has been detected early (van't Veer *et al.*, 2002). Khan *et al.* (2001) found 96 genes to classify small, round, blue-cell cancers. Ben-Dor *et al.* (2000) used 173 to 4375 genes to classify various cancers. Alon *et al.* (1999) used 2000 genes to classify colon cancers.

A major bottleneck with any classification scheme based on gene expression data is that while the sample size is small (numbering in the hundreds), the feature space is much larger, running into tens of thousands of genes. Using too many genes as classifiers results in overfitting, while using too few leads to underfitting. Thus, the main difficulty of this effort is one of scale: the number of genes is much larger than the number of samples. The consensus is that genes numbering between 10 and 50 may be sufficient for good classification (Golub *et al.*, 1999; Kim *et al.*, 2002).

In Unger and Chor (2010), computational geometry tools were used to test the linear separability of gene expression data by pairs of genes. Applying their tools to 10 different publicly available gene-expression data sets, they determined that

7 of these are highly separable. From this, they inferred that there might be a functional relationship "between separating genes and the underlying phenotypic classes." Their method of linear separability, applicable to pairs of genes only, checks for separability incrementally. For separable data sets, the running time is quadratic in the sample size m.

Alam *et al.* (2010), in a short abstract, proposed a different geometric tool for testing the separability of gene expression data sets. This is based on a linear programming algorithm of Megiddo (Dyer, 1984; Megiddo, 1982, 1984) that can test linear separability with respect to a fixed set of genes in an amount of time proportional to the size of the sample set.

In this chapter, we extend this work to testing separability with respect to triplets of genes. Since most gene sets do not separate the sample expression data, we have proposed and implemented an incremental version of Megiddo's scheme that terminates as soon as linear inseparability is detected. The usefulness of such an incremental algorithm to detect inseparability in a gene expression data set is also observed (Unger and Chor, 2010). The performance of the incremental version turned out to be better than the offline version, where we tested the separability of five different data sets by pairs/triplets of genes. Here, we also have conclusively demonstrated that linear separability can be put to good use as a feature for classification. The chapter also reformulates Unger and Chor's method as a linear programming framework. A conference version of the paper is appeared in the proceedings of ICCSA 2013 (Panigrahi *et al.*, 2013).

In a study, Anastassiou (2007) reveals that diseases (*e.g.*, cancer) are due to the collaborative effect of multiple genes within complex pathways, or to combinations of multiple single-nucleotide polymorphisms (SNPs). In reaction to this, here we illustrate the effect of the separability property of a gene to build a good classifier. In order to do so, this chapter introduces a gene selection strategy based upon the individual ranking of a gene. The ranking scheme uses these geometric tools and exploits class distinction of a gene by testing separability with respect to pairs and triplets of genes.

An important biological consequence of perfect linear separability in low dimensions is that the participating genes can be used as biomarkers. These genes can be used in clinical studies to identify samples from the input classes. This objective of linear separability in low dimensions can be achieved in an efficient way by an adaptation of Megiddo's algorithm. Since the total number of possible combination of genes in gene expression data sets that may be considered for good classification is too high, we are justified in confining ourselves to separability in low dimensions and limiting the group size to pairs and triplets. Furthermore, taking a cue from the observation (Unger and Chor, 2010) that most gene pairs are not separating, we have placed a particular emphasis on an incremental version of Megiddo's algorithm that is more efficient in this situation than an offline one. For any classification purpose, as groups of two or three genes may lead to underfitting, we also discuss a feature selection method by using this geometric tool of linear separability.

The major contributions described here can be summarized as follows:

- An offline adaptation of Megiddo's algorithm to test separability by gene pairs/ triplets, fully implemented and tested
- An incremental version of Megiddo's algorithm that is particularly useful for gene expression data sets, fully implemented and tested
- Demonstration of the usefulness of linear separability as a tool to build a good classifier with application to concrete examples
- Reformulation of Unger and Chor's method in a linear programming framework

For completeness, in the following section, we briefly discuss LP formulation of separability (Alam *et al.*, 2010; Panigrahi *et al.*, 2013).

2 LP FORMULATION OF SEPARABILITY

In this scenario, we have m samples, m_1 from a cancer type C_1, and $m_2(=m-m_1)$ from a cancer type C_2 [*e.g.*, m_1 from ALL and m_2 from AML (Golub *et al.*, 1999)]. Each sample is a point in a d-dimensional Euclidean space, whose coordinates are the expression values of the samples with respect to the d selected genes. This d-dimensional space is called the *primal space*. If a hyperplane in this primal space separates the sample points of C_1 from those of C_2, then the test group of genes is a linear separator and the resulting linear program in dual space has a feasible solution. Suppose that there is a separating hyperplane in primal space and the sample points of C_1 are above this plane while the sample points of C_2 are below it [Figure 12.1(a) is a two-dimensional (2D) illustration of this]. Figure 12.1 (b) shows that the separating line maps to a point inside a convex region. The set of all points inside this convex region make up the feasible region of a linear program in dual space and correspond to all possible separating lines in primal space.

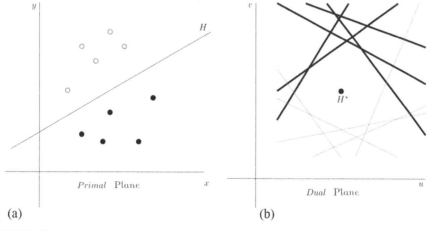

(a)   (b)

FIGURE 12.1

A separating line **H** in primal space is a feasible solution **H*** in dual space.

Thus, there is a separating hyperplane in primal space if the resulting linear program in dual space has a feasible solution. Note, however, that we will have to solve two linear programs since it is not known *a priori* if the m_1 samples of C_1 lie above or below the separating hyperplane H. Therefore, if $d = 2$ and the selected genes are g_1 and g_2, then the gene pair $\{g_1, g_2\}$ is a linear separator of the m_1 samples from C_1 and the m_2 samples from C_2.

Now we reformulate this problem as a linear program in dual space. This is another d-dimensional Euclidean space such that points (planes) in the primal space are mapped to planes (points) in this space, such that if a point is above (below) a plane in the primal space, the mapping preserves this point-plane relationship in the dual space. For $d = 2$, substitute all occurrences of the word *plane* with *line* in all the previous text.

For $d = 2$ (see O'Rourke, 1994), one such mapping of a point p and a line l in the primal space (x, y) to the line p^* and the point l^*, respectively, in the dual space (u, v) is

$$
\begin{aligned}
p &= (p_x, p_y) \rightarrow p^* : v = p_x u - p_y \\
l &: y = l_u x - l_v \rightarrow l^* = (l_u, l_v).
\end{aligned}
\tag{12.1}
$$

It is straightforward to extend this definition to more than two dimensions.

Formally, one of these linear programs in d-dimensional dual space $(u_1, u_2, \ldots, u_d)$ is shown here:

minimize u_d

$$
\begin{aligned}
p_1^i u_1 + \ldots + p_{d-1}^i u_{d-1} - u_d - p_d^i &< 0, \, i = 1, \ldots, m_1 \\
p_1'^i u_1 + \ldots + p_{d-1}'^i u_{d-1} - u_d - p_d'^i &> 0, \, i = 1, \ldots, m_2,
\end{aligned}
\tag{12.2}
$$

where $(p_1^i, p_2^i, \ldots, p_d^i)$ is the ith sample point from C_1 and the first set of m_1 linear inequalities expresses the conditions that these sample points are above the separating plane, while the second set of m_2 linear inequalities express the condition that the sample points $(p_1'^i, p_2'^i, \ldots, p_d'^i)$ from C_2 are below this plane. The linear inequalities given here that describe the linear program are called *constraints,* and we will use this term throughout the rest of this discussion.

Megiddo (1982, 1984) and Dyer (1984) both proposed an ingenious prune-and-search technique for solving this linear program that, for fixed d (dimension of the linear program), takes time linear in (proportional to) the number of constraints. In the next two sections, we discuss how this LP-framework achieve the more limited goal of testing the separability of the samples from the two input classes by an offline algorithm and an incremental one, both of which are based on an adaptation of Megiddo's and Dyer's technique.

This approach is of interest for two reasons: (a) in contrast to the algorithm of Unger and Chor (2010), the worst running time of this algorithm is linear in its sample size; and (b) in principle, it can be extended to study the separability of the sample classes with respect to any number of genes. In what follows, we adopt a coloring scheme to refer to the points that represent the samples: those in the class C_1 are colored blue and make up the set S_B, while those in C_2 are colored red and make up the set S_R.

If a pair of genes separates the sample classes, then a blue segment that joins a pair of blue points is disjoint from a red segment that joins a pair of red points. Unger and Chor (2010, p. 375), suggests an algorithm to test separability by testing if each blue segment is disjointed from a red segment. Figure 12.2 shows that this test succeeds even when the point sets are not separable. The conclusions of Unger and Chor (2010) on separability by pairs of genes, however, is based on an incremental algorithm that works correctly. Its extension to testing separability by three or more genes is not obvious.

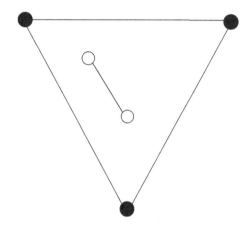

FIGURE 12.2

A counterexample

3 OFFLINE APPROACH

As Megiddo's algorithm is central to this discussion, we briefly review this algorithm for $d = 2$ and refer to Megiddo (1984) for the cases $d \geq 3$. A bird's-eye view is that in each of log m iterations, it prunes away at least a quarter of the constraints that do not determine the optimum (minimum, in our formulation), at the same time reducing the search space (an interval on the u-axis) in which the optimal solution lies.

Definition: If $f_1, f_2, \ldots, f_n$ is a set of real, single-valued functions defined in an interval $[a, b]$ on the real line, their pointwise minimum (maximum) is another function f such that for every $x \in [a, b]$,

$$f(x) = min\left(f_1(x), f_2(x), \ldots, f_n(x)\right) \left(f(x) = max\left(f_1(x), f_2(x), \ldots, f_n(x)\right)\right)$$

Let us call the pointwise minimum (maximum) of the heavy (light) lines in Figure 12.1(b) the *min-curve (max-curve)*, respectively. These are also called the *upper* and *lower envelope*, respectively.

Assume that after i iterations, we determined that the minimum lies in the interval $[u_1, u_2]$. Let us see how to prune redundant constraints from the set of constraints that determine the min-curve. We make an arbitrary pairing of the bounding lines of these constraints. With respect to the interval $[u_1, u_2]$, the intersection of such a constraint pair can lie as shown in Figure 12.3(a). For the ones that lie to the left (right) of the line $u = u_1$ ($u = u_2$), we prune the constraint whose bounding line has a larger (smaller) slope. Likewise, we can prune redundant constraints from the set of constraints that determine the max-curve.

In order to further narrow down the interval on the u-axis where the minimum lies, for all other pairs of constraints whose intersections lie within the interval $[u_1, u_2]$, we find the median u_{med} of the u-coordinates of the intersections and let $l : u = u_{med}$ be the line with respect to which we test for the location of the minimum. We make this test by examining the intersections of the min-curve and max-curve with l. This is accomplished by using the residual constraint sets that implicitly define the min-curve and max-curve. From the relative positions of these intersections and the slopes of the bounding lines of the constraints that determine these intersections, we can determine on which side of l, the minimum lies (see Figure 12.3(b)). Next, we prune a constraint from each pair whose intersections lie within $[u_1, u_2]$ but on the side opposite to which the minimum lies. Because of our choice of the test-line, we are guaranteed to throw a quarter of the constraints from those that determine these intersections. We now reset the interval that contains the minimum to $[u_{med}, u_2]$ or $[u_1, u_{med}]$.

This algorithm allows us to determine feasibility as soon as we have found a test line such that the intersection of the min-curve with l lies above its intersection with the max-curve. We implemented this offline algorithm both in two and three dimensions from scratch. Ours is probably the first such implementation in three dimensions. Refer to Megiddo (1984) for details.

Offline algorithms are effective for determining linear separability. However, as most of the gene-pairs and gene-triplets are not linearly separating, incremental algorithms would be more efficient than offline ones. This was also observed by Unger and Chor (2010). In view of this fact, in the next section, we discuss in detail an incremental version of this algorithm.

4 INCREMENTAL APPROACH

The following obvious but useful theorem (which is true in any dimension $d \geq 1$) underlies our algorithm in dual space:

Theorem 12.1 Let S_B' and S_R' be arbitrary subsets of S_B and S_R, respectively. If S_B' and S_R' are linearly inseparable, then so are S_B and S_R.

Proof: Straightforward: if S_B and S_R are linearly separable, then so are S_B' and S_R'.

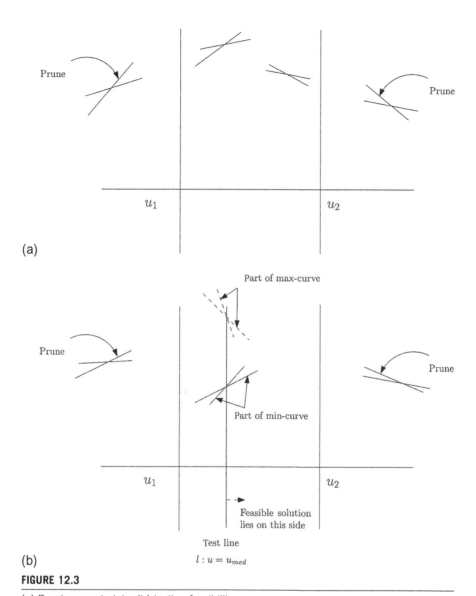

FIGURE 12.3

(a) Pruning constraints; (b) testing feasibility.

4.1 INCREMENTAL APPROACH—2D

First, we choose a small constant number of lines from each of the duals of S_R and S_B and use the offline approach described in the previous section to determine if there is a feasible solution to this constant-size problem. If not, we declare infeasibility (Theorem 12.1) and terminate. Otherwise, we have an initial feasible region and a test line $l : u = \bar{u}$.

We continued, adding a line from one of the residual sets S_A^* or S_B^*, which was also chosen randomly. Several cases can arise as a result. This line (a) becomes a part of

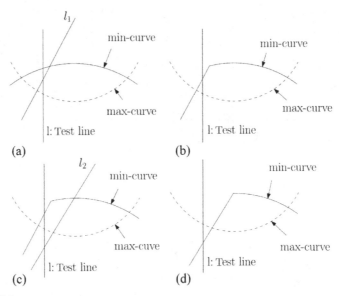

FIGURE 12.4

Updating of min-curve: (a) addition of line l_1; (b) the test line continues to pass through the feasible region on updating of the min-curve; (c) addition of line l_2; (d) test line goes out of the feasible region on updating of the min-curve.

the boundary of the feasible region, (b) leaves it unchanged, or (c) establishes infeasibility, in which case the algorithm terminates. Case (a) spawns two subcases, as shown in Figure 12.4. (a.1) the test line l still intersects the feasible region (see Figure 12.4 (a) and (b)). (a.2) the test line l goes outside the feasible region (see Figure 12.4 (c) and (d)). The lines belonging to the case (b) always leads to a condition mentioned in (a.1).

If the test line l goes outside the feasible region, constraint-pruning is triggered. This consists of examining pairs of constraints whose intersections lie on the side of l that does not include the feasible region. One of the constraints of each such pair does not intersect the feasible region and therefore is eliminated from further consideration. However, if l lies inside the new feasible interval, we continue to add new lines.

If we are able to add all lines without case (c) occurring, then we have a feasible region, and hence a separating line in the primal space.

A formal description of the iterative algorithm is as follows:

Algorithm IncrementallySeparatingGenepairs
Input: Line duals S_R^* and S_B^* of the point sets S_R and S_B.
Output: LP feasible or infeasible.

1: Choose $S_R^{*\prime} \subset S_R^*$ and $S_B^{*\prime} \subset S_B^*$ so that $\left|S_R^{*\prime}\right| = \left|S_B^{*\prime}\right| = 2$.

2: Apply the offline approach to $S_R^{*\prime}$ and $S_B^{*\prime}$. We have the following cases:
Case 1: If infeasible, then report this and halt.
Case 2: If feasible, then return the vertical test line l and continue with step 3.
3: Repeatedly add a line from $\left|S_R^* - S_R^{*\prime}\right|$ or $\left|S_B^* - S_B^{*\prime}\right|$ until no more lines remain to be added or there exists no feasible point on the test line l.
4: If there is a feasible point on the test line l we report separability and halt.
5: If there is no feasible point on the test line l, determine on which side of l the feasible solution lies.
6: Update $S_R^{*\prime}$ and $S_B^{*\prime}$ by eliminating a line from each pair whose intersection does not lie in the feasible region and was earlier used to determine l.
7: Update $S_R^{*\prime}$ and $S_B^{*\prime}$ by including all those lines added in step 3 and go to step 2.

When S_R and S_B are linearly separable (LS), the running time of the incremental algorithm is linear in the total number of inputs. Otherwise, as the algorithm terminates when a line added that reveals inseparability, the time complexity for this case is linear in the number of lines added so far.

Theorem 12.2 If m is the total number of samples, then time complexity of the incremental algorithm is $O(m)$.
Proof: In each iteration, the algorithm prunes one-quarter of the constraints (*i.e.*, samples) from the current set $S_R^{*\prime} \cup S_B^{*\prime}$. The time complexity of each iteration is $O(m)$. The run time $T(m)$ satisfies the recurrence $T(m) = O(m) + T\left(\frac{3m}{4}\right)$, whose solution is $T(m) = O(m)$.

4.2 INCREMENTAL APPROACH—3D

Suppose that constraints (*i.e.*, planes) belong to a three-dimensional (3D) Cartesian coordinate system with axes labeled as U, V, and Z, and the position of any point in 3D space is given by an ordered triple of real numbers (u_1, u_2, u_3). These numbers give the distance of that point from the origin measured along the axes.

First, we applied a 3D offline approach on a small constant number of constraints (*i.e.*, planes) from each dual of S_R and S_B. If this constant size problem is infeasible, then we report infeasibility and terminate (see Theorem 12.1). Otherwise, we have a vertical test plane that passes through the feasible region. This vertical test plane is parallel to either the VZ-plane (say $\bar{U}$) or the UZ-plane (say $\bar{V}$) and chosen suitably, as suggested by Megiddo.

A formal description of the iterative algorithm is as follows:

Algorithm IncrementalySeparatingGeneTriplets
Input: Plane duals S_R^* and S_B^* of the point sets S_R and S_B.
Output: LP feasible or infeasible.
1: Initialize $S_R^{*\prime} \subset S_R^*$ and $S_B^{*\prime} \subset S_B^*$. We can choose $\left|S_R^{*\prime}\right| = \left|S_B^{*\prime}\right| = 4$.

2: Apply Megiddo's approach to $S_R^{*\prime}$ and $S_B^{*\prime}$. We have the following cases:

Case 1: If infeasible, then report the inseparability and halt.

Case 2: If feasible, then return a vertical test plane $\bar{U}$ (or $\bar{V}$) and continue with step 3.

3: Repeatedly add a constraint from $\left|S_R^* - S_R^{*\prime}\right|$ or $\left|S_B^* - S_B^{*\prime}\right|$ and initiate an incremental 2-D approach on vertical test plane $\bar{U}$ (or $\bar{V}$). We distinguish with following cases:

Case 1: If the test plane $\bar{U}$ (or $\bar{V}$) is feasible after all the constraints are considered, then report separability and halt.

Case 2: If the test plane $\bar{U}$ (or $\bar{V}$) is infeasible, then solve two 2D linear programs to determine on which side of test plane the feasible region lies.

    Case 2.1: If any one of 2D linear program is feasible, then identify the side of feasible solution and continue with step 4.

    Case 2.2: If both 2D linear program are not feasible or both are feasible, then report the inseparability and halt.

4: Identify a second vertical test plane $\bar{V}$ (or $\bar{U}$) and initiate an incremental 2D approach by resuming the addition of constraints from $\left|S_R^* - S_R^{*\prime}\right|$ or $\left|S_B^* - S_B^{*\prime}\right|$, excluding those which are already being considered with $\bar{U}$ (or $\bar{V}$). If we do not have any second vertical test plane, then continue with step 5. We distinguish with the following cases:

Case 1: If the test plane $\bar{V}$ (or $\bar{U}$) is feasible after all the constraints are considered, then report separability and halt.

Case 2: If the test plane $\bar{V}$ (or $\bar{U}$) is infeasible, then solve two 2D linear programs to determine on which side of test plane the feasible region lies.

    Case 2.1: If any one of 2D linear program is feasible, then identify the side of feasible solution and continue with step 5.

    Case 2.2: If both 2D linear program are not feasible or both are feasible, then report the inseparability and halt.

5: Update $S_R^{*\prime}$ and $S_B^{*\prime}$ by eliminating a constraint from each coupled line which does not pass through the feasible quadrant $\bar{U}$ and $\bar{V}$.

6: Update $S_R^{*\prime}$ and $S_B^{*\prime}$ by including all those constraints considered in step 3 and step 4.

7: Repeat the algorithm for the updated set of $S_R^{*\prime}$ and $S_B^{*\prime}$.

4.3 LINEAR PROGRAMMING FORMULATION OF UNGER AND CHOR'S INCREMENTAL ALGORITHM

Unger and Chor (2010) proposed an incremental algorithm for testing separability with respect to gene pairs. They considered $m_1.m_2$ vectors obtained by joining every point in the class S_R (or S_B) to every point of the class S_B (or S_R) (see Figure 12.5). The directions corresponding to these vectors map to $m_1.m_2$ points on a unit circle, with the center at O. In this formulation, the sample classes S_R and S_B are LS if the points on the unit circle span arc are less than π.

We can reformulate this in our linear programming framework. Let $p_i(x_i, y_i), 1 \leq i \leq m_1 * m_2$ be the coordinates of the points corresponding to all the directions on the perimeter of the unit circle. We make the following observation:

Observation. The points $p_i(x_i, y_i), 1 \leq i \leq m_1 * m_2$, span an angle less than π if there exists a line, l, through O such that all the points lie on one side of it.

   maximize/minimize u

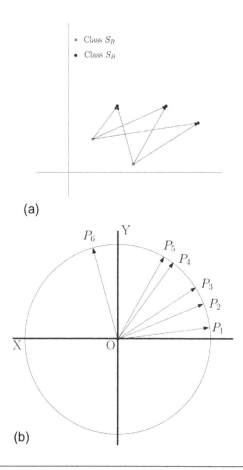

(a)

(b)

FIGURE 12.5

Linear programming formulation of the 180 strict containment condition. (a) Construction of vectors; (b) projection of the vectors onto a unit circle;

(Continued)

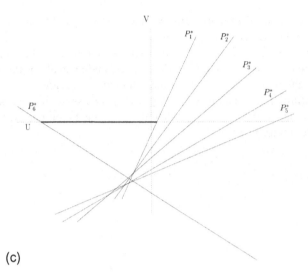

(c)

FIGURE 12.5, CONT'D

(c) mapping of points on the unit circle to a dual plane.

$$u > \frac{y_i}{x_i}, x_i > 0$$
$$u < \frac{y_i}{x_i}, x_i < 0$$

(12.3)

or

maximize/minimize u

$$u < \frac{y_i}{x_i}, x_i > 0$$
$$u > \frac{y_i}{x_i}, x_i < 0$$

(12.4)

We summarize this discussion with the following claims:

Claim 1. If $\exists u$, then $l^*(u,0)$ is a point in a dual plane such that it is either above or below of all the lines $p_i^*(v = u.x_i - y_i), 1 \leq i \leq m_1.m_2$.

Equivalently,

Claim 2. If $\exists u$, then $l(y = ux)$ is a line in a primal plane such that all the points $p_i(x_i, y_i), 1 \leq i \leq m_1.m_2$ lie on one side of this line.

The incremental implementation based on the abovementioned LP formulation is as simple as the one in Unger and Chor (2010), and it also provides early termination when inseparability is detected. In the worst case, the running time of both formulations is quadratic in the sample size m.

---

5 GENE SELECTION

Gene selection is an important preprocessing step for the classification of the gene expression data set. This helps (a) to reduce the size of the gene expression data set and improve classification accuracy; (b) to cut down the presence of noise in the gene expression data set by identifying informative genes; and (c) to improve the computation by removing irrelevant genes that not only add to the computation time, but also make classification harder.

5.1 BACKGROUND

In this subsection, we briefly discuss some popular score functions used for gene selection and compare them with our gene selection method, proposed in the next section. A simple approach to feature selection is to use the correlation between gene expression values and class labels. This method was first proposed by Golub *et al.* (1999). The correlation metric defined by Nguyen and Rocke (2002) and by Golub *et al.* reflects the difference between the class mean relative to standard deviation within the class. The high absolute value of this correlation metric favors those genes that are highly expressed in one class as compared to the other class, while their sign indicates the class in which the gene is highly expressed. We have chosen to select genes based on a t-statistic defined by Nguyen and Rocke.

For the i_{th} gene, a t-value is computed using the following formula:

$$t_i = \frac{\mu_1^i - \mu_2^i}{\sqrt{\frac{{\sigma_1^i}^2}{n_1} + \frac{{\sigma_2^i}^2}{n_2}}}, \tag{12.5}$$

where n_k, μ_k^i, and ${\sigma_k^i}^2$ are the sample size, mean, and variance of the i_{th} gene, respectively, of class $k = 1, 2$.

Another important feature selection method is based on the Fisher score (Bishop, 1995; Zhang *et al.*, 2008). The Fisher score criterion (FCS) for the i_{th} gene can be defined as

$$F_i = \frac{n_1 \left(\mu_1^i - \mu^i\right)^2 + n_2 \left(\mu_2^i - \mu^i\right)^2}{n_1 \left(\sigma_1^i\right)^2 + n_2 \left(\sigma_2^i\right)^2}, \tag{12.6}$$

where n_k, μ_k^i, and σ_k^{i2} are the sample size, mean, and variance of the ith gene, respectively, of class $k = 1, 2$, and μ^i represents the mean of the i_{th} gene.

Significance analysis of microarrays (SAM) proposed by Tusher *et al.* (2001) is another important gene filter technique for finding significant genes in a set of microarray experiments. The SAM score for each gene can be defined as

$$M_i = \frac{\mu_2^i - \mu_1^i}{s_i + s_0}. \tag{12.7}$$

For simplicity, the correcting constant s_0 is set to 1 and s_i is computed as follows:

$$s_i = \left[\left(\frac{1}{n_1} + \frac{1}{n_2} \right) \frac{\left\{ \sum_{j \in C_1} \left(x_j^i - \mu_1^i \right)^2 + \sum_{j \in C_2} \left(x_j^i - \mu_2^i \right)^2 \right\}}{(n_1 + n_2 - 2)} \right]^{\frac{1}{2}} \tag{12.8}$$

where x_j^i is the j_{th} sample of the i_{th} gene. The classes 1 and 2 are represented by C_1 and C_2. Similarly, n_k, μ_k^i, and σ_k^{i2} are the sample size, mean, and variance of the i_{th} gene, respectively, of class $k = 1, 2$.

For the purpose of generating significant genes by SAM, we have used software written by Chu *et al.* (2001), which is publicly available at http://www-stat.stanford.edu/tibs/clickwrap/sam/academic.

6 A NEW METHODOLOGY FOR GENE SELECTION

To find a set of genes that are large enough to be robust against noise and small enough to be applied to the clinical setting, we propose a simple gene selection strategy based on an individual gene-ranking approach. This consists of two steps: *coarse filtration*, followed by *fine filtration*.

6.1 COARSE FILTRATION

The purpose of coarse filtration is to remove most of the attributes that contribute to noise in the gene expression data set. This noise can be categorized into (i) biological noise and (ii) technical noise (Lu and Han, 2003). *Biological noise* refers to the genes in a gene expression data set that are irrelevant for classification. *Technical noise* refers to errors incurred at various stages during data preparation.

For coarse filtration, we follow an established approach based upon the *t*-metric discussed in the previous section. Following a general consensus (Golub *et al.*, 1999; Kim *et al.*, 2002), we chose to select a sufficient number of genes that can be further considered for fine filtration. This is a set of 100 genes obtained by taking 50 genes with the largest positive *t*-values and another 50 genes with the smallest negative *t*-values.

6.2 FINE FILTRATION

One of the problems with the abovementioned correlation metric is that the t-value is calculated from the expression values of a single gene, ignoring the information available from the other genes. To rectify this, we propose the following scheme:

Let the set of genes $\Delta = \{g_1, g_2, ..., g_n\}$ be the output of the coarse filtration step, where n $= 100$. For a gene $g_i \in \Delta$, let $S_i = \{g_j | (g_i, g_j)$ is an LS pair, $g_j \in \Delta$ and $i \neq j\}$. In other words, S_i consists of all genes that form LS pairs with g_i. For each gene $g_i \in \Delta$, its P_i-value is set as $P_i = |S_i|$.

The intuition underlying this definition is that the informative genes have very different expression values in the two classes. If such genes exist in the gene expression data set, then this ranking strategy will assign the highest rank to those genes.

A drawback of this gene selection method is that it is applicable only to those gene expression data sets that have LS pairs. For those data sets that have few LS pairs, such as Lung Cancer (Gordon *et al.*, 2002) and Breast Cancer (van't Veer *et al.*, 2002), we can extend the definition using LS gene triplets:

For a gene $g_i \in \Delta$, set

$$Q_i = \{(g_j, g_k) | (g_i, g_j, g_k) \text{ is an LS triplet}, g_j, g_k \in \Delta, \text{ and } i \neq j \neq k\},$$

In other words, Q_i consists of all gene pairs (g_j, g_k) that make up an LS triplet with the gene g_i. For each gene $g_i \in \Delta$, define $T_i = |Q_i|$. Clearly, T_i lies between 0 and $^{n-1}C_2$.

7 RESULTS AND DISCUSSION

In this chapter, we have developed offline and incremental geometric tools to test linear separability of pairs and triplets of genes, followed by a simple gene selection strategy that uses these tools to rank the genes. Based upon this ranking, we chose a suitable number of top-scoring genes for a good classifier.

We demonstrated the usefulness of the proposed methodology by testing it against five publicly available gene expression data sets: (a) Lung Cancer (Gordon *et al.*, 2002); (b) Leukemia (Armstrong *et al.*, 2002); (c) SRBCT (Khan *et al.*, 2001); (d) Colon (Alon *et al.*, 1999); and (e) Breast Cancer (van't Veer *et al.*, 2002). Table 12.1 shows the number of samples in each data set, with the number of samples from each class in parentheses.

Table 12.1 Five Gene Expression Data Sets

	Data Set	Number. of Genes	Total Samples
1.	Lung Cancer	12533	181 (31 + 150)
2.	Leukemia	12582	52 (24 + 28)
3.	SRBCT	2308	43 (23 + 20)
4.	Colon	2000	62 (40 + 22)
5.	Breast Cancer	21682	77 (44 + 33)

The 100 genes that we selected from each of these data sets in the Coarse Filtration step effectively prunes away most of the attributes (genes) that are irrelevant for classification. On the other hand, this number is large enough to provide us with a number of attributes (genes) that may be overfitting for classifier construction.

To get the best subset of genes for good classification, we chose to populate the attribute space with 5, 10, 15, 25, and 30 genes from each data set by applying Fine Filtration. The choices of these attribute/feature-space sizes are somewhat arbitrary, but the chosen attribute/feature spaces are sufficiently large in comparison to the size of the sample spaces, as Table 12.1 shows.

The computational time of the Fine Filtration step depends upon the geometric tool that we use to check the separability of gene expression data. In this chapter, we have presented linear, time-incremental algorithms for both gene pairs and gene triplets. In order to illustrate the effectiveness of this approach, we ran both versions (offline and incremental) on each of the five data sets obtained by Coarse Filtration. The computing platform was a Dell Inspiron 1545 model–Intel Core2 Duo central processing unit (CPU), 2.00 GHz, and 2 GB RAM, running under Microsoft Windows Vista. The run-time efficiency of the incremental version over the offline one is evident from Table 12.2.

A group of genes that is being tested for linear separability may include a gene that is a perfect one-dimensional (1D) separator with a TNoM score of zero, using the terminology of Ben-Dor et al. (2000). In this case, such a group will provide a positive separability test. In order to exclude such groups, we checked for the existence of such 1D separators and found that no such genes exists in these data sets. Likewise, if a gene pair shows linear separability, then all gene triplets that include these gene pairs will also be linearly separating. In order to count gene triplets that exhibit pure 3D linear separability, we avoided testing gene triplets that included an LS pair. Thus, our 3D test results shown here include only such gene triplets. We call such gene triplets *Perfect Linearly Separable Triplet (PLSTs)*. The percentage of *Linearly Separable Pairs (LSPs), Linearly Separable Triplets (LSTs),* and *Perfect Linearly Separable Triplets (PLSTs)* are calculated using these formulas:

$$\% \text{ of LSP} = \frac{\#of\,LSP}{Total\,possible\,LSP} \times 100 = \frac{\#of\,LSP}{{}^{2}C_n} \times 100$$

$$\% \text{ of LST} = \frac{\#of\,LST}{Total\,possible\,LST} \times 100 = \frac{\#of\,LST}{{}^{3}C_n} \times 100$$

$$\% \text{ of PLST} = \frac{\#of\,PLST}{Total\,possible\,LST - ((\#of\,LSP) \times (n-2))} \times 100$$

$$= \frac{\#of\,PLST}{{}^{3}C_n - ((\#of\,LSP) \times (n-2))} \times 100,$$

where n is the total number of genes in the gene expression data set.

Table 12.2 2D and 3D Separability Test with Run Time

| Data Set | 2D Separability Test with RT | | | | 3D Separability Test with RT | | | |
	LSP (%)	RT of Offline (ms)	RT of Incr. (ms)	Impr. of Incr. over Offline (%)	PLST (%)	RT of Offline (ms)	RT of Incr. (ms)	Impr. of Incr. over Offline (%)
Lung Cancer	0.72	4617	1537	66.71	0.946	1114467	166662	85.04
Leukemia	11.92	1138	418	63.27	3.72	115791	49263	57.45
SRBCT	8.86	987	356	63.93	4.11	92825	52080	43.89
Colon	0	1328	275	79.29	0	170143	39955	76.516
Breast Cancer	0.93	1606	440	72.6	0.137	274141	83913	69.39

Note: RT: run time, Incr.: incremental, Impr.: improvement.

These formulas show that the total number of triplets relative to the *PLSTs* is much higher than the total number of pairs relative to the *LSPs*. Thus, the increase in the actual number of *PLSTs* over the number of *LSPs* is suppressed by the high value of the denominator in the former case. The separability test shows that Colon (Alon *et al.*, 1999) data set has neither any *LSPs* nor any *PLSTs*. The Lung Cancer (Gordon *et al.*, 2002) and Breast Cancer (van't Veer *et al.*, 2002) data sets have a few *LSPs*, whereas the number of *PLSTs* is 41 and 5 times (approximately) the number of *LSPs*, respectively. The Leukemia (Armstrong *et al.*, 2002) and SRBCT (Khan *et al.*, 2001) data sets show a good number of *LSPs*, while the number of *PLSTs* is 6 and 11 times (approximately) the number of *LSPs*, respectively.

The motive underlying our gene selection strategy is to identify if a gene, jointly with other genes, has the class distinction property. In the current study, we identified the class distinction property by separability tests where the group size was restricted to pairs and triplets. As the Colon data set (Alon *et al.*, 1999) did not show any positive separability result, we continued our study with the remaining four gene expression data sets. This result in Colon is not surprising at all, since according to Alon *et al.* (1999), some samples such as T2, T30, T33, T36, T37, N8, N12, and N34 have been identified as outliers and presented with an anomalous muscle-index. This confirms the uncertainty of these samples.

Next, in the Fine Filtration stage, we used the incremental version of our algorithm to test separability by gene pairs and assign a P_i value to a gene $g_i \in \Delta$. Based on the ranking, we chose a set of top-scoring genes to populate five different feature spaces of size 5, 10, 15, 20, 25, and 30. If more than one gene had the same rank, then we chose an arbitrary gene from that peer group. To compare our method with other selection methods, such as *t*-metric, FCS, and SAM, we populated similar feature spaces respectively.

For classification, we used machine learning (ML) tools supported by WEKA version 3.6.3 (Hall *et al.*, 2009). We used the following two classifiers:

1. *Support Vector Classifier*: WEKA SMO class implements John C. Platt's (Platt, 1998) sequential minimal optimization algorithm for training a support vector classifier. We used a linear kernel.
2. *Bayes Network Classifier*: The Weka BayesNet class implements Bayes network learning using various search algorithms and quality measures (Bouckaert, 2004).

We chose the Bayes Network classifier based on $K2$ for learning structure (Cooper and Herskovits, 1992). Both of these classifiers normalized the attributes by default to provide a better classification result. We used a 10-fold cross-validation (Kohavi, 1995) for prediction, as shown in Figure 12.6. As suggested (Kohavi, 1995), we have used 10-fold stratified cross-validation. In stratified cross-validation, the folds are stratified so that they contain approximately the same proportions of labels as original data sets.

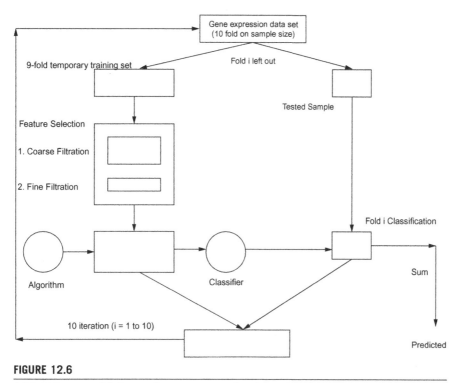

FIGURE 12.6

A 10-fold cross validation on the gene expression data set.

A comparative classification accuracy of the feature spaces generated from *P*-values, *t*-values, FCS, and SAM is shown in Figures 12.7–12.10. The results clearly show that the gene spaces generated by *P*-values yield a good classifier. Specifically, the feature spaces of sizes 10, 15, 20, 25, and 30 generated by the *P*-values perform mostly as well as or better than the feature spaces generated by the *t*-values, FCS and SAM.

To illustrate the performance of the classifiers with respect to the feature spaces generated by the *T*-values, we considered two data sets with few *LSPs*, such as Lung Cancer (Gordon *et al.*, 2002) and Breast Cancer (van't Veer *et al.*, 2002). To make sure that the data set has no *LSPs*, we removed all genes that are responsible for pair separability in the selection process. Then feature spaces of size 5, 10, 15, 20, 25, and 30 were populated based upon the *T*-values. The classification results are shown in Figures 12.7–12.10. It is interesting to note that the feature space generated from Lung Cancer (Gordon *et al.*, 2002) data set by *T*-values achieves similar or even better classification accuracy compared to *t*-values, FCS and SAM. In Figures 12.11–12.14, we have shown the classification accuracy of feature space confined to 25 and 30.

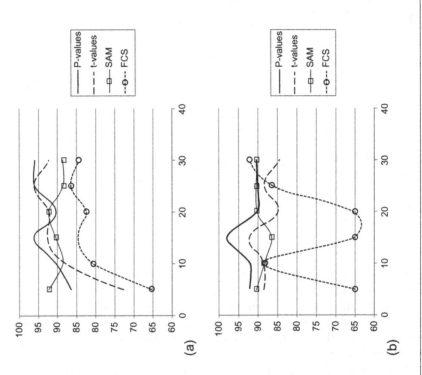

FIGURE 12.7

Accuracy versus feature space (Leukemia) (a) SVM classifier (b) Bayes Network classifier.

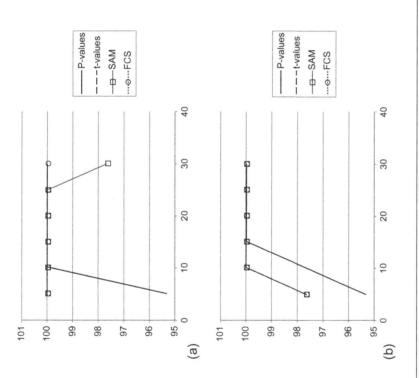

FIGURE 12.8

Accuracy versus feature space (SRBCT) (a) SVM classifier (b) Bayes Network classifier.

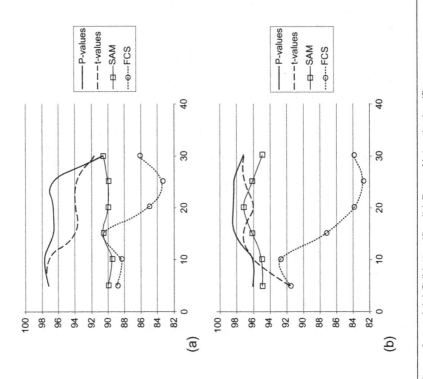

FIGURE 12.9

Accuracy versus feature space (Lung Cancer) (a) SVM classifier (b) Bayes Network classifier.

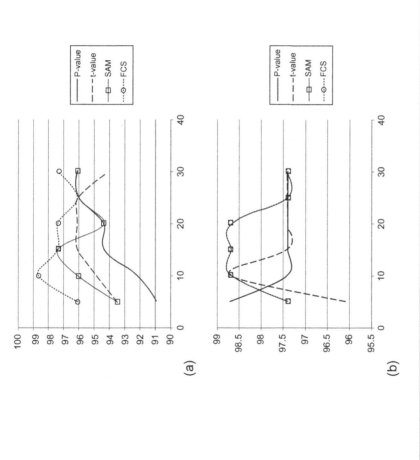

FIGURE 12.10

Accuracy versus feature space (Breast Cancer) (a) SVM classifier (b) Bayes Network classifier.

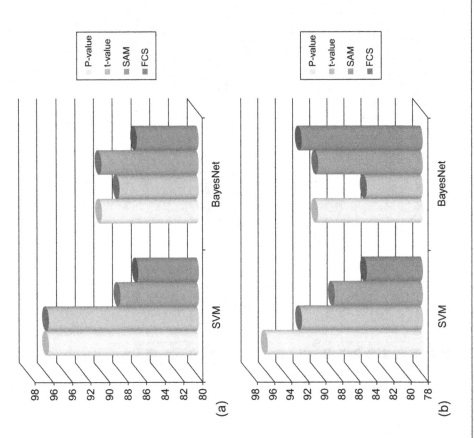

FIGURE 12.11

Classifier accuracy of gene expression data set on 25 and 30 feature space (FP) (a) 25 FS Leukemia (b) 30 FS Leukemia.

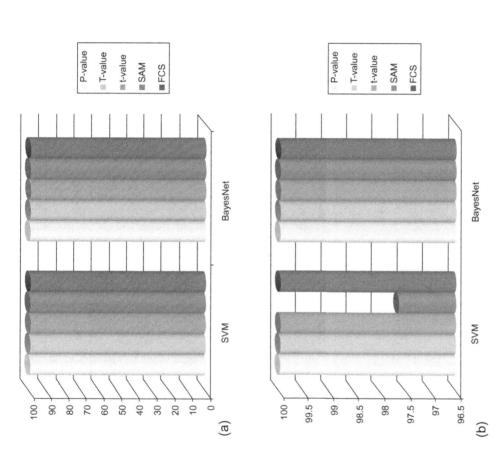

FIGURE 12.12

Classifier accuracy of gene expression data set on 25 and 30 feature space (FP) (a) 25 FS SRBCT (b) 30 FS SRBCT.

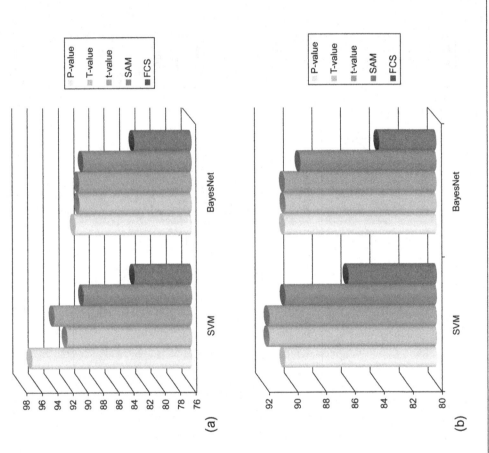

FIGURE 12.13

Classifier accuracy of gene expression data set on 25 and 30 feature space (FP) (a) 25 FS Lung Cancer (b) 30 FS Lung Cancer.

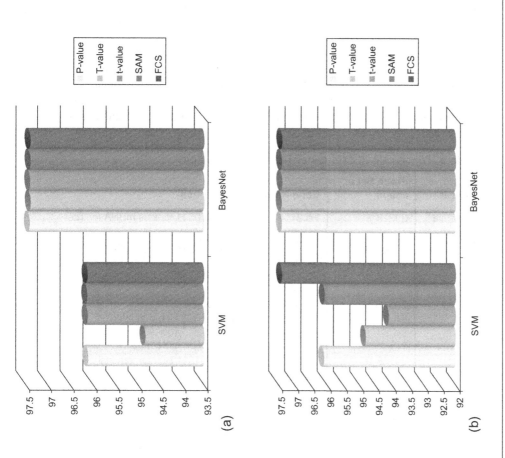

FIGURE 12.14

Classifier accuracy of gene expression data set on 25 and 30 feature space (FP) (a) 25 FS Breast Cancer (b) 30 FS Breast Cancer.

8 CONCLUSIONS

Our empirical study of the four data sets discussed in this chapter shows that the feature space generated by our methods (particularly by the use of P-values) is as good as the feature selection methods based on t-values, SAM, and FCS. Toward the broader objective of identifying important biomarkers to distinguish between input classes, we list in Table 12.3 the top 10 genes (or genes attached to a probe set in the respective microarray experiments) from each of the data sets.

We presented a gene selection strategy to achieve high classification accuracy. The gene selection strategy exploits the class-distinguishing property of genes by testing separability by pairs and triplets. To test for separability, we provided two versions of a linear time algorithm and demonstrated that the run time of the incremental version is markedly better than that of the offline version. The importance of this method lies in the fact that it can be easily extended to higher dimensions, allowing us to test if groups of more than three genes can separate the data sets. In this study, we limited the separability tests to gene pairs and triplets and used this criteria to rank the genes.

Table 3 Top ten significant genes based upon P-values

Dataset	Probe Set or Image	Gene Name or Description
Leukemia Data	39318_at	Hs.2484 gnl|UG|Hs#S4305 H.sapiens mRNA for Tcell leukemia
	36571_at	Hs.75248 gnl|UG|Hs#S5526 H.sapiens topIIb mRNA for topoisomerase IIb
	41462_at	Hs.11183 gnl|UG|Hs#S1055230 H.sapiens sorting nexin 2 (SNX2) mRNA, complete cds
	266_s_at	M26692 /FEATURE=exon#1 / DEFINITION=HUMLCKPR02 Homo sapiens lymphocyte-specific protein tyrosine kinase (LCK) gene, exon 1, and downstream promoter region
	34168_at	Hs.272537 gnl|UG|Hs#S1611 Human terminal transferase mRNA, complete cds
	40285_at	Hs.58927 gnl|UG|Hs#S876152 Homo sapiens nuclear VCP-like protein NVLp.2 (NVL.2) mRNA, complete cds
	40533_at	Hs.1578 gnl|UG|Hs#S1266737 tg78b04.x1 Homo sapiens cDNA, 3' end
	38017_at	Hs.79630 gnl|UG|Hs#S551444 Human MB-1 gene, complete cds
	40282_s_at	Hs.155597 gnl|UG|Hs#S779 Human adipsin
	39520_at	Hs.100729 gnl|UG|Hs#S1526847 wn60d01.x1 Homo sapiens cDNA, 3' end
Lung Cancer	33328_at	
	36533_at	
	33833_at	
	31684_at	
	41388_at	
	1662_r_at	

Table 3 Top ten significant genes based upon P-values—Cont'd

Dataset	Probe Set or Image	Gene Name or Description
	33904_at	
	36105_at	
	33245_at	
	39756_g_at	
Breast Cancer	Contig53226_RC	
	AI147042_RC	
	NM_000790	
	Contig1789_RC	
	NM_000238	
	AB037821	
	AB033007	
	NM_000353	
	NM_002073	
	AF053712	
SRBCT	770394	Fc fragment of IgG, receptor, transporter, alpha
	377461	caveolin 1, caveolae protein, 22kD
	1435862	antigen identified by monoclonal antibodies 12E7, F21 and O13
	814260	follicular lymphoma variant translocation 1
	866702	protein tyrosine phosphatase, non-receptor type 13 (APO-1/CD95 (Fas)-associated phosphatase)
	52076	olfactomedinrelated ER localized protein
	357031	tumor necrosis factor, alpha-induced protein 6
	43733	glycogenin 2
	207274	Human DNA for insulin-like growth factor II (IGF-2); exon 7 and additional ORF
	898219	mesoderm specific transcript (mouse) homolog

ACKNOWLEDGMENTS

This research is supported by an NSERC discovery grant to the third author.

REFERENCES

Alam, M., Panigrahi, S., Bhabak, P., Mukhopadhyay, A., 2010. A multi-gene linear separability of gene expression data in linear time. In: Short Abstracts in ISBRA 2010: 6th International Symposium on Bioinformatics Research and Applications, Connecticut. pp. 51–54.

Alon, U., et al., 1999. Broad patterns of gene expression revealed by clustering analysis of tumor and normal colon tissues probed by oligonucleotide arrays. Proc. Natl. Acad. Sci. U. S. A. s.l.:s.n., pp. 6745–6750.

Anastassiou, D., 2007. Computational analysis of the synergy among multiple interacting genes. Mol. Syst. Biol. 3(83).

Armstrong, S.A., et al., 2002. Mll translocations specify a distinct gene expression profile that distinguishes a unique leukemia. Nat. Genet. 30 (June), 41–77.

Ben-Dor, A., et al., 2000. Tissue classification with gene expression profiles. J. Comput. Biol. 7 (3–4), 559–583.

Bishop, C.M., 1995. Neural Networks for Pattern Recognition. Oxford University Press, Oxford.

Bouckaert, R.R., 2004. Bayesian Network Classifiers in Weka.

Cooper, G., Herskovits, E., 1992. A Bayesian method for the induction of probabilistic. Mach. Learn. 9, 308–347.

Dyer, M.E., 1984. Linear time algorithms for two- and three-variable linear programs. SIAM J. Comput. 13 (1), 31–45.

Chu, G., et al., 2001. Significance Analysis of Microarrays Users Guide and Technical Document, s.l.: Stanford CA 94305: Stanford University.

Golub, T.R., et al., 1999. Molecular classification of cancer: class discovery and class prediction by gene expression monitoring. Science 286 (5439), 531–537.

Gordon, G.J., et al., 2002. Translation of microarray data into clinically relevant cancer diagnostic tests using gene expression ratios in lung cancer and mesothelioma. Cancer Res. 62, 4963–4967.

Hall, M., et al., 2009. The WEKA data mining software: an update. ACM SIGKDD Explorations Newsletter 11 (1), 10–18.

Khan, J., et al., 2001. Classification and diagnostic prediction of cancers using gene expression profiling and artificial neural networks. Nat. Med. 7 (6), 673–679.

Kim, S., et al., 2002. Strong feature sets from small samples. J. Comput. Biol. 9 (1), 127–146.

Kohavi, R., 1995. A Study of Cross-Validation and Bootstrap for Accuracy Estimation and Model Selection. s.l., s.n., pp. 1137–1145.

Lu, Y., Han, J., 2003. Cancer classification using gene expression data. Inf. Syst. 28 (4), 243–268.

Megiddo, N., 1982. Linear-Time Algorithms for Linear Programming in R^3 and Related Problems. s.l., IEEE Computer Society, pp. 329–338.

Megiddo, N., 1984. Linear programming in linear time when the dimension is fixed. J. ACM 31 (1), 114–127.

Nguyen, D.V., Rocke, D.M., 2002. Tumor classification by partial least squares using microarray gene expression data. Bioinformatics 18 (1), 39–50.

O'Rourke, J., 1994. Computational Geometry in C. s.l.: Cambridge University Press.

Panigrahi, S.C., Alam, M., Mukhopadhyay, A., 2013. An incremental linear programming based tool for analyzing gene expression data. In: Murgante, B. et al., (Ed.), Computational Science and Its Applications – ICCSA 2013. s.l.: Springer Berlin Heidelberg, pp. 48–64.

Platt, J., 1998. Fast training of support vector machines using sequential minimal optimization. In: Schlkopf, B., Burges, C., Smola, A. (Eds.), Advances in Kernel Methods – Support Vector Learning. MIT Press, Cambridge, MA, pp. 42–65.

Tusher, V.G., Tibshirani, R., Chu, G., 2001. Significance analysis of microarrays applied to the ionizing radiation response. Proc. Natl. Acad. Sci. 98 (9), 5116–5121.

Unger, G., Chor, B., 2010. Linear separability of gene expression data sets. IEEE/ACM Trans. Comput. Biology Bioinform. 7 (2), 375–381.

van 't Veer, L.J., et al., 2002. Gene expression profiling predicts clinical outcome of breast cancer. Nature 415 (6871), 530–536.

Zhang, D., Chen, S., Zhou, Z.-H., 2008. Constraint score: a new filter method for feature selection with pairwise constraints. Pattern Recogn. 41 (5), 1440–1451.

The Big ORF Theory: Algorithmic, Computational, and Approximation Approaches to Open Reading Frames in Short- and Medium-Length dsDNA Sequences

13

Steven M. Carr[1,2,4], H. Dawn Marshall[1], Todd Wareham[2], and Donald Craig[3]

Department of Biology, Memorial University of Newfoundland, St. John's NL, Canada[1]
Department of Computer Science, Memorial University of Newfoundland, St. John's NL, Canada[2]
eHealth Research Unit (Faculty of Medicine), Memorial University of Newfoundland, St. John's NL, Canada[3]
Terra Nova Genomics, Inc., St. John's NL, Canada[4]

1 INTRODUCTION

The cracking of the genetic code by means of a rapid series of experiments and logical inferences is arguably the first instance of a "big science" approach in the history of molecular genetics (Judson, 1996). Theoretical considerations had already indicated that any nucleic acid code words must comprise a minimum of three letters (Crick, 1966). After it was demonstrated in 1961 that an artificial poly-U RNA template directs incorporation of the amino acid proline into a polypeptide, and thus that UUU was the code for PRO, Marshall Nirenberg's lab had by 1963 deduced an incomplete "dictionary" of 50 three-letter code words (Nirenberg *et al.*, 1965), and a substantially complete genetic code table was created by 1965 (Nirenberg *et al.*, 1966; also see Figure 13.1). The iconic 4 × 4 × 4 table is now a standard

1st Base	2nd Base				3rd Base
	U	C	A	G	
U	PHE*	SER*	TYR*	CYS*	U
	PHE*	SER*	TYR*	CYS	C
	leu*?	SER	TERM?	cys?	A
	leu*, f-met	SER*	TERM?	TRP*	G
C	leu*	pro*	HIS*	ARG*	U
	leu*	pro*	HIS*	ARG*	C
	leu	PRO*	GLN*	ARG*	A
	LEU	PRO	gln*	arg	G
A	ILE*	THR*	ASN*	SER	U
	ILE*	THR*	ASN*	SER*	C
	ile*	THR*	LYS*	arg*	A
	MET*, F-MET	THR	lys	arg	G
G	VAL*	ALA*	ASP*	GLY*	U
	VAL	ALA*	ASP*	GLY*	C
	VAL*	ALA*	GLU*	GLY*	A
	VAL	ALA	glu	GLY	G

FIGURE 13.1

The genetic code, 1965. Note that uncertainties still existed as to the coding properties of UGA (a TERM or stop codon) and UGG (a Leu codon).

feature of biology textbooks and has been incorporated into bioinformatic computational schemes as a fundamental feature.

In this chapter, we consider properties of short segments of the genetic code that are of interest both theoretically, as unexplored computational challenges, and practically, bearing on the evolution and function of the code and coding molecules. Taken together, the solution of these challenges at the intersection of computational and biological science provides reciprocal illumination to each.

2 MOLECULAR GENETIC AND BIOINFORMATIC CONSIDERATIONS

2.1 MOLECULAR GENETICS OF DNA → RNA → PROTEIN

DNA is famously a double-stranded molecule (dsDNA) that comprises two polymeric sequences of four bases (A, C, G, and T) in an aperiodic order that conveys bioinformation. The two strands are arranged in antiparallel 5'→3' directions that are implicit in the deoxyribose component. The strands are held together by noncovalent hydrogen bonds between paired A+T or C+G base pairs. The antiparallel arrangement and base pairing rules ensure that the alternative strands are complementary to each other. This relationship is the basis of DNA as a self-replicating molecule.

One DNA strand, designated the *template strand*, serves as a template for 5'→3' synthesis (transcription) of a complementary messenger RNA (mRNA) molecule, where RNA differs from DNA in being single-stranded and substituting base U for T. The mRNA molecule is translated in the 5'→3' direction into a polymer comprising a sequence of amino acids (a *polypeptide*), according to a genetic code (Figure 13.1). In the code, each of the 64 possible three-letter base sequences (*codons*) reads 5'→3' and specifies a particular amino acid, except that three codons (UAA, UAG, and UGA) do not specify any amino acid and therefore serve as terminators (known as *stops*) to polypeptide synthesis. A common genetic code is universal for the nuclear genomes of all organisms.

2.2 BIOINFORMATIC DATA-MINING

Because the mRNA sequence is complementary to that of the DNA template strand, it necessarily has the same base sequence in the same 5'→3' direction as the DNA strand complementary to the template strand, except for the substitution of U for T. This DNA strand, designated the *sense strand*, may therefore be read directly from the genetic code table, substituting T for U. As a bioinformatic process, it is straightforward to read the polypeptide sequence directly from the DNA sense strand, without the intermediate molecular steps of mRNA transcription and subsequent translation via tRNA. (By definition, codons occur only in mRNA: the equivalent three-letter sequences in the DNA sense strand are designated as *triplets*. Hereafter in this discussion, we adopt the National Center for Biotechnology Information (NCBI) bioinformatic convention and use a DNA triplet alphabet.)

Any dsDNA molecule may be read from six potential starting points, designated as *reading frames (RFs)*, which are three-base windows that commence at the first, second, or third base from the 5' end of one strand, after which each frame repeats; or from the 5' end of the other strand starting at the opposite end of the molecule. Full-length DNA sequences of several hundred to more than a thousand bases that specify protein sequences that are hundreds of amino acids long are expected to show that only one of these RFs is an Open Reading Frame (ORF); that is, that it does not include a stop triplet over the required length of the polypeptide. As three out of 64 triplets are stops (TAA, TAG, and TGA), the five alternative RFs are expected to include multiple random stops at expected intervals of about 20 triplets: the first occurrence of a stop closes the RF. We designate this the *5&1 condition*. Commercial DNA software programs perform this process as a matter of routine, either from novel data or data mined from online resources such as GenBank.

3 ALGORITHMIC AND PROGRAMMING CONSIDERATIONS

An introduction to the theory of data mining for such ORFs typically begins with the propounding of short dsDNA sequence exemplars of length $L = 15 \sim 25$ base pairs that are constrained by the 5&1 condition. A practical algorithmic generator of such exemplars must be able to access the entire space of dsDNA sequences that satisfy the 5&1 condition for a specified L, sample that space in an at least approximately random manner, and be efficient in terms of both central processing unit (CPU) run time and required memory space. We developed two such algorithms (Carr *et al.*, 2014a), the first based on a two-level recursive search that generates a dsDNA skeleton with at least one stop codon in each of five frames, and then completes the remainder of the dsDNA sequence by adding bases at random to the skeleton so as to produce an ORF exemplar in which the 5&1 condition is maintained. An app that generates dsDNA sequence exemplars that satisfy the 5&1 condition for $L \leq 100$ is available at http://www.ucs.mun.ca/~donald/orf/biocomp/. We provide a more complete discussion of the pedagogical use of the web application in a previous study (Carr *et al.*, 2014b). The second algorithm used an exhaustive search that enumerated all those dsDNA sequences of length L that satisfied the 5&1 condition without storing the results as exemplars.

The recursive and exhaustive algorithms show that there are no solutions for $L = 5 \sim 10$, and 96 for $L = 11$ (Figure 13.2, after Carr *et al.*, 2014a). Enumerations from

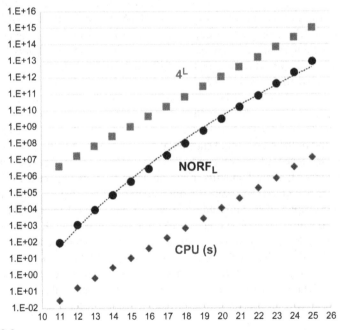

FIGURE 13.2

Semilogarithmic plot of the enumerated number of ORF exemplars of length L ($NORF_L$) for $L = 11 \sim 25$. The total number of possible dsDNA sequences of length L is 4^L (■). Required CPU time for the exhaustive algorithm is given in seconds (◆); CPU is log-linear with respect to L, as $CPU = 0.613(\log_{10} L) - 11.736$ ($r^2 = 0.9998$). After Figure 3 in Carr *et al.* (2014a).

the two methods agree for $11 \leq L \leq 19$, at which point the recursive algorithm succumbs to memory limitations. For $L < 22$, CPU usage for the exhaustive algorithm was measured on a single, quad-core PC. For $L \geq 22$, CPU usage was measured over a network of such machines: by $L = 25$, exact CPU usage is obscured by competing demands from other users on the same network. Calculation of the number of 5&1 solutions for $L > 25$ with the resources available to us would require several days.

4 ANALYTICAL AND RANDOM SAMPLING SOLUTIONS TO L > 25 SEQUENCES: TRIPLET-BASED APPROXIMATIONS

Given these limitations, we have developed a simplified analytical formulation of the 5&1 problem, in which the 64 triplets in the universal genetic code comprise $C = 61$ coding and $S = (64 - C) = 3$ stop triplets. If we disregard the actual nucleotide composition of coding and noncoding triplets and the overlapping nature of the six RFs, the probability that any given triplet is a coding triplet is $C = 61/64$. Next, the probability that a string of T triplets will be an ORF is simply calclulated as

$$p(\text{ORFT}) = C^T, \tag{13.1}$$

and the probability that such a string will include at least one stop is calculated as

$$p(\text{stop}) = 1 - C^T. \tag{13.2}$$

Then, an approximation of the probability that a string of triplets satisfies the 5&1 condition p(NORFT) is the joint probability that RF1 is open *and* RFs 2-5 are all closed, *or* that any of RF2, RF3, ... RF6 is open and the other five RFs closed. Thus,

$$p(5\&1T) = (6)(C^T)(1 - C^T)^5 \tag{13.3}$$

Figure 13.3 shows a simultaneous plot of Eqs. (13.1), (13.2), and (13.3). Where Eq. (13.3) has a constant factor $K = 6$ and p(stop) enters the function as its fifth power, p(5&1 T)] initially tracks p(stop) toward the enumerable limit of $L = 25$ as observed, but the function maximizes at $T = 37$ ($L = 111$) at $p = 0.4$ of a 5&1 solution.

Thus, and counterintuitively, the scarcity of 5&1 solutions for smaller values of T ($T < 37, L < 111$) is determined by the low probability of exactly five simultaneously stopped frames $(1 - C^T)^5$, rather than the relative scarcity of ORFs ($C^T/4^L$). For larger $T >> 37$, any given ORF is almost certainly accompanied by five frames with multiple stops.

We evaluated Eq. (13.3) as an estimator of p(5&1) by sampling for each of $L = 3 \sim 450$ (mod 3) a set 10^6 random dsDNA sequences, and ascertaining the fraction that satisfied the 5&1 condition under the universal genetic code. Figure 13.4 shows that Eq. (13.3) very slightly overestimates the proportion of 5&1 solutions in the Monte Carlo simulation for $L < 37$. This is to be expected given the absence of constraints in the triplet approximation (triplet assignments, overlapping RFs, etc.), and otherwise the equation provides a close upper bound.

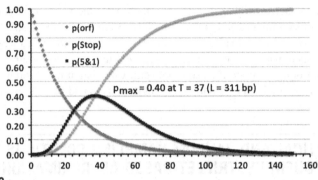

FIGURE 13.3

Plot of the three components of the triplet approximation of the 5&1 solution in Eq. (13.3) {p (5&1)], for T=1...150 (L=3...450). Note that p(ORF) as a simple exponential (C^T) starts high but declines log-linearly toward zero as T increases, and p(stop)=$(1-C^T)$ starts low but converges on 1.

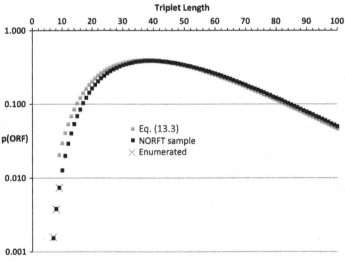

FIGURE 13.4

Probability of a 5&1 solution in triplet strings of length T=6...100, as estimated by the approximation in Eq. (13.3) (red) and by random sampling of 10^6 dsDNA sequences of length L=3 T (black). Crosses indicate exact enumerations for T=6, 7, and 8, corresponding to L =18, 21, and 24 in Figure 13.2.

5 ALTERNATIVE GENETIC CODES

Besides the universal code with three stop triplets (Figure 13.1), there are several variant codes with one, two, or four stops (Itzkovitz and Alon, 2007). Figure 13.5 shows simultaneous plots of Eq. (13.3) with $S=1$, 2, or 4, such that $C=63/64$, 62/64, and 60/64, respectively. All variants have the same $p_{max}=0.40$ as the three-stop code, at $L=342$, 168, and 84, respectively. This maximum arises as the zero (horizontal) slope of the first derivative of Eq. (13.3) when $C^T=1/6$. Substituting this back into Eq. (13.3) gives $p=0.40$. Because C is a constant for any one model of the code and co-occurs with T only in the form C^T, the derivative

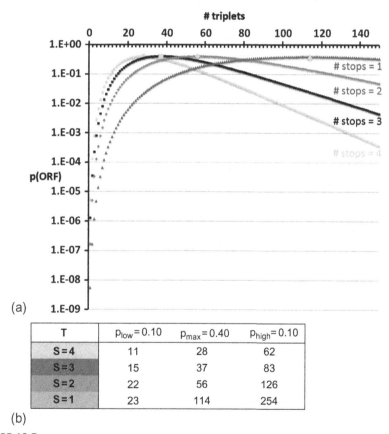

T	$p_{low}=0.10$	$p_{max}=0.40$	$p_{high}=0.10$
S=4	11	28	62
S=3	15	37	83
S=2	22	56	126
S=1	23	114	254

(b)

FIGURE 13.5

(a) Probability function of p(5&1T) for alternative genetic codes with different numbers of stop codons. The universal code has three stops (black), for which a sequence T=37 triplets (L=111) has the highest probability ($p_{max}=0.4$) of providing a 5&1 solution. (b) Upper and lower bounds for p(5&1T)=0.1, and $p_{max}=0.4$, for alternative genetic codes with S=4, 3, 2, and 1 stop triplets, respectively.

of p(NORFT) is necessarily identical for different values of C. The equation for p_{max} can then be rearranged and solved to predict T, as

$$T = \log(1/6) / (\log C) = -0.7782 / (\log C) \tag{13.4}$$

The upper bound on a 10% cutoff for p(5&1) increases rapidly as the number of stops decreases: for example, at the upper 10% probability bound, there are more than three times as many solutions with a one-stop (L=254, T=762) as with a three-stop code (L=83, T=249).

6 IMPLICATIONS FOR THE EVOLUTION OF ORF SIZE

Broad conservation of the universal code in nuclear genomes indicates that a three-stop code optimizes some selective advantage (Itzkovitz and Alon, 2007), whereas retention of an unstopped TGA in the common ancestor of all Metazoan mitochondrial DNA (mtDNA) codes suggests that there is some advantage for a two-stop code, and the relatively recent evolution of the four-stop code in Chordata offers some advantage over a three-stop intermediate (Cannaozzi and Schneider, 2012). We have shown here that short random DNA sequences have a high probability of including single ORF over certain size ranges, and that this probability is inversely proportional to the number of stops in the genetic codes used. Might size variation of ORF coding sequences across genetic codes be subject to natural selection?

A recent model of stop codon evolution (Johnson *et al.*, 2011) proposes that multi-stop codes provide a backstop against readthrough, balanced against an increased probability of random stop mutations. Like ours, the model predicts an inverse relationship between the number of stop triplets and the length of coding sequences. Consistent with this, their sampling of NCBI data shows a marked (though nonsignificant) relationship between longer coding sequence and fewer stops, for pairs of genomes in the same taxon alternatively decoded with one- versus two-, one- versus three-, or two- versus three-stop codes. There is no such trend for the two- versus four-stop Chordata comparison. Johnson *et al.* (2011) note a previous suggestion that reassignment of TGA from sense to stop has occurred frequently in association with the evolutionary reduction of genome size in mtDNA genomes, in apparent contradiction to the predicted direction. However, a phylogenetic perspective on the various mtDNA codes shows that this reassignment has occurred only once, in the shared ancestral code of all Animalia and Yeast (Ophisthokonta); this will be considered elsewhere.

In their data, coding sequences for genomes with three-stop codes are in the range of 250~400 bp, with animal mtDNA at about 300 bp: these are rather longer than our optimal of 111 or 84 bp for S=3 or 4, respectively, but they are well within the range of reasonable probability (Figure 13.5). A longer coding sequence might also be assembled from several shorter single-ORF fragments, so long as the individual ORFs were assembled in the same RF. Recall that fragments shorter than the optimum are more likely to have multiple ORFs. Selection could then act to modify the function of the corresponding polypeptide product while maintaining a single ORF. DNA sequences 5' or 3' to the ORF region can be added easily, since there is a high probability that any 3-bp sequence added in the open frame also will be open [$\sim(61/64)^3 = 0.87$], while the other five frames are already stopped. The fewer the stops, the longer the likely candidate sequences are. For example, in a four-stop code, there is less than 1% chance that an approximately 300-bp DNA will contain one and only one ORF, whereas for a one-stop code, there is a far greater than 10% chance that a sequence of many hundreds of base pairs will do so.

Are short, random DNA sequences with single ORFs of utility in evolution? It has recently been demonstrated that some free-living bacteria can take up *ex vivo*, fragmented DNA from the environment and incorporate it into their genomes by replication-dependent transformation (Overballe-Petersen *et al.*, 2013). Fragments of $20 \sim 100$ bp were most efficiently transformed at higher rates than larger fragments. We have shown that random fragments of just this size are most likely to include a single ORF, which might mediate the success of any such horizontal transfer and its incorporation into the host genome as a functional coding sequence. Overballe-Petersen *et al.*, 2013 hypothesize that "rates of molecular evolution in naturally transformable species may be influenced by the diversity of free environmental DNA." Our results suggest that one type of evolutionary diversity in random DNA may be the varying high probability that small fragments of various lengths will include unique ORFs subject to modification by natural selection.

ACKNOWLEDGMENTS

S. M. Carr, H. D. Marshall, and T. Wareham were supported by NSERC Discovery Grants during the preparation of this chapter. We thank K. Tahlan for pointing out the implications for lateral gene transfer in bacteria. We thank H. Arabnia for his leadership of the BioComp conferences, and his support for the preparation of this manuscript. SMC dedicates this chapter to Professor William D. Stansfield of California Polytechnic State University, San Luis Obispo, in recognition of his long service in genetics education.

REFERENCES

Cannaozzi, G., Schneider, A., 2012. Codon Evolution, Mechanisms and Models. Oxford University Press, Oxford.

Carr, S.M., Wareham, H.T., Craig, D., 2014a. An algorithmic and computational approach to open reading frames in short dsDNA sequences: evaluation of "Carr's Conjecture". In: Arabnia, H.R., Tran, Q.-N., Yang, M.Q. (Eds.), Proceedings of the International Conference on Bioinformatics and Computational Biology, pp. 37–43.

Carr, S.M., Craig, D., Wareham, H.T., 2014b. A web application for generation of DNA sequence exemplars with open and closed reading frames in genetics and bioinformatics education. CBE Life Sci. Educ. 13, 373–374.

Crick, F.H.C., 1966. The genetic code, yesterday, today, and tomorrow. Cold Spring Harbor Symp. Quant. Biol. 31, 3–9.

Itzkovitz, S., Alon, U., 2007. The genetic code is nearly optimal for allowing additional information within protein-coding sequences. Genome Res. 17, 405–412.

Johnson, L., Cotton, J., Lichtenstein, C., Elgar, G., Nichols, R., Polly, D., Le Comber, S., 2011. Stops making sense: translational trade-offs and stop codon reassignment. BMC Evol. Biol. 11, 227.

Judson, H., 1996. The Eighth Day of Creation, second ed. Cold Spring Laboratories, Cold Spring Harbor, New York.

Nirenberg, M., Leder, P., Bernfield, M., Brimacombe, R., Trupin, J., Rottman, F., O'Neal, C., 1965. RNA codewords and protein synthesis VII. On the general nature of the RNA code. Proc. Natl. Acad. Sci. U. S. A. 53, 1161–1168.

Nirenberg, M., Caskey, T., Marshall, R., Brimacombe, R., Kellogg, D., Doctor, B., Hatfield, D., Levin, J., Rottman, F., Pestka, S., Wilcox, M., Anderson, F., 1966. The RNA code and protein synthesis. Cold Spring Harbor Symp. Quant. Biol. 31, 11–24.

Overballe-Petersen, S., Harms, K., Orlando, L., Mayar, J., Rasmussen, S., Dahl, T., Rosing, M., Poole, A., Sicheritz-Ponten, T., Brunak, S., Inselmann, S., de Vries, J., Wackernagel, W., Pybus, O.G., Nielsen, R., Johnsen, P., Nielsen, K., Willerslev, E., 2013. Bacterial natural transformation by highly fragmented and damaged DNA. Proc. Natl. Acad. Sci. U. S. A. 110, 19860–19865.

Intentionally Linked Entities: A Detailed Look at a Database System for Health Care Informatics*

14

V. Kantabutra

Department of Electrical Engineering, Idaho State University, Pocatello, USA

1 INTRODUCTION

This chapter introduces a database system called Intentionally Linked Entities (ILE), which links data entities in a more robust and efficient way than the relational database system. ILE also stores data in a more organized fashion than the relational system, and is more efficient at searches. These positive qualities of ILE present the possibility of improving the reliability and correctness of health care databases, and may therefore lead to improved and more efficient patient care and database analysis. By storing information more accurately and in a more organized fashion than the relational database system, ILE may help health care providers avoid mistakes that can compromise patient health, patient confidentiality, or other aspects of high-quality patient care. The improved data modeling afforded by ILE may also lead to improved epidemiological data modeling, intended to aid epidemiological discoveries.

A major motivation for developing the ILE database system is the importance of implementing data linking in a better, more robust way. The importance of data linking in health care databases is eloquently described in Trotter and Uhlman (2013, p. 55):

> Data linking is all about the way data in one part of a patient's record relates to data in another part of the record. When data linking fails, the data in an EHR [electronic health record] for a patient is at war with itself. The simplest way to ensure that data is well-linked is to try and ensure that data is always linked correctly,

---

*This is an extended version of a conference paper previously presented and published in the proceedings (Kantabutra, 2014).

The authors also pointed out that when the information from a health care database is used for making dangerous decisions such as drug dosing and administration, even a seemingly minuscule error rate such as 0.02% may mean several tragic errors because of the volume of cases handled in a large medical facility. Patients with the same or similar names are routinely confused in health care facilities. Such confusion may lead to serious health risks such as improperly handling drug allergies, inappropriate medicine or medical/surgical procedures, a compromise of patient confidentiality, or inefficient or inaccurate health care database analysis. This is why linking errors have to be eliminated as much as possible.

The relational database system, first developed by Edgar F. Codd in the early 1970s, remains the most popular type of database system for health care informatics today (Wager *et al.*, 2005). Despite its name, a significant problem with the relational database system is relationship linkage, which refers to the physical linking of data entities that are supposed to be related to each other via a relationship. More specifically, the relational database system determines whether two data entries are the same by comparing data field values, values that are entered separately by the users, often without a stringent check to make sure that entries that supposed to match actually match each other.

The problem with the relational database's value comparison scheme is that any misspelling, including the inclusion of extraneous blanks or invisible control characters, can cause an absence of linkage. Less likely, but also possible, is the situation where two entries are inadvertently spelled the same and therefore linked when they should not be.

Another problem with the relational database system is that it is not a natural means of modeling complex data. Researchers and practitioners have noticed this fact since the 1980s, including in computer-aided design (CAD; Stajano, 1998) and in electronic medical records (Speckauskiene and Lukosevicius, 2008). As stated correctly in Kalet (2014, p. 134), the relational database model is appropriate for use when data logically match the idea of many identically structured records with a relatively simple structure, or a collection of such structures.

The relational database system is also well known to suffer from data redundancy and data fragmentation. Data redundancy can be reduced by not permitting duplicate entries and by normalization. However, checking for duplicates reduces efficiency in a large database, and normalization can be quite difficult to do correctly. Additionally, many users and database practitioners prefer nonnormalized databases because the tables of a nonnormalized database can be much easier to use, having all or much of the desired information in one table.

Using an object-oriented database (OODB) would solve the abovementioned linking problem inherent in the relational database system. Using a network database, such as its new form, the graph database, would solve the linking problem as well. This is because both the OODB and network database systems use object references or pointers for linkage, and linking to a nonexistent object is automatically not permitted. From Chaudhri and Zicari (2001), it can be seen that Object-Oriented databases have often become the database paradigm of choice for bioinformatics, or least for genomic computations.

However, the OODB system has two limitations that make it far less than optimum for health care informatics, or at least the part of it that deals with the treatment of diseases by health care providers working with patients and institutions like hospitals. One limitation is the lack of a query language in the original versions of the OODB. It is argued that the OODB is more often used in programs, and therefore what is important is an application programming interface (API), not a query language. However, by the turn of the millennium, OODB vendors have realized that users normally require a query language, and thus the vendors responded by providing query languages. In fact, vendors went further and permitted relational features in their systems, resulting in the object-relational database system. The other, more important limitation of the OODB is that it only supports relationships with two roles (that is, binary relationships, or relationships with arity $=2$). Basically, the only means the OODB has for relating objects is to use object-valued attributes with references to other objects (Kim, 1993; Schlegelmilch, 1996). Thus, researchers had to come up with various, nonnative ways to augment the OODB system to handle relationships of higher arity, that is, relationships with three or more roles played by entities (Schlegelmilch, 1996).

As mentioned earlier, the graph database would also solve the linkage problem. However, like the OODB, this style of database system also restricts the arity of the relationships to 2. Furthermore, many-many relationships, which are binary (arity-2) relationships, are also not natively supported. Therefore, only relationships that are binary and one-to-one or many-to-one are natively supported by the OODB. Additionally, in an OODB system, there are no physical objects (in the object-oriented sense) representing the entity sets, and likewise no physical objects representing the relationship sets. As detailed in this chapter, ILE, on the contrary, does use objects to represent entity sets and relationship sets, as well as entities and relationships.

Lee *et al.* (2013) studied using Extensible Markup Language (XML) and certain tabular NoSQL approaches as alternatives to the relational approach for storing medical records. In brief, they found that the NoSQL approach is a "viable alternative" to the relational approach, whereas the XML is a "promising solution" that is "not yet ready for prime-time usage." We will consider these approaches and compare them with the ILE approach in section 4 of this chapter.

As stated before, this chapter introduces the author's Intentionally Linked Entities (ILE) data model and the corresponding ILE database system as a better alternative to the electronic health record (EHR) than the relational, objected-oriented, tabular NoSQL systems, or the graph database system. The ILE database system was reported by this author in Kantabutra (2007). How ILE can be used in social network analysis and other applications in the digital humanities was explored in Kantabutra *et al.* (2010, 2014).

ILE uses object-reference-based data structures to link entities that play various roles in each relationship. The ILE database system natively supports relationships of all arities, meaning binary, ternary, quaternary, etc. In addition, there is no restriction on how many other entities each entity could be related to in a relationship. So, for example, many-many relationships, which are binary, are supported. Additionally, each role in a relationship can be played by an entire set of entities if that capability is needed. No other database system or model supports such general types of relationships, and that fact makes ILE more suited to the complex relationships found in health care situations. ILE was conceived as a direct implementation of the Entity/Relationship (E/R) database model. However, as it stands now, ILE is more general in some important ways than E/R.

At the time of Kantabutra (2007), ILE was not implemented. Since then, however, a prototype has been implemented in Ruby, an object-oriented programming language that is particularly good for handling complex data structures and algorithms. However, lately the Treetop library for interpreting the commands and queries has been broken. The Treetop package is not easy to work with anyway, so the author decided to rewrite the command interpreter. The ILE code itself, implementing all the data structures, remains intact, and a new command interpreter is being written using a different package, Parslet, which, in the author's opinion, is much easier to work with than Treetop.

This chapter extends the author's earlier BIOCOMP conference paper (Kantabutra, 2014) by adding a new section on modeling an epidemiological database with ILE and another section surveying other nonrelational approaches in keeping medical records.

2 INTRODUCING ILE FOR HEALTH CARE APPLICATIONS

The best way to think of ILE is that it is a direct, straightforward implementation of the E/R model. There are differences and extensions, but we can deal with those as they come up.

As can be concluded from the previous discussion, the relational model favors relatively simple data models, even when these models are not necessarily as realistic as one would like. As an example, consider a relational model from a database for JMTZ Bee Healthcare, Inc., of a relationship between a provider (a doctor in this case) and a patient, shown in Figure 14.1 (Jin, 2000).

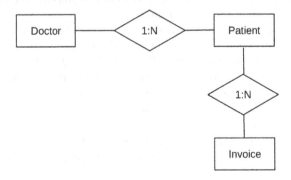

FIGURE 14.1

A partial E/R diagram showing the provider-patient relationship in a relational database for JMTZ Healthcare, Inc.

Suppose that we want to model the fact that a relationship between a provider and a patient comprises a set of visits. There are database models for the patient-provider relationship where the two people are related by a "visit" relationship. In such a representation, each visit is a separate relationship, and there is nothing that really binds all the visits of one patient to the same provider together.

In ILE, we can easily model both individual visits and the longer-term relationship between a provider and a patient. The most natural way to do this is shown in Figure 14.2.

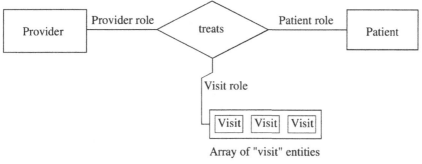

FIGURE 14.2

A possible provider-patient relationship in ILE.

This can be easily implemented in ILE as a ternary relationship, where the roles are patient, provider, and visits. The third role, visits, is actually a set or an array. In relational databases, arrays are usually not permitted. For example, MySQL does not permit array data types. Workarounds are necessary; for example, see MySQL 5.7 reference manual, section 11.1 (n.d.). Oracle, which has some features that are beyond those of plain Relational databases, does have an array data type called ARRAY, and a variant of that data type called VARRAY (see the definition of ARRAY, in the Oracle database system, n.d.), but the elements don't appear to be full-fledged entities that can be conveniently linked in relationships as individuals or first-class citizens of the database.

As another example to use in comparing the various kinds of databases, we can look at prescriptions. In JMTZ's relational database, a prescription is an entity with two binary relationships, as shown in Figure 14.3.

One of these relationships is with an invoice, and the other with one or more medicines. An invoice may have 0, 1, or more prescriptions.

The relational data model used by JMTZ allows for relationships with arbitrary arity. However, many designers of relational databases favor binary relationships because in a binary relationship, entities can be linked directly, without an extra table representing the relationship, and also because joins can be expensive, especially joins of more than two tables. Even query optimization can take considerable time. If this situation were to be modeled using a graph database or a pure OODB, then the type of relationships used would most likely be binary because only binary relationships are natively supported.

ILE, as opposed to these other database schemes, comfortably and natively supports relationships of practically any finite arity. Figure 14.4 shows how we can model a prescription in ILE as a relationship of arity 4.

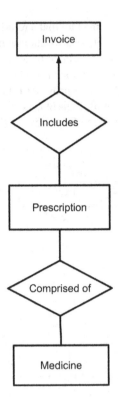

FIGURE 14.3

Representing the Prescription relationship for JMTZ Healthcare, in an E/R diagram meant for implementation as a relational database

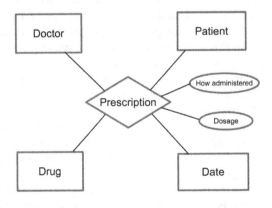

FIGURE 14.4

The Prescription relationship in ILE.

In section 5 of this chapter, we will discuss, among other things, how such relationships are implemented in ILE using relationship objects that securely link the various entities playing the roles in each relationship so that navigation from the entities playing one set of roles to the entities playing another set of roles is direct and efficient.

3 ILE AND EPIDEMIOLOGICAL DATA MODELING

One important use of health care databases that doesn't seem to have been thoroughly explored, judging from the lack of well-cited papers in that area, is the use of such databases in epidemiology, including using databases to facilitate making epidemiological discoveries. Here again, researchers have been using the relational model. In particular, we will examine the database model introduced in Winnenburg *et al.* (2006), shown in Figure 14.5.

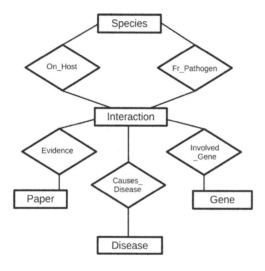

FIGURE 14.5

E/R diagram meant for a relational database for an epidemiology database from Winnenburg *et al.* (2006).

In this E/R model, it is clear that each member of the entity set Interaction actually has the meaning of a relationship that relates entities in several other entity sets, namely, Species (host and pathogen), Paper, and Gene.

For a good correspondence between data representation and data model semantics, Interaction should really be modeled as a relationship between these other entities. However, as observed earlier, relational database designers favor binary relationships over relationships with arity greater than 2, which explains why we have binary relationships here, forcing Interaction to be an entity set rather than a relationship set. It is not difficult to see why relational database designers prefer binary relationships when working with this example. If Interaction were to be represented directly as a relationship, it would need to be a quinary relationship; that is, a relationship with five roles. A relational table representing such a relationship would be large, and a query on this relational database would involves a join of up to six tables, with one table representing the relationship set Interaction and one table for each of the five roles.

Actually, even representing Interaction as an entity set and implementing the set as a table in the relational model may not save on the complexity of queries. If fields from all the entity sets are queried at the same time, then we still need to join multiple tables.

In Figure 14.6, we show the ILE alternative; that is, the ILE modeling of the same database.

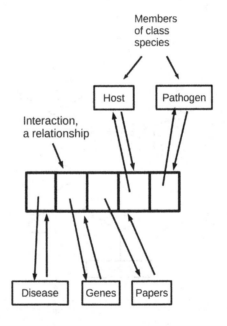

FIGURE 14.6

ILE database for the same epidemiology database as in Figure 14.5.

Since ILE naturally supports relationships of arbitrary arities, we represent the interactions between the true entities in the database—namely, Species (host and pathogen), Paper, and Gene—as a set of quinary relationships. Each relationship object has direct object references to the objects representing the entities involved in the relationships, and each of the entity objects likewise has direct object references to all the relationship, as well as to all the other relationships that the entity is involved in. No expensive table joins are required at all.

4 OTHER NONRELATIONAL APPROACHES TO KEEPING MEDICAL RECORDS

This section will describe another paper that introduces nonrelational database models for use in storing health records, and compare those approaches with the ILE model presented here. In particular, we will discuss the approaches discussed by Lee *et al.* (2013). Two approaches were considered in that paper: namely, table-based NoSQL and XML. For the XML approach, two options were considered: the option of using native XML and the option of using Microsoft SQL Server and its XML data type.

According to Lee, Tang, and Choi, each medical consultation (which we call a "visit" elsewhere in this chapter) results in a medical note. This note is then organized into a hierarchical structure, as shown in Figure 14.7.

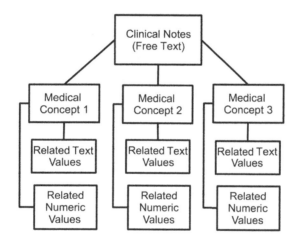

FIGURE 14.7

Lee, Tang, and Choi's conceptual model of medical notes.

Such medical records can be represented in XML as shown in Figure 14.8.

The same paper also gives the actual XML code snippet for this. The header in that code contains patient information, whereas the body contains elements representing a subset of a wide variety of possible medical concepts, which we could also call "medical conditions" or "attributes," such as fever, nausea, vomiting, or paralysis.

Our critique of the XML approach favored by Lee and colleagues is that XML most naturally supports hierarchical relationships, even though other relationships can be represented by identifying an element with an attribute of type *ID* and then referring to such an element with an attribute of type *IDREF* (Garcia-Molina *et al.*, 2008). This general-graph capability of XML only naturally supports one-to-one and

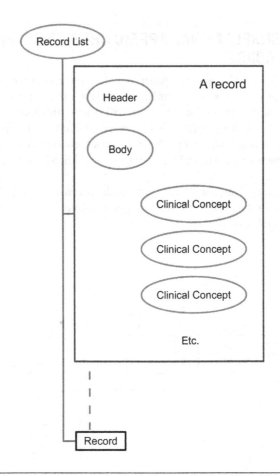

FIGURE 14.8

XML database model for medical records containing the same information as in Figure 14.7.

many-to-one binary relationships, like the graph database system. Many-to-many binary relationships and relationships with arity greater than 2 are not supported. Perhaps higher-arity relationships can be supported somewhat awkwardly in XML by simulation. On the contrary, ILE supports multiple-arity relationships natively, as explained previously.

An additional result in the Lee *et al.* study shows that the XML approach, whether using native XML or the XML data type in a relational server, is currently much slower than using tabular NoSQL approaches.

The other approach for storing medical record data suggested by Lee and colleagues is to use a table-based NoSQL database. Four options (a, b, c, and d) for this approach are shown in Figure 14.9.

Cough Table

Consult ID	Severity	Duration	Unit	Time	....	....
1	Light	2	Day	1200	....	....

Fever Table

Consult ID	Temp	Duration	Unit	Time	....	....
1	37.5	3	Day	1000	....	....

Dyspnea* Table

Consult ID	Severity	Duration	Unit	Time	....	....
1	Medium	2	Day	1200	....	....

(a)   One concept per table (3 concepts)

Consult ID	Fever	Cough	Temp.	Vomit	Chills	....
1	Yes	Medium*	40*	No	No	....

(b)   Fixed column names

Consult ID	Key1	Value1	Key2	Value2	....	....
1	Fever	Yes	Temp.	37.5C	....	....

(c)   Fixed key-value pairs

Consult ID	Key	Value1	SubKey1	SubKey Value 1	....
1	Fever	Yes	Duration	4 days	....
1	Temp.	37.7	Unit	C	....
1	Cough	Yes	Yes	3 days	....

(d)   Generalized key-value pairs

FIGURE 14.9

Various possible ways to represent medical records using tabular NoSQL, where each medical visit involves clinical notes with a widely varying set of clinical concepts. The asterisk entries are the one that are edited because the original entries are inappropriate. For example, the table label *Dyspnea* appeared as *Dyposea* in Lee, Tang, and Choi.'s paper.

These NoSQL approaches, being based on tables storing values, suffer from the same linkage problem described in this paper as belonging to relational databases. By this, we mean that such linkages implemented by matching character strings are error prone.

Additionally, these tabular NoSQL approaches suffer from data fragmentation (namely, the same data fragmentation suffered by relational systems. More specifically, there is no one place where all data pertaining to one entity can be found.

Figure 14.10 shows how to model the same database in ILE. Here, linking is more secure because the links are done with relationship objects and object references. Data fragmentation is also nonexistent because all information pertaining to each entity is linked securely.

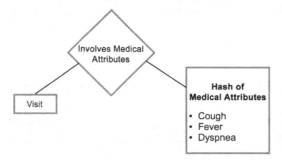

FIGURE 14.10

ILE database model for medical records fashioned after the examples shown in Lee *et al.* (2013) and containing the same information as in Figures 14.8 and 14.9.

Using ILE makes it much easier to tie together all the instances of the same medical condition because they all belong to the same entity set. The concept of entity set doesn't really exist in either XML or in the NoSQL models used by Lee, Tang, and Choi. Additionally, because the medical conditions are full-fledged entities in ILE, we can potentially link them to other entities via ILE relationships. This could be very useful in making epidemiological discoveries.

5   INSIDE THE ILE DATABASE SYSTEM

This section will look more deeply into the ILE system. Before we do that, though, let us note that the main idea is to be able to represent each relationship as an object that links the related entities together by means of links (object references or pointers) that go in both directions (namely, from the relationship object to each entity and from each entity to the relationship object). For example, the prescription relationship illustrated earlier in Figure 14.4 would be linked as illustrated in Figure 14.11.

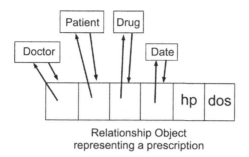

Relationship Object
representing a prescription

FIGURE 14.11

Showing links used in the Prescription relationship, as in Figure 14.4 in ILE.

While the idea behind this relationship linkage is simple enough, the actual implementation is not so simple. This is because each entity may be involved in more than one relationship, and maybe even more than one type of relationship. Therefore, instead of using one object reference to go from an entity to a relationship object, we will use an aggregate data structure to hold such object references. This and other details will be the subject of the rest of this section.

The top-level structure of ILE is actually a database set, implemented as a database set object. The database set contains its databases in a hash. This setup will permit cross-database searches within a database set, to be implemented in the future if there appears to be a need for such searches. Each database is also implemented as an object. The database set object has a hash whose data values are references to the database objects representing the databases of the database set. Each database object also has a reference back to the database set object.

Within an ILE database are four different sets of components:

- Entity sets
- Entities
- Relationship sets, also known as *relsets*
- Relationships

Each of these components is implemented as an object. The database object keeps track of the database's entity sets and relationship sets, and each entity set and each relset in turn has direct references back to the database to which they belong.

Note that the current version of ILE is value-oriented, not object-oriented, though arbitrary classes of entities are permitted simply because ILE's implementation language, Ruby, is object-oriented. In the near future it may be a good idea to extend ILE to allow full object-oriented features. Being a value-oriented database system, ILE requires the entities of each entity set to have at least 1 field serving as the primary key. This concept should be familiar to readers who use the relational database model.

The principal function of an entity set object is to keep all the entities belonging to the entity set together, as well as to facilitate searches for members of the entity set. The components of the entity set object are shown in Figure 14.12:

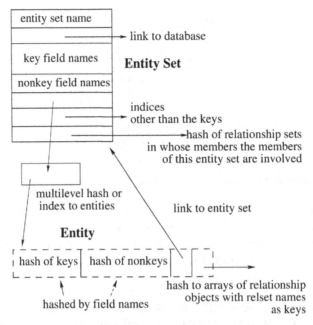

FIGURE 14.12

An entity set object and an entity object in ILE, including details of the contents of each object.

- *Entity set name.* This is any string, but of course, it is meant to describe the entities in the entity set.
- *Link to database.* This is just an object reference back to the database to which this entity set belongs.
- *Key field names.* The current version of ILE is value-oriented like the relational database system, not object-oriented, even though it is implemented with an object-oriented language and permits use of nonelementary objects such at Date, or anything else for that matter. Anyway, the fact that the ILE system is value-oriented means that all entities in an entity set have key fields. The entities may also have nonkey fields just like the entities in a relational database.
- *Multilevel hash or index to the entities belonging to this entity set.* Every entity set uses a multilevel hash as the primary way to access the entities. Another indexing scheme could be used, especially if the database is large enough that the entities mainly reside in secondary storage or somewhere on a computer network. The current index, the multilevel hash, is structured so that each level corresponds to a key field.
- *A hash of relsets to whose members the members of this entity set are involved.* This is a useful aid for performing queries on the database.

An entity object contains the following fields:

- A hash of key values.
- A hash of nonkey values.

- A link back to the entity set object representing the entity set to which this entity belongs.
- A hash to arrays of relationship objects with relset names as hash keys. For each relset, there may be more than one relationship in which this entity participates, thus explaining the use of an array of relationship objects for each relset.

We now explain relationship set (relset) objects and relationship objects, as shown in Figure 14.13.

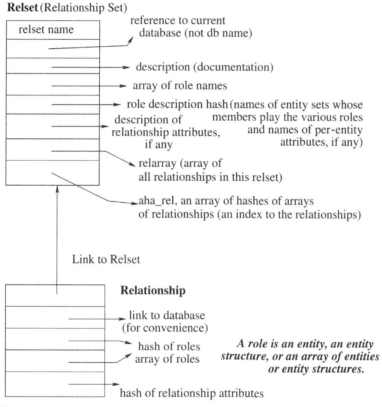

FIGURE 14.13

A relset object and a relationship object in ILE, including details of the contents of each object.

A relationship set object, or relset object, contains the following fields:

- A field for the relset name, which is any string but should represent a descriptive name.
- An object reference back to the database object.
- A verbal description of the relationship set.
- A set of role names.

- A description of relationship attributes, if any. This should be upgraded in later versions of ILE to be a more structured container for such attributes.
- Relarray, an array of all relationships in this relset.
- A data structure called aha_rel, which is an *array* of *hashes* of *arrays* of *rel*ationships in this relset. This is a complex and efficient index of all the relationships.

A relationship object has the following fields:

- A link to the database.
- A hash of roles, hashed by role name.
- An array of roles, so that one could access the roles in numerical order. Since both the hash and the array really contain object references, it is not much of a waste of space to have both the hash and the array.
- A hash of relationship attributes, if any.

A role belonging to a relationship can be of different types (see Figure 14.14).

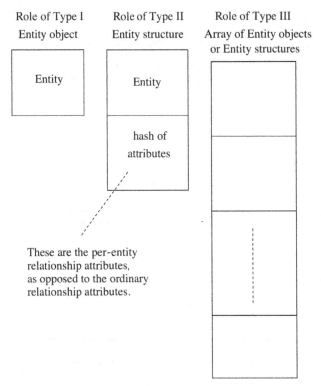

FIGURE 14.14

The three types of role objects in a relationship.

The simplest type of role is just an entity object, representing the entity that plays that role. However, in case there is a per-entity relationship attribute, then we need such attributes to be attached to the entity, forming an *entity structure* object.

But what is a per-entity relationship attribute? The concept behind this kind of attribute was inspired by a historical database, where merchants and their clients came together to sign a contract in the presence of a notary back in the 1500s in Spain. There were some cases where the person wasn't present but had someone sign the contract instead.

The contract was modeled as a relationship in ILE, and each merchant and each client played roles in this relationship. A Boolean flag was used to indicate whether or not the person was present in person to sign the contract. This flag was modeled as a per-entity relationship attribute, so that each person had a different flag. The flags could have been modeled as a bit array serving as an ordinary relationship attribute. However, it appears that the modeling of these flags as per-entity relationship attributes was a more natural, intuitively appealing choice.

We have now discussed the first two possibilities for a role as shown in Figure 14.14. The third possibility is that a role can be an array (representing a set) with each array element being either an entity object or an entity structure object.

As an example of a relationship linking roles, Figure 14.15 shows how three roles can be linked by a relationship object in ILE.

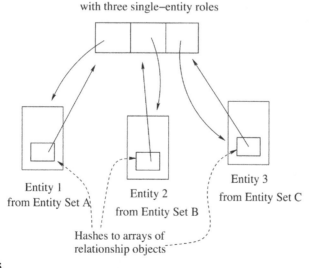

Role structure of a relationship object
with three single–entity roles

Entity 1
from Entity Set A

Entity 2
from Entity Set B

Entity 3
from Entity Set C

Hashes to arrays of
relationship objects

FIGURE 14.15

Linking three roles with a relationship object.

6 AN EXAMPLE OF THE IMPORTANCE OF AN EHR IMPLEMENTED IN ILE

We close this chapter by examining how the sophisticated data modeling afforded by ILE can make for an EHR for a hospital admission that would make it easier for hospital epidemiologists or infection control practitioners to track down how an infectious disease or agent, such as staph, tuberculosis, Ebola, or pneumonia, is being spread or may be spread in a hospital. Nosocomial infections are one of the hazards of hospitalization. Minimizing the chances of harmful nosocomial infections being spread is essential to patient health and health care administration and a robust ILE patient EHR can help with this. A robust EHR implemented in ILE can also make it easier to track which health care workers may have been exposed to a particular infectious disease.

One solution is to model hospital admissions as a relationship set. Each hospital admission then becomes a relationship in this set. This relationship is very complex because it relates entities from many entity sets. In particular, it relates a patient with a set of doctors, a set of nurses, certified nursing assistants (CNAs), technicians of various sorts, equipment, doctor's orders, patient diagnosis or diagnoses, rooms occupied, what diet the patient is eating, and other factors. If the patient has an infectious disease, the room and patient could be flagged to indicate this fact with a per-entity relationship attribute. If a particular infectious disease agent is spreading, the epidemiologist or infection control practitioner can look at the database of ILE EHRs to see if there is a common factor or factors, such as a particular health care worker, that is found in many of the patients contracting a nosocomial infection. Other database system types would have difficulty modeling such a complex set of entities and relationships about health care admissions and may be more error prone and present more difficulties with analyzing the health care data.

7 CONCLUSIONS

This chapter introduced Intentionally Linked Entities (ILE) and explains why it may be a better database system than the existing relational, graph, object-oriented, and other NoSQL database systems for managing health care information. ILE links data entities in a more robust and efficient way than the relational database system. With the embodiment of the entity sets, entities, relationship sets, and relationships as objects, ILE stores data in a more organized fashion than the relational or the graph database system. ILE is also capable of expressing more general relationships among data entities than the OODB system because the pure OODB system only natively supports binary relationships when more complex relationships may need to be represented, such as in the hospital epidemiology example described in this text. Object-relational database systems have the same pitfall in linking general relationships of arity higher than 2 as the relational database system does. ILE is designed to make more complex relationships between data entities easy to represent and analyze. All these desirable properties of the ILE database system may lead to better management of health care information and therefore possibly improved patient care, better protection of patients, hospital health care workers, support staff, and visitors from infectious disease, more efficient health care operations, and better health care database analysis.

ACKNOWLEDGMENTS

The author gratefully acknowledges the support of U.S. National Science Foundation CDI Type II award no. NSF-0941371, as well as the support of an internal Idaho State University College of Science and Engineering grant. The author is also grateful for the help of his wife, Deborah Arnold, for essential input to this project stemming from her knowledge of the health care field. Finally, thanks are also due to J. B. "Jack" Owens for his general support of this project, including the inclusion of this project into a larger project that was being funded by the NSF.

REFERENCES

ARRAY (definition of, in the Oracle database system), n.d. URL: http://psoug.org/definition/ARRAY.htm.

Chaudhri, A.B., Zicari, R., 2001. Succeeding with Object Databases. Wiley.

Garcia-Molina, H., Ullman, J.D., Widom, J., 2008. Database Systems: The Complete Book, second ed. Prentice Hall.

Jin, Y., 2000. Healthcare Management System. JMTZ Bee Healthcare, Inc. PDF document distilled from PowerPoint slides. URL:http://www.angelfire.com/ny4/yjin/Healthcare/Healthcare-ppt.pdf See also: http://www.angelfire.com/ny4/yjin/Healthcare/Healthcare-doc.pdf.

Kalet, I.J., 2014. Principles of Biomedical Informatics, second ed. Elsevier.

Kantabutra, V., 2007. A new type of database system: Intentionally Linked Entities-a detailed suggestion for a direct way to implement the entity-relationship data model. In: CSREA EEE. pp. 258–263.

Kantabutra, V., 2014. Intentionally Linked Entities: a database system for health care informatics. In: Proc. BIOCOMP, p. 14.

Kantabutra, V., Owens, J.B., Ames, D.P., Burns, C.N., Stephenson, B., 2010. Using the newly created ILE DBMS to better represent temporal and historical GIS data. Trans. GIS 14, 39–58.

Kantabutra, V., Owens, J.B., Crespo-Solana, A., 2014. Intentionally Linked Entities: a better database system for representing dynamic social networks, narrative geographic information, and general abstractions of reality. In: Crespo Solana, A., Alonso García, D. (Eds.), Spatio-Temporal Narratives: HGIS and the Study of Trading Networks (1500 - 1800). Cambridge Scholars Press, Cambridge, U.K.

Kim, W., 1993. Object-oriented database systems: promises, reality, and future. In: Proc. of the 19th VLDB, pp. 652–687.

Lee, K.K.-Y., Tang, W.-C., Choi, K.-S., 2013. Alternatives to relational database: comparison of NoSQL and XML approaches for clinical data storage. Comput. Meth. Programs Biomed. 110.

MySQL 5.7 reference manual, section 11.1, n. d. URL: http://dev.mysql.com/doc/refman/5.7/en/data-type-overview.html.

Schlegelmilch, J., 1996. An Advanced Relationship Mechanism for Object-Oriented Database Systems. Department of Computer Science, University of Rostock, Germany.

Speckauskiene, V., Lukosevicius, A., 2008. The use of object-oriented technologies for medical data storing and retrieving. European Journal for Biomedical Informatics, 4(1).

Stajano, F. 1998. A gentle introduction to relational and object-oriented databases. ORL Technical Report TR-98-2.

Trotter, F., Uhlman, D., 2013. Hacking Healthcare. O'Reilly.

Wager, K.A., Lee, F.W., Glaser, J.P., 2005. Managing Health Care Information Systems, A Practical Approach for Health Care Executives. Jossey-Bass, San-Francisco.

Winnenburg, R., Baldwin, T.K., Urban, M., Rawlings, C., Köhler, J., Hammond-Kosack, K.E., 2006. PHIbase: a new database for pathogen host interactions. Nucleic Acids Research, 34.

Region Growing in Nonpictorial Data for Organ-Specific Toxicity Prediction

Ray R. Hashemi[1], Azita A. Bahrami[2], Mahmood Bahar[3], Nicholas R. Tyler[4], and Daniel Swain, Jr.[1]

Department of Computer Science, Armstrong State University, Savannah, GA, USA[1]
IT Consultation, Savannah, GA, USA[2]
Department of Physics, Islamic Azad University, Tehran North Branch, Tehran, Iran[3]
School of Pharmacy, University of Georgia, Athens, GA, USA[4]

1 INTRODUCTION

Region growing is a well-established concept in the field of image processing. It is used to identify a group of neighboring pixels within an image (pictorial data) that have the same features. To accomplish the region growing, a pixel is selected as the "seed" and all the pixels that satisfy two criteria of being neighbors of the seed and having a common set of features with the seed are added to the region. Each added pixel, in turn, acts as a new seed and the process of region growing continues until no more pixels can be added to the region (Hashemi, 2001). Selections of the features of interest along with the neighborhood radius are subjective and defined by the region grower. An image may have several regions. The regions, among other things, can be used effectively in mining of pictorial data. Examples are numerous, including mining of abnormalities in medical images, image content discovery, image understanding, and vision (Sahu *et al.*, 2012; Antonie *et al.*, 2001; Megalooikonomou *et al.*, 2000; Smith *et al.*, 2013).

The intriguing question is whether one can grow regions for the nonpictorial data and the grown regions can effectively contribute to the mining of such data. By *nonpictorial data*, we mean a data set comprising a set of objects (records) free of pixel-based data. There are four major challenges when exploring such an intriguing question: establishing foundation of region growing, creating a vehicle for delivering regions, building a mining methodology using the regions, and comparing the effect of such methodology with the known existing ones.

The goal of this research effort is to investigate and provide for all these challenges. To meet the goal, after defining the basic foundation, we specifically introduce a new version of the self-organizing map (SOM) neural network (Kohonen, 1982), named *Neighborly SOM,* which is able to deliver the regions for a nonpictorial data set. The data set of interest includes the structure activity relationships (SAR) of a set of chemical agents and their features. A new prediction methodology is introduced based on the delivered regions that will be used to examine the prediction of the chemical agents' liver toxicity.

The remaining organization of this chapter is as follows. Related research in this area is covered in section 2. The basic foundation is presented in section 3. The methodology of the study is introduced in section 4, and the empirical results are discussed in section 5. Our conclusions and implications for future research is covered in section 6.

2 RELATED WORKS

There is a large body of research about the concepts of neighborhood and closeness. When it comes to numerical data, Euclidean distance is often the choice of measuring the closeness of objects. However, two objects that are close together, due to their small Euclidean distance, are not necessarily *neighbors*. To explain this concept further, the sum of the Euclidian distances among the n attributes of the two objects (which is only one value) is the deciding factor for determining closeness. In other words, n attributes have a collective effect on the Euclidean distance, whereas the deciding factor for having two objects as neighbors is every individual attribute distance (*i.e.,* n values) (Lin, 1997). To deliver the neighborhood for a given object, we introduce a modified version of the SOM neural network. To the best of our knowledge, using a neural network to deliver neighbors of an object (and not its close objects) has not been explored before.

The neighborhood concept as a tool for defining the granularity of data was explored by the soft computing community (Lin, 1997; Hashemi *et al.*, 1998; Yao and Zhong, 2002). Recently, there are some attempts to use the neighborhood system as a foundation for prediction (Hashemi *et al.*, 2013, 2014; Yao, 2000). We try to build such a tool using our previous experiments (Hashemi *et al.*, 2013, 2014).

3 BASIC FOUNDATION

An object with n attributes ($A_1, \ldots, A_n$) may be represented as a point in an n-dimensional space. In such a space, object O_i is the neighbor of object O_j, if O_i is within the n-sphere neighborhood of O_j. This n-sphere is centered on O_j and its radius (r) is the neighborhood radius of O_j. Therefore, O_i is the neighbor of O_j if for every attribute A_k, the distance of $|O_j.A_k - O_i.A_k| \leq r$ (for $k = 1$ to n) (Hashemi *et al.*, 2004, 2013; Yao, 2000). Two objects within the neighborhood n-sphere of O_j are not necessarily neighbors of each other. For example, the data set in Figure 15.1(a) has three objects and the objects are described by two attributes of A_1 and A_2. Consider the neighborhood radius of $r=1$, the objects of O_2 and O_3 are neighbors of O_1, but they cannot be neighbors of each other because the distance between O_2 and O_3, at least for one attribute, is greater than r [see Figure 1(b)]. If one creates the two-sphere of object O_3, it does not include O_2.

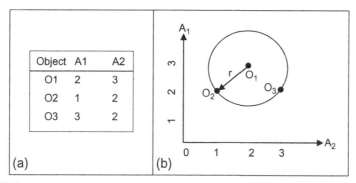

Object	A1	A2
O1	2	3
O2	1	2
O3	3	2

(a)

(b)

FIGURE 15.1

Neighborhood concept: (a) A data set and (b) the neighborhood two-sphere of object O_1.

In an image, region growing starts with a pixel as a seed, p_j, and any pixel, p_i, that satisfies the following two criteria is added to the region of p_j (Hashemi *et al.*, 2002):

Criterion I: p_i is the neighbor of p_j and
Criterion II: p_i satisfies some features

The same steps are followed to grow a region for nonpictorial data. However, due to the physical boundaries of the pixels (manifested as their coordinates), a pixel has maximum of eight *immediate* neighbors (8-Neighbor), whereas an object may have many immediate neighbors.

In other words, the first condition of region growing from a given pixel (seed) has a maximum of eight immediate candidates for further expansion, but an object may have a large number of candidates. Eventually, a pixel may participate in maximum of one region. In contrast, an object has a potential of participating in several regions. Such a potential may dilute those features of a given region that contribute to an effective data mining. Consequently, the multiple region inclusion of the same object needs to be controlled.

As part of the basic foundation, two issues need to be addressed. The first issue is about the second condition of region growing. In pictorial data, the features that a pixel can satisfy are determined through applying a function on the pixel value, the pixel's coordinates, values of the neighboring pixels, coordinates of the neighboring pixels, or any combination of these. One may ask what can be used to determine features for objects of a nonpictorial data set. The response to this question comes from the nature of data itself. To explain it further, let us divide the nonpictorial data sets into two large groups as follows. Every object in a data set of the first and the second groups are composed of *n* attributes (descriptive attributes) and n+1 attributes (n descriptive attributes and one decision attribute), respectively. Only the members of the second group are fit for region growing. As a result, the features that an object can satisfy are determined through applying a function on all or a subset of these attributes. The subset always includes the decision attribute. The descriptive and decision attributes are also known as the independent and dependent variables.

The second issue is about the differences between a *cluster* and a *region*. By definition, objects of a cluster have great similarity in comparison with each other but are very dissimilar to the objects in other clusters (Han and Kamber, 2006). This is not true for a region. An object in one region may also be a member of another region. In fact, the objects within a region are only similar to the seed and not necessarily to each other. Considering Figure 15.1 again, the objects of O_2 and O_3 are in the region of O_1. However, O_2 and O_3 are not neighbors of each other, and they are dissimilar in comparison to each other, which contradicts the definition of a cluster. In other words, a cluster includes the objects that are close to the centroid of the cluster, whereas a region includes all the neighbors of a given object.

4 METHODOLOGY

First, a new version of the SOM neural network, Neighborly SOM, is presented as the methodology for delivering regions of nonpictorial data. Second, a new prediction methodology is introduced based on the delivered regions. The details of the methodologies are covered in the following two subsections.

4.1 NEIGHBORLY SOM

The traditional SOM is a two-layer neural network, introduced by Kohonen (1982), which cluster the records of an input data set. The weight vector for each output node, representing a cluster, is generated randomly, and each input vector (O_i) fires an output node (B_j) such that the Euclidean distance between O_i and weight vector (W_j) of B_j is the minimum, calculated as follows:

$$D(B_j) = \sum_i (W_j - O_i)^2 \tag{15.1}$$

The weight vectors of the fired node and those nodes close to the fired one [within a local radius] are modified by a portion of the differences between the input and the weight vectors. The portion is decided by the learning rate, calculated as follows:

$$W_j(new) = W_j(old) + \eta [O_i - W_j(old)], \tag{15.2}$$

where O_i is an input vector, W_j is the weight vector of a node within the locale of the winner node, and η is the learning rate ($0 < \eta < 1$).

After a predefined number of epochs, both the local radius and the learning rate are reduced. The process repeats until the input vectors cannot change the size of the clusters.

Three elements shape the architecture and behavior of the Neighborly SOM and they are the nature of the input data, shortcomings of SOM (Hashemi *et al.*, 2005), and neighborhood concept influence. The nature of data was addressed in section 2 of this chapter. In building the Neighborly SOM, the remedies for shortcomings of the traditional SOM were pointed out as needed. The influence of the neighborhood concept changes the SOM from a cluster builder to a region grower.

4.1.1 Architecture of Neighborly SOM

The traditional SOM performs the clustering of the objects of a given data set. However, we are not interested in the clusters for a given set of seeds; instead, we are interested to grow regions for them. As a result, we introduce changes to the traditional SOM to support the growth of regions by adopting the same two criteria for region growing in images (introduced earlier in this chapter in section 3).

The first departure from the traditional SOM is in the number of output nodes. The number of output nodes is initially equal to 1, and the first object of the data set is considered as the weight vector of the output node. Any object of the data set that is not able to fire the existing output nodes will serve as the weight vector of a new output node. By doing so, the number of output nodes is dictated by the objects of the data set and their weight vectors are not generated randomly. Clearly, this modification is in response to some of the SOM shortcomings. (For details about these shortcomings, consult Hashemi *et al.*, 2005.)

The second departure from the traditional SOM is caused by providing for the first criterion of the region growing. Eq. (15.1) is replaced by Eqs. (15.3) and (15.4). We assume that both input and weight vectors have n elements:

$$D(B_j) = \frac{P(B_j)}{Q(B_j)}, \tag{15.3}$$

where

$$P(B_j) = \sum_i^n |w_{ij} - o_i|, \tag{15.4}$$

and $Q(B_j)$ is the number of terms of $|w_{ij} - o_i|$ in Eq. (4) that are not zero.

The winner node is the one for which

$$D(B_j) \leq r + \delta, \tag{15.5}$$

where r is the neighborhood radius and δ is a small value (usually equal to $1/10$ of r). The purpose of having δ is to inject some small flexibility into the size of the radius. This flexibility is needed due to changes in the weight vector.

Just as a reminder, using Eq. (15.1) will put both O_1 and O_3 of the nonpictorial data set of Figure 15.1(a) in the same cluster, whereas Eq. (15.5) puts O_1 and O_3 in different neighborhoods, correctly.

The last departure from the traditional SOM is caused by providing the second criterion of region growing. Having the same decision value for the overwhelming majority of the objects of a region is considered the common feature among the objects. The dilution of the common feature is measured and represented by the *dilution factor, DF,* of the region. Let R be a region with k objects and weight vector of W. Let us also assume that k_1 objects in R have the same decision value as W, k_2 objects have different decisions from W, and $k=k_1+k_2$. The dilution factor for R is defined as follows:

$$DF_R = \frac{k_1}{k} \tag{15.6}$$

It is obvious that if k_2 increases, the feature of the region R is more diluted. When an object can be a part of more than one region, it decreases the dilution factor for those regions whose decision value of their weight vectors is not the same as the object's decision value. However, if increases in k_2 are too small, then dilution can be tolerated. Both prevented dilution and tolerated dilution are used to handle the case of multiple-region membership for a given object. Of course, the enforcement of the prevented dilution has a priority over the tolerated dilutions.

Consequently, when more than one output node can be fired, the one that the decision attribute of its weight vector matches the decision attribute of the object is chosen to be fired (prevented dilution). If a tie was not resolved, then the output node whose region has the largest cardinality is fired. If the tie persists, a winner node is randomly chosen. The cardinality of a region that is used in tie breaking may be calculated using recent memory or past memory. The recent memory cardinality refers to the number of objects added to a given region during the current epoch, whereas the past memory cardinality is the number of unique objects that were a part of the region during at least one of the epochs starting from the first epoch through the current one.

As an example, let us concentrate on two output nodes of B_1 and B_2 and the first two consecutive epochs of 1 and 2. The objects firing B_1 and B_2 during each epoch which make their regions are shown in Table 15.1.

Usually, the use of recent memory is preferred when the training set is large; oth-

Table 15.1 Use of Recent and Past Memories in Calculating the Cardinality of a Region

Epochs and Cardinality	Objects in B_1 Region	Objects in B_2 Region
Epoch 1	$\{O_5, O_2, O_9, O_6\}$	$\{O_8, O_1, O_4\}$
Epoch 2	$\{O_5, O_1, O_9, O_6, O_4\}$	$\{O_8, O_2\}$
Card(Region)-Recent Memory	5	2
Card(Region)-Past Memory	6	4

erwise, use of past memory is preferred.

The locale radius in Neighborly SOM is always zero to discourage firing of multiple output nodes. These changes in the traditional SOM are encapsulated in the following algorithm:

Algorithm

Neighborly_SOM

Given: A nonpictorial data set, D, with $n+1$ attributes (n descriptive attributes and 1 decision attribute). Neighborhood radius r and δ, $(0 < \delta < 0.1*r)$. Learning rate of η, $(0 < \eta < 1)$, and β factor for decreasing η as needed. A chosen number of epochs, E.

Objective: Growing regions of the data set D.

```
Step 1—Repeat while number of epochs<E;
    Step 2—Repeat for every randomly chosen object, Oi = (o_i1...o_in) from D
    until D is exhausted;
        Step 3—Repeat for each output node, B_j, with weight vector of
        W_j = (w_i1...w_in);
            P(W_j)=Σ Abs(w_jm-o_im) (for m=1 to n);
            Q(W_j)=the number of terms (w_jm-o_im)≠0 (for m=1 to n);
            Dist(W_j) = P(W_j)/Q(W_j);
            If (Dist(W_j)≤r+δ
            Then  Add Bj to the candidateList;
        Step 4—If (Card(candidateList)=0)
            Then  Add a new output node, B_k, to the SOM;
                  Set W_k←O_j;
                  Add O_i to the region for the new output node; go to step 2;
            If (Card(candidateList) >1)
            Then  Tie breaking rules and their orders of precedence for
            selecting a winner node are:
                  a—The winner node must have the same decision value as O_i;
                      a1—If more than one such node exist, then select the
                          one with the highest cardinality of its region as
                          the winner;
                      a2—If more than one such node exist, then randomly
                          select a winner node among the ones that their
                          cardinalities are the same;
                  b—If rule (a) fails, then fire the node with the minimum
                  cardinality.
        Step 5—For the winner node, B_g, Do:
            a—Add O_i to the region for B_g;
            b—W_gm (new)=W_gm(old)+η[O_im - W_gm(old)] (for m=1 to n);
            c—The decision value of Wg is set to the dominant decision among
            the objects in the region of B_g.
    Step 6—η(new)=β * η(old) ;
Step 7—End;
```

4.2 A REGION-BASED PREDICTION METHODOLOGY

After the training of the Neighborly SOM is completed, it identifies the final set of regions $(R_1, \ldots, R_n)$, their corresponding output nodes $(B_1, \ldots, B_n)$, and their corresponding weight vectors $(W_1, \ldots, W_n)$. To turn the Neighborly SOM into a prediction tool, some adjustments are necessary. The adjustment rules are listed below based on their precedence, from highest to lowest:

If $v \neq v'$, then set $v \leftarrow v'$, where v and v' are the values for the decision attribute of Wi and dominant decision value of R_i, respectively.

If $W_i = W_j$, then replace B_i and B_j with a new output node of B_y such that $W_y = W_i = W_j$ and $R_y = R_i \cup R_j$. R_y may have a dilution factor that is different from both Ri and Rj.

If $DF_{Ri} < T_{df}$, ($\forall$ i), then remove output of node B_i, its region, and its weight vector. T_{df} is a threshold value.

If the $Card(R_i) = 1$, then remove the output node B_i, its region, and its weight vector.

The Neighborly SOM is now ready to act as a predictive tool. The features of the regions are their weight vectors. A test object that has not been previously seen by the system is fed to the system only once. A degree of neighborhood between the test object and each weight vector (say, W_j), is calculated using Eq. (15.7):

$$\text{Degree of neighborhood} = \sum_{i=1}^{n} Z_i, \qquad (15.7)$$

where $n = Card(W_j)$ and

$$Z_i = \begin{vmatrix} 1, & \text{if}(|w_{ij} - o_i| \leq r + \delta \\ 0, & \text{Otherwise} \end{vmatrix}$$

The winner node is the one that has the largest degree of neighborhood. The value of the decision attribute of the winner node's weight vector is the predicted decision for the test object. If more than one node is fired, then the dominant decision value among the weight vectors of the fired nodes is the predicted decision for the test object. If there is no dominant decision, then the test object cannot be predicted.

5 EMPIRICAL RESULTS

John Young and his research team in the National Center for Toxicological Research (NCTR) have investigated the properties of more than a thousand chemical agents (Young et al., 2004). The purpose of such investigation was to provide a means for rapidly predicting organ-specific toxicity of new chemicals. As the first step, there was a need for building a data set based on the structure activity relationships (SAR) of the chemical agents. Two main sources that contributed to the building of the SAR data set were the Carcinogenic Potency Database (CPDB) (Gold et al., 1984) and research findings reported in the literature. With regard to the first source, CPBD, a chemical agent may have several records representing studies for different genders, species, rout of administration, and organ-specific toxicity. Such group of records was mapped onto a single record for the SAR data set. A single value for the agent toxicity was also concluded using the different toxicity level of the agent. In addition, elements that could either cause inaccuracy or structural inconsistency were removed. With regard to the second resource, the findings reported in the literature were verified by Young's research team, duplicating the reported experiments.

After structural cleanup of the agents, SAR data set included 999 chemical agents (objects). Each object had 140 attributes, including a decision attribute that its value indicated whether the agent causes cancer in liver or not. The value for decision attribute was either 1 (toxin) and 0 (nontoxin). We used the proposed methodology to build a system to predict the organ-specific toxicity of the agent using its descriptive and decision attributes.

Building of the predictive system was started by identifying and removal of those descriptive attributes that are redundant. A redundant attribute does not strongly contribute to the decision. An entropy approach (Natt *et al.*, 2012) was used to complete the task that resulted in the identification of only seven descriptive attributes as nonredundant. Removal of the redundant attributes generated many duplicates and contradictory objects. Two contradictory objects have the same values for their descriptive attributes, but different values for their decision attributes. As part of the preprocessing of the SAR data set, one copy of the duplicated objects was kept and the contradictory objects were removed from data set. After the preprocessing of SAR data set was completed, it contained 426 objects.

To measure the prediction accuracy of the Neighborly SOM, the repeated random sub-sampling, RRSS, cross-validation was used. For this validation, 10 pairs of training and test sets were carved from the preprocessed SAR data set as follows. A total of 10% of the SAR objects were randomly selected as a test set. From the remaining records in SAR, the maximum number of objects was selected as a training set, such that the number of objects with decision 1 and with decision 0 in the training set were the same. The reason for having the same number of objects for each decision value was to make sure the trained Neighborly SOM was not biased toward one of the decisions. Since only 10% of the SAR objects were chosen as a test set, 10 pairs of the training and test sets were created, such that each test object appeared in only one test set.

For each pair of training and test sets, the Neighborly SOM was trained by the training set and its prediction accuracy was tested by the corresponding test set. The average results for the 10 test set along with the specificity and sensitivity are shown in Table 15.2.

Table 15.2 Prediction Results for Neighborly SOM, Traditional SOM, and C4.5 Using 10 Pairs

Methodology	% of Correct Predictions	% False Negatives	% False Positives	% Sensitivity	% Specificity	% of Failed Predictions
Neighborly SOM	77	7.62	4.3	78.3	88.7	13
Traditional SOM	63.57	29.8	6.67	72	60.94	0
C4.5	36.2	8.3	25.5	26.7	76.7	30

Table 15.3 Prediction Results for Neighborly SOM, Traditional SOM, and C4.5 Using LOO Cross-Validation

Methodology	% of Correct Predictions	% False Negatives	% False Positives	% Sensitivity	% Specificity	% of Failed Predictions
Neighborly SOM	78.2	8.5	5.9	72.5	88.1	7.5
Traditional SOM	69	25.4	6.6	70.1	67.9	0
C4.5	67.8	0.24	17.2	57.8	99.5	14.8

It is logical to compare the prediction accuracy of the Neighborly SOM with the prediction accuracy of the traditional SOM. To complete the task, we repeated the following process for each pair of the training and test set using the traditional SOM:

1. The initial possible number of output nodes was selected to be 20, for which 20 weight vectors were randomly generated (one per output node). The number of epochs remained the same so as the initial values of η and β. After the clusters of the training set were produced, the dominant decision for each cluster was calculated.
2. During the test process, the decision value of the test object was compared with the dominant decision of the cluster of the fired node.

The average results for all 10 pairs are shown in Table 15.2.

The prediction accuracy of the Neighborly SOM was also compared with the prediction accuracy of the well-known approach of C4.5 (Quinlan, 1993) using the same 10 pairs of training and test sets. These results are also shown in Table 15.2.

In addition, we compared the performance of the three predictive methods of the Neighborly SOM, traditional SOM, and C4.5, using leave-one-out (LOO) cross-validation (Kohavi, 1995). In this cross-validation, one object of the data set was set aside as a test set, and from the remaining objects, a training set was carved such that the number of objects in the training set was the same for all the decision values. The process was repeated for every object of the data set and then the prediction accuracy results for each model were averaged. The results are shown in Table 15.3.

6 CONCLUSIONS AND FUTURE RESEARCH

Neighborly SOM generates regions of the input data set, whereas the traditional SOM clusters the input data set. It is important that the differences between the region and cluster be pointed out one more time. Similar objects make a new cluster; however, neighbor objects make a new region. In clustering, the similarity function produces one value as a base for identifying similar objects. In region growing, the neighborhood function produces several values as a base for identifying neighbors of an object. As a result, two similar objects are not necessarily neighbors of each other, but two neighbor objects are similar.

The results of this study revealed that the regions delivered by the Neighborly SOM for a nonpictorial data set were effective in mining such data, and the sensitivity of the prediction methods showed that the Neighborly SOM is more robust than the other two methods. Results in Tables 15.2 and 15.3 also disclose that Neighborly SOM is less sensitive to the size of the training set.

For the sake of observation, the training and test process for the traditional SOM was repeated under the conditions that the number of outputs and the original weight vectors were exactly the same as the ones for Neighborly SOM. In fact, the set of output nodes and their initial weight vectors generated in the first epoch of Neighborly SOM were used in the traditional SOM. This condition improved the overall performance of the traditional SOM to some degree. However, the sensitivity was reduced and specificity increased.

Currently, investigations of several variations of the Neighborly SOM are in progress for development of nested regions. The ultimate goal is to use nested regions for subpartitioning a given problem space.

REFERENCES

Antonie, M.L., Zaiane, O.R., Coman, A., 2001. Application of data mining techniques for medical image classification. J. MDM/KDD 2001 (August), 94–101.

Gold, L.S., Sawyer, C.B., Magaw, R., Backman, G.M., de Veciana, M., Levinson, R., Hooper, N.K., Havender, W.R., Bernstein, L., Peto, R., Pike, M.C., Ames, B.N., 1984. A carcinogenic potency database of the standardized results of animal bioassays. Environ. Health Persp. 58, 9–319.

Han, J., Kamber, M., 2006. Data Mining: Concepts and Techniques. Morgan Kauf- mann Publishers.

Hashemi, R., Danley, J., Bolan, B., Tyler, A., Slikker, W., Paule, M., Oct. 1998. Information granulation and super rules. In: Georgiou, G., Janikow, C., Yao, Y. (Eds.), Proceedings of the Fourth International Joint Conference on Information Sciences. Research Triangle Park, NC, pp. 383–386.

Hashemi, R., Epperson, C., Jones, S., Jin, L., Smith, M., Talburt, J., August 2001. Boundary Detection in Yellow page documents. In: Ishii, N., Mizuno, T., Lee, R.Y. (Eds.), Proceedings of The 2001 Conference on Software Engineering, Artificial Intelligence, Networking and Parallel/Distributed Computing (SANPD'01)pp. 479–486, Nagoya, Japan.

Hashemi, R., Epperson, C., Jones, S., Jin, L., Smith, M., Talburt, J., June 2002. Identifying and removing extraneous graphics in a commercial OCR operation. In: Jamshidi, M., Hata, Y., Fathi, M., Homaifar, A., Jamshidi, J.S. (Eds.), Proceedings of The 2002 World Automation Congress (WAC'02). TSI Press, Orlando, Florida, pp. 389–394.

Hashemi, R., Agustino, S.D., Westgeest, B., June, 2004. Data granulation and formal concept analysis. In: Dick, S., Kurgan, L., Musilek, P., Pedrycz, W., Reformat, M. (Eds.), Proceedings of the 2004 International Conference of North American Fuzzy Information Processing Society (NAFIPS'04), pp. 79–83, Sponsored by IEEE, Banff, Alberta, Canada.

Hashemi, R., Bahar, M., De Agustino, S., Oct. 2005. An extended self-organizing map (ESOM) for hierarchical clustering. In: Jamshidi, M., Tunstel Jr., E., Anderson, G., Fathi, M., Dozier, G., Johnson, M., Chen, P. (Eds.), The 2005 IEEE International Conference on Systems, Man, and Cybernetics (CSM'05), The Big Island, Hawaii, pp. 2856–2860.

Hashemi, R., Bahrami, A., Smith, M., Tyler, N., Antonelli, M., Clapp, S., July 2013. Discovery of predictive neighborly rules from neighborhood systems. In: International Conference on Information and Knowledge Engineering (IKE'13), Las Vegas, Nevadapp. 119–125.

Hashemi, R., Bahrami, A., Tyler, N., Antonelli, M., Dahlqvist, B., August, 2014. Property preservation in reduction of data volume for mining: a neighborhood system approach. In: Laux, F., Pardalos, P.M., Crolotte, A. (Eds.),. The Third International Conference on Data Analytics (DATA ANALYTICS 2014), pp. 105–111, Rome, Italy.

Kohavi, R., August, 1995. A study of cross-validation and bootstrap for accuracy estimation and model selection. In: Mellish, C.S. (Ed.), In: Proceedings of the 14th International Joint Conference on Artificial Intelligence, vol. 2. Morgan Kaufmann Publishers Inc, Montreal, Quebec, Canada, pp. 1137–1145.

Kohonen, T., 1982. Self organizing formation of topologically correct feature maps. Biol. Cybern. 43, 59–69.

Lin, T.Y., Sept. 1997. Granular computing: from rough sets and neighborhood systems to information granulation and computing in words. In: European Congress on Intelligent Techniques and Soft Computing.pp. 1602–1606.

Megalooikonomou, V., Ford, J., Shen, L., Makedon, F., Saykin, A., 2000. Data mining in brain imaging. J. Stat. Methods Med. Res. 9 (4), 359–394.

Natt, J., Hashemi, R., Bahrami, A., Bahar, M., Tyler, N., Hodgson, J., April 2012. Predicting future climate using algae sedimentation. In: The Ninth International Conference on Information Technology: New Generation (ITNG-2012), pp. 560–565, Sponsored by IEEE Computer Society, Las Vegas, Nevada.

Quinlan, J.R., 1993. C4.5: Programs for Machine Learning. Morgan Kaufmann Publishers.

Sahu, M., Shrivastava, M., Rizvi, M.A., Nov. 2012. Image mining: a new approach for data mining based on texture. In: Proceedings of 2012 Third International Conference on Computer and Communication Technology (ICCCT), Allahabad, India, pp. 7–9.

Smith, M., Hashemi, R., Bahrami, A., July 2013. Intelligent mobile app for identifying skin pigments. In: The International Conference on Information and Knowledge Engineering (IKE'13), Las Vegas, Nevada, pp. 108–113.

Yao, Y., 2000. Information Tables with Neighborhood Semantics, Data Mining and Knowledge Discovery: Theory, Tools, and Technology II, vol. 4057, Published by the international society for optics and photonics, pp. 108-116.

Yao, Y., Zhong, N., 2002. Granular computing using information tables. In: Lin, T.Y., Yao, Y., Zadeh, L.A. (Eds.), Data Mining, Rough Sets and Granular Computing. Physica-Verlag, Heidelberg, pp. 102–124.

Young, J., Tong, W., Fang, H., Xie, Q., Pearce, B., Hashemi, R., Beger, R., Cheeseman, M., Chen, J., Chang, Y., Kodell, R., 2004. Building an organ-specific carcinogenic database for SAR analyses. Int. J. Toxicol. Environ. Health A 67 (June), 1363–1389.

Contribution of Noise Reduction Algorithms: Perception Versus Localization Simulation in the Case of Binaural Cochlear Implant (BCI) Coding

16

Arnaud Jeanvoine[1,2,4], Dan Gnansia[4], Eric Truy[1,2,5], and Christian Berger-Vachon[1,2,3]

INSERM U1028, Lyon Neuroscience Research Center, DYCOG Team/ PACS Group (Speech, Audiology, Communication Health), Lyon, France[1]
CNRS UMR5292, Lyon Neuroscience Research Center, DYCOG Team/ PACS Group (Speech, Audiology, Communication Health), Lyon, France[2]
University Lyon 1, Lyon, France[3]
Neurelec, Vallauris, France[4]
Audiology and ORL Department, Edouard Herriot Hospital, Lyon, France[5]

1 INTRODUCTION

Hearing in humans has two important purposes: communication (speech recognition) and warning (acoustic source localization). The influence of assistive technology (deafness rehabilitation) on these two basic functions is worth studying. This feature can be seen also with cochlear implants (CIs). Nowadays, CIs are widely used for profound deafness rehabilitation, but speech perception in noisy environments still remains a challenge for hearing-impaired subjects and for persons using a CI (implantees) (Dunn *et al.*, 2010); a lot of work is presently done in this field of hearing rehabilitation (Blauert, 2013; van Dijk *et al.*, 2012; Yousefian and Loizou, 2013).

Binaural hearing uses two main acoustic cues: interaural time difference (ITD) and interaural level difference (ILD) (Doerbecker and Ernst, 1996; Francart *et al.*, 2011):

- ITD is the delay between both ears. It is efficient for low frequencies (below 850 Hz). It is due to the envelope of the signal reaching the two ears. It can be reminded that a sound coming from the side at 90° has an ITD of 0.6 ms. When the source is situated in the front (azimuth 0°), the so-called front target, the ITD is 0 ms.
- ILD is related to the intensity reaching the two ears. The signal is more or less attenuated by the head shadow. This effect is mostly perceptible with high frequencies (above 3 kHz). ILD is 0 for the front target.

In the case of binaural cochlear implants (BCIs), two CIs are used, and only one processor drives them. The ITD can be employed in a coordinated process (van Hoesel et al., 2009; Lawson et al., 1998).

Several noise reduction algorithms favor the signal coming from the front (Van den Bogaert et al., 2008, 2009). The aim of noise reduction algorithms is to improve speech intelligibility, but localization should be considered as well; when an algorithm improves speech perception (for instance, by focusing on a source situated in the front), the localization of other sound sources may be affected. Furthermore, some reinjection of the input signal has been suggested by Van den Bogaert in the case of hearing aids (Van den Bogaert et al., 2008), in order to restore some source localization of the sound source; this effect will be seen in the current work. This strategy is worthy in the case of CI coding (Loizou, 2006).

Several binaural algorithms are classically used for noise reduction, such as the Beamformer, which favors a direction through delay (Bouchard et al., 2009; Kompis and Dillier, 2001). Spectral subtraction, based on the estimation of the noise, followed by the attenuation of the band spectrum containing the noise by widely used Wiener filtering, may improve the signal-to-noise ratio (SNR) (Van den Bogaert et al., 2009; Kallel et al., 2012; Yang and Fu, 2005).

In the case of CIs, an additional processing is needed to adapt the acoustic signal to the CI electric stimulation. In the current study, a vocoder simulation was taken to simulate CI coding (Loizou, 2006). Cochlear implantees cannot use some localization cues, such as the ITD (Dorman and Loizou, 1997; Lawson et al., 1998), which is lost. In our study, subjects with normal hearing were looked at to estimate the influence of the noise reduction algorithms after CI coding. Ultimately, the results will have to be seen with implantees when enough subjects wearing the BCI are available, leading to a homogeneous population. Coding of the signal, according to CI processing, with a homogeneous population of normal hearing listeners is worthy to be considered (Dorman and Loizou, 1997; Kerber and Seeber, 2012).

The goal of the present study is to evaluate the influence of the noise-reduction systems suggested by Matthias Döerbecker in the localization of a sound source, in a BCI context, compared to the beamformer algorithm. Doerbecker's processing is classically used in normal hearing aids. A sine vocoder has been considered to simulate BCI speech processing.

The technical aspects are indicated in section 2. Results are then presented and discussed in sections 3 and 4. Finally, salient features are outlined in the conclusion of the chapter.

2 MATERIALS AND METHODS
2.1 SIGNAL PROCESSING
2.1.1 Overall organization

The synoptic representation of the acquisition of the signal is represented in Figure 16.1. The speech signal was emitted by the front loudspeaker (0°), and the noise was presented from a loudspeaker (LS) array. The LSs were situated at angles θ ranging from −90° to 90°. The acoustic signal is captured by the microphones (m_1 and m_2).

In addition, a percentage (α) of the input signal was reinjected after the noise reduction algorithms (Van den Bogaert *et al.*, 2008). The values of α were fixed to 0.0, 0.2, and 0.4 (0%, 20% and 40%).

The basic reinjection formula used in this work was

$$s'(t) = (1 - \alpha).s(t) + \alpha.e(t), \tag{16.1}$$

where *e(t)* is the input signal, *s(t)* is the signal leaving the noise reduction processor, *s'(t)* is the signal output, (entering the vocoder), α is the reinjection (0%, 20%, 40%), and *s''(t)* is the output signal presented to the listeners.

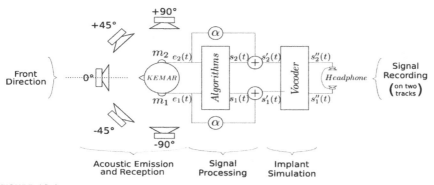

FIGURE 16.1

Synoptic of the experiment; the algorithm used is the Beamformer or either of Doerbecker's strategies.

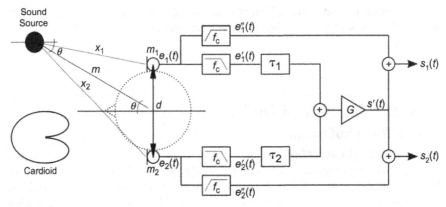

FIGURE 16.2

Synoptic representation of the beamformer algorithm

2.1.2 Beamformer

The schematic representation of the Beamformer is presented on Figure 16.2.

The signal emitted by the sound source is captured by two microphones, m_1 and m_2 (right and left), situated on the ears of a Knowles Electronics Manikin for Acoustical Research (KEMAR) head. The classical Beamformer (BF) response is a cardioid centered on the front loudspeaker, LS3 (Bouchard *et al.*, 2009). The BF algorithm is presented next, and it favors the front target (0° azimuth); the experiment was in the horizontal plane.

The input signal reaching the two ears $e(t)$ can be represented (complex plane) in the case of a sine wave by

$$e(t) = A.e^{j\omega(t-\tau)} = A.e^{j\omega\left(t-\frac{x}{c}\right)} = A.e^{j\left(\omega t-\frac{2\pi x}{c T}\right)} = A.e^{j\left(\omega t\frac{2\pi x}{\lambda}\right)} = A.e^{j(\omega t - \Phi)} \quad (16.2)$$

where A is the signal magnitude, x is the distance between the source and the microphones (x_1 and x_2), c is the sound velocity in air (340 m/s), λ is the wavelength, τ is the propagation time between the source and the microphones, d is the distance between the two ears (20 cm), Φ is the phase delay between the source and the microphones, and θ is the orientation angle of the sound source.

The phase difference between the signals reaching the two ears is

$$\Delta\Phi = \frac{2\pi}{\lambda}(x_1 - x_2) \approx \frac{2\pi.d}{\lambda}\sin(\theta)$$

The beamformer algorithm (based on the phase information) is mainly helpful when

$$\Delta\Phi = \frac{2\pi.d}{\lambda} \leq \pi,$$

leading to fc ≤ 850 Hz (850 Hz is obtained for $\theta = \pi/2$). The maximum delay between the two ears represents about 10 samples at the sampling frequency fs$= 16$ kHz.

In the Beamformer strategy, the low-frequency part of the signal (below 850 Hz) is processed and the signals coming from the two microphones are added. Then the high-frequency components of the signal are restored for further treatment.

2.1.3 Doerbecker's processing

Doerbecker's processing is a noise reduction procedure enhancing the sound coming from the front; it is based on a spectral subtraction followed by an adaptive Wiener filtering (Figure 16.3). It begins by the estimation of the noise. Doerbecker's strategy is mostly based on spectrum consideration.

In Doerbecker's processing, the noise estimation follows one of two methods. The first is referred to as the *Ephraim and Malah correction* (Ephraim and Malah, 1984), which is a binaural process reducing the musical noise introduced by the spectral subtraction. The second is *Scalart's correction* (Scalart and Filho, 1996), which selects, on each channel, the best SNR, which is similar to Wiener's algorithm (Van den Bogaert *et al.*, 2009).

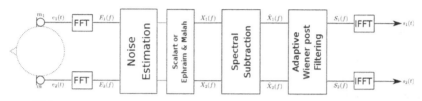

FIGURE 16.3

The main steps of the Doerbecker's algorithm.

The steps of Doerbecker's processing are as follows:

1. A short-term fast Fourier transform (FFT) is applied to the signal captured by the two microphones m_1 and m_2, leading to two processing lines, one on each side:

$$E_1(f) = FFT(e_1(t))$$

$$E_2(f) = FFT(e_2(t))$$

where $E_1(f)$ and $E_2(f)$ are the spectrum components at a frequency f (amplitude and phase) in the complex plane.

2. The estimation of the noise spectrum is obtained by subtracting the cross-power spectrum to the power spectra as follows:

Power spectra:

$$\Phi_{x_1 x_1}(f) = |E_1(f)|^2$$
$$\Phi_{x_2 x_2}(f) = |E_2(f)|^2.$$

Cross-power spectrum (scalar product):

$$\Phi_{x_1 x_2}(f) = |E_1(f).E_2(f)|.$$

3. Noise estimation (on line 1) is given by

$$\Phi_{nn1}(f) = \Phi_{x_1 x_1}(f) - \Phi_{x_1 x_2}(f)$$

If $\Phi_{nn}(f)$ is negative, $\Phi_{nn}(f)$ is set to zero; this action is called the *musical noise*. A similar formula is used on line 2.

It can be seen that if $X_1(f) = X_2(f)$, then $\Phi_{nn}(f) = 0$ (no noise) for the frequency f.

4. Ephraim and Malah correction

The Ephraim and Malah formula (Ephraim and Malah, 1984) introduces a spectrum amplitude correction for the speech signal in order to minimize the mean-square error of the log spectra. It attenuates the musical noise and represents a smoothing between the time frames:

$$G = \frac{\sqrt{\pi}}{2} \sqrt{\left(\frac{1}{1+R_{post}}\right)\left(\frac{R_{prio}}{1+R_{prio}}\right)} * M\left[(1+R_{post})\left(\frac{R_{prio}}{1+R_{prio}}\right)\right] \qquad (16.3)$$

where G is the gain that is applied to each short time spectrum; R_{post} is the *a posteriori* SNR, which is the local estimate of the SNR computed from the current data in the current short time frame; R_{prio} is the *a priori* SNR, which corresponds to the information on the spectrum magnitude gathered from previous frames (this value defines the attenuation of the musical noise and is widely discussed in Cappe, 1994); and M represents the Bessel functions of zero and first order.

5. Scalart correction

The Scalart formula was developed to improve the SNR in the frequency domain (Scalart and Filho, 1996):

$$G(f) = \sqrt{\frac{SNR(f)-1}{SNR(f)}} = \sqrt{1 - \frac{1}{SNR(f)}} \qquad (16.4)$$

$G(f)$ weights the frequencies of the signal and is set to zero if $SNR(f) < 1$. Thus, frequencies with a low SNR are disadvantaged.

6. Spectral subtraction

In the next step, a spectral subtraction is performed (Yang and Fu, 2005):

$$\text{Right side (ear)} : \overline{X}_1(f) = \sqrt{\Phi_{x_1 x_1}(f) - \Phi_{nn}(f)} \qquad (16.5a)$$

$$\text{Left side (ear)} : \overline{X}_2(f) = \sqrt{\Phi_{x_2 x_2}(f) - \Phi_{nn}(f)} \qquad (16.5b)$$

This strategy disadvantages the frequencies where $X_1(f)$ is different from $X_2(f)$.

7. Wiener filtering

A general Wiener coefficient $W_s(f)$ is calculated (Van den Bogaert et al., 2009; Doerbecker and Ernst, 1996), indicating the percentage of noise, for each frequency (Figure 16.3):

$$Ws(f) = \frac{4|\Phi_{x_1 x_2}(f)|^2}{(|\Phi_{x_1 x_1}(f)| + |\Phi_{x_2 x_2}(f)|)^2},$$

with $W_s(f) = 1$ if $X_1(f) = X_2(f)$.

Then, each frequency f of the input signal is corrected by W_s, on each way, as follows:

$$|S_1(f)| = \sqrt{|\Phi_{X_1 X_1}(f)| * W_s(f)}$$
$$|S_2(f)| = \sqrt{|\Phi_{X_2 X_2}(f)| * W_s(f)}$$

(16.6)

Finally, the processed signal is reconstructed using an inverse fast Fourier transform (IFFT).

2.1.3 Vocoder

CI coding was represented by a classical vocoder (Figure 16.4) (also see Loizou, 2006) performing the channel simulation.

For this application, the Neurelec BCI parameters have been taken:

1. Sampling frequency (fs): 16 kHz
2. Frame length: 8 ms (128 time samples); a 75% overlap between the frames was used, leading to the signal refreshing every 2 ms. Spectral bins (spectral lines) were calculated using a FFT; then the 64 bins were grouped according to the bark scale in order to build up the channels (Table 16.1). The bark scale follows the cochlea lin-log properties of the cochlea.
3. The spectrum was parted into 12 frequency bands, (12 channels, corresponding to the 12 electrodes) on each ear. According to the short-term FFT theory, bin spacing was 125 Hz.
4. The eight highest energy channels were selected Dorman and Loizou, 1997; Friesen *et al.*, 2001). For each channel, a sine wave, taken at the center frequency of each band, was multiplied by the energy of the frequency band. The four remaining (nonselected) channels were eliminated.

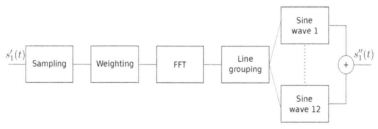

FIGURE 16.4

Synoptic of the vocoder.

2.2 PHONEME RECOGNITION SESSION

2.2.1 Phonetic material

The noise was obtained from a speech signal analyzed by a FFT and reconstructed with a random phase. The signal was the phonetically balanced Lafon's lists (www.extpdf.com/lafon-pdf/html) classically used in the French clinical tests. Each list has 17 three-phoneme words, leading to 51 phonemes. A total of 20 lists are available.

Table 16.1 Representation of the 12 Frequency Bands (Channels)

Channel	1	2	3	4	5	6	7	8	9	10	11	12
F_m (Hz)	325	473	641	836	1067	1344	1675	2087	2585	3195	3945	4866
f_M (Hz)	473	641	836	1067	1344	1675	2087	2585	3195	3945	4866	6000

Note: f_m and f_M represent the low and the high cutoff frequencies of the corresponding bandpass, respectively.

The noise was presented at the input of the system, from one of the five loudspeakers (Figure 16.1). The input angle was θ. Lafon's lists were always presented from the front LS (θ=0°).

Then, the signal was recorded on the KEMAR head. Consequently, the ITD and the ILD effects were present. The distance head-LS was 1 m; azimuth ranged from −90° to 90°, with five positions (−90°, −45°, 0°, 45°, 90°). A sample frequency was fs = 44.1 kHz; then it was downsampled to fs = 16 kHz. The intensity was 70 dB SPL, allowing a good dynamic for the recording. The recorded signal was then processed and the final signal, represented by $s_1''(t)$ and $s_2''(t)$ in Figure 16.1, was burned on a CD. All subjects followed two successive stages: first, a training session; and second, an assessment (test) session.

2.2.2 Training session

Each subject listened to the vocoded speech (VOC) with no noise added, and was asked to repeat each three-phoneme word. The percentage of correct recognition of phonemes (PCRPs) was recorded for each of the 20 lists. This training task lasted until each subject reached a performance of at least 80% of correctly repeated phonemes. The training session for all the subjects lasted less than 15 min.

2.2.3 Phoneme recognition test

Then, subjects were instructed to listen to a total of 150 lists; each list corresponded to a given experimental condition (as described next). The lists were chosen randomly in the data bank (the 20 Lafon's lists), and each list was equally represented throughout the different 150 conditions indicated here:

1. Three algorithms: Beamformer (BF), Doerbecker+Ephraim and Malah (DOEM), and Doerbecker+Scalart (DOS)
2. Three reinjection percentages: α=0% (denoted 00), 20% (20), and 40% (40)
3. Five angles for the noise: θ= -90°, -45°, 0°, +45° and +90°
4. Three SNRs: −6 dB, 0 dB, and 6 dB

This leads to $3 \times 3 \times 5 \times 3 = 135$ situations. Consequently, the parameters of the study were the algorithm, the reinjection, the noise angle, and the SNR. The corresponding condition codes were BEAM00, BEAM20, BEAM40, DOEM00, DOEM20, DOEM40, DOS00, DOS20, and DOS40, indicating the algorithm and the reinjection.

Furthermore, speech perception was tested in the VOC situation, yielding another 15 experimental conditions (3 SNRs * 5 noise angles). At the beginning of a session, a test was made without any processing to stand up as a reference (UNPROC).

The whole listening experiment lasted 3 h, including at least one break per hour (and more upon the subjects' request). Programs were developed on Matlab® software and graphical user interface (GUIDE).

2.3 LOCALIZATION TASK

Subjects listened to the noise signal delivered by one of the loudspeakers, and they had to locate the source among the five directions (Figure 16.1). They listened to 165 stimulations (the 11 conditions indicated in subsection 2.2.3, the five angles; three stimulations occurred for each condition-angle situation, and the average value was taken.

The duration of this session was about 0.5 h. Each sound lasted 5 s, and then the subject had to press a button indicating which LS he or she thought the signal was coming from. The percentage of correct localization (PCL) was recorded.

2.4 LISTENERS

A total of 26 subjects (14 males and 12 females), aged from 20 to 26 years (average age 24 years), participated in the experiment. None of the subjects had any hearing problems; they were checked in the ORL Department of the Edouard-Herriot Hospital prior to the experiment. Normal pure tone thresholds (hearing thresholds) were lower than 20 dB HL (Hearing Level) for the octave frequencies ranging from 125 Hz to 8 kHz.

This study was performed according to the French laws that apply to biomedical research and was approved by the Ethics Committee (CPP, 0100630314037, Léon-Bérard Center, Lyon).

3 RESULTS

3.1 LOCALIZATION

PCLs indicating the source localization, with and without the reinjection, are represented in Figure 16.5; standard deviations are also indicated.

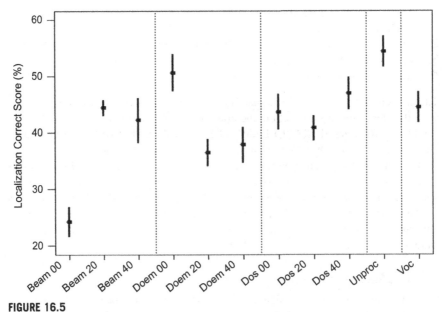

FIGURE 16.5

Source localization according to the strategy; BF, DOEM, DOS, UNPROC, VOC.

In Figure 16.5, percentages are indicated when the signal is directly presented to the listeners with the vocoder only situation (VOC), and without processing (UNPROC) for comparison purposes.

Mean values (over the reinjection) are given in Table 16.2. It can be clearly seen that UNPROC led to the best results.

Table 16.2 PCL According to the Strategy (Mean Values)

Strategy	Beam	DOEM	DOS	VOC	UNPROC
Average PCL	36	41	43	44	54

3.2 PHONEME RECOGNITION

3.2.1 Full recognition

The full recognition percentages of the phonemes PCRP (Percentage Correct Recognition Phoneme) are presented in Table 16.3. These results will be analyzed and compared to the source localization.

3.2.2 Specific recognition

As the angle of the noise perturbation did not strongly affect the percentage recognition, the results indicated here were averaged on θ (Table 16.4) for clarity purposes. Table 16.5 shows the mean values (over the SNRs) according to the algorithm and the reinjection. The corresponding value for "Voc only" was 33%.

The overall representation of the reinjection is shown in Figure 16.6.

In order to show the influence of the algorithms, PCRPs are reorganized as shown in Figure 16.7, after averaging on the SNR and on the noise angle.

4 DISCUSSION

Results can be discussed from different points of view; the following subsections give several of them.

4.1 SOURCE LOCALIZATION (PCL)

Figure 16.5 indicated the localization of the acoustic source. The Beamformer, mostly without reinjection, led to worse results.

With $\alpha = 0$ (no reinjection), DOEM presented the best percentage (50%). When a reinjection was done (20% and 40%), the results obtained with the three methods were equivalent. In this case, the percentages reached those seen with the vocoder alone.

It is worth noting that the unprocessed signal (UNPROC) led to the best localization. The vocoder showed results lower than those obtained with the unprocessed

Table 16.3 PCRPs

SNR	-6					0					6				
θ	-90	-45	0	45	90	-90	-45	0	45	90	-90	-45	0	45	90
Beam 00	16	32	25	33	27	38	45	48	52	52	52	56	58	61	60
Beam 20	18	34	24	37	30	38	49	44	53	55	57	61	58	66	66
Beam 40	20	36	29	43	33	52	56	51	59	60	67	66	70	68	69
DOEM 00	15	14	20	18	16	30	40	35	39	42	53	54	54	60	58
DOEM 20	15	20	25	24	22	50	49	62	44	52	64	61	67	67	67
DOEM 40	27	29	25	34	30	55	55	62	57	59	67	66	67	69	71
DOS 00	7	7	5	13	11	30	21	30	27	37	32	36	55	38	42
DOS 20	30	29	22	31	27	44	41	44	43	45	47	61	63	59	60
DOS 40	33	17	22	32	29	40	52	45	49	49	57	61	67	66	66
VOC	30	26	37	27	31	34	22	29	24	39	40	33	38	37	43

Table 16.4 PCRP According to Strategy and Reinjection, Related to the SNR

SNR		-6		0		6	
Beam	0	1	27	1	47	1	57
	20		29		48		62
	40		32		56		68
DOEM	0	2	17	1	37	1	56
	20		21		51		65
	40		19		58		68
DOS	0	3	9	3	29	3	41
	20		28		43		58
	40		27		47		63
VOC			30		30		38

Table 16.5 Mean PCRPs According to Strategy (Algorithm and Reinjection)

α	00	20	40
Beam	44	46	52
DOEM	37	46	48
DOS	26	43	46

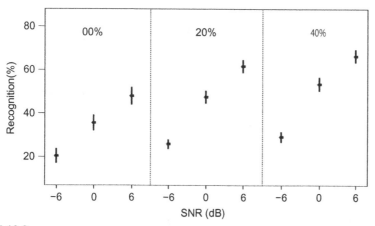

FIGURE 16.6

Percentage recognition according to the reinjection percentage (mean results).

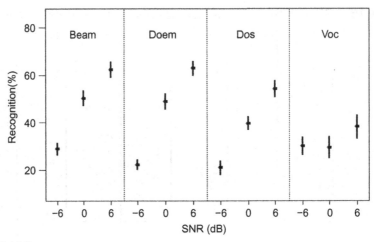

FIGURE 16.7

Recognition scores seen with the different algorithms.

signal. This is consistent with the findings of Van den Bogaert (2009); he indicated that signal reinjection had a positive action in restoring the localization ability.

4.2 RECOGNITION (PCRP)

4.2.1 Influence of the algorithms

Beam and DOEM led to the best PCRP (Figure 16.7). Results were clearly above those obtained with the vocoder only (VOC). The difference between Beam and DOEM was very small, suggesting that time strategy and spectrum processing present similar behaviors.

The Adaptive Directional Microphone (ADM) strategy was clearly an advantage for the sounds coming in front of the listener (Van den Bogaert *et al.*, 2008).

4.2.2 Influence of SNR

When no reinjection was done, the beamformer algorithm led to the best PCRPs (Table 16.4). When a reinjection was introduced, the recognition was improved with all the algorithms, but BEAM stayed ahead. (Note: SNR = − 6 dB.) In this adverse condition (low SNR), the algorithms were not efficient (compared to VOC).

In the case of SNR = 0, recognition led to better results (the noise and the signal were at the same level). Without reinjection, BEAM results were the best. With reinjection, DOEM PCRPs were greatly improved (Table 16.4).

Compared to the VOC (vocoder only) situation, PCRP recognition percentages were clearly better when a noise reduction strategy was used; reinjection leveled the recognition percentages among the algorithms.

In the case, of SNR = 6 dB, the results obtained with the different strategies were rather equivalent (Table 16.4). Reinjection had a positive influence (α starting from 20%). The VOC situation was far inferior. Similarily, Kokkinakis and Loizou (2010) indicated that when SNR was high, the improvements according to the strategies were leveled.

4.3 OTHER INFLUENCES

4.3.1 Reinjection

The reinjection factor α improved the phoneme recognition (Figure 16.6). It is interesting to point out that the best results were always obtained with $\alpha = 40\%$ in PCRP recognition.

About localization, reinjection favored the beam strategy but lowered the PCRPs obtained with the DOEM algorithm (Figure 16.5). Consequently, α improved the perception results PCs (PCRPs and PCLs) with the beam processing, which is based on the temporal properties of the signal, in both localization and recognition.

If we consider spectrum processing (Doerbecker), α lowered the source localization ability with DOEM and improved the phoneme recognition. Using DOEM processing, the choice seems to be that either we want to recognize or we want to localize—improving one reduced the other. For DOS, the results were more even with α for the localization and similar to DOEM for phoneme recognition (improvement), compared to VOC.

4.3.2 Noise angle

The noise angle (Table 16.3) did not change the behavior drastically in all the conditions. Nevertheless, it may be seen that results were slightly better when the noise was stimulating the right ear rather than to the left ear ($\theta > 0$). Is it linked to the brain hemisphere preference? The noise reaching the right ear goes mostly to the left hemisphere, which is more specialized in terms of language. The left brain may be more efficient to separate noise and speech. The ear preference is an interesting issue (Poeppel, 2003; Saoud *et al.*, 2012).

4.4 SIMULATION WITH NORMAL HEARING LISTENERS

The aspect of perception and localization, with normal-hearing listeners (NHLs) and with implantees, has been addressed by several studies. Dorman and Loizou (1997) considered this subject. They stated that performances obtained with NHLs establish a benchmark for how well implanted patients could perform if electrode arrays were able to reproduce, by artificial electrical stimulation, the stimulation produced by auditory stimulation of the cochlea.

Kerber (2012) studied the localization performances of CI users as opposed to NHLs; they indicated that the use of both ears is an advantage for helping hearing-impaired patients as well as implantees. They reached the same conclusion as Dorman.

Finally, taking NHLs in simulation instead of CI users must be considered. Results cannot be transposed carelessly from one category of people to the other, but they can be used as an indication.

5 CONCLUSIONS

The improvement in acoustic source localization and in phoneme recognition brought by noise reduction strategies (Doerbecker and Beamformer algorithms) in a simulated binaural CI coding environment has been discussed in this chapter.

Without any signal processing, listeners can localize the acoustic source. Similarly, with the binaural CI processing alone (VOC), a fairly acceptable localization was maintained. The influence of speech processing on the acoustic source localization is interesting. With the beamformer, the localization (which was poor at the beginning) was really improved when a signal reinjection was introduced. On the contrary, reinjection altered the DOEM algorithm performance. With DOS, an influence of the reinjection was not clearly seen.

Thus, with respect to the VOC situation, it can be seen that signal processing did not improve the source localization ability.

For recognition, the Beamformer and Doerbecker's strategies showed similar behavior. They increased the phoneme perception percentages in good noise situations (SNR = 0 or 6 dB) compared to the VOC situation; the average improvement was around 20%. Amelioration was poor for the worst value of the SNR (−6 dB).

Without reinjection, the Beamformer algorithm led to the best recognition (PCRP) results mostly when the SNR was low. Compared to the VOC situation, the increase brought by the Beamformer algorithm was about 30% when the SNR was 0 or 6 dB. Doerbecker's processing also improved the phoneme perception; the Ephraim and Malah's correction showed better percentages than the Scalart's strategy. A reinjection (20% or 40%) of the input signal raised the phoneme recognition results in our experiment. When the reinjection percentage grew from 20% to 40%, the performances were not deeply modified.

Finally, this work indicates that the Beamformer algorithm and Doerbecker's processing improved phoneme recognition, but they lowered the source localization. Reinjection had a positive effect on recognition, and on the localization with the Beamformer; it was less helpful for the localization with the Doerbecker's processing.

Now these indications should be revisited with cochlear implantees; investigating the noise reduction in a noisy environment still remains a challenge.

ACKNOWLEDGMENTS

This work was supported by a French CIFRE contract with the Neurelec society and the CNRS. The Phonak company supplied the KEMAR head. We are grateful to the listeners who participated in this experiment. We thank Professors Lionel Collet, Hung Thai Van and Olivier Bertrand, as well as Dr. Evelyne Veuillet for providing the facilities to conduct this experiment. We also appreciated the useful discussions with the PACS group members. Finally, our gratitude goes to the anonymous referees; their comments greatly helped us improve the manuscript.

REFERENCES

Blauert, J., 2013. The Technology of Binaural Listening. Springer, Berlin.

Bouchard, C., Havelock, D.I., Bouchard, M., 2009. Beamforming with microphone arrays for directional sources. J. Acoust. Soc. Am. 125 (4), 2098–2104.

Cappe, O., 1994. Elimination of the musical noise phenomenon with the Ephraim and Malah noise suppressor. IEEE Trans. Speech Audio Process. 2 (2), 345–349.

Doerbecker, M., Ernst, S., 1996. Combination of two-channel spectral subtraction and adaptive wiener post-filtering for noise reduction and deverberation. In: European Signal Processing Conference, Trieste, Italy, pp. 995–998.

Dorman, M.F., Loizou, P.C., 1997. Speech intelligibility as a function of the number of channels of stimulation for normal-hearing listeners and patients with cochlear implants. Am. J. Otol. 18 (6, Suppl.), S113–S114.

Dunn, C.C., Noble, W., Tyler, R.S., Kordus, M., Gantz, B.J., Ji, H., 2010. Bilateral and unilateral cochlear implant users compared on speech perception in noise. Ear Hear. 31 (2), 296–298.

Ephraim, Y., Malah, D., 1984. Speech enhancement using a minimum mean-square error short-time spectral amplitude estimator. IEEE Trans. Acoust. Speech Signal Process. 32 (6), 1109–1121.

Francart, T., Lenssen, A., Wouters, J., 2011. Enhancement of interaural level differences improves sound localization in bimodal hearing. J. Acoust. Soc. Am. 130 (5), 2817–2826.

Friesen, L.M., Shannon, R.V., Baskent, D., Wang, X., 2001. Speech recognition in noise as a function of the number of spectral channels: comparison of acoustic hearing and cochlear implants. J. Acoust. Soc. Am. 110 (2), 1150–1163.

Kallel, F., Frikha, M., Ghorbel, M., Hamida, A.B., Berger-Vachon, C., 2012. Dual-channel spectral subtraction algorithms based speech enhancement dedicated to a bilateral cochlear implant. Appl. Acoust. 73, 12–20.

Kerber, S., Seeber, B.U., 2012. Sound localization in noise by normal-hearing listeners and cochlear implant users. Ear Hear. 33 (4), 445–457.

Kokkinakis, K., Loizou, P.C., 2010. Multi-microphone adaptive noise reduction strategies for coordinated stimulation in bilateral cochlear implant devices. J. Acoust. Soc. Am. 127 (5), 3136–3144.

Kompis, M., Dillier, N., 2001. Performance of an adaptive beamforming noise reduction scheme for hearing aid applications. I. Prediction of the signal-to-noise-ratio improvement. J. Acoust. Soc. Am. 109 (3), 1123–1133.

Lawson, D.T., Wilson, B.S., Zerbi, M., van den Honert, C., Finley, C.C., Farmer, J.C., McElveen, J.T., Roush, P.A., 1998. Cochlear implants controlled by a single speech processor. Am. J. Otol. 19 (6), 758–761.

Loizou, P.C., 2006. Speech processing in vocoder-centric cochlear implants. Adv Otorhinolaryngol. 64, 109–143.

Poeppel, D., 2003. The analysis of speech in different temporal integration windows: cerebral lateralization as 'asymmetric sampling in time. Speech Comm. 41, 245–255.

Saoud, H., Josse, G., Bertasi, E., Truy, E., Chait, M., Giraud, A.-L., 2012. Brain–speech alignment enhances auditory cortical responses and speech perception. J. Neurosci. 32, 275–281.

Scalart, P., Filho, J.V., 1996. Speech enhancement based on a priori signal to noise estimation. In: Proc. Conf. IEEE Int Acoustics, Speech, and Signal Processing ICASSP-96, pp. 629–632.

van den Bogaert, T., Doclo, S., Wouters, J., Moonen, M., 2008. The effect of multimicrophone noise reduction systems on sound source localization by users of binaural hearing aids. J. Acoust. Soc. Am. 124 (1), 484–497.

van den Bogaert, T., Doclo, S., Wouters, J., Moonen, M., 2009. Speech enhancement with multichannel Wiener filter techniques in multimicrophone binaural hearing aids. J. Acoust. Soc. Am. 125 (1), 360–371.

van Dijk, B., Moonen, M., Wouters, J., 2012. Speech understanding performance of cochlear implant subjects using time-frequency masking-based noise reduction. IEEE Trans. Biomed. Eng 59 (5), 1363–1373.

van Hoesel, R.J.M., Jones, G.L., Litovsky, R.Y., 2009. Interaural time-delay sensitivity in bilateral cochlear implant users: effects of pulse rate, modulation rate, and place of stimulation. J. Assoc. Res. Otolaryngol. 10 (4), 557–567.

Yang, L.-P., Fu, Q.-J., 2005. Spectral subtraction-based speech enhancement for cochlear implant patients in background noise. J. Acoust. Soc. Am. 117 (3 Pt 1), 1001–1004.

Yousefian, N., Loizou, P.C., 2013. A dual microphone algorithm that can cope with competing talkers scenarios. IEEE Trans. Audio Speech Lang. Process. 21 (1), 145–155.

Lowering the Fall Rate of the Elderly from Wheelchairs

17

Thomas Goulding[1], Leonidas Deligiannidis[2], Peter Sylvester[2], and Bo Kim[3]

Department of Mathematics and Computer Science, Lawrence Technological University, Southfield, MI, USA[1]
ElderSafe Technologies, Inc., Harvard, MA, USA[2]
Division of Computer Science, Daniel Webster College, Nashua, NH, USA[3]

1 INTRODUCTION

According to the Centers for Disease Control and Prevention (CDC), the annual direct and indirect cost of falls among the elderly will reach $67.7 billion by 2020 (CDC, 2014a). At the end of this decade, falls will remain the leading cause of injury and death among the expected 150+ million elderly in Europe and 50+ million in the United States. Over 70 million will fall annually, and 12 million will visit an emergency room as a result. Of elderly people who fall, 25% will subsequently be admitted to a hospital, and many will never live independently again. Most of these will then spend the majority of their waking time in wheelchairs (CDC, 2013, 2014a,b). Figure 17.1 shows the enormous growth in the senior population in the United States, as reported by the U.S. Department of Health and Human Services (USDHHS, 2011).

1.1 THE FUNDAMENTAL PROBLEM

What is the fundamental issue that needs to be addressed in order to solve this intractable health care problem? Much of the research on elderly falls has focused on the ambulatory elderly, while little effort has been spent looking into wheelchair-related falls (Gavin-Dreschnack *et al.*, 2005). Unlike patients who can walk about a facility without caregiver assistance, a high fall risk patient must remain in his/her wheelchair. Wheelchair bound high fall risk patients must of necessity be left alone for long periods due to staff workloads; they participate in fewer activities; they have less human engagement and thus, they are less able to communicate to staff members about their needs, such as when toilet visits are needed. The person is liable to become impatient and attempt to get up without aid (Nyberg and Gustafson, 1996). For any number of age-related (Vlahov *et al.*, 1990) or medical conditions (*Merck Manual*, 2011), when people living in nursing homes and assisted-living facilities or rehabilitation centers (Nyberg and Gustafson, 1995) stand without the

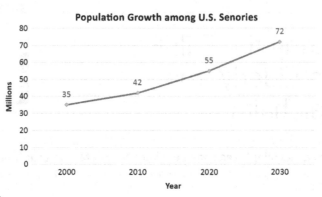

FIGURE 17.1

Actual and projected growth of the senior population in the United States in the 21st century.

assistance they need, they frequently fall. Some of the risk factors that could lead an elderly person to fall include muscle weakness, history of falling, arthritis, depression, and impairment in gait, balance, cognition, and vision (Shobha, 2005). Without continuous observation, an accurate assessment that an egress is imminent, and a method of rapid caregiver notification, the problem cannot be solved. Nevertheless, we believe that the high fall rate among community-dwelling seniors can (Greenwich Hospital, 2013) and will be solved once the full power of technology and the collective creativity found in human minds is brought to bear on the problem.

1.2 AN IMAGINED SOLUTION

Let's imagine that an elderly wheelchair occupant is continuously watched by a vigilant observer. This observer is informed about the occupant's urinary tract infection and also knows that the occupant has dementia and suffers from sundown effect, which has been shown to be a factor associated with falls (Teasell *et al.*, 2002; Granek *et al.*, 1987). Suppose that the observer is also aware that it is 4 PM, and the last scheduled toilet assistance visit by a staff member is long overdue. Finally, suppose that the observer can quickly detect that the occupant is exhibiting atypical restless behavior or risky movement, and that he has the capability to immediately summon and capture the attention of a distant, distracted, and very busy caregiver. Would the excessively high fall rates among the elderly be significantly lowered? The answer is obviously, yes; however, as explained next, using a human as the vigilant observer has generally yielded poor results.

2 CURRENT SOLUTIONS

Various forms of the abovementioned solution have been attempted using humans, such as sitters, remote video feed attendants, increased staff coverage, and more frequent rounds. There are some reports that human monitoring, augmented by video cameras, has lowered the fall rate of the elderly and medically impaired, but this low-tech strategy has not been widely adopted (USDHHS, 2011). Many of these approaches are cost prohibitive. Compounding the problem of using human attendants is the fact that electrical pathways in the human brain are often impaired by boredom, overwork, or lapses in concentration. As a result, human attendants often miss risks unfolding right before their eyes, as well as audio alerts that are blaring in their ears. To be successful, a human-centric approach has to be supplemented with a strong training program, frequent rounds, and staff task reassignment to avoid fatigue (USDHHS, 2011).

Technology solutions have tended to focus on just a small portion of the imagined solution. Fall detection technologies and local audio alarms are 50 years old, but they still dominate the marketplace today. The pressure cushion, in particular, is still widely used on wheelchairs to detect that an occupant has left the chair. A local buzzer remains the primary notification technology. Under the best of conditions, though, these are ineffective in preventing falls. Pressure cushions notify caregivers primarily after the occupant has left the chair. Consequently, the caregiver frequently finds the elderly person on the floor. Complicating the effectiveness of pressure cushions is their inherent false alarm rate due to the fact that simple patient movement or repositioning can set off an alarm. High false alarm rates eventually encourage caregivers to simply ignore the alarms (Moyer, 2012).

Lanyards are also widely used in elder-care and rehabilitation facilities, but they also have little hope of lowering fall rates. When the lanyard is severed, a local or remote buzzer notifies caregivers, but often too late to prevent a fall. Similarly, disappointing results have occurred with wearable devices, vibration sensors, cameras, and accelerometers, all of which have been combined with passive or patient-activated local and remote notification technologies (Noury et al., 2007). None detect an emerging risk soon enough, nor do they effectively capture caregiver attention in time for the caregiver to return and prevent an unassisted egress.

Several patents have been awarded for wheelchair-monitoring devices designed to assist caregivers in fall risk assessment and staff notification. One, based on assessing an occupant's proximity to an imaging sensor, did not result in a commercially viable solution, and therefore the patent was allowed to expire (U.S. Patent Sparks, 2001). The invention used a single proximity sensor that measured the distance from the sensor to the upper body of the chair occupant. We believe that the inventor's idea had promise, but a single sensor provides insufficient information to adequately assess occupant position, posture, and movement. Our research has shown that an additional sensor, appropriately positioned to the side, provides the needed additional information.

Another patent centered on a probabilistic assessment algorithm that processes inputs from multiple pressure devices located on the seat and back of a wheelchair. Notification was limited to communication with the nurse station, and thus the caregivers that were nearest and most likely able to prevent a fall would not be notified of an emerging risk. This project did not lead to a commercialized product (U.S. Patent Knight et al., 2012). Without test data and a costed bill of material, it is not possible to fully understand the effectiveness or limitations of this invention. We can speculate why this invention has not yet appeared in the marketplace. Our studies convinced us that we should avoid pressure-based solutions. The false alarm and "too-late" alarm problems endemic with commercialized pressure-based solutions convinced us to look elsewhere. Low complexity and low cost were also the primary design goals of our solution, the Sparrow (Goulding *et al.*, 2014) system (patent pending), discussed next, whereas the many sensors utilized in this invention clearly introduce cost, hardware complexity, and software complexity. Finally, we believed that notification to a nurses' station disregards the fact that the caregiver closest to the patient at risk needs to be the one to receive the alert.

3 A SYSTEMS SOLUTION

What is needed is not another technology, but a multifaceted systems-based solution that observes an elderly person's movement while alone, that anticipates that the elderly person is about to attempt an unassisted exit from a wheelchair, that alerts busy and distracted caregivers, and that provides sufficient time for the caregiver to respond before the occupant leaves the chair. This is what we believe is necessary to lower the fall rates among the elderly.

So is there an architecture that can provide busy caregivers with real-time updates about the movement of an unattended, unobserved occupant in a chair? Figure 17.2 illustrates the cloud-based architectural strategy that has the potential of answering this question. The Sparrow system monitors the patient and sends sensor data to the server on the cloud. The server then can notify devices that subscribe to notifications from Sparrow. These devices can be tablets, smart phones, high-definition televisions (HDTVs) with custom hardware installed, and even the Sparrow system itself.

A team of scientists, professors, physicians, and engineers located in Harvard, Massachusetts, is introducing a system called Sparrow that has the promise of lowering the

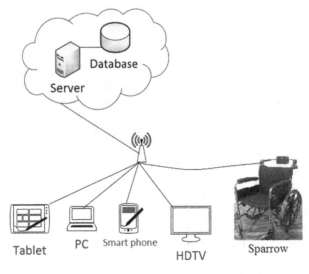

FIGURE 17.2

The Sparrow cloud-based architecture.

fall rates among the elderly. Sparrow fuses imaging sensor inputs, microprocessor power, Internet technologies, mobile devices and innovative multimodal notification strategies into a simple to use tool to aid in fall prevention, not just fall detection.

4 THE SPARROW DESIGN

Figure 17.3 shows the second-generation Sparrow prototype, which is used for laboratory testing and field demonstrations by ElderSafe Technologies Inc. (located in Harvard, Massachusetts), a startup company that has emerged from the Sparrow research project. The Sparrow system vigilantly monitors an unattended occupant seated in a wheelchair using imaging sensors. It assesses an occupant's activity, position, and posture in the chair and makes a preliminary determination of whether an egress from the chair is imminent.

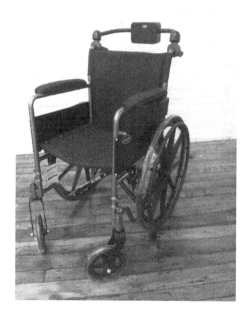

FIGURE 17.3

Sparrow prototype P-II.

The preliminary assessment is sent across the Internet, or locally to a server application depending on the facility's requirements. The server application refines the preliminary assessment and then notifies nearby health care professionals or family members that the occupant may be attempting an unassisted egress from the chair.

Notification of caregivers is accomplished using a multimodal strategy. The nursing staff can be notified of an imminent exit through a variety of Internet and other wireless technologies, including mobile tablets, PCs dedicated to monitoring, smart phones, and HDTVs located around the facility. In addition, a paging- or Internet-based notification can be integrated with the Sparrow system to notify nursing staff through a pager or iOS mobile device carried by nursing or support staff. The mobile notification devices support verbal announcements, flashing lights, vibrations, buzzers, and text messaging that identifies the occupant at risk. The chair location also could be sent to the staff in future releases of the product.

System installation and setup is designed to require minimal training and administration as well. Access to the facility's WiFi network is established at the time of delivery of the chair to the facility. A simple web application will be used to associate a patient with a specific chair ID. Afterward, the nurse staff only has to turn the system on with the power button.

Once turned on, Sparrow is controlled by a single pause-track button in order to minimize caregiver interactions with the system. In the current prototype, the button is located on top of the rear sensor box. This box also contains the sensor controller hardware. Two cables run through the rear sensor bar, one to a side sensor and one to the analytic. The system is removable as a unit by simply detaching it from the wheelchair handles and uncoupling the side sensor.

The third-generation Sparrow prototype (P-III), which is in development, will eliminate the electronics box on the back bar, reduce the size and cost of the analytic processor by 80%, and involve a redesign of the mounting apparatus in order to incorporate all the industry standards for safety, cleaning, and reliability required by a medical facility.

Multifacility outcome tracking will be an additional byproduct of the Sparrow architectural refinement (shown in Figure 17.4). If desired, fall risk management and fall reduction outcomes can be aggregated across an entire health-care network.

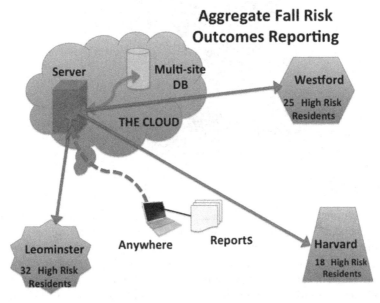

FIGURE 17.4

Multifacility outcomes

5 ASSESSMENT ALGORITHM

The simplicity of the Sparrow algorithm is what makes the system effective. The algorithm imitates the simple decision logic that resides within the human brain.

A human attendant knows that the occupant of a wheelchair is unlikely to exit the chair so long as his or her posterior is positioned in close proximity to the back of the chair. The occupant can even lift himself or herself up off the seat and still be safe under these conditions. A human attendant would not raise an alarm in such cases. Sparrow imitates this response and would not set off an alarm, as opposed to pressure cushions, which frequently set off a false alarm in response to such a stimulus.

Preliminary testing with nursing home patients indicates that the position, posture, movement (PPM) algorithm need not be customized for each patient. Field testing shows that the system works best where there is some reasonable latency between initial movement toward egress and final leaving of the chair. There is a certain type of elderly or medically impaired person who can immediately launch out of a chair; however, such patients cannot be helped by Sparrow or any other advanced notification technology, since the latency between intent and actual egress in such cases is measured in milliseconds.

It is also quite common for the elderly to assume postures that are rather severely bent forward. They may be asleep, depressed, or simply lack the energy and strength to maintain a normal sitting position. The typical attendant would not believe that this leaning forward is a precursor to an egress from a wheelchair unless the patient was reaching forward, causing his or her center of gravity to move dangerously beyond the forward edge of the seat. Rarely, if ever, would an elderly person fall out of a wheelchair if the center of gravity was behind the forward edge of the chair seat. Sparrow would not raise an alarm in such cases unless it were configured to do so.

However, a human attendant would make an entirely different assessment if the occupant slid his or her posterior forward. Most nursing professionals have indicated to the research team that this movement is a precursor to an egress; therefore, notification of this movement is usually requested by the staff. Field testing confirms the wisdom of early notification in these situations. When an advanced posterior position is also combined with a forward-leaning posture, nursing staff would become even more alarmed, and therefore, so does Sparrow. Sparrow imitates a caregiver's assessment of such situations and provides an urgent alert when an occupant is in a posterior forward–lean forward (PF-LF) posture. The Sparrow basic decision logic imitates a simple decision tree or logic ladder based on anatomical posture divergence from reference constants that are set prior to activation of the system.

6 ASSESSMENT DECISION ALGORITHM

The algorithm incorporates the following steps, to be repeated continuously:

1. The Sensor Controller (SC) receives sensor inputs from back sensors (BSs) and side sensors (SSs).
2. SC converts sensor data to reference data called BS_measured and SS_measured.

3. SC sends measured reference data to an analytic microprocessor (AM).

4. AM makes body position and posture assessment using patient-specific or generic threshold values: BS_Safe_T, BS_UnSafe_T, and SS_Safe_T.

The following test cases are considered:

Case 1: Safe
```
if (BS_measured <= BS_Safe_T && SS_measured <= SS_Safe_T)
```
Case 2: Low-risk
```
if (BS_measured > BS_Safe_T && SS_measured <= SS_Safe_T)
```
Case 3: Low-risk
```
if (BS_measured <= BS_Safe_T && SS_measured > SS_Safe_T)
```
Case 4: High-risk
```
if (BS_Safe < BS_measured <= BS_UnSafe_T && SS_measured > SS_Safe_T)
```
Case 5: Low-Risk
```
if (BS_measured > BS_UnSafe_T && SS_measured <= SS_Safe_T)
```
Case 6: Fell
```
if (BS_measured > BS_UnSafe_T && SS_measured > SS_Safe_T)
```

The assessment algorithm produces one of four different results, and AM creates color-coded alert based on the assessment result, as follows:

- *Green* (safe)
- *Yellow* (low-risk)
- *Red* (high-risk)
- *Blue* (fell)

The AM forward state changes to the web application (WA) for refinement of egress indicators. The WA factors patient pathology, environmental factors, and caregiver-engagement into the final assessment and elevates or reduces the assessment accordingly.

A whole host of devices, such as HDTVs, tablets, smart phones, PCs, and mobile iOS devices, can subscribe to these alerts. Thus, everyone on the caregiver team who has an active Internet connection can be reached, and there is nowhere the signal cannot go.

7 THE FUTURE

In more advanced versions, Sparrow can fuse preliminary risk assessment with environmental data, occupant medical pathology, and caregiver responsiveness in order to refine and tailor risk assessment to individual patients (Tsur and Segal, 2010). The system also can record caregiver-occupant engagement, log occupant "abandonment" intervals, measure alarm-response latency, and incorporate time of day and pathology into assessments. Thus, fall tracking and fall reduction outcomes reports for supervisors and administrators become an important by-product of the Sparrow architecture. These features are incorporated into the current architecture but will not be introduced until the efficacy of the algorithm is well established through extensive field testing.

Medical professionals on the Sparrow team believe that patient- and care-specific information can improve human caregiver assessment of egress risk; likewise, it is expected that incorporation of this knowledge into the Sparrow assessment will improve outcomes. For example, a dementia patient who has been unattended for 3 h who suffers from a urinary tract infection and who becomes an even greater fall risk at sundown will undoubtedly be placed at the highest alert state possible when observed in a PF-LF posture. Experienced caregivers will expect Sparrow to do this. However, it has yet to be established in the field that incorporating patient pathology and caregiver engagement into the egress assessment algorithm can be accomplished without creating an unacceptable administrative burden for caregivers and administrators. Further field testing will determine whether these features will be activated for general distribution.

8 CONCLUSION

Sparrow shows great promise in both laboratory tests and demonstrations in skilled nursing facilities. The system has been received with great enthusiasm and hope by medical professionals and caregivers. Nevertheless, the efficacy of this solution has yet to be validated beyond anecdotal observation. In 2015, we hope to complete formal clinical trials that will provide us with statistical evidence and guidance as to the future direction of our efforts.

ACKNOWLEDGMENTS

We thank the many facilities, executive directors, nursing staff, caregivers, and elderly who have observed or participated in our field demonstrations. Their feedback and encouragement has kept all the members of the Sparrow team energized and together for three years.

REFERENCES

Center for Disease Control and Prevention (CDC), September 2013. Hip Fractures among Older Americans. Home and Recreational Safety. http://www.cdc.gov/home andrecreationalsafety/falls/adulthipfx.html, Retrieved Oct., '14.

Center for Disease Control and Prevention (CDC), September 2014a. Falls among Older Adults: An Overview. Home and Recreational Safety. http://www.cdc.gov/home andrecreationalsafety/falls/adultfalls.html, Retrieved October 6, 2014.

Center for Disease Control and Prevention (CDC), September 2014b. Falls in Nursing Homes. Home and Recreational Safety. http://www.cdc.gov/homeandrecreationalsafety/falls/nursing.html Retrieved Oct. 6, '14.

Gavin-Dreschnack, D., Nelson, A., Fitzgerald, S., Harrow, J., Sanchez-Anguiano, A., Ahmed, S., Powell-Cope, G., 2005. Wheelchair-related falls: current evidence and directions for improved quality care. J. Nurs. Care Qual. 20 (2), 119–127.

Goulding, T.L., Deligiannidis, L., Sylvester, P., 3/18/2014. Intelligent Wheel Chair Accessory for Monitoring Occupant to Assess Whether an Unassisted Egress from Chair is Intended. Patent pending for Sparrow, Number: 61/954,724, USPTO.

Granek, E., Baker, S.P., Abbey, H., et al., 1987. Medication and diagnosis in relation to.falls in a long-term care facility. J. Am. Geriatr. Soc. 35, 503–511.

Greenwich Hospital, Yale New Haven Health, News room, April 2013. https://www.greenhosp.org/news/articles.aspx?id=194&sid=1&nid=111&showBack=true&PageIndex=0&showAC=true Retrieved October 6, 2014.

Moyer, V.A., 2012. Prevention of falls in community-dwelling older adults: U.S. "Preventive Services Task Force recommendation statement" Ann. Intern. Med. 157 (3), 197–204.

Noury, N., Fleury, A., Rumeau, P., Bourke, A., Laighin, G., Rialee, V., Lundy, J., Aug. 23–26 2007. Fall detection – principles and methods. In: Proceedings of the 29th Annual International Conference of the IEEE Engineering in Medicine and Biology (EMBS) pp. 1663–1666.

Nyberg, L., Gustafson, Y., 1995. Patient falls in stroke rehabilitation a challenge to rehabilitation strategies. Stroke 26, 838–842.

Nyberg, L., Gustafson, Y., 1996. Using the downtown index to predict those prone to falls in stroke rehabilitation. Stroke 27, 1821–1824.

Shobha, S.R., 2005. Prevention of falls in older patients. American Academy of Family Physicians 72 (1), 81–88.

Teasell, R., McRae, M., Foley, N., Bhardwaj, A., 2002. The incidence and consequences of falls in stroke patients during inpatient rehabilitation: factors associated with high risk. Arch. Phys. Med. Rehabil. 83 (3), 329–333.

The Merck Manual, Falls in the Elderly. 2011. http://www.merckmanuals.com/home/older_peoples_health_issues/falls/falls_in_the_elderly.html Retrieved October 7, 2014.

Tsur, A., Segal, Z., April 2010. Falls in stroke patients: risk factors and risk management. Isr. Med. Assoc. J. 12, 216–219.

U.S. Department of Health and Human Services (USDHHS), Administration for Community Living, Administration on Aging (AoA), A Profile of Older Americans. Dec. '11 http://www.aoa.gov/Aging_Statistics/Profile/2011/4.aspx Retrieved Oct. 6, '14.

US Patent Knight et al., Patent No US 8,203,454 B2 Date: June 19, 2012 Wheel Chair Alarm System Heather-Marie Callanan Knight, Lexington, MA (US); Jae-KyuLee, Cambridge, MA (US); HongshenMa, Delta(CA); ULaurenKattany, Natick, MA (US).

US Patent Sparks, Patent No. US 2,204,767 B1 Date March 20, 2001 Chair Monitor Brian J Sparks, Milwaukee, W.

Vlahov, D., Myers, A.H., Al-Ibrahim, M.S., 1990. Epidemiology of falls among patients in a rehabilitation hospital. Arch. Phys. Med. Rehabil. 71, 8–12.

Occipital and Left Temporal EEG Correlates of Phenomenal Consciousness

18

Vitor Manuel Dinis Pereira

LanCog (Language, Mind and Cognition Research Group), Philosophy Centre, University of Lisbon,
Lisbon, Portugal

1 INTRODUCTION

If there are occipital and temporal correlates of a stimulus about which we have no consciousness, our unconsciousness will involve not only not having access, but also not having a phenomenal experience (Block, 2005), despite the fact that there is electrical activity in the occipital and temporal lobes co-occurring with these stimuli.

The occipital and temporal electrical activity co-occurring with humans' visual experience of a stimulus will need to co-occur with consciousness, but an explanation of a contrast in access (*e.g.,* correct and incorrect responses; namely, the interval between the termination of a target and of a mask), does not explain a contrast in phenomenology (*e.g.,* degrees of visibility; namely, the mean rank within a interval of degrees of visibility), and occipital and temporal electrical activity co-occurring with a stimulus about which we have no consciousness (if any) will have to be distinguished from access and from phenomenal consciousness.

2 PARTICIPANTS

The participants were 22 adults with normal vision or corrected to normal, without neurological or psychiatric history, The participants were naive about the experimental purposes.. Five participants were excluded due to excessive electroencephalograph (EEG) artifacts (3) or insufficient trials (2). The experimental protocol was approved by the doctoral program in cognitive science at the University of Lisbon.

3 APPARATUS AND STIMULI

There were two types of targets: square (1.98 cm side) and diamond (for 45° rotation of the square), and two types of masks: masks and pseudo-masks. The width of the mask is 3.05 cm, and its inner white portion (RGB 255-255-255) is 8 mm wider than

FIGURE 18.1

Stimulus and screen response targets, respectively mask/pseudo-mask

the black (RGB 0-0-0) target stimulus. The width of the pseudomask is 3.10 cm, and its inner white portion is circular (2.63 cm diameter).

Despite the different sizes, the color black exists in the same area, both in mask and pseudomask, and its luminance is identical. This was expected to be important to make the masks produce similar event-related potentials (ERPs) when presented alone.

All stimuli are presented on a gray background (RGB 173-175-178). (See Figure 18.1.)

4 PROCEDURE

The first task is to recognize which of the targets—square or diamond—is presented. The second task is to evaluate the visibility of the targets. The answers are given using the keyboard or the mouse.

In the first task, recognition of targets, participants respond if "they seemed to have seen something" by pressing 8 for yes and 9 for no. A negative response completes the trial and starts the next. An affirmative answer shows the subjects a screen of 16 stimuli to signal with the mouse what they have identified. The position on the screen indicated by the participant will be recorded informatically as coordinate system $<X,Y>$.

In the second task (evaluation of visibility), we used a Likert scale from 1 to 5: "not visible at all" (1 key), "barely visible" (2 key), "visible, but obscure" (3 key), "clear but not quite visible" (4 key) and "perfectly clear and visible" (5 key).

Experiments were held by the psychology faculty in a slightly darkened silent room. Participants were seated in a reclining chair at 32-in distance from the 20-in. monitor.

It is expected that the running of experiment train the volunteer. The beginning of the behavioral and EEG recording is unknown to the volunteer.

The SuperLab program for Microsoft Windows from Cedrus, which is PC-compatible and connected to a Super Video Graphics Array (SVGA) color monitor, manages the presentation of stimuli, randomizes their sequence (the trials in each block), the exposure times, the record of the response, triggers the trigger synchronize with the system acquisition of physiological signals, MP100 and EEG amplifiers, AcqKnowledge program, both from Biopac.

Statistical analysis of neuroelectric signals and behavioral data was performed using the SPSS Statistics PASW 18.

5 EEG RECORDING

Silver chloride electrodes were placed on the scalp, according to International System 10/20. Data were recorded with a referential montage, with three channels of EEG, occipital (Oz), left temporal (T5), and right temporal (T6), which were referred to the left mastoid.

The impedance of all electrodes was kept below 5 k Ohm. The EEG records have a duration of 1150 ms, divided into 150 ms before the stimulus (baseline) and 1000 ms after its occurrence.

If the ERP is an evoked signal (*i.e.,* a signal superimposed upon and independent of the ongoing noise EEG), and not a phase alignment of the ongoing signal EEG or some combination of the two (a clear conceptual exposition of the difference is provided, for example, by Pfurtscheller and Lopes da Silva, 1999), it makes perfect sense, after visual inspection and rejection of artifacts in EEG samples for each type of stimuli sequence, to calculate the average and make the regression for the 150-ms baseline, measuring the amplitude and latency of the waveforms thus collected.

6 EXPERIMENT I

Eight volunteers (aged 18–46 years, M = 22.50, SD = 9.562, 7 females) participated in the first trial. The target and the masks will be presented for 17 ms. The mask (or pseudomask) appears 1 ms after the presentation of the target [*i.e.,* the interstimulus interval (ISI), which is the interval between the termination of the target and the onset of the mask]. These ISIs (1 ms) correspond to 18-ms stimulus-onset asynchrony (SOA), the interval between the onset of the target and the mask, with rounded values. The participants responded by clicking on a screen of 16 onscreen stimuli, among which were the mask and pseudomask. Note that the subject not performed a forced-choice task, for example, reading any question either "Diamond or Square?" or "Square or Diamond?", even if counterbalanced across participants (contrast with, for example, Lau and Passingham, 2006).

In the second trial, masks were presented for 17 ms, and answers were signaled by clicking on a screen of 16 stimuli, among which are the mask and pseudomask.

Second block. Trial: targets were presented for 17 ms, and answers were given by clicking on a screen of 16 stimuli, among which were the targets. (See Figures 18.2 and 18.4.)

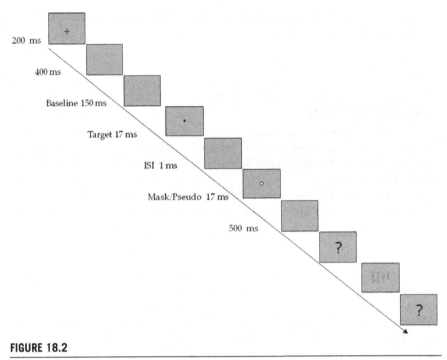

200 ms
400 ms
Baseline 150 ms
Target 17 ms
ISI 1 ms
Mask/Pseudo 17 ms
500 ms
?
?

FIGURE 18.2

Experiment I, target-mask presentations

7 EXPERIMENT II

The second experiment involved 9 volunteers (aged 20–26 years, $M = 21.22$, $SD = 2.224$; 5 females). The target will be presented for 17 ms (like Experiment I), but the mask (or pseudomask) will be presented for 167 ms (unlike Experiment I). Note that in all these experiments, targets were shown for 17 ms and were never replaced (for example, by a blank screen with the same duration of 17 ms). Contrast this, for example, with Del Cul *et al.* (2007).

Unlike Experiment I, the target was intercalated between two presentations of the mask/pseudomask (each at 167 ms): one earlier, paracontrast; the other after target, metacontrast.

The mask (or pseudomask) appears 0 ms before (forward masking) and 1 ms after (backward masking) the presentation of the target (*i.e.,* the ISI). These ISIs (1 ms) correspond to 18-ms SOA, and to 168-ms stimulus-termination asynchrony (STA), the interval between the termination of the target and of the mask (with rounded values). Unlike Experiment I, the answers in the first trial were signaled by clicking 16 onscreen stimuli, among which were the targets.

In the second trial, like Experiment I, masks were presented for 17 ms, and answers were signaled by clicking on a screen of 16 stimuli, among which were the mask and pseudo-mask.

Second block, like experiment I. Trial: targets will be presented for 17 ms, and answers are signaled by clicking on a screen of 16 stimuli, among which were the targets. (See Figures 18.3 and 18.4.)

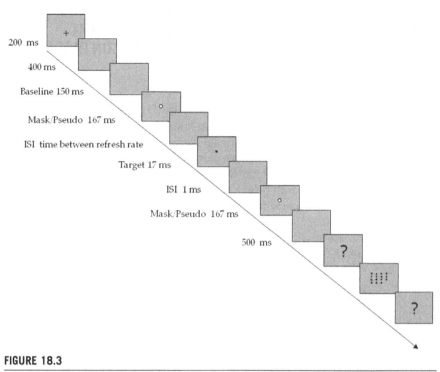

FIGURE 18.3

Experiment II, target-mask presentations

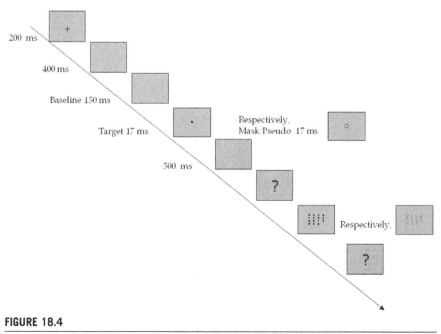

FIGURE 18.4

Experiment I and II, isolated presentations

8 THE GRAND AVERAGE OCCIPITAL AND TEMPORAL ELECTRICAL ACTIVITY CORRELATED WITH A CONTRAST IN ACCESS

8.1 ERP DATA

The Oz and T5 maximum positive amplitudes (300–800 ms) of the ERPs for Experiment II are greater compared to those of Experiment I for combined target-mask presentations than for isolated presentations. The repeated measures ANOVA with Experiment I/Experiment II as between-subject factors and electrophysiological maximum positive amplitudes (300–800 ms) related to combined target-mask/ isolated presentations as within-subject factors gave the following significant (Greenhouse/Geisser correction for sphericity violations) results for Oz [$F_{(2.557, 38.349)} = 3.348$, $p < 0.035$] and T5 [$F_{(3.700, 55.507)} = 4.066$ $p < 0.007$], but there were no significant results for T6 [$F_{(1.223, 18.342)} = 0.774$ $p < 0.416$]. (See Figures 18.5 and 18.6.)

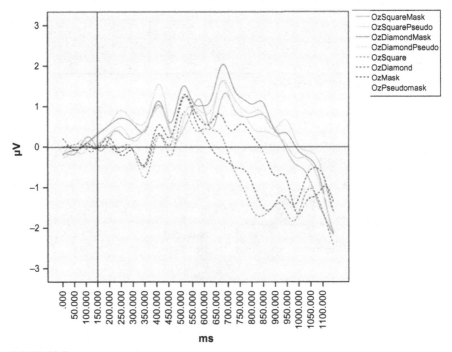

FIGURE 18.5

Derivation Oz, Experiment I, ERPs grand-average eight healthy subjects. Calibration ranges and time indicated in the figure. Black vertical line marks the beginning of the presentation of stimuli. Dot, isolated presentations; lines, target-mask presentations.

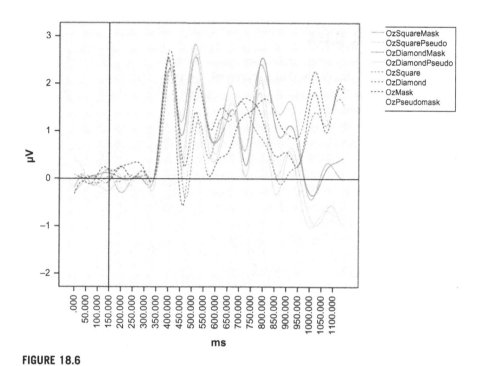

FIGURE 18.6

Derivation Oz, Experiment II, ERPs grand-average nine healthy subjects. Calibration ranges and time indicated in the figure. Black vertical line marks the beginning of the presentation of stimuli. Dot, isolated presentations; lines, target-mask presentations.

Computation of SSE 0, $_\Delta$BIC, the Bayes factor, and the posterior probabilities for the null and alternative hypotheses from inputs consisting of n (number of independent observations), $k1 - k0$ (the difference between the two models with respect to the number of free parameters), sum of squares for the effect of interest, and sum of squares for the error term associated with the effect of interest (SSE 1), as implemented in Microsoft Excel by Masson (2011), from the repeated measures ANOVA for the ERPs collected in Experiments I and II, for Oz results in $n=119$, df_effect $=2.557$,   Sseffect $=27.716$,   Sserror $=124.195$,   SSE1 $=124.1954$, SSE0 $=151.9119$, deltaBIC $=-11.7536$, BF01 $=0.002804$, p(H0|D) $=0.002796$, and p(H1|D) $=0.997204$.

For T5 is $n=119$, df_effect $=3.700$, Sseffect $=12.735$, Sserror $=46.98398$, SSE1 $=124.1954$, SSE0 $=59.71874$, deltaBIC $=-10.8557$, BF01 $=0.004392$, p (H0|D) $=0.004373$, and p(H1|D) $=0.995627$.

For T6 is $n=119$, df_effect $=1.223$, Sseffect $=36.397$, Sserror $=705.457$, SSE1 $=705.4575$, SSE0 $=741.8546$, deltaBIC $=-0.1427$, BF01 $=0.931137$, p (H0|D) $=0.48217$, and p(H1|D) $=0.51783$.

9 BEHAVIORAL DATA

The subjects gave more correct responses than incorrect responses (the first task, as described earlier in this chapter) in Experiment I (correct responses 94.47%; incorrect 5.52%) than in Experiment II (correct responses 33.67%; incorrect 66.32%). (See Figures 18.7 and 18.8.)

The target-mask presentations hinder the task of stimuli recognition in Experiment II from 5.52% (when, in Experiment I, the correct discrimination would be mask or pseudomask, depending on what the subject was shown) to 66.32% of incorrect responses (when, in Experiment II, the correct discrimination would be square or diamond, depending on what the subject was shown). The target-mask presentations in Experiment II has a higher incidence of incorrect responses than Experiment I.

Given that in Experiment II, the target (presented for 17 ms) is paracontrast and metacontrast by the mask/pseudomask (presented for 167 ms), it is the 168-ms (rounded values) interval between the termination of the target and of the mask that explains why (at least, with the design of Experiments I and II) the subject response is very often "none of the 15 stimuli presented" (the dot in the right bottom of the answers screen), none of the targets, despite that in all experiments, targets are always shown.

In other words, information about whether the target is paracontrast and metacontrast by the mask/pseudomask, 18 ms SOA, and 168 ms STA helped improve our prediction of the stimulus discrimination by 43,9% in Experiment II (the lambda

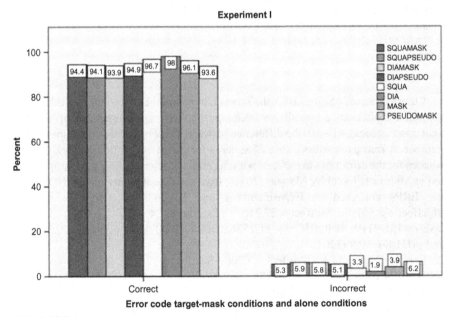

FIGURE 18.7

The subjects gave a higher percent of correct responses in target-mask Experiment I: correct responses 94.47%, incorrect 5.52%.

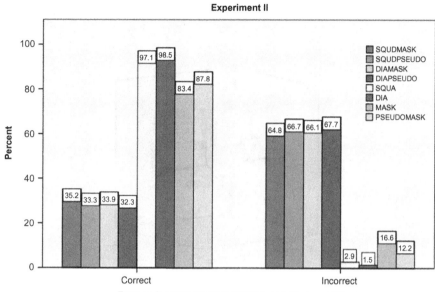

FIGURE 18.8

The subjects gave a higher percent of incorrect responses in target-mask Experiment II: correct responses 33.67%, incorrect 66.32%.

asymmetric measure of association is 0.439), and information about if the target is metacontrast by the mask/pseudomask and 18 ms SOA helped improve our prediction of the stimulus discrimination by 0% in Experiment I (the lambda asymmetric measure of association is 0.000). That is, the proportion of relative error in predicting stimulus discrimination that can be eliminated by knowledge of the way stimulus are display is 0.439 for Experiment II and is 0.000 for Experiment I.

Information about stimulus discrimination helped improve our prediction that the target is paracontrast and metacontrast by the mask/pseudomask, 18 ms SOA, and 168 ms STA by 9.3% in Experiment II (the lambda asymmetric measure of association is 0.093), and information about stimulus discrimination helped improve our prediction that the target is metacontrast by the mask/pseudomask, 18 ms SOA, by 0.5% in Experiment I (the lambda asymmetric measure of association is 0.005). That is, the proportion of relative error in predicting the way that stimulus are displayed that can be eliminated by knowledge of stimulus discrimination is 0.093 for Experiment II and is 0.005 for Experiment I.

Thus, the contrast in Oz and T5 between higher positive amplitudes (300–800 ms in combined stimuli presentations for Experiment II than for Experiment I correlates with the statistically significant contrast in stimuli discrimination between more incorrect responses in Experiment II [$\chi(7) = 2370.368$, p$=0.000$; 0 cells (0%) have an expected count of less than 5; the minimum expected count is 293.80] than in Experiment I [$\chi(7) = 27.029$, p$=.006$; 0 cells (0%) have an expected count of less than 5; the

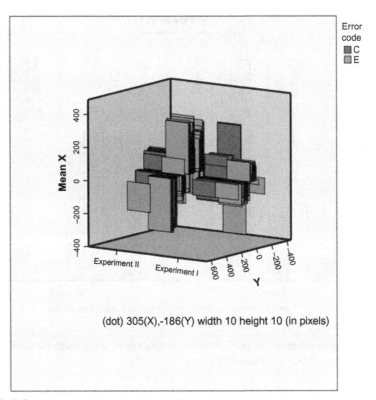

FIGURE 18.9

In target-mask experiment II, the subject response is very often "none of the fifteen stimuli presented" (the dot in the right bottom of answers screen, see Procedure), none of the targets, despite that in all experiments, targets are always shown.

minimum expected count is 29.83] and so correlate with contrast in access (the grand average ERPs correlated with correctly identified stimuli would be the correlate of the access). The Chi square test χ^2 is carried out on the actual number of correct and incorrect responses, not on percentages, proportions, means, or other derived statistics of correct and incorrect responses. (See Figures 18.10 and 18.11.)

The grand average Oz ERP positive amplitudes (300–800 ms) for the combined presentations is 3.678 μV for Experiment II and 2.5145 μV for Experiment I. And the grand average T5 ERP positive amplitude (300–800 ms) for the combined presentations is 3.139 μV for Experiment II and 2.582 μV for Experiment I.

10 THE GRAND AVERAGE OCCIPITAL AND TEMPORAL ELECTRICAL ACTIVITY CORRELATED WITH A CONTRAST IN PHENOMENOLOGY

Notwithstanding, in target-mask presentations of Experiment II, the degree of visibility (the second task, as described earlier) ranges from 19.27% "clear but not quite visible" responses to 62.22% "perfectly clear and visible" responses. (See Figure 18.12.)

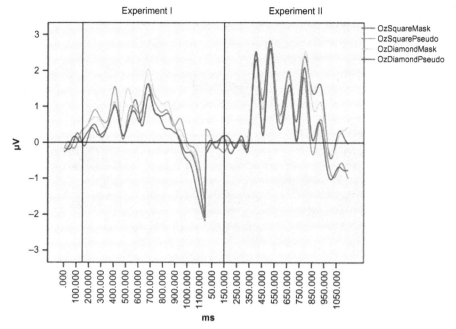

FIGURE 18.10

The contrast in Oz between higher positive amplitude (300-800 ms) in combined stimuli presentations for Experiment II than for Experiment I correlate with the contrast between more incorrect responses in Experiment II [×(7)=2370.368, p=.000] than in Experiment I [×(7)=27.029, p=.006] and so correlate with the contrast in access.

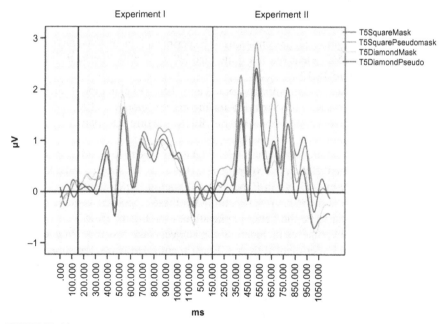

FIGURE 18.11

The contrast in T5 between higher positive amplitude (300-800 ms) in combined stimuli presentations for Experiment II than for Experiment I correlate with the contrast between more incorrect responses in Experiment II [×(7)=2370.368, p=.000] than in Experiment I [×(7)=27 .029, p=.006] and so correlate with the contrast in access.

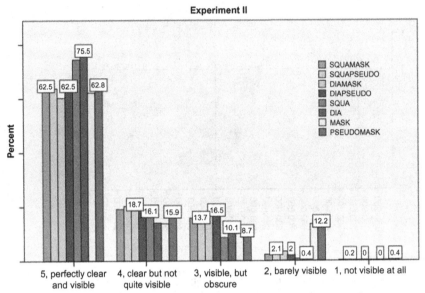

FIGURE 18.12

In target-mask presentations of Experiment II, the visibility range from 19.27% "clear but not quite visible" (key 4) to 62.22% "perfectly clear and visible" (key 5).

However, in target-mask presentations of Experiment I, the results range is much smaller: from 31.05% "clear but not quite visible" to 32.52% "perfectly clear and visible." (See Figure 18.13.)

The average reaction time appears not to be the better explanation: Experiment I (RT for correct responses, 1055 ms; RT for incorrect responses, 1129 ms); Experiment II (RT for correct responses, 1338 ms; RT for incorrect responses, 1715 ms). (See Figure 18.14.)

One hypothesis should be that the subjects take less time to respond incorrectly on average in Experiment II than in Experiment I. However, the subjects take longer to respond incorrectly on average in Experiment II than in Experiment I.

Even if we look at the mean reaction times for these responses, average reaction time does not appear to be the better explanation. (See Figure 18.15.)

Other possible hypotheses include that the subjects take less time on average to press keys 4 or 5 in Experiment II than in Experiment I. However, the subjects take longer on average to make these responses in Experiment II than in Experiment I.

Meanwhile, the difference between the two experiments in mean rank within the interval of degrees of visibility is statistically significant either if the targets combined with masks or with pseudomasks were incorrectly or correctly identified [H (1) = 290.908, p = 0.000, with a mean rank of 1848.19 for Experiment I, and a mean rank of 2393.18 for Experiment II (according to the Kruskal-Wallis test)]; or if the

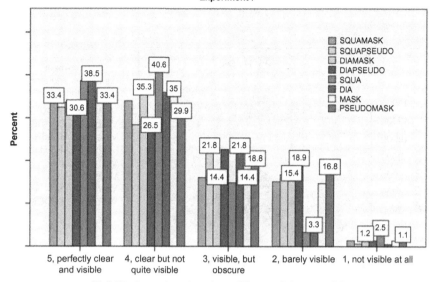

FIGURE 18.13

In target-mask presentations of Experiment I, the visibility range from 31.05% "clear but not quit visible" (key 4) to 32.52% "perfectly clear and visible" (key 5).

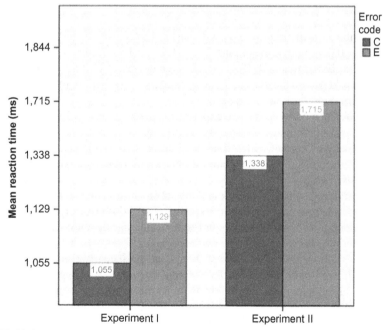

FIGURE 18.14

Mean stimuli discrimination reaction times do not appear to be the better place to look: Experiment I [RT for correct responses, 1055 ms; RT incorrect responses, 1129 ms]; Experiment II [RT for correct responses, 1338 ms; RT for incorrect responses, 1715 ms].

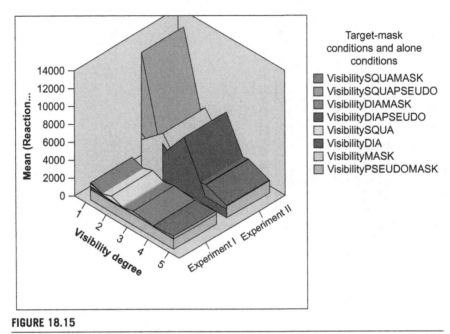

FIGURE 18.15

Visibility degree reactions times.

targets combined with masks or pseudomasks were correctly identified [$H(1) =$ 817.157, $p = 0.000$, with a mean rank of 3761.52 for Experiment I, and mean rank of 5055.58 for Experiment II]. Note that the high degree of visibility is not assigned to the target asked to do the identification in combined target-mask presentations, but to the mask/pseudomask that was seen.

If the difference between the two experiments in mean rank within the interval of degrees of visibility remains statistically significant between the two experiments in target presentations correctly identified, the interval between the termination of the target and of the mask does not explain the contrast in mean rank within the interval of degrees of visibility.

The second trial of the first block and the second block, in which the stimuli are presented in isolation, are the same in Experiments I and II. Thus, it is expected that the discrimination of stimuli that are not statistically significant contrast in correct and incorrect responses between the two experiments.

In isolated presentations of targets, there is no statistically significant contrast in stimuli discrimination between Experiment II [$\chi(1) = 3.492$, $p = .062$; 0 cells (0%) have an expected count of less than 5; the minimum expected count is 17.47] and Experiment I [$\chi(1) = 3.160$, $p = .075$; 0 cells (0%) have an expected count of less than 5; the minimum expected count is 20.38]. In addition, the contrast in stimuli discrimination between more correct responses in Experiment II (square correct 97.1%, incorrect 2.9%; diamond correct 98.5%, incorrect 1.5%)

than in Experiment I (square correct 96.7%, incorrect 3.3%; diamond correct 98.1%, incorrect 1.9%) is not statistically significant. Therefore, there is no statistically significant difference between correct responses in Experiment II than in Experiment I (the block in which the targets are presented in isolation is the same in both experiments). The access does not significantly change between Experiment II and Experiment I.

However, in mask or pseudomask isolated presentations, there is a statistically significant contrast in stimuli discrimination in Experiment II [$\chi(1)=6.256$, $p=.012$; 0 cells (0%) have an expected count of less than 5. The minimum expected count is 112.36], contrary to there being no statistically significant contrast in stimuli discrimination in Experiment I [$\chi(1)=3.682$, $p=.055$; 0 cells (0%) have an expected count of less than 5; the minimum expected count is 33.35].

In mask or pseudomask isolated presentations, the incorrect responses are significantly greater in Experiment II (mask incorrect 16.6%, pseudomask incorrect 12.2%) than in Experiment I (mask incorrect 3.9%, pseudomask incorrect 6.2%), and the correct responses are not significantly greater in Experiment I (mask correct 96.1%, pseudomask correct 93.6%) than in Experiment II (mask correct 83.4%, pseudomask correct 87.8%).

Arguably, because the second trial is randomized in the first block with the first trial where the correct identification of stimuli are targets in combined presentations in Experiment II (depending on whether the subject had been shown a square or a diamond) but is randomized in the first block with the first trial where the correct identification of stimuli are masks in combined presentations in Experiment I (depending on whether the subject had been shown a mask or a pseudomask).

The difference between the two experiments in mean rank within the interval of degrees of visibility remains statistically significant between the two experiments in target presentations correctly identified [$H(1)=336.045$, $p=0.000$), with a mean rank of 1081.05 for Experiment I, and a mean rank of 1522.38 for Experiment II (according to the Kruskal-Wallis test)]. The interval between the termination of the target and of the mask does not explain the contrast in mean rank within the interval of degrees of visibility. The better explanation for this is the phenomenology. Since the access is the same (see Figure 18.16), and since there is a statistically significant difference in mean rank within the interval of degrees of visibility, the better explanation is a difference in phenomenology.

Thus, the contrast between higher positive amplitude (300–800 ms) in target presentations for Experiment II than for Experiment I (Oz, square/diamond and T5, diamond) and in T5 between higher positive amplitude (300–800 ms) in square target presentations for Experiment I than for Experiment II (because there are more incorrect responses in mask or pseudomask isolated presentation for Experiment II than Experiment I) correlates with the contrast between higher mean rank within the interval of degrees of visibility in target presentations for Experiment II than for Experiment I, and thus correlate with the contrast in phenomenology (in isolated presentations of targets, there is no statistically significant contrast in correct responses between the two experiments). (See Figures 18.17–18.20.)

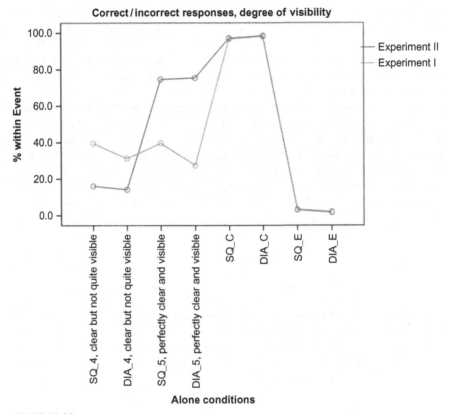

FIGURE 18.16

If the access is the same (SQ_C, DIA_C) and if, as there are, there are a statistically significant difference in mean rank within the interval of degrees of visibility "4" and "5", the better explanation is a difference in phenomenology.

11 THE GRAND AVERAGE OCCIPITAL AND TEMPORAL ELECTRICAL ACTIVITY CO-OCCURRING WITH UNCONSCIOUSNESS

Given that the subject response in Experiment II is very often "none of the 15 stimuli presented," they have no access to the targets, and given that the subject assigned a high degree of visibility to the mask/pseudomask they saw, they have no visual experience of the targets, the contrast in Oz and T5 between higher positive amplitude (300–800 ms) in combined stimuli presentations for Experiment II than for Experiment I is not a contrast between access and phenomenal consciousness of the targets. Rather, it is a contrast in access—namely, if the mask/pseudomask EEG signal is subtracted from the target-mask Experiment II EEG signal, the result is (at least arguably) the occipital and left temporal electrical activity co-occurring with the targets about which we have no consciousness. (See Figures 18.21 and 18.22.)

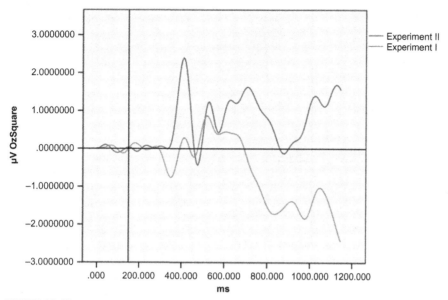

FIGURE 18.17

The contrast in Oz between higher positive amplitude (300-800 ms) in square presentations for Experiment II than for Experiment I correlate with the contrast between high mean rank degrees of visibility in target presentations for Experiment II than for Experiment I and so correlate with the contrast in phenomenology.

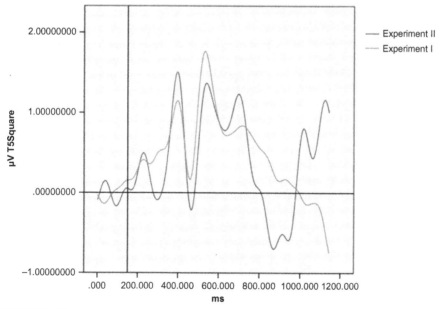

FIGURE 18.18

The contrast in T5 between higher positive amplitude (300-800 ms) in square presentations for Experiment I than for Experiment II correlate with the contrast between high mean rank degrees of visibility 4 and 5 in square presentations for Experiment II than for experiment I and so correlate with the contrast in phenomenology.

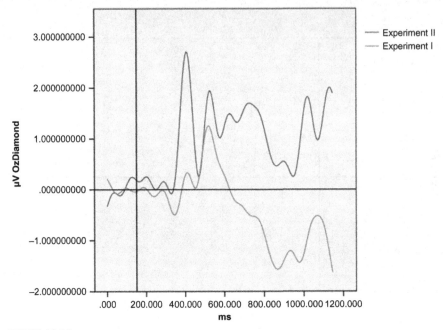

FIGURE 18.19

The contrast in Oz between higher positive amplitude (300-800 ms) in diamond presentations for experiment II than for Experiment I correlate with the contrast between high mean rank degrees of visibility 4 and 5 in diamond presentations for Experiment II than for Experiment I and so correlate with the contrast in phenomenology.

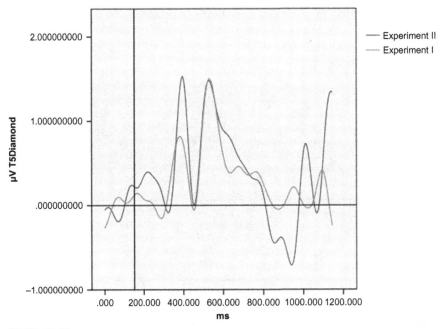

FIGURE 18.20

The contrast in T5 between higher positive amplitude (300-800 ms) in diamond presentations for Experiment II than for experiment I correlate with the contrast between high mean rank degrees of visibility 4 and 5 in diamond presentations for Experiment II than for Experiment I and so correlate with the contrast in phenomenology.

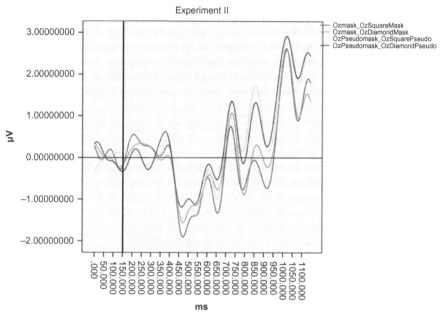

FIGURE 18.21

The occipital electrical activity co-occurring with the targets about which we have no consciousness.

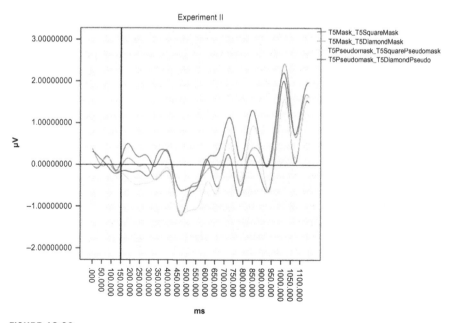

FIGURE 18.22

The left temporal electrical activity co-occurring with the targets about which we have no consciousness.

ACKNOWLEDGMENTS

I wish to acknowledge my mother, Maria Dulce; João Carneiro; and Susana Lourenço; several faculty members of the psychology department at the University of Lisbon, Ana Marques, Inês Raposo, Inês Reis, and Isabel Barahona; and, from LanCog (Language, Mind and Cognition Research Group), Philosophy Centre, University of Lisbon, Adriana Graca; João Branquinho; Ricardo Santos. My research would not have been possible without their help.

REFERENCES

Block, N., 2005. Two neural correlates of consciousness. Trends Cognit. Sci. 9, 46–52.

Del Cul, A., Baillet, S., Dehaene, S., 2007. Brain dynamics underlying the nonlinear threshold for access to consciousness. PLoS Biol. 5, 2408–2423 (Late positivity, LP, 500-600 ms).

Lau, H.C., Passingham, R.E., 2006. Relative blindsight in normal observers and the neural correlate of visual consciousness. Proc. Natl. Acad. Sci. U. S. A. 103, 18763–18768.

Masson, M.E.J., 2011. A tutorial on a practical Bayesian alternative to null–hypothesis significance testing. Behav. Res. Meth. 43, 679–690.

Pfurtscheller, G., Lopes da Silva, F.H., 1999. Event-related EEG/MEG synchronization and desynchronization: basic principles. Clin. Neurophysiol. 110, 1842–1857.

Chaotic Dynamical States in the Izhikevich Neuron Model

19

Sou Nobukawa[1], Haruhiko Nishimura[2], Teruya Yamanishi[1], and Jian-Qin Liu[3]

Department of Management Information Science, Fukui University of Technology, Fukui, Japan[1]
Graduate School of Applied Informatics, University of Hyogo, Hyogo, Japan[2]
National Institute of Information and Communications Technology, Hyogo, Japan[3]

1 INTRODUCTION

In recent years, according to the development of brain measurement technology, it has been recognized that information is transmitted among neurons by the spike timing of neurons instead of the firing rate. Therefore, spiking neuron models, which can describe spike timing, have been attracting a lot of attention. The Hodgkin-Huxley (HH) model is known as the most important spiking neuron model to simulate neurodynamics by describing the capacitance of membrane and characteristics of ion channel resistance (Hodgkin and Huxley, 1952). However, because of its complexity, many neuron models that are simpler than the HH model have been proposed to focus on the membrane potential behavior (*i.e.,* spiking activity), such as the integrate-and-fire neuron model and the FitzHugh-Nagumo neuron model (Rabinovich *et al.*, 2006). Among these models, the Izhikevich neuron model (Izhikevich, 2004a) can reproduce major spike patterns observed experimentally, and its biological variety is the highest in comparison with other models (Izhikevich, 2004b). For this reason, this model has attracted our attention.

Stochastic resonance (SR) is a phenomenon in which the presence of noise helps a nonlinear system to amplify a weak (under-barrier) signal and can be observed in many kinds of systems, such as global climate (Benzi *et al.*, 1981) and neural systems (Moss and Wiesenfeld, 1995; Gammaitoni *et al.*, 1998; Hänggi, 2002; Mori and Kai, 2002; McDonnell and Lawrence, 2011). On the other hand, fluctuating activities in the deterministic chaos also cause a phenomenon like SR, which is known as *chaotic resonance (CR)* (Carrol and Pecora, 1993; Crisanti *et al.*, 1994; Nicolis *et al.*, 1993; Sinha and Chakrabarti, 1998; Anishchenko *et al.*, 2002). Recently, the study of CR has been proceeding in neural systems, such as the chaotic neural network (Aihara *et al.*, 1990; Adachi and Aihara, 1997; Nishimura *et al.*, 2000; Nobukawa *et al.*, 2012a) and the inferior olive neuron system (Schweighofer *et al.*, 2004; Tokuda *et al.*, 2010, 2013; Nobukawa *et al.*, 2011a; Nobukawa and Nishimura, 2013a, 2013b; Schweighofer *et al.*, 2013). However, there has been no fundamental study that investigates the signal responses of CR in some chaotic states existing in the spiking neural system.

In this chapter, we examine and classify the chaotic characteristics for the Izhikevich neuron model. Since the Izhikevich neuron model includes the state-dependent jump in its resetting process, an ordinary Lyapunov exponent on the system trajectory cannot be applied (Kim, 2010; Bizzarri *et al.*, 2013). Nowadays, several methods have been proposed to evaluate the chaos in the system with the state-dependent jump, such as a Lyapunov exponent inserting a salutation matrix (Bizzarri *et al.*, 2013; Bernardo, 2008) and the 0-1 test (Kim, 2010; Gottwald and Melbourne, 2004). As one of these methods, we introduce using the Lyapunov exponent on the Poincaré section (PS-Lyapunov exponent), not on the system trajectory. And then, following up on our previous work (Nobukawa *et al.*, 2011b, 2012b), we evaluate the signal response of CR on the classified chaotic states through computer simulations. In section 2 of this chapter, as a preliminary step, we introduce the concepts of SR, CR, and the Izhikevich neuron model. In section 3, we introduce the evaluation indices to check the neuron state and investigate the chaotic characteristics for this model. In section 4, an extended Izhikevich neuron model with weak periodic signal and the evaluation indices for the signal response are introduced, and the characteristics of CR are examined.

2 FUNDAMENTAL DESCRIPTION

In this section, we give fundamental descriptions of SR, CR, and the Izhikevich neuron model.

2.1 SR AND CR

Figure 19.1(a) shows the general condition, where the applied signal is too weak for the state of system to exceed the barrier or threshold and therefore the signal cannot be detected. Then, in the SR case, the state happens to exceed the barrier or threshold according to the weak signal, with the help of appropriate noise; that is, the signal can be detected as shown in Figure 19.1(b). Originally, the concept of SR was introduced to reveal the mechanism of the periodically recurrent Ice Ages (Benzi *et al.*, 1981), but nowadays, SR can be observed in many kinds of systems, which have three ingredients: the form of barrier/threshold, the source of noise, and the weak input signal, such as biological reactions and brain activities (Moss and Wiesenfeld, 1995; Gammaitoni *et al.*, 1998; Hänggi, 2002; Mori and Kai, 2002). As examples of the biological reaction, a crayfish and a paddlefish detect slight movement of predators and preys, respectively (Moss and Wiesenfeld, 1995; Gammaitoni, 1998; Hänggi, 2002; Mori and Kai, 2002). As an example of brain activity, SR arises in the visual processing area of the human brain on the experiment of the entrainment of brain wave by light stimuli (Mori and Kai, 2002; McDonnell and Lawrence, 2011).

On the other hand, fluctuating activities in the deterministic chaos also cause CR, a phenomenon that is similar to SR. In the CR phenomenon, under the condition where no additive noise exists, the system responds to the weak input signal by the effect of the intrinsic chaotic activities, as shown in Figure 19.1(c). At first, its characteristic was investigated on simple models, such as the one-dimensional cubic map and Chua's circuit (Carrol and Pecora, 1993; Crisanti *et al.*, 1994; Nicolis *et al.*, 1993; Sinha and Chakrabarti, 1998; Anishchenko *et al.*, 2002). These systems have a chaotic attractor separated into two attractors, which induces a phenomenon called *chaos-chaos intermittency*. If the weak signal inputs to these systems, the chaos-chaos switching is synchronized to the signal; that is, CR arises. Focusing on the neural system, it has been observed that chaos exists on several hierarchical levels, from the electrical response of an ion channel to the activity of the brain as the neuron

Table 19.1 Chaos on Several Hierarchical Levels in Neural Systems

Hierarchical Level	Example
internal neuron	ion channel
single neuron	onchidium verruculatum, squid giant axon hippocampal pyramidal cell of rat
neuron assembly	brain wave in olfactory bulb of rabbit brain wave of human

Sources: Hayashi et al., 1982; Matsumoto, 1987; Skarda and Freeman, 1987; Freeman, 1988, 1992; Ikeguchi et al., 1990; Hayashi and Ishizuka, 1995.

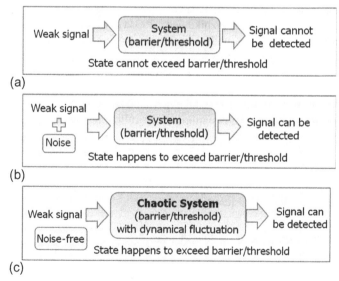

(a)

(b)

(c)

FIGURE 19.1

Concept of SR and CR. (a) System condition: weak signal cannot be detected. (b) SR: weak signal is detected with the help of noise. (c) CR: weak signal is detected by the effect of the intrinsic chaotic activities.

assembly, as shown in Table 19.1 (Hayashi *et al.*, 1982; Matsumoto *et al.*, 1987; Skarda and Freeman, 1987; Freeman, 1988, 1992; Ikeguchi *et al.*, 1990; Hayashi and Ishizuka, 1995). Recently, the study of CR has been proceeding in neural systems, such as the chaotic neural network (Aihara *et al.*, 1990; Adachi and Aihara, 1997) with several chaotic attractors (Nishimura *et al.*, 2000; Nobukawa *et al.*, 2012a). It is also reported that CR arises in excitable systems, such as spiking neural systems, which lack some attractors (Schweighofer *et al.*, 2004, 2013; Tokuda *et al.*, 2010, 2013; Nobukawa *et al.*, 2011b, 2012b; Nobukawa and Nishimura, 2013a, 2013b). In this chapter, we deal with CR in the spiking neural system.

2.2 IZHIKEVICH NEURON MODEL

The Hodgkin-Huxley (HH) model (Hodgkin and Huxley, 1952) is known as the most important spiking neuron model to simulate neurodynamics by describing the capacitance of membrane and characteristics of ion channel resistance. This model consists of four equations and many physiological parameters regarding membrane potential, activation of Na and K currents, and inactivation of Na current. It can reproduce almost all spiking activity observed in the neural system by tuning the parameters. However, because of the complexity of the physiological parameters, many neuron models with a small number of parameters, which are simpler than the HH model, have been proposed to focus on the membrane potential behavior (spiking activity), such as the integrate-and-fire neuron model and the FitzHugh-Nagumo neuron model (Rabinovich *et al.*, 2006). Among these models, the Izhikevich neuron model (Izhikevich, 2004a), which combines continuous spike-generation mechanisms and a discontinuous resetting process after spikes, can reproduce major spike patterns observed experimentally by tuning a few parameters. And the variety of their spiking properties is higher than that of other models (Izhikevich, 2004b).

The Izhikevich neuron model (Izhikevich, 2004a, 2004b) is a two-dimensional system of ordinary differential equations of the following form:

$$v' = 0.04v^2 + 5v + 140 - u + I, \tag{19.1}$$

$$u' = a(bv - u), \tag{19.2}$$

with the auxiliary after-spike resetting:

$$\text{if } v \geq 30[\text{mV}], \text{ then } \begin{matrix} v \leftarrow c \\ u \leftarrow u + d \end{matrix}. \tag{19.3}$$

Here, v and u represent the membrane potential of the neuron and a membrane recovery variable, respectively; v and the time t have [mV] and [ms] scales, respectively; and I is the input dc-current. Parameters a and b describe the time scale and the sensitivity of u, respectively. Spiking behaviors such as regular spiking (RS), intrinsically bursting (IB), and chattering (CH) are reproduced using this model. In our simulation, this model is discretized with the difference interval $\Delta t = 10^{-4}$ ms to achieve enough numerical precision to evaluate the chaotic spiking activity (Izhikevich, 2004b), which is much smaller than $\Delta t = 0.5$ ms adopted for reproducing only the periodic spiking in Izhikevich (2004a).

Let us demonstrate the time evolution of $v(t)$ in the cases of RS $(a = 0.02, b = 0.2, c = -65, d = 8)$, IB $(a = 0.02, b = 0.2, c = -55, d = 4)$, and CH $(a = 0.02, b = 0.2, c = -50, d = 2)$. When the dc-current $I = 10$ is input to RS neurons as shown at the bottom of Figure 19.2(a), the neuron fires a few spikes with short inter-spike periods, and then the periods become long. This spiking behavior is the most typical in the cortex. There are not only spiking neurons like RS neurons, but also bursting neurons like IB and CH in the cortex. Figure 19.2(b) shows that the IB neuron bursts at the beginning of $I = 10$ and then bursting changes to spiking. On the other hand, CH neuron bursts during $I = 10$, and the interburst frequency can be as high as about 40 Hz, as shown in Figure 19.2(c).

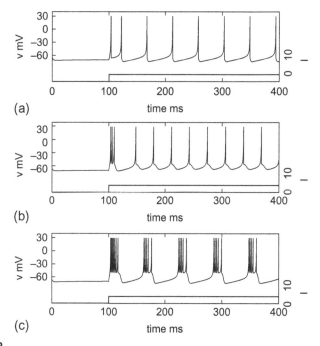

FIGURE 19.2

Firing patterns in the Izhikevich neuron model. (a) Regular spiking (RS) $(a = 0.02, b = 0.2, c = -65, d = 8)$. (b) Intrinsically bursting (IB). $(a = 0.02, b = 0.2, c = -55, d = 4)$. (c) Chattering (CH) $(a = 0.02, b = 0.2, c = -50, d = 2)$.

Next, we will explain the mechanism of firing by using the RS case. Figure 19.3 shows v-nullcline (dashed line), u-nullcline (dotted line), and the vector field of v and u (arrows), which are given by $v' = 0$, $u' = 0$, and the values of (v', u') on the $v - u$

phase plane, respectively. In the input dc-current $I = 0$ case (a), v -nullcline and u-nullcline cross at $(v, u) = (-70, -14)$ (filled circle) and $(-50, -10)$ (open circle). At $(v, u) = (-70, -14)$, the real parts of eigenvalues of Jacobian in Eqs. (19.1) and (19.2) are negative; *i.e.,* the system state is drawn to this point, called the *stable fixed point*. Meanwhile, the real parts of eigenvalues at $(v, u) = (-50, -10)$ are positive and the system state disengages from this point, which is called the *unstable fixed point*. In the input dc-current $I = 10$case (b), v-nullcline and u-nullcline do not cross. Due to the extinct of the stable fixed point, the system state moves through the vector filed and leads to the firing ($v > 30$ mV), as shown in Figure 19.4. After firing, the system state (v, u) follows the resetting process given by Eq. (19.3) and jumps to the point $((v, u) \approx (-65, 0.3)$ discontinuously.

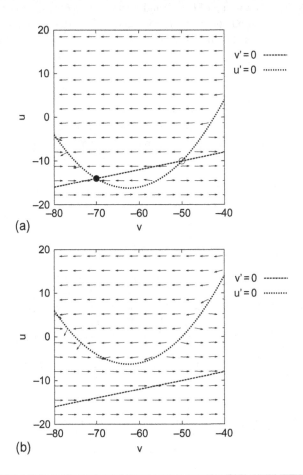

FIGURE 19.3

v-nullcline ($v' = 0$), u-nullcline ($u' = 0$), and vector field of v and u (v', u'), indicated by dashed line, dotted line, and arrows, respectively. (a) Input dc-current $I = 0$ case. (Filled circle: stable fixed point, open circle: unstable fixed point.) (b) Input dc-current $I = 10$ case.

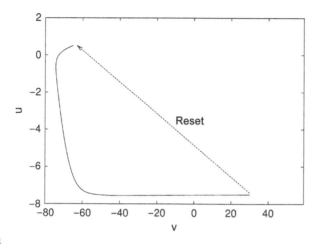

FIGURE 19.4

RS trajectory (solid line), including state-dependent jump in the (v, u) phase plane. $(a = 0.02, b = 0.2, c = -65, d = 8, l = 10.)$

3 CHAOTIC PROPERTIES OF IZHIKEVICH NEURON MODEL

In this section, focusing on the uniformity of neuron spikes and the Lyapunov exponent on the Poincaré section, we examine and classify the chaotic behavior in the Izhikevich neuron model. First, the evaluation indices are introduced. Second, the chaotic behaviors are investigated using these indices.

3.1 EVALUATION INDICES

To evaluate the uniformity of neuron spikes, we adopt the normalized fluctuations of spike durations (Pikovsky and Kurths, 1997):

$$R = \frac{\sqrt{Var(T_k)}}{\langle T_k \rangle}. \tag{19.4}$$

T_k is the kth spike interval ($T_k = t_{k+1} - t_k$). $Var(T_k)$ and $< T_k >$ are the variance and the mean of T_k, respectively. Here, R becomes 0 in the periodic state and positive in the aperiodic state, including the chaotic state.

As a straightforward index to check whether the state is chaotic, ordinarily we would use the maximum Lyapunov exponent for the system with the continuous trajectory, which is calculated by

$$\lambda_1 = \frac{1}{\tau N} \sum_{k=1}^{N} \ln \left(\frac{|d^k(t_l = \tau)|}{|d^k(t_l = 0)|} \right). \tag{10.5}$$

Here, $|d^k(t_l = 0)|$ ($k = 1, 2, ..., N$) are N perturbed initial conditions applied at $t_l \in [0 : \tau]$ and $d^k(t_l = \tau)$ are their time evolution for t_l (Parker and Chua, 1989).

Let us consider the case that a neuron fires at $t_l = t_s$, $k = i$. Since the time evolution of the system trajectory is discontinuous in the resetting process [Eq. (19.3)], then $d^i(t_s)$ receives the interruption and $|d^i(\tau)|$ becomes irrelevant. Due to this influence, λ_1 loses its validity for such a situation. Therefore, trials for new measures of such a system are needed (Kim, 2010; Bizzarri *et al.*, 2013; Bernardo, 2008; Gottwald and Melbourne, 2004). In our simulation, in order to overcome this problem, we introduce the Lyapunov exponents λ_v and λ_u on the Poincaré section instead of the system trajectory, which is introduced in the next section of this chapter

3.2 CHAOTIC BEHAVIORS IN IZHIKEVICH NEURON MODEL

The Izhikevich neuron model can reproduce major firing patterns, such as regular spiking, intrinsically bursting, chattering, and fast spiking (Izhikevich, 2004a, 2004b). Moreover, it is suggested that this model can produce a chaotic behavior with appropriate parameter values $(a = 0.2, b = 2, c = -56, d = -16, I = -99)$ in Eqs. (19.1) and (19.2) (Izhikevich, 2004b). Figures 19.5(a, b) show the chaotic time evolution of $v(t)$ and the strange attractor in a phase plane (v, u), respectively. We now examine the strange attractor in more detail using the Poincaré sections: Φ_v $(v > v_-^*, u = u_-^*)$ and Φ_u $(v = v_-^*, u > u_-^*)$, where $(v_-^*, u_-^*) \approx (-57.0, -114.0)$ is one of the solutions $(v_\pm^*, u_\pm^*)$ obtained by $v' = 0, u' = 0$. Note that both solutions $(v_\pm^*, u_\pm^*)$ are unstable fix points. The dynamics of $(v_1, v_2, ..., v_N)$ and $(u_1, u_2, ..., u_N)$, which are time evolutions of v and u on the Φ_v and Φ_u, are defined as Poincaré mapping $v_{n+1} = \emptyset_v(v_n)$ and $u_{n+1} = \emptyset_u(u_n)$.

The resulting Poincaré return map of v_n and u_n in Figure 19.5(c) shows that the strange attractor of Figure 19.5(b) has the stretching and folding structure.

Next, we calculate the PS-Lyapunov exponents of v and u. The points after m times passing through the Φ_v and Φ_u from v_n and u_n are given by

$$v_{n+m} = \emptyset_v^m(v_n)$$ (19.6)

$$u_{n+m} = \emptyset_u^m(u_n)$$ (19.7)

By introducing a small difference δ_0 to v_n and u_n, the evolutions of Eqs. (19.6) and (19.7) are perturbed after mth mapping:

$$v_{n+m} + \delta_m^n = \emptyset_v^m(v_n + \delta_0)$$ (19.8)

$$u_{n+m} + \delta_m^n = \emptyset_u^m(u_n + \delta_0)$$ (19.9)

Then, the Lyapunov exponents of v_n and u_n are calculated by

$$\lambda_v = \frac{1}{L} \sum_{i=1}^{L-1} \log \frac{\delta_m^{i+mi}}{\delta_0},$$ (19.10)

$$\lambda_u = \frac{1}{L} \sum_{i=1}^{L-1} \log \frac{\delta_m^{i+mi}}{\delta_0}.$$ (19.11)

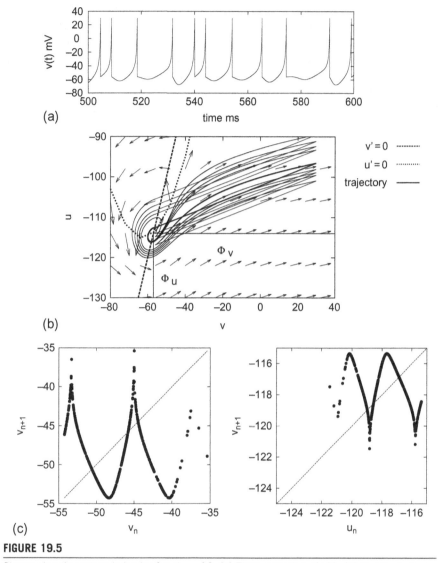

FIGURE 19.5

Strong chaotic system behavior for $d = -16$. (a) Time evolution of $v(t)$. (b) Its return map in the (v, u) phase plane. Dashed line is v-nullcline ($v' = 0$) and dotted line is u-nullcline ($u' = 0$). Arrows indicate the vector field of v and u. (c) Poincaré return map of v_n and u_n in the strong chaotic state ($a = 0.2$, $b = 2$, $c = -56$, $d = -16$, $I = -99$).

By setting the initial difference $\delta_0 = 0.1$ and $m = 1$, the PS-Lyapunov exponents become $\lambda_v \approx 1.20 > 0$ and $\lambda_u \approx 1.14 > 0$. This indicates that the behavior in Figure 19.5 is chaotic.

Next, we investigate the system behavior in detail by enlarging the parameter region on I and d including the values of and $I = -99$ and $d = -16$, used in Figure 19.5 following Izhikevich (2004b). Figure 19.6 shows the dependence of λ_v and λ_u on I obtained under the condition that the values of other parameters are fixed to the ones in Figure 19.5. There is chaotic region ($\lambda_{v,u} > 0$) in a certain range on either side of $I = -99$ ($-104.5 \lesssim I \lesssim -94.5$). Also, the system becomes rest (nonfiring) in $I \lesssim -104.5$, while it becomes periodic, firing in $I \gtrsim -94.5$.

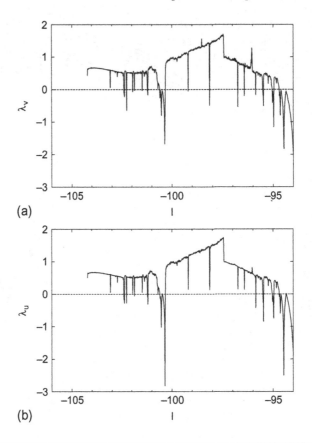

(a)

(b)

FIGURE 19.6

Dependence of the Lyapunov exponent $\lambda_{v,u}$ on the input dc-current I.
($a = 0.2$, $b = 2$, $c = -56$, $d = -16$, $A = 0, \delta_0 = 0.1$).

Fixing I to -99, we investigate the bifurcation by changing d with a bifurcation diagram that consists of $(v_1, v_2, \ldots, v_N)$ and $(u_1, u_2, \ldots, u_N)$. Figures 19.7(a) and (c) are the bifurcation diagram of v_n and λ_v as the function of d, respectively. The chaotic trajectory is distributed extensively in $d \lesssim -11.9$, and the system seems to be periodic ($\lambda_v < 0$) in $d \gtrsim -11.9$. A similar result appears in the case of the bifurcation diagram of u_n [Figure 19.7(b)] and $\lambda_u < 0$ [Figure 19.7 (d)].

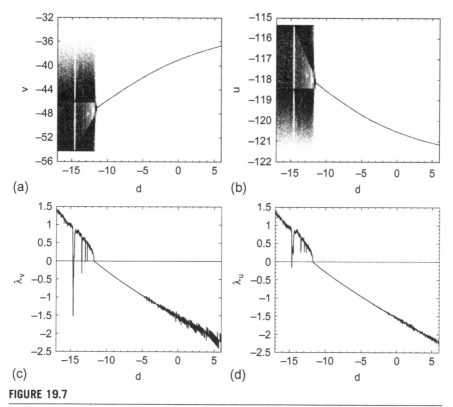

FIGURE 19.7

d dependence of bifurcation. (a) Bifurcation diagram of v. (b) Bifurcation diagram of u.
(c) Lyapunov exponent λ_v. (d) Lyapunov exponent λ_u.
($a = 0.2$, $b = 2$, $c = -56$, $I = -99$, $\delta_0 = 0.1$).

In $d \gtrsim -11.9$, the system seems to be periodic; however, the normalized fluctuation R in Eq. (19.4) indicates the slightly fluctuated spike interval ($R \gtrsim 10^{-5}$) in $-11 \lesssim d \lesssim 0$, as shown in Figure 19.8(a). This slight fluctuation's behavior can be checked with $\lambda_{v,u}$ by using a smaller initial perturbation such as $\delta_0 = 10^{-6}$ (hereinafter written as $\lambda_{v,u}|_{\delta_0=10^{-6}}$). Figure 19.8(b) shows that the values of $\lambda_{v,u}$ in $-11.9 \lesssim d \lesssim 0$ indicate that this slight fluctuation is chaotic ($\lambda_{v,u}|_{\delta_0=10^{-6}} > 0$). This means that the slightly fluctuated trajectory looks stable in the large scale with $\delta_0 \sim 0.1$, but the trajectory exhibits chaotic behavior in the small scale, with $\delta_0 \sim 10^{-6}$. For example, Figure 19.9 shows that this chaotic state in the case of $d = -11$ has almost periodic time evolution of $v(t)$ (a) and stable trajectory (b), while slight fluctuation appears in the limited region from the result of the Poincaré return map (c).

In this chapter, the extensively fluctuated chaos ($\lambda_{v,u}|_{\delta_0=0.1} > 0$) and $\lambda_{v,u}|_{\delta_0=10^{-6}} > 0$) is called *strong chaos,* and the slightly fluctuated chaos

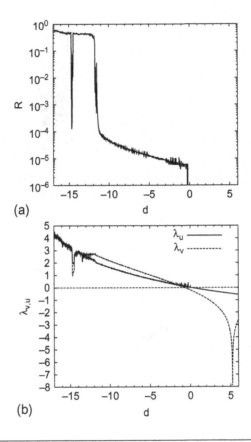

FIGURE 19.8

(a) d dependence of normalized fluctuations of spike duration R. (b) Lyapunov exponent $\lambda_{v,u}$ with initial value for parturition $\delta_0 = 10^{-6}$. ($a = 0.2$, $b = 2$, $c = -56$, $l = -99$).

($\lambda_{v,u}|_{\delta_0=0.1} < 0$) and $\lambda_{v,u}|_{\delta_0=10^{-6}} > 0$) is called *weak chaos*. It is also confirmed that the weak chaotic state is invariably sustained, even though the difference interval Δt is set to be less than 10^{-4}.

4 RESPONSE EFFICIENCY IN CHAOTIC RESONANCE

In this section, to reveal the high efficiency of the signal response in the chaotic state, we investigate the response to a periodic signal with weak strength, which cannot be detected in the nonchaotic state. First, we introduce the extended Izhikevich neuron model with a signal. Second, to measure the efficiency of the response to the weak periodic signal, evaluation indices of mutual correlation and mutual information are defined. Third, the dependence of the signal response efficiency on the parameter d and the signal strength is evaluated by using these evaluation indices.

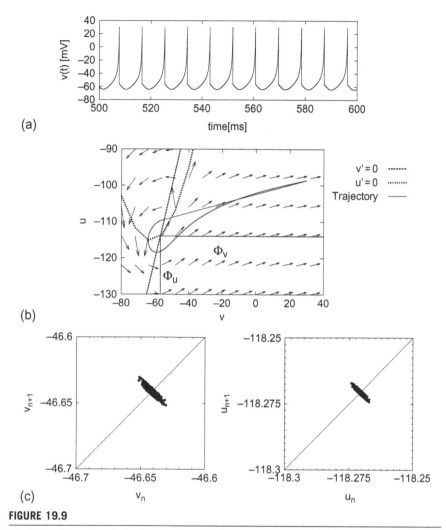

FIGURE 19.9

Weak chaotic system behavior for $d = -11$. (a) Time evolution of $v(t)$. (b) Its return map in the (v, u) phase plane. (c) Poincaré return map of v_n and u_n. $(a = 0.2, b = 2, c = -56, I = -99, S(t) = 0)$.

4.1 EXTENDED IZHIKEVICH NEURON MODEL WITH A PERIODIC SIGNAL

Eqs. (19.1), (19.2), and (19.3) are extended with a weak periodic signal $S(t)$ as follows:

$$v' = 0.04v^2 + 5v + 140 - u + I + S(t), \tag{19.12}$$

$$u' = a(bv - u), \tag{19.13}$$

with the auxiliary after-spike resetting

$$\text{if } v \geq 30\,\text{mV, then} \quad \begin{matrix} v \leftarrow c \\ u \leftarrow u + d \end{matrix}, \tag{19.14}$$

where we adopt $S(t) = A\sin 2\pi f_0 t$. It is noted that the sinusoidal signal has been utilized merely as a typical example of the signal in the neural system. In the following simulation, we set the parameter values to $(a, b, c, I) = (0.2, 2, -56, -99)$, as well as the values in Figures 19.7 and 19.8 and $f_0 = 0.1$.

We evaluate the timing of spikes against the signal $S(t)$ by using the cycle histogram $F\left(\tilde{t}\right)$. $F\left(\tilde{t}\right)$ is a histogram of firing counts at $t_k \bmod(T_0)$ ($k = 1, 2, ..$) against the signal $S\left(\tilde{t}\right)$ with a period $T_0 (= 1/f_0), 0 \leq \tilde{t} \leq T_0$. For example, in the case of the spike times $t_k = 2, 6, 12, 16, 26$, the values of the $t_k \bmod(T_0)$ are $2, 6, 2, 6, 6$ ($T_0 = 10$), and then the cycle histogram becomes $F(2) = 2$ and $F(6) = 3$.

To quantify the signal response, we use the following indices. The mutual correlation $C(\tau)$ between the cycle histogram $F\left(\tilde{t}\right)$ of the neuron spikes and the signal $S\left(\tilde{t}\right)$ is given by

$$C(\tau) = \frac{C_{SF}(\tau)}{\sqrt{C_{SS}C_{FF}}}, \tag{19.15}$$

$$C_{SF}(\tau) = \left\langle \left(S\left(\tilde{t} + \tau\right) - \left\langle S\left(\tilde{t}\right) \right\rangle \right) \left(F\left(\tilde{t}\right) - \left\langle F\left(\tilde{t}\right) \right\rangle \right) \right\rangle. \tag{19.16}$$

For the time delay factor τ, we check $\max_\tau C(\tau)$, i.e., the largest $C(\tau)$ between $0 \leq \tau \leq T_0$. In our simulation, we set the width of the bin of the cycle histogram to 20 times the difference interval Δt and use 4.0×10^6 ms as the evaluation duration.

As an extensively used index for evaluating the information transmission, we use mutual information, which is the information transmitted from input S to output F:

$$MI(F; S) = H(F) - H(F|S). \tag{19.17}$$

Here, S and F consist of $m_s (s_1, s_2, ..., s_{m_s})$ and $m_f (f_1, f_2, ..., f_{m_f})$ event states into which $S\left(\tilde{t}\right) (-A \sim A)$ and $F\left(\tilde{t}\right) (0 \sim$ its maximum value) are divided equally, respectively. $H(F)$ and $H(F|S)$ are given by

$$H(F) = -\sum_j P\left(f_j\right)\log_2 P\left(f_j\right), \tag{19.18}$$

$$H(F|S) = -\sum_i\sum_j P(s_i)P\left(f_j|s_i\right)\log_2 P\left(f_j|s_i\right), \tag{19.19}$$

where $P(s_j)$ and $P(f_j)$ are the occurrence probability of s_j and f_j, and $P\left(f_j|s_i\right)$ is the conditional probability for f_j and s_i. In our simulation, we set $m_s = m_f = 20$, but if the maximum value of $F\left(\tilde{t}\right)$ is less than m_f, m_f is set to the maximum value because $F\left(\tilde{t}\right)$ is an integer of firing counts.

4.2 DEPENDENCE ON PARAMETER d

This section concerns the response of the system in Eqs. (19.12)–(19.14). Figure 19.10 shows the time series of $v(t)$ and the corresponding cycle histogram $F\left(\tilde{t}\right)$ of firing counts. In case (a), $d = -16$, the neuron fires aperiodically and the

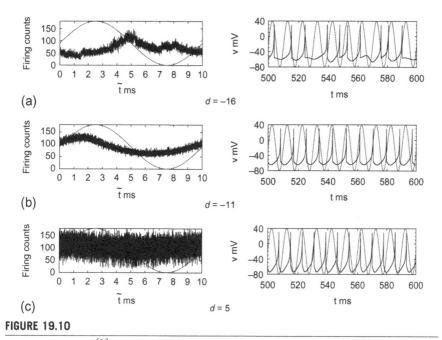

FIGURE 19.10

Cycle histogram $F\left(\tilde{t}\right)$ (left) and time series of $v(t)$ (right) in the cases of (a) $d = -16$, (b) $d = -11$, and (c) $d = 5$ in CR. Dotted lines are the input signal $S\left(\tilde{t}\right)$. ($a = 0.2$, $b = 2$, $c = -56$, $I = -99$, $A = 0.3$, $f_0 = 0.1$.)

cycle histogram $F\left(\tilde{t}\right)$ responds to the signal $S\left(\tilde{t}\right)$ with some time delay $\tau \approx 8$ ms. In case (b), $d = -11$, the neuron fires more periodically than (a) and the cycle histogram $F\left(\tilde{t}\right)$ fits the signal $S\left(\tilde{t}\right)$ with $\tau \approx 1.5$ ms well. However, by changing d to the periodic region, the neuron fires periodically and the cycle histogram $F\left(\tilde{t}\right)$ does not respond to the signal $S\left(\tilde{t}\right)$, as shown in (c) $d = 5$.

As mentioned in section 3, the system ($-17 \lesssim d \lesssim 0$) sees chaotic activity in the region ($-17 \lesssim d \lesssim 0$), and this region is divided into the strong chaotic region ($-17 \lesssim d \lesssim -11.9$), in which the spike timing is not uniform, and the weak chaotic region ($-11.9 \lesssim d \lesssim 0$), where the spike timing is seemingly uniform. Now, we evaluate the $\max_\tau C(\tau)$ and $MI(F; S)$ for the system. As shown in Figure 19.11(a), $\max_\tau C(\tau)$ becomes high (≈ 0.9) in the region of ($-17 \lesssim d \lesssim 0$), except for $d = -12$, where the system has chaotic activity. Thus, CR arises in this region.

Note that the delay τ given in the top of Figure 19.11(a) suggests that CR in the weak chaotic region has a prompt response ($\tau < 1.5$ ms) in comparison with the strong chaotic region ($\tau > 8$ ms). Similar to $\max_\tau C(\tau)$, $MI(F; S)$ also keeps a high value ($\gtrsim 0.5$) in the region ($-17 \lesssim d \lesssim -11$), but it has the tendency to decrease from ($d \gtrsim -11$), despite neurons having chaotic activity, as shown in Figure 19.11 (b).

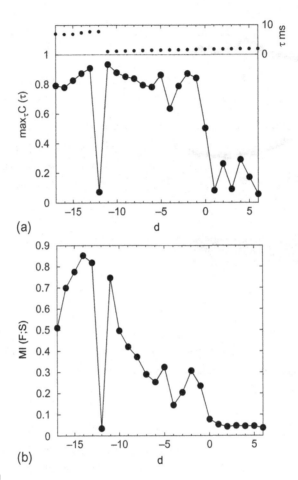

FIGURE 19.11

Dependence on parameter d in CR. (a) d dependence of $\max_\tau C(\tau)$ between cycle histogram $F\left(\tilde{t}\right)$ and input signal $S\left(\tilde{t}\right)$. (b) d dependence of $MI(F; S)$ between cycle histogram $F\left(\tilde{t}\right)$ and input signal $S\left(\tilde{t}\right)$. ($a = 0.2, b = 2, c = -56, l = -99, A = 0.3, f_0 = 0.1$.)

This is because decreasing of the $F\left(\tilde{t}\right)$ range, such as in Figure 19.10(b), makes the values of $P(f_i)$ biased compared to values of $P(s_i)$.

In addition, there is a good reason for decreasing the values of $\max_\tau C(\tau)$ and $MI(F; S)$ at $d = -12$ as in Figure 19.11. Figure 19.12 is the bifurcation diagram of v (a) and u (b) around $d = -12$ under the same conditions as in Figure 19.11. In $d \lesssim -12.04$, the trajectories of v and u expand in a wide range, but in $-12.04 \lesssim d \lesssim -11.15$, they are confined in the two limited regions corresponding to almost period-2 state synchronous to $S(t)$, which still have a weak chaotic fluctuation [$(\lambda_{v,u}|_{\delta_0 = 10^{-6}} > 0$]. Thus, the frequency of the cycle histogram $F\left(\tilde{t}\right)$ focuses on two specific bins, and the values of $\max_\tau C(\tau)$ and $MI(F; S)$ drastically decreases.

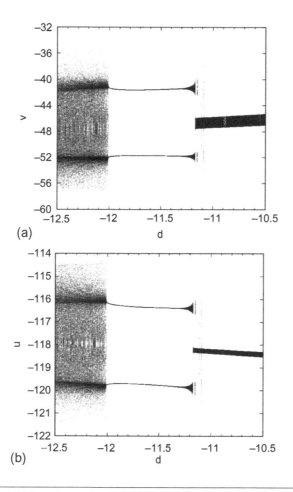

FIGURE 19.12

(a)d dependence of bifurcation under signal $S(t)$. (a) bifurcation diagram of v. (b) bifurcation diagram of u. ($a = 0.2$, $b = 2$, $c = -56$, $I = -99$, $A = 0.3$, $f_0 = 0.1$.)

4.3 DEPENDENCE ON SIGNAL STRENGTH *A*

We also examine the dependence on the signal strength A in CR. Figure 19.13 shows A dependence of $\max_\tau C(\tau)$ (a) and $MI(F; S)$ (b) in the strong chaotic ($d = -16$), the weak chaotic ($d = -11$), and the periodic ($d = 5$) cases. The strong and weak chaotic states have higher values of $\max_\tau C(\tau)$ and $MI(F; S)$ than the periodic state in the signal strength region ($A \lesssim 1$). Especially, as shown in Figure 19.13(a), $\max_\tau C(\tau)$ is higher and τ is smaller in the weak chaotic state than those in the strong chaotic state in ($0.03 < A < 0.7$). This result indicates that the weak chaotic state has higher sensitivity and a prompter response against the weak signal than the strong chaotic state.

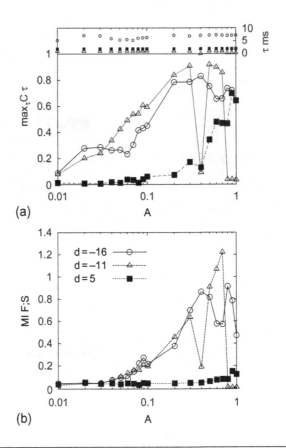

FIGURE 19.13

Dependence on signal strength A in CR. (a) signal strength A dependence of $\max_\tau C(\tau)$. (b) signal strength A dependence of $MI(F; S)$. ($a = 0.2$, $b = 2$, $c = -56$, $I = -99$, $f_0 = 0.1$)

5 CONCLUSIONS

In this chapter, the fundamental descriptions of SR, CR, and the Izhikevich neuron model were introduced. Next, we examined the chaotic characteristics of the Izhikevich neuron model in detail by using the PS-Lyapunov exponent and found the existence of two distinctive states: strong and weak chaotic states. In order to evaluate the signal response of CR on these classified states, we introduced the extended Izhikevich neuron model with a weak periodic signal, and defined the cycle histogram of neuron spikes and the corresponding mutual correlation and mutual information. Through computer simulations, we confirmed that both strong and weak chaotic states in CR can respond to the weak signal sensitively, and moreover, the weak chaotic state has a much prompter response than the strong chaotic state.

From the results in this work, we can expect that the PS-Lyapunov exponent can be applied to other reset systems with the state jump, such as control systems and models in social and financial science, as the index to distinguish whether they are chaotic or not. With regard to the CR phenomena, it might be inferred that CR plays an important role in the information transmission of the actual nervous systems. From the engineering viewpoint, the high signal response efficiency in CR can be utilized to develop a device to detect weak signals.

A further intent of this study is to evaluate the signal response in neuron assemblies consisting of strong chaotic, weak chaotic, and periodic neurons. We explored the coupling strength dependency of signal response in the neuron assemblies and found the preliminarily result that they maintain a similar signal response efficiency with the single-neuron case over a wide range of coupling strengths. We are now working to confirm the result in more detail.

REFERENCES

Adachi, M., Aihara, K., 1997. Associative dynamics in a chaotic neural network. Neural Network. 10 (1), 83–98.

Aihara, K., Takabe, T., Toyoda, M., 1990. Chaotic neural networks. Phys. Lett. 144 (6), 333–340.

Anishchenko, V.S., Astakhov, V.V., Neiman, A.B., Vadivasova, T.E., Schimansky-Geier, L., 2002. Nonlinear Dynamics of Chaotic and Stochastic System. Springer.

Benzi, R., Sutera, A., Vulpiani, A., 1981. The mechanism of stochastic resonance. J. Phys. Math. Gen. 14 (11), 453–457.

Bernardo, M.D. (Ed.), 2008. Piecewise-Smooth Dynamical Systems: Theory and Applications. Springer.

Bizzarri, F., Brambilla, A., Gajani, G.S., 2013. Lyapunov exponents computation for hybrid neurons. J. Comput. Neurosci. 35 (2), 201–212.

Carrol, T.L., Pecora, L.M., 1993. Stochastic resonance and crises. Phys. Rev. Lett. 70, 576–579.

Crisanti, A., Felcioni, M., Paladin, G., Vulpiani, A., 1994. Stochastic resonance in deterministic chaotic system. J. Phys. Math. Gen. 27, 597–603.

Freeman, W.J., 1988. Strange attractors that govern mammalian brain dynamics shown by trajectories of electroencephalographic (EEG) potential. IEEE Trans. Circ. Syst. CAS-35 (7), 781–783.

Freeman, W.J., 1992. Tutorial on neurobiology: from single neurons to brain chaos. Int. J. Bifurcat. Chaos 2 (03), 451–482.

Gammaitoni, L., Hänggi, P., Jung, P., Marchesoni, F., 1998. Stochastic resonance. Rev. Mod. Phys. 70 (1), 223–287.

Gottwald, G.A., Melbourne, I., 2004. A new test for chaos in deterministic systems. Proc. Roy. Soc. Lond. A Math. Phys. Eng. Sci. 460, 603–611.

Hänggi, P., 2002. Stochastic resonance in biology. Chem. Phys. Chem 3, 285–290.

Hayashi, H., Ishizuka, S., 1995. Chaotic responses of the hippocampal CA3 region to a mossy fiber stimulation in vitro. Brain Res. 686 (2), 194–206.

Hayashi, H., Ishizuka, S., Ohta, M., Hirakawa, K., 1982. Chaotic behavior in the Onchidum giant neuron under sinusoidal stimulation. Phys. Lett. 88, 435–438.

Hodgkin, L., Huxley, A.F., 1952. A quantitative description of membrane current and application to conduction and excitation in nerve. J. Physiol. 117, 500–544.

Ikeguchi, T., Aihara, K., Itoh, S., Utsunomiya, T., 1990. An analysis on the lyapunov spectrum of electroencephalographic (EEG) potentials. Trans. IEICE E73 (6), 842–847.

Izhikevich, E.M., 2004a. Simple model of spiking neurons. IEEE Tran. Neural Network. 14 (6), 1569–1572.

Izhikevich, E.M., 2004b. Which model to use for cortical spiking neurons? IEEE Trans. Neural Network. 15 (5), 1063–1070.

Kim, Y., 2010. Identification of dynamical states in stimulated Izhikevich neuron models by using a 0-1 test. J. Korean Phys. Soc. 57 (6), 1363–1368.

Matsumoto, G., Aihara, K., Hanyu, Y., Takahashi, N., Yoshizawa, S., Nagumo, J., 1987. Chaos and phase locking in normal squid axons. Phys. Lett. 123 (4), 162–166.

McDonnell, M.D., Lawrence, M.W., 2011. The benefits of noise in neural systems: bridging theory and experiment. Nat. Rev. Neurosci. 12 (7), 415–426.

Mori, T., Kai, S., 2002. Noise-induced entrainment and stochastic resonance in human brain waves. Phys. Rev. Lett. 88 (21), 218101–218105.

Moss, F., Wiesenfeld, K., 1995. The benefits of background noise. Sci. Am. 273 (2), 66–69.

Nicolis, G., Nicolis, C., McKernan, D., 1993. Stochastic resonance in chaotic dynamics. J. Stat. Phys. 70, 125–139.

Nishimura, H., Katada, N., Aihara, K., 2000. Coherent response in a chaotic neural network. Neural Process. Lett. 12 (1), 49–58.

Nobukawa, S., Nishimura, H., 2013a. Signal response in Velarde-Llinás model of inferior olive neuron. IEICE J96-A (1), 1–11 (in Japanese).

Nobukawa, S., Nishimura, H., 2013b. Characteristic of signal response in coupled inferior olive neurons with Velarde-Llinás model. In: Proceedings of SICE Annual Conference (SICE2013), pp. 1367–1374.

Nobukawa, S., Nishimura, H., Katada, N., 2011a. Efficiency analysis of signal response in coupled inferior olive neurons with Velarde-Llinás model. In: Proceedings of 2011 International Symposium on Nonlinear Theory and its Applications (NOLTA2011) 8147, pp. 423–426.

Nobukawa, S., Nishimura, H., Yamanishi, T., Liu, J.-Q., 2011 bb. Signal response efficiency in Izhikevich neuron model. In: Proceedings of SICE Annual Conference (SICE2011), pp. 1242–1247.

Nobukawa, S., Nishimura, H., Katada, N., 2012a. Chaotic resonance by chaotic attractors merging in discrete cubic map and chaotic neural network. IEICE J95-A (4), 357–366 (in Japanese).

Nobukawa, S., Nishimura, H., Yamanishi, T., Liu, J.-Q., 2012b. Chaotic resonance in Izhikevich neuron model and its assembly. In: Proceedings of the 6th International Conference on Soft Computing and Intelligent Systems, the 13th International Symposium on Advanced Intelligent Systems (SCIS-ISIS2012), pp. 49–54.

Parker, T.S., Chua, L.O., 1989. Practical Numerical Algorithms for Chaotic Systems. Springer-Verlag, New York Inc.

Pikovsky, A.S., Kurths, J., 1997. Coherence resonance in a noise-driven excitable system. Phys. Rev. Lett. 78 (5), 775–778.

Rabinovich, M.I., Varona, P.A., Selverston, I., Abarbanel, H.D.I., 2006. Dynamical principles in neuroscience. Rev. Mod. Phys. 78 (4), 1213–1265.

Schweighofer, N., Doya, K., Fukai, H., Chiron, J.V., Furukawa, T., Kawato, M., 2004. Chaos may enhance information transmission in the inferior olive. Proc. Natl. Acad. Sci. U. S. A. 101 (13), 4655–4660.

Schweighofer, N., Lang, E.J., Kawato, M., 2013. Role of the olivo-cerebellar complex in motor learning and control. Front. Neural Circ. 7, article 94.

Sinha, S., Chakrabarti, B.K., 1998. Deterministic SR in a piecewise linear chaotic map. Phys. Rev. E 58, 8009–8012.

Skarda, C.A., Freeman, W.J., 1987. How brains make chaos in order to make sense of the world. Behav. Brain Sci. 10, 161–195.

Tokuda, I.T., Han, C.E., Aihara, K., Kawato, M., Schweighofer, N., 2010. The role of chaotic resonance in cerebellar learning. Neural Netw. 23 (7), 783–938.

Tokuda, I.T., Hoang, H., Schweighofer, N., Kawato, M., 2013. Adaptive coupling of inferior olive neurons in cerebellar learning. Neural Netw. 47, 42–50.

Analogy, Mind, and Life

20

Vitor Manuel Dinis Pereira

LanCog (Language, Mind and Cognition Research Group), Philosophy Centre, University of Lisbon, Lisbon, Portugal

1 INTRODUCTION

The analogy between life and information—for example, pattern recognition, with hierarchical structure and suitable weightings for constituent features (Kurzweil, 2012)—seems to be central to the effect that artificial mind may represents an expected advance in the evolution of life in the universe, since information (namely, pattern recognition) is supposed to be the essence of mind and is implemented by the same basic neural mechanisms. And since we can replicate these mechanisms in a machine, there is nothing to prevent us from setting up an artificial mind. We just need to install[1] the right pattern recognizers.

2 THE ARTIFICIAL MIND AND COGNITIVE SCIENCE

The area of artificial mind research can be described as including the following: machine learning, reasoning, knowledge representation, restriction fulfillment, search, planning, and scheduling, agents, robotics, philosophical foundations, natural language processing, perception and vision, cognitive modeling, knowledge, and applications engineering. The main core consists of the first three: machine learning, reasoning, and knowledge representation. Now let's look at the area of cognitive science research.

Consider the following items: perception and action, memory, attention and consciousness, so-called nuclear knowledge, classification, lexicon and ontology, learning, language and representation, choice, rationality and decision, culture, and social awareness. The area of study that includes these concepts is explored by cognitive science research, with artificial mind research as a major part of it. In a way, cybernetics, computer sciences, language sciences, neurosciences, brain sciences,

---

[1]To create a mind, as argued by Kurzweil (2012), we need to create a machine that recognizes patterns, such as letters and words. Consider the task of translating a paper. Despite our best efforts to develop artificial universal translators, humans are still very far from being able to express what we write in another language.

psychology, biology, philosophy, mathematics, physics, and engineering sciences all contribute to the study of human cognition.

Artificial mind research is a way of discovering, describing, and modeling some of the main features of consciousness—specifically cognitive ones. Artificial mind researchers assist cognitive science researchers in explaining how consciousness emerges or could emerge (*i.e.,* be caused) by nonconscious entities and processes (a explanatory question), or if it makes any difference for the performance/operation of the systems in which it is present; and if so, why and how this occurs (a functional question).

A central notion in artificial mind research is that of the agent. An *agent* is defined as an ongoing and autonomously operating entity in an environment in which there are other processes and agents. We are interested in knowing how a mind agent is designed. The usual questions are the following: How does it perceive, rationalize, decide, learn? How does it perform independently in a mutual environment of problems (specific agents for certain intervention domains)? In this discussion, we are interested in multiplying those agents and ask how it happens that an enormous variety of those agents can articulate coherently in a multiagent system (interaction and organization). The combination of these questions (and their answers) can be designated by the term *distributed artificial intelligence.*

3 CONSCIOUSNESS

Consciousness can be classified in the following ways (Block, 2002):

- *Access consciousness:* That is, we have access consciousness of something if we have its representation, it can be transmitted to each part of the brain, and in this way, it can be used in our reasoning and rational control of our actions. It is likely that this is the type of consciousness that can be implemented in a machine. But we have the problem of debating whether the machine actually "experiences" something (and in this case, "actually" is not clearly defined).
- *Phenomenal consciousness:* That is, x is in a phenomenal conscious state if x experiences something that characterizes that state. The criterion widely used to talk about phenomenal consciousness is that of "there is something it is like to be in that state." For example, if we are phenomenally conscious of a bright blue sky, then it is because we are experiencing something that makes that mental state a phenomenal conscious state. This experience is the key concept of phenomenal consciousness.

Block identifies the following three differences between access consciousness and phenomenal consciousness:

- Access consciousness is completely defined by a representation (such as a logical agent clause that represents a concept or a fact). Phenomenal consciousness can also have a representational component, but what identifies it is that the experience of x (an agent) is such that were x not in this phenomenal conscious state, it would not have the experience that it de facto has.

- Access consciousness characterizes a mental state as a conscious state because their relations with other modules (in other words, access consciousness uses a functional way of classifying mental states as a conscious state). Being aware is being capable of reasoning and acting, and of being stimulated and responding to those stimuli.
- Phenomenal consciousness identifies types of conscious states. For example, all the sensations of pain are phenomenal conscious states of the same type (*i.e.,* pain). But if we consider pain from the perspective of access consciousness, each pain is a different conscious state because it causes different reactions, memories, and inferences.

To better illustrate the difference between access and phenomenal consciousness, Block describes cases of access without phenomenal (a) and phenomenal without access (b):

(a) An individual can have his visual cortex damaged (*i.e.,* have suffered an injury in the V1 area), there are things in his field of vision that he cannot see, the so-called blind spots. Even so, he responds with an elevated exactness to questions concerning the properties of those visual stimuli. This pathology, called *blind-sight* (Holt, 2003), exemplifies the case of access consciousness without phenomenal consciousness. Phenomenologically, it is not aware of anything, but this does not preclude it from representing those stimuli. Are your representations that enable it to respond to such visual stimuli?

However, we can still give another example: the Belief-Desire-Intention agent, which does not have experiences: he is presumably "aware" of everything in front of him but does not experience any of it. A discussion related to this example is the thought experiment of the Chinese Room by Searle (1980). His alleged "consciousness" is presumably "access," not phenomenal consciousness.

(b) One case of having phenomenal consciousness without access consciousness is a situation in which we experience a normally disruptive sound, but because we are so used to living with it, we do not represent it. Perhaps a friend of yours, used to the silence of the countryside, could find it strange how you are able to live in the noise of the city. The reason, though, is that you do not have access consciousness of these noises even though you are phenomenally conscious of them.

Self-awareness is the state of something when there is an internal representation of oneself. For example, a chimpanzee or a two-year-old baby is capable of recognizing itself in the mirror, but a dog is not. It is likely when a dog looks at the reflected image of itself in the mirror, it is conscious of the phenomenal, but it interprets the representation to which it has conscious access as another dog.

Coelho (2008) asserts the need of a theory of subjectivity and a theory of the body. The difficulty of the subjectivity theory can be illustrated in the following way: we are not capable of having the sensations of a bat (Nagel, 1974) because we are not bats. And the difficult thing about the theory of the body is that robotic "organs" are not organs from natural selection, but our brain is (Edelman, 2006).

The main difficulty with phenomenal consciousness is the so-called hard problem of consciousness (Chalmers, 1995). There is nothing we know more intimately than the conscious experience, but there is nothing more difficult to explain. However, this problem is far from being exclusive to artificial mind research. For example, in neuroscience, the best one can do is find the neural correlates of access consciousness.

In other words, *access consciousness* refers to the possibility of a mental state to be available to the rest of the cognitive system (to be available, for example, to our production system language, such as when we try to describe the stinging of a pinprick, the taste of chocolate, or the vibrant red of a fire truck). The access is representational in a way that phenomenology is not: the contrast is between feeling that sting, savoring that chocolate, or seeing that red, and associated representations such that we may not access these representations (not being in possession of relevant concepts). But if we have an experience, we have the experience that in fact we have (for example, see the red of the truck in contrast with seeing that this truck is red).

In artificial mind research, the alleged "consciousness" that one gets are also presumably "access," and agents have "representations of" their "own internal states," the so-called self-awareness. Examples of these agents are Homer, implemented by Vere and Bickmore (1990), and the Conscious Machine (COMA) project by Schubert *et al.* (1993).

Architectures such as Soar (originally stood for State, Operator And Result), IDA (Intelligent Distribution Agent), and ACT-R (Adaptive Control of Thought—Rational) are computational models of human cognition (for example, real processing time). However, researchers working in those areas do not explicitly attempt to build an agent with access consciousness.

Other research projects involve the construction of androids. These have provided an experimental device for various debates: the debate about the relationship between mind and body (unifying the psychological and biological), the relationship of the social interaction with internal mechanisms (unifying social sciences and cognitive psychology), reductionism in neurosciences (the so-called theories of creation of artificial intelligence), connectionism versus modularity in cognitive science (the architectures that produce responses similar to human ones), and nature versus creation (the relative importance of innateness and learning in social interaction). The construction of androids could very well provide experimental data to the study of subjectivity.

Here, we must note the following: missing a theory of subjectivity is not missing information; rather, this information may be available (presumably provided by researchers in artificial mind) but still lack a theory of subjectivity. For example, consider what happens when you look at a Necker (1832) cube: suddenly it flips, and although the retinal image and visible two-dimensional (2D) structure are unchanged, the three-dimensional (3D) interpretation is different. Lines (or, rather, cube edges) that once sloped down away from the viewer now slope up (but still away from the viewer), and the vertical square cube face that was previously farther away is now nearer.

The Necker flip in what it's like to see the pattern of lines as a cube is likely to occur in visually sophisticated robots under appropriate conditions. There can be no reason for which that variation in what it is like to see these lines as a cube could not take place in robots that are visually sophisticated (in the appropriate conditions).

However, whether we are well informed about this x or not, it is a epistemological problem, not a ontological problem. In this sense, of information not being a ontological problem, Sloman (1996) said say that in this area— subjectivity—there is no philosophical problem.

We have information about, but not a theory of, subjectivity because here, we are confusing two things: epistemology and ontology. The first is the science of how we know things; the other is what things are.

Artificial mind research contributes to the study of human cognition, as well as to the study of subjectivity: contributes not exhausted the study of subjectivity.

The so-called Turing (1950) test assumed, in its evaluation of intelligence, that the mental does not have to be embodied. However, Alan Turing was wrong regarding the nature of the mental. The so-called total Turing test (TTT) preserves the idea that the mental has to be embodied (Harnad, 1991). The candidate for the TTT has to be capable of doing, in the world of objects and persons, all they can do, and do them in a way that is indistinguishable (to people) from their workings. The environment and the set design about which Coelho writes in 2008 (Coelho, 2008).

So, arguably, we have the experimental grounds to build androids. By implementing neuron-cognitive mechanisms in androids, evaluating their interactions with human beings, researchers can hope to build a bridge, for example, between neuroscience and behavioral sciences: with androids, we have an experimental apparatus for tests of subjectivity, our subjectivity being the same as theirs (even if they do not have subjectivity, we put our subjectivity in them experimentally).

We need a working hypothesis about the study of the human mind, a theory of subjectivity, and a theory of the body. Human beings have the mind they have because they have the body they have, and there are no disembodied minds outside the environment (as instantiated by humans). The mind, even if the mind is a distinct substance from the body, gets most of its stimulation from the body. Furthermore, the mind acts through the body. Given that so much of mental activity arises from bodily stimulation and so much of it is designed to contribute to bodily movement, the human mind is radically unlike, say, the mind of a pure intellect like God (if indeed God exists). Taking this seriously, it seems that the human mind could not exist without a body.

The consciousness of human beings is both access and phenomenal. Our problem is that there is no place for a necessary connection with physiology in the space of possible development defined by the concept of the mind. Although such conceptual expansion does not imply a contradiction with the essential nature of the subjective experience, nothing precludes an expanded concept of mind from preserving the features of the former concept and allowing the discovery of this connection (Nagel, 1998, 2002).

Homer and COMA (to cite the examples given previously), as a working hypothesis about the study of the human cognition, presumably have access consciousness (representations of) but not phenomenal consciousness (subjectivity). Presumably, "access consciousness" of agents as Homer and COMA cannot be separated from the body (Total Turing Test). However, this body cannot be any aggregate of matter; rather, a body must be indistinguishable from humans to humans: human beings looking at these bodies and confusedly process them as other humans. The phenomenological properties of the bodies of these agents, the way they appear to us, being indistinguishable from the phenomenological properties of human bodies.

The phenomenological properties of the bodies of these agents—that is, the way they appear to us—are indistinguishable from the phenomenological properties of human bodies. Our brain processes androids [note that the sophisticated robots discussed in Sloman (1996) have a body very different from ours] as human for 2 s. There are studies, such as Ishiguro (2005), showing that this is the case for 70% of participants). It is for this reason that we need a theory of subjectivity and a theory of the body as working hypotheses about the study of the human mind.

Notwithstanding, the kind of analogy between life and information argued for by authors such as Davies (2000), Walker and Davies (2013), Dyson (1979), Gleick (2011), Kurzweil (2005, 2012), and Ward (2009)—which seems to be central to the effect that the artificial mind may represents an expected advance in the life evolution in the universe—is like the design argument. If the design argument is unfounded and invalid, the argument to the effect that the artificial mind may represents an expected advance in the evolution of life in the universe is also unfounded and invalid.

4 THE CLASSIC WATCHMAKER ANALOGY

The design argument presented and criticized, for example, by Hume (1779) in his dialogues concerning natural religion can be formulated as the classic watchmaker analogy as follows.

1. The clock, for its complexity and the way is ordered, is a machine that has to have an intelligent author and builder, with proportional capacities to his work—a human watchmaker.
2. The world, for its complexity and the way is ordered, is like a clock.
3. Therefore, the world also has to have a smart author and builder, with proportional capacities to his work—the divine watchmaker (*i.e.,* God).

Basically, this argument holds that given the similarities between a watch and the world, just as we can assume that an intelligent entity built a clock in a specific way and for a specific purpose, we can do the same for the world. While in the first case, the most plausible hypothesis for the builder of the clock would be a human watchmaker, in the second, the most plausible hypothesis for the builder of the world would be a "divine watchmaker" because only such a being could be capable of this work.

This argument is an analogy, but, as we shall see next, it raises several problems. Consider this: it is obvious that the world is complex and has an order, and natural events have a regularity, but the analogy with the watch is fragile, remote, and reductive.

5 THE CLASSIC WATCHMAKER ANALOGY IS FRAGILE, REMOTE AND REDUCTIVE

The first issue with the watchmaker analogy is that it is fragile. While a clock is a perfect machine, the world is a "machine" full of imperfections and irregularities that go beyond their usual order or regularity. Next, it is remote, because any similarities between the watch and the world can only be regarded as very distant and only in some aspects. That is, one cannot say with certainty that the world order is similar to the order of the clock, because while we are sure, by our experience, that the clock and their order were created according to an end, we have no certainty (not having had any experience of this) that the world and its order were even created, much less that it occurred in accordance with an end (that would be divine) and not just by natural accident (the latter explanation is, moreover, the scientific explanation). Third, the analogy is reductive because while the clock is a machine with limited complexity to its small dimensions, the world is a machine not comparable to the dimensions of the watch, so its complexity cannot be compared with that of the clock.

Now, an analogy can be established from an example that is similar in a relevant aspect — in the case of the watchmaker analogy, the example would be the clock and the relevant aspect would be the complexity of the clock comparable to the complexity of the world. And we have seen that the watchmaker analogy does not fulfill these conditions, so we conclude that the analogy is neither founded nor valid. Therefore, the argument is unfounded and invalid and should not be considered as good proof of the existence of God.

The analogy between mental life and information is the same kind of analogy involved in the argument from design. From the fact that there are mental operations as thought and intention in some parts of nature, particularly in humans and other animals, it does not follow that this may be the rule of the whole (that is, of the nature).

The analogy between life and information takes a part (information) from the whole (life). The idea that a natural biological function of the brain is processing information has not been established empirically, by cognitive neuroscience, is a metaphor. The concepts of processing and information are concepts of folk psychology that seems scientifically rigorous, but are not scientifically rigorous. Concepts like pattern recognition does not exhaust all mental activity: if any mental activity falls under the concept of pattern recognition is only part of the activity of the mind.

In what way does thinking co-occur with a stimulus and categorizing it? When I am thinking about Waltham (Massachusetts) while in Lisbon (Portugal), I am not recognizing any presented stimulus as Waltham (Massachusetts) since I am not perceiving it with my senses. There is no perceptual recognition going on at all in thinking about an absent object. So concepts as pattern recognition although some part of what there is to say about the nature of thought—such as when I am perceiving Waltham (Massachusetts) with my senses—is far from all there is to say about the nature of thought.

Reach to the explanation of the whole [nature, as in the discussion of the argument from design by Hume; life, as in the discussion of the analogy between life and information by authors such as Davies (2000), Walker and Davies (2013), Dyson (1979), Gleick (2011), Kurzweil (2005, 2012), Ward (2009) starting with just one part (humans and other animals, as in the discussion of the argument from design by Hume; or information, as in the discussion of the analogy between life and information), without more, makes these arguments very weak: to the effect of the existence of God (criticized by Hume); and to the effect of the analogy between life and information (argued by authors such as Davies 2000; Walker and Davies 2013; Dyson 1979; Gleick 2011; Kurzweil 2005, 2012; Ward 2009).

At the same time, as Hume says, if we are prepared to admit (though we should not do) this method of reasoning as valid, why then choose the part of nature that says more about us, and not another? Or, as I say, why then choose specifically some of the cognitive features of consciousness, not subjectivity? In other words, why then choose the part of mental life that says more about perceptual cases and not emotion, imagination, reasoning, willing, intending, calculating, silently talking to oneself, feeling pain and pleasure, itches, and moods—the full life of the mind? Certainly, they are nothing like the perceptual cases on which the analogy between life and information rest.

According to science, a succession of chances (without any special or divine plan, although according to the "laws of nature") led to the creation of the world and its existence as we know it. Thus, even before being able to dream even with Darwinian theories and how they revolutionized scientific knowledge, Hume, through his character Philo, already objected to the argument from design that he could not imagine as having a scientific basis of the most devastating effects against such an argument from design —namely, the watchmaker analogy.

Indeed, the hypothesis of Hume of a succession of chances, besides being more logical and plausible than the theistic hypothesis, is one that most closely matches Darwinian theories of evolution by natural selection, which would arise a century later (namely, in the 19th century), as well as approaches all subsequent scientific discoveries, not only of biology, but also of chemistry, and physics, regarding the possible certainties that we can have about the creation of the universe.

6 THE ANALOGY BETWEEN LIFE AND INFORMATION SEEMS TO SUGGEST SOME TYPE OF REDUCTIONISM

The analogy between life and information, if we are prepared to accept (supposing that you do not agree that the kind of analogy between life and information is like the design argument) that this method of reasoning as valid (though we should not), seems to suggest some type of reductionism of life to information. However, biology, chemistry, and physics are not reductionist, contrary to what seems to be suggested by the analogy between life and information.

On the biological level, for example, molecular genetics cannot provide a derivation base for evolutionary biology (Lewontin, 1983; Levins, 1968) or even for classical genetics (Kitcher, 1984). Particularly, Kitcher (1984, p. 350) writes: "the molecular derivation forfeits something important. [...] The molecular account objectively fails to explain because it cannot bring out that feature of the situation which is highlighted in the [biological] cytological story." Richard Lewontin (quoted in Callebaut, 1993, p. 261), in its turn, claims: "Any textbook or popular lecture on genetics will say: 'The gene is a self-reproducing unit that determines a particular trait in an organism.' That description of genes as self-reproducing units which determine the organism contains two fundamental biological untruths: The gene is not self-replicating and it does not determine anything. I heard an eminent biologist at an important meeting of evolutionists say that if he had a large enough computer and could put the DNA sequence of an organism into the computer, the computer could 'compute' the organism. Now that simply is not true. Organisms don't even compute themselves from their own DNA. The organism is the consequence of the unique interaction between what it has inherited and the environment in which it is developing (*cf.* Changeux, 1985; Edelman, 1988a, 1998b), which is even more complex because the environment is itself changed in the consequence of the development of the organism." So, as exemplified by these two quotes from people working in the field, biology is not reductionist. Neither chemistry nor physics is reductionist, either. On the chemical level, for example, the reduction of chemistry to quantum mechanics (Cartwright, 1997; Primas, 1983) is a case of failed or incomplete reduction.

And the presumed reductionism in physics is also no more successful than biology or chemistry (on a physical level, for example); it is not always possible to combine models of gravitation and electromagnetic forces in a coherent way: they generate inconsistent or incoherent results when applied to dense matter, for example. This is the main problem currently driving people searching for a unified field theory.

---

7 CONCLUSION

Things in the world are not representational; intentional mental states about them are that they are representational, but phenomenological, physical, and functional characteristics of mental states (certain type of nerve cell activation co-occurring with our view of the world) also are not representational; rather, they are sensations and experiences.

Cognitive mental states represent, but sensations do not represent anything: if certain things out there stimulate nerve cells, this stimulation of nerve cells are not representations.

Semantics is out there, things out there stimulate nerve cells, but the co-occurring configuration of these nerve cells with that stimulation, if they claim to be representational or informational or coding, is just a misuse and overuse of terms like *representation:* neurons, their synapses, neurotransmitters, molecular receptors, etc., are cellular organisms more than we can access because there is no information or representation to explain what in fact we felt and experienced.

The idea that neurons (their chemistry and physics) "encode" or represent "information" is wrong (cf. Burock, 2010). If neurons encode or represent, is starting to take for granted what is intended to show: there is no difference between saying that certain BOLD[2] (fMRI) or electroencephalogram (EEG) signal correlates with certain information and saying that certain BOLD (fMRI) or EEG signal is correlated with certain conscious mental states (phenomenal or access). What's there here is question-begging. A fallacy, because they assume "information," they study "consciousness": but someone already showed what neurons encode or represent.

The metaphor of information or representation is the same kind of fallacy. Neurons neither encode nor represent anything or nothing: what the human voice is encoding or representing? Certain sound waves.

Expressions such as *neural code* are not neurons, are us talking about them. They are to be things out there, they are being represented by us, but they themselves are not representations. Expressions like *information* and *representation* can be eliminated, that what the relevant discipline says about neurons (and related) remains informative. And if information is a certain kind of frequency, the frequency is enough! We telephoned someone, and the listener understands us. But we do not say that the signal between these devices, represents, encodes, or is information.

A book about oceans is not an ocean: we can bathe ourselves in parts of the ocean without have any concept of *ocean* or of *part,* we can see red things without seeing that they are red (*i.e.,* not having the concept of *red*).

Having information about living organisms does not make this information living organisms—they can be "automata" (as Descartes said in the second of his *Meditations on the First Philosophy,* 1641). By definition, for example, an artificial plant (information about the way plants look) is not a living organism—it is not a plant. In the same vein, the artificial mind is not a mind and cannot represent an expected advance in the evolution of life in the universe in a way suggested by the analogy between life and information. But as a tool, pattern recognition can help us to have more information about humans and other animals in perceptual cases.

For example, methodological concerns of animal experiments as the problem of disparate animal species and strains, with a variety of metabolic pathways and drug metabolites, lead to variations in efficacy and toxicity or as the problem of length of the follow-up before determination of disease outcome varies and may not correspond to disease latency in humans (Pound *et al.*, 2004) and given the third of the four Rs (reduction, refinement, replacement, and responsibility), namely replacement the use of nonliving systems and computer simulation (Schechtman, 2002; Hendriksen, 2009; Arora *et al.*, 2011) pattern recognition can substitute animals in research (for example, drug research and vaccines).

---

[2]Blood oxygenation level dependent (for example, Ogawa *et al.*, 1992).

ACKNOWLEDGEMENTS

I wish to acknowledge my mother, Maria Dulce.

REFERENCES

Arora, T., Mehta, A.K., Joshi, V., Mehta, K.D., Rathor, N., Mediratta, P.K., Sharma, K.K., 2011. Substitute of animals in drug research: an approach towards fulfillment of 4R's. Indian J. Pharmaceut. Sci. 73 (1), 1–6.

Block, N., 2002. Some concepts of consciousness in Chalmers. In: David, J. (Ed.), Philosophy of Mind: Classical and Contemporary Readings. Oxford University Press, pp. 206–218.

Burock, M., 2010. Evidence for Information Processing in the Brain. [Preprint] http://philsci-archive.pitt.edu/id/eprint/8845 [1 March 2015].

Callebaut, W., 1993. Taking the Naturalistic Turn, or, How Real Philosophy of Science Is Done. University of Chicago Press, Chicago.

Cartwright, N., 1997. Why Physics? In: Penrose, R., Shimony, A., Cartwright, N., Hawking, S. (Eds.), The Large, the Small and the Human Mind. Cambridge University Press, Cambridge.

Chalmers, D.J., 1995. Facing up to the problem of consciousness. J. Conscious. Stud. 2 (3), 200–219.

Changeux, J.-P., 1985. Neuronal Man: The Biology of Mind. Oxford University Press, Oxford.

Coelho, H., 2008. Teoria da Agência, Arquitectura e Cenografia [Theory of Agency, Architecture and Set Design].

Davies, P., 2000. The Fifth Miracle: The Search for the Origin and Meaning of Life. Simon & Schuster.

Descartes, R., 1641. Meditations on First Philosophy. http://www.wright.edu/~charles.taylor/descartes/meditation2.html [12 June 2015].

Dyson, F.J., 1979. Time without end: physics and biology in an open universe. Rev. Mod. Phys. 51, 447–460.

Edelman, G.M., 1988a. The Remembered Present: A Biological Theory of Consciousness. Basic Books, New York.

Edelman, G.M., 1988b. Topobiology: An Introduction to Molecular Embryology. Basic Books, New York.

Edelman, G.M., 2006. Second Nature - Brain Science and Human Knowledge. Yale University Press.

Gleick, J., 2011. The Information: A History, A Theory, A Flood. Vintage.

Harnad, S., 1991. Other bodies, other minds: a machine incarnation of an old philosophical problem. Mind. Mach. 1, 43–54.

Hendriksen, C.F., 2009. Replacement, reduction and refinement alternatives to animal use in vaccine potency measurement. Expert Rev. Vaccines 8, 313–322.

Holt, J., 2003. Blindsight and the Nature of Consciousness. Broadview Press, Ontario.

Hume, D., 1779. Dialogues Concerning Natural Religion. http://www.davidhume.org/texts/dnr.html [12 June 2015].

Ishiguro, H., 2005. Android science: toward a new cross-disciplinary framework. In: Cogsci - 2005 Workshop: Toward Social Mechanisms of Android Science, pp. 1–6.

Kitcher, P., 1984. 1953 and all that: a tale of two sciences. Phil. Rev. 93, 335–373.

Kurzweil, R., 2005. The Singularity is Near: When Humans Trascend Biology. Penguim Books.

Kurzweil, R., 2012. How to Create a Mind: The Secret of Human Thought Revealed. Viking Adult.

Levins, R., 1968. Evolution in Changing Environments. Princeton University Press, Princeton, NJ.

Lewontin, R.C., 1983. Biological Determinism. Tanner Lectures on Human Values. University of Utah Press, Salt Lake City.

Nagel, T., 1974. What is it like to be a bat? Phil. Rev. 83 (4), 435–450.

Nagel, T., 1998. Conceiving the impossible and the mind-body problem. Philosophy 73 (285), 337–352.

Nagel, T., 2002. Concealment and Exposure and Other Essays. Oxford University Press, New York.

Necker, L.A., 1832. Observations on some remarkable optical phaenomena seen in Switzerland; and on an optical phaenomenon which occurs on viewing a figure of a crystal or geometrical solid. London and Edinburgh Philosophical Magazine and Journal of Science 1 (5), 329–337.

Ogawa, S., Tank, D.W., Menon, R., Ellermannn, J.M., Kim, S.-G., Merkle, H., Ugurbil, K., 1992. Intrinsic signal changes accompanying sensory stimulation: functional brain mapping with magnetic resonance imaging. Proc. Natl. Acad. Sci. U. S. A. 89, 5951–5955.

Pound, P., Ebrahim, S., Sandercock, P., Bracken, M.B., Roberts, I., Reviewing Animal Trials Systematically (RATS) Group, 2004. Where is the evidence that animal research benefits humans? Br. Med. J. 328 (7438), 514–517.

Primas, H., 1983. Chemistry, Quantum Mechanics, and Reductionism. Springer-Verlag, Berlin.

Schechtman, L.M., 2002. Implementation of the 3Rs (refinement, reduction, and replacement): Validation and regulatory acceptance considerations for alternative toxicological test methods. J. Infect. Dis. 43 (Suppl.), S85–S94.

Schubert, L.K., Schaeffer, S., Hwang, C.H., de Haan, J., 1993. EPILOG: The Computational System for Episodic Logic. USER GUIDE. .

Searle, J., 1980. Minds, brains, and programs. Behav. Brain Sci. 3, 417–424.

Sloman, A., 1996. What is like to be a rock?. URL: http://www.cs.bham.ac.uk/research/projects/cogaff/misc/like_to_be_a_rock/rock.html [1 March 2015].

Turing, A.M., 1950. Computing machinery and intelligence. Mind 59, 433–460.

Vere, S., Bickmore, T., 1990. A basic agent. Comput. Intell. 6 (1), 41–60.

Walker, S., Davies, P., 2013. The algorithmic origins of life. J. R. Soc. Interface 10 (79), 1–9.

Ward, P., 2009. The Medea Hypothesis: Is Life on Earth Ultimately Self-Destructive? Princeton University Press.

Copy Number Networks to Guide Combinatorial Therapy of Cancer and Proliferative Disorders

21

Andy Lin and Desmond J. Smith

Department of Molecular and Medical Pharmacology, David Geffen School of Medicine, University of California, Los Angeles, USA

1 INTRODUCTION

The challenge of discovering new drugs is confronted by rising costs and diminishing success rates. In response to these obstacles, genome and network data have been used to reposition drugs outside their usual domain or to design novel drug combinations. The networks used in these efforts typically consist of transcriptional coexpression networks (Ahn *et al.*, 2009; Zhang and Horvath, 2005), protein-protein interaction networks (Geva and Sharan, 2011; Giot *et al.*, 2003; Venkatesan *et al.*, 2009; Vidal *et al.*, 2011; Yu *et al.*, 2008) or, in nonvertebrate model organisms, genetic interactions (Costanzo *et al.*, 2010; Lehner *et al.*, 2006). However, these networks have many false positives and false negatives (Bruckner *et al.*, 2009; Mackay *et al.*, 2007) and also suffer from bias (Coulomb *et al.*, 2005). Less effort has been devoted to constructing mammalian networks at the level of the gene. Here, we focus on genetic interactions in mammalian cells identified from correlated patterns of unlinked copy number alterations (CNAs). These networks represent an opportunity for the design of novel treatments and are particularly relevant to antiproliferative therapies in disorders such as cancer and autoimmunity.

2 A DIMINISHING DRUG PIPELINE

Small organic molecules continue to be the mainstay of medical therapies, though prominent niche roles are being taken by macromolecules, such as interfering RNA, gene therapy, and therapeutic antibodies. Regardless of modality, it is increasingly difficult to gain approval for new drugs, leading to blocked therapeutic pipelines (Csermely *et al.*, 2013; Gupta *et al.*, 2013; Pujol *et al.*, 2010; Zou *et al.*, 2013). New drugs can fail at multiple steps in the testing process, often because of unexpected safety or toxicological concerns. Another relevant factor is the enormous development costs of new drugs. Eroom's Law (*i.e.*, Moore's Law backwards) says that the number of therapies developed per research dollar has halved every nine years for decades (Scannell *et al.,* 2012; Wobbe, 2008).

3 USING GENOME DATA TO REPLENISH THE PIPELINE BY DRUG REPOSITIONING

To open up the pipeline, there is a growing interest in using genomic and network data to design new drug therapies and minimize side effects. For example, one recent study combined transcript profiling data from many studies to identify CD44 gene expression as strongly correlated with type II diabetes mellitus (Kodama *et al.,* 2012). Introducing CD44 deficiency into mouse models blunted the effects of diabetes, suggesting that targeting this molecule will have useful therapeutic effects.

In addition to identifying new drug targets, networks can be used to redeploy drugs from other disorders (Gupta *et al.,* 2013; Zou *et al.,* 2013). This approach is called *drug repositioning* or *repurposing.* One strategy uses multidimensional readouts of drug-exposed cells to construct networks of drug-drug similarities. Modules of interconnected drugs can then predict compounds that will have efficacy in novel settings (Gottlieb *et al.,* 2011; Iorio *et al.,* 2010; Iskar *et al.,* 2013). Drug repositioning has also been explored by evaluating protein interactions common to different drugs, constructing personalized drug networks from genomewide association studies, and using drug side effects to suggest novel therapeutic areas (Csermely *et al.,* 2013; Pujol *et al.,* 2010).

4 THE SMALL-WORLD PROPERTIES OF NETWORKS EXPEDITE COMBINATION THERAPIES

Biological networks display "small-world" properties, whereby any two genes are separated by only a small number of links (Watts and Strogatz, 1998). If each gene interacts with 30 others, a gene connects with 900 genes in two steps (*i.e.,* 30^2), and with all genes within three steps ($30^3 > 20{,}000$ genes). In fact, the average path length in biological networks (the number of links between any two genes) varies between roughly two to four interactions. Thus, nearly all genes are linked within a short number of steps to all other genes (Albert, 2005; Albert and Barabási, 2002; Tsaparas *et al.,* 2006; Vidal *et al.,* 2011; Xu *et al.,* 2011; Zou *et al.,* 2012).

There are nearly 3000 Food and Drug Administration (FDA)–approved drugs (http://www.fda.gov). After accounting for overlapping targets, it is estimated that these drugs affect approximately 1000 different gene products (Overington *et al.,* 2006), meaning that approximately 1 in 20 genes is a target for an FDA-approved drug. Within one step, each gene will thus interact with 1–2 drug targets, and within two steps, 45 targets. Therefore, even if no drug is available for a disease gene, the gene can still be targeted by directing approved drugs in single, double, and triple combinations to interacting genes.

Despite the relatively small number of FDA-approved compounds, network approaches are a general, effective, and accessible strategy for disease treatment (Kwong *et al.*, 2012; Lin and Smith, 2011, 2014; Nijman and Friend, 2013; Pujol *et al.*, 2010; Yang *et al.*, 2010; Zou *et al.*, 2013). Drug combinations also exhibit greater efficacy, with fewer side effects and decreased toxicity, than individual therapies (Sun *et al.*, 2013).

In fact, the small-world properties of biological networks may explain the common phenomenon in which unexpected therapeutic effects are obtained for drugs normally used in other diseases. For example, thalidomide was initially developed as a sedative, which unfortunately caused birth defects when taken by pregnant women, but is now used to treat cancer (Sissung *et al.*, 2009). Further, employing approved/developed drugs diminishes the need for preclinical testing. Many orphan diseases, in particular, have no available drugs (Sardana *et al.*, 2011). Network-guided therapy may provide options for these disorders.

5 MOLECULAR NETWORKS CAN BE USED TO GUIDE DRUG COMBINATIONS

The small-world properties of biological networks have been used to design combination therapies for disorders including cancer, diabetes, neurodegenerative disorders, and infectious diseases (Csermely *et al.*, 2013; Kwong *et al.*, 2012; Nijman and Friend, 2013; Pujol *et al.*, 2010; Yang *et al.*, 2010; Zou *et al.*, 2013). One study used highly time-resolved transcript profiles and cell-based phenotypes to show that epidermal growth factor receptor (EGFR) inhibition reactivated apoptotic networks in breast cancer cells (Lee *et al.*, 2012). These apoptotic pathways left the malignant cells susceptible to subsequent treatment with genotoxic drugs. Another investigation examined already-employed therapeutic drug combinations and merged these data with known drug-target interactions and protein–protein interactions (Zou *et al.*, 2012). The integrated data could be used to successfully predict new drug combinations.

A different approach employed an algorithm that incorporated previously reported drug-drug interactions to predict new interactions (Guimera and Sales-Pardo, 2013). Stochastic block models that used the notion of group-dependent interactions were employed to infer networks in which the interaction between any drug pair was predicted by the group in which the pair resides. Another study increased the efficiency of discovery for drug pairs with synergistic interactions by combining pre-existing data from empirically determined interacting drugs with other data, such as protein interactions. The investigation used the matrix algebraic technique based on cyclical projections onto convex sets (Gerlee *et al.*, 2013).

6 COPY NUMBER ALTERATIONS AS A DISEASE DRIVER

For cancer, in particular, it is well established that amplification or deletion of genes plays a causative role. Amplification of the *c-Myc* and *EGFR* genes, for example, have been strongly implicated in non-small-cell lung cancer (NSCLC)

(Sos *et al.,* 2009), as well as a variety of other cancers (Beroukhim *et al.,* 2010). Systematic surveys of DNA copy number alterations (CNAs) have linked cancer with a broad array of genes, both oncogenes and tumor suppressor genes. Further, the mechanisms by which the CNAs drive proliferation can be dissected using genomic techniques. For example, CNAs in glioblastoma have been connected to altered gene expression, which in turn has been related to survival (Jornsten *et al.,* 2011). However, individual oncogenes have generally been studied in isolation. Coinheritance patterns for pairs of amplified and deleted genes, particularly those distant from each other in the genome, have been subjected to more limited scrutiny.

7 USING CORRELATED COPY NUMBER ALTERATIONS TO CONSTRUCT SURVIVAL NETWORKS

Recent investigations have sought genetic interaction networks for cancer by seeking correlated patterns of unlinked CNAs. Genetic survival networks identified using correlated CNAs have been found in glioma cells (Bredel *et al.,* 2009; Rapaport and Leslie, 2010) and ovarian cancer cells (Gorringe *et al.,* 2010). Correlated patterns of CNAs in cancer that span entire chromosome arms have also been identified (Kim *et al.,* 2013). However, the chromosome arm network highlights a problem of charting CNA interactions in cancer—namely, amplifications and deletions are not distributed randomly over the genome. Rather, CNAs are flanked by hot spots for DNA rearrangement and can incorporate many genes (Beroukhim *et al.,* 2010; Hsiao *et al.,* 2013). This poor resolution can make the identification of causative gene pairs difficult.

8 A PAN-CANCER CNA INTERACTION NETWORK

In a relevant study, the resolution of identified CNA interactions was improved by combining data from over 4000 different cancers across 11 different varieties (Zack *et al.,* 2013). For each cancer type, there was a median of 74 consistent CNAs, summing to a total of 770 CNA regions over all varieties. Pan-cancer CNAs were identified by looking for alterations present in all cancers. The size of the significant CNAs decreased from 1.4 Mb in the individual cancers to 0.7 Mb in the pan-cancer CNAs, improving the resolution with which causative genes were mapped. Yet, by imposing the criterion that the CNAs were found in all cancers, the number of detectable events was diminished about fivefold. Further, most pan-cancer CNAs still harbored more than 1 gene (often more than 200). It was possible to construct a network by looking for correlated CNAs in the pan-cancer data. Not surprisingly, however, the size of the resulting network was small, with only 436 nodes.

9 MAPPING GENETIC SURVIVAL NETWORKS USING CORRELATED CNAs IN RADIATION HYBRID CELLS

Our group has used radiation hybrid (RH) panels to map genetic interactions critical for cell survival. RH mapping was invented to determine the relative locations of genes within mammalian genomes (Cox *et al.,* 1994; Goss and Harris, 1975). RH panels are constructed by lethally irradiating cells, causing the DNA to fragment into small pieces. The irradiated cells are then fused to living hamster cells, which incorporate the DNA fragments into their genomes. The resulting hybrid cells each contain extra copies of a random assortment of genes (about 25% of the genome), which are triploid rather than diploid. Genes in close proximity tend to be coinherited in the RH clones, while genes far apart tend to be inherited independently. The small size of the DNA fragments affords the technique very high resolution—in fact, to within a single gene.

We showed that extra copies of distinct genes, unlinked triploid pairs, may enhance the survival of an RH cell (Lin *et al.,* 2010). Because of the hardiness of the RH clones, statistically significant patterns of coinherited genes pointed to the cell's survival mechanism. Over 7.2 million statistically significant interactions were identified using the RH data, including genes that partner specifically with oncogenes. The RH network was mapped at a single-gene resolution (<150 kb) (Figure 21.1A), and the fact that the network was Gaussian rather than scale-free indicated that nearly all of the network has been charted. In fact, the RH survival network overlaps significantly with other protein–protein interaction networks, while being hundreds of times more comprehensive.

10 A SURVIVAL NETWORK FOR GBM AT SINGLE-GENE RESOLUTION

We explored the existence of survival networks in cancer (Lin and Smith, 2011). Correlated patterns of CNAs for distant genes in glioblastoma multiforme (GBM) brain tumors were identified using the same method employed to construct the RH survival network. We analyzed public data on 301 GBM brain tumors, which had been assessed for CNAs using array comparative genomic hybridization (aCGH) with 227,605 markers (TCGA Research Network, 2008). The tumors had a mean amplification length of 5.35 Mb and a mean deletion length of 5.87 Mb. A total of 11.2% genes were amplified in more than 5% of the glioblastomas, and 0.9% were deleted. Copy number variations found in the normal population were excluded.

Pairs of amplified genes in the tumors were identified that were separated by more than the corresponding upper limit of the amplification lengths in the genome. Pairs of distant genes, both of which were deleted, were also identified, as well as pairs of genes where one was amplified and the other deleted. We tested whether the amplification and deletion of the widely separated genes occurred simultaneously

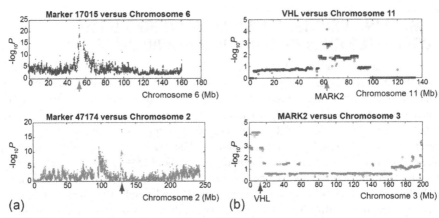

FIGURE 21.1 Genetic interactions in RH and GBM cells.

(a) an interaction between a gene on chromosome 6 (arrow, 57 Mb) and a gene on chromosome 2 (arrow, 130 Mb) in the RH network (Lin *et al.*, 2010). The ordinate shows the significance value ($-\log_{10}P$) for coretention. (b) An interaction between the *MARK2* gene on chromosome 11 (arrow, 64 Mb) and the *VHL* gene on chromosome 3 (arrow, 10 Mb) in the GBM network.

at a rate greater than chance. A total of 436,302 interactions were found in the GBM network at a false discovery rate (FDR) of less than 5% (Benjamini and Hochberg, 1995). An example of gene interaction between the Von Hippel–Lindau (VHL) tumor suppressor gene and the MAP (microtubule-associated protein)/Microtubule Affinity-Regulating Kinase 2 (MARK2) gene is shown in Figure 21.1B. Unlike the RH interaction peaks, the GBM interaction peaks have multiple plateaus representing nonrandom break points in the tumor DNA. This phenomenon decreases mapping resolution for interacting genes.

The GBM and RH survival networks overlapped significantly ($P = 3.7 \times 10^{-31}$, the one-sided Fisher's exact test), validating the cancer network. We therefore exploited the high-resolution mapping of the RH data to obtain single-gene specificity in the GBM network. We identified overlapping interactions in the two networks to construct a cancer network featuring 5439 genes and 13,846 interactions (FDR < 5%). This network suggested novel approaches to the therapy of GBM. An example featuring the EGFR oncogene is discussed next.

11 USING CNA NETWORKS TO GUIDE COMBINATION THERAPIES

CNA networks represent a new opportunity to design combination therapies based on direct genetic interactions rather than proxy measures of interaction, such as correlated gene expression levels. We focus on the single-gene resolution CNA networks deduced from the RH and GBM data sets. The principal therapeutic opportunity using these networks is for disorders of cell proliferation, including cancer, autoimmunity, and atherosclerosis.

In the following sections, we illustrate three strategies by which CNA interaction networks can be used to design network guided combinatorial therapies: (1) using subnetworks to identify multiple drug targets that interact with a disease gene (Figure 21.2); (2) using drugs to target multiple genes in a disease pathway (Figure 21.3); and (3) using drugs to target genes in parallel pathways converging on a disease process (Figure 21.4). Drug/gene interactions in the examples were obtained from a number of databases, including DrugBank (http://www.drugbank.ca; Knox *et al.*, 2011), the Drug Gene Interaction Database (DGIdb; http://dgidb.genome.wustl.edu; Griffith *et al.*, 2013), GeneCards (www.genecards.org; Safran *et al.*, 2010), the Pharmacogenomics Knowledge Database (PharmGKB, http://www.pharmgkb.org; Whirl-Carrillo *et al.*, 2012), and the Therapeutics Targets Database (http://bidd.nus.edu.sg/group/ttd/ttd.asp; Zhu *et al.*, 2012). Other databases can also be employed (Csermely *et al.*, 2013; Sun *et al.*, 2013; Zou *et al.*, 2012).

12 TARGETING MULTIPLE DRUGS TO SINGLE-DISEASE GENES IN CANCER

The *c-Myc* oncogene plays a major role in a wide variety of cancers (Wang *et al.*, 2011). No approved compounds are available that specifically inhibit *c-Myc*, but a strategy that targets genes interacting with this gene product may be fruitful (Yang *et al.*, 2010). In the RH survival network, 45 genes were linked with statistical significance (FDR $< 10^{-4}$) to *c-Myc*. Of the genes that interacted with *c-Myc*, 12 (27%) happened to be specific targets for already-existing drugs, though not necessarily for cancer treatment (Figure 21.2A). For example, the BMI1 polycomb ring finger oncogene product (PCGF4) is a subunit of an E3 ubiquitin ligase and is inhibited by the compound PRT4165 (Alchanati *et al.*, 2009). Similarly, MAP2K5 (MEK5/ERK5) is a dual-specificity protein kinase belonging to the MAP kinase kinase family and is inhibited by the compounds BIX02188 and BIX02189 (Tatake *et al.*, 2008).

The *EGFR* oncogene is frequently activated in GBM and other cancers. Medications that target the *EGFR* oncogene include the monoclonal antibody cetuximab (Erbitux) and the kinase inhibitors erlotinib (Tarceva) and gefitinib (Iressa; Stinchcombe *et al.*, 2010). Eventually, however, resistance to these treatments occurs (Dhomen *et al.*, 2012).

A total of 46 genes were identified that interacted with *EGFR* in the combined GBM/RH survival network (FDR < 0.05), of which 10 (22%) happened to be targets for existing drugs (Figure 21.2B). For example, butyrylcholinesterase (BCHE) is inhibited by donepezil, an anticholinesterase employed in treatment of Alzheimer's disease (Anand and Singh, 2013). SLC2A9 is a high-capacity urate transporter and is inhibited by the uricosuric agent benzbromarone, which is used to treat gout

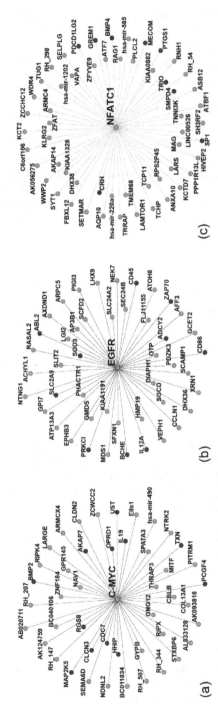

FIGURE 21.2 Using subnetworks to target individual node genes.

(a) Subnetwork for *c-Myc* and all genes one edge away in the RH survival network (FDR < 10⁻⁴). Genes with dark shading are targets for existing drugs. (b) A subnetwork for the *EGFR* gene in the combined RH/GBM network (FDR < 0.05). (c) Subnetwork for the T cell activation gene *NFATc1* and all genes one edge away in the RH network (FDR < 10⁻⁴).

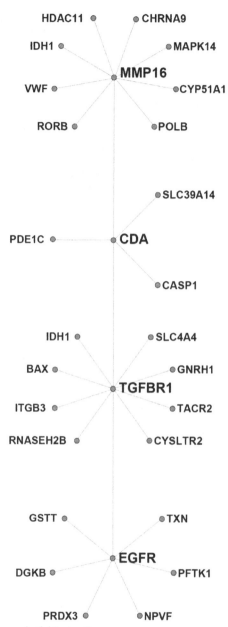

FIGURE 21.3 Targeting an individual pathway.

A pathway leading to the *EGFR* oncogene in the RH network. All genes shown are targets for existing drugs. Genes that are nondrug targets are not indicated. (FDRs for interacting genes: MMP16 $< 10^{-5}$, CDA $< 10^{-4}$, TGFB1 $< 10^{-5}$, EGFR $< 10^{-6}$.)

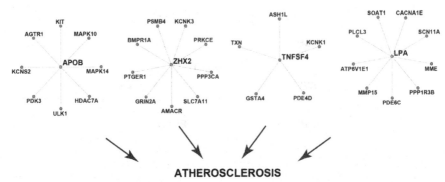

FIGURE 21.4 Targeting parallel pathways.

Genes that conspire to promote atherogenesis in the RH network. All genes shown (dark shading) are targets for existing drugs, except for the node genes *APOB*, *ZHX2*, and *LPA* (light shading), which are not drug targets. (FDRs for interacting genes $< 10^{-4}$.)

(Caulfield *et al.*, 2008; Doring *et al.*, 2008; Vitart *et al.*, 2008). These observations suggest that a flank attack strategy that strikes at both *EGFR* and its partner genes in the GBM survival network may be an effective approach for treatment of these tumors.

Patient-to-patient variations exist in disease networks. For instance, a variety of oncogenes are activated in different cancers (TCGA Research Network, 2008; Zack *et al.*, 2013). Our strategy of using correlated CNAs to guide combination therapies can account for individual variations in disease networks, providing a foundation for personalized medicine.

13 TARGETING MULTIPLE DRUGS TO A SINGLE-DISEASE GENE IN AUTOIMMUNITY

We have also used correlated CNA networks to design combination treatments centered on *NFATc1*. This gene plays a key role in T cell activation, an important cellular response in autoimmune disorders (Bartelt *et al.*, 2009; Kannan *et al.*, 2012; Smith-Garvin *et al.*, 2009). In the RH survival network, 56 genes were linked with statistical significance (FDR $< 10^{-4}$) to NFATc1 (Figure 21.2C). No approved compounds exist that specifically target *NFATc1*. However, of the genes that interact with *NFATc1*, 9 (16%) happen to be specific targets for already-existing drugs. One unsurprising example is PTGS1 (cyclooxygenase 1). This enzyme is involved in prostaglandin synthesis and is a target for nonsteroidal inflammatory drugs (NSAIDs; Dinarello, 2010). Another plausible example is the MECOM oncoprotein, which is specifically degraded by arsenic trioxide (ATO), perhaps explaining the promise of this compound in the treatment of autoimmune syndromes

(Bobe *et al.*, 2006; Shackelford *et al.*, 2006). Other interacting genes and their cognate pharmaceuticals were more unexpected and have yet to be used to treat autoimmune conditions. The enzyme SMPD4 (sphingomyelin phosphodiesterase 4) is inhibited by the compound GW4869 (Chipuk *et al.*, 2012). Similarly, the *TRIO* gene encodes a rho guanine nucleotide exchange factor, which is specifically inhibited by the compound ITX3 (Bouquier *et al.*, 2009).

14 TARGETING MULTIPLE GENES IN A SINGLE PATHWAY FOR CANCER

The second strategy to design drug combinations with CNA network information targets gene products that participate in a single pathogenic pathway. One such pathway in the RH survival network ends on the *EGFR* oncogene (Figure 21.3). (Note that this subnetwork does not incorporate information from the glioblastoma CNA network and may be a more general network than shown in Figure 21.2B.) A total of 22 genes interacted with the *EGFR* gene in the RH network (FDR $< 10^{-6}$), of which seven (32%) happened to be targets for existing compounds (Figure 21.3). For example, R59022 inhibits diacylglycerol kinase β (DGKB; Batista *et al.*, 2005; Kamio *et al.*, 2010) and RGB-286147 inhibits PFTAIRE protein kinase 1 (PFTK1) (Caligiuri *et al.*, 2005).

A trio of gene products that interacted with *EGFR* had antioxidant activity (Figure 21.3). Thioredoxin reductase (TXN) is inhibited by the gold compound, auranofin (Cox *et al.*, 2008; Liu *et al.*, 2012), which is also employed to treat autoimmune conditions such as rheumatoid arthritis. Peroxiredoxin 3 (PRDX3) is inhibited by thiostrepton, a thiazole antibiotic that shows activity against tumor cells (Newick *et al.*, 2012). Glutathione-S-transferase (GSTT) is inhibited by α tocopherol, a form of vitamin E (Van Haaften *et al.*, 2001), as well as by ellagic acid and curcumin, which are plant polyphenolic compounds (Hayeshi *et al.*, 2007). There has been rising interest in inhibiting reduction/oxidation pathways for cancer treatment since these pathways are required for cell proliferation (Kwok *et al.*, 2008; Newick *et al.*, 2012; Tew and Townsend, 2011). One mechanism by which these pathways might exert their therapeutic effects may be exemplified by interactions with oncogenes such as *EGFR*.

The transforming growth factor β receptor 1 gene (*TGFBR1*) also interacted with *EGFR* (Figure 21.3). *TGFBR1* is a target for a number of kinase inhibitors, including SB525334 and SD-208 (Akhurst, 2006; Mohammad *et al.*, 2011; Thomas *et al.*, 2009). A total of 72 genes interacted with *TGFBR1* (FDR $< 10^{-5}$), of which 9 (12.5%) represented targets for available drugs. One of these genes was cysteinyl leukotriene receptor 2 (CYSLTR2), which is inhibited by available leukotriene inhibitors such as zafirlukast and zileuton. These compounds are used clinically as anti-inflammatory agents (Scow *et al.*, 2007). Another gene that interacted with *TGFBR1* was tachykinin receptor 2 (*TACR2*). Antagonists of this receptor include ibodutant and saredutant (Santicioli *et al.*, 2013).

TGFBR1 also interacted with cytidine deaminase (CDA), which in turn interacted with matrix metalloproteinase-16 (MMP16) (FDR $< 10^{-4}$). CDA is inhibited by chemotherapeutic drugs such as tetrahydrouridine (Beumer *et al.*, 2008) and zebularine (Lemaire *et al.*, 2009). MMP16 is inhibited by marimastat (Wong *et al.*, 2013). Both CDA (interactors FDR $< 10^{-4}$) and MMP16 (interactors FDR $< 10^{-5}$) were linked with a number of additional genes whose products can be antagonized by available drugs (Figure 21.3). The wide variety of existing drugs that target the *EGFR* pathway suggest that combinations of these compounds might have therapeutic benefits in applications in which this oncogene is a key node driving proliferation.

15 TARGETING GENES IN PARALLEL PATHWAYS CONVERGING ON ATHEROSCLEROSIS

The third strategy that employs CNA networks to design combination therapies exploits parallel disease pathways. An example of this approach targets the multiple pathways that have been implicated in atherogenesis (Figure 21.4) (Lusis, 2012; Lusis *et al.*, 2004). Apolipoprotein B (APOB) is the major protein constituent of low-density lipoprotein (LDL) and elevated LDL concentrations are associated with increased atherosclerotic risk. Lipoprotein(a) (LPA) is a lipoprotein that also raises the risk of atherosclerosis through unknown mechanisms. The zinc fingers and homeoboxes 2 gene (*ZHX2*) and the Ox40 ligand (TNFSF4) have been implicated in atherosclerosis through genetic studies in mice and humans. There are no available drugs that directly affect any of these proteins. However, each of these atherogenic genes interact with between 5 and 9 genes (FDR $< 10^{-4}$) that are affected by existing compounds. Some of these drugs are already employed as anti-atherogenic agents.

For example, ZHX2 interacts with the prostaglandin E receptor 1 gene (*PTGER1*). NSAIDs such as aspirin and naproxen inhibit the synthesis of the prostaglandin ligands for this receptor. These drugs are also widely used as prophylactic drugs to protect against atherosclerosis. The APOB gene interacts with the tyrosine kinases c-Kit (KIT) and MAPK14. KIT can be inhibited by kinase inhibitors such as imatinib and dasatinib (Ashman and Griffith, 2013). Similarly, phosphorylation of MAPK14 can be blocked using the kinase inhibitor sorafinib (Chapuy *et al.*, 2011). The inference that kinase inhibitors may be beneficial in atherosclerosis is supported by recent studies (Grimminger *et al.*, 2010; Hilgendorf *et al.*, 2011).

The network connections of drug targets may explain their unexpected therapeutic effects in atherosclerosis. The angiotensin II receptor, type 1 (AGTR1) is significantly linked to APOB in the RH network (Figure 21.4). The angiotensin converting enzyme (ACE) inhibitors (*e.g.*, enalapril), and the angiotensin receptor blockers (ARBs) (*e.g.*, losartan) are effective in combating atherosclerosis (Patarroyo Aponte and Francis, 2012). The connection of AGRT1 with APOB might explain part of the efficacy of angiotensin pathway-blocking agents as anti-atherosclerotic drugs as well as antihypertensive agents.

16 USING CNA NETWORKS TO SYNERGIZE DRUG COMBINATIONS AND MINIMIZE SIDE EFFECTS

Network-guided combination therapies might allow the use of multiple high-efficacy drugs at low concentrations, or alternatively, combinations of low-efficacy drugs. One potential example of this synergistic strategy is provided by marimastat, which inhibits MMP16 in the RH pathway terminating on *EGFR* (Figure 21.3). Marimastat is not used clinically because of unacceptable side effects (Wong *et al.*, 2013). By combining marimastat at low concentrations with other drugs in a network-guided strategy, it might be possible to maximize their common therapeutic effects while minimizing the divergent adverse effects. Nevertheless, accumulating side effects will eventually set limits to polypharmacy. The optimal balance between therapeutic synergism and gathering side effects will require empirical investigation.

Based on network data alone, it is not always possible to predict the direction of a drug effect. For example, APOB interacts with histone deacetylase 7A (HDAC7A; Figure 21.4). HDAC7A, a class II HDAC, is a target for inhibition by histone deacetylation inhibitors (HDIs). In fact, recent studies indicate that HDIs show promise in the therapy of atherosclerosis (Ordovas and Smith, 2010; Xu *et al.*, 2012; Zhou *et al.*, 2011). However, the HDI trichostatin A targets HDAC7A, but is proatherogenic in mouse models (Choi *et al.*, 2005), underlining the necessity of experimental testing. Nevertheless, the strategy of CNA network-guided combinatorial therapy promises to be a useful approach to advancing novel treatments for a wide variety of common and uncommon disorders.

17 DISCLAIMER

The authors declare no conflict of interest.

ACKNOWLEDGMENTS

This work was supported by the University of California Cancer Research Coordinating Committee.

REFERENCES

Ahn, S., Wang, R.T., Park, C.C., Lin, A., Leahy, R.M., Lange, K., Smith, D.J., 2009. Directed mammalian gene regulatory networks using expression and comparative genomic hybridization microarray data from radiation hybrids. PLoS Comput. Biol. 5, e1000407.

Akhurst, R.J., 2006. Large- and small-molecule inhibitors of transforming growth factor-beta signaling. Curr. Opin. Investig. Drugs 7, 513–521.

Albert, R., 2005. Scale-free networks in cell biology. J. Cell Sci. 118, 4947–4957.

Albert, R., Barabási, A.L., 2002. Statistical mechanics of complex networks. Rev. Mod. Phys. 74, 47–97.

Alchanati, I., Teicher, C., Cohen, G., Shemesh, V., Barr, H.M., Nakache, P., Ben-Avraham, D., Idelevich, A., Angel, I., Livnah, N., et al., 2009. The E3 ubiquitin-ligase Bmi1/Ring1A controls the proteasomal degradation of Top2alpha cleavage complex - a potentially new drug target. PLoS One 4, e8104.

Anand, P., Singh, B., 2013. A review on cholinesterase inhibitors for Alzheimer's disease. Arch. Pharm. Res. 36, 375–399.

Ashman, L.K., Griffith, R., 2013. Therapeutic targeting of c-KIT in cancer. Expert Opin. Investig. Drugs 22, 103–115.

Bartelt, R.R., Cruz-Orcutt, N., Collins, M., Houtman, J.C., 2009. Comparison of T cell receptor-induced proximal signaling and downstream functions in immortalized and primary T cells. PLoS One 4, e5430.

Batista Jr., E.L., Warbington, M., Badwey, J.A., Van Dyke, T.E., 2005. Differentiation of HL-60 cells to granulocytes involves regulation of select diacylglycerol kinases (DGKs). J. Cell. Biochem. 94, 774–793.

Benjamini, Y., Hochberg, Y., 1995. Controlling the false discovery rate: a practical and powerful approach to multiple testing. J. R. Stat. Soc. Ser. B Methodol. 57, 289–300.

Beroukhim, R., Mermel, C.H., Porter, D., Wei, G., Raychaudhuri, S., Donovan, J., Barretina, J., Boehm, J.S., Dobson, J., Urashima, M., et al., 2010. The landscape of somatic copy-number alteration across human cancers. Nature 463, 899–905.

Beumer, J.H., Eiseman, J.L., Parise, R.A., Florian Jr., J.A., Joseph, E., D'Argenio, D.Z., Parker, R.S., Kay, B., Covey, J.M., Egorin, M.J., 2008. Plasma pharmacokinetics and oral bioavailability of 3,4,5,6-tetrahydrouridine, a cytidine deaminase inhibitor, in mice. Cancer Chemother. Pharmacol. 62, 457–464.

Bobe, P., Bonardelle, D., Benihoud, K., Opolon, P., Chelbi-Alix, M.K., 2006. Arsenic trioxide: a promising novel therapeutic agent for lymphoproliferative and autoimmune syndromes in MRL/lpr mice. Blood 108, 3967–3975.

Bouquier, N., Vignal, E., Charrasse, S., Weill, M., Schmidt, S., Leonetti, J.P., Blangy, A., Fort, P., 2009. A cell active chemical GEF inhibitor selectively targets the Trio/RhoG/Rac1 signaling pathway. Chem. Biol. 16, 657–666.

Bredel, M., Scholtens, D.M., Harsh, G.R., Bredel, C., Chandler, J.P., Renfrow, J.J., Yadav, A.K., Vogel, H., Scheck, A.C., Tibshirani, R., et al., 2009. A network model of a cooperative genetic landscape in brain tumors. JAMA 302, 261–275.

Bruckner, A., Polge, C., Lentze, N., Auerbach, D., Schlattner, U., 2009. Yeast two-hybrid, a powerful tool for systems biology. Int. J. Mol. Sci. 10, 2763–2788.

Caligiuri, M., Becker, F., Murthi, K., Kaplan, F., Dedier, S., Kaufmann, C., Machl, A., Zybarth, G., Richard, J., Bockovich, N., et al., 2005. A proteome-wide CDK/CRK-specific kinase inhibitor promotes tumor cell death in the absence of cell cycle progression. Chem. Biol. 12, 1103–1115.

Caulfield, M.J., Munroe, P.B., O'Neill, D., Witkowska, K., Charchar, F.J., Doblado, M., Evans, S., Eyheramendy, S., Onipinla, A., Howard, P., et al., 2008. SLC2A9 is a high-capacity urate transporter in humans. PLoS Med. 5, e197.

Chapuy, B., Schuelper, N., Panse, M., Dohm, A., Hand, E., Schroers, R., Truemper, L., Wulf, G.G., 2011. Multikinase inhibitor sorafenib exerts cytocidal efficacy against Non-Hodgkin lymphomas associated with inhibition of MAPK14 and AKT phosphorylation. Br. J. Haematol. 152, 401–412.

Chipuk, J.E., McStay, G.P., Bharti, A., Kuwana, T., Clarke, C.J., Siskind, L.J., Obeid, L.M., Green, D.R., 2012. Sphingolipid metabolism cooperates with BAK and BAX to promote the mitochondrial pathway of apoptosis. Cell 148, 988–1000.

Choi, J.H., Nam, K.H., Kim, J., Baek, M.W., Park, J.E., Park, H.Y., Kwon, H.J., Kwon, O.S., Kim, D.Y., Oh, G.T., 2005. Trichostatin A exacerbates atherosclerosis in low density lipoprotein receptor-deficient mice. Arterioscler. Thromb. Vasc. Biol. 25, 2404–2409.

Costanzo, M., Baryshnikova, A., Bellay, J., Kim, Y., Spear, E.D., Sevier, C.S., Ding, H., Koh, J.L., Toufighi, K., Mostafavi, S., et al., 2010. The genetic landscape of a cell. Science 327, 425–431.

Coulomb, S., Bauer, M., Bernard, D., Marsolier-Kergoat, M.C., 2005. Gene essentiality and the topology of protein interaction networks. Proc. Biol. Sci. 272, 1721–1725.

Cox, D.R., Green, E.D., Lander, E.S., Cohen, D., Myers, R.M., 1994. Assessing mapping progress in the Human Genome Project. Science 265, 2031–2032.

Cox, A.G., Brown, K.K., Arner, E.S., Hampton, M.B., 2008. The thioredoxin reductase inhibitor auranofin triggers apoptosis through a Bax/Bak-dependent process that involves peroxiredoxin 3 oxidation. Biochem. Pharmacol. 76, 1097–1109.

Csermely, P., Korcsmaros, T., Kiss, H.J., London, G., Nussinov, R., 2013. Structure and dynamics of molecular networks: a novel paradigm of drug discovery: a comprehensive review. Pharmacol. Ther. 138, 333–408.

Dhomen, N.S., Mariadason, J., Tebbutt, N., Scott, A.M., 2012. Therapeutic targeting of the epidermal growth factor receptor in human cancer. Crit. Rev. Oncog. 17, 31–50.

Dinarello, C.A., 2010. Anti-inflammatory agents: present and future. Cell 140, 935–950.

Doring, A., Gieger, C., Mehta, D., Gohlke, H., Prokisch, H., Coassin, S., Fischer, G., Henke, K., Klopp, N., Kronenberg, F., et al., 2008. SLC2A9 influences uric acid concentrations with pronounced sex-specific effects. Nat. Genet. 40, 430–436.

Gerlee, P., Schmidt, L., Monsefi, N., Kling, T., Jornsten, R., Nelander, S., 2013. Searching for synergies: matrix algebraic approaches for efficient pair screening. PLoS One 8, e68598.

Geva, G., Sharan, R., 2011. Identification of protein complexes from co-immunoprecipitation data. Bioinformatics 27, 111–117.

Giot, L., Bader, J.S., Brouwer, C., Chaudhuri, A., Kuang, B., Li, Y., Hao, Y.L., Ooi, C.E., Godwin, B., Vitols, E., et al., 2003. A protein interaction map of Drosophila melanogaster. Science 302, 1727–1736.

Gorringe, K.L., George, J., Anglesio, M.S., Ramakrishna, M., Etemadmoghadam, D., Cowin, P., Sridhar, A., Williams, L.H., Boyle, S.E., Yanaihara, N., et al., 2010. Copy number analysis identifies novel interactions between genomic loci in ovarian cancer. PLoS One 5, e11408.

Goss, S.J., Harris, H., 1975. New method for mapping genes in human chromosomes. Nature 255, 680–684.

Gottlieb, A., Stein, G.Y., Ruppin, E., Sharan, R., 2011. PREDICT: a method for inferring novel drug indications with application to personalized medicine. Mol. Syst. Biol. 7, 496.

Griffith, M., Griffith, O.L., Coffman, A.C., Weible, J.V., McMichael, J.F., Spies, N.C., Koval, J., Das, I., Callaway, M.B., Eldred, J.M., et al., 2013. DGIdb: mining the druggable genome. Nat. Methods 10, 1209–1210.

Grimminger, F., Schermuly, R.T., Ghofrani, H.A., 2010. Targeting non-malignant disorders with tyrosine kinase inhibitors. Nat. Rev. Drug Discov. 9, 956–970.

Guimera, R., Sales-Pardo, M., 2013. A network inference method for large-scale unsupervised identification of novel drug-drug interactions. PLoS Comput. Biol. 9, e1003374.

Gupta, S.C., Sung, B., Prasad, S., Webb, L.J., Aggarwal, B.B., 2013. Cancer drug discovery by repurposing: teaching new tricks to old dogs. Trends Pharmacol. Sci. 34, 508–517.

Hayeshi, R., Mutingwende, I., Mavengere, W., Masiyanise, V., Mukanganyama, S., 2007. The inhibition of human glutathione S-transferases activity by plant polyphenolic compounds ellagic acid and curcumin. Food Chem. Toxicol. 45, 286–295.

Hilgendorf, I., Eisele, S., Remer, I., Schmitz, J., Zeschky, K., Colberg, C., Stachon, P., Wolf, D., Willecke, F., Buchner, M., et al., 2011. The oral spleen tyrosine kinase inhibitor fostamatinib attenuates inflammation and atherogenesis in low-density lipoprotein receptor-deficient mice. Arterioscler. Thromb. Vasc. Biol. 31, 1991–1999.

Hsiao, T.H., Chen, H.I., Roessler, S., Wang, X.W., Chen, Y., 2013. Identification of genomic functional hotspots with copy number alteration in liver cancer. EURASIP J. Bio. inform. Syst. Biol. 2013, 14.

Iorio, F., Isacchi, A., di Bernardo, D., Brunetti-Pierri, N., 2010. Identification of small molecules enhancing autophagic function from drug network analysis. Autophagy 6, 1204–1205.

Iskar, M., Zeller, G., Blattmann, P., Campillos, M., Kuhn, M., Kaminska, K.H., Runz, H., Gavin, A.C., Pepperkok, R., van Noort, V., et al., 2013. Characterization of drug-induced transcriptional modules: towards drug repositioning and functional understanding. Mol. Syst. Biol. 9, 662.

Jornsten, R., Abenius, T., Kling, T., Schmidt, L., Johansson, E., Nordling, T.E., Nordlander, B., Sander, C., Gennemark, P., Funa, K., et al., 2011. Network modeling of the transcriptional effects of copy number aberrations in glioblastoma. Mol. Syst. Biol. 7, 486.

Kamio, N., Akifusa, S., Yamashita, Y., 2010. Diacylglycerol kinase alpha regulates globular adiponectin-induced reactive oxygen species. Free Radic. Res. 45, 336–341.

Kannan, A., Huang, W., Huang, F., August, A., 2012. Signal transduction via the T cell antigen receptor in naive and effector/memory T cells. Int. J. Biochem. Cell Biol. 44, 2129–2134.

Kim, T.M., Xi, R., Luquette, L.J., Park, R.W., Johnson, M.D., Park, P.J., 2013. Functional genomic analysis of chromosomal aberrations in a compendium of 8000 cancer genomes. Genome Res. 23, 217–227.

Knox, C., Law, V., Jewison, T., Liu, P., Ly, S., Frolkis, A., Pon, A., Banco, K., Mak, C., Neveu, V., et al., 2011. DrugBank 3.0: a comprehensive resource for 'omics' research on drugs. Nucleic Acids Res. 39, D1035–D1041.

Kodama, K., Horikoshi, M., Toda, K., Yamada, S., Hara, K., Irie, J., Sirota, M., Morgan, A.A., Chen, R., Ohtsu, H., et al., 2012. Expression-based genome-wide association study links the receptor CD44 in adipose tissue with type 2 diabetes. Proc. Natl. Acad. Sci. U. S. A. 109, 7049–7054.

Kwok, J.M., Myatt, S.S., Marson, C.M., Coombes, R.C., Constantinidou, D., Lam, E.W., 2008. Thiostrepton selectively targets breast cancer cells through inhibition of forkhead box M1 expression. Mol. Cancer Ther. 7, 2022–2032.

Kwong, L.N., Costello, J.C., Liu, H., Jiang, S., Helms, T.L., Langsdorf, A.E., Jakubosky, D., Genovese, G., Muller, F.L., Jeong, J.H., et al., 2012. Oncogenic NRAS signaling differentially regulates survival and proliferation in melanoma. Nat. Med. 18, 1503–1510.

Lee, M.J., Ye, A.S., Gardino, A.K., Heijink, A.M., Sorger, P.K., MacBeath, G., Yaffe, M.B., 2012. Sequential application of anticancer drugs enhances cell death by rewiring apoptotic signaling networks. Cell 149, 780–794.

Lehner, B., Crombie, C., Tischler, J., Fortunato, A., Fraser, A.G., 2006. Systematic mapping of genetic interactions in Caenorhabditis elegans identifies common modifiers of diverse signaling pathways. Nat. Genet. 38, 896–903.

Lemaire, M., Momparler, L.F., Raynal, N.J., Bernstein, M.L., Momparler, R.L., 2009. Inhibition of cytidine deaminase by zebularine enhances the antineoplastic action of 5-aza-2'-deoxycytidine. Cancer Chemother. Pharmacol. 63, 411–416.

Lin, A., Smith, D.J., 2011. A genetic survival network for glioblastoma multiforme. Genome Biol. 12 (Suppl. 1), 14.

Lin, A., Smith, D.J., 2014. Copy number networks to guide combinatorial therapy for cancer and other disorders. bioRxiv. http://dx.doi.org/10.1101/005942.

Lin, A., Wang, R.T., Ahn, S., Park, C.C., Smith, D.J., 2010. A genome-wide map of human genetic interactions inferred from radiation hybrid genotypes. Genome Res. 20, 1122–1132.

Liu, Y., Li, Y., Yu, S., Zhao, G., 2012. Recent advances in the development of thioredoxin reductase inhibitors as anticancer agents. Curr. Drug Targets 13, 1432–1444.

Lusis, A.J., 2012. Genetics of atherosclerosis. Trends Genet. 28, 267–275.

Lusis, A.J., Fogelman, A.M., Fonarow, G.C., 2004. Genetic basis of atherosclerosis: part I: new genes and pathways. Circulation 110, 1868–1873.

Mackay, J.P., Sunde, M., Lowry, J.A., Crossley, M., Matthews, J.M., 2007. Protein interactions: is seeing believing? Trends Biochem. Sci. 32, 530–531.

Mohammad, K.S., Javelaud, D., Fournier, P.G., Niewolna, M., McKenna, C.R., Peng, X.H., Duong, V., Dunn, L.K., Mauviel, A., Guise, T.A., 2011. TGF-{beta}-RI kinase inhibitor SD-208 reduces the development and progression of melanoma bone metastases. Cancer Res. 71, 175–184.

Newick, K., Cunniff, B., Preston, K., Held, P., Arbiser, J., Pass, H., Mossman, B., Shukla, A., Heintz, N., 2012. Peroxiredoxin 3 is a redox-dependent target of thiostrepton in malignant mesothelioma cells. PLoS One 7, e39404.

Nijman, S.M., Friend, S.H., 2013. Cancer. Potential of the synthetic lethality principle. Science 342, 809–811.

Ordovas, J.M., Smith, C.E., 2010. Epigenetics and cardiovascular disease. Nat. Rev. Cardiol. 7, 510–519.

Overington, J.P., Al-Lazikani, B., Hopkins, A.L., 2006. How many drug targets are there? Nat. Rev. Drug Discov. 5, 993–996.

Patarroyo Aponte, M.M., Francis, G.S., 2012. Effect of Angiotensin-converting enzyme inhibitors and Angiotensin receptor antagonists in atherosclerosis prevention. Curr. Cardiol. Rep. 14, 433–442.

Pujol, A., Mosca, R., Farres, J., Aloy, P., 2010. Unveiling the role of network and systems biology in drug discovery. Trends Pharmacol. Sci. 31, 115–123.

Rapaport, F., Leslie, C., 2010. Determining frequent patterns of copy number alterations in cancer. PLoS One 5, e12028.

Safran, M., Dalah, I., Alexander, J., Rosen, N., Iny Stein, T., Shmoish, M., Nativ, N., Bahir, I., Doniger, T., Krug, H., et al., 2010. GeneCards Version 3: the human gene integrator. Database (Oxford) baq020.

Santicioli, P., Meini, S., Giuliani, S., Catalani, C., Bechi, P., Riccadonna, S., Ringressi, M.N., Maggi, C.A., 2013. Characterization of ibodutant at NK(2) receptor in human colon. Eur. J. Pharmacol. 702, 32–37.

Sardana, D., Zhu, C., Zhang, M., Gudivada, R.C., Yang, L., Jegga, A.G., 2011. Drug repositioning for orphan diseases. Brief. Bioinform. 12, 346–356.

Scannell, J.W., Blanckley, A., Boldon, H., Warrington, B., 2012. Diagnosing the decline in pharmaceutical R&D efficiency. Nat. Rev. Drug Discov. 11, 191–200.

Scow, D.T., Luttermoser, G.K., Dickerson, K.S., 2007. Leukotriene inhibitors in the treatment of allergy and asthma. Am. Fam. Physician 75, 65–70.

Shackelford, D., Kenific, C., Blusztajn, A., Waxman, S., Ren, R., 2006. Targeted degradation of the AML1/MDS1/EVI1 oncoprotein by arsenic trioxide. Cancer Res. 66, 11360–11369.

Sissung, T.M., Thordardottir, S., Gardner, E.R., Figg, W.D., 2009. Current status of thalidomide and CC-5013 in the treatment of metastatic prostate cancer. Anticancer Agents Med. Chem. 9, 1058–1069.

Smith-Garvin, J.E., Koretzky, G.A., Jordan, M.S., 2009. T cell activation. Annu. Rev. Immunol. 27, 591–619.

Sos, M.L., Michel, K., Zander, T., Weiss, J., Frommolt, P., Peifer, M., Li, D., Ullrich, R., Koker, M., Fischer, F., et al., 2009. Predicting drug susceptibility of non-small cell lung cancers based on genetic lesions. J. Clin. Invest. 119, 1727–1740.

Stinchcombe, T.E., Bogart, J., Wigle, D.A., Govindan, R., 2010. Annual review of advances in lung cancer clinical research: a report for the year 2009. J. Thorac. Oncol. 5, 935–939.

Sun, X., Vilar, S., Tatonetti, N.P., 2013. High-throughput methods for combinatorial drug discovery. Sci. Transl. Med. 5, 205rv201.

Tatake, R.J., O'Neill, M.M., Kennedy, C.A., Wayne, A.L., Jakes, S., Wu, D., Kugler Jr., S.Z., Kashem, M.A., Kaplita, P., Snow, R.J., 2008. Identification of pharmacological inhibitors of the MEK5/ERK5 pathway. Biochem. Biophys. Res. Commun. 377, 120–125.

Tew, K.D., Townsend, D.M., 2011. Redox platforms in cancer drug discovery and development. Curr. Opin. Chem. Biol. 15, 156–161.

The Cancer Genome Atlas (TCGA) Research Network, 2008. Comprehensive genomic characterization defines human glioblastoma genes and core pathways. Nature 455, 1061–1068.

Thomas, M., Docx, C., Holmes, A.M., Beach, S., Duggan, N., England, K., Leblanc, C., Lebret, C., Schindler, F., Raza, F., et al., 2009. Activin-like kinase 5 (ALK5) mediates abnormal proliferation of vascular smooth muscle cells from patients with familial pulmonary arterial hypertension and is involved in the progression of experimental pulmonary arterial hypertension induced by monocrotaline. Am. J. Pathol. 174, 380–389.

Tsaparas, P., Marino-Ramirez, L., Bodenreider, O., Koonin, E.V., Jordan, I.K., 2006. Global similarity and local divergence in human and mouse gene co-expression networks. BMC Evol. Biol. 6, 70.

Van Haaften, R.I., Evelo, C.T., Penders, J., Eijnwachter, M.P., Haenen, G.R., Bast, A., 2001. Inhibition of human glutathione S-transferase P1-1 by tocopherols and alpha-tocopherol derivatives. Biochim. Biophys. Acta 1548, 23–28.

Venkatesan, K., Rual, J.F., Vazquez, A., Stelzl, U., Lemmens, I., Hirozane-Kishikawa, T., Hao, T., Zenkner, M., Xin, X., Goh, K.I., et al., 2009. An empirical framework for binary interactome mapping. Nat. Methods 6, 83–90.

Vidal, M., Cusick, M.E., Barabasi, A.L., 2011. Interactome networks and human disease. Cell 144, 986–998.

Vitart, V., Rudan, I., Hayward, C., Gray, N.K., Floyd, J., Palmer, C.N., Knott, S.A., Kolcic, I., Polasek, O., Graessler, J., et al., 2008. SLC2A9 is a newly identified urate transporter influencing serum urate concentration, urate excretion and gout. Nat. Genet. 40, 437–442.

Wang, C., Tai, Y., Lisanti, M.P., Liao, D.J., 2011. c-Myc induction of programmed cell death may contribute to carcinogenesis: a perspective inspired by several concepts of chemical carcinogenesis. Cancer Biol. Ther. 11, 615–626.

Watts, D.J., Strogatz, S.H., 1998. Collective dynamics of 'small-world' networks. Nature 393, 440–442.

Whirl-Carrillo, M., McDonagh, E.M., Hebert, J.M., Gong, L., Sangkuhl, K., Thorn, C.F., Altman, R.B., Klein, T.E., 2012. Pharmacogenomics knowledge for personalized medicine. Clin. Pharmacol. Ther. 92, 414–417.

Wobbe, C.R., 2008. Project management and the productivity of novel small molecule drug discovery. Pharmaceutical SIG Newsletter, 5–9, December 2008.

Wong, M.S., Sidik, S.M., Mahmud, R., Stanslas, J., 2013. Molecular targets in the discovery and development of novel antimetastatic agents: current progress and future prospects. Clin. Exp. Pharmacol. Physiol. 40, 307–319.

Xu, K., Bezakova, I., Bunimovich, L., Yi, S.V., 2011. Path lengths in protein-protein interaction networks and biological complexity. Proteomics 11, 1857–1867.

Xu, S.S., Alam, S., Margariti, A., 2012. Epigenetics in vascular disease - therapeutic potential of new agents. Curr. Vasc. Pharmacol. 12, 77–86.

Yang, D., Liu, H., Goga, A., Kim, S., Yuneva, M., Bishop, J.M., 2010. Therapeutic potential of a synthetic lethal interaction between the MYC proto-oncogene and inhibition of aurora-B kinase. Proc. Natl. Acad. Sci. U. S. A. 107, 13836–13841.

Yu, H., Braun, P., Yildirim, M.A., Lemmens, I., Venkatesan, K., Sahalie, J., Hirozane-Kishikawa, T., Gebreab, F., Li, N., Simonis, N., et al., 2008. High-quality binary protein interaction map of the yeast interactome network. Science 322, 104–110.

Zack, T.I., Schumacher, S.E., Carter, S.L., Cherniack, A.D., Saksena, G., Tabak, B., Lawrence, M.S., Zhang, C.Z., Wala, J., Mermel, C.H., et al., 2013. Pan-cancer patterns of somatic copy number alteration. Nat. Genet. 45, 1134–1140.

Zhang, B., Horvath, S., 2005. A general framework for weighted gene co-expression network analysis. Stat. Appl. Genet. Mol. Biol. 4, Article17.

Zhou, B., Margariti, A., Zeng, L., Xu, Q., 2011. Role of histone deacetylases in vascular cell homeostasis and arteriosclerosis. Cardiovasc. Res. 90, 413–420.

Zhu, F., Shi, Z., Qin, C., Tao, L., Liu, X., Xu, F., Zhang, L., Song, Y., Liu, X., Zhang, J., et al., 2012. Therapeutic target database update 2012: a resource for facilitating target-oriented drug discovery. Nucleic Acids Res. 40, D1128–D1136.

Zou, J., Ji, P., Zhao, Y.L., Li, L.L., Wei, Y.Q., Chen, Y.Z., Yang, S.Y., 2012. Neighbor communities in drug combination networks characterize synergistic effect. Mol. Biosyst. 8, 3185–3196.

Zou, J., Zheng, M.W., Li, G., Su, Z.G., 2013. Advanced systems biology methods in drug discovery and translational biomedicine. Biomed Res. Int. 2013, 742835.

DNA Double-Strand Break–Based Nonmonotonic Logic

22

Andrei Doncescu[1] and Pierre Siegel[2]

University Paul Sabatier – INSERM – CNRS, CRCT, France[1]
Aix Marseille University, CNRS, LIF, Marseille, France[2]

1 INTRODUCTION

E-cell simulation is a very useful tool in the drug discovery process. The simulation programs can be divided into two areas: dynamic simulation and knowledge-based discovery programs (KBDPs). In the first, the model is based on differential equations and has the capacity to predict biological states. In the other, the consistency of the model is checked. The most efficient KBDP is based on first-order logic (FOL).

A particularly and difficult field is cancer. The causal graph representation used in this area requires an appropriate evaluation of sure knowledge, corroborated with the available experimental data in order to represent existing knowledge and discover new knowledge. The key mechanism of cancer is DNA double-strand breaks (DSBs), which could be viewed as a complex system constituting protein-protein interactions, protein-DNA interactions, and gene regulation, where the input is the DNA DSBs and the output is apoptosis or cancer.

Cancer can be seen as a pathological alteration of the signaling networks of the cell. The study of signaling events appears to be one important key of biological, pharmacological, and medical research. For over a decade, signaling networks have been studied using analytical methods based on the recognition of proteins by specific antibodies. Parallel DNA chips (microarrays) are widely used to study the coexpression of candidate genes to explain the etymology of certain diseases, including cancer. This huge amount of data allows the modeling of gene interactions. Biologists look for evidence of interactions between metabolites or genes.

From the standpoint of artificial intelligence, cells are sources of information that include a large amount of intracellular and extracellular inputs and outputs. Therefore, representation by graphs is the best way to understand biological systems. The graph representation has mathematical properties and for this application the presence of positive and negative loops are the representation of genetic regulatory function. Biochemical reactions are often a series of events instead of one elementary action. We suppose even the biological cycles could be discretized according some events. Therefore, one direction of research in system biology is to capture or describe the series of steps called *pathways* by metabolic engineering. Any reaction that allows the transformation of one initial molecule to a final one constitutes a metabolic pathway. Any compound that participates in different metabolic pathways is grouped under the term *metabolite*.

The challenges of analysis and modeling of causal graphs have been well identified and studied in artificial intelligence over the last 30 years. Indeed, the description of signaling pathway is never complete: biological experiments prove a number of biological interactions, but certainly not all of them. On the other hand, the complexity and the burden of some experiments can lead to uncertain and imprecise information. Some data may be erroneous and must be corrected or revised. Finally the information from different sources and experiences can be contradictory. It is the goal of different nonclassical logics, and particularly nonmonotonic logics, to handle these kinds of situations. Afterward, these graphs of interactions must be validated by biological experiments. Of course, these experiments are time consuming and expensive, but less so than some exhaustive experiments.

This chapter focuses on three main problems: conflicts that can occur in gene representation, completing the signaling pathway using new interactions, and handling the complexity of the algorithms. The solutions to these problems allow a great number of inferences be made with the aim of discovering gene mechanisms.

Our approach uses default logic, which allows us to deal with incomplete information. Abductive reasoning is used to complete the missing information from the signaling pathway. The last part is dedicated to a new language of representation, which seems to be the key to handling algorithm complexity.

2 DNA DSBs

DNA double- and single-strand breaks are not formed as a consequence of direct perturbation of DNA. Rather, they form due to attempts to repair DNA damage. It is a common event in eukaryotic cells, and there are two major pathways for repairing them: homologous recombination and nonhomologous DNA end joining.

The regulation of the cellular cycle is the process deciding the cell's survival, containing the detection and repairing of genetic damage. The cell cycle is involved in uncontrollable cell division. Two classes of molecules, cyclins and kinase-dependent cyclins (CDKs), determine cellular dynamics. It was showed that CDK, CDK-activating kinase generate dynamical behaviors including limit cycles. By the term *cellular dynamics,* we mean the molecule concentrations in a specific signaling pathway according the time when different stimuli are applied. In a general way, the cell can receive information by protein interactions that will transduce signals. First, the information is discovered by sensor proteins, which will recruit some other mediator proteins whose function is to participate to all interactions between the sensors and the transducers. These transducers are proteins that will amplify the signal by biochemical methods such as phosphorylation. In the end, the signal will be sent to effectors that will engage important cell processes.

Cell responses to DNA DSBs of DNA have been studied for some years, but the ATM-dependent signaling pathway has only been clarified since the discovery of H2AX (Bassing and Alt, 2004), the phosphorylated form of histone H2AX. All the protein interactions of this pathway have been reported by Pommier et al. (2005, 2006). Figures 22.1 and 22.2 (Pommier et al., 2005, 2006), including the signaling of the DSB (involving important proteins such as H2AX, MDC1, BRCA1, and the MRN complex) but also for the checkpoint mechanisms (involving p53, the

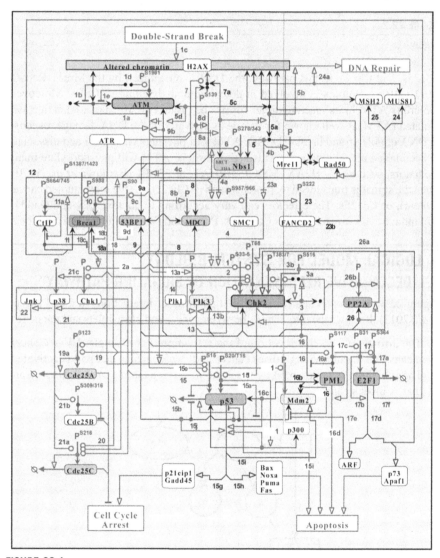

FIGURE 22.1

Signaling pathway of DNA DSBs.

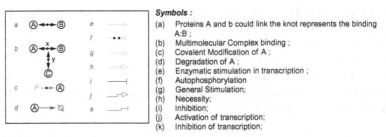

FIGURE 22.2

Legend TK

Cdc25s, and Chk2). In this pathway, the DSB is recognized by the Mre11-Rad50-Nbs1 (MRN) complex is involved in detection and signaling of DSBs. Moreover, it recruits ATM in its inactive dimer form. The protein kinase ataxia-telangiectasia mutated (ATM) is well known for its role as activator of the DNA damage response to DNA double-strand breaks (DSBs). ATM will phosphorylate itself and dissociate to become an active monomer. This active form of ATM will phosphorylate many mediators, such as $\gamma - H2AX$, MDC1, BRCA1, or 53BP1 (Bartkova *et al.*, 1970). Then the signal is transduced by proteins such as Chk2, p53 (the most studied cancer protein), or Cdc25s. The effectors can vary according to context: p21 and Gadd45 will induce cycle arrest, whereas Box, Nas, Puma, and Fas will induce cell apoptosis.

3 LOGICAL MODEL FOR SYSTEM BIOLOGY

3.1 DECLARATIVE REPRESENTATION OF SIGNALING PATHWAY

Figure 22.3 presents a classical simplified pathway of interactions in a cell (Inoue *et al.*, 2013). It shows the interactions between cancer and ultraviolets and the genes:

- The arrow $\rightarrow$ shows the direction of the activation. For example, $UV \rightarrow Cancer$ means that the ultraviolet causes cancer, but $\rightarrow p53$ means that *p53* is activated.
- The inhibition is represented by the symbol $\dashv$. For example, $A \dashv Cancer$ means that A blocks cancer.

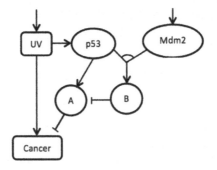

FIGURE 22.3

The simplified model of a DSB.

- The binding means that two genes bind together to create a compound, such as *p53* and *Mdm2*. This compound activates B.

From a biological point of view, *Mdm2* is a cellular antagonist of *p53* that maintains a balanced cellular level of *p53*. The two proteins are linked by a negative regulatory feedback loop and physically bind to each other via a putative helix formed by residues 18–26 of *p53* transactivation domain (TAD).

Intuitively, the causal graph represented in Figure 22.3 shows through different mechanisms (not shown) that an ultraviolet (UV) drives the cell to develop cancer. This is represented by an arrow: $UV \rightarrow cancer$. On the other hand, the UV activates the protein P53: $UV \rightarrow P53$. Protein B activates protein A: $P53 \rightarrow A$, and protein A blocks cancer: $A \dashv cancer$. In addition, Mdm2 binds protein P53, the complex activates B, and B blocks A.

Obviously, this explication lacks coherence. If it is known that UV is an active input and *mdm2* is not, then the cancer is triggered. But, if *p53* is activated, then A is activated and cancer is inhibited or blocked. Therefore, the cancer is both activated and blocked, which is inconsistent.

This example is very simple, but it is helpful to explain our representation for gene networks and the algorithms used for biological knowledge discovery. To analyze real biological systems, which contain many pathways with thousands of genes, it is obvious that computational complexity has to be handled.

3.2 LOGIC REPRESENTATION

A biological function is not the result of only one macro-molecule. Indeed, a group of macromolecules including genes and proteins acts simultaneously and results in the activation of one or more signaling pathways. In this logical model, genes and proteins are considered i the same object, even though they are different biologically (Tran and Baral, 2007).

In this chapter, biological events are often described using propositional logic. However, to design a new plan of experiments, the study of interactions is based on queries. Queries are used to ask whether something is a logical consequence of a knowledge base or not. With propositional queries, a user can ask yes-or-no questions. Queries with variables allow the system to return the values of the variables that make the query a logical consequence of the knowledge base. Therefore, the representation of concentration changes. It is possible, for example, using predicates such as *increased* or *decreased*, and the query is whether the concentration of protein *A* increases or decreases. Some of these queries fall outside the scope of propositional logic, but the basic problems are the same: the protein concentration is rarely precise, and often in practice, the experiments encounter some difficulty in defining thresholds.

The dynamic aspect of protein interactions is based on first-order logic and propositional logic. For example, *stimulation(UV)* means that the DNA is subjected to ultraviolet, and *GlassScreen* $\rightarrow \neg$ *stimulation(UV)* means a glass screen protects against ultraviolet light.

The advantage of such a logical framework is the possibility of representing almost everything in a very natural way that is close to natural language. The tradeoff of this first-order language representation is the combinatorial complexity algorithms. Therefore, it is essential to reduce the expressive power of language.

3.3 CAUSALITY AND CLASSICAL INFERENCE

Interactions between genes can be seen as a very simple form of causality (Kayser and Levy, 2004). To express basic interactions in logic, it is common to use two binary relations, *trigger*(A, B) and *block*(A, B), as well as the ternary relation *bind*(A, B, C). The first relation means that the protein A triggers or stimulates or activates the production of protein B. The second relation is the inhibition. These two relations are graphically represented by $A \rightarrow B$ and $A \dashv B$. The third relation means that A and B bind to produce C (in Figure 22.3, for instance, $p53$ and $Mdm2$ bind to produce B).

These relations are a basic form of causality. The main purpose of causality is to distinguish between what is caused and what is true. That means that not all inferences obtained are true in the case of biological systems.

In this chapter, we describe and use the simplest logical form of causality, and show that cell modeling can be validated by either biological knowledge or biological experiments. This approach could be improved or replaced by Bayesian approaches or much better probabilistic logics (Sato and Kameya, 2003), and another option is modal logics.

The inferences of classical logic $A \rightarrow B$ or $A \vdash B$ are fully described formally, with all the so-called good logic properties (tautology, noncontradiction, transitivity, contraposition, etc.). But the causality cannot be seen as a classical logic relation. A basic example is "If it rains, the grass is wet." In classical logic, the formula $Rain \rightarrow LawnWet$ means that if it rains, the grass is always wet. But this formula is too strong. Indeed, there may be exceptions to this rule (say, if the lawn is under a shed).

In the first approach, the biological events can be expressed naturally as follows:

1. If A trigger B and A is true, then B is true.
2. If A blocks B and A is true, then B is false.

Depending on the context, *true* can mean what is known, certain, believed, or proved. The first idea is to express these laws in classical logic by two formulas:

$$f_1 = \text{trigger}(A, B) \wedge A \rightarrow B$$
$$f_2 = \text{block}(A, B) \wedge A \rightarrow \neg B$$

But this formulation is problematic when there is conflict. Unfortunately, this is often ignored. For example, if we add the three pieces of information: A trigger B, A blocks B and A is true, there is a conflict (inconsistency in logic). These three information are represented by a set of three propositional formulas:

$$F = \{A, trigger(A, B), blocks(A, B)\},$$

From F, implies B and $\neg B$. This is inconsistent. To solve such incongruencies, we can try to use methods inspired by constraint programming, such as the use of negation by failure of the Prolog programming language. It is also possible to use nonmonotonic logic.

The first method, negation by failure, poses many theoretical and technical problems beyond the simplest examples. These problems are often solved by adding properties to the formal system in keeping with the domino principle. We find here all the classic problems that arise when one wants to try to formalize and use of negation by failure in programming languages such as Prolog or Solar (Nabeshima *et al.*, 2010).

Therefore, we will use here a classical nonmonotonic formalism: the default logic of Reiter (Reiter 1980).

3.4 CAUSALITY AND NONMONOTONIC LOGICS

To solve the conflict problem action/reaction simultaneously, the intuitive idea is to weaken the previous formulation as follows:

1. If A triggers B, if A is true, and it is *possible* that B, then B is *true*.
2. If A blocks B, if A is true, and it is *possible* that B is false, then B is *false*.

The problem is to formally describe what is meant by "possible". This question began to arise in the study of artificial intelligence 30 years ago, and led to investigations of new types of reasoning. In this type of reasoning, one has to deal with incomplete, uncertain information that is subject to revision and sometimes is false. On the other hand, we must often choose between several possible contradictor conclusions.

One basic example is:

Penguins are birds.
Birds fly.
Penguins do not fly.

In classical logic, we have a contradiction if we know that Tweety flies, and the system is inconsistent. This inconsistency can be accounted for if we can handle the exception by replacing *"Birds fly"* with *"Typically, birds fly"*. The nonmonotonic logics formally describe the modes of reasoning that take into account these phenomena.

Classical logic, as first-order logic or modals logic, are monotonic: if it adds information or a formula F to a formula E, everything which was deduced from E will be deducted from $E \cup F$. In other words, for monotonic logic, anything that is deduced from information will always be true if we add new information. This property of monotonicity generates inconsistent or revisable information. Indeed, in real life, it will be common to invalidate previously established conclusions when new information is added or changed. Nonmonotonic logic allows us to eliminate the monotony property of the classical logic: conclusions can be revised with the addition of new knowledge.

3.5 DEFAULT LOGIC

In this section, we use default logic (Reiter, 1980), which is the nonmonotonic logic most frequently used. This logic can be seen as an improvement and a generalization of the negation by failure in Prolog. It is also a generalization of answer set programming (ASP) formalisms, which appear years later.

Default logic is defined by $\Delta = (D, W)$. The set W is a set of facts that are always true information represented by formulas of propositional logic or first-order logic. The set D is a set of defaults that are inference rules with specific content, which expresses the uncertainty. A default is an expression of the form

$$d = \frac{A(X) : B(X)}{C(X)},$$

where $A(X)$, $B(X)$, and $C(X)$ are formulas and X is a set of variables. $A(X)$ is the prerequisite, $B(X)$ is the justification, and $C(X)$ is the consequent. The set X is the set of free variables in d.

Intuitively, the default d means that if $A(X)$ is true, and if it is possible that $B(X)$ is true, then $C(X)$ is true. If $B(X) = C(X)$, the default is normal. Normal default means that normally, A implies B. In this chapter, a default is seminormal if its justification entails its conclusion. The default logic used transforms the previous rules, which are expressed as follows:

1. If A trigger B, if A is true and if B *is not contradictory*, then B is true.
2. If A blocks B, if A is true and if ¬B *is not contradictory,* then ¬B is true.

And these rules can be represented by normal defaults, without variables:

$$d1 = \frac{trigger(A, B) \wedge A : \neg B}{B}$$

$$d2 = \frac{blocks(A, B) \wedge A : \neg B}{\neg B}$$

Therefore, a signaling pathway is represented here using a default theory $\Delta = \{W, D\}$, where W is a set of classical logic formula and D is the set of defaults.

3.6 EXTENSIONS AND CHOICE OF EXTENSIONS

The goal of default logic is to find extensions of a default theory $\Delta = \{W, D\}$. An extension E is a consistent set of formulas obtained by adding to W, under specific conditions, a maximal set of consequents of D. An extension can for example, represent a subgraph of the gene pathways constituted in network without conflict. The definition of extension is based on the utilization of W and a subset of defaults D.

Formally, E is an extension of Δ if and only if

$$E = \bigcup_{i=0}^{\infty} E_i,$$

With

$$1)\, E_0 = W$$

$$2)\, E_{i+1} = Th(E_i) \cup C / \left\{ d = \frac{A : B}{C} D, A \in E_i, \neg B \notin E \right\}.$$

Here, $Th(E_i)$ is the set of formulas derived from E_i in classical first-order logic.

The previous definition is difficult to use in practice. Indeed, in the latter condition, $\neg B \notin E$ supposes that E is known, while E is not yet calculated. In this case, an extension is a fixed point. But if all defaults are normal, the last condition can be replaced by $\neg B \notin Th(E_i)$. The verification of the condition is possible and extension to build. In practical terms, an extension is built starting with W and adds a maximal consistent set of consequents of D. The condition to use a normal default $d = \dfrac{A : B}{B}$ starts by checking if, in the current state, the prerequisite A is verified as B, and B does not lead to contradiction. In a simple manner, B does not lead to contradiction, meaning $\neg B$ (the negation of B) is not verified. If this request is *True*, we add the consequent B to W, and the algorithm is restarted until all defaults have been used or rejected.

For example, if we consider $\triangle = \{W, D\}$ with

$$W = \{A, \text{trigger}(A, B), \text{block}(A, B)\}$$

and

$$D = \{d1, d2\} \text{ given above,}$$

it is impossible to use $d1$ and $d2$ in the same extension. Indeed, if $d1$ is used, B is added to the extension, and it is impossible to use $d2$ because $\neg \neg B = B$ is verified. Similarly, if $d2$ is used, it is impossible to use $d1$. However, it is possible to use a single default. Therefore, we obtain two extensions: $E1$, which contains B, and $E2$, which contains $\neg B$:

$$E1 = \{A, \text{trigger}(A, B), B\} \text{ if } d1 \text{ is used.}$$

$$E2 = \{A, \text{block}(A, B), \neg B\} \text{ if } d2 \text{ is used.}$$

By using default logic, the conflict is resolved, and we obtain two contradictory solutions.

But it is not possible to rank the extensions: Is B true or false? In fact, this will depend on the context. For biologists, sometimes the negative interactions are preferred to the positive ones (or vice versa). Another possibility is to use probabilistic or statistical methods to weigh each extension based on the evaluation of the knowledge. From an algorithmic viewpoint, the ranking of extensions also can be evaluated through the calculation of these extensions; and even offline ranking is preferred.

4 COMPLETING THE SIGNALING PATHWAYS BY DEFAULT ABDUCTION

In Figure 22.3, earlier in this chapter, we showed a simple example that sums up the question "How could we block cancer by preventing B?" One analytical solution is to activate protein C, which blocks B, and to consider that protein X is for binding with *p53* or *mdm2*. This simple reasoning reflects the biologist's approach (Inoue *et al.*, 2013). Therefore, in this case, it is possible to set up some experiments that prove this hypothesis. It is well known that experiments are time consuming and expensive. It is obvious that in the case of Big Data, it is necessary to automate the process, taking into account all available information. In so doing, we can consider how it is possible to find, *in silico,* a molecule (*i.e.,* a future drug) that might act effectively by blocking some pathways. In terms of logic, drug discovery is a problem of abduction.

Classical logic uses the deduction $F \vdash R$, which says that result R is inferred from an information (formula) F. Abduction generalizes deduction. The information F is incomplete, and abduction amounts to adding to F a set of hypotheses H such that $F \land H \vdash R$ and $F \land H$ is consistent.

Abduction is an important topic in artificial intelligence. The difficulty lies with implementation of the algorithms. Abduction algorithms are far too high in terms of computational complexity. Even limited to propositional calculus, the theoretical complexity revolves around $\sum_2^p$ which is totally unacceptable beyond very small examples. Many theoretical studies have been done on the complexity of abduction and research the sublanguage of propositional calculus where complexity is reduced. These sublanguages most often cover the Horn clauses and renaming. But even here, the complexity is too great and can be considered NP-complete (all known algorithms are exponential in the worst case). Conversely, existing polynomial classes provide only a low power of expression on issues to be addressed. On the other hand, for many real applications, experience shows that it is not necessary to use the full expressive power of logic.

In the case of signaling pathways, abduction is used mainly to search missing interactions. The predicate $trigger(\alpha, X)$ is used inside the default without prerequisite:

$$d = \frac{: trigger(\alpha, X)}{trigger(\alpha, X)}.$$

Here, α is a variable, which could be instantiated by any protein. This can be generalized to all predicates.

For the example given by Figure 22.3, by calculating the extensions that contains the predicate *block*(*cancer*), we obtained eight extensions, but only two contains $p53$ and $mdm2$. These two extensions are represented by Figure 22.4:

- In Figure 22.4, all the original rules (black arrows) are given as defaults rules.
- The red arrows show links automatically found by abduction.
- The right portions of the figures, list the default rules used for the extensions that block cancer. Here, the sign - is the negation $\neg$.
- As UV and Mdm2 are activated, is indeed obtained that cancer is blocked.
- Note that for the 2 cases, it is impossible to use a additional default rule: we get an inconsistent set of formulas.

5 LOGIC REPRESENTATION OF A SIGNALING PATHWAY WITH THE GOAL OF REDUCING COMPUTATIONAL COMPLEXITY

Today, no programming language exists that allows the abduction reasoning under the incomplete and uncertain information. We present in this section the outlines of a language dedicated to the discovery of biological interactions responding to these

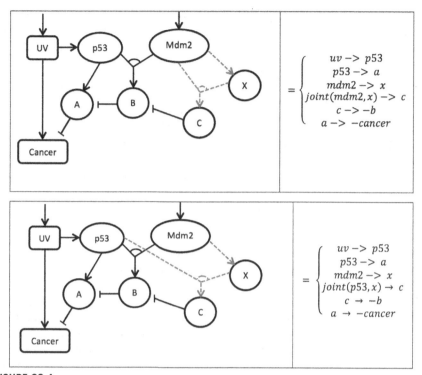

FIGURE 22.4

(a) The explanation using Default Logic (extension 1): the protein X joints mdm2. (b) The explanation using Default Logic (extension 2): the protein X joints p53.

requests. This formalism uses the default logic and also has a dynamic approach that consists of considering the time as a succession of events. The syntax is inspired from Prolog, and it is described next.

5.1 CLAUSES AND HORN CLAUSES

The logic plays with atoms building relation $R(A1, .., An)$. If the atoms are signed, they are called *literals:* positives $R(A1, .An)$ or negatives $\neg R(A1, ..An)$.

In our representation, *product*(P53) is an atom. It is also a positive literal, meaning that the protein p53 increases in concentration. The $\neg product$(P53) is a negative literal, which means that it is not possible to determine if the p53 concentration increasing. In this model, activation is related to the increase in concentration. The dynamic of the system, for example, can be specified by *concentration* $(p53,100,T)$, which means the concentration of p53 at the time T equals 100 a.u., and $\neg concentration$(P53,*sup*(200),$T+3$) says that at the time $T+3$, the concentration of p53 is not greater than 200 a.u.

Clauses are the simplest type of formula. Formally, a *clause* is a disjunction of literals $1 \lor .. \lor ln$. If the connectors are forgetters, a clause is a set or a list of literals. For example $\{a, \neg b, \neg c, d\}$ or $a \neg b \neg c d$ represents $a \lor \neg b \lor \neg c \lor d$. A *Horn clause* is a clause with a maximum of one positive literal. The clauses a and $\neg b \lor \neg c \lor d$ and $\neg b \lor \neg c$ are Horn clauses, and $a \lor b$ is not. For the rest, we use Horn clauses, which are interesting for two reasons.

First, using Horn clauses is a natural way to represent knowledge. In fact, the formula $a \land b \land c \land d \rightarrow d$ is equivalent to the Horn clause $\neg a \lor \neg b \lor \neg c \lor d$. Similarly, the formula $\neg(a \land b)$ (a and be cannot be true simultaneously) is equivalent to the negative Horn clause $\neg a \lor \neg b$.

The second advantage of Horn clauses, which is fundamental in this discussion, is that their use drastically reduces the computational complexity. Indeed, any logical formula can be rewritten as a set of clauses, so complexity problems may arise in terms of clauses. In propositional calculus, the basic problem is whether a set of clauses is consistent. This is the Satisfiability problem, which is NP-complete. Otherwise, all known algorithms are exponential in the worst case. On the other hand, if all clauses are Horn causes, algorithms can be linear proportional to the size of the data. For gene pathways, the use of Horn clauses provides practically usable algorithms.

Clearly, Horn clauses cannot represent all formulas. In particular, $a \lor b$ is not a Horn clause. But this type of positive disjunctive information is quite rare in practice. To be more explicit, in the case of DNA DSBs, all biological reactions can be represented using Horn clauses. Even in the case of non-Horn clauses, it is possible to solve the problem by using efficient techniques, which come from constraint programming and from practical algorithms for solving NP-complete problems. These techniques may be, for example, using cardinalities, symmetries (Benhamou and Siegel, 2008) (Benhamou *et al.*, 2010), and strong backdoors (Ostrowski *et al.*, 2010).

In fact, the use of Horn clauses and default logic has been studied for an application with the DCNS group (DCNS is the main French group that designs, builds, and supports surface combatants, submarines, systems, and equipment). The problem was to simulate the decisions of a commander aboard a submarine in wartime. This is a problem of incomplete information because a submarine is "blind" and almost "deaf," but it must make quick decisions, so to speak. Using Horn clauses, default logic, mutual exclusion, and simple management of the temporal aspect, it was possible to simulate several hours of fighting in seconds (Toulgoat *et al.*, 2010a, 2010b; Toulgoat, 2011).

5.2 LANGUAGE SYNTAX

A signaling pathway is described by a set of rules. A rule can be either a hard rule, a default. Pratically a rule is a triplet (<type>, <corps>, <weight>) for which:

- < *type* > can take two values: *hard* and *def*. If the value is hard, the rule is a hard rule and represents a Horn clause, which is sure and nonrevisable. If the value is *def,* the rule represents a normal default.

- $<$ *weight* $>$ weighs the rule, which makes it possible to choose between the different extensions proposed by the algorithm.
- $<$ *corps* $>$ is a couple (L, R). The left element L is a set of literals $(l1, ..ln)$ eventually empty. This set is identified to $l1 \wedge .. \wedge ln$. The right element R is either a single literal or empty. If the rule is hard, the couple (L, R) represents the formula $L \rightarrow R$. If the rule is a default, the couple represents a normal default $d = \dfrac{L : R}{R}$ Increased attention is made given these two cases.

5.3 HARD RULES AND DEFAULT RULES

5.3.1 Hard rules

A hard rule (L, R) represents the formula $L \rightarrow R$, where L is a conjunction of literals and R a literal. As we decided to restrict our algorithm to Horn clauses, all literals of L are positive. The literal R can be positive or negative. Here, we describe two special cases:

1. L is empty. Therefore, the rule represents a positive or negative unary clause. Unary clauses are elementary sources of information. They do not contain variables, they are ground clauses. This allows the decidability of the algorithm. However the other clauses can contain variables, making possible to leave the pure propositional calculus.
2. R is empty. For this empty consequence, the rule $L \rightarrow \varnothing$ is equivalent to $\neg L$, which in turn is equivalent to a negative clause. For example, we can use such a clause to represent a mutual exclusion: "It is impossible to trigger and to block a protein at the same time."

5.3.2 Default rules

If (L, R) is a default rule, then it represents a normal default, the prerequisite is L, and R is the justification and the consequent. If the prerequisite is empty, the default is without justification. According to the definition of the defaults, it is impossible to have an empty consequence. Unlike hard rules, the prerequisite R can contain negative literals.

5.4 CELL SIGNALING PATHWAY REPRESENTATION

We have based our work on the bibliographic data of the response to DSBs represented on a signaling pathway (see Figure 22.2 earlier in this chapter), given by Pommier *et al.* (2005). The drawback of this representation is that it is very difficult to add a new interaction or protein without full reassessment. In particular, the management of conflicts (such as simultaneous trigger and block interactions) is very difficult. We worked on the translation of this interaction map in our logic language. Initial results have translated this signaling pathway, and some algorithms have been tested (Doncescu and Siegel, 2012; Doncescu *et al.*, 2012a, 2013, 2014a, 2014b).

Today, the signaling pathway is translated by 206 rules in a very natural way, without having to tweak the predicates or the rules. The rules are expressed in the syntax given previously in this chapter. These rules can be hard rules or defaults. The syntax used is very simple, and it is possible to change the nature of these rules to test different configurations. We can calculate the extensions in a very short time. As it turns out, the use of non-Horn clauses was not necessary. This reinforces our opinion that it is possible to use a nonmonotonic logic and abduction and time on real applications.

In the case of signaling pathways, we consider a predicate to be a biological reaction or the production and activation of proteins. For example:

- product(P), binding(P, Q, R), block-binding(P, Q), stimulation(P),
- phosphorylation(P) , dissociation, transcription-activating,
- increase(P), decrease(P)...
- concentration(P, > 1000), where 1000 is a threshold if it is possible to measure it.

The logical model of DNA DSB contains two types of rules: facts (*hard*) and defaults (*def*). For example:

- *hard*: *stimulate(dsb, dna)* that is an elementary fact (a ground unary clause) says that DSB stimulates ADN.
- *def*: *stimulate(dsb, dna) → product(altered-dna)*. This default rule means, "(Generally when dsb (double-strand breaks) stimulates DNA, an altered DNA is produced). For example, during replication, a thymine nucleotide might be inserted in place of a guanine nucleotide. With base substitution mutations, only a single nucleotide within a gene sequence is changed, so only one codon is affected."
- *hard*: *product(p-atm-atm-bound) → ¬product(atm-atm)* that is a negative clause. *def*: *product(p-s15-p53-mdm2) ∧ product(p-chk1). → phosphorylation(p-chk1, →p-s15-p53-mdm2)*.

Using a simple logic formalism can express much of what biologists need to represent.

6 ALGORITHM AND IMPLEMENTATION

The algorithm is written with SWI-Prolog, which is an implementation of Prolog. A rule:

(< type >, < corps >, < weight >)

is represented by a unary Prolog clause:

rule(< type >, < corps >, < weight >).

Thus, the rules and the algorithm are in the same Prolog program, which is very practical. Another advantage to using Prolog is that the unification, the backtracking, and the list management are well optimized. Of course, Prolog is interpreted, so it is slower than compiled languages (but not significantly). On the other hand, Prolog programs are short and simple, which saves a lot of time to testing programs and heuristics.

Our algorithm calculates the extensions. As the clauses are Horn clauses, and as the defaults are normal, the research tree is optimized. It is easy to calculate extensions without duplicating (*i.e.,* we do not calculate the same extension several times). For algorithms, we can also use a weak form of negation as failure (Benhamou and Siegel, 2012).

For initial tests, given by the map of the entire signaling pathway of Pommier *et al.* (2005), we calculate all extensions in a short time. For example, with most of the rules, there are two extensions by default. The calculation time takes 500,000 logicals inference per second (LIPS) and 0.4 seconds of central processing unit (CPU) time on MacBook. The temporal aspect of gene networks has been tested for small examples, but the scaling has not yet been done. Our experiments on submarines application (Toulgoat *et al.*, 2010a, 2010b; Toulgoat, 2011) suggest that it should work. For the abduction, it is similar. The algorithm has been tested on small examples, and scaling up, with the greatest exemples, remains to be done, but again, that should be possible. There are not theoretical problems.

7 RESULTS

It has been well established that loss of function of the p53 tumor suppressor protein is a major step in the development of cancer. This can be obtained by direct mutation of the *p53* gene, but also by alterations in *p53* regulators, downstream targets, or both. Moreover, it has been established that the Mdm2 protein is an essential regulator of p53 during embryonic development. The p53 protein family, which consists of p53, p63, and p73, plays a pivotal role in the regulation of multiple cellular mechanisms, including apoptosis, cell cycle control, and DNA damage repair. The role of p53 in human studies is relatively well studied, but less is known about p73 and p63. Using our e-cancer model, we found several hypotheses about the activity of p73. Introducing time in defaults (the prerequisite considered at time t and the conclusion at time $t+1$), we obtained a simplified map of Pommier *et al.* (2005). The DNA DSB generated automatically showed that the p73 protein is not directly implicated to trigger apoptosis, which is one of the key points of our knowledge discovery (Figure 22.5a).

Therefore, our main result is a new DNA DSB map containing only the main reactions. This result, obtained automatically using default logic (Figure 22.5a), has been compared with the simplified biological model of Pommier (Figure 22.5b). This model was obtained manually using a reasoning based on biological deductions. The difference is a few proteins.

At first, we used Hypothesis-Logic (Siegel 1990; Siegel and Schwind, 1991, 1993; Schwind and Siegel, 1994), which is a modal generalization of default logic but the computational complexity was too high. We also used and tested the concepts of production fields (Siegel, 1987) of characteristic clauses (Bossu and Siegel, 1985) and a consequence-finding algorithm (Siegel, 1987; Boi *et al.*, 1992), based on production fields. Again, the computational complexity is not of interest here.

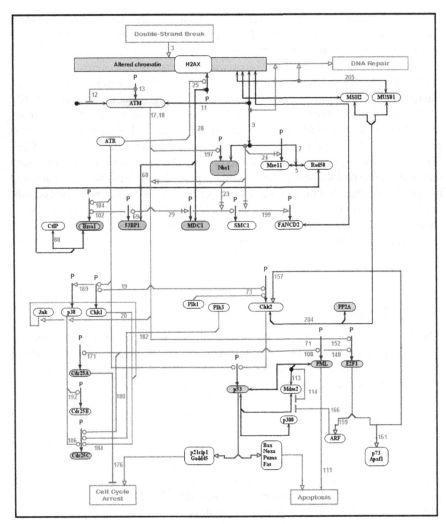

FIGURE 22.5

(a) DNA DSB map generated automatically.

(Continued)

Our algorithm has been compared with SOLAR (Nabeshima *et al.*, 2010). SOLAR is based on production fields, and the consequence-finding algorithm is used to produce new clauses (Doncescu *et al.*, 2002, 2007a, 2007b). The great complexity of these algorithms does not allow real examples to be set up (Inoue, 2004).

We compared this with the ASP formalism. Again, the impression is mixed. Indeed, ASP deals mainly with normal defaults, without prerequisites. Obtaining all the power representations of defaults with prerequisites is possible by rewriting techniques. But the drawback of this approach is a loss of clarity and efficiency.

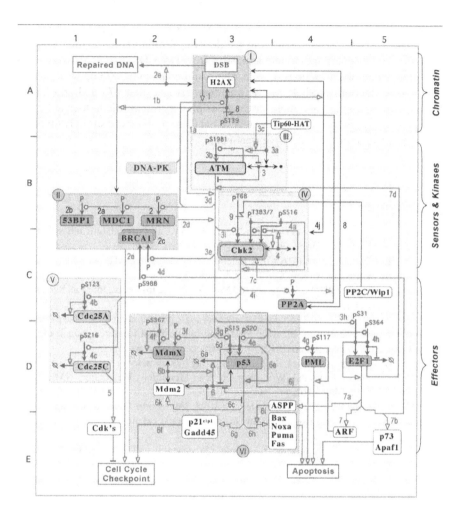

FIGURE 22.5, CONT'D

(b) DNA DSB map generated by Pommier (Pommier *et al.*, 2006).

For ASP, a new semantic (Benhamou and Siegel, 2012), seems to work reasonably well in practice.

8 CONCLUSIONS

Most researchers attempt to complete the signaling pathway. In our approach, the map is simplified as the main reactions, which is very useful for biological experiments. In this chapter, an algorithm based on default logic is proposed to check the consistency of DNA DSB maps. First, we define the representation, which is concise and adequate. Our representation keeps the flow of information represented by gene expression and receptor and protein structures from DNA DSBs to apoptosis and all main proteins involved in the cell cycle. Our result concerning p73 opens new avenues of investigation. Furthermore, it was demonstrated that p73 and p63 family interact with each other, and these interactions play a critical role in human tumorigenesis. Our experimental data also suggest that these proteins are strongly involved in a response to anticancer curative treatment.

REFERENCES

Bartkova, J., Horejsi, Z., et al., 1970. DNA damage response as a candidature anticancer barrier in early human tumorigenesis. Nature 434, 864–870, 2005.

Bassing, C.H., Alt, F.W., 2004. H2AX may function as an anchor to hold broken chromosomal DNA ends in close proximity. Cell Cycle 3, 149–153.

Benhamou, B., Siegel, P., 2008. Symmetry and Non-monotonic inference. In: Proc. Symco'08, Sydney, Australia, Sept. 2008.

Benhamou, B., Siegel, P., 2012. A new semantics for logic programs capturing and extending the stable model semantics. In: IEEE Proc. 24th International Conference on Tools with Artificial Intelligence, ICTAI 2012, Athens, Greece, November 2012.

Benhamou, B., Nabhani, T., Siegel, P., 2010. Reasoning by symmetry in nonmonotonic logics. In: Proc. 13th International Workshop on Non-Monotonic Reasoning, NMR 2010, Toronto, Canada, May 2010.

Boi, J.M., Innocenti, E., Rauzy, A., Siegel, P., 1992. Production fields: a new approah to deduction problems and two algorithms for propositional calculus. Revue d'Intelligence Artificielle 25 (3), 235–255.

Bossu, G., Siegel, P., 1985. Saturation, nonmonotonic reasoning and the closed world assumption. Artif. Intell. 25 (1), 13–63.

Doncescu, A., Weisman, J., Richard, G., Roux, G., 2002. Characterization of bio-chemical signals by inductive programming. Knowl. Base. Syst. 15 (1), 129–137.

Doncescu, A., Yamamoto, Y., Inoue, K., 2007. Biological systems analysis using Inductive Logic Programming. In: Proc. of the 21st International Conference on Advanced Information Networking and Applications (AINA 2007). EEE Computer Society, pp. 690–695.

Doncescu, A., Inoue, K., Yamamoto, Y., 2007b. Knowledge-based discovery in systems biology using CF-induction. New trends in applied artificial intelligence. In: Proc. 20th International Conference on Industrial, Engineering and Other Applications of Applied Intelligent Systems (IEA / AIE 2007), Lecture Notes in Artificial Intelligence, vol. 4570. Springer, pp. 395–404.

Doncescu, A., Le, T., Siegel, P., 2012. Default logic for diagnostic of discrete time systems. In: Proc. BWCCA-2013 - 8th International Conference on Broadband and Wireless Computing, Communication and Applications, pp. 488–493, Compiegne, France, Oct 2012.

Doncescu, A., Siegel, P., 2012. The logic of hypothesis generation in kinetic modeling of system biology. In: Proc.23rd IEEE International Conference on Tools with Artificial Intelligence, pp. 927–929 Boca Raton, Florida, USA, Nov. 2012.

Doncescu, A., Le, T., Siegel, P., 2013. Utilization of default logic for analyzing a meta-bolic system in discrete time. In: Proc.13th International Conference on Computational Science and Its Applications, ICCSA 2013, pp. 130–136, Ho Chi Min, Vietnam, June 2013.

Doncescu, A., Siegel, P., Le, T., 2014a. Relevance of information in cell signaling pathways using default logic. BIOCOMP'14. In: Proceedings of the International Conference on Bioinformatics and Computational Biology, ISBN 1-60132-265-8, pp. 16–22.

Doncescu, A., Siegel, P., Le, T., 2014b. Representation and efficient algorithms for the study of cell signaling pathways ICAI'14. In: Proceedings of the International Conférences on Artificial Intelligence, vol. 1. ISBN 1-60132-274-7, pp. 504–510 21–24, July 2014.

Inoue, K., 2004. Induction as consequence finding. Mach. Learn. 55 (2), 109–135.

Inoue, K., Doncescu, A., Nabeshima, H., 2013. Completing causal networks bymeta-level abduction. Mach. Learn. 91 (2), 239–277.

Kayser, D., Levy, F., 2004. Modeling symbolic causal reasoning. Intellecta 1, 38, 291–232.

Nabeshima, H., et al., 2010. SOLAR: An automated deduction system for consequence find-ing. AI Commun. 23 (2–3), 183–203.

Ostrowski, R., Paris, L., Sais, L., Siegel, P., 2010. Computing horn strong backdoor sets thanks to local search. In: Proc International Conference on Tools with Artificial Intelligence, ICTAI'06. IEEE Computer Society, Washington D.C., US, pp. 139–143, nov. 2006.

Pommier, Y., et al., 2005. Targeting Chk2 Kinase: molecular interaction map and therapetic rationale. Curr. Pharm. Des. 11 (22), 2855–2872.

Pommier, Y., et al., 2006. Chk2 molecular interaction map and rationale for Chk2 inhibitors. Clin. Canc. Res. 12 (9), 2657–2661.

Reiter, R., 1980. A logic for default reasoning. Art Int. 13 (1–2), 81–132.

Sato, T., Kameya, Y., 2003. PRISM: a language for symbolic-statistical modeling. Int. Joint Conf. Artif. Intell. 15, 1330–1339.

Schwind, C., Siegel, P., 1994. Modal logic for hypothesis theory. Fundam. Inform, col 21, n° 1-2 89-101.

Siegel, P., 1987. Représentation et utilisation de la connaissance en calcul propositionnel. Thèse de Doctorat d'état en Informatique, Université d'Aix-Marseille II, juillet 1987.

Siegel, P., 1990. A modal language for nonmonotonic reasonning. In: Proc. Workshop DRUMS/CEE Marseille 24-27 Février 1990.

Siegel, P., Schwind, C., 1991. Hypothesis theory for nonmonotonic reasoning. In: First International Proc. Workshop on Nonstandard Queries and Answers, Toulouse, July 1991.

Siegel, P., Schwind, C., 1993. Modal logic based theory for nonmonotonic reasoning. J. Appl. Non classical Logic 3 (1), 73–92.

Toulgoat, I., 2011. Modélisation de combat humain dans les simulations de combat naval. Thèse de doctorat, Université de Toulon 31, Janvier 2011.

Toulgoat, I., Siegel, Lacroix, Y., Botto, J., 2010a. Operator decision in naval action's simu-lation. In: 13th International Workshop on Non-Monotonic Reasoning, NMR'10, Sydney, May 2010.

Toulgoat, I., Siegel, P., Lacroix, Y., Botto, J., 2010b. Operator decision modeling: application to a scenario involving two submarines. In: Computer Application and Information Tech-nology in the Maritine Industries, COMPIT10 Gubbio Italy, 12–14 April 2010.

Tran, N., Baral, C., 2007. Hypothesizing and reasoning about signaling networks. J. Appl. Logic 7, 253–274.

An Updated Covariance Model for Rapid Annotation of Noncoding RNA

23

Yinglei Song[1] and Junfeng Qu[2]

School of Electronics and Information Science, Jiangsu University of Science and Technology, Zhenjiang, Jiangsu, China[1]
Department of Computer Science and Information Technology, Clayton State University, Morrow, GA, USA[2]

1 INTRODUCTION

Noncoding RNA (ncRNA) plays an important role in a variety of biological processes, including RNA modification, gene regulation, and choromosome replication (Frank and Pace, 1998; Luo and Zhou, 2001; Mitchels and Bensaude, 2001). In general, the biological functions of ncRNA are determined by its secondary structure. Recently, due to the large amount of available genome data, computational approaches have been developed to search genomes to identify new ncRNAs (Jones and Eddy, 2001; Lowe and Eddy, 1997). Most of these approaches use a structure model to describe the secondary structure of an ncRNA family and use sequence-structure alignment to determine whether a given sequence segment belongs to the ncRNA family.

Most software tools (Lowe and Eddy, 1997; Klein and Eddy, 2003) that can search genomes for ncRNAs use the covariance model (CM) (Eddy and Durbin, 1994) to model the secondary structure of an ncRNA family. Similar to the Hidden Markov model (HMM), CM uses the statistical profiles of all single and paired positions in the sequence to describe both the primary sequence and the secondary structure of an ncRNA family. The sequence-structure alignment between a sequence and a structure model can be performed by a dynamic programming algorithm (Eddy and Durbin, 1994). Based on the statistical profiles of single and paired positions, the algorithm can find the alignment with the maximum probability. The value of this probability is then used to decide whether the sequence is part of the family. The CM-based sequence structure alignment has been successfully used to identify a variety of ncRNAs in the genomes of many species.

The dynamic programming algorithm that can optimally align a sequence to a CM needs a computation time of $O(WN^3)$, where N is the number of nucleotides in the sequence and W is the size of the CM. The size of the CM is often proportional to the length of the sequences in the ncRNA family that it models. When the length of the sequence is long, CM-based searching becomes inefficient due to the time complexity needed to perform the sequence-structure alignment and the size of the genome. For example, a genome of moderate size contains around one million nucleotides and the annotation of an ncRNA that contains 300 nucleotides in such a genome may need a few days of computation time.

In this chapter, we develop a new model to describe the secondary structure of an ncRNA molecule. In particular, based on the length distribution of a structure unit in the secondary structure, we restrict the number of insertions and deletions that may occur in the structure unit during the evolution. We show that the computation time needed to align a sequence to this new model can be significantly reduced. The increase in speed that can be achieved by our model is significant for sequences that contain a large number of nucleotides.

We implemented this approach using a computer program and tested its performance in searching a few ncRNAs in genomes. We compared both the accuracy and computational efficiency of our approach with those of the CM-based search. The testing results showed that our approach can achieve search accuracy comparable with that of the CM-based search, while significantly reducing the amount of computation time needed to search through a genome.

2 METHOD

2.1 CONVENTIONAL CM

A conventional CM usually contains two types of elements: states and transition rules that define the possible transitions among states in the model. Each state is used to describe a single unpaired position or two paired positions in the secondary structure. Each state is associated with a set of emission probability values that describe the probability for each nucleotide or base pair to appear in the position or positions. Each transition rule is also associated with a probability value that describes the probability for the transition to occur. A well-known fact regarding the conventional CM is that it is an extension to the HMM, such that a base pair in a secondary structure can be described by emitting the nucleotides that form the base pair simultaneously. A CM is equivalent to stochastic context-free grammar (SCFG). The optimal alignment between a sequence and a conventional CM is thus computed with a dynamic programming algorithm that is similar to the CYK algorithm.

2.2 THE UPDATED CM

In our new structural model, the secondary structure of an RNA family contains a few basic structure units, each of which is a stem or a loop. Each structure unit is associated with a pair of integers. One of the integers is the minimum length of the structure unit, and the other is its maximum length. In other words, we restricted the length of each structure unit to a small interval. We describe the method that we used to determine the length restrictions for a structure unit later in this chapter. In addition to the length restrictions for the structure units, we used a CM to model the secondary structure of the family.

2.3 SEQUENCE-STRUCTURE ALIGNMENT

The sequence-structure alignment between a sequence **L** and a structure model **M** can be performed with a dynamic programming algorithm similar to the CYK algorithm used to align a sequence to a conventional CM. Since each structure unit has its own length restrictions, we are able to compute for each state in the CM the range of the lengths of the subsequences that can be derived from it. The dynamic programming for each state is then performed only within the range. For the conventional CM, the dynamic programming algorithm for sequence-structure alignment computes the probabilities for each state to derive all subsequences of **L.** Our structure model, therefore, can lead to a significant improvement in the computational efficiency of sequence-structure alignment.

2.4 COMPUTING THE LENGTH RESTRICTIONS

Each structure unit in the structure model is associated with a pair of integers that describe the range of its length in an ncRNA sequence. Given the training sequences in an ncRNA family, we could construct an HMM **M** for each structure unit **S** in the secondary structure of the family. In addition, we computed the average length and the base composition of the subsequences that form **S** in the training sequences. We used **A** to denote the average length of **S** in the training sequence, and using the base composition to randomly generate **N** subsequences of length **L**, we then aligned all these generated subsequences to **M** and obtained **N** different alignment scores. These **N** alignment scores together formed a distribution of the alignment scores of subsequences from the given base composition. We computed the mean **m** and the standard deviation **d** of these **N** alignment scores.

We were then ready to compute the upper bounds and lower bounds for the length of **S**. Next, we describe an approach that can compute both bounds given a statistical confidence value **p**. In particular, starting with L' = L + 1, we randomly generated **N** different subsequences of length **L'** using the same base composition and align each of them to **M**. N alignment scores could be generated by performing these alignments. These **N** alignment scores formed a new distribution. We computed the mean of these alignment scores and used **m'** to denote its value. We then checked whether the difference between this new distribution and the one obtained on subsequences of length L was statistically significant. To this end, we checked whether the difference between **m** and **m'** is larger than **cd** or not, where **c** was a constant that depends on the statistical confidence value **p**. If that were the case, **L'** would be the upper bound for the structure unit. Otherwise, we incremented the value of **L'** by 1. We repeated this procedure until we found an **L'** that could lead to a distribution statistically different from the one obtained on subsequences of length **L**. The lower bound can be obtained with a similar approach.

3 TEST RESULTS

We performed experiments to test the accuracy and efficiency of our approach and compared the performance of our approach with that of the conventional CM. The training data were obtained from the Rfam database. For each family, we chose up to 60 sequences, with their pairwise identities lower than 80% of the total number of nucleotides in each sequence. We inserted several RNA sequences from the same family into a random background generated with the same base composition as the sequences in the family. We then used both our algorithm and a CM-based searching algorithm to search for the inserted sequences.

In order to compute the length restrictions for each structure unit, we assumed that the lengths of each structure unit form a normal distribution and choose a confidence value of $p = 0.01$. The value of constant c, thus, is 3.0. We compared the sensitivity and specificity of both approaches used with several different RNA families, and the results are shown in Table 23.1. It is not difficult to see from this table that the search accuracy of our approach is comparable to that of the CM-based searching algorithm in terms of sensitivity and specificity. Table 23.2 compares the computation time of our approach with that of the CM-based search algorithm. It is not difficult to see that our approach is significantly faster than the CM-based approach for all tested ncRNA families. In particular, our approach only needs around 1.1% of the computation time needed by the CM-based search algorithm to search for Lin_4, while achieving the same search accuracy in terms of sensitivity and specificity.

Table 23.1 Sensitivity and Specificity of Our Approach and the CM-based Search Algorithm

RNA	Average Length	Sensitivity of Our Approach	Specificity of Our Approach	Sensitivity of CM-based Search Algorithm	Specificity of CM-based Search Algorithm
Entero_CRE	61	0.78	0.97	**0.81**	1
Entero_OriR	73	0.95	1	**1**	1
Let_7	84	1	1	1	1
Lin_4	72	1	1	1	1
Purine	103	**0.96**	0.97	0.93	**1**
SECIS	68	0.95	0.89	**1**	**0.97**
S_box	112	0.93	1	**1**	1
Tymo_tRNA-like	86	1	**1**	1	0.97

Table 23.2 Computation Time Needed to Search All ncRNA Families

RNA	Computation Time for CM-based Search Algorithm (s)	Computation Time for Our Approach (s)	The Amount of Speed-up Using Our Approach
Entero_CRE	57.96	2.41	24.05X
Entero_OriR	103.08	3.72	27.71X
Let_7	157.11	10.81	14.53X
Lin_4	132.51	1.46	**90.76X**
Purine	179.29	3.62	55.00X
SECIS	185.21	7.25	25.54X
S_box	756.27	24.52	30.84X
Tymo_tRNA-like	185.05	3.23	57.29X

4 CONCLUSIONS

In this chapter, we developed a new structure model that can be used to significantly speed up the sequence-structure alignment for ncRNAs. This new model is based on the conventional CM, which describes the sequences of an ncRNA family and their secondary structure with a statistical model. In addition to employing a CM to describe the primary sequence content and the secondary structure of sequences in an ncRNA family. Our model imposes length restrictions on each structure unit in the secondary structure. Using the length restrictions of structure units, the dynamic programming algorithm for sequence-structure alignment is significantly faster than that of the conventional CM. We showed that the length restrictions of a structure unit can be computed from the training data based on a statistical confidence value. Our testing results showed that this approach can significantly speed up the search of ncRNAs in genomes while achieving a search accuracy comparable to that of the conventional CM-based approach.

One disadvantage of our approach is that it cannot be used to model the ncRNA family, where some sequences do not contain certain structure units that are present in other sequences. In other words, some structure units are missing in these sequences. Although a missing structure unit can be accurately modeled by a conventional CM, our model may have difficulty doing that. The difficulty is largely because a missing structure unit can generate a sudden change in the range of lengths for some states in the CM. This sudden change cannot be accurately described by the length restrictions without significantly increasing the amount of computation time. The development of new approaches or models that can also handle the missing structure units is one of the directions we are taking in our future work.

So far, our approach has been used only to search for ncRNAs that do not contain pseudoknots. Pseudoknots contain crossing stems and are more difficult to model than secondary structure that does not contain crossing stems. Our previous work

(Song *et al.*, 2006; Song and Chi, 2015; Song *et al.*, to come, 2014) has developed methods and models that can estimate the parameters associated with structural models and search for ncRNAs that contain pseudoknots. Our future may extend this approach to modeling ncRNAs that contain pseudoknot structures. In addition, approaches based on data mining and statistical principles (Qu *et al.*, 2007, 2008, 2009; Qu and Arabnia, 2005a, 2005b; Song *et al.*, 2014; Song and Qu, 2014) have been proved to be effective for solving problems from a large number of areas. Combining our techniques with the techniques that are already available in these areas to further improve the accuracy of our approach is another possible direction for our future work.

REFERENCES

Eddy, S., Durbin, R., 1994. RNA sequence analysis using covariance models. Nucleic Acids Res. 22, 2079–2088.

Frank, D.N., Pace, N.R., 1998. Ribonuclease p: unity and diversity in a tRNA procesing ribozyme. Annu. Rev. Biochem. 67, 153–180.

Jones, E.R., Eddy, S.R., 2001. Computational identification of noncoding RNAs in *E. Coli* by comparative genomics. Curr. Biol. 11, 1369–1373.

Klein, R.J., Eddy, S.R., 2003. Rsearch: finding homologs of single structured RNA sequences. BMC Bioinformatics 4, 44.

Lowe, T.M., Eddy, S.R., 1997. tRNASCAN-SE: a program for improved detection of transfer RNA genes in genomic sequence. Nucleic Acids Res. 25, 955–964.

Luo, Z.Y., Zhou, Q., 2001. The 7sk small nuclear rna inhibits the cdk9/cyclin t1 kinase to control transcriptions. Nature 414, 317–322.

Mitchels, V., Bensaude, O., 2001. 7sk small nuclear rna binds to and inhibits the activity of cdk9/cyclin t complexes. Nature 414, 322–325.

Qu, J., Arabnia, H.R., 2005a. Mining structural changes in financial time series with gray system. In: Proceedings of the 2005 International Conference on Data Miningpp. 173–180.

Qu, J., Arabnia, H.R., 2005b. A novel short-term stock price predicting system. In: Proceedings of the 2005 International Conference on Information & Knowledge Engineering, pp. 25–31.

Qu, J., Arabnia, H.R., Song, Y., Rasheed, K., Houston, J., 2007. Time series similarity with a new distance measure. In: Proceedings of the 2008 International Conference on Information & Knowledge Engineering, pp. 183–189.

Qu, J., Song, Y., Arabnia, H.R., Jeff, B., 2008. Knowledge retrieval in financial domain. In: Proceedings of the 2008 International Conference on Information & Knowledge Engineering, pp. 140–144.

Qu, J., Rahman, M.A., Song, Y., Zhu, L., Wei, Y., Hong, W., Arabnia, H.R., 2009. PaperGuard: a support vector machine approach for screening machine generated papers. In: Proceedings of the 2009 International Conference on Information & Knowledge Engineering, pp. 433–438.

Song, Y., Chi, A., 2015. A new approach for parameter estimation in the sequence-structure alignment in noncoding RNAs. J. Inform. Sci. Eng. 31 (2), 593–607.

Song, Y., Qu, J., 2014. A graph theoretic approach for protein threading. In: Proceedings of the 10th International Conference on Intelligent Computing, pp. 501–507.

Song, Y., Liu, C., Malmberg, R.L., Pan, F., Cai, L., 2005. Tree decomposition based fast search of RNA structures including pseudoknots in genomes. In: Proceedings of the Fourth International IEEE Computational Systems Bioinformatics Conferences, pp. 223–234.

Song, Y., Liu, C., Huang, X., Malmberg, R.L., Xu, Y., Cai, L., 2006. Efficient parameterized algorithms for biopolymer structure-sequence alignment. IEEE/ACM Trans. Comput. Biol. Bioinform. 3 (4), 423–432.

Song, Y., Wang, C., Qu, J., 2014. A parameterized algorithm for predicting transcription factor binding sites. In: Proceedings of the 10th International Conference on Intelligent Computing, pp. 339–350.

Song Y., Liu C., Wang, Z., A machine learning based approach for accurate annotation of non-coding RNAs. IEEE/ACM Transactions on Computational Biology and Bioinformatics, to appear.

SMIR: A Web Server to Predict Residues Involved in the Protein Folding Core

24

Ruben Acuña[1], Zoé Lacroix[1], Jacques Chomilier[2,3], and Nikolaos Papandreou[4]

Scientific Data Management Laboratory, Arizona State University, Tempe, AZ, USA[1]
IMPMC, Sorbonne Universités, Université Pierre et Marie Curie, CNRS, MNHN,
IRD, Paris, France[2]
RPBS, Université Paris Diderot, Paris, France[3]
Department of Biotechnology, Agricultural University of Athens, Athens, Greece[4]

1 INTRODUCTION

Amino acids involved in interresidue contacts may play a role in the compactness of the protein; hence are called Most Interacting Residues (MIR). The MIR method was first introduced to simulate the origin of protein folding (Chomilier *et al.*, 2004). Starting from a random conformation, the folding process can be dynamically simulated in a discrete space (a lattice). Successive residues that collapse and form a local compact structure (linked to another one by an extended polypeptide chain) form a *fragment*. The MIR method focuses exclusively on the early steps of the folding process. In its very first implementation, it aimed to delineate the fragments formed at this stage. For this reason, the method was calibrated with time limits to maximize the number of fragments before the folding process reaches a single compact domain. It assigned a score between 2 and 8 to each residue, corresponding to the mean number of non-covalent neighbors in the lattice. A high score indicates that the residue is buried, thus belongs to a fragment. A low score indicates a low interacting residue belonging to a piece of the chain that links two consecutive fragments. A correspondence between fragments and regular secondary-structure elements (SSEs) was demonstrated on a set of 42 proteins, representative of various folds (Chomilier *et al.*, 2004). However, it has been shown that a pertinent analysis of globular protein structures with respect to folding properties consists of describing them as an ensemble of contiguous closed loops (Berezovsky *et al.*, 2000) or tightened end fragments (TEFs; Lamarine *et al.*, 2001). This description reveals that the ends of TEFs are fold elements crucial for the formation of stable structures and for navigating the very process of protein folding. Meanwhile, the MIR algorithm evolved, and newer versions (including the actual presented one) aim to locate individual residues with a very high mean number of neighbors (typically ≥ 6), which are called MIRs. In the other limit, individual residues with a low mean number of neighbors (typically 2) are Least Interacting Residues (LIRs).

Therefore, the residues identified as MIRs have the tendency to be buried at the early stages of the folding process. The comparison of MIR positions with the positions of the limits of closed loops, in proteins of known three-dimensional (3D) structures, showed a statistically significant agreement. MIRs also significantly correlate with topohydrophobic positions; i.e., positions in multiple alignments of sequences of common fold occupied only by hydrophobic amino acids, and correlated to the folding nucleus (Poupon and Mornon, 1998), thereby giving a route to simulations of the protein folding process (Papandreou *et al.*, 2004). Thus, MIR is a potential method for an ab initio estimation of the residues that are important for folding and consequently, significantly sensitive to mutations.

It is important to keep in mind the difference between a protein core and a nucleus. *Core* is a static concept, and it results from the fact that a globular protein is a micelle, with an internal phase of hydrophobic character, and an external phase of hydrophilic character, statistically. The core of a protein can be derived by a simple accessible surface area calculation, or with more sophisticated methods (Bottini *et al.*, 2013). In contrast, *nucleus* is a dynamic concept that relies on a model of folding—namely, the nucleation condensation model (Abkevich *et al.*, 1994, Itzhaki *et al.*, 1995). In a few words, a small set of dispersed amino acids come into contact during the folding because of the thermal vibrations of the molecule. They are hydrophobic, and once they form such a nucleus, the rest of the structure can be formed. Among proteins sharing the same fold, part of the nucleus is conserved. In addition, it is now documented that nonnative contacts are necessary for the folding, and they disappear once the stability is sufficient. Figure 24.1 illustrates the difference between core and nucleus in the case of a fibronectin.

The knowledge of the residues constituting the folding nucleus is important for instance in the annotation of misfolding-related pathologies, but their experimental determination is not 100% secure. The role of prediction, at this moment, is a

FIGURE 24.1

The difference between the core (left) and nucleus (right) of type III fibronectin (Lappalainen *et al.*, 2008; Billings *et al.*, 2008).

valuable complementary approach. The literature commonly admits that the number of residues involved in the folding nucleus is typically less than 10% of the sequence length, roughly one-third of the hydrophobic residues. Initial MIR calculation slightly overpredicts the nucleus. One guideline to improve prediction can be to produce a smoothing of the curve of NCN as a function of the sequence. This is one of the major improvements proposed with the Smoothed Most Interacting Residues (SMIR) method.

The SMIR method presented in this chapter aims at improving the accuracy of MIR in the prediction of residues involved in the folding nucleus. Indeed, it has been shown that MIR overestimates the folding nucleus of numerous proteins. The SMIR method is implemented and available as a server that supports the submission and the analysis of protein structures with MIR2.0 and SMIR. The server offers a dynamic interface with the display of results in a 2D graph.

2 METHODS

The MIR method is an extension of previous simulations performed on cubic lattices, devoted to the complete folding of globular domains (Papandreou *et al.*, 1998). The MIR algorithm is a topological calculation resulting from a series of energy-driven simulations of a protein backbone, where the mean number of noncovalent contacts is deduced for each residue. The analysis is performed at the early steps of folding and provides the number of noncovalent neighbors (NCNs) for each residue in the sequence.

The simulation of the early steps of the folding is designed in the following manner. First, an extended initial conformation is produced for an alpha-carbon-only simplified representation of the polypeptide chain. Each alpha carbon is placed at random (while constrained as a chain) on the nodes of a lattice. An extension of a cubic lattice, namely (2, 1, 0), originally proposed by Skolnick and Kolinski (1991) is used (see Figure 24.2). Compared to the simple cubic lattice, it allows a wider range of backbone angles, from 64° to 143°, among three contiguous alpha carbons. The number of first neighbors is also higher: 24 instead of 6. Side chains are discarded in the present simulation. Folding is produced by randomly selecting one amino acid and submitting it to one of two available moves: an end move for the

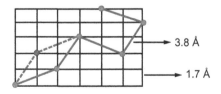

3.8 Å

1.7 Å

FIGURE 24.2

Details of the (2, 1, 0) lattice, with respect to the underlying cubic lattice. The dotted line indicates a possible move to a free node (Acuña *et al.*, 2014).

N or C terminal positions, or a corner move otherwise. The crankshaft move is no longer permitted with the (2, 1, 0) lattice. The new position can be occupied if it was previously empty, and the energy of the new conformation is computed by means of a statistical potential of mean force taken from the literature (Miyazawa and Jernigan, 1996). The Metropolis criterion is applied to accept or reject the new conformation.

The process is stopped when roughly 10^6 to 10^7 Monte Carlo steps are reached, depending on the length of the query sequence. The full process is repeated 100 times, starting from 100 different initial conformations. The number of NCNs is recorded during each complete simulation. Two noncovalently bound residues are considered to interact if the distance between their respective alpha carbons does not exceed the upper limit of 5.9 Å. The mean NCN is calculated at the end of the process and for all the initial conformations. The distribution of NCN along the sequence presents maxima and minima. We paid most of our attention to the maxima because we were aiming to predict the core contacting residues, expected to be crucial for the formation of secondary structures (Kirster and Gelfand, 2009) and whose prediction allows for determining the fold (Jones et al., 2012). Therefore, a residue i is accepted as a MIR if NCN(i) is equal or higher than 6. The result is that more than 90% of the MIRs are hydrophobic (Acuña et al., 2014).

It has been demonstrated that for each protein, residues identified as MIRs constitute a nontrivial subset of the hydrophobic residues. Among families of folds (several domains per family, similar structure, potentially different functions, and very divergent sequences), MIRs occupy equivalent positions in the multiple alignments. Therefore, among families, a small number of hydrophobic positions are conserved as hydrophobic. They are compulsory for the folding to occur; they are deeply buried. For these reasons, it seems reasonable to question whether they constitute the folding nucleus of the various folds. The answer is positive, as proposed by the presently available studies. They concern a very small number of families because experimental evidence of the folding nucleus is not obvious and can show strong biases. Demonstration has been extensively proposed on two complete families, the immunoglobulins (56 structures of divergent sequences) and flavodoxins (43 structures).

One limitation of the MIR algorithm was the number of MIRs identified by the threshold—typically around 15% of the amino acids—while the rate of amino acids expected to belong to the folding nucleus lies roughly in the range of 5% to 10% This limitation also relates to the overall sharp variation in the graph. The SMIR extension addresses these issues, and it uses a Pascal triangle method to give smooth results. We also adjust the maxima that are identified in the smoothed graph to nearby (within three residues) hydrophobic positions based on the accepted precision of the algorithm (Chomilier et al., 2006). This is coherent with the expected accuracy for protein residue contact prediction of the contact prediction session of the Critical Assessment of (protein) Structure Prediction (CASP) experiments (Eickholt and Cheng, 2013). Hence, we continue to identify minima with a threshold but validate the extrema against the actual amino acids.

3 RESULTS

3.1 MODEL

We model a protein as a chain of evenly spaced C_α atoms placed on a lattice (Chomilier *et al.*, 2004). We define a lattice unit (lu) to be 1.7 Å. Hence, C_α atoms are connected by vectors of the form (2,1,0), these vectors are $5^{1/2}$ lu in length which corresponds to 3.8 Å—the mean distance between adjacent C_α atoms. This results in 24 immediate neighbor positions for each point in the lattice. This represents the intersection of a $4 \times 4 \times 4$ segmented cube with a sphere of radius 3.8 Å ($5^{1/2}$ lu).

The model does not take into account the presence of side chains; therefore, the required separation is modeled with the 3.8 Å minimum distance requirement. Based on chain geometry, we limit the angle between some C_αs at positions i and $i+2$ by requiring the distance between them to range from 4.1 to 7.2 Å (or from $6^{1/2}$ to $18^{1/2}$ lu). This corresponds to angles from 66° to 143°, which is closer to the real angles in alpha and beta conformations. This is illustrated in Figure 24.3, where a residue i is fixed at [0, 0, 0] and all 24 possible positions for residue $i+1$ are represented as black vectors. There is a choice of 23 possible vectors for residue $i+2$. For the sake of clarity, only one position [0, 1, 2] (the green and red vectors) is shown. Red vectors are those that violate the distance (angle) restriction.

To initiate the simulations, 100 different starting models within this lattice are used. Figures 24.3 and 24.4 display a sample of five and all models, respectively,

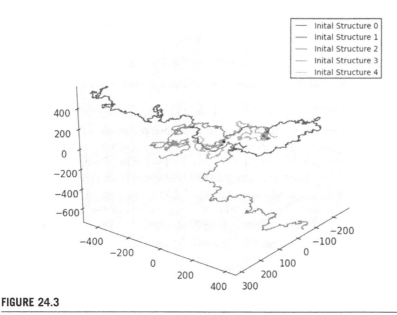

FIGURE 24.3

The first five initial models (Acuña *et al.*, 2014).

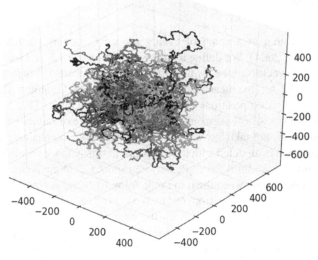

FIGURE 24.4

All initial models (Acuña *et al.*, 2014).

as a comprehensive plot. These models were computed randomly offline for chains of 1100 residues. For the initial models, our only requirement is that they have some level of noncompactness (Papandreou *et al.*, 2004). Starting from the first residue, located at position [0, 0, 0], the first *n* positions in the seed model will be used for an input model with *n* residues—any additional residues in the random sequence will be discarded.

3.2 SMIR

The MIR method was first developed in 2004 (Chomilier *et al.*, 2004; Papandreou *et al.*, 2004), and MIR 1.0 was first made available online as a function of the Ressource Parisienne en Bioinformatique Structurale (RPBS) server in 2005 (Alland *et al.*, 2005). The present SMIR server exploits MIR2.2 implemented with Fortran for server-side simulation and a SMIR JavaScript front end for interactive analysis. The input to the MIR algorithm is a FASTA file containing a sequence using standard amino acids. The input file is either provided by the user or automatically retrieved from RCSB via a Protein Data Bank (PDB) ID. The output consists of a table associated with each residue: AA letter, NCN, MIRs, and LIRs. NCN is an integer while MIR and LIR are Boolean flags.

Server-side computation time is quadratic on the length of the sequence and may be modeled by $6.062\text{E} - 5x^2 - 0.0138x + 0.843$ hours, where x is the number of residues, on an Intel Core 2 Duo E6600 computer. The results are stored in a MySQL 5.1 database running on Ubuntu 13.04 LTS. The new SMIR smoothing method is implemented in JavaScript with D3 (Bostock *et al.*, 2011) and has been primarily tested in Google Chrome 33. Firefox 18 and Safari 6 have also been tested. Microsoft Internet Explorer is not currently supported. It has been found that the computation time for SMIR, once MIR results are available, is negligible on Intel Core 2 Duo–based computers. A browser-based implementation allows users to retrieve this new analysis for any existing protein without the need to resubmit the entry to our submission server.

3.3 SUBMITTING A PROTEIN

The SMIR interface illustrated in Figure 24.5 supports the submission of a PDB ID, a list of PDB IDs, or a FASTA file. In the latter case, the user will also enter a four-letter alphanumeric code to identify the submission and later retrieve the results. The submission of an e-mail address is optional. Should one be submitted, it will be used only for the purpose of informing the user of the availability of the results in the database with a reminder of the code. After submission, the server returns a SMIR status window (see Figure 24.6). Here, the window displays the status for five proteins of PDB codes: 1AMM, 1DX5, 1I5I, 1QUC, and 1ZAC. At the top of the status windows are listed the PDB IDs that have already been analyzed by MIR. Each PDB (e.g., 1AMM, 1DX5, or 1I5I) is listed with a bullet. If a protein has more than one chain, each available chain will be listed on that PDB's line and enclosed in parentheses [e.g., 1DX5(A), 1DX5(I), etc.]. The middle part of the window lists invalid retrieval PDB codes (e.g., 1QUC). The last part consists of the proteins that will be submitted to the server (e.g., 1ZAC). In this case, the PDB IDs will be added to the server queue for processing. Each protein submitted to the server is displayed in the status window

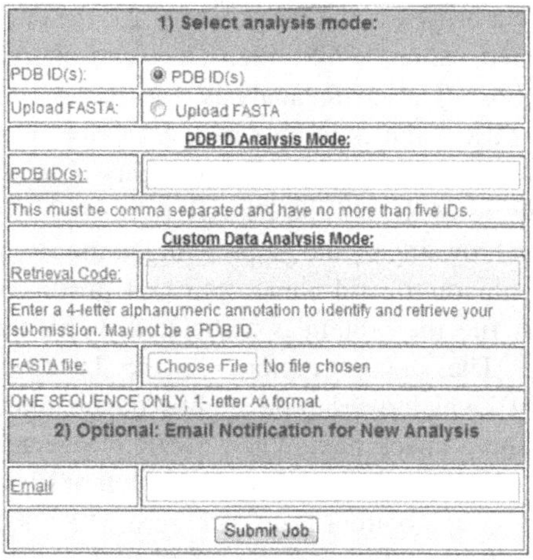

FIGURE 24.5

MIR interface.

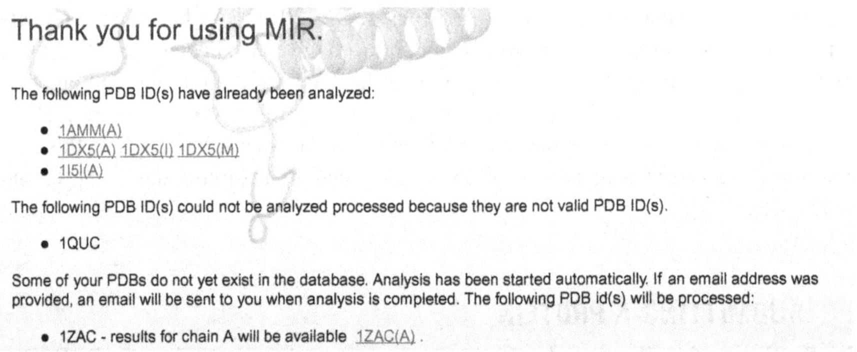

Thank you for using MIR.

The following PDB ID(s) have already been analyzed:

- 1AMM(A)
- 1DX5(A) 1DX5(I) 1DX5(M)
- 1I5I(A)

The following PDB ID(s) could not be analyzed processed because they are not valid PDB ID(s).

- 1QUC

Some of your PDBs do not yet exist in the database. Analysis has been started automatically. If an email address was provided, an email will be sent to you when analysis is completed. The following PDB id(s) will be processed:

- 1ZAC - results for chain A will be available 1ZAC(A) .

FIGURE 24.6

MIR submission status.

with the retrieval link to access the data once the execution is completed. If an e-mail address was entered on the previous screen, a notification with a link will be sent upon completion. The proteins listed at the top of the SMIR status window are immediately viewable with a 2D graph (see Figure 24.7). If a PDB ID is not in the list of available proteins, it will be automatically submitted for analysis. Once the user's protein is ready to be analyzed, the server downloads the information associated with that PDB ID from the PDB and runs MIR. After execution, the user may use the retrieval link or return to MIR query mode and enter that PDB ID to access the SMIR results. Additionally, the information that was generated for the new PDB ID is now available to other researchers for further use.

The graphical representation illustrated in Figure 24.7 is composed of three areas: legend for the MIR interface (top left), 2D display graph (top right), and data download (bottom). On recent browsers, such as Chrome 24, the data can be downloaded with a comma-separated values (CVS) file. They can alternately be copied and pasted from a text box. The MIR analysis for protein 1amm(A), shown in Figure 24.8, displays MIR residues in blue as a 2D graph. Dark blue vertical bars indicate which residues are MIRs, while dark red bars indicate LIRs (note that no LIR was shown in Figure 24.8). All the bars plot the NCN count at a position on the vertical axis. When browsing on the graph with the mouse, a black pop-up information box displays the amino acid name, its exact position in the protein (with respect to the FASTA file the protein is associated with), the number of NCNs, and the MIR status. The orange regions in the background indicate TEFs (Chomilier et al., 2004), which overlap on slightly darker orange areas. The SMIR method is activated with a check box. When SMIR is selected, the 2D graph will show dynamically how MIR predictions (see the top left of Figure 24.8) are replaced by SMIR predictions (see the bottom right of Figure 24.8). When in smooth mode (i.e., when SMIR is selected), the dark blue and dark red bars indicate SMIRS and SLIRS (smoothed LIR, which are minima in the NCN curves) respectively. Note that two SMIRS are shown for protein 1amm(A) in Figure 24.8.

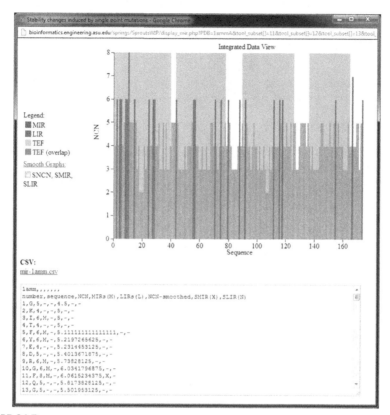

FIGURE 24.7

MIR results for protein 1AMM(A).

3.4 USE CASE AND DISCUSSION

John Orban's group has demonstrated how a single point mutation could have a transformative impact on the protein fold (He *et al.*, 2005, 2012; Alexander *et al.*, 2007, 2009). They first considered two short domains G_A and G_B with low sequence similarity (because their sequence identity is 16%, we will use the notations GA16 and GB16, respectively, for G_A and G_B in the rest of this discussion). The two wild types (WTs) GA16 and GB16 were not entered in PDB, but their sequences shown in Table 24.1 were published by He and colleagues in 2005. They engineered two proteins, 2LHC (also referred to as GA98) and 2LHD (also referred to as GB98), of length 56, with 98% sequence identity. Their sequences only differ by one residue on position 45, as displayed in Table 24.2. Although these two sequences show very high sequence identity, the structures display significantly different structures. 2LHC contains three alpha helices, while 2LHD contains four beta sheets and one alpha helix, as illustrated in Figure 24.9. A single mutation at the 45th residue (leucine toward tyrosine) changes dramatically the folded conformation.

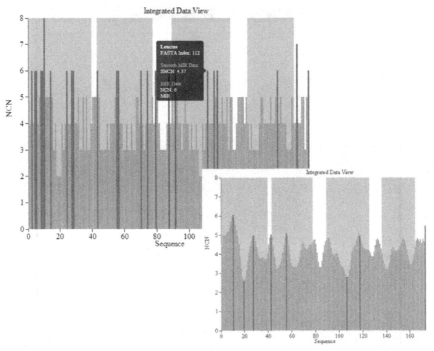

FIGURE 24.8

SMIR dynamic results (bottom right) activated for 1amm(A).

We conducted a SMIR analysis on the 14 proteins presented, including the 2 WTs, 10 intermediate engineered proteins, and 2LHC and 2LHD. The SMIRs and SLIRs collected are displayed in Table 24.3 and illustrated in Figure 24.10. The SMIR method is sensitive to structure conservation, which relies more on the concept of a protein seen as a micelle, with a hydrophobic core and an outer shell, mainly hydrophilic. Structure conservation when transferred into sequence space, can be approached as conservation of a class of amino acids. Usually, two classes are proposed, called H and P classes in the literature. Class H is the class of hydrophobic (FILMVYW) amino acids. The reasons for the transformation from one fold to another has been the object of much conjecture, for instance in the so-called Paracelsus challenge in the 1990s. Following this idea, John Orban and colleagues proposed to keep the initial fold of a set of two proteins, each one being mutated with the purpose of increasing the sequence identity with the partner. In execution, they used two domains of 56 amino acids each, from the *Streptococus celle* surface G. In a series of papers, starting from the WT pair at 16% identity, they progressively increased identity up to one single mutation, but with two folds—namely, three helices on one hand (called G_A) and a four-stranded sheet plus one helix on the other (called G_B).

Table 24.1 Sequences of WT proteins GA (ga16A) and GB (gb16A) and Engineered Proteins Until 98% Sequence Identity, Reached with GA98 (2lhcA) and GB98 (2lhdA)

%	A (albumin-binding)	ID	B (IgG-binding)	ID
98	TTYKLILNLKQAKEEAIKELVDAGTAEKYFKLIANAKTVEGVWTLKDEIKTFTVTE	2lhcA	TTYKLILNLKQAKEEAIKELVDAGTAEKYFKLIANAKTVEGVWTYKDEIKTFTVTE	2lhdA
95	TTYKLILNLKQAKEEAIKELVDAGTAEKYIKLIANAKTVEGVWTLKDEIKTFTVTE	2kdlA	TTYKLILNLKQAKEEAIKEAVDAGTAEKYFKLIANAKTVEGVWTYKDEIKTFTVTE	2kdmA
91	TTYKLILNLKQAKEEAIKELVDAGTAEKYIKLIANAKTVEGVWTLKDEILTFTVTE	ga91a	TTYKLILNLKQAKEEAIKEAVDAGTAEKYFKLIANAKTVEGVWTYKDEIKTFTVTE	2kdmA
88	TTYKLILNLKQAKEEAIKELVDAGIAEKYIKLIANAKTVEGVWTLKDEILTFTVTE	2jwsA	TTYKLILNLKQAKEEAITEAVDAGTAEKYFKLYANAKTVEGVWTYKDEIKTFTVTE	gb88A
77	TTYKLILNLKQAKEEAIKELVDAGIAEKYIKLIANAKTVEGVWTLKDEILKATVTE	ga77A	TTYKLILNGKQLKEEAITEAVDAATAEKYFKLYANAKTVEGVWTYKDETKTFTVTE	gb77A
59	MYYLVVNKQQNAFYEVLNMPNLNEDQRNAFIQSLKDDPSQSANVLAEAQKLNDVQA	ga59A	MYYLVVNKGQNAFYETLTKAVDAETARNAFIQSLKDDGVQGVWTYDDATKTFTVQA	gb59A
WT	MDNKFNKEQQNAFYEVLNMPNLNEDQRNGFIQSLKDDPSQSANVLAEAQKLNDAQA	ga16A	MTYKLVINGKTLKGETTTKAVDAETAEKAFKQYANDNGVDGVWTYDDATKTFTVTE	gb16A

Table 24.2 Sequences of 2lhc(A) and 2lhd(A) with 98% Sequence Identity, with a Single Mutation on Residue 45

2LHC(A)	TTYKLILNLKQAKEEAIKELVDAGTAEKYFKLIANAKTVEGVWTLKDEIKTFTVTE
2LHD(A)	TTYKLILNLKQAKEEAIKELVDAGTAEKYFKLIANAKTVEGVWTYKDEIKTFTVTE

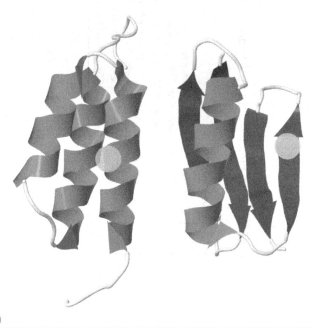

FIGURE 24.9

PDB structures for 2LHC (GA98), on the left, and 2LHD (GB98), on the right. The colored dot indicates the position of the 45th residue in both sequences.

Figure 24.10 shows the smoothed NCN on the pairs of mutated proteins, starting from the WT, until the two sequences at 98% identity (*i.e.,* different by a single mutation). If one looks at the left column of the figure, with the fold with three helices, some peaks appear in the NCN distribution, but one peak remains at the same location all over the proteins: the one at 30–31. Since some structures are available, such as 1ZXG for the protein GA59, one can see that positions 30–31 are in the middle of the second helix. The second observation that one can make on the set of proteins from the mixed fold (right column of Figure 24.10) is that most of the peaks are displaced when the number of mutations increases, at the exception of the one around 30–31, which remains a maximum in the NCN distribution throughout the set of proteins. Analysis of the structure with the PDB code 1ZXH, corresponding to the sequence GB59 in Figure 24.10, shows that positions 30–31 are also in the middle of the sole helix of this fold. Therefore, we may hypothesize that these positions are

Table 24.3 SMIR results for 14 proteins: WTs GA16 and GB16 (He *et al.*, 2005) with 16% sequence identity, intermediate engineered proteins with pairwise increased sequence identity GA59 and GB59 (He *et al.*, 2005), followed by GA77, GB77, GA88, GB88, GA91, GB91, GA95, GB95 (Alexander *et al.*, 2009) and the final sequences GA98 (2LHC) and GB98 (2LHD) (He *et al.*, 2012) with 98% sequence identity.

Protein	SLIR residue position		SMIR residue position					
GA16 or G$_A$	25	38	1	13	45	51		
GB16 or G$_B$			1 5 7		43		52	54
GA59	25	37		16	45	51		54
GB59	24			14	45			
GA77	14	37	7		45	49		
GB77			7	32	45		52	54
GA88	14	37	7			49		
GB88	14	37	7	32		49		
GA91	14	37	7			49		
GB91	14		7	32		49		
GA95	13	37	7		45			
GB95	14		7	32		49		
GA98	14	37	7		45	49		
GB98	13	37	7			49		

crucial for the formation of a helix, independent of the rest of the structure. It is not arbitrary if position 30 is occupied by a hydrophobic residue, F, in both WTs. Moreover, if one looks thoroughly at this position all along the sequences of either the A or the B fold (shown in Figure 24.10), there is either F or I at this position, and it is known to belong to the core of the GA protein (He *et al.*, 2012). One must also remember that these lab proteins are rather unstable, as noticed by the authors.

For a possible understanding of the SMIR prediction in the context of this set of experiments, one may somehow consider a degenerate alphabet. We used the most common one in the field of lattice simulation of folding by two classes of amino acids: FILMVYW as the hydrophobic group (Callebaut *et al.* 1997), named H, and the rest denoted as P. It is noticeable that the profiles of smoothed NCN are sensitive to point mutation. Considering the A fold scenario, increasing the number of mutations in order to look like the B fold, one starts with a landscape of three main and clear peaks, roughly centered on the three alpha helices. So long as mutations are performed, a new peak appears at both terminal ends, although it is much clearer at the N terminus. This is the bulk of the discussion proposed by John Orban's group in successive papers. There is an equilibrium between the two folds, at least when one single mutation separates the two proteins, and the two ends play a critical role. If the folding nucleates around position 30, producing the presence of a helix under the local interactions, the rest of the fold will depend on long-range interactions. In the case of a Leu at position 45, as is the case for GA98, this will favor the formation

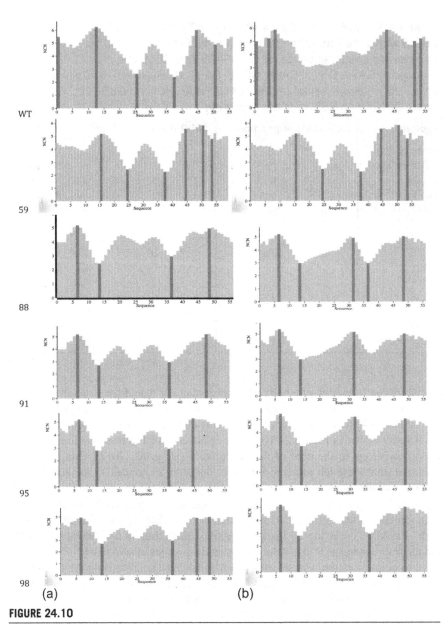

WT

59

88

91

95

98

(a)   (b)

FIGURE 24.10

SMIR results for 14 proteins: WTs GA16 and GB16 (He *et al.*, 2005) with 16% sequence identity are shown at the top (GA16 on the left, GB16 on the right), intermediate engineered proteins with pairwise increased sequence identity GA59 and GB59 (He *et al.*, 2005), followed by GA77, GB77, GA88, GB88, GA91, GB91, GA95, and GB95 (Alexander *et al.*, 2009) and the final sequences GA98 (2lhc) and GB98 (2lhd) (He *et al.*, 2012), with 98% sequence identity.

of a helix because Leu propensity is highest for helices. In addition, this is the most frequent residue predicted as a MIR. This second helix formation will guide the rest of the fold toward the alpha type. Otherwise, if there is a Tyr, the small difference in propensity to form helices and to be involved in numerous side chain interactions, is sufficient to drive the folding toward a beta fold. MIR simulation on its own is insufficient to provide a complete and correct prediction; nevertheless, it can help in obtaining a better understanding of the steps followed by the proteins along their folding pathways.

As a particular case of interpreting the SMIR results for generations of similar sequences, consider A91–A95. The main effect in A95 compared to A91 occurs at the place of the mutation, 50: the peak disappears, enhancing the 45 peak. In A95, position 30 is mutated, which is a peak in the smoothed NCN. The mutation is I30F. The frequencies of Ile and Phe as MIR (Acuña *et al.*, 2014) are similar; thus, they should not significantly modify the number of local interactions. According to Alexander *et al.*, the core of A95 contains 9 AA, with 5 hydrophobic interacting residues located at 16, 20, 30, 33, and 49. If we assume that we have a low resolution, it means that we have three interacting clusters: 20, 30, and 45. It is also indicated that the three positions 20, 30, and 45 can either produce a core and therefore an alpha class (with LIL at these positions) or a sheet with AFY. One can assume that the two leucines, which have a higher propensity for helices, drive the pathway. We predict these peaks, although we have an extra one at the N terminus. Looking at the structure (PDB 2KDL) for A95, we see that I6 is very close in distance from V39 (6.1 Å), even if it is in a loop. This is noted by Alexander *et al.* since both ends are loops in the A form and strands in the B form.

4 CONCLUSION

Based on previous work (Chomilier *et al.*, 2004; Papandreou *et al.*, 2004), we have presented the fundamental MIR algorithm and a method for increasing the readability and accuracy of residue interaction data. Our contribution over the previous MIR implementations is twofold: we have presented SMIR, an algorithm involving Pascal Triangle smoothing and hydrophobic residue analysis to calculate smoothed data. We have also implemented this algorithm in a new, dynamic 2D graphical interface. Users may now view the smoothed MIR data for all proteins already existing in the SPROUTS database without needing to resubmit the protein for processing. These contributions refine the MIR technique to make MIR results more intuitive and useful to the scientific community.

One practical aspect of the prediction of MIR that can be important for wet biologists can be in cases where they face the production of inclusion bodies during the process of expression and purification. One of the ways used to circumvent this difficulty is to practice random mutations. The use of this server can be a suggestion not to mutate some positions suspected to be important for the structure, and consequently for the function (specifically MIR). MIR and SMIR methods are also integrated into the SPROUTS workflow, where they can be compared with stability analysis (Acuña *et al.*, 2015).

SMIR is free and open to all users as a functionality of the Structural Prediction for pRotein fOlding UTility System (SPROUTS) with no login requirement at http://sprouts.rpbs.univ-paris-diderot.fr/mir.html. SMIR is hosted at the Université Paris Diderot on the RPBS server which provides scientists with a large range of resources devoted to the analysis of protein structure (Alland *et al.*, 2005). SMIR is also available for integrated analyses of point mutation on the protein structure (Lonquety *et al.*, 2008).

ACKNOWLEDGMENTS

We acknowledge Pierre Tufféry for his help with using the RPBS resources, Dirk Stratmann for exciting discussions on benchmarks and method comparison and integration, and Elodie Duprat for sharing her results on the beta/gamma-crystallin superfamily. Mathieu Lonquety and Christophe Legendre contributed to the SPROUTS database where SMIR results are stored, and Fayez Hadji tested a preliminary version of the server. They are all thanked for their help. We also wish to acknowledge our collaborators at ASU: Rida Bazzi, who is working with us on issues related to scientific workflow updates; Antonia Papandreou-Suppappola and Anna Malin, who have worked on an alternative MIR method; and Banu Ozkan, for evaluating SPROUTS functionalities and discussing future improvements.

Funding: This work was partially supported by the National Science Foundation (grants IIS 0431174, IIS 0551444, IIS 0612273, IIS 0738906, IIS 0832551, IIS 0944126, and CNS 0849980), and by an invitation of the Université Pierre et Marie Curie.

Disclaimer: Any opinion, finding, and conclusion or recommendation expressed in this material are those of the authors and do not necessarily reflect the views of the National Science Foundation.

REFERENCES

Abkevich, V.I., Gutin, A.M., Shakhnovich, E.I., 1994. Specific nucleus as the transition state for protein folding: evidence from the lattice model. Biochemistry. 33 (33), 10026–10036.

Acuña, R., Lacroix, Z., Papandreou, N., Chomilier, J., 2014. Protein intrachain contact prediction with most interacting residues (MIR). Bio. Algorithm Med.-Syst. 10 (4), 227–242.

Acuña, R., Lacroix, Z., Chomilier, J., 2015. SPROUTS 2.0: a database and workflow to predict protein stability upon point mutation. In: European Conference on Computational Biology 2014, 7 - 10 Sep 2014, E01.

Alexander, P.A., He, Y., Chen, Y., Orban, J., Bryan, P.N., 2007. The design and characterization of two proteins with 88% sequence identity but different structure and function. Proc. Natl. Acad. Sci. U. S. A. 104 (29), 11963–11968.

Alexander, P.A., He, Y., Chen, Y., Orban, J., Bryan, P.N., 2009. A minimal sequence code for switching protein structure and function. Proc. Natl. Acad. Sci. U. S. A. 106 (50), 21149–21154.

Alland, C., Moreews, F., Boens, D., Carpentier, M., Chiusa, S., Lonquety, M., Renault, N., Wong, Y., Cantalloube, H., Chomilier, J., et al., 2005. RPBS: a web resource for structural bioinformatics. Nucleic Acids Res. 33, W44–W49.

Berezovsky, I.N., Grosberg, A.Y., Trifonov, E.N., 2000. Closed loops of nearly standard size: common basic element of protein structure. Febs Lett. 466, 283–286.

Billings, K., Best, R., Rutherford, T., Clake, J., 2008. Crosstalk between the protein surface and hydrophobic core in a swapped fibronection type III domain. JMB 375, 560–571.

Bostock, M., Ogievetsky, V., Heer, J., 2011. D-3: Data-Driven Documents. IEEE Trans. Vis. Comput. Graph. 17, 2301–2309.

Bottini, S., Bernini, A., De Chiara, M., Garlaschelli, D., Spiga, O., Dioguardi, M., Vannuccini, E., Tramontano, A., Niccolai, N., 2013. ProCoCoA: a quantitative approach for analyzing protein core composition. Comput. Biol. Chem. 43, 29–34.

Callebaut, I., Labesse, G., Durand, P., Poupon, A., Canard, L., Chomilier, J., Henrissat, B., Mornon, J.P., 1997. Deciphering protein sequence information through hydrophobic cluster analysis (HCA): current status and perspectives. Cell. Mol. Life Sci. 53, 621–645.

Chomilier, J., Lamarine, M., Mornon, J.P., Torres, J.H., Eliopoulos, E., Papandreou, N., 2004. Analysis of fragments induced by simulated lattice protein folding. C. R. Biol. 327, 431–443.

Chomilier, J., Lonquety, M., Papandreou, N., Berezovsky, I., 2006. Towards the prediction of residues involved in the folding nucleus of proteins. In: Proc. DIMACS Workshop on Sequence, Structure and System Approaches to Predict Protein Function, May 3-5, 2006. Center for Discrete Mathematics and Theoretical Computer Science (DIMACS) Center, Rutgers University. http://dimacs.rutgers.edu/Workshops/ProteinFunction/slides/chomilier.pdf.

Eickholt, J., Cheng, J., 2013. A study and benchmark of DNcon: a method for protein residue contact prediction using deep networks. BMC Bioinformatics 14 (Suppl), 512.

Fersht, A., Sato, S., 2004. Φ-value analysis and the nature of protein folding transition states. Proc. Natl. Acad. Sci. U. S. A. 101, 7976–7981.

Garbuzynskiy, S.O., Finkelstein, A.V., Galzitskaya, O.V., 2005. On the prediction of folding nuclei in globular proteins. Mol. Biol. 39 (6), 906–914.

Hamill, S., Steward, A., Clarke, J., 2000. The folding of an immunoglobulin like Greek key protein is defined by a common core nucleus and regions constrained by topology. J. Mol. Biol. 297, 165–178.

He, Y., Yeh, D.C., Alexander, P.A., Bryan, P.N., Orban, J., 2005. Solution NMR structures of IgG binding domains with artificially evolved high levels of sequence identity but different folds. Biochemistry 44 (43), 14055–14061.

He, Y., Chen, Y., Alexander, P.A., Bryan, P.N., Orban, J., 2012. Mutational tipping points for switching protein folds and functions. Structure 20 (2), 283–291.

Itzhaki, L.S., Otzen, D.E., Fersht, A.R., 1995. The structure of the transition state for folding of chmotrypsin inhibitor 2 analysed by protein engineering methods: evidence for a nucleation condensation mechanism for protein folding. J. Mol. Biol. 25, 260–288.

Jones, D., Buchan, D., Cozzetto, D., Ponti, M., 2012. PSICOV : precise structural contact prediction using spase inverse covariance estimation on large multiple sequence alignments. Bioinformatics 28, 184–190.

Kister, A., Gelfand, I., 2009. Finding of residues crucial for supersecondary structure formation. Proc. Natl. Acad. Sci. U. S. A. 106, 18996–19000.

Lamarine, M., Mornon, J.P., Berezovsky, I.N., Chomilier, J., 2001. Distribution of tightened end fragments of globular proteins statistically matches that of topohydrophobic positions: towards an efficient punctuation of protein folding? Cell. Mol. Life Sci. 58, 492–498.

Lappalainen, I., Hurley, M.G., Clarke, J., 2008. Plasticity within the obligatory folding nucleus of an immunoglobulin-like domain. J. Mol. Biol. 375, 547–559.

Lonquety, M., Lacroix, Z., Papandreou, N., Chomilier, J., 2008. SPROUTS: a database for the evaluation of protein stability upon point mutation. Nucleic Acids Res.. 37 (Database issue), D374-9.

Miyazawa, S., Jernigan, R.L., 1996. Residue-residue potentials with a favorable contact pair term and an unfavorable high packing density term, for simulation and threading. J. Mol. Biol. 256, 623–644.

Papandreou, N., Kanehisa, M., Chomilier, J., 1998. Folding of the human protein FKBP. Lattice Monte-Carlo simulations. Comptes Rendus De L'Académie Des Sciences Série Iii-Sciences De La Vie-Life Sciences 321, 835–843.

Papandreou, N., Berezovsky, I.N., Lopes, A., Eliopoulos, E., Chomilier, J., 2004. Universal positions in globular proteins - From observation to simulation. Eur. J. Biochem. 271, 4762–4768.

Poupon, A., Mornon, J.P., 1998. Populations of hydrophobic amino acids within protein globular domains: Identification of conserved "topohydrophobic" positions. Proteins-Structure Function and Genetics 33, 329–342.

Skolnick, J., Kolinski, A., 1991. Dynamic Monte Carlo Simulations of a New LAttice Model of Globular Protein Folding, Structure and Dynamics. J. Mol. Biol. 221, 499–531.

Predicting Extinction of Biological Systems with Competition

25

Branko Ristic and Alex Skvortsov

Defence Science and Technology Organisation, Melbourne, VIC, Australia

1 INTRODUCTION

Predicting the risk of population extinction is one of the central themes in population biology (Lande *et al.*, 2003; Ovaskainen and Meerson, 2010; Ladle, 2009). Population extinction is influenced by many unpredictable factors, such as the environmental conditions (*e.g.,* food/water availability, climate change) and demographic variability (*e.g.,* genetic diversity, different fitness of individual species); see Bartlett (1961, 2000), McLaughlin *et al.* (2002), and Lande and Orzack (1988). Understanding and predicting the time to extinction is important in the context of the conservation of biodiversity, control of epidemics and for planning a responsible consumption of natural resources (Davidson *et al.*, 2009; Brook *et al.*, 2000). Extinction studies are also relevant in a broader context of complex systems exhibiting multiagent interacting dynamics: stock market trading (Sprott, 2004), biochemical reactions (Wilkinson, 2013), brain activity networks (Rabinovich *et al.*, 2008), and particle systems with complex pair interaction (Krapivsky *et al.*, 2010).

The events of species extinction and survival are inherently stochastic. Stochasticity becomes the dominant factor of system evolution, particularly when the number of species becomes very low. This implies that when the fluctuating population size of the system falls below a certain threshold, then the demographic noise (*i.e.,* noise induced by finite population size) drives the system to extinction (Ovaskainen and Meerson, 2010; Dennis *et al.*, 1991).

The theoretical prediction of a population extinction event, therefore, involves the theory of stochastic processes, Ovaskainen and Meerson (2010), Dennis *et al.* (1991). More specifically, the population dynamics are modelled as a stochastic birth-and-death process and the theory predicts the evolution of the probability distribution function of the system state in a multidimensional state space (Kolmogorov or Fokker-Plank equations). The event of population extinction occurs when the system trajectory crosses the surface of a given population threshold in the state space. The extinction time then simply corresponds to the *first-passage time* of the underlying random process. A plethora of theoretical methods exists for studying the first-passage time problems; see Gardiner (2010) and Redner (2001). Depending on the complexity of the underlying birth-and-death process, the first-passage time approach may lead to closed-from analytical expressions, which relate the extinction time and the parameters of the model. These expressions can be used as a foundation for development of an algorithm for prediction of population extinction, based on the temporal observation of the species count, followed by the estimation of system model parameters.

For the case of no interaction among the species (*i.e.,* a single species in isolation), it has been found that the population size undergoes a random walk, leading to the inverse Gaussian distribution of extinction times; see Lande and Orzack (1988) and Dennis *et al.* (1991). For the case of structured populations consisting of multiple interactive groups, the estimation of extinction time becomes much more challenging. This is due to the temporal correlations between population groups, which drives a complex and versatile set of extinction scenarios (Ovaskainen and Meerson, 2010). Close to extinction, the system exhibits strong fluctuations and becomes analytically intractable. The conventional approach to overcome this difficulty is to invoke simplifying assumptions (*e.g.,* moments closure scheme or mean-field theories (Allen, 2003; Holyoak *et al.*, 2000). While these assumptions lead to a tractable problem, they often have limited validity—for comments on inconsistency of the moment closure approach, see Gardiner (2010); or impose a significant constraint on model parameters—*e.g.,,* diffusion approximation is valid only for large population sizes (Gardiner, 2010). A novel approach to this problem was reported in recent studies, which demonstrated that the longtime phenomenology of population extinction can be described by methods borrowed from quantum mechanics (Goldenfeld, 1984; Dykman *et al.*, 1994; Doering *et al.*, 2005). These methods recently helped to understand the extinction of dynamic systems consisting of two interacting species [*e.g.,* SIS compartmental model of an epidemic outbreak (Ovaskainen and Meerson, 2010) and predator-prey model (Parker and Kamenev, 2009, 2010).

In this chapter, we go a step further and study the extinction of a complex biological system consisting of many species that compete for a finite set of resources. The problem is cast in the framework of a stochastic multiple-predator single-prey Lotka-Volterra (LV) system (Rabinovich *et al.*, 2008). In this context, the prey population plays the role of a finite supply of food or resources, for which the predators compete. Extinction is the event when either the resources are exhausted or all the competing predators die out.

The theoretical predictions of extinction time build upon the previous work of Parker and Kamenev (2009, 2010) for the classical LV system (one predator and one prey). We extend these studies by introducing a concept of an aggregated predator, whose effect in the multipredator system is approximately equivalent to the combined effect of all predators. This coarse approximation of the multipredator LV system removes all the irrelevant information on predators (including their total number and the specifics of each group) resulting in a significant simplification of estimation algorithms (the reduced state space and independence of the variety of predator-species).

The chapter also develops a practical algorithm for forecasting extinction. Given noisy and sporadic observations of the prey count (the quantity of resources), it is capable of predicting the timing of extinction event in a probabilistic manner. Remarkably, in doing so, it does not have to know how many predators are competing for resources. The first phase of this algorithm is parameter estimation: observations of the quantity of finite resources are used to estimate the unknown system parameters via a Bayesian method known as *particle Markov Chain Monte Carlo (pMCMC)* (Andrieu *et al.*, 2010). These estimated parameters, along with the analytical expressions derived here, are then used in the second phase of the algorithm to compute the probability density function (PDF) of extinction time. Validation of the resulting, theoretically predicted, PDF of extinction time is carried out numerically against the actual extinction statistics.

2 A MODEL OF COMPETING SPECIES

As a model of competing species, we adopt the multipredator, single-prey LV system. Let x be the prey population that acts as the food for n competing predators y_i, $i = 1, \cdots, n$. Assuming that the population sizes are continuous-valued and the system evolution is deterministic, it can be described by $n + 1$ ordinary differential equations (Korobeinikov, 1999):

$$\dot{x} = \alpha x \left(1 - \sum_{i=1}^{n} \beta_i \gamma_i \right) \tag{25.1}$$

$$\dot{y}_i = \beta_i x y_i - \gamma_i y_i \tag{25.2}$$

for $\alpha, \beta_i, \gamma_i > 0$ and $i = 1, \cdots, n$. In this model, the prey species reproduces at the rate α, while the predator species i die (by natural causes) at rate γ_i. By consuming the prey, predator i reproduces at the rate β_i. Note that according to this model, predator species do not interact directly; *i.e.,* they do not target each other. Each predator is thus characterized by the survival capacity (fitness) β_i/γ_i. Korobeinikov (1999) showed that an unsuccessful predator, with the smallest survival capacity, will be extinct in finite time. However, the overall LV system [Eqs. (25.1)–(25.2)] is stable, providing that all survival capacities are different. The system [Eqs. (25.1)–(25.2)], with the state space $(x, y_1, \cdots, y_n)$, has $n + 1$ equilibria: the trivial one at the origin, and n solutions in coordinate planes $x - y_i$, given by: $\left(\dfrac{\gamma_1}{\beta_1}, \dfrac{\alpha}{\beta_1}, 0, \cdots, 0 \right)$, $\left(\dfrac{\gamma_2}{\beta_2}, 0, \dfrac{\alpha}{\beta_2}, 0, \cdots, 0 \right)$, $\cdots$, $\left(\dfrac{\gamma_n}{\beta_n}, 0, \cdots, 0, \dfrac{\alpha}{\beta_n} \right)$.

An extinction event (in this case, when either the prey becomes extinct or all the competing predators die out) can happen only if the system is modelled in a discrete-stochastic manner (Ullah and Wolkenhauer, 2011). For this purpose, let us represent the single-prey, multipredator LV system (abbreviated to LV-1n) by a system of $2n + 1$ biochemical reactions:

$$X \xrightarrow{\alpha} 2X \tag{25.3}$$

$$X + Y_i \xrightarrow{\beta_i} 2Y_i \tag{25.4}$$

$$Y_i \xrightarrow{\gamma_i} 0 \tag{25.5}$$

for $i = 1, \cdots, n$. Stochastic fluctuations (demographic noise) in the LV-1n system [Eqs. (25.3)–(25.5)] will inevitably force it to extinction, regardless of the initial count of species and the values of rate parameters $\alpha, \beta_1, \cdots, \beta_n, \gamma_1, \cdots, \gamma_n$.

Figure 25.1 shows two trajectories of the LV-1n system for $n = 2$ in the (x, y_1, y_2) space, using parameters $\alpha = 15$, $\beta_1 = 0.02$, $\beta_2 = 0.015$, $\gamma_1 = 5$ and $\gamma_2 = 4$ with initial conditions $x(0) = 150$, $y_1(0) = 225$ and $y_2(0) = 112$. The plot in Figure 25.1(a) is generated using the continuous-deterministic model [Eqs. (25.1)–(25.2)]; note that the population of the second predator gradually dies out due to its lesser survival capacity; the system reaches an equilibrium in the form of a closed orbit in the $(x, y_1, 0)$ plane, describing the stable periodic oscillations of the first predator and the prey. The trajectory in Figure 25.1(b) is created using the discrete-stochastic model [Eqs. (25.3)–(25.5)], implemented using the Gillespie algorithm (Gillespie, 1977; Ullah and Wolkenhauer, 2011). Note that extinction happens when the trajectory touches one of the axes of the state space (x, y_1, y_2).

3 DENSITY FUNCTION OF EXTINCTION TIME

In order to derive the PDF of extinction time for the LV-1n system, first we conceptually reduce the original model given by Eqs. (25.1)–(25.2) in the continuous-deterministic form or [Eqs. (25.3)–(25.5)] in the discrete-stochastic form, by introducing an aggregated predator y. Then the original LV-1n model [Eqs. (25.1)–(25.2)] can be mapped to the classical LV-11 model with one prey and one predator (*i.e.*, with $n = 1$) as follows:

$$\dot{x} = \alpha x(1 - \beta y) \tag{25.6}$$

$$\dot{y} = \beta xy - \gamma y. \tag{25.7}$$

Similarly, Eqs. (25.3)–(25.5) can be represented by three reactions:

$$X \xrightarrow{\alpha} 2X, \; X + Y \xrightarrow{\beta} 2Y, \; Y \xrightarrow{\gamma} 0. \tag{25.8}$$

Note that we have introduced the effective parameters β and γ of the aggregated predator y, which are related to the (unknown) original parameters $\beta_i, \gamma_i, i = 1, \cdots, n$.

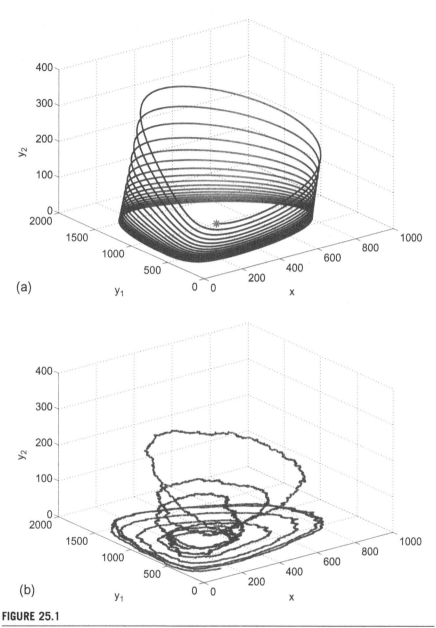

(a)

(b)

FIGURE 25.1

Trajectory of the single-prey, two-predator LV system, with parameters $\alpha = 15$, $\beta_1 = 0.02$, $\beta_2 = 0.015$, $\gamma_1 = 5$, $\gamma_2 = 4$ and initial state $x(0) = 150$, $y_1(0) = 225$ and $y_2(0) = 112$: (a) deterministic model [Eqs. (25.1)–(25.2)]; (b) stochastic model (with demographic noise) [Eqs. (25.3)–(25.5)]. The red asterisk marks the initial state of the system. Extinction occurs when the random system trajectory hits one of the axes.

For the classic LV-11 model with a single predator [*cf.* Eq. (25.8)], analytical results for extinction time exist. According to Parker and Kamenev (2009, 2010), the PDF of the rescaled dimensionless extinction time $\tilde{T} = T/\tau$ can be presented in terms of a parameter-free inverse Gaussian distribution (note that the standard inverse Gaussian distribution, derived as the first-passage time of the Brownian motion with a drift, has two parameters):

$$P\left(\tilde{T}\right) = \frac{a}{\sqrt{\pi \tilde{T}^3}} exp\left[-\left(\tilde{T} - a\right)^2 / \tilde{T}\right],\tag{25.9}$$

where $a \approx 0.5$ is a constant, found empirically and specific to the LV model [Eq. (25.8)]. The characteristic extinction time τ is a function of reaction rates α, β, γ and the initial state of the aggregated system $x(0)$, $y(0)$. It is given by

$$\tau = \frac{1}{\beta} \frac{B(s)}{\epsilon^2 + 1/\epsilon^2},\tag{25.10}$$

where $\epsilon = \sqrt{\alpha/\gamma}$ is the prey-predator asymmetry parameter and the dimensionless function $B(s)$ specifies the dependence on the initial condition $s = G_o/\sqrt{\alpha\gamma}$, with

$$G_o = \beta y(0) - \alpha - \alpha \ln\left(\frac{y(0)\beta}{\alpha}\right) + \beta x(0) - \gamma - \gamma \ln\left(\frac{x(0)\beta}{\gamma}\right).\tag{25.11}$$

$B(s)$ is approximately given by

$$B(s) \approx \frac{1 + Qs^2}{1 + Qs\cosh(s)},\tag{25.12}$$

with $Q(\epsilon) = \left(\epsilon^2 + \frac{1}{\epsilon}\right)/\left(\epsilon + \frac{1}{\epsilon}\right)$.

In summary, we can theoretically predict the PDF of extinction time T of the population system with competing predator species if we can determine the characteristic time τ of the equivalent LV-11 model. Since τ is the known function of reaction rates α, β, γ and the initial conditions $x(0)$ and $y(0)$, our next task is to compute the estimates of these quantities [*i.e.*, $\hat{\alpha}, \hat{\beta}, \hat{\gamma}, \hat{x}(0), \hat{y}(0)$]. Estimation needs to be carried out using the noisy counts of prey species (food, resources) collected occasionally during an observation period.

4 ESTIMATION OF PARAMETERS

Let an observation (count) of prey species of the LV-1n system at time t_k be denoted as z_k. Observations are modeled as random draws from the Poisson distribution whose parameter is the true count of prey species at time t_k. Let us denote all observations collected during the observation period as a time series $z_{1:K} = \{z_k\}_{1 \leq k \leq K}$, with index k referring to the sampling time t_k. Note that prediction is carried *after* the observation period; that is, starting from time t_K, when the last observation z_K is reported. This means that the initial time for prediction in Eq. (25.11)—that is, $t = 0$ —refers to time t_K. Hence, we are after the estimates $\hat{x}(t_K), \hat{y}(t_K)$, in addition to $\hat{\alpha}, \hat{\beta}, \hat{\gamma}$.

Parameter estimation is carried out in the Bayesian framework assuming the reduced LV-11 model. Let $\boldsymbol{\theta} = [\alpha\ \beta\ \gamma]^T$ denote the unknown parameter vector and $\boldsymbol{x}_t = [x(t)\ y(t)]^T$ the (unknown) state vector of the LV-11 system during the observation interval; *i.e.*, $t_1 \leq t \leq t_K$. The goal in the Bayesian framework is to compute the posterior distribution $p(\boldsymbol{\theta}, \boldsymbol{x}_{t_1 \leq t \leq t_K})$, which provides the complete probabilistic description of all unknown quantities. From this posterior, one can extract the marginal distributions $p(\boldsymbol{\theta}|z_{1:K})$ and $p(\boldsymbol{x}_{t_K}|z_{1:K})$, and subsequently point estimates $\hat{\alpha}, \hat{\beta}, \hat{\gamma}, \hat{x}(t_K), \hat{y}(t_K)$, which are required for the computation of the characteristic time τ. Since the state of the LV system is time-varying and its dynamics is highly nonlinear, estimation will be carried out using the sequential Monte Carlo method. However, the straightforward sequential Monte Carlo estimation on the joint space $(\boldsymbol{\theta}, \boldsymbol{x}_{t_1 \leq t \leq t_K})$, where part of the state vector are fixed parameters, is known to be inefficient due to "particle degeneracy" (Liu and West, 2001). Instead, it is more efficient to perform estimation separately on $\boldsymbol{\theta}$ and $\boldsymbol{x}_{t_1 \leq t \leq t_K}|\boldsymbol{\theta}$ spaces, using the pMCMC method (Andrieu *et al.*, 2010).

For a given $\boldsymbol{\theta}$, estimation of the posterior $p(\boldsymbol{x}_t|z_{1:K}, \boldsymbol{\theta})$ in interval $t_1 \leq t \leq t_K$ is carried out using the standard particle filter (PF) (Ristic *et al.*, 2004; Cappé *et al.*, 2007), developed for the stochastic dynamic model specified by reactions [Eq. (25.8)]. The main feature of this PF is that it uses the Gillespie algorithm (Gillespie, 1977; Ullah and Wolkenhauer, 2011) as an exact discrete-time stochastic simulation method to predict the transition of particles from t_k to t_{k+1}. In the update step of the PF, the Poisson distribution acts as the likelihood function of observations $z_{1:K}$. The PF performs two roles. First, at each time t (where $t_1 \leq t \leq t_K$), it provides a random sample $\left\{ x_t^{(1)}, \cdots, x_t^{(N)} \right\}$, which approximates the posterior $p(\boldsymbol{x}_t|z_{1:K}, \boldsymbol{\theta})$; here, N is the number of random samples or particles (recall that only the last random sample, corresponding to the time t_K, is required for the estimation of τ). Second, the PF provides an estimate of the marginal likelihood $g(z_{1:K}|\boldsymbol{\theta})$ by integrating out the state $\boldsymbol{x}_t$ at each time step (Cappé *et al.*, 2007). This marginal likelihood $g(z_{1:K}|\boldsymbol{\theta})$ is required in the MCMC Metropolis-Hastings (MH) scheme (Robert and Casella, 2004) for estimation of the posterior $p(\boldsymbol{\theta}|z_{1:K})$ according to the Bayes rule: $p(\boldsymbol{\theta}|z_{1:K}) \propto g(z_{1:K}|\boldsymbol{\theta})\pi(\boldsymbol{\theta})$. Here, $\pi(\boldsymbol{\theta})$ is the prior distribution of the parameter vector $\boldsymbol{\theta}$ (reflects our prior knowledge of rate parameters). Thus, the PF plays a double role in the pMCMC method. Note that at every iteration of the MH algorithm, it is necessary to run the PF in order to obtain the estimate of $g(z_{1:K}|\boldsymbol{\theta})$. The output of the MH algorithm is a random sample of parameter vectors, $\left\{ \boldsymbol{\theta}^{(j)} \right\}_{1 \leq j \leq M}$, which approximates the posterior $p(\boldsymbol{\theta}|z_{1:K})$; here, M is the number of samples generated by the MH algorithm.

5 NUMERICAL RESULTS

A numerical study was carried out for the LV-1n system with $n=3$ competing predators. Figure 25.2 shows the count of species for the considered LV-13 system during an observation period that lasts 3 units of time. Red squares indicate the

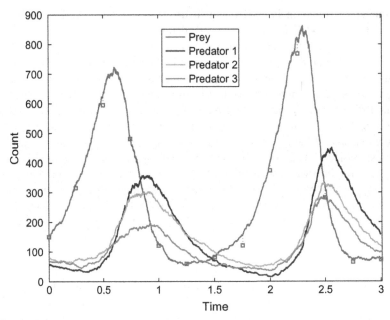

FIGURE 25.2

Input data for the numerical study: the count of prey (red line) and three competing predators (blue, green, and black lines); the red squares are the observations of prey species used by the pMCMC algorithm to estimate the parameters.

observations of prey species collected every 0.25 units of time. The parameters of this LV-13 system are $\alpha=5$, $\beta_1=0.15$, $\beta_2=\beta_3=0.01$, $\gamma_1=4$, and $\gamma_2=\gamma_3=3$. The state vector at the final observation time $t_K=3$ is $x_o=[x(t_K)\ y_1(t_K)\ y_2(t_K)\ y_3(t_K)]^T=[73\ 161\ 120\ 101]^T$.

Figure 25.3 shows (a) the empirical PDF and (b) the corresponding cumulative distribution function (CDF) of extinction time (black solid lines). The PDF was obtained by the kernel density estimation (Silverman, 1986), based on 1000 samples of extinction time. The samples of extinction time were generated by running the LV-13 system with true parameters $\alpha=5$, $\beta_1=0.15$, $\beta_2=\beta_3=0.01$, $\gamma_1=4$, $\gamma_2=\gamma_3=3$ and identical initial state $x(0)$, until either the prey count or the sum count of all predators equals zero.

Figure 25.3 also shows 100 overlaid theoretical PDFs and CDFs computed using 100 pMCMC-generated samples of estimates $\hat{\alpha},\hat{\beta},\hat{\gamma},\ \hat{x}(0),\hat{y}(0)$. The number of particles in the PF of the pMCMC was $N=1000$. The MH algorithm of pMCMC was run $M=1000$ times, but only the last 100 samples were used in plotting the theoretical PDFs of extinction time. We can observe from Figure 25.3 that there is a good match between the theoretically predicted PDFs/CDFs and the empirical PDF/CDF, which verifies the proposed method. The theoretically predicted PDFs/CDFs are computed

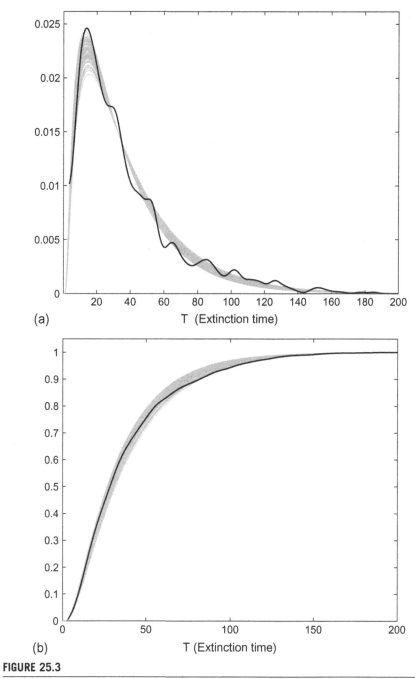

(a)

(b)

FIGURE 25.3

PDFs (a) and CDFs (b) of extinction time: empirical (black solid lines) and theoretically predicted (blue lines) for each of the 100 pMCMC-generated samples.

without knowledge of the number of predator species competing for the prey, because all predator species are treated as one aggregated predator.

6 SUMMARY

This chapter described an extinction process in a complex biological system with competition. To model this process, we used a generalized version of the stochastic LV system (multiple-predator and single-prey). Given noisy and sporadic observations of the prey count only, collected during an observation period, the proposed method is capable of predicting the timing of extinction in a probabilistic manner. Remarkably, in doing so, this method does not require prior knowledge of how many predators are competing for food (*i.e.,* prey). The key idea is to treat the competing predator species as a single, aggregated predator, for which the theoretical PDF of extinction time has been derived using the mathematical tools of the first-passage-time studies.

The LV system is used as a canonical model in many areas of population biology and, by a well-known mapping procedure (Bomze, 1995), can be related to the replicator equation that is an important part of a modeling framework in evolutional studies (Hofbauer and Sigmund, 1998). From this perspective, the presented study can be seen as a step toward the goal of long-term prediction of abrupt changes (catastrophic events) in complex dynamic stochastic systems, operating under supply-demand constraints (*e.g.,* emerging epidemic, virus mutation, stock-market crash, network traffic jam).

ACKNOWLEDGMENTS

The authors would like to thank Alex Kamenev for helpful and stimulating discussions.

REFERENCES

Allen, L.J.S., 2003. Risk of population extinction due to demographic stochasticity in population models'. Comments Theor. Biol. 8, 433–454.

Andrieu, C., Doucet, A., Holenstein, R., 2010. Particle Markov chain Monte Carlo methods. J. R. Statis. Soc. B 72 (Part 3), 269–342.

Bartlett, M.S., 1961. Stochastic Population Models in Ecology and Epidemiology. Wiley, New York.

Bartlett, M.S., 2000. Stochastic Epidemic Models and Their Statistical Analysis. Springer, New York.

Bomze, I.M., 1995. Lotka-Volterra equation and replicator dynamics: new issues in classification'. Biol. Cybern. 72, 447–453.

Brook, B.W., O'Grady, J.J., Chapman, A.P., Burgman, M.A., Akakaya, H.R., Frankham, R., 2000. Predictive accuracy of population viability analysis in conservation biology'. Nature 404, 385–387.

Cappé, O., Godsill, S.J., Moulines, E., 2007. An overview of existing methods and recent advances in sequential Monte Carlo. Proc. IEEE 95 (5), 899–924.

Davidson, A.D., Hamilton, M.J., Boyer, A.G., Brown, J.H., Ceballos, G., 2009. Multiple ecological pathways to extinction in mammals. Proc. Natl. Acad. Sci. U. S. A.. 106(26).

Dennis, B., Munholland, P.L., Scott, J.M., 1991. Estimation of growth and extinction parameters for endangered species. Ecol. Monogr. 61, 115–143.

Doering, C.R., Sargsyan, K.V., Sander, L.M., 2005. Extinction times for birth-death processes: exact results, continuum asymptotics, and the failure of the Fokker-Planck approximation. Multiscale. Model. Simul. 3, 283–299.

Dykman, M.I., Mori, E., Ross, J., Hunt, P.M., 1994. Large fluctuations and optimal paths in chemical kinetics. J. Chem. Phys. 100, 5735.

Gardiner, C., 2010. Stochastic Methods: A Handbook for the Natural and Social Sciences, fourth ed. Springer, Berlin.

Gillespie, D.T., 1977. Exact stochastic simulation of coupled chemical reactions. J. Phys. Chem. 81 (25), 2340–2361.

Goldenfeld, N., 1984. Kinetics of a model for nucleation-controlled polymer crystal growth. J. Phys. A 17, 2807–2821.

Hofbauer, J., Sigmund, K., 1998. Evolutionary Games and Population 0044ynamics. Cambridge University Press.

Holyoak, M., Lawler, S.P., Crowley, P.H., 2000. Predicting extinction: progress with an individual-based model of protozoan predators and prey. Ecology 81, 3312–3329.

Korobeinikov, A., 1999. Global properties of the three-dimensional predator-prey Lotka-Volterra systems'. J. Appl. Math. Decis. Sci. 3 (2), 155–162.

Krapivsky, P.L., Redner, S., Naim, E.B., 2010. A Kinetic View of Statistical Physics. Cambridge University Press.

Ladle, R.J., 2009. Forecasting extinctions: uncertainties and limitations. Diversity 1, 133–150.

Lande, R., Orzack, S.H., 1988. Extinction dynamics of age structured populations in a fluctuating environment. Proc. Natl. Acad. Sci. U. S. A. 85, 7418–7421.

Lande, R., Engen, S., Saether, B.E., 2003. Stochastic Population Dynamics in Ecology and Conservation. Oxford University Press.

Liu, J., West, M., 2001. Combined parameter and state estimation in simulation-based filtering. In: Doucet, A., de Freitas, F., Gordon, N. (Eds.), Sequential Monte Carlo Methods in Practice. Springer, chapter 10.

McLaughlin, J.F., Hellmann, J.J., Boggs, C.L., Ehrlich, P.R., 2002. Climate change hastens population extinctions. Proc. Natl. Acad. Sci. U. S. A. 99, 6070–6074.

Ovaskainen, O., Meerson, B., 2010. Stochastic models of population extinction. Trends Ecol. Evol. 25, 643–652.

Parker, M., Kamenev, A., 2009. Extinction in the Lotka-Volterra model. Phys. Rev. E 80, 021129.

Parker, M., Kamenev, A., 2010. Mean extinction time in predator-pray model. J. Stat. Phys. 141, 201–216.

Rabinovich, M.I., Huerta, R., Varona, P., Afraimovich, V.S., 2008. Transient cognitive dynamics, metastability and decision making. PLoS Comput. Biol.. 4(5).

Redner, S., 2001. A Guide to First Passage Processes. Cambridge University Press.

Ristic, B., Arulampalam, S., Gordon, N., 2004. Beyond the Kalman Filter: Particle Filters for Tracking Applications. Artech House.

Robert, C.P., Casella, G., 2004. Monte Carlo Statistical Methods, second ed. Springer.

Silverman, B., 1986. Density Estimation for Statistical and Data Analysis. Chapman and Hall.

Sprott, J.C., 2004. Competition with evolution in ecology and finance. Phys. Lett. A 325, 329–333.

Ullah, M., Wolkenhauer, O., 2011. Stochastic Approaches for Systems Biology. Springer.

Wilkinson, D.J., 2013. Stochastic Modelling for Systems Biology, second ed. Taylor & Francis Group.

Methodologies for the Diagnosis of the Main Behavioral Syndromes for Parkinson's Disease with Bayesian Belief Networks

26

Iyad Zaarour[1], Ali Saad[2,3], Abbass Zein Eddine[2], Mohammad Ayache[3], François Guerin[2], Paul Bejjani[4], and Dimitri Lefebvre[2]

Doctoral School of Science and Technology, Lebanese University, Beirut, Lebanon[1]

Laboratory of GREAH (Groupe de Recherche en Electrotechnique et Automatique), University of Le Havre, Le Havre, France[2]

Islamic University of Lebanon, Khaldeh, Lebanon[3]

Associate Professor of Neurology, Director of the Parkinson's Disease and Memory Center, Notre Dame de Secours Hospital, Byblos, Lebanon[4]

1 INTRODUCTION

Parkinson's disease (PD) is a progressive neurological disorder caused by the loss of dopaminergic and other subcortex neurons. It affects motor control, such as walking, body balancing, writing, and speaking (Morris and Iansek,1996) (Saad *et al.*,2012), and it causes chronic and progressive loss of muscle control. The distinctive signs of PD include tremor in the hands, swallowing and speech difficulties, and emotional fluctuations (Noth *et al.*, 2011; Aarsland *et al.*, 1999). The authors (Muller *et al.*, 2001) (Rosenbek and Jones, 2007) (Leopold and Kagel, 1997) suggest that anywhere from 40% to 95% of persons with PD have motor speech disorder. PD is also characterized by a number of motor and nonmotor complications and symptoms that have a significant impact on the quality of life. One usual PD symptom is freezing, which may occur during gait, speaking, or a repetitive movement like handwriting. The incidence of occurrence of PD has been reported as 1% of the population over the age of 50, and 10% of occurrence over the age of 65 (Okuma and Yanagisawa, 2008). It has been shown that 80% of PD patients suffer from movement disorders, 10% with wild symptoms, while 80% of severely affected patients experience freezing. Over half of patients with PD eventually develop freezing of gait (FoG) (Nutt et al., 2011). Furthermore, there is no objective diagnosis for PD; since there is no specific and decisive laboratory tests that detect PD, the disease must be diagnosed based on clinical criteria (Jankovic, 2008).

This study describes reliable methodologies for diagnosing and detecting multiple PD syndromes based on Bayesian belief network (BBN) formalism. More specifically, the syndromes that we tackled consist of (1) FoG episodes, (2) handwriting disorders, and (3) speech difficulties. The methodology of the FoG modeling approach consists of data acquired from acceleration sensors placed on the ankle, knee, and hip of PD patients during walking, and used to search for FoG diagnosis and causality in the context of Bayesian naïve classifier (BNC); For handwriting and speech skills (HSS), we used digitizer tablets and microphone headsets to acquire kinematic and speech features from PD traces and sentence phonations. The structure components of BBN consist of a layered architecture and hidden variable hierarchy, and a probabilistic inference is applied in an unsupervised classification manner.

The second section of this chapter is about FoG diagnosis. The third section concerns the diagnosis of handwriting and speech syndromes. The fourth section illustrates how heterogeneous syndromes may be combined and integrated with a common architecture in the framework of modeling and diagnosing PD syndromes. Finally, the fifth section presents our conclusions and planned future work in this area.

2 DIAGNOSIS OF FoG

FoG can be defined as "a brief, episodic reduction of forward progression of the feet despite the intention to walk," and is often described by patients as if their feet are glued to the floor for a short period of time (Giladi et al., 1992). FoG is a phenomenon that affects the gait most commonly, in the form of an intermittent failure to initiate or maintain walking that is often associated with shaky legs or sudden immobility (Saad et al., 2013). FoG aspects of PD do not respond well to dopaminergic drugs, as it is one of the symptoms that often result from nondopaminergic pathology (Okuma and Yanagisawa, 2008). FoG is one of the most common, disturbing, and least understood symptoms in advanced stages of PD; it often results in falls (Bloem et al., 2004) and consequent injuries impairing quality of life. Its unpredictable occurrence and sensitivity to external factors such as medication, environmental triggers, or cues make it hard to detect FoG in a clinic or research laboratory (Giladi and Nieuwboer, 2008). Although some studies have suggested that longer duration of dopaminergic treatment is associated with FoG, the disease progression alone may be responsible for its development (Okuma and Yanagisawa, 2008). FoG occurs more frequently in men than in women, especially those who report tremor symptoms (Moore et al. (2007)). Accurate detection and rating of both the severity and impact of FoG is therefore important (Snijders et al., 2008; Fahn, 1995). A gold standard measurement and diagnosis of FoG is currently unavailable.

Our proposal is a modeling approach that focuses on a specific class of the Probabilistic Graphical Model (PGM), the directed[1] one (*i.e.,* BBN).The followed approach consists of the following: (1) assessing the framework of the BBN model, we tried to identify if this is a traditional BBN case (Pearl, 1986, 1988) or a causal one (Glymour and Cooper, 1988; Pearl, 2000); (2) by means of the assessed model, a classification tool is built to judge the FoG episodes of PD patients. This classification model can be inferred to diagnose/forecast issues based on Internet data that is acquired from acceleration sensors placed on the ankle, knee, and hip of PD patients during walking. In the next section, we will briefly describe our methodology, which consists of preparation of the data, extracting features, and a description of the modeling approach dimensions that are based on FoG causality and the diagnosis of FoG by BNC.

2.1 DATA ACQUISITION AND PREPARATION

In previous research, Marc Bächlin and colleagues developed an assistant for PD patients that detects FoG by analyzing frequency components inherent in the body movements. They used measurements from acceleration sensors worn on the body (Bächlin *et al.*, 2010). Their detection algorithm was based on the principle illustrated by Moore *et al.* (2008) that introduced a freeze index (FI) to evaluate the gait condition of PD patients. The *FI* is a ratio defined as the power in the "freeze" band [3–8 Hz] divided by the power in the "locomotor" band [0.5–3 Hz]. The FoG detection is performed by defining a freeze threshold, where values above it are considered as FoG events.

To confirm and improve this approach, a multisensor device has been proposed in our previous work (Saad *et al.*, 2014). This device acquires heterogeneous signals (*i.e.,* from different types of sensors). The integrated sensors in the device are the goniometer, the telemeter, and the accelerometer. The variation of the step distance is measured using the telemeter sensor. From the PD expert's point of view, this measurement defines the FoG phenomenon, since during a FoG episode, the patient's step distance decreases significantly while maintaining movement. From the signals of the sensors, new features that are related to FoG were introduced to the FoG domain. Designing a system that is able to detect and diagnose a patient's FoG episodes accurately would lead to discovering the actions that must be taken to overcome and correct each FoG episode.

The approach has been tested with simulation data that are generated by imitating the behavior of PD patients in normal walking and during FoG. The scenario is to wear the multisensor device, then walk with normal short steps for 10 s, and then simulating FoG for 5 s, and finally another 5 s of normal short steps. The short steps

---

[1]The alternative classes of the PGM are undirected Markov networks and hybrid graphs (Lauritzen, 1996); those families of classes are better adapted to statistical physics and computer vision (Messaoud, 2012).

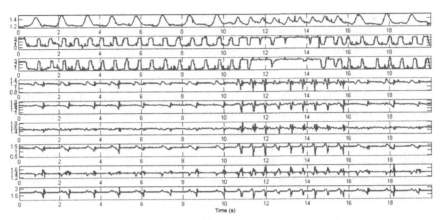

FIGURE 26.1

Signals (V) from all sensors during a randomly picked run. Starting from top to bottom: goniometer, upper telemeter, lower telemeter, x-axis shin accelerometer, y-axis shin accelerometer, z-axis shin accelerometer, x-axis foot accelerometer, y-axis foot accelerometer, z-axis foot accelerometer.

simulated the normal gait of PD patients. The mentioned scenario is repeated 10 times in order to extract the optimal features where abrupt changes in signals occur during FoG. Figure 26.1 shows signals from all sensors during one run of the above-mentioned scenario.

Figure 26.2a shows a significant increasing of the mean frequency for the goniometer when an episode of FoG occurred. As for FI, one should notice that all previous studies applied this feature only with acceleration sensors. But our results show that this feature can be used to detect FoG using the goniometer as well. Signals of both upper and lower telemeter sensors showed a significant change of their mean during FoG episodes (Figure 26.2b). This result is very advantageous, especially in order to design a system for online detection of FoG, since the mean of the telemeter signal, which is a time domain feature, needs less computational time. Thus, an online detection system can be implemented with a minimal latency period. For the shin acceleration data, the features that allow to detect FoG in both the x- and y-axis are the standard deviation (time domain), power spectral density (PSD) power, and FI (frequency domain). It is worth mentioning that FI has the most significant change during FoG when compared to the other two indicators (Figure 26.2c). On the other hand, the z-axis of the shin accelerometer shows less significance than the other two axes. With respect to the foot accelerometer (Figure 26.2d), FI is the best indicator that can be used to detect FoG. Furthermore, standard deviation and PSD power can be considered, but they have much less significance. The changes of all three indicators in the foot accelerometer during FoG are less than those in the shin accelerometer. Positioning the accelerometer on the shin is better than placing it on the foot. Table 26.1 summarizes the best indicators for each sensor that can be used to detect FoG.

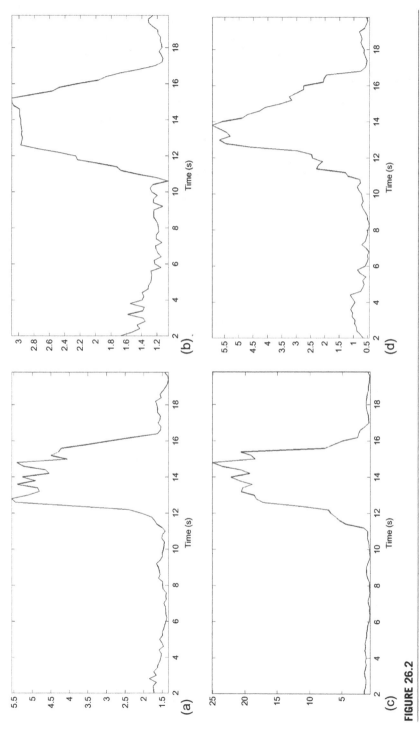

FIGURE 26.2

Different features as functions of time: (a) mean frequency (Hz) of goniometer data; (b) mean (V) of telemeter data; (c) FI of x-axis shin acceleration data; (d) FI of x-axis foot acceleration data.

To conclude, this study confirms that the FI is a relevant feature for FoG detection. It also highlights the benefit to introduce simple features as the mean frequency of the goniometer for real-time detection. Finally, it shows that the multisensor device can be used to improve detection of FoG episodes. Referring to the data obtained by Bächlin *et al.* (2010) from 10 PD patients with FI, we incorporated these values into our probabilistic model in an attempt to predict upcoming FoG episodes.

Table 26.1 Summary of All Indicators That Best Detect Fog

Feature	Best Indicators (*with less significance)
Goniometer	Mean frequency
	FI*
Upper and lower telemeter	Mean
	Standard deviation*
Shin accelerometer	FI
	Standard deviation*
	PSD power*
Foot accelerometer	FI
	Standard deviation*
	PSD power*

2.2 CAUSALITY AND METHODOLOGY

Inferring the causal structure of a set of random variables is a challenging task. In the causality domain, the variables of interest are not just statistically associated with each other, and yet there is a causal relationship between them. The famous slogan "correlation does not imply causation" is recognized and seems approved by researchers in empirical and theoretical sciences. Formerly, Spirtes *et al.*, 1990 stated that "one of the common aims of empirical research in social sciences is to determine the causal relations among a set of variables, and to estimate the relative importance of various causal factors." Recently, the philosophical wisdom of this quote is broadly discussed, specifically in the medical and health fields, more precisely in the context of symptoms/disease episodes (Russo and Williamson, 2007; Frumkin, 2006; Lagiou, Adam, and Trichopoulos, 2005; Thagard, 1998).

In particular, Lagiou *et al.* (2005) stated: "A factor is a cause of a certain disease when alterations in the frequency or intensity of this factor, without concomitant alterations in any other factor, are followed by changes in the frequency of occurrence of the disease, after the passage of a certain time period (incubation, latency, or induction period)." In order to highlight the causal trends of our FoG problem, and from an epidemiological point of view, we will explicitly illustrate the FoG model (Figure 26.3) by applying the Hills Criteria of Causation (Hill, 1956). Hill's work was recently validated by Kundi (2006) as a valuable tool, since both mechanistic and probabilistic aspects were considered. The first step for examining our causal proposal was to test if our study is consistent with Hill's criteria. Table 26.2 summarizes the nine criteria defined by Hill and the observations when applying it to the FoG case with respect to FI. It can be clearly observed that not all of the criteria hold in our case, where criteria 4 and 9 did not apply.

Table 26.2 Observations Based on Hill's Criteria for FoG

Criterion	FoG Correlation with FI
1. Strength of association	As FoG episodes occur, the value of the FI in higher than that when normal gait is happening.
2. Temporality	FoG in the vast majority of cases occurs when the FI increases.
3. Consistency	Several studies were applied on different patients, which produced the same results. The relationship also appeared for different genders.
4. Theoretical plausibility	We do not have an explained biological theory stating a theoretical relationship between FI and FoG.
5. Coherence	The conclusion (that accretion of FI causes FoG) made sense, given the knowledge about the algorithm for calculating the FI with respect to FoG occurrence.
6. Specificity in the causes	FI is one of the clinical features (not the only one) that can be used to predict FoG.
7. Dose response relationship	Extracted data showed a direct relationship between the value of the FI and the occurrence of FoG episodes.
8. Experimental evidence	The experimental data collected clinically from patients made certain that FoG occurs when the FI increases.
9. Analogy	In this case, contrasting similar phenomena could not be applied because the approach of detecting causality of FoG is novel.

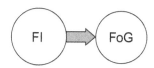

FIGURE 26.3

FoG causal model.

2.3 MODELING WITH BNCs

The first step of our learning protocol is to divide the acceleration data into learning (nine data sets for each different patient) and the rest for testing. Each data set consists of nine signals: the x, y, and z components from the ankle accelerometer, the x, y, and z components from the knee accelerometer, and the x, y, and z components from the hip accelerometer. For each component, FI is calculated. Thus, we built nine BNC models for nine different patients. For this purpose, nine belief network graphs were constructed (Figure 26.4), where the class node (FoG) was the parent of the three FI nodes (FI nodes represented the magnitude of the FI components for each acceleration sensor). Although the data intended to learn each BNC model was divided into 70% learning data and 30% testing data. Continuous variables were discretized based on Akaike's criterion (Song et al., 2011) before learning the BNC structure. The learning experiments were conducted with a random ten fold validation; each fold takes a random 70% from the data set for learning and the remaining 30% for testing.

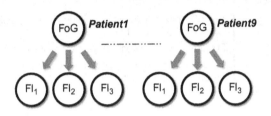

FIGURE 26.4

Nine BNC models for each PD patient.

After learning each fold, a classical confusion matrix was calculated (Table 26.3) using the test data. This table represents the true positives (TP), false positives (FP), false negatives (FN), and true negative (TN). From the confusion matrix, we evaluated three important values: FoG-precision, NoFoG-precision, and Accuracy.

Table 26.3 Confusion Matrix Calculated for Each Random Fold

	Model classification		
Real classification	FoG	True	False
	True	TP	FN
	False	FP	TN

After calculating these values for each fold, we choose the learning that holds the highest three values based on the priority of each value (FoG-precision was the highest priority, followed by NoFoG-precision, and finally Accuracy). After choosing the nine BNC models for nine different patients, the other data sets was introduced to each BNC model as testing data sets for the purpose of testing the degree of generalization of our models.

2.4 RESULTS AND DISCUSSION

Following the learning and testing protocol, data sets were represented by S<patient number>R<test or run number>. It is seen when testing S01R01 (patient 1, first run) that the FoG precision value was apparently high in all nine classifiers. We can see that the best results were for the data sets S01R02 (FoG-precision = 70.67% and NoFoG-precision = 84.74%) and S03R01 (FoG-precision = 73.68% and NoFoG-precision = 79.13%); the first data set was for the same patient but on a different run, while the second data set was for another patient. This finding shows that both patients may be correlated in freezing behavior. As for data set S02R02, some results had low FoG-precision; this may be due to the different walking behavior of patients, knowing that S02R01 (same patient, but different run) showed an acceptable result for NoFoG-precision and a very high result for FoG-precision (92.85%). Table 26.4 presents the average accuracy, FoG-precision, and noFoG-precision for different data sets.

Table 26.4 Average for Accuracy, FoG-Precision and NoFoG-Precision

Average	NoFoG-Precision (%)	FoG-Precision (%)	Accuracy (%)
S01R01	59.07	81.20	60.10
S02R02	85.22	50.31	80.87
S05R02	71.42	39.20	65.10
S06R01	61.23	66.66	61.40
System accuracy	**69.24**	**59.34**	**66.87**

3 DIAGNOSIS OF HANDWRITING AND SPEECH

Handwriting is a very active area of research, bringing together psycholinguists, psychologists, and specialists in motor control and artificial intelligence. It is a complex skill that depends on the maturation and integration of cognitive ability, perceptual and psychometric abilities, and motor control (Sage and Zesiger, 2010; Zaarour et al., 2005, 2004b, p. 78). Also, speaking, as a basic mode of communication, is the most complex motor skill that humans can perform. Disorders of speech and language are the most common symptom of brain disease or injury (Maassen and van Lieshout, 2007). PD is a disorder of the central nervous system that has an effect on controlling muscles; thus, it influences movement, speech, and handwriting of patients (Pahwa, Lyons, and Koller, 2007). The handwriting of a PD patient (PDP) is often characterized by micrographia, a reduction of letter size during continuous writing (Teulings and Stelmach, 1991). It has also been reported that kinematic features (e.g., speed, acceleration, and stroke duration) of handwriting movements are affected by PD (Teulings and Stelmach, 1991; Tucha et al., 2006; Flash et al., 1997; Longstaff et al., 2001). Moreover, Parkinsonian speech is characterized by reduced vocal loudness, monotone, a breathy or hoarse voice, and imprecise hypokinetic articulation (Factor and Weiner, 2008).

3.1 EXPERIMENTAL PROTOCOL

A total of 10 subjects diagnosed with PD were recruited. Using a digitizer tablet, each patient was asked to write four traces: (1) the letter *l* written in cursive manner with one stroke (Figure 26.5, left), (2) the number 8, (3) the infinity symbol (∞), and (4) the sentence "the killing bullet is fast" (Figure 26.5, right). The extracted kinematic parameters that fit to the characteristics of different handwriting traces are the mean velocity, fluidity, fluency, mean pressure, pause in duration, and the number of strokes.

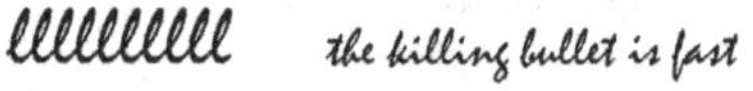

FIGURE 26.5

Trace examples.

The acoustic feature measurements of the PDPs were done by quantifying several vocal phonations. Using a noise-canceling microphone, they were asked to emit a sustained vowel *a* and a short sentence in Arabic. The use of sustained vowel phonations was to assess the degree of vocal symptoms in the acquired voice. We applied the Praat software package, which has been widely and recently used (Rusz *et al.* 2011; Little *et al.*, 2009) as a speech feature extractor, and specifically as a PD speech diagnosis. Features extracted from the vowel included the maximum phonation time (MPT), frequency perturbation (jitter), intensity perturbation (shimmer), and harmonic/noise ratio (HNR). While the standard deviation of the intensity (STD intensity) and the voice breaks were extracted from the phrase.

3.2 CLUSTERING WITH BBNs

Currently, attractive requests of graphical models, particularly in the form of BBN classifiers, can be found in many disciplines, such as finance (risk evaluation and stress test) (Rebonato, 2010; Meucci, 2008), network diagnosis (Khanafar *et al.*, 2008), and for medical applications (Intan and Yuliana, 2011; Sacha, Goodenday, and Cios, 2002; Gong, Zhang and Gao, 2009). BBNs are high-level representation of probability distributions over a set of variables that are used for building a model of the problem domain. It provides a compact and natural representation, an effective inference, and efficient learning (Friedman, 1997; Borgelt, Steinbrecher, and Krus, 2009). Based on BBN framework models—more specifically, the Hierarchical Latent Class (HLC) models anticipated in Zhang and Kocka (2004a), Wang and Zhang (2004), and Zhang (2004) and used in Zaarour *et al.* (2004a, 2005, 2010)— we modeled our problem with HLC. Those are tree-structured BBNs where leaf nodes are observed while internal nodes are hidden. We represented the physiological brain structure (*i.e.*, PPN[2]) by a hidden variable that influences both

---

[2]The pedunculopontine nucleus (PPN) has been highlighted as a target for deep brain stimulation for the treatment of freezing of postural instability and gait disorders in PD and progressive supranuclear palsy (Ramig *et al.*, 2008).

handwriting and speech measuring variables. Continuous variables have been discretized based on Akaike's criterion (Song *et al.*, 2011) before learning the BBN structures.

The fundamental hypothesis published by Zaarour *et al.* (2003, 2004b, p. 78, 2010) assumes that if features of writing (or speech) of a set of PD pupils are similar with respect to a given metric, then these pupils nearly share the same handwriting (or speech) pattern. Part of our work, therefore, aims at identifying and studying patterns by clustering PDPs according to their HSS. Thus, the discovered PD clusters can serve as a fundamental reference for future assistance, such as a motor diagnosis tool based on HSS. We used the EM algorithm, which is a broadly applicable approach to the iterative computation of maximum likelihood (ML) estimates, useful in a variety of incomplete-data problems (McLachlan and Ng, 2009; Han and Kamber, 2006). Typically, the bottom layer is the visible one, containing the observable data variables, and the top layer is the hidden one, representing latent variables.

There are no justified theoretical selection criteria for HLC models in particular and BBNs with latent nodes (Wang and Zhang, 2004; Zhang and Kocka, 2004b). The challenge is that both the BBN structure and the number of clusters partially depend on the neurologist expert knowledge, and the parameters (*i.e.*, conditional probabilities between children and their parents) are estimated by the EM algorithm. The missing data in this challenge are hidden variables treated as a new unlabeled pattern in the outline of unsupervised learning (*i.e.*, clustering). After clustering, we attempted to split the feature values into a set of nominal values based on a percentage scale. This methodology lead to more informative results interpretation for each discovered cluster (Zaarour, Labiche, and Meillier, 2010; Naim *et al.*, 2008). Thus, using the scale shown in Figure 26.6, each feature value was categorized according to five levels.

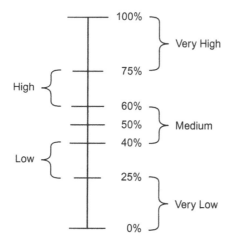

FIGURE 26.6

Percentage scale.

The results of our voice diagnosis model classified patients according to their ability to control their voice, which is related to the extent that they utilize their voice in their daily activity. The results of the handwriting diagnosis models showed that traces l, 8, and ∞ clustered patients according to their ability of controlling the handwriting of each trace. Moreover, the trace phrase clustered patients with respect to their response ability to hand-motor physiotherapy. The result obtained from this trace reveals that clinical physiotherapy leads to more effective improvements for PD patients' motor abilities than if it were done at home (Saad *et al.*, 2012).

4 TOWARD A GLOBAL METHODOLOGY FOR PD

Recent research reports have suggested that modulation of the activity of an area in the brainstem, the pedunculopontine nucleus (PPN) is beneficial in the treatment of axial symptoms (Mazzone *et al.* 2005). Furthermore, PPN is a brainstem locomotive center that is involved in the processing of sensory and behavioral information (Hamani, Moro, and Lozano, 2010). The HSS of PD patients can appear as axial symptoms; thus, it has been assumed in this chapter that PPN influences these symptoms. Therefore, PPN was represented by a hidden variable in the framework of BBN formalism. The hidden variable is evaluated according to HSS measured features that are collected from PDPs via a particular experimental protocol. Our aim is to identify patterns, by clustering PDPs according to their HSS. The discovered PDP clusters represent a coherent unity that is more easily identifiable and more informative at the level of handwriting and acoustic features. These can serve as a fundamental reference for future critical assistance, such as a motor diagnosis tool based on HSS of PDP.

4.1 HANDWRITING AND SPEECH LINK

On the way of building our HLC model, we considered the obtained handwriting and speech patterns (local diagnosis models) as leaf nodes for a new latent class that is a source influencing and acting on both types of patterns (pattern of speech and writing). Each local prototype has its own particular motor abilities represented by hidden discrete variables. This model is conceptualized as a global diagnosis model that deals with each local diagnosis model (Figure 26.7). The only assumption we make is that these abilities are independent but conditionally dependent on a hidden global class, which is the missing data in this case. For this reason, we used the EM algorithm for calculating the conditional probabilities between local classes and the global class, knowing that the previously calculated conditional probabilities between features (handwriting or speech) and their corresponding class was predetermined for the global model.

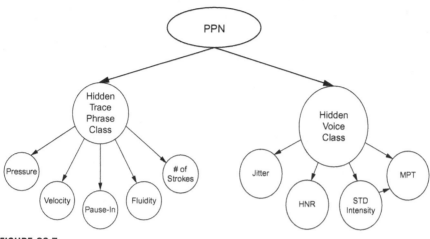

FIGURE 26.7

Handwriting and speech global structure.

4.2 RESULTS AND DISCUSSION

After the modeling and learning phase, the global BBNs were used as an inference tool. For instance, through inference, we can make tradeoffs between traces and voice parameters: What is the probability that a PDP has such difficulty in handwriting, knowing that this person has such a fixed pattern of speech? Our approach had resulted in classification into three groups, as shown in Figure 26.8.

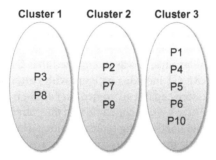

FIGURE 26.8

Clustering results for the global structure.

In Table 26.5, the common feature characteristics of each cluster are summarized, where each feature was characterized according to resulting output measurements in the form of low (L), high (H), and medium (M) with respect to the percentage scale shown in Figure 26.6.

Table 26.5 Common Characteristics of Global Structure Clusters

	Trace I	Trace 8	Trace ∞	Trace Phrase	Voice	
Cluster 1						
Velocity	M	L	L	M	MPT	H
Pause-in	>Zero	H	H	M	Jitter	L
Fluidity	H	L	L	M	HNR	H
Number of Strokes	>One	L	H	M	STD Intensity	H
Pressure				M		
Cluster 2						
Velocity					MPT	M
					Jitter	M
Pause-in	Zero					
Fluidity	V.H		H		HNR	
Number of Strokes	One	L	L		STD Intensity	
Cluster 3						
Velocity	M	H		M	MPT	M
Pause-in				M	Jitter	M
Fluidity				M	HNR	M
Number of Strokes				M	STD Intensity	
Pressure				M		

After tabulating these groups, it was recognized that C1 includes two patients (P3 and P8) (Figure 26.8). C1 includes patients with better acoustic features. On the other hand, patients were capable of controlling all their writing abilities while writing each trace test. Thus, we can conclude that the patients in C1 are capable of controlling their voice and handwriting motor abilities. Probably, based on demographic data of the patients, those results may be because the patients (P3 and P8) are in the early stages of the disease (3–4 years). As for C2 patients, they have low voice quality with respect to the extracted acoustic features. On the other hand, they showed little ability to control axiomatic traces (trace L). Also, they negatively responded to hand-motor physiotherapy (trace Phrase). Hence, C2 patients were not able to control their handwriting or acoustic abilities. This may be linked to their belated disease duration (11–15 years). Finally, the common feature characteristics of C3 patients are moderate kinematic features during hand-motor physiotherapy (trace Phrase) and moderate acoustic features acquired from the sustained vowel. In addition, we noticed that C3 patients have a disease duration of 2–6 years. Hence, our global methodology consists of diagnosing PD by clustering patients with respect to their behavior. The PD behavior is represented by a set of features. Each cluster will be simply labeled by experts in neurology and motor control domain using the classical percentage scale. In the case of handwriting and speech syndromes, characteristics are gathered in the same experiments. To expand this methodology to new PD syndromes, a new experimental protocol must be introduced concerning the new syndromes. For example, the FoG syndrome can be integrated into our methodology by acquiring handwriting and speech data from patients before, during, and after FoG episodes. Next, by constructing and learning our BBN, we can discover a specific prototype (or cluster) of handwriting and speech linked to the FoG episodes.

5 CONCLUSIONS AND FUTURE WORK

In this chapter, we have described a global methodology for the modeling and diagnosis of the main behavioral syndromes for PD with BBNs. The first contribution establishes the causality in the FoG/FI system by making an epidemiological study. This approach resulted in weak or no causality in the FoG/FI system. Next, we built nine different BNC models for different patients in a classical, supervised classification manner. This approach showed a fluctuating percentage of accuracy, FoG-precision, and NoFoG-precision. Our classifier had the ability to detect FoG with up to 86% accuracy.

In order to expand our study to diagnose a wide range of syndromes of PD, we also investigated two new syndromes: handwriting and speech. We have described a new way for labeling handwriting and acoustic prototypes of PD patients. A method based on BBN formalism, combined with a Bayesian clustering algorithm that integrates a priori knowledge provided by experts, has been developed. We represented the physiological brain structure (*i.e.,* PPN) by a hidden variable that influences both handwriting and speech measuring variables. The results, therefore, should appeal to neurologists and doctors who are interested in the PDP development of axial symptoms.

Our future work is to improve the diagnosis of FoG by creating a new prototype that integrates heterogeneous data from different types of sensors: accelerometers, telemeters, and goniometers obtained with the multisensor device developed by our team. An extended diagnosis model that combines different useful information from the statistical studies with the PD experts' knowledge will be proposed.

Another important perspective is to generate a global diagnosis model for PD syndromes. Depending on the results of the handwriting and speech global diagnosis model, and based on the recent studies that shows a relationship between the frequency of freezing episodes during gait (FoG) and during a bimanual task (like handwriting; see Nieuwboer *et al.*, 2009), a global probabilistic model can be created (Figure 26.9), that integrates the three different symptoms of PD (FoG,

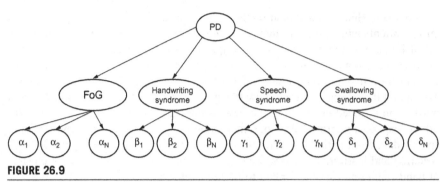

FIGURE 26.9

Toward a global diagnosis methodology for PD.

handwriting, and speech). By using the inference tool of BBN, the developed model can be used to evaluate different probabilities that link each syndrome to the other. It can be used, for example, to calculate the probability of a patient having a freezing episode if it is known that the patient has a specific behavior of writing. And so it will be possible to predict the harshness staging of a PDP using both motor (*i.e.*, handwriting and FoG) and nonmotor (speech) syndromes. Many new PD syndromes can be integrated into our model to achieve a global assessment for PD, such as swallowing as a neuromuscular activity that influences dysphagia[3] (Figure 26.9).

REFERENCES

Aarsland, D., et al., 1999. Range of neuropsychiatric disturbances in patients with Parkinson's disease. J. Neurol. Neurosurg. Psychiatry 67 (4), 492–496.

Bächlin, M., et al., 2010. Wearable assistant for Parkinson's disease patients with the freezing of gait symptom. IEEE Trans. Inf. Technol. Biomed. 14 (2), 436–446.

Bloem, B.R., et al., 2004. Falls and freezing of gait in parkinson's disease: a review of two interconnected, episodic phenomena. Mov. Disord. 19 (8), 871–884.

Borgelt, C., Steinbrecher, M., Krus, R., 2009. Graphical Models: Representations for Learning, Reasoning and Data Mining. John Wiley & Sons Ltd., United Kingdom.

Factor, S., Weiner, W., 2008. Parkinson's Disease: Diagnosis and Clinical Management, second ed. Demos Medical Publishing LLC., New York.

Fahn, S., 1995. The freezing phenomenon in parkinsonism. Adv. Neurol. 67, 53–63.

Flash, T., et al., 1997. Kinematic analysis of upper limb trajectories in Parkinson's disease. Exp. Neurol. 118 (2), 215–226.

---

[3]Dysphagia in PD can result in serious health issues, including aspiration pneumonia, malnutrition, and Dehydration (Tjaden, 2008).

Friedman, N., 1997. Learning Bayesian Networks in the Presence of Missing Values and Hidden Variables. In: Proceedings of the Fourteenth International Conference on Machine Learning. D. Fisher, San Francisco, California.

Frumkin, H., 2006. Causation in Medicine [lecture]. Emory University, Rollins School of Public Health, Public Health. Emory University, Atlanta, Georgia.

Giladi, N., Nieuwboer, A., 2008. Understanding and treating freezing of gait in Parkinsonism, proposed working definition and setting the stage. Mov. Disord. 23 (2), 23–25.

Giladi, N., et al., 1992. Motor blocks in Parkinson's disease. Neurology 42 (3), 333–339.

Glymour, C., Cooper, G., 1988. Computation, Causation, and Discovery. MIT Press, Cambridge, MA.

Gong, Y.B., Zhang, N.L., Gao, S.H., 2009. A study of symptom distribution regularities of Type II Diabetes using latent structure models. J. World Sci. Technol. Mod. Tradit. Chin. Med. Mater. Med. 4 (4), 516–521.

Hamani, C., Moro, E., Lozano, A., 2010. The pedunculopontine nucleus as a target for deep brain stimulation. J. Neural Transm. 118 (10), 1461–1468.

Han, J., Kamber, M., 2006. Data Mining: Concepts and Techniques, second ed. Morgan Kaufman Publishers, Oxford.

Hill, B., 1956. The environment of disease: association or causation? Proc. R. Soc. Med. 58 (5), 295–300.

Intan, R., Yuliana, O.Y., 2011. Fuzzy bayesian belief network for analyzing medical track record. Journal of Advances in Intelligent Information and Database Systems Studies in Computational Intelligence 283, 279–290.

Jankovic, J., 2008. Parkinson's disease: clinical features and diagnosis. J. Neurol. Neurosurg. Psychiatry 79 (4), 368–376.

Khanafar, R.M., et al., 2008. Automated diagnosis for UMTS networks using a bayesian network approach. IEEE Trans. Veh. Tech. 57 (4), 2451–2461.

Kundi, M., 2006. Causality and the interpretation of epidemiological evidence. Environ. Health Perspect. 114 (7), 969–974.

Lagiou, P., Adam, H.O., Trichopoulos, D., 2005. Causality in cancer epidemiology. Eur. J. Epidemiol. 20 (7), 565–574.

Lauritzen, S.L., 1996. Graphical Models. Clarendon Press, Oxford, UK.

Leopold, N.A., Kagel, M.C., 1997. Pharyngo-esophageal dysphagia in Parkinson's disease. Dysphagia 12 (1), 11–18.

Little, M.A., et al., 2009. Suitability of dysphonia measurements for telemonitoring of Parkinson's disease. IEEE Trans. Biomed. Eng. 56 (4), 1015–1020.

Longstaff, M., et al., 2001. Continuously Scaling a Continuous Movement: Parkinsonian Patients Choose a Smaller Scaling Ratio and Produce More Variable Movements Compared to Elderly Controls. In: Proceedings of the 10th Biennial Conference of the International Graphonomics Society. Nijmegen, The Netherlands, 6th to 8th August 2001, pp. 84–89.

Maassen, B., van Lieshout, P. (Eds.), 2007. Speech Motor Control New Developments in Basic and Applied Research. OUP Oxford, Oxford.

Mazzone, P., et al., 2005. Implantation of human pedunculopontine nucleus: a safe and clinically relevant target in Parkinson's disease. Neuroreport 16 (17), 1877–1881.

McLachlan, G.J., Ng, S.K., 2009. The Top Ten algorithm in Data Mining. In: Xindong, W., Kumar, V. (Eds.), CRC Press Taylor & Francis Group, New York.

Messaoud, B.M., 2012. SemCaDo: An Approach for Serendipitous Causal Discovery and Ontology Evolution. Ph.D thesis, Ecole Polytechnique de l"Université de Nantes.

Meucci, A., 2008. Fully flexible views: theory and practice. Risk 21 (10), 97–102.

Moore, O., Peretz, C., Giladi, N., 2007. Freezing of gait affects quality of life of peoples with Parkinson's disease beyond its relationships with mobility and gait. Move. Dis. 22 (15), 2192–2195.

Moore, S.T., MacDougall, H.G., Ondo, W.G., 2008. Ambulatory monitoring of freezing of gait in Parkinson's disease. J. Neurosci. Methods 167 (2), 340–348.

Morris, M.E., Iansek, R., 1996. Characteristics of motor disturbance in Parkinson's disease and strategies for movement rehabilitation. Hum. Mov. Sci. 15 (5), 649–669.

Muller, J., et al., 2001. Progression of dysarthria and dysphagia in postmortem-confirmed parkinsonian disorders. Arch. Neurol. 58 (2), 259–264.

Naim, P., et al., 2008. Réseaux Bayésiens. In: Groupe Eyrolles (Ed.), third ed. ISBN : 978-2-212-11972-5.

Nieuwboer, A., et al., 2009. Upper limb movement interruptions are correlated to freezing of gait in Parkinson's disease. Eur. J. Neurosci. 29 (7), 1422–1430.

Noth, E., Stemmmer, G., Ruzickova, H., 2011. Detection of Persons with Parkinson's Disease by Acoustic, Vocal, and Prosodic Analysis. In: Automatic Speech Recognition and Understanding. Waikoloa, 11th to 15th December 2011. IEEE, Waikoloa, pp. 478–483.

Nutt, J.G., et al., 2011. Freezing of gait: moving forward on a mysterious clinical phenomenon. Lancet Neurol. 10 (8), 734–744.

Okuma, Y., Yanagisawa, N., 2008. The clinical spectrum of freezing of gait in parkinson's disease. Mov. Disord. 23 (2), 26–30.

Pahwa, R., Lyons, K., Koller, W., 2007. Handbook of Parkinson's Disease: Neurological Disease & Therapy, fourth ed. Informa Healthcare USA Inc., New York.

Pearl, J., 1986. Fusion, propagation, and structuring in belief networks. Artif. Intell. 29 (3), 241–288.

Pearl, J., 1988. Probabilistic Reasoning in Intelligent Systems: Networks of Plausible Inference. Morgan Kaufmann Publishers Inc., San Francisco, USA.

Pearl, J., 2000. Causality: Models, Reasoning and Inference. Cambridge University Press, Cambridge, MA.

Ramig, L.O., Fox, C., Sapir, S., 2008. Speech treatment for Parkinson's disease. Expert Rev. Neurother. 8 (2), 299–311.

Rebonato, R., 2010. A bayesian approach to stress testing and scenario analysis. J. Invest. Manag. 8 (3), 1–13.

Rosenbek, J.C., Jones, H.N., 2007. Dysphagia in Patients with Motor Speech Disorders. In: Weismer, G. (Ed.), Motor Speech Disorders. Plural Publishing Inc., San Diego, CA.

Russo, F., Williamson, J., 2007. Interpreting causality in the health sciences. Int. Stud. Philos. Sci. 21 (2), 157–170.

Rusz, J., et al., 2011. Quantitative acoustic measurements for characterization of speech and voice disorders in early untreated Parkinson's disease. J. Acoust. Soc. Am. 129 (1), 350–367.

Saad, A., et al., 2012. Handwriting and speech prototypes of parkinson patients: belief network approach. Int. J. Comput. Sci. Issues 9 (3), 499–505.

Saad, A., et al., 2013. About Detection and Diagnosis of Freezing of Gait. In: International Conference on Advances in Biomedical Engineering. IEEE, Tripoli, Lebanon, pp. 117–120, Tripoli, Lebanon 11th to 13th September 2013.

Saad, A., et al., 2014. Sensoring and Features Extraction for the Detection of Freeze of Gait in Parkinson Disease. In: Multi-Conference on Systems, Signals & Devices. IEEE, Barcelona, Spain, pp. 1–6 Barcelona, Spain, 11th to 14th February 2014.

Sacha, J.P., Goodenday, L., Cios, kJ., 2002. Bayesian learning for cardiac SPECT image interpretation. J. Artif. Intell. Med. 26 (1-2), 109–143.

Sage, I., Zesiger, P., 2010. Profils de scripteurs âgés de 8 à 12 ans. L'écriture et ses pratiques du 8 au 10 Novembre 2010 - Université de Poitiers.

Snijders, A.H., et al., 2008. Clinimetrics of freezing of gait. Move. Dis. 23 (2), 68–74.

Song, D., et al., 2011. Multivariate Discretization for Bayesian Network Structure Learning in Robot Grasping. In: International Conference on Intelligent Robots and Systems. IEEE, Shanghai, pp. 20–27, Shanghai, 9th to 13th May 2011.

Spirtes, P., Glymour, C., Scheines, R., 1990. Causality from probability. Dietrich college of humanities and social sciences. Department of Philosophy. 236.

Teulings, H., Stelmach, G., 1991. Control of stroke size, peak acceleration, and stroke duration in parkinsonian handwriting. Hum. Mov. Sci. 10 (2–3), 315–334.

Thagard, P., 1998. Explaining disease: correlations, causes, and mechanisms. J. Mind. Mach. 8 (1), 61–78.

Tjaden, K., 2008. Speech and swallowing in Parkinson's disease. Top. Geriatr. Rehabil. 24 (2), 115–126.

Tucha, O., et al., 2006. Kinematic analysis of dopaminergic effects on skilled handwriting movements in Parkinson's disease. J. Neural Transm. 113 (5), 609–623.

Wang, Y., Zhang, N.L., 2004. Latent tree models and approximate inference in bayesian networks. J. Artif. Intell. Res. 32 (21), 879–900.

Zaarour, I., et al., 2003. A Probabilistic Modeling of the Writing Strategies Evolution for Pupils in Primary Education. In: 11th Conference of the International Graphonomics Society, pp. 174–177, Scottsdale, Arizona, 2nd to 5th November 2003.

Zaarour, I., et al., 2004a. Clustering and bayesian network approaches for discovering handwriting strategies of primary school children. Int. J. Pattern Recogn. Artif. Intell. 18 (7), 1233–1251.

Zaarour, I., et al., 2004b. Modelling of Handwriting Prototypes in Graphonomics : Bayesian Network Approach. In: 5th EUROSIM Congress on Modelling and Simulation, p. 78, Marne-la- Vallée, France, 6th to 10th September 2004.

Zaarour, I., et al., 2005. Une modélisation de haut niveau des stratégies d'écriture motrice d'enfants en scolarité primaire : approche bayésienne. Journal de Physique 124 (4), 230–236.

Zaarour, I., Labiche, J., Meillier, D., 2010. Classification de l'Écriture des Groupes d'Enfants Typiques. In: 3rd International Conference: EMedical Systems, Fes, Morocco, 12th to 14th May 2010.

Zhang, N.L., 2004. Hierarchical latent class models for cluster analysis. J. Mach. Learn. Res. 5 (1), 697–723.

Zhang, N.L., Kocka, T., 2004a. Efficient learning of hierarchical latent class models, Tools with Artificial Intelligence. J. Mach. Learn. Res. 5 (5), 697–723.

Zhang, N.L., Kocka, T., 2004b. Effective dimensions of hierarchical latent class models. J. Artif. Intell. Res. 21 (1), 1–17.

Practical Considerations in Virtual Screening and Molecular Docking

27

Michael Berry[1], Burtram Fielding[2], and Junaid Gamieldien[1]

South African National Bioinformatics Institute, University of the Western Cape, Cape Town, South Africa[1]

Department of Medical Biosciences, University of the Western Cape, Cape Town, South Africa[2]

1 INTRODUCTION

In silico virtual screening, or high-throughput virtual screening (HTVS), has yielded an excellent complement to the time-consuming and expensive experimental techniques of high-throughput screening. The ability to virtually screen compound libraries to improve enrichment of ligands progressed to experimental validation has provided countless lead compounds. HTVS computationally screens large databases of virtual compounds that either possess similarity toward a known inhibitor (ligand-based) or complementarity toward the solved receptor structure (structure-based; Shoichet, 2004). This allows researchers to screen large databases or compound libraries in order to identify a highly focused subset from which actives can be confirmed experimentally (Ripphausen *et al.*, 2011) and, in the case of molecular docking, can predict the binding pose, thereby simplifying future lead optimization (Joseph-McCarthy *et al.*, 2007). HTVS is especially attractive to academic facilities, occasionally in parallel with HTS, as fiscal expenses of pure HTS screens are often too large for academic budgets (Zhu *et al.*, 2013). Improvements in computer hardware and the availability of relatively inexpensive clusters have also increased the speed of HTVS, contributing to its gain in popularity (Anderson, 2003). Because it mostly eliminates cost-of-ownership associated with computing infrastructure, it is likely that cloud computing will further contribute to this uptake.

Molecular docking was first described in 1982 (Kuntz *et al.*, 1982) and has since become the central idea in structure-based virtual screening. It comprises two major tasks for which separate algorithms are used. The sampling algorithm predicts the many confirmations, referred to as *poses,* which the ligand can assume within the binding or active pocket. A scoring function then predicts the binding energies between the ligand and receptor for each predicted pose. The generated binding poses are then ranked based on their binding energies, where the top-ranked pose should correspond to the correct confirmation of the ligand. Scoring functions are, therefore, also capable of filtering through, and ranking, large databases of compounds in virtual screening, where the highest-ranked binding energies should correspond to a potential lead (Phatak *et al.*, 2009).

Used on its own, molecular docking is, however, plagued with weaknesses. The static nature of the receptor is a primary fault where the dynamic nature of the biological structures is not considered. Limitations in sampling algorithms and imperfections in scoring functions also lead to the generation of both false positives and false negatives (Lill, 2011; Wang *et al.*, 2003; Brooijmans and Kuntz, 2003; Alvarez, 2004) and the requirement for training sets in various algorithms often leads to accuracy being highly target dependent (Warren *et al.*, 2006). These inherent flaws are further exacerbated by user oversights and errors. This chapter will detail several practical aspects to consider prior to commencing a virtual screening study, while simultaneously providing a theoretical explanation of docking and scoring. This review will provide guidelines, but there is no "one-rule-fits-all" in molecular docking. Most docking programs have varying methods to deal with each topic discussed and describing details of each program is outside the scope of this review. It must also be taken into account that every receptor is different and the ability to replicate experimental and physiological findings is highly system dependent.

2 RECEPTOR STRUCTURE PREPARATION

Although most receptor preparation tools accurately complete processes that were not undertaken during X-ray crystal structure refinement, it is important to understand these processes and make adjustments where necessary. The most common receptor preparation procedures include adding hydrogens and atom-type charges, but it is also important to ensure that missing side-chains are added, missing bonds and molecule chain breaks are detected and fixed, bond orders are assigned, and where alternate locations are present, the atoms with highest frequencies must be selected. Other, more complicated, procedures in receptor preparation include accurate prediction of protonation states and identifying which water molecules (if any) should remain in the receptor structure. All of these procedures maximize the biological realism in the modeled system, which leads to the identification of a higher proportion of true bioactives.

2.1 PROTONATION STATES

The resolution of most crystal structures does not provide information on the location of hydrogens, commonly referred to as the *protonation state* (ten Brink and Exner, 2009). The accurate prediction of the correct protonation state, especially within the binding interface, is crucial to accurately predict the correct binding mode and, to a greater extent, binding affinity (Kalliokoski *et al.*, 2009; Fornabaio *et al.*, 2003; Onufriev and Alexov, 2013). This incorrect prediction of binding mode and affinity will inevitably lead to the identification of false positives, while true bioactives are missed (Onufriev and Alexov, 2013). It is notable to point out that force field–based scoring functions are more susceptible to incorrect protonation states in comparison to knowledge-based scoring functions (Onufriev and Alexov, 2013). Assigning the incorrect protonation states further alters the state of hydrogen bond donors and acceptors, which substantially limits the accurate prediction of protein-ligand interactions (Polgár and Keserü, 2005).

Side-chains of ionizable amino acids can further vary their protonation states within a receptor depending on the local environment and pH. Ligand binding can also be accompanied by proton gain or release (Petukh *et al.*, 2013) but this is almost never incorporated into a molecular docking study (Onufriev and Alexov, 2013). One study pointed out that a residue's protonation state cannot be accurately replicated, as protons are not static and are readily transferred between molecules (Fornabaio *et al.*, 2003). The quantum mechanical simulations necessary to replicate proton movements are far beyond the scope and capabilities of molecular docking and at best, the protonation state, or an ensemble of protonation states, that is most suitable to ligand binding must be identified.

Histidine (His) provides a unique problem in terms of residue protonation, as it can be protonated in three different conformations. The imidazole ring of the His side-chain can be protonated in a neutral confirmation at the ε-nitrogen or the δ-nitrogen or in a charged (+1) conformation where both the ε- and δ-nitrogens are protonated (Kim *et al.*, 2013). To further complicate the correct conformation of the imidazole side-chain ring, ambiguities in crystal structures often switch the carbon and nitrogen, creating an additional three rotameric conformations, termed "flipped" (Glusker *et al.*, 1994). His also represents a weaker base, and for this reason, determining the protonation state is more complicated than for other ionizable residues and must be determined individually (Waszkowycz *et al.*, 2011). In the case of His, analysis of hydrogen bonding networks is likely to yield the most detail about the correct side-chain protonation.

The dynamic nature of a receptor means the protonation states of ionizable residues are constantly changing. In order to accurately predict the conformation of a ligand binding to a receptor, the protonation state of the receptor must be relevant to the bound conformation and in correspondence with crystal data (*i.e.,* absence of steric clashes and hydrogen bonds occurring at expected locations) and in accordance with the pH of the experimental conditions. Assigning protonation states to Asp, Glu, Arg, and Lys during receptor preparation is generally straightforward, with deprotonated acids (Asp and Glu) and protonated bases (Arg and Lys) (Kim *et al.*, 2013; Waszkowycz *et al.*, 2011). This is, however, a generalization and not a rule, and the microenvironment of the residue and physiological pH of the receptor must be taken into careful consideration. Calculating the theoretical pK_a of these residues at the physiological pH is possibly the most straightforward mechanism to determine or estimate their protonation state (Polgár and Keserü, 2005).

As scoring functions are highly dependent on the correct receptor protonation state, it can be assumed that a scoring function will favor the correct protonation state by scoring it above the incorrect state (Onufriev and Alexov, 2013). This provides a mechanism to accurately predict the correct protonation state within an ensemble of pregenerated receptor states. The correct replication of hydrogen bond positions between ligand and receptor, as seen in the crystal structure or detailed in the literature, will further suggest the accurate placement of residue protons (Krieger *et al.*, 2012; Hooft *et al.*, 1996). Observable steric clashes between a ligand and receptor, after protonation, will further suggest incorrect proton placement (Word *et al.*, 1999; Krieger *et al.*, 2012). This approach will only account for ionizable groups within the binding interface and will not be able to account for the entire receptor, but this remains a far more attractive strategy than ignoring the issue entirely.

In summary, in order to accurately approximate a receptor's protonation state, the identification of its physiological pH is key. Second, calculated pK_a values for ionizable residues enables determination of the protonation state according to the given pK_a at the specified pH. Third, crystal structures and known, experimentally identified bioactives can yield a wealth of knowledge on the protonation state of a receptor by scoring function analysis and inspection of steric clashes and hydrogen bonding networks between ligand and receptor. Given these guidelines, the techniques used to accurately predict the correct protonation state of a receptor are largely dependent on the class of receptor being studied. For this reason, the techniques applied must be accurately verified for the receptor under investigation before virtual library screening.

2.2 SELECTING IMPORTANT ACTIVE SITE WATER MOLECULES

Active site water molecules are key determinants in ligand-receptor binding (Thilagavathi and Mancera, 2010; Barillari *et al.*, 2007). Not only can they mediate hydrogen bonding between ligand and receptor, but their contribution to entropic and enthalpic changes are significant (Lie *et al.*, 2011; Cheng *et al.*, 2012; Kroemer, 2007). In a virtual screening context, the addition of water (an explicit solvent) is frequently neglected, as the intensive computational simulations required does not permit the rapid screening required for large libraries, often seen in high-throughput virtual screens, and accounting for water molecules in docking remains a significant challenge (Cheng *et al.*, 2012; Huang and Shoichet, 2008; Schneider and Fechner, 2005).

The position of water molecules within an active site are also highly variable (Santos *et al.*, 2009), and to account for them as static in nature would be biased toward ligands that complement the specific orientation and prejudice those that would physiologically replace the water molecules, leading to a drastic increase in false negatives (Kroemer, 2007). Several reports claim to more accurately predict the binding mode of crystal structure inhibitors by incorporating water molecules within the active site (Lemmon and Meiler, 2013). While these studies do possess a high degree of merit, the inclusion of waters within the active site greatly decreases the volume of the pocket and thereby the possible conformations that the ligand may assume, which is further biased toward the correct conformation (Lie *et al.*, 2011; Hartshorn *et al.*, 2007). As there is a constant compromise between speed and accuracy in a high-throughput virtual screen, however, the presence of active site waters can greatly increase ligand enrichment. It is, therefore, important to determine which waters, if any, must be kept during a virtual screen and exclude those that are nonessential.

An initial step to assess the importance of active site waters would be to attempt to replicate the binding mode of experimental structures in the absence of explicit waters. If the accuracy is diminished by the absence of waters in the binding site, it is important to select which waters are pivotal to binding. Waters that are not hydrogen bonded to the receptor, and those that are located outside the binding pocket (more than 5Å), will obviously have little effect on ligand binding and can therefore be removed (Huang and Shoichet, 2008). Waters that possess three hydrogen bonds with the receptor, or those with low B-factors, are likely to be highly stable within the pocket and should be included in docking studies, as these waters may prove difficult to displace by ligand binding and likely function to stabilize the protein binding site (Yang *et al.*, 2006; Hornak *et al.*, 2006). Waters that form hydrogen bond bridges between the ligand and receptor are also likely to be important in ligand binding. This may, however, be highly ligand-specific and its importance in virtual screening, where a diverse set of ligand classes are under study, must be properly assessed and validated. Where essential water molecules are included in a virtual screen they should, ideally, be treated as flexible (Huang and Shoichet, 2008). It is also important to bear in mind that the accuracy of a docking algorithm may be highly dependent on the parameterization of the algorithm and suitability toward the class of receptor and inhibitor, which will be discussed later in this chapter.

3 ACCURATELY PREDICTING THE POSE OF SOLVED CRYSTAL STRUCTURES AND DIFFERENTIATING DECOYS FROM ACTIVES

It is commonly accepted that there is no "first-in-class" algorithm or molecular docking software for the prediction of correct ligand-binding pose or relative free energy of binding. Molecular docking algorithms are often calibrated on a training set of experimental ligand-protein complexes and accuracy of these docking programs is often highly dependent on the training set used (Ballester and Mitchell, 2010). This highlights the importance of confirming that the docking software used for virtual screening is capable of replicating the binding mode of known, experimental inhibitors for the class of receptor studied (Lim *et al.*, 2011; Kroemer, 2007). To improve ligand enrichment in a virtual screening context, the docking algorithm selected must be properly validated for the class of receptor under investigation. Of course, in a virtual screen, where hundreds of thousands to millions of compounds are potentially being screened, validating for each class of potential inhibitor would be impossible, but accurate validation must be undertaken with the largest obtainable data set of true experimental leads, where the binding pose is known. A root-mean-square deviation (RMSD) below 2Å for heavy atoms (excluding hydrogens) between the experimental structure and predicted pose of docking is a well-defined benchmark to assess the accuracy of molecular docking sampling algorithms (Houston and Walkinshaw, 2013).

A highly useful benchmarking strategy and metric to gauge the success of a molecular docking program is the ability to differentiate true actives from decoys. The Database of Useful Decoys–Enhanced (DUD-E; http://dude.docking.org/gener ate) can generate decoys for an active compound (Mysinger et al., 2012). DUD generates decoys based on cheminformatic properties, including molecular weight, logP, number of rotatable bonds, and number of hydrogen bond donors and acceptors. As these decoys are not intended to bind to the target receptor, they are topologically distinct from the active inhibitors, thereby serving as suitable negative controls. The enrichment of the docking program can be assessed by its ability to rank true actives above decoy ligands (Mysinger et al., 2012).

4 SIDE-CHAIN FLEXIBILITY AND ENSEMBLE DOCKING

Virtual screening simulations are typically performed on static structures, and it has previously been demonstrated that the use of a *holo* (ligand-bound) conformation provides better enrichment when compared to *apo* or homology modeled receptors (McGovern and Shoichet, 2003). Given this, addressing protein flexibility can substantially improve enrichment but remains one of the most challenging aspects of molecular docking. There are currently two approaches to incorporate the dynamic nature of protein structures; flexible receptor docking and ensemble docking (Lill, 2013). These approaches have shown to improve enrichment in docking studies (Craig et al., 2010), but the compromise between speed and accuracy must be heavily weighted in high-throughput virtual screens.

Flexible docking most often only incorporates side-chains of residues within the active site and therefore does not cover the dynamic range of protein conformations (Meng et al., 2011). It has been demonstrated that only a small number of side-chains within a binding pocket undergo structural changes upon ligand binding. This study suggested that, within 85% of studied receptors, only three or fewer side-chains exhibited movements upon ligand binding and further developed a scale of side-chain flexibility (Lys > Arg, Gln, Met > Glu, Ile, Leu > Asn, Thr, Val, Tyr, Ser, His, Asp > Cys, Trp, Phe; Najmanovich et al., 2000). Utilizing this scale, it may be possible to identify which side-chains within a pocket must be made flexible and which may be left static, although the ability to accurately enrich active ligands must be displayed.

In ensemble docking, the ensemble of rigid structures can be generated by a molecular dynamic simulation where snapshots are isolated from the trajectory or when several structures are available from crystallography or nuclear magnetic resonance (NMR) experimental studies. There are two distinct classes of ensemble docking. In the first method, several protein conformations are generated prior to a docking screen and each ligand is docked into each receptor independently (Carlson, 2002; Carlson and McCammon, 2000; Barril and Morley, 2005), thereby introducing receptor flexibility by multiple docking runs (Henzler and Rarey, 2010). This is, of course, computationally inefficient and the time required to conduct a screen increases with every protein structure included in the ensemble. The conformational diversity is also limited to the conformational representations included in the ensemble (B-Rao et al., 2009). The second method assesses an ensemble of protein structures in a single docking screen (B-Rao et al., 2009). This method either unites ensemble structures or uses a receptor grid averaged over all protein structures, and therefore reduces computational cost considerably (Totrov and Abagyan, 2008; Knegtel et al., 1997; Henzler and Rarey, 2010). To identify a suitable ensemble of structures to incorporate in a docking run, an enrichment docking screen of known actives can be performed. Both ensemble and flexible receptor docking is described in greater detail in several reviews (Cavasotto and Abagyan, 2004; Carlson, 2002; Therrien et al., 2014; Henzler and Rarey, 2010).

Molecular dynamic (MD) simulations is considered to be the most accurate method to determine the stability of a ligand within a binding pocket, while accounting for full side-chain and backbone flexibility and incorporating solvent effects (Marco and Gago, 2007; Alonso et al., 2006). Several docking studies have utilized MD simulations to confirm results obtained from docking studies. However, the intense computational costs make it practical for only a small set of ligands (Österberg and Åqvist, 2005; Han, 2012; Mukherjee et al., 2011; Segura-Cabrera et al., 2013).

5 CONSENSUS DOCKING

Scoring functions have been highlighted as the major weakness of molecular docking (Yang et al., 2005; Warren et al., 2006; Wang et al., 2003). As these functions are solely responsible for selecting and ranking the correct ligand pose within the binding site from the many possible conformations generated by the sampling algorithm, it can potentially lead to identification of an incorrect pose. The integration of a consensus approach to sampling and scoring, incorporating several algorithms to each task, has shown to greatly improve ligand enrichment in virtual screening and identifying the correct pose of experimental structures (Teramoto and Fukunishi, 2007; Houston and Walkinshaw, 2013; Kukol, 2011; Yang et al., 2005; Charifson et al., 1999; Plewczynski et al., 2011). Consensus scoring compensates for deficiencies in individual scoring functions and thereby improves the overall performance (Teramoto and Fukunishi, 2007), with the inclusion of a single extra scoring function being sufficient to improve binding affinity predictions (Chang et al., 2010). A similar technique to consensus scoring is the approach of consensus sampling, which is less well characterized. A recent study by Houston and Walkinshaw, 2013 utilized three sampling algorithms from Dock (Ewing et al., 2001), Autodock (Morris et al., 2009), and Autodock Vina (Trott and Olson, 2010) to identify the experimental pose of a diverse set of ligands. The study achieved an accuracy of 82%, compared to the 55%–64% accuracy of using a single algorithm (Houston and Walkinshaw, 2013). In this study, a consensus result was confirmed when independently predicted poses were within an RMSD cutoff of 2Å, the same distance defined as correct sampling in comparison to experimental structures (Houston and Walkinshaw, 2013).

The approach of employing several algorithms to identify the correct pose with subsequent consensus scoring to identify top-ranked ligands can greatly improve the enrichment rate in a virtual screening context. The major cost of this approach is the increase in false negatives, which are therefore missed and do not progress to experimental testing. In an academic setting, or a lab where resources are limited, this is an acceptable consequence, as the quality of the results is more vital in a virtual screening context. The improvement in the identified hit list, with a decrease in false positives and subsequent decrease in resource waste, would largely compensate for the increase in false negatives (Houston and Walkinshaw, 2013).

6 MM-GBSA

Various elements of binding free energy, including long-range electrostatics, desolvation upon binding, and entropic contributions, are poorly defined in conventional scoring functions utilized in molecular docking (Rastelli *et al.*, 2010a). These terms are better defined by more rigorous and computationally intensive calculations included in techniques such as free energy perturbation (FEP; Kollman, 1993), thermodynamic integration (TI; Lybrand *et al.*, 1986), linear response (LR; Åqvist *et al.*, 1994), molecular mechanics Poisson-Boltzmann/surface area (MM-PBSA; Kuhn and Kollman, 2000) and molecular mechanics generalized-Born/surface area (MM-GBSA; Kollman *et al.*, 2000). Of these, MM-PBSA and MM-GBSA are faster by several orders of magnitude, making them favorable techniques for the rescoring and reranking of hit lists identified by virtual screening. As these techniques are computationally efficient and yield high correlations with experimental binding energies, the general opinion that docking results should be further analyzed by more advanced approaches is increasing (Rastelli *et al.*, 2010a, Sgobba *et al.*, 2012).

MM-PBSA and MM-GBSA previously required an ensemble of snapshots, generated by an MD simulation of the protein-ligand complex in water. This has been replaced by the use of a continuum implicit solvent model with a single minimized protein-ligand structure. This technique has given excellent correlations with experimental data (Guimarães and Cardozo, 2008; Greenidge *et al.*, 2013) and is comparable with the more time-consuming and computer-intensive approach of averaging MD simulations in water (Rastelli *et al.*, 2010a). The use of a single energy-minimized structure with a continuum implicit solvent has further improved the enrichment of virtual screens and can successfully discriminate between true binders and decoys (Rastelli *et al.*, 2010a). Explicit solvent models have further shown to decrease this correlation (Greenidge *et al.*, 2013).

MM-PBSA and MM-GBSA are force field–based methods that use a combination of molecular mechanics (MM) energies, polar and nonpolar solvation terms, and an entropy term to calculate the free energy of binding (ΔG_{bind}; Massova and Kollman, 2000; Kollman *et al.*, 2000) from the change between the bound complex (ΔG_{com}) and unbound receptor (ΔG_{rec}) and ligand (ΔG_{lig}) in solution [Eq. (27.1); Rastelli *et al.*, 2010a; Guimarães and Cardozo, 2008]:

$$\Delta G_{bind} = \Delta G_{com} - \Delta G_{rec} - \Delta G_{lig}. \qquad (27.1)$$

Each of these terms are decomposed into gas-phase MM energy (ΔE_{MM}), polar and nonpolar solvation terms (ΔS_{solv}), and an entropy term (ΔS) at a predefined temperature (T) [Eq. (27.2)].

$$\Delta G_{(com/rec/lig)} = \Delta E_{MM} + \Delta G_{solv} - T.\Delta S. \qquad (27.2)$$

E_{MM} is calculated by the sum of chemical bonds, angles, and torsion terms (E_{bat}) predefined by the force field and van der Waals (E_{vdW}) and Coulombic terms (E_{coul}). The G_{solv} terms are further decomposed into a polar ($G_{solv,p}$) contribution and nonpolar ($G_{solv,np}$) contribution. The polar contributions are calculated by generalized-Born (GB) approximations in MM-GBSA (Kollman *et al.*, 2000; Greenidge *et al.*, 2013) and a Poisson-Boltzamn (PB) distribution in MM-PBSA (Kuhn and Kollman, 2000), where the nonpolar contribution is usually calculated as a linear function of the solvent accessible surface area (Hou *et al.*, 2011a; Greenidge *et al.*, 2013). With these functions, the binding free energy (ΔG_{bind}) is calculated:

$$\Delta G_{(com/rec/lig)} = \Delta E_{bat} + \Delta E_{vdW} + \Delta E_{coul} + \Delta G_{solv,p} + \Delta G_{solv,np} - T.\Delta S. \qquad (27.3)$$

In most studies, the entropy (T. ΔS) term is neglected, as its calculation can be a major source of error (Rastelli *et al.*, 2010b) and does not always improve the prediction accuracy (Hou *et al.*, 2011a; Guimaraes, 2012); however, some researchers do still advocate its use (e.g., Lafont *et al.*, 2007).

When comparing the PB and GB methods in calculation of solvation terms, the PB model is theoretically more rigorous and computationally intensive than GB but does not always give a stronger correlation with experimental binding free energy. The GB model is also more efficient and faster at ranking binding affinities of ligands, making it more suitable in a virtual screening context (Hou *et al.*, 2011a, 2011b; Huang *et al.*, 2010; Li *et al.*, 2010). MM-GBSA has further been shown to be a more attractive option than the computationally heavy FEP and TI methodologies, as it can be as accurate and computationally more efficient, and handle structurally more diverse ligands because it requires no training set (Guimarães and Cardozo, 2008). In conclusion, MM-GBSA provides excellent correlation with experimental binding energy, improved enrichment in virtual screening of compound databases, is computationally suitable for medium-throughput screening or reranking a defined hit list and provides more accurate docking poses (Hou *et al.*, 2011b). With this, the rescoring of docking complexes using MM-GBSA has emerged as a computationally important approach in structure-based drug design (Guimaraes, 2012).

7 INCORPORATING PHARMACOPHORIC CONSTRAINTS WITHIN THE VIRTUAL SCREEN

A *pharmacophore* is defined as an ensemble of structural features that are necessary for molecular recognition (Guner, 2000). These features predominantly include hydrophobic moieties and hydrogen bond donors and acceptors, but may also include aromatic rings, cations, and anions. A pharmacophore model can be used prior to a docking study to reduce the size of a ligand library, or it can be used to filter hits following a virtual screen. These pharmacophoric features can be defined by an ensemble of known, active inhibitors where features that are frequently repeated are included in the pharmacophore model (Yang, 2010), or they can be defined by the natural substrate. Identifying ligands that are able to replicate the interactions made between the natural substrate and a receptor can greatly improve the success and enrichment of a virtual screen. An example of substrate derived pharmacophoric constraints is the three chymotrypsin-like protease (3CL^{pro}) of coronaviruses. The S$_1$ pocket in this family of proteases has an absolute specificity for glutamine, which is mediated by a hydrogen bond between the substrate and His163, deep in the pocket. The S$_2$ pocket forms a deep hydrophobic region that displays preference for a hydrophobic moiety and the Glu166 residue increases substrate specificity via an additional hydrogen bond (Zheng *et al.*, 2007; Chuck *et al.*, 2011; Shoichet, 2004; Schapira *et al.*, 2003). These pharmacophoric features have been extensively used to identify novel inhibitors of the 3CL^{pro} (Jacobs *et al.*, 2013).

8 CONCLUSION

Despite its limitations, molecular docking has yielded the discovery of novel leads (Shoichet and Kobilka, 2012; Wang and Ekins, 2006) and, if used correctly, the speed and cost effectiveness at which molecular docking screens can be conducted can provide an excellent starting point in a project with few to no compelling leads (Alvarez, 2004). Possibly the most important consideration to make when commencing a structure-based drug design study is a question of project design, especially if the user is a beginner in the field. The more prior knowledge and availability of published data, the greater the chance of success in the project where proper scrutiny of available literature is essential. The availability of high-resolution crystals or NMR structures of the receptor are paramount prior to a virtual screen, as homology models have been proven to yield low enrichment when compared to *holo* or *apo* experimental structures. *Holo* structures have further proven to improve enrichment, and the state of the experimental structure should therefore be taken into account (McGovern and Shoichet, 2003). Efficient characterization of the active or allosteric binding site is essential. Detailed understanding of the location and flexibility of side-chains within the pocket, the presence or absence of active site waters, and protonation states of ionisable residues will contribute greatly to enrichment in a virtual screen. The availability of known actives will also allow for essential benchmarking, validation, and potential generation of an effective pharmacophore model. It is important to characterize what class of inhibitors these actives belong to. Molecular docking is not capable of replicating covalent interactions between ligand and receptor, and therefore covalent inhibitors should be excluded. Large peptidomimetics are also difficult to dock with conventional docking methodologies. This is directly related to the inaccuracy of docking algorithms to predict the correct conformation of compounds with increased number of rotatable bonds. With each rotatable bond, the conformational space that must be sampled increases dramatically and thereby reduces the chance of successfully predicting the correct pose. Ligands in a molecular docking screen, therefore, should be limited to eight rotatable bonds (Houston and Walkinshaw, 2013). A final consideration covered in this chapter is the use of consensus scoring and sampling. This has been shown to greatly improve enrichment with MM-GBSA rescoring, yielding high correlations with experimental evidence and should be considered in a virtual screening context (Teramoto and Fukunishi, 2007; Chang et al., 2010; Houston and Walkinshaw, 2013; Hou et al., 2011b).

REFERENCES

Alonso, H., Bliznyuk, A.A., Gready, J.E., 2006. Combining docking and molecular dynamic simulations in drug design. Med. Res. Rev. 26, 531–568.

Alvarez, J.C., 2004. High-throughput docking as a source of novel drug leads. Curr. Opin. Chem. Biol. 8, 365–370.

Anderson, A.C., 2003. The Process of Structure-Based Drug Design. Chem. Biol. 10, 787–797.

Åqvist, J., Medina, C., Samuelsson, J.-E., 1994. A new method for predicting binding affinity in computer-aided drug design. Protein Eng. 7, 385–391.

Ballester, P.J., Mitchell, J.B., 2010. A machine learning approach to predicting protein–ligand binding affinity with applications to molecular docking. Bioinformatics 26, 1169–1175.

Barillari, C., Taylor, J., Viner, R., Essex, J.W., 2007. Classification of water molecules in protein binding sites. J. Am. Chem. Soc. 129, 2577–2587.

Barril, X., Morley, S.D., 2005. Unveiling the full potential of flexible receptor docking using multiple crystallographic structures. J. Med. Chem. 48, 4432–4443.

B-Rao, C., Subramanian, J., Sharma, S.D., 2009. Managing protein flexibility in docking and its applications. Drug Discov. Today 14, 394–400.

Brooijmans, N., Kuntz, I.D., 2003. Molecular recognition and docking algorithms. Annu. Rev. Biophys. Biomol. Struct. 32, 335–373.

Carlson, H.A., 2002. Protein flexibility and drug design: how to hit a moving target. Curr. Opin. Chem. Biol. 6, 447–452.

Carlson, H.A., Mccammon, J.A., 2000. Accommodating protein flexibility in computational drug design. Mol. Pharmacol. 57, 213–218.

Cavasotto, C.N., Abagyan, R.A., 2004. Protein flexibility in ligand docking and virtual screening to protein kinases. J. Mol. Biol. 337, 209–225.

Chang, M.W., Ayeni, C., Breuer, S., Torbett, B.E., 2010. Virtual screening for HIV protease inhibitors: a comparison of AutoDock 4 and Vina. PLoS One 5, e11955.

Charifson, P.S., Corkery, J.J., Murcko, M.A., Walters, W.P., 1999. Consensus scoring: a method for obtaining improved hit rates from docking databases of three-dimensional structures into proteins. J. Med. Chem. 42, 5100–5109.

Cheng, T., Li, Q., Zhou, Z., Wang, Y., Bryant, S.H., 2012. Structure-based virtual screening for drug discovery: a problem-centric review. AAPS J. 14, 133–141.

Chuck, C.-P., Chow, H.-F., Wan, D.C.-C., Wong, K.-B., 2011. Profiling of substrate specificities of 3C-like proteases from group 1, 2a, 2b, and 3 coronaviruses. PLoS One 6, e27228.

Craig, I.R., Essex, J.W., Spiegel, K., 2010. Ensemble docking into multiple crystallographically derived protein structures: an evaluation based on the statistical analysis of enrichments. J. Chem. Inf. Model. 50, 511–524.

Ewing, T.J., Makino, S., Skillman, A.G., Kuntz, I.D., 2001. DOCK 4.0: search strategies for automated molecular docking of flexible molecule databases. J. Comput. Aided Mol. Des. 15, 411–428.

Fornabaio, M., Cozzini, P., Mozzarelli, A., Abraham, D.J., Kellogg, G.E., 2003. Simple, intuitive calculations of free energy of binding for protein-ligand complexes. 2. Computational titration and pH effects in molecular models of neuraminidase-inhibitor complexes. J. Med. Chem. 46, 4487–4500.

Glusker, J.P., Lewis, M., Rossi, M., 1994. Crystal Structure Analysis for Chemists and Biologists. John Wiley & Sons.

Greenidge, P.A., Kramer, C., Mozziconacci, J.C., Wolf, R.M., 2013. MM/GBSA binding energy prediction on the PDBbind data set: successes, failures, and directions for further improvement. J. Chem. Inf. Model. 53, 201–209.

Guimaraes, C.R., 2012. MM-GB/SA Rescoring of Docking Poses. Computational Drug Discovery and Design. Springer.

Guimarães, C.R., Cardozo, M., 2008. MM-GB/SA rescoring of docking poses in structure-based lead optimization. J. Chem. Inf. Model. 48, 958–970.

Guner, O.F., 2000. Pharmacophore Perception, Development, and Use in Drug Design. International University Line, La Jolla, CA, 29.

Han, S.-H., 2012. Docking and molecular dynamics simulations of celastrol binding to p23. Bulletin of the Korean Chemical Society 33, 322–324.

Hartshorn, M.J., Verdonk, M.L., Chessari, G., Brewerton, S.C., Mooij, W.T., Mortenson, P.N., Murray, C.W., 2007. Diverse, high-quality test set for the validation of protein-ligand docking performance. J. Med. Chem. 50, 726–741.

Henzler, A.M., Rarey, M., 2010. Pursuit of Fully Flexible Protein-Ligand Docking: Modeling the Bilateral Mechanism of Binding. In: Molecular Informatics, 29, pp. 164–173.

Hooft, R.W., Sander, C., Vriend, G., 1996. Positioning hydrogen atoms by optimizing hydrogen-bond networks in protein structures. Proteins: Structure, Function, and Bioinformatics 26, 363–376.

Hornak, V., Okur, A., Rizzo, R.C., Simmerling, C., 2006. HIV-1 protease flaps spontaneously close to the correct structure in simulations following manual placement of an inhibitor into the open state. J. Am. Chem. Soc. 128, 2812–2813.

Hou, T., Wang, J., Li, Y., Wang, W., 2011a. Assessing the performance of the molecular mechanics/Poisson Boltzmann surface area and molecular mechanics/generalized Born surface area methods. II. The accuracy of ranking poses generated from docking. J. Comput. Chem. 32, 866–877.

Hou, T., Wang, J., Li, Y., Wang, W., 2011b. Assessing the performance of the MM/PBSA and MM/GBSA methods. 1. The accuracy of binding free energy calculations based on molecular dynamics simulations. J. Chem. Inf. Model. 51, 69–82.

Houston, D.R., Walkinshaw, M.D., 2013. Consensus docking: improving the reliability of docking in a virtual screening context. J. Chem. Inf. Model. 53, 384–390.

Huang, N., Shoichet, B.K., 2008. Exploiting ordered waters in molecular docking. J. Med. Chem. 51, 4862–4865.

Huang, S.Y., Grinter, S.Z., Zou, X., 2010. Scoring functions and their evaluation methods for protein-ligand docking: recent advances and future directions. Phys. Chem. Chem. Phys. 12, 12899–12908.

Jacobs, J., Grum-Tokars, V., Zhou, Y., Turlington, M., Saldanha, S.A., Chase, P., Eggler, A., Dawson, E.S., Baez-Santos, Y.M., Tomar, S., Mielech, A.M., Baker, S.C., Lindsley, C.W., Hodder, P., Mesecar, A., Stauffer, S.R., 2013. Discovery, synthesis, and structure-based optimization of a series of N-(tert-butyl)-2-(N-arylamido)-2-(pyridin-3-yl) acetamides (ML188) as potent noncovalent small molecule inhibitors of the severe acute respiratory syndrome coronavirus (SARS-CoV) 3CL protease. J. Med. Chem. 56, 534–546.

Joseph-Mccarthy, D., Baber, J.C., Feyfant, E., Thompson, D.C., Humblet, C., 2007. Lead optimization via high-throughput molecular docking. Curr. Opin. Drug Discov. Devel. 10, 264–274.

Kalliokoski, T., Salo, H.S., Lahtela-Kakkonen, M., Poso, A., 2009. The effect of ligand-based tautomer and protomer prediction on structure-based virtual screening. J. Chem. Inf. Model. 49, 2742–2748.

Kim, M.O., Nichols, S.E., Wang, Y., Mccammon, J.A., 2013. Effects of histidine protonation and rotameric states on virtual screening of M. tuberculosis RmlC. J. Comput. Aided Mol. Des. 27, 235–246.

Knegtel, R., Kuntz, I.D., Oshiro, C., 1997. Molecular docking to ensembles of protein structures. J. Mol. Biol. 266, 424–440.

Kollman, P., 1993. Free energy calculations: applications to chemical and biochemical phenomena. Chem. Rev. 93, 2395–2417.

Kollman, P.A., Massova, I., Reyes, C., Kuhn, B., Huo, S., Chong, L., Lee, M., Lee, T., Duan, Y., Wang, W., 2000. Calculating structures and free energies of complex molecules: combining molecular mechanics and continuum models. Acc. Chem. Res. 33, 889–897.

Krieger, E., Dunbrack Jr., R.L., Hooft, R.W., Krieger, B., 2012. Assignment of Protonation States in Proteins and Ligands: Combining Pka Prediction with Hydrogen Bonding Network Optimization. Computational Drug Discovery and Design. Springer.

Kroemer, R.T., 2007. Structure-based drug design: docking and scoring. Current Protein and Peptide Science 8, 312–328.

Kuhn, B., Kollman, P.A., 2000. Binding of a diverse set of ligands to avidin and streptavidin: an accurate quantitative prediction of their relative affinities by a combination of molecular mechanics and continuum solvent models. J. Med. Chem. 43, 3786–3791.

Kukol, A., 2011. Consensus virtual screening approaches to predict protein ligands. Eur. J. Med. Chem. 46, 4661–4664.

Kuntz, I.D., Blaney, J.M., Oatley, S.J., Langridge, R., Ferrin, T.E., 1982. A geometric approach to macromolecule-ligand interactions. J. Mol. Biol. 161, 269–288.

Lafont, V., Armstrong, A.A., Ohtaka, H., Kiso, Y., Mario Amzel, L., Freire, E., 2007. Compensating enthalpic and entropic changes hinder binding affinity optimization. Chem. Biol. Drug Des. 69, 413–422.

Lemmon, G., Meiler, J., 2013. Towards ligand docking including explicit interface water molecules. PLoS One 8, e67536.

Li, Y., Liu, Z., Wang, R., 2010. Test MM-PB/SA on true conformational ensembles of protein – ligand complexes. J. Chem. Inf. Model. 50, 1682–1692.

Lie, M.A., Thomsen, R., Pedersen, C.N., Schiøtt, B., Christensen, M.H., 2011. Molecular docking with ligand attached water molecules. J. Chem. Inf. Model. 51, 909–917.

Lill, M.A., 2011. Efficient incorporation of protein flexibility and dynamics into molecular docking simulations. Biochemistry 50, 6157–6169.

Lill, M., 2013. Virtual screening in drug design. Methods Mol. Biol. 993, 1–12.

Lim, S.V., Rahman, M.B.A., Tejo, B.A., 2011. Structure-based and ligand-based virtual screening of novel methyltransferase inhibitors of the dengue virus. BMC bioinformatics 12, S24.

Lybrand, T.P., Mccammon, J.A., Wipff, G., 1986. Theoretical Calculation of Relative Binding Affinity in Host-Guest Systems. In: Proceedings of the National Academy of Sciences, 83, pp. 833–835.

Marco, E., Gago, F., 2007. Overcoming the inadequacies or limitations of experimental structures as drug targets by using computational modeling tools and molecular dynamics simulations. ChemMedChem 2, 1388–1401.

Massova, I., Kollman, P.A., 2000. Combined molecular mechanical and continuum solvent approach (MM-PBSA/GBSA) to predict ligand binding. Perspect Drug Discov Des 18, 113–135.

Mcgovern, S.L., Shoichet, B.K., 2003. Information decay in molecular docking screens against holo, apo, and modeled conformations of enzymes. J. Med. Chem. 46, 2895–2907.

Meng, X.-Y., Zhang, H.-X., Mezei, M., Cui, M., 2011. Molecular docking: a powerful approach for structure-based drug discovery. Curr. Comput. Aided Drug Des. 7, 146.

Morris, G.M., Huey, R., Lindstrom, W., Sanner, M.F., Belew, R.K., Goodsell, D.S., Olson, A.J., 2009. AutoDock4 and AutoDockTools4: automated docking with selective receptor flexibility. J. Comput. Chem. 30, 2785–2791.

Mukherjee, P., Shah, F., Desai, P., Avery, M., 2011. Inhibitors of SARS-3CLpro: virtual screening, biological evaluation, and molecular dynamics simulation studies. J. Chem. Inf. Model. 51, 1376–1392.

Mysinger, M.M., Carchia, M., Irwin, J.J., Shoichet, B.K., 2012. Directory of useful decoys, enhanced (DUD-E): better ligands and decoys for better benchmarking. J. Med. Chem. 55, 6582–6594.

Najmanovich, R., Kuttner, J., Sobolev, V., Edelman, M., 2000. Side-chain flexibility in proteins upon ligand binding. Proteins: Structure, Function, and Bioinformatics 39, 261–268.

Onufriev, A.V., Alexov, E., 2013. Protonation and pK changes in protein–ligand binding. Q. Rev. Biophys. 46, 181–209.

Österberg, F., Åqvist, J., 2005. Exploring blocker binding to a homology model of the open hERG K$^+$ channel using docking and molecular dynamics methods. FEBS Lett. 579, 2939–2944.

Petukh, M., Stefl, S., Alexov, E., 2013. The role of protonation states in ligand-receptor recognition and binding. Curr. Pharm. Des. 19, 4182.

Phatak, S.S., Stephan, C.C., Cavasotto, C.N., 2009. High-Throughput and in Silicon Screenings in Drug Discovery.

Plewczynski, D., Lazniewski, M., Von Grotthuss, M., Rychlewski, L., Ginalski, K., 2011. VoteDock: consensus docking method for prediction of protein-ligand interactions. J. Comput. Chem. 32, 568–581.

Polgár, T., Keserü, G.M., 2005. Virtual screening for β-secretase (BACE1) inhibitors reveals the importance of protonation states at Asp32 and Asp228. J. Med. Chem. 48, 3749–3755.

Rastelli, G., Del Rio, A., Degliesposti, G., Sgobba, M., 2010a. Fast and accurate predictions of binding free energies using MM-PBSA and MM-GBSA. J. Comput. Chem. 31, 797–810.

Rastelli, G., Rio, A.D., Degliesposti, G., Sgobba, M., 2010b. Fast and accurate predictions of binding free energies using MM-PBSA and MM-GBSA. J. Comput. Chem. 31, 797–810.

Ripphausen, P., Nisius, B., Bajorath, J., 2011. State-of-the-art in ligand-based virtual screening. Drug Discov. Today 16, 372–376.

Santos, R., Hritz, J., Oostenbrink, C., 2009. Role of water in molecular docking simulations of cytochrome P450 2D6. J. Chem. Inf. Model. 50, 146–154.

Schapira, M., Raaka, B.M., Das, S., Fan, L., Totrov, M., Zhou, Z., Wilson, S.R., Abagyan, R., Samuels, H.H., 2003. Discovery of Diverse Thyroid Hormone Receptor Antagonists by High-Throughput Docking. In: Proceedings of the National Academy of Sciences, 100, pp. 7354–7359.

Schneider, G., Fechner, U., 2005. Computer-based de novo design of drug-like molecules. Nat. Rev. Drug Discov. 4, 649–663.

Segura-Cabrera, A., García-Pérez, C.A., Guo, X., Rodríguez-Pérez, M.A., 2013. Repurposing of FDA-approved drugs for the discovery of inhibitors of dengue virus NS2B-NS3 protease by docking, consensus scoring, and molecular dynamics simulations. Biophys. J. 104, 404a.

Sgobba, M., Caporuscio, F., Anighoro, A., Portioli, C., Rastelli, G., 2012. Application of a post-docking procedure based on MM-PBSA and MM-GBSA on single and multiple protein conformations. Eur. J. Med. Chem. 58, 431–440.

Shoichet, B.K., 2004. Virtual screening of chemical libraries. Nature 432, 862–865.

Shoichet, B.K., Kobilka, B.K., 2012. Structure-based drug screening for G-protein-coupled receptors. Trends Pharmacol. Sci. 33, 268–272.

Ten Brink, T., Exner, T.E., 2009. Influence of protonation, tautomeric, and stereoisomeric states on protein – ligand docking results. J. Chem. Inf. Model. 49, 1535–1546.

Teramoto, R., Fukunishi, H., 2007. Supervised consensus scoring for docking and virtual screening. J. Chem. Inf. Model. 47, 526–534.

Therrien, E., Weill, N., Tomberg, A., Corbeil, C.R., Lee, D., Moitessier, N., 2014. Docking Ligands into Flexible and Solvated Macromolecules. 7. Impact of Protein Flexibility and Water Molecules on Docking-based Virtual Screening Accuracy.

Thilagavathi, R., Mancera, R.L., 2010. Ligand – Protein cross-docking with water molecules. J. Chem. Inf. Model. 50, 415–421.

Totrov, M., Abagyan, R., 2008. Flexible ligand docking to multiple receptor conformations: a practical alternative. Curr. Opin. Struct. Biol. 18, 178–184.

Trott, O., Olson, A.J., 2010. AutoDock Vina: improving the speed and accuracy of docking with a new scoring function, efficient optimization, and multithreading. J. Comput. Chem. 31, 455–461.

Wang, B., Ekins, S., 2006. Computer Applications in Pharmaceutical Research and Development. John Wiley & Sons.

Wang, R., Lu, Y., Wang, S., 2003. Comparative evaluation of 11 scoring functions for molecular docking. J. Med. Chem. 46, 2287–2303.

Warren, G.L., Andrews, C.W., Capelli, A.-M., Clarke, B., Lalonde, J., Lambert, M.H., Lindvall, M., Nevins, N., Semus, S.F., Senger, S., 2006. A critical assessment of docking programs and scoring functions. J. Med. Chem. 49, 5912–5931.

Waszkowycz, B., Clark, D.E., Gancia, E., 2011. Outstanding challenges in protein–ligand docking and structure-based virtual screening. Wiley Interdisciplinary Reviews: Computational Molecular Science 1, 229–259.

Word, J.M., Lovell, S.C., Richardson, J.S., Richardson, D.C., 1999. Asparagine and glutamine: using hydrogen atom contacts in the choice of side-chain amide orientation. J. Mol. Biol. 285, 1735–1747.

Yang, S.-Y., 2010. Pharmacophore modeling and applications in drug discovery: challenges and recent advances. Drug Discov. Today 15, 444–450.

Yang, J.-M., Chen, Y.-F., Shen, T.-W., Kristal, B.S., Hsu, D.F., 2005. Consensus scoring criteria for improving enrichment in virtual screening. J. Chem. Inf. Model. 45, 1134–1146.

Yang, H., Bartlam, M., Rao, Z., 2006. Drug Design targeting the main protease, the Achilles heel of Coronaviruses. Curr. Pharm. Des. 12, 4573–4590.

Zheng, K., Ma, G., Zhou, J., Zen, M., Zhao, W., Jiang, Y., Yu, Q., Feng, J., 2007. Insight into the activity of SARS main protease: molecular dynamics study of dimeric and monomeric form of enzyme. Proteins 66, 467–479.

Zhu, T., Cao, S., Su, P.C., Patel, R., Shah, D., Chokshi, H.B., Szukala, R., Johnson, M.E., Hevener, K.E., 2013. Hit identification and optimization in virtual screening: practical recommendations based on a critical literature analysis. J. Med. Chem. 56, 6560–6572.

Knowledge Discovery in Proteomic Mass Spectrometry Data

28

Michael Netzer[1], Michael Handler[1], Bernhard Pfeifer[1], Andreas Dander[2], and Christian Baumgartner[1,3]

Institute of Electrical and Biomedical Engineering, UMIT, Hall in Tirol, Austria[1]
Division for Bioinformatics, Biocenter, Innsbruck Medical University, Innsbruck, Austria[2]
Institute of Heath Care Engineering with European Notified Body of Medical Devices, Graz University of Technology, Graz, Austria[3]

1 INTRODUCTION

In proteomics, mass spectrometry (MS) allows the identification of hundreds to thousands of proteins in cells, tissues, and biofluids (Gerszten *et al.*, 2011). Changes in the concentration of proteins may indicate pathologic processes. Very recent examples include new biomarkers in coronary artery disease (Lee *et al.*, 2015), breast (Suh *et al.*, 2012; Bouchal *et al.*, 2013), bladder (Lindén *et al.*, 2012), liver (Poté *et al.*, 2013), or prostate cancer (Pallua *et al.*, 2013; Mantini *et al.*, 2007), pancreatic beta cell injury (Brackeva *et al.*, 2015), as well as in neurodegenerative diseases such as Alzheimer's disease (Ringman *et al.*, 2012).

In general, the biomarker discovery process includes several steps: experimental study design and execution, sample collection, preparation and separation, MS analysis, biomarker identification, and biological interpretation and validation (Handler *et al.*, 2011).

After the raw MS data is available, a technical review is necessary due to background signals caused by electronic and chemical noise or ions from unknown fragments in the sample (Cerqueira *et al.*, 2009). To treat background signals, sophisticated computational methods for preprocessing raw data are necessary to provide quality-assured data for further analysis. Such methods include baseline correction, normalization, and quality assessment.

In the next analysis step, highly discriminatory biomarker candidates—at this stage presented by mass-to-charge (m/z) ratio values in the spectra—are identified from the preprocessed spectra. However, the bioinformatic-driven search for relevant markers is challenging, as the spectra are characterized by a huge number of features (hundreds or thousands of m/z values; Osl *et al.*, 2008).

Basically, features can be identified either by calculating a specific score indicating the predictive value of features and selecting those that have a score beyond a certain threshold (filter approaches; John *et al.*, 1994) or by searching the space of feature sets in combination with a learning strategy (*e.g.*, classifier) to select a set of highly discriminating candidates (the wrapper approach; Kohavi and John (1998). Because of the huge amount of possible feature sets, wrapper approaches have higher computational costs, and yet they yield a higher performance compared to filter approaches. In addition, the combination (pooling) of feature selection methods are proposed as described in Netzer *et al.* (2009) or Saeys *et al.* (2007). Recently, network-based methods have also been suggested for the identification of metabolic biomarker candidates (Netzer *et al.*, 2011), taking into account the kinetics of circulating analytes.

In this chapter, we present a comprehensive computational workflow for the identification of biomarker candidates using proteomic mass spectrometry data. The first step of the workflow is comprised of complex data preprocessing modalities necessary to transform "noisy" raw spectra into adjusted spectra, followed by a three-step feature selection approach for biomarker identification that combines the advantages of the efficient filter and effective wrapper techniques. This analysis strategy was integrated into the software package, which has been published as the Knowledge Discovery in Databases (KD^3) Designer by our group (Dander *et al.*, 2011).

The chapter is structured as follows: Section 1, "Technical Background," gives a brief survey on MS profiling technologies. In section 2, "Computational Workflow," we describe the proposed bioinformatic approach for proteomic biomarker identification. In section 3, "Analysis Tool," we present KD^3 as a software tool for data analysis facilitating high usability of all processing steps. Section 4 presents a brief conclusion.

2 TECHNICAL BACKGROUND

This section delineates the technical background of MS-based profiling technologies, which have become a key analysis platform in proteomics. In general, a mass spectrometer consists of three components (Aebersold and Mann (2003)): (i) an ion source, (ii) a mass analyzer that measures the mass-to-charge (m/z) ratio of the ionized molecules, and (iii) a detector that counts the ions at each m/z value.

Matrix-assisted laser desorption/ionization (MALDI; Karas and Hillenkamp, 1988) and electro spray ionization (ESI; Fenn *et al.*, 1989) are two commonly used methods to produce ions from macromolecules such as proteins (Aebersold and Mann (2003)).

In this chapter, we focus on MALDI technology and data, which is generally used to ionize dry samples, whereas ESI is also coupled with liquid-based separation platforms (Aebersold and Mann, 2003). In MALDI, a laser and an ultraviolet (UV)–absorbing chemical compound are used to vaporize and ionize the analytes (Parker *et al.*, 2010). MALDI is usually coupled with time-of-flight (TOF) analyzers that measure the mass of intact peptides based on the TOF of molecules in an electric field. Finally, a detector amplifies and counts the arriving ions (Aebersold and Mann,

2003). The resulting spectrum presents mass identities over m/z values; however, mass signals in the spectrum ("true" peaks) can be contaminated by diverse chemical and physical noise (Satten *et al.,* 2004; Mantini *et al.,* 2007). These disturbances in the signal may lead to baseline drift, which is the trend of the signal generated if no material was introduced, and background noise caused by electronic disturbances and fragments varying over small mass ranges randomly (Mantini *et al.,* 2007).

In the next section, we present a coupled computational workflow to denoise raw mass spectra and to identify putative biomarker candidates in the adjusted data.

3 COMPUTATIONAL WORKFLOW

In this section, a workflow for data preprocessing and proteomic biomarker identification is presented, which has been recently introduced to identify highly dis- criminatory masses when comparing diseased and harmless forms of samples (Handler *et al.,* 2011; Pallua *et al.,* 2013). All steps of this workflow were implemen- ted as plug-ins for the software package KD^3 (Dander *et al.,* 2011), providing a user- friendly assembly of the different processing steps to configurable workflows.

This discussion aims to provide additional information about our previously pub- lished workflow (Handler *et al.,* 2011, Pallua *et al.,* 2013), together with a description of the parameters, which need to be defined for the modules implemented in KD^3.

3.1 PREPROCESSING

In order to compare mass spectra for the identification of proteomic biomarkers, mul- tiple steps need to be performed to standardize all given spectra to a common format. Therefore, a preprocessing pipeline is used for the transformation of data into a proper format for analysis (shown in Figure 28.1) (Handler *et al.,* 2011).

Some of the modules in this workflow use the PROcess library (Li, 2005) of the Bioconductor R package (R Development Core Team, 2009). For the integration of

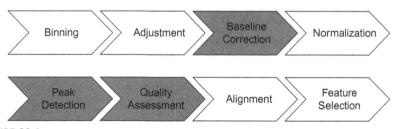

FIGURE 28.1

Preprocessing and evaluation steps (gray boxes indicate the direct use of algorithms of the R/Bioconductor (R Development Core Team, 2009) library PROcess (Li, 2005). Note that binning, adjustment, and normalization need to be repeated after the alignment step for equally spaced, consistent, and normalized spectra.

processing steps into KD^3 submodules (functional objects), a parallel execution of the algorithms was made possible, which can efficiently compute numerous MALDI spectra on systems with multiple cores, for example, on a computational cluster or workstation. The figures demonstrating the preprocessing results were created using the JFreeChart library (JFreeChart, 2012).

Binning of m/z values Due to unequally distributed m/z values in the compared spectra, a direct comparison between intensities of different spectra is difficult. In our approach, therefore, we included a binning step to map the intensities of the given spectra onto equally distributed m/z bins. In particular, the dimension (number of m/z values) of high-resolution spectra can be reduced using this step (Ressom *et al.*, 2005).

Using the Binning module, the width w of the resulting bins and the method for calculation of the bin representative can be selected. As intensity value of the bin representative $I(x)$ at m/z value x the mean/maximum intensity of all intensities in the range $\left[x - \frac{w}{2}; x + \frac{w}{2}\right)$ is calculated. Furthermore, the user can choose whether the intensities of empty bins should be linearly interpolated by neighboring intensities or set to 0.

After setting these parameters, spectra can be assigned to this module. As a result, the Binning module delivers spectra with equally distributed m/z bins (see Figure 28.2).

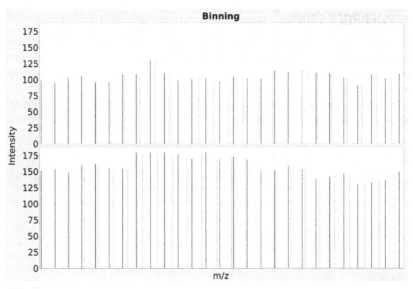

FIGURE 28.2

Binning: The m/z values of mass intensities differ between the two plots (gray lines). After binning, the mass intensities of both spectra are located on equally distributed m/z bins (black lines).

Adjustment of m/z ranges Spectra with different m/z ranges cannot be matched with each other over the whole m/z domain. To use most of the spectra for further preprocessing, the adjustment step is applied, which removes all values from the spectra outside the boundary of the highest common minimal m/z value x_{min} and the lowest common maximum m/z value x_{max} of all spectra.

The Adjustment module allows the user to set the values x_{min} and x_{max} manually. The user can also decide individually whether spectra are selected for further preprocessing that do not lie within the defined boundaries. If, for example, a spectrum starts at a higher m/z value as defined by x_{min}, this spectrum can be filtered out by this step. The m/z lower and upper bounds of residual spectra are equalized by removing all m/z bins outside the defined boundaries. Therefore, after this step, the m/z range of all spectra is now equal and consistent (see Figure 28.3).

Baseline subtraction Chemical noise in the energy absorbing molecule solution and ion overload can lead to an elevated baseline within the spectra (Li *et al.*, 2005). Different algorithms are available for effective removal of baselines from spectra. For example, Ressom *et al.* (2005) used a spline approximation on local minima of a spectrum to estimate its baseline. In this work, the baseline subtraction algorithm described by Li *et al.* (2005) was implemented, which estimates the baseline by local regression to the points below a certain quantile or to local minima of a moving window. After the baseline is estimated, it is subtracted from the original spectrum. The Baseline subtraction module allows the configuration of parameters, which are directly passed to the *bslnoff* operation of the PROcess package of R (Li, 2005). The user can set parameters such as the number of breaks on the log m/z scale

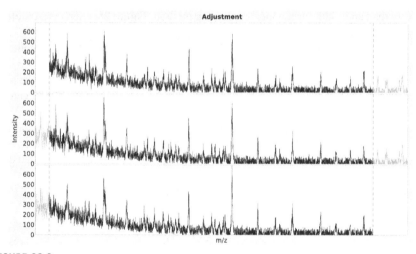

FIGURE 28.3

Adjustment: The dashed lines represent the position of the common minimal and common maximal m/z values of the three given spectra. Adjusted spectra with m/z values within the two boundaries are used for further processing.

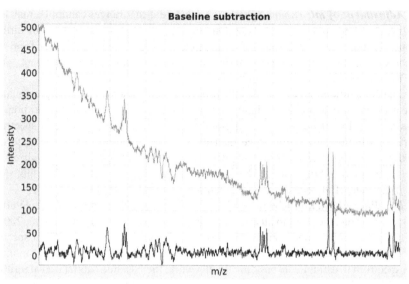

FIGURE 28.4

Baseline subtraction: A spectrum before baseline subtraction (gray) and after baseline subtraction (black) is shown.

for finding the local minima or intensity values below a defined quantile necessary for local regression calculation. Basically, it can be selected between local regression or linear interpolation for smoothing the estimated baseline. The user can also specify the bandwidth for the local regression method. Figure 28.4 depicts a baseline corrected spectrum returned by this module.

Normalization Effects of experimental noise can cause variations in the amplitude of spectra. To remove this artifact from spectra the total ion normalization procedure was used (Li *et al.*, 2005) to rescale intensity values of the spectra. In this step, the area under the curve (AUC) is calculated for each spectrum above a user-defined cutoff. This cutoff is relevant because of high noise signals at low m/z values. The AUC of a spectrum is calculated as the sum of all intensities of a spectrum (considering the given cutoff value) if the intensities are represented by equally distributed m/z bins (Li *et al.*, 2005). A normalized spectrum N_i based on the spectrum U_i is calculated as

$$N_i(x) = U_i(x) \cdot \frac{AUC_M}{AUC(U_i)}, \tag{28.1}$$

where

$$AUC(U_i) = \sum_{j=1}^{n} U_i(j) \tag{28.2}$$

defines the AUC of the spectrum U_i, n is the number of m/z values in the spectrum U_i, and AUC_M defines the median AUC of all spectra (see Figure 28.5). Alternatively, the user has the possibility to define the AUC as a parameter directly.

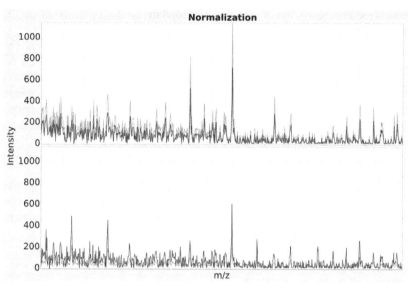

FIGURE 28.5

Normalization: Gray spectra indicate spectra before normalization. The normalized spectra are depicted in black. The AUC of the upper spectrum is higher than the AUC of the lower spectrum before normalization. After normalization, the AUC of both spectra is equal. Note that only a cutout of the entire m/z range of the spectra is presented here.

Peak detection Peaks in the spectra represent specific, abundant polypeptides in the sample (Li *et al.*, 2005). These peaks define reasonable intensities compared to intensities of other m/z values, which appear as noise (Ressom *et al.*, 2005). To identify peaks in the spectra, the function *isPeak* of the PROcess package is used (Li, 2005). Three different parameters are considered for the selection of the peaks:

- The signal-to-noise ratio (SNR), defined as the local smooth divided by the local estimate of variation
- A detection threshold below which the intensities of the spectrum are considered as zero
- The shape ratio, which is defined as the ratio between the area under the curve within a small distance of a peak candidate, as already identified by the first two criteria, and the maximum of all such peak areas of a spectrum

In addition to these parameters, the user can define window widths for the estimation of local variance, for smoothing the spectrum before peak detection, and for the calculation of the area under the peak, which are passed to the *isPeak* operation of the PROcess library.

Quality assessment Spectra of poor quality may cause reduction of statistical significance of selected masses. Therefore, a quality assessment step on preprocessed spectra is recommended. In our workflow, we used the *quality* operation of the PRO-cess package (Li, 2005).

The quality of a spectrum is evaluated using the following three measures: Quality, Retain, and Peak. For computation of the Quality and Retain measures, a noise envelope is used, which is computed as follows: First, the noise is estimated as the difference between the spectrum and its moving average with a window size of 5 points starting from a user-defined cutoff value. Afterward, the noise envelope is computed as three times the standard derivation of the previously calculated noise in a 250-point window.

For the computation of the *Peak* measure, the peak information retrieved by the previous step is required.

The three measures for the quality estimation are defined as follows (Li *et al.*, 2005):

- *Quality:* The measure of the separation of signal from noise, defined as the ratio of the AUC before and after subtraction of the noise envelope.
- *Retain:* The number of high peaks in a spectrum is quantified by comparing the number of intensities more than five times the noise envelope over the total number of points in a spectrum.
- *Peak:* The number of peaks of the current spectrum is compared to the average number of peaks in all spectra.

The boundary parameters for the three measurements can be defined by the user. If a spectrum does not exceed any of the defined boundaries, the spectrum is removed.

Alignment to internal standards Because of measurement variations, peaks in different spectra that correspond to the same protein may be located at different m/z values (Li *et al.*, 2005). In the peak alignment of spectra, peaks are identified across spectra, which are likely to represent the same protein. For the alignment, different algorithms are available (*e.g.*, Li *et al.*, 2005; Ressom *et al.*, 2005). In our workflow, a method for peak alignment was integrated that used internal standards as reference points in the spectrum. By definition, an internal standard is a compound added to a sample in known concentration to facilitate the qualitative identification and/or quantitative determination of the sample components (Ettre, 1993). In this approach, two internal standards are used. To align a spectrum by using this method, corresponding peaks have to be found close to the defined m/z values of the internal standards. Either the closest peak or the peak with maximal intensity in a user-defined window is chosen. The m/z values of the aligned spectrum are subsequently calculated by linear interpolation:

$$\hat{x} = (x - IS_l) \cdot \frac{\widehat{IS}_u - \widehat{IS}_l}{IS_u - IS_l} + \widehat{IS}_l \qquad (28.3)$$

where x is the original m/z value, $\hat{x}$ is the aligned m/z value, IS_l and IS_u denote the m/z values of the corresponding lower and upper internal standard peaks of the processed spectra, and $\widehat{IS}_l$ and $\widehat{IS}_u$ denotes the m/z values of the lower and upper internal standard (see Figure 28.6).

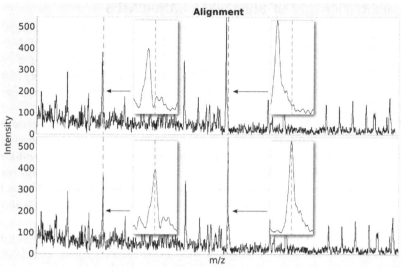

FIGURE 28.6

Alignment: In the upper panel, an unaligned spectrum and the areas around the internal standards (dashed lines) are depicted. The lower panel shows the aligned peaks of this spectrum.

The peak information and the m/z values of two internal standards, including a defined window size around the standards, are required for running the alignment. If no peaks are found with a smaller or equal distance than half of the window, the spectrum is removed and is not considered for further analysis. Note that the maximum peak or the closest peak within a window can be chosen as an internal standard for the alignment.

Recalibration of preprocessed spectra Due to the alignment to internal standards, parts of the initial preprocessing modality (*i.e.*, binning, adjustment, and normalization) need to be repeated to ensure that the m/z values of the remaining spectra are (i) equally binned, (ii) within the same m/z bounds, and (iii) have the same AUC.

Generation of mean spectra If multiple spectra per sample are available, these spectra can be averaged to a mean spectrum by calculating the mean intensities over the entire m/z value range. By this action, the noise can be reduced and the SNR significantly improved. Note that spectra of the same sample are identified by the file name of the spectra that included the sample IDs.

Formatting of spectra for feature selection approach For the biomarker identification, some algorithms from the Weka software package are used (Hall *et al.*, 2009). To assign the spectra to different classes and transform the spectra information into ARFF (Attribute-Relation File Format), two additional modules were implemented (class assignment by file name and conversion to ARFF).

3.2 IDENTIFICATION OF BIOMARKER CANDIDATES

After preprocessing, the spectra have comparable m/z and intensity values and can be defined as a set of tuples, $T = \{(c_j, m) \mid c_j \in C, m \in M\}$ with $C = \{case, control\}$, where C is the set of class labels and M is the set of features (m/z values in the spectrum). In order to identify those masses in M that show highest discriminatory ability according to class C, we adjusted an algorithm previously published by our group (Plant *et al.,* 2006).

In the first step, a filter approach is used to select relevant features (m/z values). The resulting features from step 1, however, contain regions of adjacent features that are highly correlated, as most of them are redundant, representing the same information of the spectra. Consequently, in step 2, we identify a representative for every region in the spectra. Finally, in step 3, a wrapper approach further reduces the dimensionality of the result set of step 2 by optimizing the discriminatory ability using a classifier.

Note that for evaluating these analysis steps, synthetic spectra were created using the spectrum generator of mMass 5.0 (Strohalm *et al.,* 2010). Overall, we generated 50 case and 50 control spectra and inserted randomly two artificial, well-discriminating m/z regions.

Step 1: Selecting relevant features In this work, we used a Student t-test as a filter approach. In addition to the resulting P-value, we calculated a second parameter Δ representing the ratio of the mean intensities in each class $\bar{x}_{c_i}$ relative to the maximum intensity I_{max} in all spectra. The parameter Δ was defined by

$$\Delta = \frac{|\bar{x}_{c_1} - \bar{x}_{c_2}|}{I_{max}} \tag{28.4}$$

This parameter is important to ensure that differences in the intensity can also be technically detected. A feature is defined as relevant if the following two conditions are fulfilled:

$$P - value < \alpha$$

$$\Delta > \Gamma.$$

The parameters α and Γ are set by the user.

Step 2: Selecting region representatives We used a forward selection strategy to identify a representative for every region in the spectra. The representative feature is the feature with the highest quality (*i.e.*, the discriminatory ability according to the filter method applied in step 1) within the region. The size s of the region depends on the index of the feature representing the m/z value, which is due to technical reasons, as different fragments of peptides with low molecular weight cause many narrow peaks in the spectral region of low m/z values.

Step 3: Selecting the best features To further reduce the number of features, a wrapper-based approach is used, including a classifier and a search strategy to find a smaller feature subset while keeping the discriminatory ability at least constant.

We apply logistic regression (Le Cessie and Van Houwelingen, 1992) as the classifier and a modified binary search (MBS) (Plant *et al.*, 2006) as the search strategy. The area under the receiver operating characteristic (ROC) curve is selected as the measure for assessing the discriminatory ability. As introduced, selected features using this approach represent highly discriminating m/z values in the spectra. Finally, the local maximum in the neighborhood of a selected m/z value is determined to ensure that the selected mass represents a real peak in the spectra. Figure 28.7 demonstrates a snapshot of two matched spectra when comparing two different groups of mass spectrometry data (*e.g.*, cases versus controls). This three-step strategy is able to identify highly discriminating mass peaks between the spectra (in this example, with superior sensitivity and specificity). In particular, in this example, we were able to identify our two predefined artificial biomarker candidates.

After applying this computational strategy, identified well-discriminating mass peaks need to be verified and validated as biomarkers by subsequent database verification, lab experiments, and clinical trials before selected biomarker candidates can go into clinical application.

4 ANALYSIS TOOL

As the analysis of MALDI data comprises several steps, and a variety of methods are available for each of those steps, the analysis of such data is challenging. Knowledge Discovery in Databases (KDD) is a process to manage and analyze huge amounts of data. Fayyad *et al.* (1996) splits the KDD process into several steps from storing data via selection, preprocessing and transformation to data mining methods. An interpretation and evaluation step follows this series of tasks, which is performed by experts in the individual field. One major point here is that the entire KDD process is iterative, which results in reanalyzing the raw data set or intermediate results with small or large changes in the analytical workflow. To overcome this hurdle of using different applications for those steps, KD^3 has been developed by our group (Dander *et al.*, 2011).

The following sections describe the KD^3 Composition, KD^3 Functional Object, and KD^3 Workflow based on Pfeifer *et al.* (2008).

4.1 KD^3 COMPOSITION

The implemented KD^3 application consists of four main parts. A screenshot of the application is depicted in Figure 28.8. The application can be divided into four parts. The first part shows the available functional objects, which are loaded using the Java reflection application programming interface (API) and are grouped using a hierarchical structure. In a workspace window, the user can drop functional objects and parameterize them by setting up annotated constructors and methods. In the center of the window, the workflow is visualized.

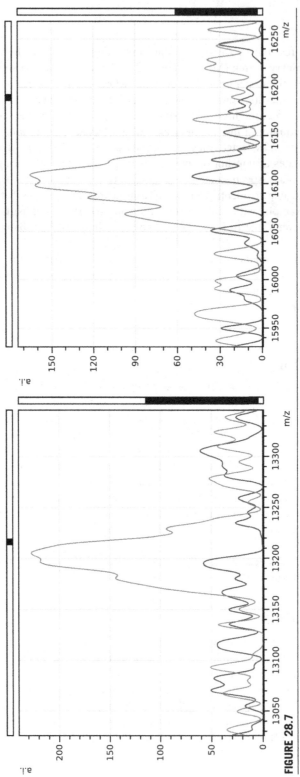

FIGURE 28.7

Identified mass peaks when comparing two different groups of mass spectrometry data using our synthetic data. These two mass peaks were classified as highly discriminatory features.

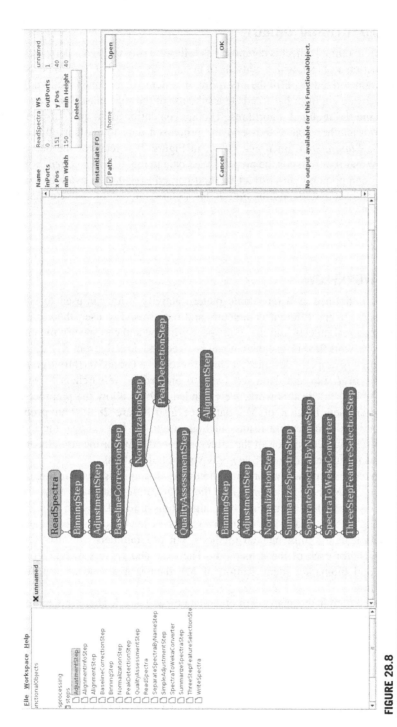

FIGURE 28.8

A screenshot of the complete preprocessing and biomarker identification workflow modeled in KD³.

4.2 KD³ FUNCTIONAL OBJECT

In general, a functional object is composed as follows: From the user's perspective, a task is a functional object, which consists of in- and out-ports that have to be assembled and parameterized to fulfill their purpose. In order to extend the functionality of KD³, the software engineer has to create a subclass of the superclass *FunctionalObject* containing the required algorithms. The abovementioned in- and out-ports get the data from another object and send the processed data to another object. For instance, the *BinningStep* functional object in Figure 28.8 receives the data from *ReadSpectra* and finally sends the preprocessed data to the *AdjustmentStep*. For performing the computation, an abstract method named *execute()* is available, which must be overridden in derived *FunctionalObject* classes in order to solve a specified problem.

4.3 KD³ WORKFLOW

A *workflow* is defined as a repeatable pattern activity, which is used to solve a defined process using different parameters and data sets. The user, therefore, can drop the functional objects into the workspace window and can specify the parameters. After the workflow is designed, it can be executed directly from KD³. Finally, if the workflow is properly designed, it can be saved as a GraphML (http://graphml. graphdrawing.org/) file and deployed (*e.g.*, to biomedical researchers to analyze newly available data). In this work, we extended KD³ to allow the preprocessing and biomarker identification of MS data (see also Figure 28.8). Our proposed workflow-oriented architecture results in high usability. KD³ allows the user to exchange different methods for all the aforementioned steps, or the straightforward implementation and integration of newly developed algorithms.

As the integration of new algorithms should be as simple as possible, the developer has to develop the new algorithm in the programming language Java. Therefore, the only need for integrating new algorithms into KD³ is an elementary understanding of Java. KD³ automatically generates the graphical user interface (GUI) for each of the implemented methods, but programmers can also develop a specific GUI for each of those methods. The extended version of KD³ for preprocessing and biomarker identification of MS data is available at http://www. umit.at/kd3ms.

KD³ can be used in the analyses of other data types as well. Therefore, more than 100 different methods and algorithms have been integrated into this application. As our group mainly deals with research questions in computational biomarker discovery, we applied KD³ successfully in several research projects, such as addressing the search for metabolic biomarkers in cardiovascular disease or the identification of human breath gas markers in liver disease using ion-molecule reaction-mass spectrometry (Pfeifer *et al.*, 2007; Netzer *et al.*, 2009, 2011; Baumgartner *et al.*, 2010; Millonig *et al.*, 2010).

5 CONCLUSION

In this chapter, we have presented a comprehensive computational workflow for the identification of proteomic biomarker candidates using mass spectrometry data. The proposed approach includes the preprocessing of raw spectra coupled by a three-step-feature selection approach that combines the advantages of filter- and wrapper-based methods. We could illustrate the power of our approach in identifying predefined "biomarker candidates" using a synthetic MS data set for demonstration purposes. It is important to note that the selected filter and wrapper methods can generically be replaced by alternative feature selection methods. Only small parts of the entire workflow need to be modified to treat other types of MS data generated in proteomic and metabolomic experiments. The integration of the presented methods into KD^3 results in high usability and accessibility, allowing a targeted search for highly predictive biomarker candidates in MS data.

REFERENCES

Aebersold, R., Mann, M., 2003. Mass spectrometry-based proteomics. Nature 422 (6928), 198–207.

Baumgartner, C., Lewis, G.D., Netzer, M., Pfeifer, B., Gerszten, R.E., 2010. A new data mining approach for profiling and categorizing kinetic patterns of metabolic biomarkers after myocardial injury. Bioinformatics 26 (14), 1745–1751.

Bouchal, P., Dvorakova, M., Scherl, A., Garbis, S.D., Nenutil, R., Vojtesek, B., 2013. Intact protein profiling in breast cancer biomarker discovery: protein identification issue and the solutions based on 3D protein separation, bottom-up and top-down mass spectrometry. Proteomics 13 (7), 1053–1058.

Brackeva, B., De Punt, V., Kramer, G., Costa, O., Verhaeghen, K., Stangé, G., Sadones, J., Xavier, C., Aerts, J.M.F.G., Gorus, F.K., Martens, G.A., 2015. Potential of UCHL1 as biomarker for destruction of pancreatic beta cells. J. Proteomics 117, 156–167.

Cerqueira, F.R., Morandell, S., Ascher, S., Mechtler, K., Huber, L.A., Pfeifer, B., Graber, A., Tilg, B., Baumgartner, C., 2009. Improving phosphopeptide/protein identification using a new data mining framework for MS/MS spectra preprocessing'. J. Proteomics Bioinform. 2, 150–164.

Dander, A., Handler, M., Netzer, M., Pfeifer, B., Seger, M., Baumgartner, C., 2011. [KD^3] A Workflow-Based Application for Exploration of Biomedical Data Sets. In: Hameurlain, A., Küng, J., Wagner, R., Böhm, C., Eder, J., Plant, C. (Eds.), 'Transactions on Large-Scale Data- and Knowledge-Centered Systems IV', Lecture Notes in Computer Science. Berlin Heidelberg: Springer, pp. 148–157.

Development Core Team, R., 2009. R: A Language and Environment for Statistical Computing. R Foundation for Statistical Computing, Vienna, Austria.

Ettre, L.S., 1993. Nomenclature for chromatography (IUPAC Recommendations 1993). Pure Appl. Chem. 65 (4), 819–872.

Fayyad, U., Piatetsky-Shapiro, G., Smyth, P., 1996. From data mining to knowledge discovery in databases'. AI Magazine 17 (3), 37–54.

Fenn, J.B., Mann, M., Meng, C.K., Wong, S.F., Whitehouse, C.M., 1989. Electrospray ionization for mass spectrometry of large biomolecules. Science 246 (4926), 64–71.

Gerszten, R.E., Asnani, A., Carr, S.A., 2011. Status and prospects for discovery and verification of new biomarkers of cardiovascular disease by proteomics. Circ. Res. 109 (4), 463–474.

Hall, M., Frank, E., Holmes, G., Pfahringer, B., Reutemann, P., Witten, I.H., 2009. The WEKA data mining software: an update. SIGKDD Explor Newsl 11 (1), 10–18.

Handler, M., Pallua, J.D., Schäfer, G., Netzer, M., Osl, M., Seger, M., Pfeifer, B., Becker, M., Meding, S., Rauser, S., Walch, A., Klocker, H., Bartsch, G., Huck, C.W., Baumgartner, C., Bonn, G.K., 2011. A Workflow for Preprocessing and Proteomic Biomarker Identification on Mass-Spectrometry Data. In: Baumgartner, C. (Ed.),; Proc. 8th Int. Conf. on Biomedical Engineering (Biomed'2011). ACTA Press, pp. 181–187.

JFreeChart, 2012. JFreeChart. http://sourceforge.net/projects/jfreechart.

John, G.H., Kohavi, R., Pfleger, K., 1994. Irrelevant Features and the Subset Selection Problem. In: Cohen, W.W., Hirsh, H. (Eds.), In: Proceedings of the 11th International Conference on Machine LearningMorgan Kaufmann Publishers, pp. 121–129.

Karas, M., Hillenkamp, F., 1988. Laser desorption ionization of proteins with molecular masses exceeding 10,000 daltons. Anal. Chem. 60 (20), 2299–2301.

Kohavi, R., John, G.H., 1998. The Wrapper Approach. In: Liu, H., Motoda, H. (Eds.), 'Feature Extraction, Construction and Selection: A Data Mining Perspective', Vol. 453 of The Springer International Series in Engineering and Computer Science. Kluwer Academic Publishers, pp. 33–50.

Le Cessie, S., Van Houwelingen, J.C., 1992. Ridge estimators in logistic regression. Appl Statist 41 (1), 191–201.

Lee, M.-Y., Huang, C.-H., Kuo, C.-J., Lin, C.-L.S., Lai, W.-T., Chiou, S.-H., 2015. Clinical proteomics identifies urinary CD14 as a potential biomarker for diagnosis of stable coronary artery disease. PLoS One 10 (2), e0117169.

Li, X., 2005. PROcess: ciphergen SELDI-TOF processing. R package version. 1(24).

Li, X., Gentleman, R., Lu, X., Shi, Q., Iglehart, J.D., Harris, L., Miron, A., 2005. SELDI-TOF Mass Spectrometry Protein Data. In: Gentleman, R., Carey, V.J., Huber, W., Irizarry, R.A., Dudoit, S. (Eds.), 'Bioinformatics and Computational Biology Solutions Using R and Bioconductor', Statistics for Biology and Health. Springer, New York, pp. 91–109.

Lindén, M., Lind, S.B., Mayrhofer, C., Segersten, U., Wester, K., Lyutvinskiy, Y., Zubarev, R., Malmström, P.-U., Pettersson, U., 2012. Proteomic analysis of urinary biomarker candidates for nonmuscle invasive bladder cancer. Proteomics 12 (1), 135–144.

Mantini, D., Petrucci, F., Pieragostino, D., Boccio, P.D., Nicola, M.D., Ilio, C.D., Federici, G., Sacchetta, P., Comani, S., Urbani, A., 2007. LIMPIC: a computational method for the separation of protein MALDI-TOF-MS signals from noise. BMC Bioinformatics 8, 101.

Millonig, G., Praun, S., Netzer, M., Baumgartner, C., Dornauer, A., Mueller, S., Villinger, J., Vogel, W., 2010. Non-invasive diagnosis of liver diseases by breath analysis using an optimized ion-molecule reaction-mass spectrometry approach: a pilot study. Biomarkers 15 (4), 297–306.

Netzer, M., Millonig, G., Osl, M., Pfeifer, B., Praun, S., Villinger, J., Vogel, W., Baumgartner, C., 2009. A new ensemble-based algorithm for identifying breath gas marker candidates in liver disease using ion molecule reaction mass spectrometry. Bioinformatics 25 (7), 941–947.

Netzer, M., Weinberger, K.M., Handler, M., Seger, M., Fang, X., Kugler, K.G., Graber, A., Baumgartner, C., 2011. Profiling the human response to physical exercise: a computational strategy for the identification and kinetic analysis of metabolic biomarkers. J. Clin. Bioinforma. 1 (1), 34.

Osl, M., Dreiseitl, S., Pfeifer, B., Weinberger, K., Klocker, H., Bartsch, G., Schäfer, G., Tilg, B., Graber, A., Baumgartner, C., 2008. A new rule-based algorithm for identifying metabolic markers in prostate cancer using tandem mass spectrometry. Bioinformatics 24 (24), 2908–2914.

Pallua, J.D., Schäfer, G., Seifarth, C., Becker, M., Meding, S., Rauser, S., Walch, A., Handler, M., Netzer, M., Popovscaia, M., Osl, M., Baumgartner, C., Lindner, H., Kremser, L., Sarg, B., Bartsch, G., Huck, C.W., Bonn, G.K., Klocker, H., 2013. MALDI-MS tissue imaging identification of biliverdin reductase b overexpression in prostate cancer. J. Proteomics 91, 500–514.

Parker, C.E., Warren, M.R., Mocanu, V., 2010. Mass Spectrometry for Proteomics. In: Alzate, O. (Ed.), Neuroproteomics. CRC Press, pp. 71–92.

Pfeifer, B., Aschaber, J., Baumgartner, C., Modre, R., Dreiseitl, S., Schreier, G., Tilg, B., 2007. A Data Warehouse for Prostate Cancer Biomarker Discovery. In: Cohen Boulakia, S., Tannen, V. (Eds.), 4th International Workshop, DILS. Springer, Philadelphia, PA, USA, p. 9ff, Vol. 4544 of LNCS.

Pfeifer, B., Tejada, M.M., Kugler, K., Osl, M., Netzer, M., Seger, M., Modre-Osprian, R., Schreier, G., Tilg, B., 2008. A Biomedical Knowledge Discovery in Databases Design Tool - Turning Data Into Information. In: eHealth2008 – Medical Informatics Meets eHealth.pp. 23–28.

Plant, C., Osl, M., Tilg, B., Baumgartner, C., 2006. Feature Selection on High Throughput SELDI-TOF Mass-Spectrometry Data for Identifying Biomarker Candidates in Ovarian and Prostate Cancer. In: 'ICDMW '06: Proceedings of the Sixth IEEE International Conference on Data Mining - Workshops'. IEEE Computer Society, Washington, DC, USA, pp. 174–179.

Poté, N., Alexandrov, T., Faouder, J.L., Laouirem, S., Léger, T., Mebarki, M., Belghiti, J., Camadro, J.-M., Bedossa, P., Paradis, V., 2013. Imaging mass spectrometry reveals modified forms of Histone H4 as new biomarkers of microvascular invasion in hepatocellular carcinomas. Hepatology 58 (3), 983–994.

Ressom, H.W., Varghese, R.S., Orvisky, E., Drake, S.K., Hortin, G.L., Abdel-Hamid, M., Loffredo, C.A., Goldman, R., 2005. Analysis of MALDI-TOF Serum Profiles for Biomarker Selection and Sample Classification. In: Proceedings of the 2005 IEEE Symposium on Computational Intelligence in Bioinformatics and Computational Biology. IEEE, pp. 1–7, CIBCB'05.

Ringman, J.M., Schulman, H., Becker, C., Jones, T., Bai, Y., Immermann, F., Cole, G., Sokolow, S., Gylys, K., Geschwind, D.H., Cummings, J.L., Wan, H.I., 2012. Proteomic changes in cerebrospinal fluid of presymptomatic and affected persons carrying familial Alzheimer disease mutations. Arch. Neurol. 69 (1), 96–104.

Saeys, Y., Inza, I., Larranaga, P., 2007. A review of feature selection techniques in bioinformatics. Bioinformatics 23 (19), 2507–2517.

Satten, G.A., Datta, S., Moura, H., Woolfitt, A.R., da G. Carvalho, M., Carlone, G.M., De, B.K., Pavlopoulos, A., Barr, J.R., 2004. Standardization and denoising algorithms for mass spectra to classify whole-organism bacterial specimens. Bioinformatics 20 (17), 3128–3136.

Strohalm, M., Kavan, D., Novák, P., Volný, M., Havlíček, V., 2010. mMass 3: a cross-platform software environment for precise analysis of mass spectrometric data. Anal. Chem. 82 (11), 4648–4651.

Suh, E.J., Kabir, M.H., Kang, U.-B., Lee, J.W., Yu, J., Noh, D.-Y., Lee, C., 2012. Comparative profiling of plasma proteome from breast cancer patients reveals thrombospondin-1 and BRWD3 as serological biomarkers. Exp. Mol. Med. 44 (1), 36–44.

A Comparative Analysis of Read Mapping and Indel Calling Pipelines for Next-Generation Sequencing Data

Jacob Porter, Jonathan Berkhahn, and Liqing Zhang

Department of Computer Science, Virginia Tech, Blacksburg, VA, USA

1 INTRODUCTION

Indels are the second most common class of mutation in the human genome (Mullaney *et al.*, 2010). They consist of an insertion or deletion of one or more DNA bases into a genome. This can have far-ranging effects concerning gene expression and genetic disease (Mullaney *et al.*, 2010). Detecting and identifying indels is a multistep process in which error can be introduced at every step. Starting with a set of DNA sequence reads and a reference DNA genome, reads are first mapped to the reference genome with a mapping program and then the mapped results are inputted into indel-calling software to identify indels.

A growing variety of software is available for read mapping and indel calling. New tools are constantly being developed with an eye toward better performance and increased accuracy. As the variety of available tools and the complexity of the technologies involved in indel calling increases, it becomes increasingly important to understand the relationships between mapping software and indel calling software. While previous studies (Neumann *et al.*, 2013; Pabinger *et al.*, 2013) assessed the accuracy of indel calling by only varying mapping software or by only varying indel-calling software, we studied the accuracy of mapper and indel-calling software combinations. We evaluated the accuracy of pipelines consisting of four popular mapping programs and three indel-calling programs on simulated data based on a portion of human chromosome one. For mapping, BFAST (Homer *et al.*, 2009), Bowtie2 (Langmead and Salzberg, 2012), BWA (Li and Durbin, 2009), and SHRIMP (David *et al.*, 2011) were selected. For indel calling, we used Dindel (Albers *et al.*, 2010), FreeBayes (Wei *et al.*, 2011), and SNVer (Garrison and Marth, 2012). We varied the coverage of the reads inputted to the mappers to study the effects of different levels of read coverage on the precision and recall of called indels. We evaluated the accuracy of these pipelines on indels from 1–30 bases long.

Furthermore, pipeline accuracy was assessed with real human data from chromosome 22. The indels were validated with an alternate method described by Mill *et al.*, (2011).

The remainder of this paper is organized as follows. Section 2 discusses the read-mapping software and the indel calling software we selected. It discusses the methods we used to generate our simulated and real data sets, and the statistics that we used to evaluate the accuracy of our pipelines. Section 3 discusses the accuracy results of the pipelines and runtime on real data. Section 4 concludes.

2 MAPPING AND CALLING SOFTWARE

Read mappers use a seed-and-extend approach to mapping short reads to a reference genome. A string index, such as the Burrows-Wheeler Transform (BWT) or a hash table, is used as a string index. Typically, small portions of sequences from the read are matched to the reference genome string index. Next, different locations on the reference genome, for which the read is mapped from the seeding phase, are extended with an alignment algorithm such as the Smith-Waterman algorithm or the Needleman-Wunsch algorithm. These algorithms perform local and global alignments, respectively. Local alignment finds the most optimal similarity score between strings (DNA sequences) over all possible string lengths. Global alignment finds the optimal similarity over the entire strings. These algorithms include insertions, deletions, and point mutations, so they are ideal for DNA sequence alignment. The location with the best similarity is reported as the location to map the read.

2.1 HASH TABLES

A hash table maps a key to a value. If the value is desired, the key can be supplied to obtain the value. For mapping software, the key is a DNA sequence, and the value is the locations on the DNA string where the key occurs. Hash tables can be built in linear time in the length of the string, and looking up location values with a DNA key can be done in amortized linear time in the DNA key length. The locations give candidate locations for mapping the DNA. For example, if the DNA key is a substring of a short DNA read, and the locations are locations on the reference genome, then the locations give candidate locations on the reference genome to map the read since the key matches those locations exactly. A hash table can be implemented as an array of linked lists, together with a mapping between keys and buckets in the array. The linked list in each bucket stores the values. Hash tables are advantageous as a DNA sequence index since keys with variation and gaps relative to the indexed string can be stored (Homer *et al.*, 2009).

2.2 BWT

Both Bowtie (Langmead and Salzberg, 2012) and BWA (Li and Durbin, 2009) use the FM-Index via the BWT on the reference genome. The BWT can be constructed in the following manner. First, a character $ that is lexicographically smaller than all the other characters G in the string is concatenated to the end of a string T. All lexico-graphically sorted cyclic permutations of the string could be created together with their suffix positions in the suffix array S. The last character for each string in the sort is concatenated together to give BWT(T). For example, the BWT of T = ACAG$ can be found by first creating the sorted array [$ACAG, ACAG$, AG$AC, CAG$A, G$ACA] with suffix array $[6, 0, 2, 1, 3], and the BWT(T) = G$CAA. Notice that for a given suffix W in T, the BWT sorts all occurrences of the substring W in T together, and this is why it is useful in substring matching.

The FM-Index includes an array C(R) for R in G, the character set, that gives the number of characters in T that are lexicographically smaller than R (not including $). So, for example, C(C) = 1 for the previous example since only A is smaller than C. This array is proportional to |R|. The FM-Index also includes a two-dimensional (2D) occurrence array Occ(R, i) that counts the number of occurrences of R in G in BWT (T)[0,i]. For example, Occ(A, 4) = 1 in this example since only one occurrence of A comes before position 4 in the BWT(T). Together, a string W can be matched to T by using the C(.) and Occ(. , .) arrays to retrieve the suffix array interval of S(.) that matches W. Formulas for this are included in the BWA paper and the FM-Index paper, and there are algorithms for computing the FM-Index and the BWT in O (|T|) time. Furthermore, exact substring matching can be done in O(|W|) time (Li and Durbin, 2009).

The FM-Index allows a time-memory tradeoff since only a period of the arrays Occ(. , .) and S(.) need to be stored, and the absent values are calculated when needed. BWA stores Occ(. ,K) for every K that is a multiple of 128, and calculates absent entries of Occ(. , .) by scanning the BWT(T). BWA stores every 32nd entry in the suffix array S(.) and uses a formula for calculating the absent entries when needed. This formula uses the inverse compressed suffix array defined as $\Psi^{-1}(i) = C(BWT(T)[i]) + Occ(BWT(T)[i], i)$ (Li and Durbin, 2009). By a result from the original FM-Index paper by Ferragina and Manzini (2000), $S(k) = S((\Psi^{-1})^j(k)) + j$, where $(\Psi^{-1})^j$ means applying the Ψ^{-1} operation to its own output j times.

2.3 SMITH-WATERMAN ALGORITHM

The Smith-Waterman algorithm is a dynamic programming algorithm that builds a real or implicit array where each cell of the array represents a subproblem in the alignment problem (Smith and Waterman, 1981). For strings a and b and for mismatch scoring function $s(a,b)$ and gap score, W_i, the Smith-Waterman matrix H is

$$H(i, 0) = 0 \; H(0, j) = 0$$

$$H(i, j) = max \begin{cases} 0 \\ H(i-1, j-1) + s(a_i, b_j) \; mismatch \\ max_{k \geq 1}(H(i-k, j) + W_k) \; delete \\ max_{l \geq 1}(H(i, j-l) + W_l) \; insert \end{cases}$$

where $0 \leq i \leq n$ and $0 \leq j \leq m$, where n and m are the lengths of the strings a and b.

The cell $H(n,m)$ contains the optimal score, and the optimal alignment can be found by backtracing starting from the last cell and going in the direction that the matrix was created.

2.4 DINDEL INDEL CALLING MODEL

One of the best indel callers in this study was Dindel. Dindel works in the following manner. First, candidate SNPs and indels are repositioned to canonical positions and grouped into realignment windows of 120 bp each, where a read overlaps with at least 20 bp in the alignment window. For each window, candidate haplotypes $\{H_j\}$ are generated and each candidate haplotype for the window will be considered against the same set of reads R_i. The haplotype posterior probability given the read data, $P(H_j|R)$, is estimated with Bayes' theorem, $P(H_j|R) \propto P(R|H_j)P(H_j)$ where $P(H_j)$ is the prior probability of the candidate haplotype, and $P(R|H_j)$ is the likelihood function (Albers et al., 2010).

Candidate haplotypes can be generated by the user, but they are also created from the read-alignment file. Candidate haplotypes are sequences of DNA that comprise combinations of local blocks. Local blocks can come from the reference genome of the 120-bp realignment window. All portions of the reference genome in the 120-bp window are represented in the set of candidate haplotypes. Local blocks can also come from contiguous DNA sequences with high empirical frequency in the reads, and local blocks can be user specified. Candidate haplotypes are concatenations of local blocks that span the realignment window. For computational efficiency, Dindel defaults to eight candidate halplotypes. Candidate indels, which come from the user or from the alignment file, are inserted into each of the candidate haplotypes.

The likelihood model incorporates base-call reliability with base quality scores from the sequencing technology, read mapping quality, and indel sequencing error given the specific sequence context. The model uses something like a profile hidden Markov model (HMM) with hidden parameters that give the position and length of an insertion or a deletion. Probabilities with these hidden parameters are computed, and then the maximum likelihood is estimated with the Viterbi algorithm. The benefit of the hidden parameters is that they give an alignment for a read concerning deletions and insertions so that indel identity and position can be output (Albers et al., 2010).

3 METHODS

3.1 SOFTWARE WORKFLOW

We selected mapping software that was both widely used and that covered a variety of different algorithms. Bowtie2 (Langmead and Salzberg, 2012) and Burrows-Wheeler Aligner (BWA; Li and Durbin, 2009) were both popular tools that use the BWT to map reads. SHRiMP (David et al., 2011) and BFAST (Homer et al., 2009) are both hash-based mapping tools. SHRIMP creates a hash table index of the read sequences, but BFAST creates a hash table index of the reference sequences. For indel calling, we selected two programs that use Bayesian statistics: Dindel (Albers *et al.*, 2010) and FreeBayes (Wei *et al.*, 2011). SNVer (Garrison and Marth, 2012) is based on a frequentist model developed by the SNVer creators and reports p-values for variant calls.

All of our experiments were run on SystemG nodes. SystemG is a research cluster at Virginia Tech. Each node had two quad-core 2.8-GHz Intel Xeon processors and 8 GB of random access memory (RAM). The mappers were run with four threads when possible, but the indel callers were single-thread only.

Each tool was run with default settings since that is how it would most likely be used. The workflow consisted of creating Sequence Alignment/Map Format files (SAM files) from each read-mapper and then transforming the SAM files into a binary form (BAM files) with SAMtools. Finally, each indel-caller produced a virtual contact file (VCF) from the BAM files. The following are the version numbers for the software: bfast-0.7.0a, bowtie2-2.1.0, bwa-0.7.1, SHRiMP-2.2.3, dindel-1.01, freebayes-0.9.9, and SNVer-0.4.1. The real data workflow was similar to the simulated data workflow. The differences are that SHRiMP was run with –no-qv-check and –qv-offset 33 because the real data were Sanger traces rather than Illumina reads, and Dindel was run with –numWindowsPerFile 1000000. Dindel was not used much on real data because at one day of running, it was still not finished. The workflow and arguments used were the following.

1. Read Mapping:

   BFAST:
   bfast fasta2brg -f reference.fasta
   bfast index -f reference.fasta -m 11111111111111111111111 -w 14 -n 4
   bfast match -f reference.fasta -r reads.fastq -n 4 -t 1>
   bfast.matches.bmf 2>bfast.matches.out
   bfast localalign -n 4 -t -f reference.fasta -m
   bfast.matches.bmf 1>bfast.aligned.baf 2>bfast.aligned.out
   bfast postprocess -f reference.fasta -i bfast.aligned.baf -o 3 -a 3>align.sam

   Bowtie 2:
   bowtie2-build reference.fasta reference
   bowtie2 –p 4 -x ref -U reads.fastq -S align.sam

   BWA:
   bwa index reference.fasta
   bwa aln reference.fasta reads.fastq –t 4 > align.sai
   bwa samse reference.fasta align.sai reads.fastq > align.sam

   SHRiMP:
   gmapper -N 4 reads.fastq reference.fasta > align.sam

2. BAM Conversion:

Samtools:
samtools faidx reference.fasta
samtools view -b -S align.sam > align.bam
samtools sort align.bam align.sorted
samtools index align.sorted.bam

3. Indel Calling

Dindel:
dindel –ref reference.fasta –outputFile dindel_output –bamFile align.sorted.bam –analysis getCIGARindels
makeWindows.py –inputVarFile dindel_output.variants.txt –windowFilePrefix realign_windows –numWindowsPerFile 1000
dindel –analysis indels –bamFile align.sorted.bam –doDiploid –ref reference.fasta –varFile realign_windows.1.txt –libFile dindel_output.libraries.txt – outputFile stage3_output
echo "stage3_output.glf.txt" > list.txt
mergeOutputDiploid.py -i list.txt -o indels.vcf -r reference.fasta

FreeBayes:
freebayes –no-snps –no-mnps –no-complex -b align.sorted.bam -f reference.fasta -v indels.vcf

SNVer:
java -jar SNVerIndividual.jar -i align.sorted.bam -o indels.vcf -r reference.fasta

3.2 SIMULATED DATA

The simulated data was generated from 10 megabases of chromosome, 1 from a human genome publicly available from the National Center for Biotechnology Information. Artificial mutations were introduced using inGAP, a software tool for the manipulation of genetic data (Qi *et al;*, 2010). Single-nucleotide polymorphisms (SNPs) were inserted at a divergence rate of 0.1%, and indels were inserted at a divergence rate of 0.02%. These values were chosen since they were realistic (Mullaney *et al.*, 2010) . Indel lengths were uniformly distributed from 1 to 30 bases. A total of 10 replicates of simulated reads were produced to generate average and error statistics for the tests. Reads of uniform 50 base pair length were generated from the mutation sequences in the FASTQ file format using inGAP. Reads of length 50 were chosen because indel identification is more complex for shorter single-end reads since they "lack insert length variance" (Neumann *et al.*, 2013), so short single-end reads represented a good test of indel pipeline sensitivity. In order to study the effects of varying coverage on the accuracy of the pipelines, reads were generated for 10x, 50x, and 100x coverage for each of the mutation sequences.

At a fixed coverage of 10x, reads of 100 bp and 150 bp long were sampled from the same 10 replicates of mutated FASTA files to study read length effects on mapping.

4 REAL DATA

Applied Biosystems (Sanger) paired-end traces from the set Chr_22_7340 were identified and downloaded from the NCBI trace archive. These traces were used in a Devine lab study that searched for indels in human chromosome 22 (Mill *et al.*, 2011). The paper identified 6487 indels for the Chr_22_7340 traces.

We cleansed the traces of contamination using NCBI VecScreen, where traces with vector contamination in the middle were discarded and traces with vector contamination on the ends had the contamination trimmed off. After this, there were 217,924 traces with sizes as much as 2000 bp. Since short read mappers perform poorly with very long sequences, three samples of 10, 20, and 30 million 100bp portions of the traces were sampled with replacement in order to simulate short reads. The three sets of simulated single-end sequences were run through the pipelines with timing tracked with the Linux "date" command.

A second real data set from the 1000 genomes project (http://www.1000genomes. org/;) (McVean *et al.*, 2012) was evaluated. This project called variants by aligning short reads to a reference genome and then computationally calling indels presumably with Dindel. The phase 3 variant set (VCF file) of September 17, 2014, for human chromosome 22 was downloaded and compared to the indels called by our pipelines for reads from a randomly chosen individual, NA18647. The FASTQ file used for this individual was SRR766008_2.filt.fastq, which comprised 28,936,312 101bp reads generated with Illumina short read technology. The chromosome 22 variants for individual NA 18647 were extracted from the phase 3 variant set with Tabix (Li, 2011) and VCF-subset from VCFtools (Danecek *et al.*, 2011):

```
tabix − h file.vcf.gz 22 | perl vcf − subset − c NA18647 | bgzip − c > new.vcf.gz
```

4.1 INDEL DETECTION

A confusion matrix for each pipeline on each data set was created that recorded true positives, false positives and false negatives. Indels were recorded as true positives if the predicted indel's position was plus or minus 5 nucleotides of the actual indel's position and the predicted length was within 5% of the actual length (with all lengths set to be one if 5% of the actual length was less than 1). The indel had to be correctly classified as an insertion or a deletion marked a true positive; otherwise, it was classified as a false positive. The sequence identity of predicted and actual indels was not checked since differences in sequence identity were rare. A false positive was a predicted indel that did not meet the preceding criteria, and a false negative was an actual indel that was not identified by the indel classifier. Precision, recall, and F1-score were calculated for all pipelines to assess accuracy.

Precision is the ratio of true positives to the sum of true positives and false positives. Precision reveals the percentage of predicted indels that are genuine. *Recall* is the ratio of true positives to the sum of true positives and false negatives. Recall reveals the percentage of genuine indels that are predicted. A good indel classifier will have both high precision and high recall. F1-score is the harmonic mean of precision and recall. F1-score is 2 *(precision * recall) / (precision+recall). A perfect classifier has precision and recall (and F1-score) at 1.

Python 2.6 and Bash scripts were created to do the statistical analysis and workflow.

5 RESULTS AND DISCUSSION

5.1 ANALYSIS OF F1-SCORE AND COVERAGE ON SIMULATED DATA

In our results on simulated data with indels of size 1–30 bases, there were clearly pipelines that performed better than other pipelines as measured by the F1-score (Figure 28.1). For each pipeline, Figure 28.1 shows the average F1-score and the minimum and maximum F1-score of the 10 replicates. Most indels called had fewer than 10 bases.

Figure 28.1 shows that pipelines with 10X coverage have the best F1-scores, and that 50X and 100X coverage perform less well. This was explained by a tradeoff between precision and recall caused by both increasing false positives and increasing true positives. As coverage increased, recall increased since indel callers return more predicted indels, and thus more genuine indels. However, there were more false positives as coverage increased, so precision went down at the same time. The general downward trend of the F1-score was because precision decreased more than recall increased with increasing coverage. This suggests that there is some coverage amount that maximizes F1-score for the data, and increasing coverage is not always desirable. This result was consistent with other work that showed statistically significant precision and recall trends with increasing coverage (Neumann *et al.*, 2013).

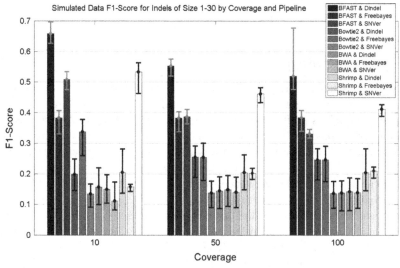

FIGURE 29.1

The F1-score of indel-calling pipelines on simulated data with reads containing indels of 1–30 bases. The results are divided into sets of 10X, 50X, and 100X coverage. The F1-score is shown with average, low and high scores.

The three top performing pipelines were BFAST-Dindel (avg F1-score 0.66), SHRIMP-SNVer (0.53), and BFAST-SNVer (0.51) in the 10X coverage for 1-30 indels. The BFAST-Dindel pipeline had the best average F1-score for all coverage amounts (Figure 29.1). SHRIMP pipelines were interesting since the F1-score varied considerably. The SHRIMP-SNVer pipeline was among the top performing, but SHRIMP-FreeBayes and SHRIMP-Dindel performed poorly. By default, SHRIMP mapped some reads to multiple positions, while other read mappers only report uniquely aligned reads by default. This could be the cause of SHRIMP's variable performance.

Read mappers use a seed and extend strategy, and BFAST's seeding strategy used a sliding window at every base. Bowtie2 used multiple 20bp seeds with an offset determined by the read length. Perhaps BFAST's seed strategy allowed it to be more accurate. All the mappers' extension phases are similar since they use local or global alignment algorithms (Langmead and Salzberg, 2012; Li and Durbin, 2009; David et al., 2011; Homer et al., 2009).

The F1-score difference for 10X coverage between the best pipeline (BFAST-Dindel) and the worst (BWA-SNVer) was about 0.546. BWA generally performed poorly, and this could be because it only supported gaps that were less than 10 bases in alignment (Li and Durbin, 2009). Even though BWA and Bowtie2 used a similar seeding strategy with the BWT, Bowtie2 pipelines usually had better F1-scores. Bowtie2's split seed approach handles some variation in the seed (Langmead and Salzberg, 2012).

Interestingly, there isn't one indel caller that clearly did the best overall. Bowtie2-SNVer was among the lowest performing, while SHRIMP-SNVer was among the best. Dindel did well with BFAST, but not very well with SHRIMP.

5.2 PRECISION AND RECALL ON SIMULATED DATA WITH SMALLER AND LONGER INDELS

Figures 29.2 and 29.3 show a comparison of the effects of longer indels on precision and recall at 10X coverage. Pipelines performed worse for data with indels of 1-30 bases (Figure 29.3) than for indels with 1-10 bases (Figure 29.2). Figure 29.3's precision-recall tuples are generally shifted left when compared to Figure 29.2. The Bowtie2-FreeBayes pipeline did noticeably better with 1–10 indel lengths.

The precision-recall plots show which pipelines are conservative, which generous, and which are balanced. The pipelines involving BWA and Bowtie2 were the most conservative with high precision but low recall. Pipelines involving FreeBayes were the most generous with low precision but higher recall. BFAST-Dindel and SHRIMP-SNVer had the most balanced precision and recall results, with (0.648,0.771) and (0.640,0.799), respectively, for indels of length 1–10. The BFAST-Dindel pipeline performed better than SHRIMP-SNVer for indels of length 1–30.

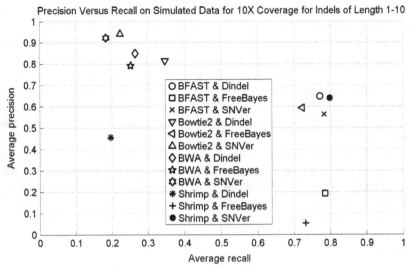

FIGURE 29.2

Average precision and average recall for 10 simulated data replicates for the indel-calling pipelines. Precision and recall was calculated for indels with only 1–10 bases at 10X coverage. The reads contained indels as large as 30 bases.

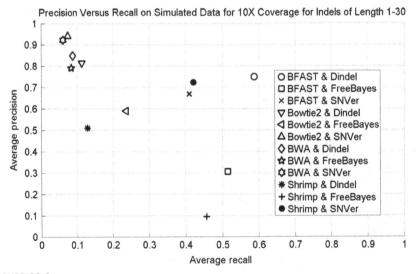

FIGURE 29.3

Average precision and average recall for 10 simulated data replicates for the indel-calling pipelines. Precision and recall was calculated for all indels. Indels had 1–30 bases at 10X coverage.

Bowtie2 pipelines generally appeared mediocre in our tests. BFAST pipelines had generally good performance with different indel callers, while SHRIMP pipeline performance varied considerably with indel-calling software. BWA pipelines performed poorly.

5.3 EFFECT OF READ LENGTH ON SIMULATED DATA

Figure 29.4 shows the F1-score of the pipelines for read lengths 50 bp, 100 bp, and 150 bp. There is a generally positive correlation with F1-score and read length for all pipelines. The results are similar to the coverage results, with pipelines involving BFAST and Dindel performing well. Interestingly, the SHRIMP-Dindel pipeline improved dramatically at 100 bp, and Bowtie2 pipelines improved as well. BWA pipelines and SHRIMP-FreeBayes did poorly.

5.4 ACCURACY OF SANGER REAL DATA

The only accurately called indels on real data were smaller than 5 bp. Figure 29.5 shows the F1-scores of the real data pipelines. SNVer pipelines had the best F1-scores. Similar to the simulated data, pipelines with FreeBayes were too generous with high recall but low precision. Average precision and recall for FreeBayes was 0.000440955 and 0.010906428, but with SNVer it was 0.00117591 and 0.001079081. Thus, SNVer was more conservative in indel calling. The SHRIMP-SNVer and Bowtie2-SNVer pipelines did the best, while BWA-FreeBayes was the worst. The choice of read mapper made little difference, and this could be because only small indels were called. True positives were few relative to indels called (Table 29.1). For the BWA mappings, Dindel completed in 6.6 h with similar precision (0.00062) and recall (0.0026) to the BFAST-SNVer pipeline (0.00079, 0.0012).

5.5 RUN-TIME PERFORMANCE ON SANGER DATA

Table 29.1 summarizes run-time performance on the 10 million read set for the pipelines for the real human chr22 data. Bowtie2 and BWA had the fastest run times at 27 and 23 min, respectively. BFAST and SHRIMP were the slowest mappers, and both used a sliding window hashing seed strategy. BFAST was about 10 min slower, but SHRIMP was 6.2 times slower than BWA, making SHRIMP pipelines the slowest. The SHRIMP read mapping% is more than 100% since it mapped some reads to multiple positions by default.

The indel callers did not have multithreading, so they were slow. FreeBayes was always faster than SNVer, and SNVer took 145 min with SHRIMP's input, making the SHRIMP-SNVer pipeline the slowest. Dindel took more than a day (except with BWA input), making it less tolerable for big indel-calling projects; however, Dindel has the ability to split its work into multiple files for manual multiprocessing.

5.6 ACCURACY OF 1000 GENOMES REAL DATA

Similar to the Sanger data, F1-scores for the 1000 genomes data were very small. Figure 29.6 summarizes the results. Interestingly, SNVer consistently performed worse than FreeBayes, which is the opposite of the Sanger data. The filtered indel

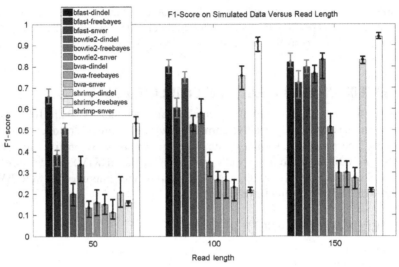

FIGURE 29.4

The F1-score for the pipelines on simulated data versus reads of length 50, 100, and 150 base pairs.

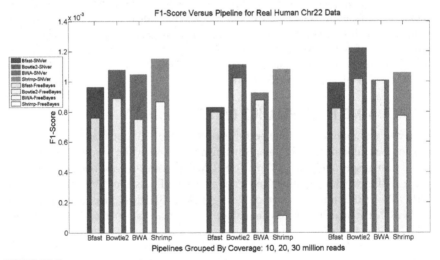

FIGURE 29.5

F1-Score for the indel calling pipelines on 10, 20, and 30 million reads on real human chromosome 22 Sanger traces.

variant file was used for SNVer to compute the F1-score to be consistent with the simulations and the Sanger data, but the unfiltered indel file for 1000 Genomes data had an F1-score on par with FreeBayes. This was the opposite for the simulations and the Sanger data. This is the only data where FreeBayes performed the best. Dindel was prohibitively slow.

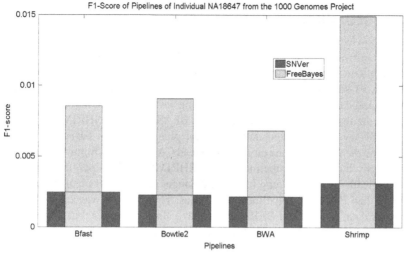

FIGURE 29.6

F1-score for the indel-calling pipelines for individual NA 18647 of the 1000 Genomes Project. Variants from the Phase 3 data were used in comparison.

Table 29.1 Mapper, Caller, Pipeline Run Time, Percent Mapped, and Indels Called on 10 Million Real Human 100-bp Reads

Mapper	Caller	Min	Total Min	% Reads Mapped	Total Indels Called	True Indels
BFAST		38		0.5437498		
	SAMtools	5				
	SNVer	18	61		20,486	8
	FreeBayes	37	80		358,574	139
Bowtie2		8		0.4850195		
	SAMtools	4				
	SNVer	19	31		9812	6
	FreeBayes	16	28		114,679	54
BWA		10		0.412648		
	SAMtools	4				
	SNVer	18	32		6388	5
	FreeBayes	9	23		30,789	14
SHRIMP		143		1.7618786		
	SAMtools	4				
	SNVer	145	292		9145	9
	FreeBayes	59	206		168,684	76

6 CONCLUSIONS

To our knowledge, this work is the first to look at the accuracy of the combination of mapping software and indel-calling software with larger (>10 nucleotides) indels. F1-scores, a measure of accuracy, fell with increased coverage, belying expectations. However, F1-scores increased with read lengths on simulations. Indel-calling accuracy depended on the combination of mapping software and indel-calling software. Some of the top-performing pipelines were BFAST-Dindel, SHRIMP-SNVer, and BFAST-SNVer on simulated data. The best pipeline had an F1-score that is 0.6 higher than the worst pipeline on simulated reads. All pipelines improved with longer read lengths, but Bowtie2 pipelines and the SHRIMP-Dindel pipeline improved dramatically with longer read lengths. On real Sanger data, SNVer pipelines were more accurate than FreeBayes pipelines in all cases. The opposite was true for the 1000 Genomes data. SNVer and SHRIMP can have slow run times, but Dindel was by far the slowest variant caller. Future work could include exploring the parameter space of the tools to observe the effects of argument selection on sensitivity.

REFERENCES

Albers, C.A., Lunter, G., MacArthur, Daniel G., McVean, Gilean, Ouwehand, Willem H., Durbin, Richard, 2010. Dindel: Accurate indel calls from short-read data. Genome Res.

Danecek, Petr, et al., 2011. The variant call format and VCFtools. Bioinformatics 27 (15), 2156–2158.

David, M., Dzamba, M., Lister, D., Ilie, L., Brudno, M., 2011. SHRiMP2: sensitive yet practical Short Read Mapping. Bioinformatics 27, 1011–1102.

Ferragina, Paolo, Manzini, Giovanni, 2000. Opportunistic Data Structures with Applications. In: Proc. 41st IEEE Symposium on Foundations of Computer Science (FOCS), Redondo Beach, CA, (USA).

Erik Garrison, Gabor Marth, 2012. Haplotype-based variant detection from short-read sequencing. ArXiv:1207.3907[q-bio.GN].

Heng, Li, 2011. Tabix: fast retrieval of sequence features from generic TAB-delimited files. Bioinformatics 27 (5), 718–719.

Homer, N., Merriman, B., Nelson, S.F., 2009. BFAST: an alignment tool for large scale genome resequencing. PLoS One 4 (11), e7767.

Langmead, B., Salzberg, S., 2012. Fast gapped-read alignment with Bowtie 2. Nat. Methods 9, 357–359.

Li, H., Durbin, R., 2009. Fast and accurate short read alignment with Burrows-Wheeler Transform. Bioinformatics 25, 1754–1760.

McVean, et al., 2012. An integrated map of genetic variation from 1,092 human genomes. Nature 491, 56–65.

Mill, Ryan E., Pittard, Stephen, et al., 2011. Natural genetic variation caused by small insertions and deletions in the human genome. Genome Res. 21, 830–839.

Mullaney, J.M., Mills, R.E., Pittard, W.S., et al., 2010. Small insertions and deletions (INDELs) in human genomes. Hum. Mol. Genet. 19, R 131-b.

Neumann, J.A., Isakov, O., Shomron, N., 2013 Jan. Analysis of insertion-deletion from deep-sequencing data: software evaluation for optimal detection. Brief. Bioinform. 14 (1), 46–55.

Pabinger, S., et al., 2013 Jan 21. survey of tools for variant analysis of next-generation genome sequencing data. Brief. Bioinform.

Qi, J., Zhao, F., Buboltz, A., et al., 2010. InGAP: an integrated next-generation genome analysis pipeline. Bioinformatics 26, 127–129.

Smith, Temple F., Waterman, Michael S., 1981. Identification of Common Molecular Subsequences. J. Mol. Biol. 147, 195–197.

Wei, Z., Wang, W., Hu, P., Lyon, G.J., Hakonarson, H., 2011 Oct. SNVer: a statistical tool for variant calling in analysis of pooled or individual next-generation sequencing data. Nucleic Acids Res. 39 (19), e132.

Two-Stage Evolutionary Quantification of *In Vivo* MRS Metabolites

30

G.A. Papakostas[1], D.A. Karras[2], B.G. Mertzios[3], D. van Ormondt[4], and D. Graveron-Demilly[5]

Department of Computer and Informatics Engineering, Eastern Macedonia and Thrace Institute of Technology, Kavala, Greece[1]
Department of Automation, Sterea Hellas Institute of Technology, Evia, Greece[2]
Department of Electrical and Computer Engineering, Democritus University of Thrace (DUTH), Greece[3]
Applied Physics, Delft University of Technology, Delft, Netherlands CN[4]
Laboratoire CREATIS-LRMN, CNRS UMR 5220, Inserm U630, Université Claude Villeurbanne, France[5]

1 INTRODUCTION

Magnetic resonance spectroscopy (MRS) has been widely used in medical diagnosis due to its advantage to provide diagnostic information about the biochemical content of the human tissues in a noninvasive manner. Among the several processing steps (in't Zandt *et al.*, 2001) applied to the MRS data, the quantification of the metabolites presented into the retrieved spectrum constitutes a significant and challenging scientific research field. The quantification of the metabolites' concentrations is achieved by measuring the area under their peaks presented into the MRS spectrum.

Depending on the processing domain where the quantification algorithms are applied, they are classified into two categories: time-domain (Vanhamme *et al.*, 2001) and frequency-domain (Mierisova and Ala-Korpela, 2001) methods. While in the time-domain algorithms, the acquired signal (MRS) is processed in its physical domain, in the frequency domain, the signal is transformed into its frequency spectrum by applying a Fourier Transform (FT). Although the proposed methodology is independent of the processing domain, the overall technique is described in the time domain.

In this work, a novel technique that encounters the quantification procedure of *in vivo* MRS metabolites as an optimization problem, which is solved by using a simple Genetic Algorithm (GA), is proposed (Weber *et al.*, 1998). The parallel nature of the GA gives it more chances to converge in a global optimum at the expense of speed. Moreover, evolutionary optimization permits the usage of objective minimization functions without the requirement to be differentiable and allows prior knowledge of the metabolite properties (such as the frequency and phase of each metabolite peak) to be easily incorporated into the overall quantification procedure.

Mainly, there are three open issues to cope with regarding the quantification of the metabolites by using evolutionary optimization: (1) the high overlapping of the metabolites' peaks that makes the separation of these peaks difficult, (2) the low convergence rate of the GA as the number of unknowns increases, due to high complex search space and (3) the low performance of the GA in noise conditions, where the presence of a noisy signal's samples increases the search space virtually.

As far as the first issue is concerned, our previous studies (Papakostas *et al.*, 2009, 2010a, 2010b) have shown that the GA is able to separate the peaks satisfactorily, and its performance is highly dependent on the noise level of the acquired MRS signal.

On the other hand, the capabilities of the GA to find a global optimum set of peak parameters that are necessary to quantify them decrease as the unknown variables are increased. One advantage of the GA-based quantification is that it permits the easy incorporation [in the form of constraints in the fitness function definition (Papakostas *et al.*, 2010a)] of any prior knowledge into the quantification procedure. In this way, the number of unknowns can be reduced by boosting the overall performance of the GA.

This phenomenon of the high complex search spaces becomes more difficult in noisy conditions. The presence of noisy samples further increases the complexity of the search space since the correlation of the desired approximated signal with the noisy one is significantly lower.

However, while the incorporation of as many as possible prior knowledge enforces the GA based optimization procedure, this amount of knowledge is not always available. In this case, the performance of the GA-based quantification is quite poor.

The main contribution of this chapter focuses on the increasing of the GA quantification performance, by alleviating the influence of the noise with the use of less prior knowledge simultaneously. This is achieved by applying an additional processing stage of noise removal and signal smoothing. For this purpose, along with a wavelet denoising by applying discrete wavelet transform, the signal separation by Singular Value Decomposition (SVD) analysis is also examined (Zhu *et al.*, 2003). These two processing steps are investigated separately and in a combinational fashion by formulating a novel, two-stage evolutionary quantification technique with improved performance.

The organization of this chapter is as follows. The main processing steps of the proposed methodology are analyzed in detail in section 2. An extensive study regarding the performance of the introduced method is described in section 3. Finally, the main conclusions are summarized in section 4.

2 PROPOSED METHODOLOGY

In this section, a model-based quantification method that tackles the problem as a curve-fitting procedure is proposed. The curve-fitting procedure is implemented by considering an optimization problem of finding the model parameter set that best fits the measured curve.

Mainly, three different line shapes are commonly used to model the magnetic resonance (MR) signals—that is, Free Induction Decays (FIDs) (Vanhamme *et al.*, 2001): the Lorentzian, Gaussian, and Voigt model line-shapes. The proposed quantification methodology considers the first line-shape model, while all the processing is taking place in the time domain, although it also can be applied with the other line shapes and in the frequency domain.

An MRS signal is composed of a set of metabolites that are exponentials, and its description according to the Lorentzian line shape is as follows:

$$y_{MRS}(t) = \sum_{k=1}^{K} a_k e^{j\varphi_k} e^{(-d_k + j2\pi f_k)t}, \tag{30.1}$$

where K represents the number of different resonance frequencies. Moreover, a_k is the amplitude, d_k the damping factor, f_k the frequency, and φ_k the phase of the kth peak component.

The quantification procedure includes the determination of the parameter set $\{a_k, d_k, f_k, \varphi_k\}$ for each peak comprising the MRS signal. Under these circumstances, the quantification procedure can be described as an optimization problem according to the following definition:

> *Find a parameter set that best fits the time-domain MRS signal in process, in terms of an error objective function.*

In this study, this optimization problem is addressed by the usage of a GA, the main operational principles of which are analyzed hereafter.

2.1 METHODOLOGY DESCRIPTION

The proposed methodology consists of two distinctive processing stages, each having a specific contribution in achieving the target, which is the accurate quantification of the metabolites comprising the MRS signal under process. A block diagram of the introduced method is illustrated in Figure 30.1.

Based on this diagram, the acquired MRS signal is preprocessed initially, before being inserted to the main quantification mechanism of the method that gives the final solution (set of model parameters).

The two processing stages of the method, along with their specific subfunctions, are described in the next sections.

2.2 STAGE 1: MRS SIGNAL PREPROCESSING

The main role of this preprocessing stage is the smoothing of the analyzed MRS signal by applying wavelet denoising, SVD signal separation, or both. This stage is of major significance since it aims to reduce the influence of the noise to the quantification procedure by providing the second stage (GA quantification) with a signal that is very close to the desired line-shape model. In this direction, three different approaches are studied, as depicted in Figure 30.2.

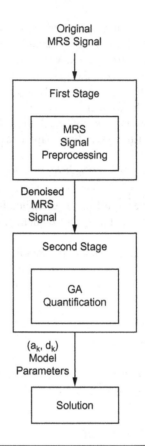

FIGURE 30.1

Block diagram of the proposed methodology.

Initially, a typical wavelet denoising procedure is applied on the real part of the time-domain MRS signal, while in the second approach, the SVD signal separation is used to discard the noisy singular values. Finally, these two methods are combined in a back-to-back operation to improve the final noise reduction.

It is worth mentioning that the order the wavelet denoising and SVD separation are applied is important. The former task gives a description of the signal in many frequency bands, and therefore, the denoising in the wavelet domain can remove more high-frequency components of the signal (and thus noise), while the coarse characteristics of the signal remain unchanged. On the other hand, SVD separation gives a more coarse description of the signal, so a possible first application of SVD could remove useful information of the signal and not as much noise. In the proposed scheme, the wavelet denoising removes many noisy components, and then, in a second phase, the SVD further smooths the already-denoised MRS signal.

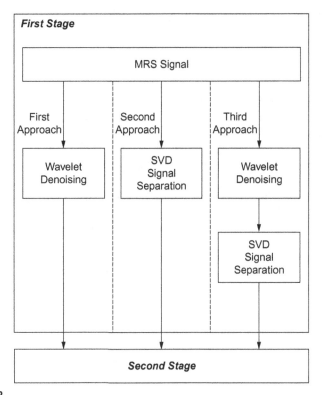

FIGURE 30.2

Examined approaches of the first processing stage.

2.2.1 Wavelet denoising

Wavelet analysis constitutes an advanced signal processing tool that enables the breaking up of a signal into shifted and scaled versions of the base wavelet, called *mother wavelet*. This description has the advantage of studying a signal on a time-scale domain by providing time and frequency (there is a relation between scale and frequency), which both are useful pieces of information about the signal, simultaneously.

The procedure of decomposition (*analysis*) into several resolutions and reconstruction (*synthesis*) of a signal f (MRS signal in this case) can be described by Eqs. (30.2) and (30.3), respectively:

$$f(t) = \sum_k u_{j_0,k} \cdot \varphi_{j_0,k}(t) + \sum_{j=j0}^{\infty} \sum_k w_{j,k} \cdot \psi_{j,k}(t) \tag{30.2}$$

$$u_{j,k} = W_\phi(f(j,k)) \, , \ w_{j,k} = W_\psi(f(j,k)), \tag{30.3}$$

where $u_{j,k}$, $w_{j,k}$ are the scaling and wavelet coefficients, respectively; j,k are indices of the translation and dilation parameters; j_0 represents the coarsest scale; and W_ψ, W_φ

are the *mother wavelet* (ψ) and *scaling function* (φ) wavelet transforms of the signal, defined as

$$W_\psi(f(k2^{-s}, 2^{-s})) = 2^{s/2} \int_{-\infty}^{\infty} f(t) \cdot \psi(2^s t - k) \, dt \qquad (30.4)$$

The scaling and wavelet coefficients are considered as the coefficients of a low-pass (signal *approximation*—low-frequency components) and a high-pass (signal *details*—high-frequency components) filter, respectively. These filters are the part of the *quadrature mirror filter* (Strang and Nguyen, 1997) that describes the one-level decomposition and reconstruction of the signal. The decomposition process can be iterated by decomposing the approximations of each level to lower resolution components, a procedure known as *multiresolution analysis (MRA)*.

Wavelet denoising applied in this research includes the one-level decomposition of the real part of the MRS signal by using the one-dimensional (1D) discrete wavelet transform (DWT), subject to a specific mother wavelet, and the thresholding of the detail coefficients by applying soft thresholding (Donoho, 1995) according to the following formula:

$$\hat{c}_i = \begin{cases} sign(c_i)(|c_i| - thr) & , |c_i| > thr \\ 0 & , |c_i| \leq thr \end{cases} \qquad (30.5)$$

where c_i is the ith detail coefficient, $\hat{c}_i$ is its compressed version, and *thr* the threshold. Soft thresholding is an extension of hard thresholding, which first sets to zero the elements whose absolute values are lower than the threshold, and then shrinks the nonzero coefficients toward 0.

The remaining coefficients are used to reconstruct the initial MRS signal by applying the 1D inverse discrete wavelet transform (IDWT). In this way, the noise components, which affect the detail part of the signal (high-frequency components) are discarded.

The wavelet denoising procedure can be described as follows:

Step 1: Apply one-level decomposition (1D DWT) on the real part of the MRS signal
Step 2: Apply soft thresholding to the detail coefficients
Step 3: Reconstruct the MRS signal by applying 1D IDWT

It must be noted that according to the MATLAB implementation (http://www.mathworks.com/) used in this study, the threshold used in step 2 is equal to

$$thr = \frac{1}{N} \sum_{i=1}^{N} |c_i|, \qquad (30.6)$$

or if this value is 0, the threshold is set to

$$thr = 0.05 \times \max\{|c_i|, i \in [1, N], \qquad (30.7)$$

where c_i is the ith detail coefficient.

After the denoising of the MRS signal using the previous procedure, the signal is expected to be smoother, with reduced noisy components able to be quantified more accurately by the GA of the second stage.

It is noted that the prescribed wavelet denoising procedure is applied by using the MATLAB implementation, consisting of the functions `dencmp()` and `wdencmp()`.

2.2.2 SVD signal separation

SVD has been applied successfully in MRS (Pijnappel *et al.*, 1992; Stamatopoulos *et al.*, 2009), to separate the signal into MRS and noise components. According to the SVD decomposition for any matrix $\mathbf{A} \in R^{m \times n}$, it takes the following form:

$$\mathbf{A} = \mathbf{U} \mathbf{S} \mathbf{V}^{\mathrm{T}}, \tag{30.8}$$

where $\mathbf{U}$ is an $m \times n$ orthogonal matrix, $\mathbf{S}$ an $n \times n$ diagonal matrix, and $\mathbf{V}$ an $n \times n$ orthogonal matrix. The diagonal values of $\mathbf{S}$ are called *singular values* of $\mathbf{A}$ and correspond to the square roots of the eigenvalues of $\mathbf{A}^T\mathbf{A}$ and $\mathbf{A}\mathbf{A}^T$.

In this work, the application of the SVD analysis aims to separate the MRS signal into the pure MRS signal and its noise component based on the following formula (Stamatopoulos *et al.*, 2009):

$$
\begin{aligned}
\mathbf{A}_{MRS} &= \mathbf{A}_{MRS\,signal} + \mathbf{A}_{MRS\,noise} \\
&= \sum_{m=1}^{M} u_m s_m v_m^T + \sum_{m=M+1}^{N} u_m s_m v_m^T,
\end{aligned} \tag{30.9}
$$

where N is the number of the singular values of the $\mathbf{A}$ matrix. In this representation, it is assumed that the original part of the MRS signal is described by the first M (with the higher value) components, while the other value, $N - M$, corresponds to the noise components of the acquired MRS signal.

As it can be seen from this discussion of the SVD analysis, this procedure is applied to a matrix representation of a signal. Therefore, its application directly on the time-domain MRS is not possible, and an intermediate transformation of the signal to a matrix form has to be performed first.

For this purpose, a matrix consisting of the coefficients derived by applying a continuous wavelet transform (CWT) on the MRS signal for various scales and positions (dilations and translations) is constructed. This signal representation is in some sense the wavelet power spectrum (the squared absolute values $|.|^2$ of the coefficients) of the MRS signal over the time and for different scales and is computed as follows:

$$C(s,p) = \int_{-\infty}^{\infty} y_{MRS}(t)\psi(s,p)dt, \tag{30.10}$$

where s and p are the scale and position, respectively.

Advantages of this signal representation include that it captures the time and frequency variations of the signal and it permits the reconstruction of the initial image by applying the inverse continuous wavelet transform (ICWT). The reconstruction of the signal by its wavelet coefficients is necessary since after the rejection of the noisy singular values ($m > M$) and the SVD composition of the modified $C^{mod}(s,p)$ coefficients, the denoised MRS signal has to be reconstructed in order to be quantified during the second stage of the methodology.

Moreover, the determination of the M value usually is performed empirically, by a trial-and-error procedure. However, in the proposed methodology, an automatic procedure for the determination of the number of the singular values that better describe the useful part of the MRS signal is also applied. The number of singular values that correspond to the useful part of the MRS signal is defined by applying cluster analysis on the overall singular values derived by the SVD process.

The well-known *k-means* (Kuncheva, 2004) clustering algorithm is used in order to group the singular values of the acquired MRS signal into two separate clusters: one with the useful signal and the other with the noise. Those singular values (M values) that belong to the signal cluster is used in the first summation of Eq. (30.9), while the remaining values ($N - M$) are used in the second summation of the same equation. The SVD signal separation procedure is shown in detail in Figure 30.3.

The SVD signal separation procedure described in this section is applied on the two approaches of the first stage, illustrated in Figure 30.2. While the role of this procedure is clearly defined in the second approach (signal denoising), its usage in combination with the wavelet denoising in the third approach aims to improve the accuracy of the k-means clustering, and therefore the fidelity of the separated signal. The produced denoised MRS signal is then fed to the second stage of the GA-based quantification process.

**SVD
Signal
Separation**

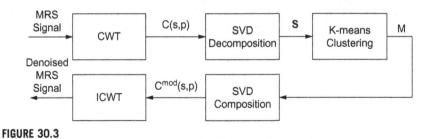

FIGURE 30.3

SVD signal separation procedure.

2.3 STAGE 2: GA QUANTIFICATION

As already mentioned in the previous section, the MRS metabolites quantification procedure can be defined as an optimization problem. In order to solve it, a simple GA is used to create a possible solution by applying repetitively a set of genetically inspired operators.

These operators try to mimic the process that characterizes the evolution of living organisms (Holland, 2001). This theory is based on the mechanism of survival of the fittest individuals in a population. In fact, some specific procedures are taking place until the predominance of the fittest individual.

In the sequel, the used terminology in the field of genetic methods for optimization and searching purposes is given (Coley, 2001):

1. *Individual (chromosome)* is a solution of a problem satisfying the constraints and demands of the system in which it belongs.
2. *Population* is a set of candidate solutions of the problem (chromosomes), which contains the final solution.
3. *Fitness* is a real number that characterizes any solution and indicates how appropriate the solution is for the problem under consideration.
4. *Selection* is an operator applied to the current population, in a manner similar to the one of natural selection found in biological systems. The fitter individuals are promoted to the next population, and poorer individuals are discarded.
5. *Crossover* is the second operator that follows *Selection*. This operator allows solutions to exchange information in such a way that the living organisms use in order to reproduce themselves. Specifically, two solutions are selected to exchange their substrings from a single point and afterward, according to a predefined probability (Pc). The resulting offspring carry some information from their parents. In this way, new individuals are produced, and new candidate solutions are tested in order to find the one that satisfies the appropriate objective.
6. *Mutation* is the third operator that can be applied to an individual. According to this operation, its single bit of an individual binary string can be flipped with respect to a predefined probability (Pm).

After the application of these operators to the current population, a new population is formed and the generational counter is increased by 1. This process will continue until a predefined number of generations are attained or some form of convergence criterion is met.

While the incorporated genetic operators are almost the same for each application, where a GA is applied to solve an optimization problem, the module of *Fitness Calculation* is application dependent and needs particular formulation. For the needs of metabolite quantification, the fitness of each candidate solution, which corresponds to a model parameter set, is measured by comparing the constructed MRS signal with the real acquired signal by means of a predefined objective function.

The general form of the chromosome coding the parameters sets of k metabolites peaks used in the case of MRS quantification is depicted in Figure 30.4.

The fitness function used to measure the strength of each candidate solution of a current population has the following form:

$$fitness = \sum_{i=1}^{N} \left(F(i) - \hat{F}(i)\right)^2 \tag{30.11}$$

where N is the number of the MRS signal's samples, and F and $\hat{F}$ the original and estimated MRS signals, respectively. Taking into account that the GA usually performs the minimization of an error function, the chromosome with the lowest fitness according to Eq. (30.11) is the optimal solution of the problem. Besides the line-shape model parameters that need to be optimized according to this definition, the number of peaks is also unknown and has to be found. To this end, the GA is applied iteratively in an early stage for different numbers of peaks (*e.g.,* 1–20) and selecting that number that shows the lowest final fitness value (Papakostas *et al.*, 2009, 2011).

3 EXPERIMENT

In order to investigate the performance of the proposed quantification methodology, a set of appropriate experiments was arranged. For the experimental purposes, specific software was developed in MATLAB, while all experiments were executed on an Intel i5 3.3GHz PC with 8 GB random access memory (RAM).

For experimental purposes, an artificial MRS signal was used; the MATLAB source code that generated it came from http://www.esat.kuleuven.be/sista/members/biomed/data005.htm. The signal consisted of 11 exponentials derived from a typical *in vivo* ^{31}P spectrum measured in a human brain. The ^{31}P peaks from brain tissue, phosphomonoesters, inorganic phosphate, phosphodiesters, phosphocreatine, gamma-ATP, alpha-ATP, and beta-ATP were presented in this simulation signal. The time-sampling interval is 0.333 ms, and the number of samples in the signal is 256. The real and imaginary parts of the artificial MRS signal are depicted in Figure 30.5, while its corresponding frequency representation (amplitude spectrum) is derived by applying the Fourier transform and takes the form shown in Figure 30.6.

It is worth mentioning that, without loss of generality, the quantification methodology proposed in this work is making use of the real part of the MRS signal. However, the methodology can be applied successfully to the complex or imaginary

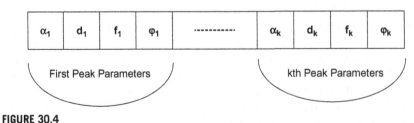

FIGURE 30.4

Chromosome structure.

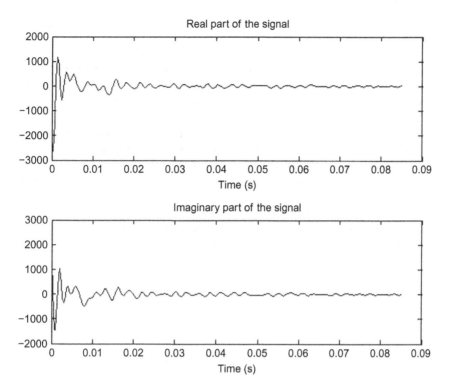

FIGURE 30.5

Real and imaginary parts of the artificial signal.

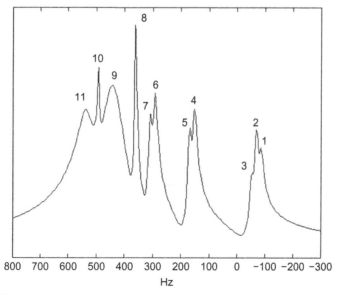

FIGURE 30.6

Frequency domain representation (amplitude spectrum) of the artificial signal, where the 11 peaks can easily be identified.

signals unchanged. Moreover, the signal is processed in the time domain, although frequency-domain processing also can be considered.

The parameters of the 11 peaks comprising the artificial MRS signal of Figure 30.5 are summarized in Table 30.1.

In order to investigate the quantification performance of the proposed methodology under the three examined approaches shown in Figure 30.2, two different experimental scenarios were considered. In the first scenario, the parameters of the peaks were almost completely known, while in the second, there was only a little information about them.

The settings of the GAs for the two scenarios are summarized in Table 30.2.

Note that these settings were not optimal. Rather, they were found by trial and error, and therefore the following results can be improved significantly by applying

Table 30.1 Parameters of the 11 Peaks of the Artificial Signal

Peak (k)	Amplitude (α_k)	Damping Factor (d_k)	Frequency (f_k)	Phase (φ_k)
1	75	50	−86	135
2	150	50	−70	135
3	75	50	−54	135
4	150	50	152	135
5	150	50	168	135
6	150	50	292	135
7	150	50	308	135
8	150	25	360	135
9	1400	285.7	440	135
10	60	25	490	135
11	500	200	530	135

Table 30.2 GA Settings

Parameter	Value	
Experiment	Scenario 1	Scenario 2
Population size	200	600
Maximum generations	2000	4000
Crossover probability (Pc)	0.8	
Mutation probability (Pm)	0.01	0.5
Selection method	Stochastic universal approximation (SUS)	
Crossover points	2 points	

a more sophisticated calibration procedure. Furthermore, the quantification accuracy of each studied method is measured through the relative error (RE) in percent, defined as

$$RE(\%) = \frac{|V_{Est} - V_{Act}|}{V_{Act}} \times 100 \qquad (30.12)$$

where V_{Act} is the actual and V_{Est} the estimated value of the parameter V, respectively.

In order to minimize the influence of the GA's randomness on the experimental results, each experiment has been executed 10 times and the mean values of them are presented. Moreover, 10 different levels [having a standard deviation (Stdv) from 5 to 50 with step 5] of Gaussian noise have been applied to the original MRS signal to construct noisy signals.

3.1 SCENARIO 1: COMPLETE PRIOR KNOWLEDGE

As already stated, in the first scenario, complete data about most of the peaks' parameters ($d, f,$ and φ) are assumed to be available, and only the amplitude (α) of each peak is unknown. In this case, the GA searches for the optimal peaks' amplitudes (α_k) that better fit the MRS signal in process.

The performance of the GA-based quantification is studied without applying the first stage of preprocessing. Some representative quantification results for the case of deviation noise Stdv values equal to 5, 15, 25, 35, and 45 are presented in Table 30.3.

By studying the results of Table 30.3, it can be concluded that the single GA-based quantification quantifies perfectly (0% RE) the artificial MRS signal in the noise-free case. However, its performance deviates in the presence of noise, and

Table 30.3 Quantification Results (% RE) When Only the Amplitudes (α_k) Are Unknown

Peak (k)	Gaussian Noise (Stdv)					
	0	5	15	25	35	45
1	0.0	0.8	2.3	3.9	5.3	6.9
2	0.0	0.8	2.4	4.1	5.8	7.6
3	0.0	0.4	1.1	1.7	2.4	3.0
4	0.0	1.1	3.5	5.9	8.4	11.1
5	0.0	0.5	1.6	2.7	3.7	4.7
6	0.0	0.2	0.5	0.9	1.3	1.6
7	0.0	0.5	1.5	2.4	3.3	4.2
8	0.0	0.1	0.3	0.5	0.6	0.8
9	0.0	0.2	0.5	0.8	1.2	1.5
10	0.0	0.7	1.9	3.1	4.3	5.6
11	0.0	0.3	0.9	1.5	2.2	2.8

as the noise level increases, the quantification fails more [the % RE varies from 0.8% (Stdv-5) to 6.9% (Stdv-45)]. This means that while the number of the unknowns remains the same, the presence of noise broadens the search space, where the GA searches the optimum solution by making it difficult to work in a satisfactory way.

Although the single GA-based quantification seems to be influenced by the presence of the noisy conditions, its performance is comparable. In some cases, it is better than other methods from previous studies (Stamatopoulos *et al.*, 2009).

It is interesting to consider that in this very simple case, due to the thoroughness of the prior knowledge, the preprocessing stage seems unable to improve the quantification performance. This is because while the only unknowns are the peak's amplitudes, any denoising or smoothing procedure may cause the corruption of the initial signal, which will deviate from the ideal model of Eq. (30.1).

3.2 SCENARIO 2: LIMITED PRIOR KNOWLEDGE

In the second experimental scenario, only limited prior knowledge is considered [namely, the frequencies and phases (f, φ)], while the other two parameters [namely, the amplitude and damping factor (α_k, d) of each peak] are unknown. The additional unknown parameter (d) causes an increase of the chromosomes' length by a factor of 2. Therefore, the population size, mutation probability, and generation number of the algorithm need to be increased, as shown in Table 30.2.

3.2.1 Performance of the first stage

However, before studying the performance of the each incorporating the denoising preprocessing stage, it is useful to investigate the denoising operation itself. The performance of each denoising approach (wavelet, SVD, wavelet+SVD), measured by the signal-to-noise ratio (SNR) in decibels for different noise levels, is summarized in Table 30.4.

From all this, it can be deduced that all the denoising approaches improve the SNR of the MRS signal, since they remove sufficient noisy components. Of the three methods, the wavelet+SVD approach shows the best results in almost all the noise levels, behavior that helps the fitting mechanism of the second stage.

Table 30.4 Performance of Each Denoising Method in Terms of SNR (dB)

Signal	Gaussian Noise (Stdv)				
	5	15	25	35	45
Noised	0.008	−0.015	−0.087	−0.206	−0.369
Wavelet	0.042	0.089	0.107	0.093	0.053
SVD	0.088	0.079	−0.089	−0.179	−0.244
Wavelet+SVD	0.121	0.055	0.069	0.105	0.060

3.2.1.1 Overall Performance

The optimization problem that the algorithm is required to solve in this case is more difficult, also due to the noisy conditions. In this scenario, the preprocessing stage of the proposed algorithm is incorporated, and the performance of the three possible approaches is investigated. In order to understand the difficulty of this optimization problem, let us look at Tables 30.5 and 30.6, which show the performance of the single GA-based quantification procedure without the preprocessing stage.

From these tables, it can be recognized that the performance of the single GA has been degraded with the addition of an extra unknown parameter for each metabolite peak. The main difficulty of the algorithm is not only the noisy conditions, as in the case of the first scenario, but the large search space formed by the number of the unknown parameters. This is justified by the contents of the first column of Table 30.5, which corresponds to the noise-free case, showing that the derived amplitudes are far enough from the desired values.

As far as the peaks' damping factors derived by the single GA method are concerned, the accuracy is better than those of the amplitudes, as can be concluded by looking at Table 30.6.

The corresponding quantification results for the case of the first approach of implementing the second stage of the proposed methodology are summarized in Tables 30.7 and 30.8.

By comparing the performance of the wavelet denoising (first approach) with that of the single GA quantification, it can highlight that it outperforms the previous one. The wavelet denoising helps the searching mechanism of the GA by reducing the influence of noise. In this way, more accurate peak parameters (amplitudes and damping factors), near the desired values, are found by the quantification stage of

Table 30.5 Quantification Results (% RE) of the Single GA When the Unknowns Are (α_k, d_k)—Values of (α_k)

Peak (k)	Gaussian Noise (Stdv)					
	0	5	15	25	35	45
1	21.7	51.6	38.3	26.0	10.3	11.3
2	31.6	69.2	38.2	19.0	1.3	7.2
3	24.5	52.9	36.4	27.7	7.6	16.4
4	5.1	5.7	0.8	1.4	6.3	12.8
5	1.1	0.3	1.9	2.1	3.1	1.9
6	3.0	0.1	19.7	20.3	36.3	35.8
7	0.1	0.9	12.3	10.9	17.6	21.5
8	3.8	4.8	10.6	15.1	21.8	25.3
9	25.1	13.4	9.9	16.8	9.9	30.0
10	1093.5	491.0	240.2	482.5	10.5	939.7
11	54.5	23.1	8.9	17.5	12.3	38.0

Table 30.6 Quantification Results (% RE) of the Single GA When the Unknowns Are (α_k, d_k)— Values of (d_k)

Peak (k)	Gaussian Noise (Stdv)					
	0	5	15	25	35	45
1	15.4	38.5	31.0	26.1	21.5	24.6
2	25.7	57.8	32.2	14.3	3.6	4.9
3	19.7	40.0	28.2	26.1	14.5	24.8
4	4.8	4.7	0.5	1.5	2.5	8.0
5	2.0	1.7	4.4	6.7	3.5	7.2
6	2.9	1.2	21.6	24.9	40.7	40.9
7	0.2	0.2	10.2	10.6	16.7	22.0
8	4.0	6.2	15.4	21.2	32.0	37.9
9	6.8	4.9	5.1	9.1	10.3	16.2
10	1474.2	733.3	541.5	745.2	24.0	1548.8
11	24.0	8.9	1.4	3.4	8.6	7.9

Table 30.7 Quantification Results (% RE) of the First Approach (Wavelet Denoising) When the Unknowns Are (α_k, d_k)—Values of (α_k)

Peak (k)	Gaussian Noise (Stdv)					
	0	5	15	25	35	45
1	50.8	41.2	60.1	21.9	41.9	17.6
2	63.1	57.5	72.9	23.7	37.3	8.6
3	52.5	42.7	61.3	16.9	42.7	19.7
4	4.1	2.3	5.4	1.8	7.8	12.2
5	7.2	6.0	0.1	5.2	0.3	5.5
6	1.7	1.0	14.9	20.1	36.5	38.1
7	0.8	1.6	8.3	13.4	23.7	19.3
8	2.9	5.9	9.3	14.7	21.4	25.0
9	11.3	7.3	5.6	22.5	25.2	14.5
10	437.8	194.7	0.3	770.5	736.2	141.2
11	21.1	11.2	0.0	44.6	42.0	14.7

the proposed methodology. For example, while the mean RE values of computing α_k with the single GA method are 64.83% and 103.63% for the 5 and 45 noise levels, respectively, the corresponding errors of the first approach are 33.74% and 28.77%—significantly less.

The quantification results of the second approach, presented in Tables 30.9 and 30.10, are better than those of the wavelet denoising for the low noise levels.

Table 30.8 Quantification Results (% RE) of the First Approach (Wavelet Denoising) When the Unknowns Are (α_k, d_k)—Values of (d_k)

Peak (k)	Gaussian Noise (Stdv)					
	0	5	15	25	35	45
1	34.3	32.2	42.9	1.3	38.5	27.6
2	52.9	47.5	64.1	24.1	32.7	6.0
3	35.7	32.0	42.7	1.2	36.4	26.1
4	3.5	2.2	3.4	0.1	4.2	6.3
5	6.0	5.5	3.1	9.1	6.3	3.5
6	1.5	1.8	18.3	24.7	40.7	43.4
7	1.0	0.5	6.8	13.0	22.9	18.9
8	3.9	8.1	12.4	21.1	31.0	36.5
9	3.3	2.8	5.5	8.3	12.3	11.3
10	697.2	433.4	3.3	1348.5	1355.0	368.6
11	6.5	0.3	2.0	13.6	10.1	2.3

Table 30.9 Quantification Results (% RE) of the Second Approach (SVD Signal Separation) When the Unknowns Are (α_k, d_k)—Values of (α_k)

Peak (k)	Gaussian Noise (Stdv)					
	0	5	15	25	35	45
1	61.9	51.1	26.7	17.5	18.7	1.2
2	58.7	46.5	9.6	2.3	8.2	9.8
3	57.3	49.1	18.1	12.3	16.3	2.1
4	4.0	2.1	0.8	3.5	9.1	17.7
5	2.1	1.5	2.0	3.9	5.5	11.5
6	4.1	3.8	6.9	11.4	17.5	33.5
7	16.1	14.5	3.4	0.2	9.7	23.7
8	8.9	10.0	14.7	21.5	27.5	29.9
9	11.3	8.3	14.0	10.6	18.9	21.8
10	202.5	27.7	296.3	0.0	341.7	504.0
11	13.5	2.4	12.4	11.1	3.6	12.1

For example, the mean absolute error values (of α_k) for the 5 and 45 noise levels are 19.71% and 69.66%, respectively.

It is worth pointing out that wavelet denoising shows better performance when the noise level is generally increased, as compared to the second approach. This means that the SVD signal separation discards fewer noisy signal's components than

Table 30.10 Quantification Results (% RE) of the Second Approach (SVD Signal Separation) When the Unknowns Are (α_k, d_k)—Values of (d_k)

Peak (k)	Gaussian Noise (Stdv)					
	0	5	15	25	35	45
1	45.5	37.9	29.7	29.1	35.0	28.3
2	44.1	36.1	4.8	0.8	4.3	9.9
3	33.2	26.5	11.7	14.8	23.3	23.0
4	3.6	3.7	4.8	5.9	8.0	12.3
5	2.4	4.1	4.2	6.8	7.7	5.0
6	6.3	4.8	8.0	15.2	24.0	40.6
7	8.6	6.5	2.3	6.6	15.2	25.8
8	10.9	12.9	17.6	25.2	33.3	37.7
9	8.1	8.2	7.3	9.1	10.8	10.9
10	314.2	20.1	519.2	8.7	695.8	1350.0
11	14.0	6.8	7.6	1.8	3.2	9.2

the first approach. On the other hand, in conditions of low noise, the first approach seems to reject useful information, where the SVD is more accurate.

The third approach, consisting of the back-to-back operation of wavelet denoising and SVD signal separation, tries to make better use of their advantages by combining them. The wavelet denoising is applied first, in order to remove the noisy components of the MRS signal, so the SVD can work more accurately by keeping the useful parts of the signal. The less noisy the signal that is guided to the SVD module, the more accurate is the procedure (*k*-means clustering) of finding the parameter *M* of SVD decomposition. Tables 30.11 and 30.12 summarize the quantification results of the third approach.

In order to better understand the impact of the proposed methodology under the several approaches examined in this experiment, the data from Tables 30.5–30.12 have been combined and displayed in Figures 30.7–30.9.

Figures 30.7 and 30.8 illustrates the mean RE in percent of the proposed methodology compared with the single GA quantification method for the case of the amplitude (a_k) and damping factor (d_k) parameters, respectively. From these figures, it can be concluded that the proposed methodology in all three approaches significantly improves the searching capabilities of the GA, by converged to the best peaks' parameter sets.

Moreover, the third approach, consisting of the combinative operation of the wavelet denoising and the SVD signal separation, shows the best performance in almost all the noise levels. This can be deduced by studying the mean RE in percent for both parameters (amplitudes and damping factors) of the methods, as depicted in Figure 30.9.

Apart from the previous quantification results, a Monte Carlo study with many different noise realizations can construct a more statistically accurate image of the methods' performances. However, due to computation limitations coming from

Table 30.11 Quantification Results (% RE) of the Third Approach (Wavelet Denoising Followed by SVD Signal Separation) When the Unknowns Are (α_k, d_k)—Values of (α_k)

Peak (k)	Gaussian Noise (Stdv)					
	0	5	15	25	35	45
1	29.1	38.8	24.0	19.7	2.5	6.3
2	16.1	27.7	10.1	12.4	12.7	19.3
3	18.8	35.2	16.0	16.5	2.1	6.4
4	6.5	6.3	2.8	12.3	9.2	16.5
5	3.7	5.5	2.3	9.8	5.9	11.7
6	0.6	3.6	10.9	13.5	18.4	27.1
7	10.9	12.1	0.3	1.0	4.9	8.7
8	7.0	8.9	14.5	19.9	27.1	34.3
9	7.2	15.1	9.4	11.5	17.9	16.4
10	42.5	429.3	21.8	13.5	239.8	7.0
11	1.0	24.1	1.2	1.2	15.6	0.8

Table 30.12 Quantification Results (% RE) of the Third Approach (Wavelet Denoising Followed by SVD Signal Separation) When the Unknowns Are (α_k, d_k)—Values of (d_k)

Peak (k)	Gaussian Noise (Stdv)					
	0	5	15	25	35	45
1	23.6	31.3	27.2	29.6	24.3	22.9
2	8.6	18.9	4.7	7.6	15.4	21.8
3	5.3	20.8	11.0	18.3	13.4	17.2
4	0.5	1.0	6.3	13.1	8.1	13.9
5	3.8	7.8	3.1	0.2	5.5	2.9
6	3.0	3.9	12.0	16.5	23.2	33.7
7	5.2	6.2	4.8	7.0	11.3	13.9
8	8.9	10.6	18.8	25.7	34.8	44.9
9	7.2	6.8	8.7	10.3	12.3	15.5
10	37.2	605.3	14.3	4.0	458.9	9.9
11	8.7	15.4	6.4	5.1	7.4	4.5

the high overhead of the GA operation, a Monte Carlo analysis with hundreds or millions of noise realizations is computationally difficult. Therefore, the 10 noise levels of the previous experiments (having Stdv from 5 to 50, with step 5) can be used to perform an analysis in this framework. Some statistical results (i.e., mean, Stdev) of this analysis are summarized in Table 30.13.

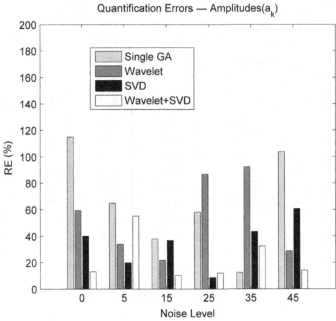

FIGURE 30.7

The various methods' quantification errors in the case of amplitude parameters (α_k).

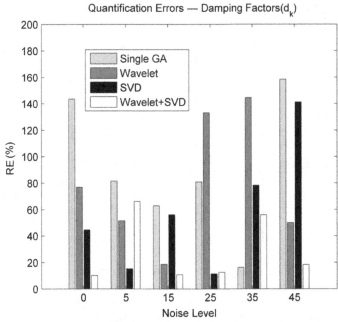

FIGURE 30.8

The various methods' quantification errors in the case of damping factor parameters (d_k).

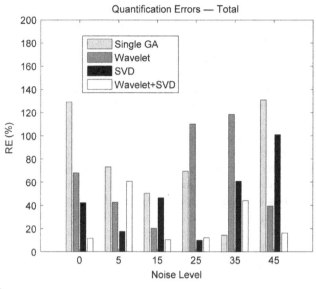

FIGURE 30.9

Total quantification errors for all the parameters (α_k, d_k) for the various methods.

Table 30.13 Statistical Results (Mean/Stdv) of Monte Carlo Analysis Quantifying the 11 Peaks for the Studied Approaches

Peak (k)	Method			
	Single GA	Wavelet	SVD	Wavelet+SVD
1	29.2/14.5	35.3/19.4	79.3/75.7	62.8/68.8
2	26.9/20.8	44.5/28.3	32.6/27.0	26.7/20.5
3	29.2/14.0	35.5/20.3	34.7/22.3	29.3/24.1
4	5.9/4.8	5.6/4.1	12.2/9.8	16.2/11.8
5	4.3/3.1	5.0/3.0	13.6/14.6	11.1/10.9
6	23.2/17.1	23.5/16.3	21.1/12.8	15.7/9.6
7	12.4/8.5	12.4/9.0	11.8/9.2	9.5/8.0
8	21.1/11.7	18.5/10.9	23.1/10.2	23.2/11.2
9	14.5/6.1	11.0/5.5	14.6/5.4	14.4/5.4
10	686.7/476.3	444.1/417.7	212.4/297.1	106.0/168.0
11	15.9/11.4	11.9/10.5	8.4/4.1	11.4/8.6
Mean	79.0/53.5	58.8/49.6	42.2/44.4	29.7/31.5

By examining these results, the superiority of the wavelet + SVD methodology can be confirmed via the statistics. Moreover, it is worth pointing out that of the 11 peaks of the simulated MRS signal, the 10th peak was not quantified with any of the approaches. A brief look at the peaks' locations (Figure 30.6) shows that the 10th peak was the highest, with two other peaks being very close. This means that all the approaches have difficulty identifying this peak due to the presence of other peaks with almost the same amplitude and frequency together.

From the precedent analysis, it can be concluded that the low quantification performance of the single GA-based quantification technique, for limited prior knowledge and noisy conditions, as proposed in previous studies (Papakostas *et al.*, 2009, 2010a, 2010b), can be improved significantly by incorporating an additional processing stage (Figure 30.1 and 30.2). Among the three approaches investigated in the context of the proposed two-stage quantification methodology, the third one, consisting of the combination of wavelet denoising with SVD analysis, shows the best overall performance. The proposed methodology of the third approach can reduce the mean RE in finding the (α_k, d_k) parameters of the artificial signal by 50% over the performance of the single GA method.

Although the introduced methodology exhibits improved quantification capabilities, further research has to be performed in order to establish it as a reliable MRS metabolite quantification procedure. The optimization of wavelet denoising by finding the most appropriate wavelet family and level of decomposition (the coiflet of an order 3 wavelet with one-level decomposition was used in our experiments), along with the studying of other clustering algorithms (such as SOM clustering and Fuzzy c-means), are some of the future research issues that have to be studied.

Furthermore, future research issues include the redesign of the proposed methodology to involve concurrent and distributed GAs (Adeli and Cheng, 1994; Adeli and S. Kumar, 1995; Hung and Adeli, 1994) to be applied in magnetic resonance spectroscopy imaging (MRSI), as well as investigations of how to extract rules using specific GA techniques (Ballesteros, 2010) in the context of MRS and MRSI. Finally, instead of uniform sampling in the definition of fitness in Eq. (30.11). it might be advantageous to investigate hybrid sampling techniques (Seiffert *et al.*, 2009) in metabolite quantification.

4 CONCLUSIONS

A novel MRS metabolites quantification methodology was proposed in this chapter. The introduced method consists of two processing stages: one for the preprocessing of the MRS signal and the other for the peaks' parameter optimization. It has shown an improved performance compared with the single GA method. The experimental results on artificial data testified that the combination of wavelet denoising and SVD signal separation in the preprocessing stage of the technique can lead to significant improvement in the quantification procedure under noisy conditions.

While the preliminary results are very promising, further research on the directions of enhancing wavelet denoising and SVD analysis, along with the application of the method in real data, is needed in order to establish it as a generic quantification procedure.

ACKNOWLEDGMENTS

This work has been partially supported by the European Project FAST—Advanced Signal Processing for Ultra-Fast Magnetic Resonance Spectroscopic Imaging, and Training, Marie Curie Research Training Network, MRTN-CT-2006-035801.

REFERENCES

Adeli, H., Cheng, N.-T., 1994. Concurrent genetic algorithms for optimization of large structures. J. Aero. Eng. ASCE 7 (3), 276–296.

Adeli, H., Kumar, S., 1995. Distributed genetic algorithms for structural optimization. J. Aero. Eng. 8 (3), 156–163.

Coley, D.A., 2001. An Introduction to Genetic Algorithms for Scientists and Engineers. World Scientific Publishing.

Donoho, D.L., 1995. De-noising by soft-thresholding. IEEE Trans. on Inf. Theory 41 (3), 613–627.

Holland, J.H., 2001. Adaptation in Natural and Artificial Systems, 6th Ed. MIT Press.

http://www.esat.kuleuven.be/sista/members/biomed/data005.htm, (accessed 01.03.15).

http://www.mathworks.com/, (accessed 02.03.11).

Hung, S.L., Adeli, H., 1994. A parallel genetic/neural network learning algorithm for MIMD shared memory machines. IEEE Trans. Neural Netw. 5 (6), 900–909.

in't Zandt, H.J.A., van der Graaf, M., Heerschap, A., 2001. Common processing of in vivo MR spectra. NMR Biomed. 14 (4), 224–232.

Kuncheva, L.I., 2004. Combining Pattern Classifiers: Methods and Algorithms. Wiley-Interscience Publiching.

Martínez-Ballesteros, M., Troncoso, A., Martínez-Álvarez, F., Riquelm, J.C., 2010. Mining quantitative association rules based on evolutionary computation and its application to atmospheric pollution. Integrated Comput. Aided Eng. 17 (3), 227–242.

Mierisova, S., Ala-Korpela, M., 2001. MR spectroscopy quantitation: a review of frequency domain methods. NMR Biomed. 14 (4), 247–259.

Papakostas, G.A., Karras, D.A., Mertzios, B.G., 11-12 May 2009. Dealing with Peaks Overlapping Issue in Quantifying Human Brain Metabolites of MRSI. In: IEEE International Workshop on Imaging Systems and Techniques (IST'09), pp. 58–62 Shenzhen – China.

Papakostas, G.A., Karras, D.A., Mertzios, B.G., van Ormondt, D., Graveron-Demilly, D., 1-2 July 2010. On Quantifying MRS Metabolites Using a Constrained Genetic Algorithm. In: IEEE International Workshop on Imaging Systems and Techniques (IST'10), pp. 46–51 Thessaloniki – Greece.

Papakostas, G.A., Karras, D.A., Mertzios, B.G., Graveron-Demilly, D., van Ormondt, D., 13-15 December 2010. A Constrained Genetic Algorithm with Adaptively Defined Fitness Function in MRS Quantification. In: International Conference on Grid and Distributed Computing, Control and Automation, (CGD/CA'10), pp. 257–268, Jeju Island – Korea.

Papakostas, G.A., Karras, D.A., Mertzios, B.G., van Ormondt, D., Graveron-Demilly, D., 2011. "*In vivo* MRS Metabolites Quantification Using Evolutionary Optimization", Measurement Science and Technology 22 (11), 114004, (9pp).

Pijnappel, W.W.F., van den Boogaart, A., de Beer, R., van Ormondt, D., 1992. SVD-based quantification of magnetic resonance signals. J. Magn. Reson. 97 (1), 122–134.

Seiffert, C., Khoshgoftaar, T.M., Van Hulse, J., 2009. Hybrid sampling for imbalanced data. Integrated Comput. Aided Eng. 16 (3), 193–210.

Stamatopoulos, V.G., Karras, D.A., Mertzios, B.G., 2009. On an efficient modification of singular value decomposition using independent component analysis for improved MRS denoising and quantification. Meas. Sci. Tech. 20, 104021, 9 pp.

Strang, G., Nguyen, T., 1997. Wavelets and Filter Banks. Wellesley-Cambridge Press.

Vanhamme, L., Sundin, T., Hecke, P.V., van Huffel, S., 2001. MR spectroscopy quantitation: a review of time-domain methods. NMR Biomed. 14 (4), 233–246.

Weber, O.M., Duc, C.O., Meier, D., Boesiger, P., 1998. Heuristic optimization algorithms applied to the quantification of spectroscopic data. Magn. Reson. Med. 39 (5), 723–730.

Zhu, X.-P., Du, A.-T., Jahng, G.-H., Soher, B.J., Maudsley, A.A., Weiner, M.W., Schuff, N., 2003. Magnetic resonance spectroscopic imaging reconstruction with deformable shape-intensity models. Magn. Reson. Med. 50 (3), 474–482.

Keratoconus Disease and Three-Dimensional Simulation of the Cornea throughout the Process of Cross-Linking Treatment

31

H. Kaya[1], A. Çavuşoğlu[2], H.B. Çakmak[3], B. Şen[1], and E. Çalık[4]

Yıldırım Beyazıt University, Department of Computer Engineering, Ankara, Turkey[1]
Scientific and Technological Research Council of Turkey, Ankara, Turkey[2]
Yıldırım Beyazıt University, Atatürk Education and Research Hospital, Ankara, Turkey[3]
Karabük University, School of Health Sciences, Karabük, Turkey[4]

1 INTRODUCTION

Keratoconus can be defined as the forward extension of the cornea (the transparent, breaker layer, like a watch glass in front of the eye) as it tapers conically (Figure 31.1). This disease is more common among women. Changing the refractive power of the cornea, it causes a moderate or severe degree of irregular astigmatism and blurred vision. In the final stages of keratoconus, corneal swelling and blanching can be seen.

Light enters the eye through the cornea, and because it provides clear vision by breaking or focusing the rays, the cornea is a very important part of the eye. In keratoconus, the shape of the cornea is changed and vision distorted as a result; therefore, it may cause problems with some activities, such as driving a car, using a computer, watching television, and reading. Especially in young people, it may lead to some serious difficulties in their education and work lives. If keratoconus is not treated, it causes serious vision problems. Therefore, early diagnosis and selecting the appropriate treatment is of great importance. Cross-Linking Treatment is suitable for the situation that the patient is in the age group of 15-35, Keratoconus is progressive, patient does not feel comfortable longer with the lenses and the cornea is thicker than 400 micrometers. The purpose of this treatment method is to stop the advance of keratoconus, to improve vision quality by reducing the refractive defect, and to eliminate the need for corneal transplantation (keratoplasty). According to several

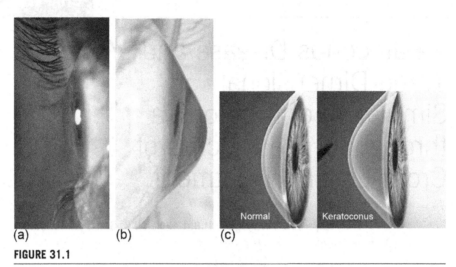

FIGURE 31.1

(a) Healthy eye, (b) eye with Keratoconus, (c) comparison of healthy cornea and cornea with Keratoconus.

studies, if the cross-linking treatment is preferred, the progression for the disease can be stopped at the rate of 90%–98%.

The disease is widespread throughout the world, but Turkey is located in the region where the disease is most prevalent. Depending on the high rate of the young population in our country and that existing in the sunny and pollen-rich climate zone, disease can be seen from 2000 to 2500 per person. The disease is genetic, and it can be seen as high astigmatism. In patients, irregular astigmatism or myopia is constantly increasing, and bilateral involvement occurs in time. The majority of patients complain of having to change their eyeglass prescriptions frequently, but eventualy, these glasses will be inadequate and visual impairment will continue that cannot be fixed with glasses. Keratoconus can be associated with corneal injury and systemic diseases. After applying excimer laser surgery to an eye thinner than 400 micrometers, due to the weakening of the vitreous of the eye, keratoconus may occur. In all cases that keratoconus is suspected, doing corneal topography before diagnosis is of great importance (Kocamış, 2011).

There is not a precise classification method in keratoconus that everyone can agree on. So far, various classification methods are used considering such parameters as conus morphology, clinical findings, visual acuity, disease progression, keratometry, topography-derived values, corneal aberrations alone, or combinations of them. First, classification based on the progression of the disease was made by Amsler (1938) and then similar reclassifications have been made (Hom and Bruce, 2006). Amsler evaluated keratoconus in four stages. For diagnosis and classification of keratoconus, various classification methods obtained from corneal topography systems have been formed. Several researchers have made classifications using corneal topography results (Rabinowitz and Donnell, 1989; Rabinowitz and Rasheed, 1999; McMahon *et al.*, 2006; Mahmoud *et al.*, 2008).

Recently, the possibility of diagnosing the disease with anterior segment parameters using the Scheimpflug camera system was proposed. The Scheimpflug camera system is a next-generation system that can record three-dimensional (3D) images as making rotation to the axis of the eye with its rotating camera. In this kind of systems, in addition to topography maps, corneal volume, anterior chamber angle, anterior chamber volume and anterior chamber depth parameters are also used to diagnose Keratoconus and to evaluate the severity of the disease. (Emre, Doğanay and Yoloğlu, 2007). These devices can record 3D images but offers in two-dimensional (2D) form to the user. Images that were made more understandable by modeling in 3D form in our study were taken from the Scheimpflug camera system.

The importance of correctly identifying and classifying keratoconus is increasing because nowadays, a variety of very effective treatment options are available. Hereafter, treatments such as collagen cross-linking used in progressive keratoconus cases can make it possible to stop the progression of the disease (Kocamış, 2011). The collagen cross-linking method has been used for keratoconus in recent years and is applied to corneas thicker than 400 μm. After treatment, a thin cornea hardens. In this way, sharpness of the cornea and the disease progression can be halted or very decelerated.

Among half of patients treated in this way, the cornea is flattened approximately 2–3 times. Raiskup-Wolf *et al.* (2008) followed the results of cross-linking on keratoconus cases in a 6-year period. In their study, at the end of the third year, a decrease of 4.84 D in corneal slope and an accompanying increase in best corrected visual acuity was reported. Various studies were conducted on the subject of how to use the treatment, current status, and monitoring of results. A number of studies have shared the effects of the treatment on the disease and the postoperative corneal changes (Utine *et al.*, 2009; Uçakhan Gündüz, 2009; Utine, 2005; Raiskup and Spoerl, 2011; Zhang, 2012; Caporossi *et al.*, 2010; Tahzib *et al.*, 2010). Using the computerized devices benefiting from 3D technologies provides support to the field experts on making the right decisions on the diagnosis in a short time, determining the most effective and results-oriented treatment, and realizing and monitoring the treatment and operations.

Nowadays, 3-D devices increase the success of the monitoring and the treatment processes in Medicine. For an instance, in cancer treatment, healthy cells are prevented from damaging by using 3-D devices because they can clearly determine the accurate tumor localization. As an example of this type of treatment, a 3D imaging device known as the Varian Linear Accelerator started to be used at the Gazi University Faculty of Medicine in order to support target-oriented radiation treatment. It contributed significantly to patients' comfort and to the treatment. In this treatment method, with the computerized planning device that collects such tumor-related information as the location, size, and precision to make a computerized simulation, it can be possible to mark the tumor and surrounding delicate tissue and determine the treatment doses.

Displaying the face in 3D form is recognized as an advance in physical modeling techniques using the engineering methods in medicine. Kumar and Vijai (2012) performed 3D modeling of the face in a different imaging approach.

In this study, a decision support system for the physician was performed on the course of keratoconus to display the cornea in 3D form. Therefore, visibility and readability of the corneal region with keratoconus increased.

2 METHODOLOGY

2.1 DATA

Our study was conducted on 749 digital images of 122 patients recorded by the Scheimpflug camera and the Placido Disc Combination from January 24, 2009, to January 24, 2012. Data were provided from the Yıldırım Beyazıt University Atatürk Education and Research Hospital by the Ethics Committee approval report 43, dated April 25, 2013.

2.2 APPLICATION

First, the data set of this study was obtained through 749 2D corneal images that were recorded by the Scheimpflug camera and Placido Disc Combination. After data cleaning and preparing, 144 images had to be discarded because of scanning problems, especially due to closed eyelids, and the final data set had 605 original 2D images. These images were cropped by our application using the Cropped Quad-Tree method. The recorded images have some unnecessary elements, like eyebrows and eyelashes, so these parts were discarded by using this cropping method.

Cropped images were grouped using Multilayer Perceptron and Logistic Regression classification methods using the thickness values that were obtained by our application. With the help of a 3D imaging application developed using the grouped 2D images obtained in the previous step, more easily interpretable 3D maps were obtained.

After modeling the 2D image data set in 3D form, we also developed comparing screens for the physician to see the pre- and post-operational forms of the cornea to follow up the results of the operation.

The steps of our study are detailed in Figure 31.2.

The application architecture of this study is seen in Figure 31.3.

In this application, the Cropped Quad-Tree method was implemented to present the corneal part in the recorded image and crop out the unnecessary parts. By the help of this method, we disregarded the parts that were out of our study's scope.

A quad-tree is a hierarchical data model that recursively decomposes a map into smaller regions. Each node in the tree has four children nodes, each of which represents one-quarter of the area that the parent represents. So, the root node represents the complete map. This map is then split into four equal quarters, each of which is represented by one child node. Each of these children is now treated as a parent, and

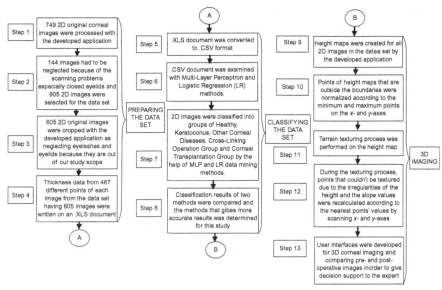

FIGURE 31.2

Application steps of the study.

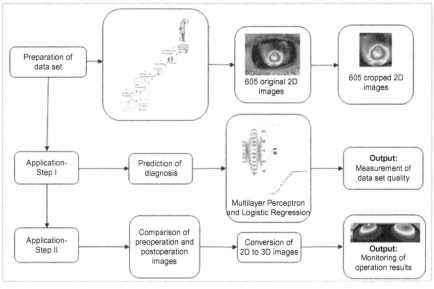

FIGURE 31.3

Application architecture.

its area is recursively split into four equal areas, and so on, until a desired depth is reached. The Cropped Quad-Tree method is the enhanced version of the Quad-Tree method. Here, the minimal screen part where the object is located is determined instead of performing operations on the entire image. Later, division operation is performed only within the window determined previously; in this way, adscititious processes are avoided. Consequently, benefits are obtained in an algorithm in terms of speed depends on the size of the object on the image (Çavuşoğlu et al., 2013). You can see how this method can be implemented in the study in Figure 31.4.

Figure 31.4 corresponds to the following quad-tree in Figure 31.5.

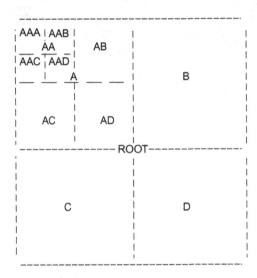

FIGURE 31.4

Diagram of Cropped Quad-Tree algorithm.

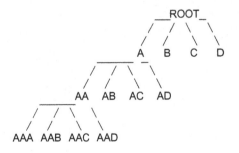

FIGURE 31.5

Representation of the quad-tree structure.

In our study, we applied the Cropped Quad-Tree method to the corneal image as implementing the algorithm:

function CropImage{Takes Points as a Parameter}
Initialize Parameters
Initialize the Reference Height Values(that represents the colour values)
Set Minimum-Maximum X-Y Coordinates
Search for Min-Max X Coordinates for All Points
Search for Min-Max Y Coordinates for All Points
Crop the Image According to the Decision bits
end function

An example screenshot from the screen dividing process can be seen in Figure 31.6. This process was conducted for the purpose of finding which areas were not necessary and cropping these unnecessary areas.

Decision bits on how to crop the image achieved by cropping the screen using the occupied parts can be seen in Figure 31.7. The tree is represented by a series of bits that indicate termination by a leaf with a 0 and branching into child nodes with a 1 based on the occupation situation. We have achieved our desired location (there is no node that is not occupied) in the fifth step, as seen in Figure 31.7.

A multilayer perceptron (MLP) is used in this study as one step of the data mining process. An MLP is a feed-forward artificial neural network model that maps sets of input data onto a set of appropriate outputs. An MLP consists of multiple layers of nodes in a directed graph, with each layer fully connected to the next (Figure 31.8). Except for the input nodes, each node is a neuron (or processing element) with a nonlinear activation function. MLP utilizes a supervised learning technique called *back-propagation* for training the network. The mathematical expression of each perceptron's computation can be expressed as

$$y = \varphi\left(\sum_{i=1}^{n} \omega_i x_i + b\right) = \varphi\left(\mathbf{w}^T \mathbf{x} + b\right), \qquad (31.1)$$

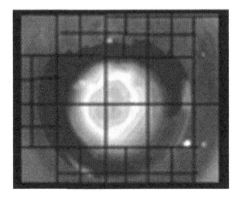

FIGURE 31.6

Quad-tree structure of original corneal image.

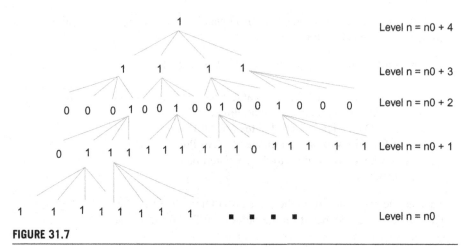

FIGURE 31.7

Decision bits encoding quad-tree structure of the corneal image.

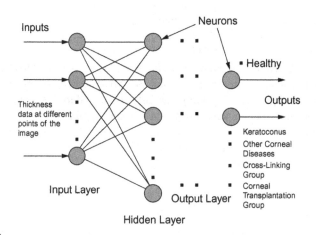

FIGURE 31.8

Structure of an MLP.

where $\mathbf{w}$ is the vector of weights, $\mathbf{x}$ is the vector of inputs, b is the bias, and φ is the activation function.

MLP (Figure 31.8) is a feed-forward network of interconnected neurons that are usually trained using the error back-propogation algorithm. This popular algorithm works by iteratively changing a network's interconnecting weights in proportion to a "training rate" set by the artificial neural network (ANN) method such that the overall error (*i.e.*, between observed values and modeled network outputs) is reduced.

The other step of our study's data mining part is logistic regression (LR). The purpose of using LR is to establish a least-variable model that is optimum fitting and can define the relationship between dependent and independent variables and that is biologically acceptable (Bircan, 2004). The logistic regression model can be expressed as

$$\ln[p/(1-p)] = a + BX + e, \qquad (31.2)$$

where **ln** is the natural logarithm, $\log_{exp}$, where exp=2.71828..; **p** is the probability that the event Y occurs; p(Y=1); **p/(1-p)** is the odds ratio; $\ln[p/(1-p)]$ is the log odds ratio, or logit; *a* is the coefficient on the constant term; *B* is the coefficients on the independent variable(s); **X** is the independent variables; and **e** is the error term.

In our study, we obtained thickness values from 467 points of 605 2D images by analyzing each image with unsupervised MLP and LR methods. A total of 70% of this data are used for training; the remaining 30% of the data is used for testing.

In order to use 3D modeling techniques in our software development process, XNA Framework dynamic-link libraries (DLLs) were added on Microsoft .NET C# platform. Microsoft XNA Framework is a tool that enables software developers developing games using Microsoft Visual Studio C# language on Microsoft Windows and Xbox 360 platforms. Standard game development procedures require a good deal of code and time; XNA Framework is intended to facilitate this process. To bring this idea to fruition, it is presented that the most important thing the programmers should take care of is the code. XNA Framework takes the items on itself that processing and designing periods take time as graphics card, resolution, image processing. Also, it creates a game window for developers. (XNA Framework, 2014). With the help of these DLLs, software codes were developed that supports the 3D transactions in the following ways:

- Creating a height map (terrain) from the red, green, blue (RGB) or grayscale corneal image using the Diamond Square algorithm
- Cleaning the image parts outside the normal range (normalizing the image according to the minimum and the maximum points)
- Terrain texturing
- During the texturing process, if some points cannot be textured due to the irregularities of the height and the slope values, recalculating these values according to the values of the nearest points by scanning the x- and y-axes, respectively

The Diamond Square algorithm that was used in creating the height map in our study includes the following steps:

1. The diamond step: Taking a square of four points, generate a random value at the square midpoint, where the two diagonals meet. The midpoint value is calculated by averaging the four corner values, plus a random amount. This gives you diamonds when you have multiple squares arranged in a grid.

2. The square step: Taking each diamond of four points, generate a random value at the center of the diamond. Calculate the midpoint value by averaging the corner values, plus a random amount generated in the same range as used for the diamond step. This results in squares again.

3. So long as the length of the side of the squares is greater than zero, keep performing the diamond and square steps for each square present and reduce the random number range.

Stages of the normalization process involve finding the points that have minimum and maximum height values, respectively, for the x- and y- axes and displaying after recalculating all points according to these values [Eq. (31.3)]. Normalization formula is as follows:

$$I : \{X \subseteq \mathbb{R}^n\} \rightarrow \{\text{Min}, .., \text{Max}\}$$
$$I_N : \{X \subseteq \mathbb{R}^n\} \rightarrow \{\text{newMin}, .., \text{newMax}\}$$
$$I_N = (I - Min)\frac{\text{newMax} - \text{newMin}}{\text{Max} - \text{Min}} + \text{newMin}.$$

(31.3)

After normalization and texturing processes on the height map shown in Figure 31.9(c), 3D corneal image in Figure 31.10 was obtained.

Our study was developed in order to provide monitoring and evaluation processes that can be done even by those who are not experienced in dealing with keratoconus, not overlooking any detail in the diagnosis process of the disease, with the help of easily readable and interpretable maps. Thanks to the system that was developed, recorded images for preoperation and postoperation in 2D form were transformed to 3D images (Figure 31.11).

In the next step, to facilitate monitoring the effects of the treatment, images were overlapping (Figure 31.12). In Figure 31.12(b), it can be seen that when the cross-links existing in the corneal layer hardened and became more resistant after the treatment, prolonged tissues were withdrawn.

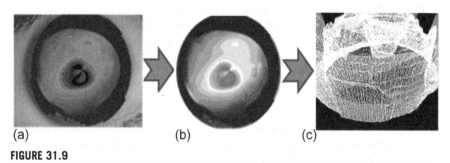

(a) (b) (c)

FIGURE 31.9

(a) RGB image, (b) grayscale image, (c) height map.

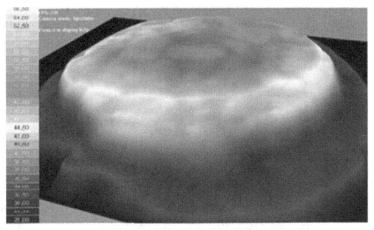

FIGURE 31.10

Textured 3-D view of the cornea.

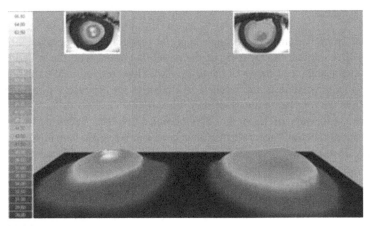

FIGURE 31.11

2-D and 3-D post-operational images of cornea.

3 CONCLUSIONS AND RECOMMENDATIONS

Early diagnosis and suitable treatment planning at the right time is extremely important for success in treating keratoconus disease. Because the disease can be treated if diagnosed early, the need for corneal transplantation can be prevented or delayed for many patients through early diagnosis. Keratoconus subsequently occurs in many of the 11-12-year-old amblyopia patients that have astigmatism in one eye and their vision cannot be increased in their past life. Because the disease cannot be identified

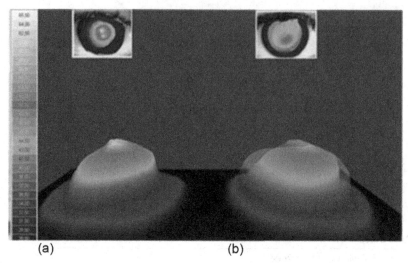

(a)(b)

FIGURE 31.12

(a) Pre-operational images, (b) Comparison of the overlapping pre-operational and post-operational images.

by routine examination in early stages, special topographic devices are needed to diagnose it. To notice the tapering of the patient's cornea with the naked eye can be available in advanced stages of the disease which require corneal transplantation. Because that special tests are needed to diagnose the disease, large number of patients live without being aware of their disease.

There is a shortage of 3D studies about corneal diseases. Because this disease is very commonly seen and accurate treatment is very important to cure it, we conducted this study. In this study, it was performed to simulate the changes occurred in the cornea by using 3D modeling techniques between preoperational and postoperational periods as selecting from the cornea images of good quality in recording by using data mining methods. With the help of the application developed and discussed here, it was made possible to monitor whether the treatment was successful in achieving the desired results, as well as monitoring the healing process in the posttreatment period. A decision support system was developed by this study for eye specialists in the diagnosis, treatment, and follow-up phases by the established system.

In our study, 605 images were selected from 749 images by data cleaning and preparing steps. Then the images in the data set were cropped using the Cropped Quad-Tree method. This method made our cropping process easier and more accurate. It is also beneficial in studies where speed is important. After the cropping process, thickness values of 467 different points of these 605 cropped images were obtained.

Thickness data obtained from the previous step were analyzed with MLP and LR methods. A total of 424 rows of data were used to train the system, and 181 rows of data were used for the classification process.

Table 31.1 Results of Classification Algorithms

Algorithm	MLP	LR
Number of input variables	**Total number of instances:** 605 **Number of training data:** 424 (70% of total 605 instances) (This data is not used for classification, only for training the system.) **Number of test and classification data:** 181 (30% of total 605 instances) (This data is used for classification of the images.)	**Total number of instances:** 605 **Number of training data:** 424 (70% of total 605 instances) (This data is not used for classification, only for training the system.) **Number of test and classification data:** 181 (30% of total 605 instances) (This data is used for classification of the images.)
The number of correctly classified instances	**176 instances** out of 181 test and classification instances **97.2376%**	**159 instances** out of 181 test and classification instances **87.8453%**
The number of incorrectly classified instances	**5 instances** out of 181 test and classification instances **2.7624%**	**22 instances** out of 181 test and classification instances **12.1547%**
Classification time	1011.16 s	6.7 s
True classification	Very Good	Good

Results of the classification methods used in the study are shown in Table 31.1. MP, with an accuracy rate of 97.2376%, is more successful than LR, with an accuracy rate of 87.8453%. A 2D data set grouped with MLP (because it has produced more correctly classified instances) was modeled in 3D form on the .NET C# platform with the help of XNA Framework DLLs. We added this framework to our .NET C# project, and by using the 3D imaging method of consisting of creating a height map, normalizing this map, and applying terrain-texturing process on the height map, we modeled 2D corneal images in 3D form. A directory of corneal images recorded by the Scheimpflug camera system can be given to this system, and it has the potential of performing the following steps:

1. Prepare the data set so as to select the appropriate ones for the study, cropping and cleaning these images.
2. Classify the images into groups of healthy, keratoconus, other corneal diseases, cross-linking and transplantation operations.
3. Convert the 2D image to a height map using the Diamond Square algorithm.
4. Normalize the height map according to the minimum and the maximum points on the x- and y-axes.

5. Texture these height maps by using the color and height correlation of the Scheimpflug camera system (that the 2D images were recorded by).
6. Give some comparisons of preoperation and postoperation 3D images with the color and height palettes. Also, in the comparison screens, there are camera applications that can change the viewpoint of the users to help them to see the image from different perspectives.

With the help of 3D images, readability of the cornea increased. This study showed that display of the disease and the healing process can be improved by using more interpretable 3D images.

ACKNOWLEDGMENTS

This study is based upon the project supported by T. C. Ministry of Science, Industry, and Technology in the scope of SAN-TEZ Project No. 0477.STZ.2013-2, with Yıldırım Beyazıt University and Akgün Software Company. Also, we would like to thank Yıldırım Beyazıt University, Ataturk Education and Research Hospital board for their permission to use the digital image data with Ethics Committee approval.

REFERENCES

Amsler, M., 1938. Le keratocone fruste au javal. Ophtalmologica 96, 77–83.

Bircan, H., 2004. Lojistik regresyon analizi: tıp verileri üzerine bir uygulama. Kocaeli Üniversitesi Sosyal Bilimler Enstitüsü Dergisi. 2004 (2), 186,189,197.

Caporossi, A., Mazzotta, C., Baiocchi, S., Caporossi, T., 2010. Long-Term results of riboflavin ultraviolet a corneal collagen cross-linking for keratoconus in italy: the siena eye cross study. Am. J. Ophthalmol. 149 (4), 585–593.

Çavuşoğlu, A., Şen, B., Özcan, C., Görgünoğlu, S., 2013. Cropped quad-tree based solid objects colouring with CUDA. Math. Comput. Appl. 18 (3), 301–312.

Emre, S., Doğanay, S., Yoloğlu, S., 2007. Evaluation of anterior segment parameters in keratoconic eyes measured with pentacam system. J. Cataract Refract. Surg. 33, 1708–1712.

Hom, M., Bruce, A.S., 2006. Manual of Contact Lens Prescribing and Fitting. Butterworth-Heinemann, London, p:503-544.

Kocamiş S.İ. (2011) Keratokonus Tanısında CLMI'nın Etkinliğinin Güncel Ölçümlerle Karşılaştırılarak Değerlendirilmesi, Thesis, Ankara Atatürk Eğitim ve Araştırma Hastanesi 1. Göz Kliniği (Thesis Advisor: Doç. Dr. Hasan Basri ÇAKMAK), Ankara.

Kumar, T.S., Vijai, A., 2012. 3D reconstruction of face from 2D CT scan images. Procedia Engineering 30, 970–977.

Mahmoud, A.M., Roberts, C.J., Lembach, R.G., Twa, M.D., Herderick, E.E., Mcmahon, T.T., 2008. CLMI: the cone location and magnitude index. Cornea 27, 480–487.

Mcmahon, T.T., Szczotka-Flynn, L., Barr, J.T., Anderson, R.J., Slaughter, M.E., Lass, J.H., Iyengar, S.K., Clek Study Group, 2006. A new method for grading the severity of keratoconus: the keratoconus severity score (KSS). Cornes 25 (7), 794–800.

Rabinowitz, Y.S., Mc Donnell, P.J., 1989. Computer-Assisted corneal topography in keratoconus. Refract. Corneal Surg. 5, 400–408.

Rabinowitz, Y.S., Rasheed, K., 1999. KISA% index: a quantitative video keratography algorithm embodying minimal topographic criteria for diagnosing keratoconus. J. Cataract Refract. Surg. 25, 1327–1335.

Raiskup, F., Spoerl, E., 2011. Corneal cross-linking with hypo-osmolar riboflavin solution in thin keratoconic corneas. Am. J. Ophthalmol. 152 (1), 28–32.

Raiskup-Wolf, F., Hoyer, A., Spoerl, E., Pillunat, L.E., 2008. Collagen cross-linking with riboflavin and ultraviolet-A light in keratoconus: long-term results. J. Cataract Refract. Surg. 34, 796–801.

Tahzib, N.G., Soeters, N., Lelij, A.V., 2010. Pachymetry during cross-linking. Ophthalmology 117 (10), 2041.

Uçakhan Gündüz, Ö.Ö., 2009. Keratokonusta alternatif tedavi yöntemleri: intrastromal halka segmentler ve kollajen çapraz bağlama: güncel durum. MN Oftalmoloji 3, 39–44.

Utine, C.A., 2005. Hafif ve Orta Derecedeki Keratokonusun Tedavisinde Radyal Keratotomi Uygulaması. Thesis, İstanbul.

Utine, C.A., Çakir, H., Altunsoy, M., 2009. Korneanın ektatik hastaliklarinin tedavisinde kollajen çapraz bağlama. T. Oft. Gaz. 39, 153–160.

XNA Framework, Retrieved on January 25, 2014 from the World Wide Web: http://www.sdtslmn.com/kodmod/xna-framework-1-xna-nedir/.

Zhang, Z.Y., 2012. Corneal thickness change in eyes undergoing corneal cross-linking. Am. J. Ophthalmol. 153 (2), 383.

Emerging Business Intelligence Framework for a Clinical Laboratory Through Big Data Analytics

32

Emad A. Mohammed[1], Christopher Naugler[2], and Behrouz H. Far[1]

Department of Electrical and Computer Engineering, Schulich School of Engineering, University of Calgary, Calgary, AB, Canada[1]
Departments of Pathology and Laboratory Medicine and Family Medicine, University of Calgary and Calgary Laboratory Services, Diagnostic and Scientific Centre, Calgary, AB, Canada[2]

1 INTRODUCTION

Clinical laboratories provide medical test services to a variety of customers. From a business perspective, providing high-quality services at lower costs mandates the need for efficient utilization of clinical resources (McDonald *et al.*, 1997). Historical and current clinical resource utilization data sets are now digitally available at almost all clinical facilities (Kessel *et al.*, 2014). The improvement of digital equipment facilitates the acquisition and storage of all kind of clinical data at a rate much faster than what can be processed using traditional processing systems (Peters and Buntrock, 2014), which give rise to the clinical Big Data era.

Clinical Big Data is the technical term used to describe massive databases with varying high volume, variety, and velocity [*e.g.,* electronic medical record (EMR) and biometrics data]. These databases present difficulties with storage, processing, and visualization (Rajaraman and Ullman, 2012; Coulouris *et al.*, 2005).

Business intelligence (BI) is defined as the use of data and dedicated processing to assist informed decisions in diverse administrative settings (Pine *et al.*, 2011). An intrinsic trait of an BI is that it integrates data from a diversity of sources, resulting in an effective information framework for clinical laboratory decision makers (Negash, 2004).

A clinical laboratory facility can have many managers with different perspectives (Bennett, 2007) (*e.g.,* clinical section manager, logistic manager, finance manager, etc.). BI can deliver assistances to clinical laboratory directors comprising effective utilization of human resources (Crist-Grundman and Mulrooney, 2010), improved process efficiency, and unnecessary cost prevention (Foshay and Kuziemsky, 2014). BI should help clinical laboratory managers with different roles in describing and diagnose current performance and predicting the future performance. To deal with these challenges, new software programming frameworks to multithread computing tasks have been developed (Coulouris *et al.*, 2005; de Oliveira Branco, 2009; Dean and Ghemawat, 2008). However, many clinical laboratory settings have not yet applied BI systems (Foshay and Kuziemsky, 2014), and there has been very limited research on the factors that contribute to the successful implementation of BI in a health care–specific context (Foshay and Kuziemsky, 2014).

Several BI applications already exist (Anon, 2014e, 2014f, 2014d, 2014b, 2014c, Publishing, 2014), however they usually suffer from two drawbacks: firstly, they offer a rigid and less flexible framework that addresses the need of a specific group of users; secondly, they adopt the scope of scenario-based simulation rather than Big Data–driven analytics.

New challenges have emerged, especially with respect to processing of the massive data sets that are being produced daily. This drives the need for a new framework that can be used by different clinical laboratory managers to support the informed decisions.

In this chapter, we explore a combination of reusable data analytics (*i.e.,* BI framework) that helps clinical laboratory managers with different roles to become more effective by supporting their decisions using the BI framework. Two real-life case studies (namely, clinical laboratory test usage pattern visualization and estimation of clinical test volumes) are designed to identify potential analytics to support decisions of laboratory managers. The objective is to identify the reusable components of a user-centered framework (*i.e.,* clinical laboratory managers with different roles and perspectives) based on Big Data analytics of clinical data sets. The implementation and validation of other framework components/analytics will be explored in future research.

2 MOTIVATION

The case studies have emerged from real-life concerns of laboratory managers. Increases in population have a stunning influence on health care, including laboratory diagnostics. Clinical laboratories in Canada have experienced substantial growth in utilization in recent years. However, in Alberta, the volumes of all types of laboratory testing are increasing at a rate much faster than population growth, with a 36% increase in chemistry test volumes between 2003 and 2009 (Di Matteo and Di Matteo, 2009). There have been repeated statements that a substantial amount of laboratory tests are tangibly redundant. A current meta-analysis assessed the proportion of redundant tests to be in the range of 30% (Zhi *et al.*, 2013). In Calgary alone, this equates to as many as 8 million potentially unnecessary laboratory tests per year, representing a cost of at least $80 million per year in direct and indirect costs. Indications that additional test utilization does not advance clinical outcomes have been reported in a number of studies that have found no association between the volume of tests ordered and clinical outcome (Daniels and Schroeder, 1977; Ashley *et al.*, 1972; Bell *et al.*, 1998; Powell and Hampers, 2003). Redundant laboratory tests not only waste valuable resources, but also may lead to patient impairment as false positives. If a healthy person is subjected to 10 unrelated (unnecessary) tests, the probability of at least 1 deviant test result is 40% (Axt-Adam *et al.*, 1993). This deviant test result may lead to unnecessary, far-reaching, expensive, and time-consuming diagnostic examinations (Lewandrowski, 2002).

The driving forces for the efforts illustrated in this chapter are derived from the literature cited above, and the current BI frameworks are based on text and flowchart process simulation for best scenario practices and optimization rather than Big Data analytics (Anon, 2014b, 2014c, Publishing, 2014). Text- and flowchart-based approaches are subjective (*i.e.*, users use different synonymous and acronyms, and different flowcharts are created for the same process). On the other hand, Big Data are more representative of the variations in a given process. Moreover, representing a complex process using text and flowcharts may be inaccurate, while complex process traits are encapsulated in the Big Data representation form. Furthermore, as more and more data are collected for the same measurement, the data model becomes more and more accurate.

Another driving motivation is that there is no efficient statistical method to highlight the overutilization or underutilization of clinical laboratory Big Data (Naugler, 2013, 2014; MacMillan, 2014). Moreover, physician test ordering patterns have no analyzing/feedback mechanism (Plebani, 1999; Plebani *et al.*, 2014; Kiechle *et al.*, 2014), and thus, a significant amount of clinical tests and resources (*e.g.*, medical equipment utilization, more technician workload, and cost, etc.) are misused. Furthermore, there is no efficient method to measure or visualize a human performance index (Wennberg, 2004; Ashton *et al.*, 1999; Monsen *et al.*, 2008)—analysis of variance. In addition, most managerial decisions are based on descriptive analytics that tell what happened, and little are based on predictive analytics that tell what is going to happen (Davenport, 2013).

3 MATERIAL AND METHODS

3.1 DATA SOURCE

Supervisors at Calgary Laboratory Services (CLS), University of Calgary (Anon, 2014g), provide different types of data sets (*i.e.*, clinical laboratory test volumes and clinical test utilization by physicians).

3.2 MAPREDUCE FRAMEWORK

A commonly implemented programming framework that depends on functional programming for massive/Big Data processing is the MapReduce framework (de Oliveira Branco, 2009; Dean and Ghemawat, 2008; Peyton Jones, 1987). MapReduce is an evolving programming framework for massive data applications proposed by Google. It is based on functional programming (Peyton Jones, 1987), where the designer defines map and reduce tasks to process large sets of distributed data. Applications of MapReduce (Dean and Ghemawat, 2008) enable many of the common tasks on massive data to be implemented on computing clusters in a way that is tolerant of hardware failures.

3.3 THE HADOOP DISTRIBUTED FILE SYSTEM

Hadoop (Bryant, 2007; White, 2012; Shvachko *et al.*, 2010) is an open-source implementation of the MapReduce framework for implementing applications on large clusters of commodity hardware (Anon, 2014k). Hadoop is a platform that affords both distributed file system (DFS) and processing capabilities. Hadoop was realized to resolve a scalability issue in the Nutch project (Shvachko *et al.*, 2010; Olson, 2010), which is an open-source crawler engine that uses the MapReduce and the Big-table (Olson, 2010). Hadoop is a distributed master-slave architecture that contains the Hadoop Distributed File System (HDFS) and the MapReduce framework. Characters intrinsic to Hadoop are data partitioning and parallel computation of massive data sets. Hadoop storage and processing capabilities balance with the addition of computing machines to the cluster, with volume sizes in the terabyte/petabyte level on clusters with thousands of machines.

3.4 THE EMERGING FRAMEWORK

Unlike other works that start with the design of the framework, we selected the empirical route to identify reusable BI analytics components. The methodology is based on conducting the case studies and identifying the commonalities between them and then extracting reusable framework elements. The results are presented next, and details about the case studies will follow.

The framework on clinical Big Data analytics emphasizes the modeling of several interacting processes in a clinical setting (*e.g.,* clinical test utilization pattern, test procedures, specimen collection/handling, etc.). This indeed can be constructed using clusters of commodity hardware and the appropriate open-source tool on top of the cluster to construct convenient processing platform for the massive clinical data. This is the basis of future laboratory informatics applications, as laboratory data are increasingly integrated and consolidated.

A main requirement of the framework is that it should adapt to the changes of users and their perspectives. Figure 32.1 shows the different perspectives of a clinical laboratory setting. The clinical section managers (*i.e.,* general pathology, clinical biochemistry, microbiology, hematology, and cytopathology) can use the framework to plan for clinical lab workload and demand forecasting. Human resources managers can use the framework to monitor staff key performance indicators (KPIs) and for capacity planning. Rewards analytics can be used by different managers to estimate the trend of award increasing/decreasing according to the desired KPIs. Environmental health and safety (EH&S) managers can use the framework to detect disease outbreaks. Planning and new business managers can use the framework analytics to simulate different investment scenarios (*e.g.,* purchase planning, effect of certain supply cutoff, etc.). Finance managers can use the framework for many different purposes, such as payroll, rewards, and fraud detection.

In some clinical facilities, the blood/tissue samples are collected by courier services from patient service centers (PSCs)—a typical scenario in the City of Calgary—and sampling handling time may play a significant role in the accuracy of test results. The logistic manager can use the system to monitor the performance of the courier service fleet drivers, estimate the sample handling time, and plan for driver routes for sampling pickup and handling. Information technology (IT) service administration managers can use this framework to estimate the potential utilization of the IT system and infrastructure, and hence plan for system maintenance and expansions.

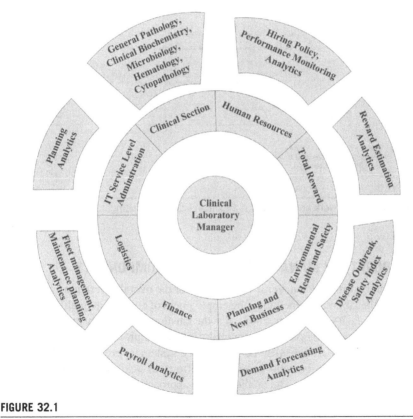

FIGURE 32.1

The different perspectives of a clinical laboratory setting.

The identified components of the framework of a clinical laboratory setting are shown in Figure 32.2. It illustrates the different analytics services that can be utilized by clinical laboratory users. Every component consists of a set of MapReduce statistical algorithms that help the lab directory with a specific concern to support undergoing decisions in a specific process through the analysis of historical Big Data (*e.g.,* hiring new staff, clinical test workload management, etc.). The design of the system is derived from clinical laboratory managers' different roles and perspectives illustrated in Figure 32.1.

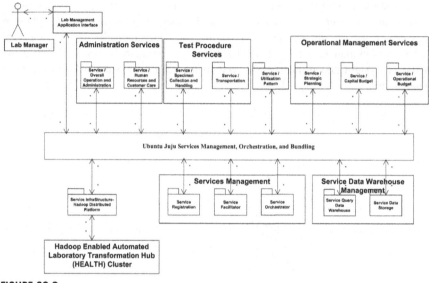

FIGURE 32.2

User-centered framework architecture in a clinical laboratory setting.

3.5 LABORATORY MANAGEMENT SYSTEM COMPONENTS

The laboratory director/manager is responsible for the overall operation and administration of the laboratory, including the employment of competent qualified personnel (Reller *et al.*, 2001; Bennett, 2007). It is the lab director's responsibility to ensure that the laboratory develops and uses a quality system approach to provide accurate and reliable patient test results. In the quality system approach, the laboratory focuses on comprehensive and coordinated efforts to achieve accurate, reliable, and timely testing services. The quality system approach includes all the laboratory policies, processes, procedures, and resources needed to achieve consistent and high-quality testing services.

As a result of the many, complex lab director/manager responsibilities, there is a pressing need toward the automation of the overall process through the development of a Big Data analytics framework that can aid a lab director to inform decisions. In the following section, different components of the system are explained.

3.6 LAB MANAGEMENT APPLICATION INTERFACE

The lab management application interface is the main screen that a lab director interacts with. It provides different groups of functionalities that process different types of Big Data (*e.g.,* clinical test, human resources, and traffic data for CLS fleet management, etc.) through the Hadoop platform. The programs are developed in MapReduce and coded in Java and R statistics packages.

3.7 ADMINISTRATION SERVICES

The laboratory director has many responsibilities related to human resources. This person must ensure that the laboratory has a suitable number of trained staff with adequate supervision to meet the loads of the laboratory service, regulations, and accreditation standards.

3.8 TEST PROCEDURE SERVICES

The laboratory director is responsible for all aspects of testing. The director guarantees the selection of suitable analyzers, reagents, supplies, calibrators, and control materials, so the test methods have performance characteristics that meet the needs of laboratory users (Simpson *et al.*, 2000).

3.9 OPERATIONAL MANAGEMENT SERVICES

The critical responsibilities of a lab director are strategic planning, organizational goal setting, capital and operational budgeting, research and development, marketing, and vendor contracting. The director must manage patients and clinicians in negotiations and decisions related to operational management.

3.10 SERVICE INFRASTRUCTURE-HADOOP PLATFORM AND HADOOP ENABLED AUTOMATED LABORATORY TRANSFORMATION HUB (HEALTH) CLUSTER

These services collectively handle connection to the computing infrastructure, as this connection handles the passage of the correct data with the required type of processing (*e.g.,* test procedure service).

3.11 DATA WAREHOUSE MANAGEMENT SERVICE

The data warehouse management service is a connection to the required data at the data centers or the associated laboratory information system (LIS).

3.12 UBUNTU JUJU AS A SERVICE ORCHESTRATION AND BUNDLING

Ubuntu Juju is an open-source service orchestration (Anon, 2014n). It consents of software to be deployed, integrated, and scaled on a cloud service or server. The underlying mechanism behind Juju is known as Charms. Moreover, Juju has an element called *Charm Bundles*. A Charm Bundle allows a group of charms, properties, and relations to be exported into a YAML file, which can be imported into another Juju environment.

3.13 TYPICAL FRAMEWORK USAGE SCENARIO IN A CLINICAL LABORATORY SETTING

The framework can be used by laboratory managers differently according to each manager's perspective. If a laboratory manager who is interested in purchase planning for test consumables (*e.g.*, different test consumables for the next 3 months), he or she can use the "lab management application interface" to set up a perspective for planning future test consumable purchasing. This will instruct the framework to search for suitable data sets and analytics algorithms to estimate the test volumes. These data sets and algorithms will be retrieved from the framework through the orchestration services "Ubuntu juju," which is facilitated by attaching every data set in the data warehouse and the analytics algorithms with a tag that can be used by the service orchestration to bundle data sets with the correct analytics algorithms. The data can be acquired from the clinical laboratory repository using the suitable data connections between platforms [*e.g.*, Oracle to Hadoop data connector (Anon, 2014i)]. This is followed by bundling the Service Infrastructure-Hadoop platform service to the retrieved data sets and algorithms. The infrastructure Hadoop platform serves as the processing platform for the framework. The framework will then provide the available services (functionalities) and data to carry on with the user demands through the "lab management application interface." If neither the right data set nor the right analytics exist, the lab management application interface will display an error message to the user asking for other keywords/tags for the requested services.

4 USE-CASES

In this section, we present the details of the two use-cases. The first reflects a typical scenario for the use of analytics for visualization of the clinical laboratory test usage problem, and the second employs Big Data analytics for prediction. Many of the typical clinical decision support use-cases fall into either of these categories.

Precisely stated, the purpose of these use-cases is to estimate the clinical test volumes of a given test per unit time—a time series analysis (*i.e.*, Alberta provincial test volume estimation). Moreover, the clinical laboratory test utilization pattern service has a novel method to visualize the individual physician usage pattern for a given test or a test panel (*i.e.*, a group of standard tests). In the following discussion, the clinical laboratory test utilization pattern visualization and provincial laboratory test volume estimation are illustrated and detailed, along with the associated design limitations.

5 CASE STUDY 1: CLINICAL LABORATORY TEST USAGE PATTERNS VISUALIZATION

Excessive usage of diagnostic tests is a key challenge in health-care systems. Data sets of clinical test volumes for individual physicians are available from hospitals' laboratory information systems (LISs). The unjustified usage of clinical tests drives the need for a tool to underline the usage pattern (utilization) of a given clinical test or test panel of a physician among his or her peers. The data sets must be normalized for different physician characteristics (*e.g.,* number of working hours, years of experience, etc.,), patient status (*e.g.,* condition of the patient, number of visits, etc.), and department workload (*e.g.,* emergency, outpatient, hospitalized patient, etc.).

6 DATA SOURCE AND METHODOLOGY

For illustration, we use a simple example representing a set of five different clinical tests with varying test volumes are acquired for 35 physicians over a 3-month time span at one medical facility at the city of Calgary. The data were anonymized to comply with the Personal Information Protection and Electronic Documents Act of Canada. (Anon, 2014j).

In this section, a novel graphical tool based on the *z*-score to identify extremes of practice variance from laboratory test ordering data is used to analyze and visualize the usage pattern of the recorded five clinical tests. This methodology can be used to assess the efficacy of a test usage control criterion (Murphy and Henry, 1978; Plebani *et al.*, 2014; Bates *et al.*, 1999). Evaluation and visualization of physician usage patterns of clinical tests could yield a beneficial tool to visualize physician utilization of clinical tests. In the following discussion, we describe a novel method for comparing the utilization patterns of different physicians using laboratory data. In order to use this method, the number of physicians in a given data set had to be greater than or equal to 30; otherwise, we used the T-test (Rosner, 2010).

The steps of the proposed method are:

1. Acquire test volumes for a group of physicians for a given test or test panel. The test volumes must be normalized per physician for a given range of physician characteristics, patient status, and department workload, as described earlier in this chapter.
2. Calculate the mean and standard deviation of the test volumes per test as shown by Eqs. (32.1) and (32.2):

$$\mu_T = \frac{1}{N}\sum_{p=N}^{p=1} X_p, \tag{32.1}$$

where μ_T is the mean of a given test (T); N is the number of physicians using test (T); and X_p is the volume of test (T) used by physician (p).

$$\sigma_T = \sqrt{\frac{\sum_{p=N}^{p=1}\left(X_p - \mu_T\right)^2}{N}}, \tag{32.2}$$

where σ_T is the standard deviation of a given test (T).

3. Calculate the z-score for each test per physician, as shown by Eq. (32.3):

$$zscore_{p|T} = \frac{X_p - \mu_T}{\sigma_T}, \tag{32.3}$$

where $zscore_{p|T}$ is the z-score of test (T), which has test volume X_p that is used by the physician (p).

The adaptation of test volumes into z-scores permits assessment of clinical laboratory tests with different average volumes.

4. Calculate the mean z-score for all tests and the standard deviation of their z-scores per physician, as shown in Eqs. (32.4) and (32.5):

$$\mu_{zscore_p} = \frac{1}{T}\sum_{i=\tau}^{i=1} zscore_{p|T_i} \tag{32.4}$$

$$\sigma_{zscore_p} = \sqrt{\frac{\sum_{i=\tau}^{i=1}\left(zscore_{p|T_i} - \mu_{zscore_p}\right)^2}{T}} \tag{32.5}$$

5. For each physician, plot the mean z-scores against the standard deviation of z-scores for that physician.
6. Define performance marker lines at the mean z-score and the mean standard deviation of z-scores to divide the z-score space into four regions. The explanation of these regions is described in Table 32.1.

Table 32.1 Categorical Classification of the z-score Space

Region/ Group	Explanation
A	Physicians with high overall usage of a specific test and low variance from their peer group
B	Physicians with both high volumes of tests and high disparity from their peer group
C	Physicians with high practice variance but lower overall usage than group B physicians
D	Physicians with both low variations from peers and low overall test volumes

7 RESULTS AND DISCUSSION

The data set for 35 physicians utilizing five different tests (*i.e.*, chemical seven test panel CH7; D-Dimer, DDEL; throat swab for beta hemolytic streptococcus, M BETA; urine culture, M URINE; and Troponin I, TNIV) were processed via the proposed method using the R statistical package (Anon, 2014m), the *z*-scores for each test were calculated, and the average *z*-score for all five tests was also calculated. Figure 32.3 illustrates the usage pattern of the CH7 test by the 35 physicians, illustrating that most of the physicians belonged to group D, a small number of physicians were in groups A and B, and only a few physicians belonged to group C. This reveals an optimal degree of usage of this test.

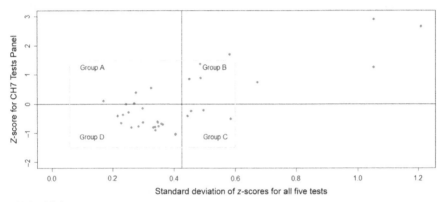

FIGURE 32.3

Usage pattern of the CH7 for 35 physicians.

The vertical, solid black line dividing the golden rectangle characterizes the mean usage pattern of the five tests (*x*-axis). A physician who equally uses the five tests is characterized as a red dot on this line. A physician who uses all five tests at a slower rate than average will be characterized by a red dot on the left side of this line, and vice versa.

The *y*-axis characterizes the usage probability of this test (*i.e.*, CH7), represented by its computed *z*-score. It would not be possible to convert the *z*-scores into probabilities unless it is assumed that the test volumes are drawn from a normal distribution. A adaptation table to transform *z*-scores into probabilities can be found in Held and Bove (2014) and Rosner (2010).

The allowed disparity within the test volumes for a given test is represented by the width of the golden rectangle, and the height represents the range of the usage probabilities. The horizontal line crossing the zero of the *y*-axis represents the usage probability of the mean of the underlined test. The golden rectangle space is divided into four groups by the intersection of the vertical line representing the mean usage pattern of the test and the zero *z*-score line. A physician with perfect average usage will be represented by a dot at the intersection of these two lines. The distribution of the points outside the rectangle represents the outliers. There are many factors that may drive the physician to utilize more tests to have a better assessment of the patient conditions, and thus, Eq. (32.3) must be normalized by these factors, if quantifiable, and the modified equation for computing the z-score becomes

$$zscoreMod_{p|T} = \frac{X_p - \mu_T}{\sigma_T * NFs} \tag{32.6}$$

where *zscoreMod* is the modified z-score and *NFs* are the product of all the normalization factors.

Figure 32.4 shows the average usage pattern for all five tests, the average usage pattern illustrates the most common group is Group D, with a wider probability of usage for all five tests.

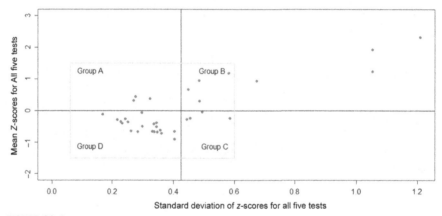

FIGURE 32.4

Average usage pattern of all five tests for 35 physicians.

8 LIMITATIONS

The visualization model assumes that the data is drawn from normal distributions to translate the z-score to the probability of usage. This visualization framework is designed to view the relative usage pattern of physicians utilizing a group of clinical tests. This framework is used to visualize practice variance, not to provide conclusive proof of redundant usage of clinical tests. The framework has some restrictions, as it does not account for prospective influencing parameters such as limited ranges of practice, patient conditions, and number of hospital visits per patient that may affect test usage characteristics, as these parameters are not quantified.

9 CASE STUDY 2: PROVINCIAL LABORATORY CLINICAL TEST VOLUME ESTIMATION

One main characteristic of any clinical laboratory BI platform is the ability to estimate clinical laboratory test volumes (El-Gayar and Timsina, 2014; Ferranti *et al.*, 2010; Ashrafi *et al.*, 2014). Accordingly, test consumables and workload can be optimized by short-term reliable forecasting. Large amounts of clinical test volume data are accessible from a variety of available data ware house in hospitals and clinical settings (Anon, 2014g). In this section, a Holt-Winters method (De Gooijer and Hyndman, 2006; Chatfield and Yar, 1988) is used to estimate the province of Alberta laboratory test volume. The results are compared to an estimation using an Auto Regressive Integrated Moving Average (ARIMA) model (Rosner, 2010).

10 DATA SOURCE AND METHODOLOGY

A huge volume of data has been queried to consolidate a data set of clinical laboratory test volume for all ordered tests over a 40-month span from all Alberta medical facilities. This data is provided by provincial laboratory utilization office, CLS, and at the University of Calgary (Anon, 2014g).

10.1 HOLT-WINTERS MODEL

The Holt-Winters method is a statistical method of prediction/estimation, applied to time series considered by the existence of trend and seasonality that is founded on the exponential weight moving average method. This is achieved by separating the data into three parts (*i.e.,* level, trend, and seasonal index). The Holt-Winters method has two types: one method for additive seasonality and the other for multiplicative seasonality. The multiplicative Holt-Winters method is described by the following equations:

$$\text{Level}: L_t = \alpha\left(\frac{Y_t}{S_{t-p}}\right) + (1-\alpha) * (L_{t-1} - b_{t-1}) \tag{32.7}$$

$$\text{Trend}: b_t = \beta * (L_t - L_{t-1}) + (1-\beta) * b_{t-1} \tag{32.8}$$

$$\text{Sesonal Index}: S_t = \gamma * \left(\frac{Y_t}{L_t}\right) + (1-\gamma) * S_{t-p} \tag{32.9}$$

$$\text{Forecast}: F_{t+k} = (L_t + k * b_t) * S_{t+k-p} \tag{32.10}$$

where p is the number of data points of the seasonal cycle. The smoothing factor are α, β, and γ where $0 \le \alpha \le 1$, $0 \le \beta \le 1$ and $0 \le \gamma \le 1$. The seasonal index demonstrates the differences between the current level and the data at the recorded point in the seasonal cycle.

The additive Holt-Winters method is described by the following equations:

$$\text{Level}: L_t = \alpha(Y_t - S_{t-p}) + (1 - \alpha) * (L_{t-1} - b_{t-1}) \tag{32.11}$$

$$\text{Trend}: b_t = \beta * (L_t - L_{t-1}) + (1 - \beta) * b_{t-1} \tag{32.12}$$

$$\text{Sesonal Index}: S_t = \gamma * (Y_t - L_t) + (1 - \gamma) * S_{t-p} \tag{32.13}$$

$$\text{Forecast}: F_{t+k} = (L_t + k * b_t) + S_{t+k-p} \tag{32.14}$$

The initial values for the level, trend, and seasonal index are estimated by carrying out a simple decomposition into trend and seasonal components using the moving averages model on the first period (*i.e.*, 12 months) (Anon, 2014m).

The goodness-of-fit of the model is evaluated using the mean square error measure (Rosner, 2010) (MSE) defined by the following equation:

$$MSE = \frac{1}{n}\sum_i^1 (Y_i - F_i)^2, \tag{32.15}$$

where Y_i is the observed value at time (i) and n is the total number of points MSE represents the goodness-of-fit of the model to the given data. Moreover, the coefficient of determination (Rosner, 2010) (R^2) value can be used to further examine the goodness-of-fit of the model. It is defined as the relative enhancement in the prediction/estimation of the model, compared to the average value of the observations (*i.e.*, representing the data with the mean model), where it designates the goodness-of-fit of the model to predict/estimate the future values.

A zero value of R^2 specifies that the model does not increase the prediction/estimation ability over the mean model, and one specifies perfect prediction/estimation. The R^2 value can be calculated as

$$R^2 = \frac{1}{n}\sum_i^1 \frac{(F_i - \bar{Y})^2}{(Y_i - \bar{Y})^2}. \tag{32.16}$$

where $\bar{Y}$ is the average value of the recorded measurements.

10.2 ARIMA MODEL

ARIMA is a hybrid model consisting of two models and a differencing parameter. The first is the autoregressive (AR) model, where the value of a variable in one cycle is related to its values in previous cycles. The second model is the moving average (MA) model, which accounts the relationship between a variable and the residual errors from previous cycles. The differencing is a technique to transform the data from non-stationary to stationary nature by taking the d difference of the data (Rosner, 2010).

The ARIMA model can be describes by the following equation:

$$y_t = \mu + \sum_{i=1}^{p} \gamma_i y_{t-i} + \epsilon_i + \sum_{i=1}^{q} \theta_i \epsilon_{t-i}, \tag{32.17}$$

where μ is a constant and γ_i is the coefficient for the lagged variable in time t-p, ϵ_i is the error due to the current observation, θ_i is the coefficient of the lagged error term in time $t - q$, and p, q are time lags associated with the AR and MR models, respectively.

The variable y_t is represented by an ARIMA (p,d,q) model, which designates an ARMA model with p autoregressive lags, q moving average lags, and a difference in the order of d.

10.2.1 Holt-Winters and ARIMA model assumption testing

The fundamental notion of the Holt-Winters and ARIMA models is that the data of time series under test is stationary (De Gooijer and Hyndman, 2006). Stationary means that it arises from a stochastic process (*i.e.,* stable process) whose parameters (*i.e.,* the mean and variance) are constant over time (Grenander and Rosenblatt, 1957). The augmented Dickey-Fuller (ADF) test (Engle and Granger, 1987) is used to test for the stationary nature of the time series.

10.2.2 Model selection criteria

Akaike information criterion (AIC) (Akaike, 1974) is a fined technique based on in-sample fit to estimate the likelihood of a model to predict/estimate the future values.

A good model is the one that has minimum AIC among all the other models. The AIC can be used to select between the additive and multiplicative Holt-Winters models.

Bayesian information criterion (BIC) (Stone, 1979) is another criteria for model selection that measures the trade-off between model fit and complexity of the model. A lower AIC or BIC value indicates a better fit.

The following equations are used to estimate the AIC and BIC (Stone, 1979; Akaike, 1974) of a model:

$$AIC = -2 * \ln(L) + 2 * k \tag{32.18}$$

$$BIC = -2 * \ln(L) + 2 * \ln(N) * k \tag{32.19}$$

where L is the value of the likelihood, N is the number of recorded measurements, and k is the number of estimated parameters.

The stationary nature of the provincial laboratory test is tested using the R statistical package (Anon, 2014m) and it is used to model the data using Holt-Winters and ARIMA models. The Holt-Winters parameters α, β, and γ is calculated based on minimizing one-step-ahead error (*i.e.,* MSE) value of each model. A set of ARIMA models are used to compare the performance of the Holt-Winters models in estimating the provincial test volume. Minimum AIC and BIC values are used as model selection criteria. The optimal model is selected based on the highest R^2 and minimum AIC and BIC.

10.3 **STATIONARY TESTING**

The ADF test is based on the null hypothesis test. The more negative the test is, the stronger the rejections of the null hypothesis, which announces the stationary nature of the time series. Table 32.2 shows the result of the ADF test and the associated ρ values.

Table 32.2 ADF Test Output

	ADF Test	
Time Series	**Dickey-Fuller statistic**	**ρ (significance <= 0.01)**
Provincial test volumes	−5.6335	0.01

Auto-correlation function (ACF) is a measure of the degree of similarity between the original time series and the time lag version of the time series. ACF can evaluate the stationary nature of a time series, high correlation resulting from high similarity, and less stationary representing a slowly decaying ACF. Figure 32.5 shows the ACF of the provincial test volumes time series, which reflects the stationary nature of the recorded data when correlated with itself for different time lags.

10.4 **ARIMA MODEL SELECTION**

The ADF test suggests the time series is of a stationary nature, and thus, the candidate ARIMA models will be reduced to ARMA models with only AR and MA with p and q lags, respectively, with no differencing variable d. The minimum AIC or BIC is used to choose the best model.

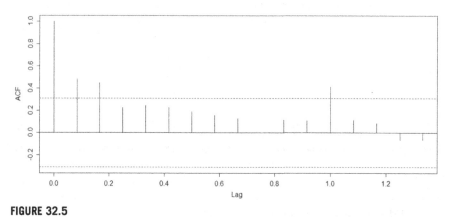

FIGURE 32.5

ACF for the provincial test volume time series.

Table 32.3 illustrates the AIC and BIC for the candidate ARIMA models with the model complexity (*i.e.,* the number of parameters associated with every mode). The selected ARIMA model is ARIMA (1,0,1) and it is used for the provincial test volume time series estimation.

Table 32.3 ARIMA Models Used to Model the Provincial Test Volumes with the Associated AIC and BIC

Time Series	ARIMA (1,0,1) Number of Calculated Parameters = 2		ARIMA (1,0,2) Number of Calculated Parameters = 3		ARIMA (2,0,1) Number of Calculated Parameters = 3		ARIMA (2,0,2) Number of Calculated Parameters = 4		ARIMA (3,0,3) Number of Calculated Parameters = 6	
	AIC	BIC	AIC	BIC	AIC	BIC	AIC	BIC	BIC	AIC
Provincial test volumes	1125.8	1132.5	1128.4	1136.9	1127.5	1135.9	1145.16	1155.3	1128.7	1142.2

The models are arranged according to the complexity of the model (i.e., number of parameters to be estimated).

10.5 PERFORMANCE COMPARISON AND MODEL SELECTION

Table 32.4 shows the MSE and R^2 values recorded for every model. The Holt-Winters multiplicative and additive model have $R^2 = 0.8791$, and 0.8619, respectively, which means that they have a better performance than the mean model; however, they have MSE $= 9.05*10^{10}$ and $8.9*10^{10}$, respectively. On the other hand. ARIMA (1,0,1) has a better MSE than both the two Holt-Winters model ($5.1*10^{10}$). However, the ARIMA model has the smallest $R^2 = 0.49541$. The main reason for this is that the ARIMA model tend to memorize the repeating monthly pattern resulting in a poor estimation of the time series.

The multiplicative and additive Holt-Winters models tend to adapt the estimation of the provinical test volume time series according to the previous samples weighted by the exponential smoothing parameters (*i.e.*, α, β, and γ). The smoothing parameters are shown in Table 32.5.

Table 32.4 Holt-Winters and ARIMA (1,0,1) Model Performance

Time Series	Mean Square Error (MSE)			R^2		
	HWA	HWM	ARIMA	HWA	HWM	ARIMA
Provincial test volumes	$8.9*10^{10}$	$9.05*10^{10}$	$5.1*10^{10}$	0.8619	0.8791	0.49541

The mean square error (MSE) signifies the goodness of the model to fit the data. The R^2 value signifies the goodness of the model to predict the variance in the data (Holt-Winters multiplicative "HWM", Holt-Winters additive "HWA", and ARIMA models).

Table 32.5 Smoothing Factors Used in the Holt-Winters Multiplicative and Additive Models

Time Series	Holt-Winters Multiplicative Model Smoothing Parameters			Holt-Winters Additive Model Smoothing Parameters		
	α	β	γ	α	β	γ
Provincial test volumes	0.32598	0	0	0.33989	0	0

11 RESULTS AND DISCUSSION

Figures 32.6, 32.7, and 32.8 show the performance of the Holt-Winters multiplicative, Holt-Winters additive, and ARIMA (1,0,1) models to fit the provincial volume time series and estimate future values with a 95% confidence interval. The observed data are represented by the black curve; the fitted/estimated data are shown in red, and the 95% confidence intervals are shown in blue. The 95% confidence intervals signify the disparities (*i.e.*, precision) of the model.

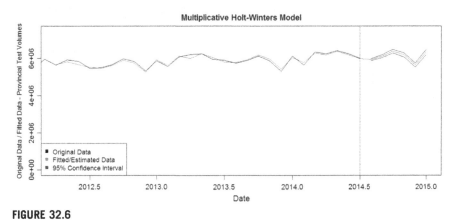

FIGURE 32.6

Holt-Winters multiplicative model for the provincial test volume time series.

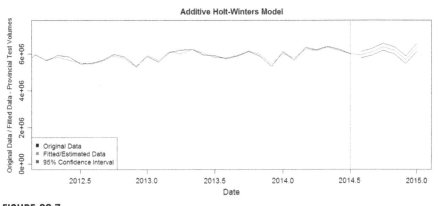

FIGURE 32.7

Holt-Winters additive model for the provincial test volume time series.

The estimation of the smoothing parameters α, β, and γ are based on minimizing one step ahead of the MSE. If these parameters are found to be near zero, it means that the model adds more weight to the previous samples, resulting in more smoothing. Nevertheless, if these parameters are found to be near 1, it means the model tends to add less weight to the previous samples and thus feature less smoothing.

Minimum AIC and BIC information criteria is used as model selection criteria whenever the performance parameters (*i.e.*, MSE and R^2) are close for the model ensemble. Table 32.6 shows the AIC and BIC values for the Holt-Winters multiplicative and additive models, along with the selected model. When $R^2 < = 0.5$, then it may be better to choose the mean model to fit and estimate the time series (De Gooijer and Hyndman, 2006), which is the case for the ARIMA (1,0,1) model with $R^2 = 0.49541$.

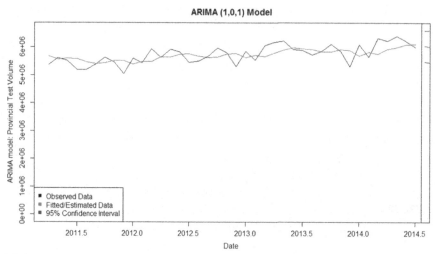

FIGURE 32.8

ARIMA (1,0,1) model for the provincial test volume time series.

Table 32.6 Information Criteria of Holt-Winters Models

Time Stamp	Holt-Winters Multiplicative Model		Holt-Winters Additive Model		Selected Model
	AIC	BIC	AIC	BIC	
Provincial test volumes	1081.416	1110.127	1075.947	1104.658	Holt-Winters additive

The best modes are selected based on the minimum AIC and BIC

Table 32.6 shows that the Holt-Winters additive model is a better model to fit and estimate the provincial test volume time series. This means that the level, trend, and the error are additive in nature. This is clearly shown in Figure 32.9, where the estimated values by the additive model (*i.e.,* xhat), level, trend, and seasonality show additive behavior.

Figure 32.10 shows the histogram of the residual error of the Holt-Winters additive model with a normal distribution curve fitted to the residual errors. The diagram shows that the error is almost centered on 0 mean, which means that the errors are uncorrelated and normally distributed. This strengthens the choosing of the additive Holt-Winters model to fit and estimate the data.

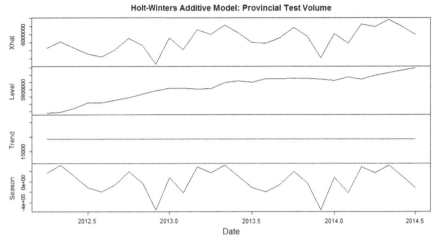

FIGURE 32.9

The individual component of the Holt-Winters additive model for fitting the provincial test volume time series. The level and trend of the time series show additive behavior.

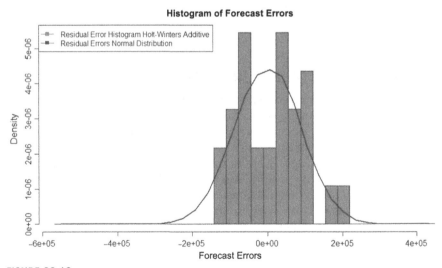

FIGURE 32.10

The residual error histogram of the additive Holt-Winters model. A normal distribution curve is fitted to the histogram showing that these residual errors are uncorrelated (centered on 0 mean).

12 LIMITATIONS

Figure 32.7 shows the estimation horizon of 6 months in the future of the additive Holt-Winters model. The estimation horizon of the 6 months in the future and the upper and lower limits (*i.e.*, precision) are shown in Table 32.7. When the estimation horizon moves forward, the 95% confidence interval becomes wider, resulting in poor precision. This drawback results from the limitation that the additive Holt-Winters model is static (*i.e.*, the exponential smoothing parameters are calculated only once from the historical data). This is due to the limited computational resources as the time series increases with time. A good solution is to implement an adaptive Holt-Winters model that utilizes the error between the estimated and exact value of the future points to update the smoothing parameters of the model; however, it may consume a good deal of computational resources.

Table 32.7 Estimation of the Provincial Test Volume for 6 Months, Starting August 2014, Using the Additive Holt-Winters Model

Date	Estimated Provincial Test Volume	Upper Limit	Lower Limit
August 2014	5,943,146	6,111,962	5,774,330
September 2014	6,101,442	6,279,742	5,923,141
October 2014	6,368,317	6,555,622	6,181,013
November 2014	6,169,616	6,365,512	5,973,721
December 2014	5,674,618	5,878,744	5,470,492
January 2015	6,310,749	6,522,786	6,098,713

13 CONCLUSION AND FUTURE WORK

This chapter presents a user-centered analytics framework as a BI platform that can be used in a clinical laboratory setting to come to an informed conclusion on questions such as "What is the usage pattern of a clinical test?" and "Can we estimate the clinical test volumes for the next month?". We selected the empirical route in order to understand and describe a BI framework for a clinical laboratory setting. The practice is based on conducting real-life case studies, identifying the commonalities between them, and extracts reusable framework elements that can be used as a BI framework to help clinical laboratory managers support their informed decisions.

This BI is composed of multiple services that can be used by clinical laboratory managers (*e.g.*, CLS managers). The BI is based on the MapReduce framework and an open-source implementation of the Hadoop is used to process the massive clinical laboratory data sets to form the basic Big Data analytics tools. The user-centered analytics framework is designed with the clinical laboratory managers in mind, resulting in the BI platform with the necessary functionalities for different laboratory manager perspectives.

The two use-case studies present the value of BI analytics framework in managing clinical laboratory test volumes (*i.e.,* usage pattern visualization and test volume estimation) utilizing the clinical databases available at the data warehouse. The analytics presented in the two use-cases present tools that can be reused by managers of different clinical laboratory settings to visualize performance and estimate resources (*i.e.,* logistic manager, who estimates a specimen handling time; financial manager, who estimates employee rewards based on the facility-specific key performance indicators).

Big Data tools (Olston *et al.,* 2008; 2014l; Chen *et al.,* 2014; Hortonworks, 2014; 2014a; 2014h) present a development of Big Data analysis imposed by the advent of large-scale databases. The Hadoop platform and the MapReduce programming framework already have a substantial base in the bioinformatics community, especially in the field of next-generation sequencing analysis, and such use is increasing.

This study makes the following contributions to the literature:

- This is the first attempt to address a user-centered analytics framework based on Big Data analytics to process massive clinical data sets.
- The application of a novel visualization tool based on the z-score to visualize the clinical test utilization.
- The application of Holt-Winters method to estimate the provincial test volume of the province of Alberta, Canada. To the best of our knowledge, this is the first attempt to develop demand-estimation analytics for the clinical laboratory test volumes in Alberta.

Future research on the clinical Big Data analytics BI framework should accentuate the modeling of whole-business interacting subprocesses (*e.g.,* clinical test utilization pattern, test procedures, specimen collection/handling, etc.). This can be assembled using inexpensive clusters of commodity hardware and the proper tool to construct a suitable processing framework for handling massive clinical data.

REFERENCES

Akaike, H., 1974. A new look at the statistical model identification. Automatic Control 19, 716–723, IEEE Transactions on.

Anon, 2014k. IBM InfoSphere Warehouse 10.1 [Online]. Available:http://www-01.ibm.com/support/docview.wss?uid=swg21585911.

Anon, 2014l. Laboratory Service Calgary - Laboratory Service Southern Alberta | Calgary Laboratory Services [Online]. Available:http://www.calgarylabservices.com/.

Anon, 2014m. The Platform for Big Data and the Leading Solution for Apache Hadoop in the Enterprise - Cloudera [Online]. Available:http://www.cloudera.com/content/cloudera/en/home.html.

Anon, 2014n. The R Project for Statistical Computing [Online]. Available:http://www.r-project.org/.

Anon, 2014a. AWS | Amazon Elastic Compute Cloud (EC2) - Scalable Cloud Hosting [Online]. Available: http://aws.amazon.com/ec2/.

Anon, 2014b. Discrete Event Simulation & Business Process Modeling Software | Manufacturing, Supply Chain & Healthcare Simulation Software | Arena Simulation [Online]. Available: https://www.arenasimulation.com/.

Anon, 2014c. Discrete Event — AnyLogic Simulation Software [Online]. Available: http://www.anylogic.com/discrete-event-simulation.

Anon, 2014d. IBM - Cognos Business Intelligence [Online]. Available: http://www-03.ibm.com/software/products/en/business-intelligence.

Anon, 2014e. IBM InfoSphere BigInsights Quick Start Edition: Hadoop [Online]. Available: http://www-01.ibm.com/software/data/infosphere/biginsights/quick-start/downloads.html.

Anon, 2014f. MAPR [Online]. Available: http://www.mapr.com/products/m3.

Anon, 2014g. Oracle Big Data Connectors | Oracle Database to Hadoop [Online]. Available: http://www.oracle.com/us/products/database/big-data-connectors/overview/index.html.

Anon, 2014h. Personal Information Protection and Electronic Documents Act [Online]. Available: http://laws-lois.justice.gc.ca/eng/acts/p-8.6/.

Anon, 2014i. The Apache Software Foundation [Online]. Available: http://apache.org/.

Anon, 2014j. Ubuntu Juju - Automate your cloud infrastructure [Online]. Available: https://juju.ubuntu.com/.

Ashley, T., Pasker, P., Beresford, J., 1972. How much clinical investigation? Lancet 299, 890–893.

Ashrafi, N., Kelleher, L., Kuilboer, J.-P., 2014. The Impact of Business Intelligence on Healthcare Delivery in the USA. Interdiscipl. J. Inform. Knowl. Manag. 9.

Ashton, C.M., Petersen, N.J., Souchek, J., Menke, T.J., Yu, H.-J., Pietz, K., Eigenbrodt, M.L., Barbour, G., Kizer, K.W., Wray, N.P., 1999. Geographic variations in utilization rates in Veterans Affairs hospitals and clinics. N. Engl. J. Med. 340, 32–39.

Axt-Adam, P., Van Der Wouden, J.C., Van Der Does, E., 1993. Influencing behavior of physicians ordering laboratory tests: a literature study. Med. Care. 784–794.

Bates, D.W., Kuperman, G.J., Rittenberg, E., Teich, J.M., Fiskio, J., Ma'luf, N., Onderdonk, A., Wybenga, D., Winkelman, J., Brennan, T.A., 1999. A randomized trial of a computer-based intervention to reduce utilization of redundant laboratory tests. Am. J. Med. 106, 144–150.

Bell, D.D., Ostryzniuk, T., Verhoff, B., Spanier, A., Roberts, D.E., 1998. Postoperative laboratory and imaging investigations in intensive care units following coronary artery bypass grafting: a comparison of two Canadian hospitals. Can. J. Cardiol. 14, 379–384.

Bennett, S.T., 2007. Role and Responsibilities of the Laboratory Director. Springer, Laboratory Hemostasis.

Bryant, R.E., 2007. Data-Intensive Supercomputing: The Case for Disc.

Chatfield, C., Yar, M., 1988. Holt-Winters forecasting: some practical issues. The Statistician 129–140.

Chen, W.-P., Hung, C.-L., Tsai, S.-J.J., Lin, Y.-L., 2014. Novel and efficient tag SNPs selection algorithms. Biomed. Mater. Eng. 24, 1383–1389.

Coulouris, G.F., Dollimore, J., Kindberg, T., 2005. Distributed Systems: Concepts and Design, Pearson Education.

Crist-Grundman, D., Mulrooney, G., 2010. Effective workforce management starts with leveraging technology, while staffing optimization requires true collaboration. Nurs. Econ. 29, 195–200.

Daniels, M., Schroeder, S.A., 1977. Variation among physicians in use of laboratory tests II. Relation to clinical productivity and outcomes of care. Med. Care. 482–487.

Davenport, T.H., 2013. Enterprise Analytics: Optimize Performance, Process, and Decisions Through Big Data. Pearson Education.

De Gooijer, J.G., Hyndman, R.J., 2006. 25 years of time series forecasting. International journal of forecasting 22, 443–473.

De Oliveira Branco, M., 2009. Distributed Data Management for Large Scale Applications. University of Southampton.

Dean, J., Ghemawat, S., 2008. MapReduce: simplified data processing on large clusters. Comm. ACM 51, 107–113.

Di Matteo, L., Di Matteo, R., 2009. The Fiscal Sustainability of Alberta's Public Health Care System. School of Public Policy, University of Calgary.

EL-Gayar, O., Timsina, P., 2014. Opportunities for Business Intelligence and Big Data Analytics in Evidence Based Medicine. System Sciences (HICSS). In: 47th Hawaii International Conference on, 2014. IEEE, pp. 749–757.

Engle, R.F., Granger, C.W., 1987. Co-integration and error correction: representation, estimation, and testing. Econometrica: journal of the Econometric Society 251–276.

Ferranti, J.M., Langman, M.K., Tanaka, D., Mc Call, J., Ahmad, A., 2010. Bridging the gap: leveraging business intelligence tools in support of patient safety and financial effectiveness. J. Am. Med. Inform. Assoc. 17, 136–143.

Foshay, N., Kuziemsky, C., 2014. Towards an implementation framework for business intelligence in healthcare. International Journal of Information Management 34, 20–27.

Grenander, U., Rosenblatt, M., 1957. Statistical Analysis of Stationary Time Series.

Held, L., Bove, D.S., 2014. Applied Statistical Inference: Likelihood and Bayes. Springer Berlin Heidelberg, Berlin, Heidelberg.

Hortonworks, 2014. Hortonworks [Online]. Available:http://hortonworks.com/.

Kessel, K.A., Bohn, C., Engelmann, U., Oetzel, D., Bougatf, N., Bendl, R., Debus, J., Combs, S.E., 2014. Five-year experience with setup and implementation of an integrated database system for clinical documentation and research. Comput. Methods Programs Biomed. 114, 206–217.

Kiechle, F.L., Arcenas, R.C., Rogers, L.C., 2014. Establishing benchmarks and metrics for disruptive technologies, inappropriate and obsolete tests in the clinical laboratory. Clin. Chim. Acta 427, 131–136.

Lewandrowski, K., 2002. Managing utilization of new diagnostic tests. Clinical leadership & management review: the journal of CLMA 17, 318–324.

Macmillan, D., 2014. Calculating cost savings in utilization management. Clin. Chim. Acta 427, 123–126.

Mcdonald, C.J., Overhage, J.M., Dexter, P., Takesue, B.Y., Dwyer, D.M., 1997. A framework for capturing clinical data sets from computerized sources. Ann. Intern. Med. 127, 675–682.

Monsen, A., Gjelsvik, R., Kaarbøe, O., Haukland, H., Sandberg, S., 2008. Appropriate use of laboratory tests--medical aspects. Tidsskrift for den Norske laegeforening: tidsskrift for praktisk medicin, ny raekke 128, 810–813.

Murphy, J., Henry, J.B., 1978. Effective utilization of clinical laboratories. Hum. Pathol. 9, 625–633.

Naugler, C., 2013. Laboratory test use and primary care physician supply. Can. Fam. Physician. 59, e240–e245.

Naugler, C., 2014. A perspective on laboratory utilization management from Canada. Clin. Chim. Acta 427, 142–144.

Negash, S., 2004. Business intelligence. The Communications of the Association for Information Systems 13, 54.

Olson, M., 2010. Hadoop: scalable, flexible data storage and analysis. IQT Quarterly 1, 14–18.

Olston, C., Reed, B., Srivastava, U., Kumar, R., Tomkins, A., 2008. Pig Latin: A Not-So-Foreign Language for Data Processing. In: Proceedings of the 2008 ACM SIGMOD international conference on Management of data. ACM, pp. 1099–1110.

Peters, S.G., Buntrock, J.D., 2014. Big Data and the Electronic Health Record. J. Ambul. Care Manage. 37, 206–210.

Peyton Jones, S.L., 1987. The Implementation of Functional Programming Languages (Prentice-Hall International Series in Computer Science). Prentice-Hall, Inc.

Pine, M., Sonneborn, M., Schindler, J., Stanek, M., Maeda, J.L., Hanlon, C., 2011. Harnessing the power of enhanced data for healthcare quality improvement: lessons from a Minnesota Hospital Association Pilot Project. Journal of healthcare management/American College of Healthcare Executives 57, 406–418, discussion 419–20.

Plebani, M., 1999. The clinical importance of laboratory reasoning. Clin. Chim. Acta 280, 35–45.

Plebani, M., Zaninotto, M., Faggian, D., 2014. Utilization management: a European perspective. Clin. Chim. Acta 427, 137–141.

Powell, E.C., Hampers, L.C., 2003. Physician variation in test ordering in the management of gastroenteritis in children. Arch. Pediatr. Adolesc. Med. 157, 978–983.

Publishing, R., 2014. Risk Analysis Software, Monte Carlo Simulation Software, Probabilistic Event Simulation - RENO [Online]. Available: http://www.reliasoft.com/reno/.

Rajaraman, A., Ullman, J.D., 2012. Mining of Massive Datasets. Cambridge University Press.

Reller, L.B., Weinstein, M.P., Peterson, L.R., Hamilton, J.D., Baron, E.J., Tompkins, L.S., Miller, J.M., Wilfert, C.M., Tenover, F.C., Thomson, R.B., 2001. Role of clinical microbiology laboratories in the management and control of infectious diseases and the delivery of health care. Clin. Infect. Dis. 32, 605–610.

Rosner, B., 2010. Fundamentals of Biostatistics. Cengage Learning.

Shvachko, K., Kuang, H., Radia, S., Chansler, R., 2010. The Hadoop Distributed File System. Mass Storage Systems and Technologies (MSST). In: IEEE 26th Symposium on, 2010. IEEE, pp. 1–10.

Simpson, R., Marichal, M., Uccini, S., 2000. European society of pathology statement on minimal requirements for a pathology laboratory. Virchows Arch. 436, 509–526.

Stone, M., 1979. Comments on model selection criteria of Akaike and Schwarz. Journal of the Royal Statistical Society. Series B (Methodological) 276–278.

Wennberg, J.E., 2004. Practice variations and health care reform: connecting the dots. HEALTH AFFAIRS-MILLWOOD VA THEN BETHESDA MA-23, VAR-140.

White, T., 2012. Hadoop: The Definitive Guide. O'Reilly Media, Inc.

Zhi, M., Ding, E.L., Theisen-Toupal, J., Whelan, J., Arnaout, R., 2013. The landscape of inappropriate laboratory testing: a 15-year meta-analysis. PLoS One 8, e78962.

A Codon Frequency Obfuscation Heuristic for Raw Genomic Data Privacy

33

Kato Mivule

Computer Science Department, Bowie State University, Bowie, MD, USA

1 INTRODUCTION

Genomic data grants clinical researchers with considerable prospects to study various patient sicknesses. Nevertheless, genomic data includes a lot of revealing information, some of which a patient might want to remain concealed. The question from such a patient-controlled data scenario becomes: How can an entity transact in full DNA sequence data while concealing certain sensitive pieces of information in the genome sequence, and yet maintaining DNA data utility? In this chapter, we respond to this question by putting forward a heuristic in which the patients might have a say about what part of their genomic information they wish to remain concealed. The rest of the chapter is organized as follows. In section 2, background definitions of bioinformatics and data privacy terms are given. In section 3, a review of related work on the subject of DNA privacy is described. In section 4, the proposed heuristic and methodology is outlined in detail. In section 5, the experiment and results are discussed, and finally, in section 6, the conclusion and future work is discussed.

2 BACKGROUND

DNA stands for deoxyribonucleic acid, a chemical substance that comprises functionality information for the make-up and growth of an organism (Genome.gov, 2014). DNA organization is an organized collection of four building blocks called nucleotide bases: namely, adenine (A), thymine (T), guanine (G), and cytosine (C), in which the adenine (A) pairs with the thymine (T), and guanine (G) with cytosine, forming a twisted, ladderlike strand, referred to as a double helix (Dnaftb.org, 2014). Genomics is the study of the genome (DNA) sequence structure, the chemical components that make up the DNA structure, including the chemical elements that hold DNA components together (Genomic.org.uk, 2014). DNA sequencing refers to the process of mapping out the nucleotide sequence of DNA (E. B. Online, 2014). Codon is a sequence of three subsequent nucleotides in the genome that map to a specific amino acid in a protein; a codon could also represent a triplet, which is the start and stop points in the DNA sequence (NIH.gov, 2014). Codon frequency table or codon usage table is the statistical representation of each codon existence in the DNA sequence (OpenWetWare.org, 2014).

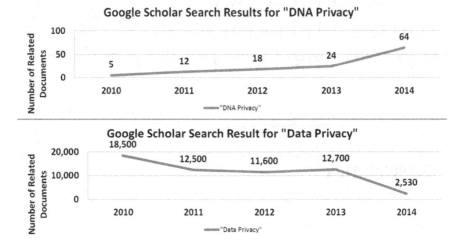

FIGURE 33.1

Google Scholar search results for "DNA Privacy."

Data obfuscation is a data privacy technique in which data is distorted, made imprecise, and indistinguishable so as to conceal information (Parameswaran and Blough, 2005). *Data shuffling* is a data privacy technique first proposed by Dalenius and Reiss (1978) as a data-swapping methodology for categorical data (Fienberg and McIntyre, 2004), and later extended by Muralidhar and Sarathy (2003) for numerical data. *Data suffling* is a data privacy procedure in which sensitive data values $v_i, \ldots v_n$, within an attribute A_i are exchanged between tuples $t_i, \ldots t_n$ in the same attribute A_i; for instance, a sensitive value v_i belonging to tuple t_i is assigned to tuple t_n and the value v_n belonging to tuple t_n is assigned to tuple t_i in the same attribute A_i (Muralidhar *et al.*, 2006).

3 RELATED WORK

In this section, we look at some work being done in the Genomics data privacy domain. Research in Genomics data privacy is relatively in the early stages, and not much work and literature exists on the subject. For instance, as illustrated in Figure 33.1., a Google Scholar search only returned 24 documents related to the "DNA Privacy" search term for 2013, compared to 12,700 related documents to the search term "Data Privacy," for 2013 (Google, 2014). However, Genomic data privacy researchers have largely focused on using cryptographic techniques in granting confidentiality to DNA data sets. Malin and Sweeney (2004) proposed employing reidentification techniques in evaluating and modeling of anonymity protection systems for genomic data; the goal was to prevent any information leakage between genomic data and named individuals in public records. Their model focused on engineering a secure and confidential data privacy transaction model for genomics without perturbing the DNA sequence structure.

However, Malin (2005b) proposed one of the first genomic data privacy models that involved the actual manipulation of the DNA sequence to enhance confidentiality. That model employed k-anonymity with generalization by ensuring that in a collection of DNA sequence data, each generalized DNA record would appear at least $k > 1$ times, to satisfy k-anonymity requirements. Additionally, Malin (2005a) provided a holistic evaluation of the current state of genomic data privacy storage and transaction systems by outlining the shortcomings and providing recommendations.

In this chapter, we take a similar approach by proposing a genomic data privacy solution that takes into consideration both the bio-bank architecture and the confidential transaction of the individual's DNA sequence. Other works have centered on employing genomics as a tools for cryptography (Guo *et al.*, 2012; El Emam, 2011). For instance, Heider and Barnekow (2007), proposed using DNA cryptographic and steganography algorithms as watermarks to detect any unauthorized use of genetically modified organisms protected by patents. Additionally, Kantarcioglu *et al.* (2008) proposed a cryptographic model in which aggregated data mining, such as frequency counts, could be done securely on genomic sequences without revealing the original, encrypted raw DNA sequence. On the other hand, El Emam (2011), in a review of deidentification technics for genomics data, observed that electronic records are increasingly being linked to DNA bio-banks, used by clinicians for genomic research, and that challenges and risks still remained despite deidentification techniques for confidentiality.

In this chapter, we argue for a holistic approach that considers privacy modeling at both the bio-bank storage level and the data transaction level among the patient, doctor, and clinical researchers. Ayday *et al.* (2013) proposed a holistic model for genomics confidentiality in which data privacy enhancing principles, using homomorphic encryption, were employed in modeling a secure bio-bank system, the DNA data transaction process, and the confidentiality of the DNA sequence. Furthermore, Ayday *et al.* (2014) proposed a privacy-preserving system to grant confidentiality using encryption to short reads of raw genomic data. In their model, Ayday *et al.* (2014), suggested storing short reads in encrypted form at a bio-bank and then allow the stackholders to securely retrieve only needed short reads.

From a bio-bank architectural privacy modeling view, we follow a similar approach to Ayday *et al.* (2014) by proposing the encryption of all medical records, including genomic data at the bio-bank level. However, in our model, the full perturbed raw DNA sequence, in which sensitive genomic information is either suppressed or altered, is retrieved. Furthermore, to prevent information leakages, the number of queries is limited for the DNA sequences. For instance, a clinical researcher in hospital A might be interested only in a set of genes responsible for cancer, while another researcher at hospital B might be interested in genes linked to diabetes. In such scenarios, information leaked from hospitals A and B could be used to reconstruct sensitive information in the DNA sequence of a patient.

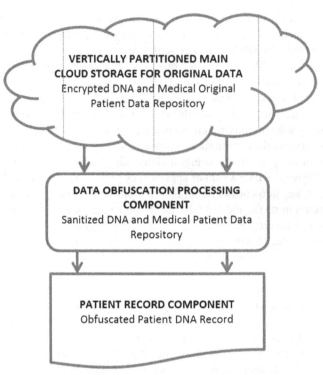

FIGURE 33.2

Overview of the bio-bank and DNA transaction model.

As another way to get around the issue of information leakage, we propose the publication of static tabulated results for noninteractive settings. In this scenario, our model would only publish or transact in predefined results that could not be changeable after the initial obfuscation. In this case, patients would publish the same privatized DNA sequence to all parties involved. This would be useful when dealing with entities such as insurance companies and clinical researchers, which are only interested in aggregated statistical analysis.

4 METHODOLOGY

In this section, we present our methodology on obfuscation of codons with highly expressed genes for privacy. In this study, we assume that the DNA data transaction will occur between the patient, data curator (bio-bank), and a clinical researcher. The goal is to obfuscate the DNA data so that the clinical researchers will not view any gene information deemed sensitive by the patient. In other words, patients control by authorization what they wish to be disclosed about themselves. Our proposed architecture, as illustrated in Figure 33.2, is composed of three components: the main original data storage component, the obfuscated data component, and the patient record component. These can be described as follows:

1. *The main original data storage component (Bio-bank)*: This acts as a main storage location for the patient medical records, including the DNA data. The original data storage component is highly restricted and all records are encrypted. Access to this data storage is enforced by documentation of who gained access, what time they gained access, how long they accessed the system, what information they accessed, and what time they exited the storage system. In this controlled environment, access to the storage requires another signatory for accountability. In other words, the system will not allow one individual to access the system without accountability from another official.

2. *The obfuscation data processing component*: This component, as illustrated in Figure 33.3, acts as a privacy layer between the patient record access component and the main original data storage component. Data generation in the obfuscated data storage is done by controlled query access on the main original data storage component. The number and type of queries run on the system are strictly limited to prevent information leakage. Obfuscation procedures are then applied to the results that are generated by the query. The only records stored or accessed in the obfuscated data storage component, are those that have been sanitized (privatized) via obfuscation and other data privacy algorithms. Access to the obfuscated data component and querying process is strictly enforced using the same security access control methods, as applied to the original data storage component. Any data transaction will only involve access to the obfuscated data storage unit. This component is responsible for generating obfuscated patient records needed for any data transaction.

3. *The patient record component*: In this component, the patient and clinical researcher have access to the obfuscated medical and DNA record. The patient can authorize time-restricted access to this record to their physician or a clinical researcher. The patient record component will document each access by a doctor, clinician, and the patient. The patient record component could be accessible using mobile devices, via secure and encrypted connectivity.

Phase I: In the first phase of the obfuscation, as illustrated in Figure 33.3, personal identifiable information (PII) is removed from the data set. After PII is removed, data shuffling is applied to the deidentified data set to increase obfuscation. In our methodology, partial data shuffling is selectively applied on the data set. All attributes undergo data shuffling with exception of the Patient ID and DNA attributes. The reason for the data shuffling is that if the controlled and restricted data falls in the hands of an attacker, it would be difficult to reconstruct the full identify of a patient. Yet this still would prevent inside attacks by those who have minimal access to the data system at various technical support levels. In our methodology, data shuffling is based on a random number generator. The rows of data values (tuples) in each attribute are aligned to a sequence of randomly generated numbers, which then get sorted. The random number generator seed is kept secret by the data curators (i.e., the bio-bank),

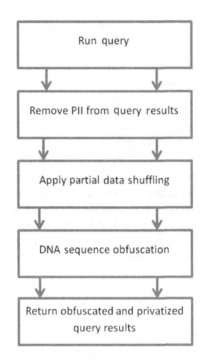

FIGURE 33.3

The obfuscated data processing component.

making it difficult for any reverse engineering attacks. In this model, each attribute is shuffled vertically and separately, and finally, all attributes are combined to generate the complete partially shuffled data set.

Phase II: In phase II, data obfuscation is done on the DNA sequence by perturbation of the codon frequency table, as illustrated in Figure 33.4. In the first step, a codon frequency table is generated for each DNA sequence in the database. A frequency analysis is then done to highlight the most frequent codons in the table—that is, codons with the most highly expressed genes in each amino acid group. The perturbation by redistribution is done within the same amino acid group. The perturbation is done on codons with high-frequency values by redistributing the frequencies among the codon values in the same amino acid group. In this way, the same amino acid could remain highly expressed while giving a form of obfuscation to the highly expressed genes in the codon.

For example, the codon GAC has a high-frequency value in the aspartic (Asp) amino acid group, with a frequency of 5, while GAT appears only once. The total frequency for the Asp amino acid group is then 6, as shown in Table 33.1. After perturbation by redistribution of the codon frequencies, the GAC codon gets a frequency value of 3, while the GAT codon has a frequency value of 3. However, the total frequency value for the Asp amino acid group remains intact, at 6, as shown in Table 33.2.

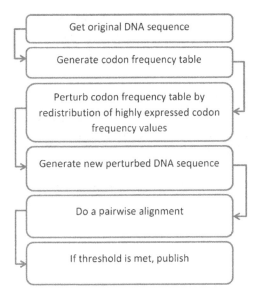

FIGURE 33.4

DNA data obfuscation overview.

Table 33.1 Codon Frequency for Asp Before Obfuscation

Asp	GAT	1
Asp	GAC	5

Table 33.2 Codon Frequency for Asp After Obfuscation

Asp	GAT	3
Asp	GAC	3

The totals of all codons in the frequency table stay the same; at this stage, the DNA sequence base pair size stays intact and remains the same as the original. After perturbation by redistribution of the codon frequencies, the new generated frequency table (privatized table) is then used to generate a new privatized DNA sequence. A pairwise alignment to compare the original DNA sequence to the privatized DNA sequence is done. Similarity values are used to determine if an acceptable threshold value is achieved. For example, a 50% similarity value might be acceptable as a threshold; if this value is not met, then a refinement is done by redistributing frequency values in the codon table. The last step is to publish the privatized DNA sequence without revealing data from highly expressed genes in codons with high frequencies. The original codon frequency values are kept encrypted at the main bio-bank storage. Therefore, this procedure could be applicable by implementing the extra layer of confidentiality on the patient DNA sequence during data transaction from one point to another.

5 EXPERIMENT AND RESULTS

Experiment Phase I: To test our hypothesis, we generated a synthetic patient records data set with 150 data points containing PII information, medical records, and the DNA sequence for each patient.

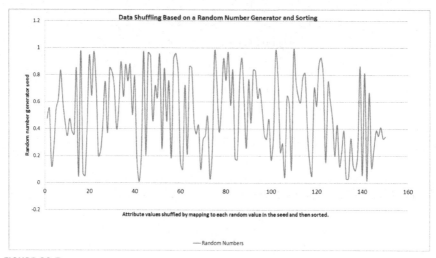

FIGURE 33.5

The random number generator seed used for shuffling.

The synthetic patient records data set was used to simulate the real original patient records data set. The synthetic patient records data set included the following set of attributes: {Patient ID, First Name, Last Name, Gender, SSN, DOB, Address, City, State, Zipcode, Country, Diagnosis Code, Diagnosis Description, PCP, and DNA}. During the first phase of the obfuscation, the following attributes were removed from the data set to satisfy PII sanitization requirements: {First Name, Last Name, SSN, Address, and City}. Data shuffling was then individually applied to each of the following remaining attributes: {Patient ID, Gender, DOB, State, Zipcode, Country, Diagnosis Code, Diagnosis Description, PCP, and DNA}.

A random number generator was used to shuffle the values in each separate attribute. The values were mapped to the randomly generated numbers between a chosen seed, in the case of our experiment, the seed was chosen as real numbers between 0 and 1. After the mapping the values in the attributes to the random numbers, sorting was done. The values in the attributes changed positions with each sorting iteration,

Patient_ID	Gender	DOB	State	Zipcode Country	Diagnosis Code	Diagnosis Description	PCP	DNA
P000001	M	1979	SD	39967 USA	298.3	Bronchitis, acute	Soo Mills	CAAGACAC
P000002	F	1991	SD	57037 USA	530.81	Asthma, extrinsic, acute exacerbat	Niverta Fulks	TACGACTC
P000003	M	1979	NH	17657 USA	300.3	Atelectasis	Ruby Banh	ATCGATTC
P000004	M	1987	NV	04456 USA	074.3	Anemia, other, unspec.	Bjorn Michalak	TCTTTGAA
P000005	F	1977	WA	15278 USA	782.8	Pain, psychogenic	Routledge Guilfo	TAGTATC
P000006	F	1979	NH	52217 USA	493.12	Asthma, cough variant	Elizabeth Ruggier	CCGTGTAT
P000007	F	1989	PA	32426 USA	298.1	Asthma, intrinsic w/o status asthm	Cyril Strohm	GGTGTGG

FIGURE 33.6

The values in red show the change in position after shuffling.

thus shuffling, as illustrated in Figure 33.6. Figure 33.6, is an illustration of returned query results displaying the effects of shuffling on the attribute values. The highlighted values in red in Figure 33.6 show the shift in each of the shuffled values from their original positions.

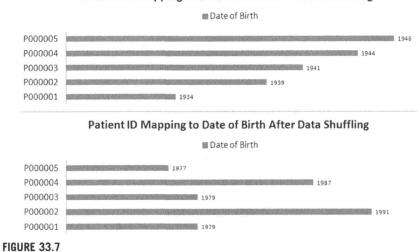

FIGURE 33.7

Shuffling results for the date of birth attribute.

It would be difficult for an attacker to reverse-engineer the process to gain the original row of data without prior knowledge, considering that the database would contain millions of data points. To ensure that the data values in each attribute were efficiently shuffled, we did a frequency distribution analysis on the date of birth attribute before and after shuffling. As illustrated in Figure 33.7, the date of birth for Patient ID P000001 was 1934 before shuffling. However as illustrated in the figure, the date of birth for the same Patient ID P000001 was substituted with 1979 after shuffling, thus offering a layer of confidentiality for Patient ID P000001.

Experiment Phase II: To further test our hypothesis, we generated synthetic DNA sequences for each of the Patient ID records in that database. For the remainder of this chapter and the context of this experiment, we shall refer to both the synthetic DNA sequence and synthetic patient records as *original data.* Each generated original DNA sequence contained 500 base pairs. The FASTA format was used in formatting the raw generated original DNA sequence. A total of 150 original DNA sequences were generated for the original patient database. In the next step of Phase II expeiment, the codon frequency of the generated original DNA sequence was completed. Codon frequency obfuscation was achieved by redistributing values of codons with highly expressed genes within the same amino acid group. For instance, as illustrated in Figure 33.8, the codon values for CAG and CAA in the Glutamine (Gln) amino acid group were 2 and 9, respectively. In the obfuscation process, the codon values for CAG and CAA after redistribution were reassigned to 5 and 6, respectively.

It is important to note that while the codon values for CAG and CAA were altered, the totals for the frequency of that particular amino acid—in this case, glutamine (Gln)—remained the same at 11. In other words, perturbation was done to the frequency values of the codons themselves, but not the frequency values of the amino acid group. As shown in Figure 33.9, the frequency of the Gln in the original DNA sequence is 11, and after obfuscation, the frequency value for the same amino acid stays the same at 11. The obfuscated codon table was then used to generate the obfuscated DNA sequence. Next, a pairwise comparison was done on both the original and obfuscated DNA sequences. A pairwise analysis was performed on both the original and obfuscated DNA sequence. The goal was to implement an obfuscation of codons with highly expressed genes in the DNA sequence. The question of data privacy versus utility still affects the outcome of the results. Too much obfuscation may alter the DNA sequence with many mutations; minimal obfuscation could also be revealing.

In the first part of our pairwise analysis, we compared the original protein sequence to the obfuscated protein sequence. Tables 33.3 and 33.4 show the protein sequences that we used for the pairwise analysis for both the original and obfuscated data.

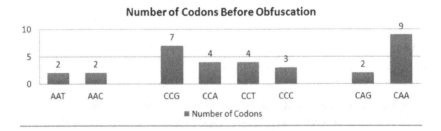

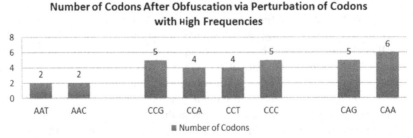

FIGURE 33.8

Codon frequencies before and after obfuscation.

Amino Acid Totals Before Obfuscation

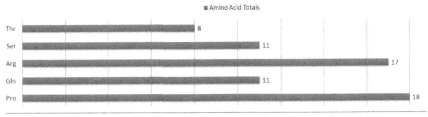

Amino Acid Totals After Obfuscation via Perturbation of Highly Expressed Codon Frequencies

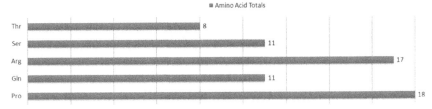

FIGURE 33.9

Amino acid frequencies before and after obfuscation.

Table 33.3 Original Protein Sequence

>EMBOSS_001_1
QDSSGLEVAPAKEDAWYSRTMKPVQRQHPHLGEPKRGIKVTFWIPETNPMVVLRLGSLSP
LGPISGNRRQVQSVFRRTMEQCG*DVLHLYPTQAGPRSARRGGAQAIDN*PPCIHYGTRD
FKPSQWSSQYRVYRILP*LTNCDPPQVKPLPLRHAVRVIM*TLRGLT

Sequence Translation tool: http://www.ebi.ac.uk/Tools/st/

Table 33.4 Obfuscated Protein Sequence

>EMBOSS_001_1
RDAQSVPGSSTVERVLGTHDTADDVIYRTSHLASLGRRDQYSTNEPNSSRPRSLPRTGAA
EPLLGGLQPRHYSRHPLRHGAWRKAGRNYKRNAQVVAFNQLSLSVRSSQPFKLSRHST*Q
LFASGTGLSD*WQPHVLL*LP**LPGPH*LGSRYRHGPCFNNQIF

Sequence Translation tool: http://www.ebi.ac.uk/Tools/st/

As shown in Figures 33.10 and 33.11, the pairwise alignment analysis for both the original and obfuscated protein sequence, generated only 18% similarity (A. S. F. *et al.*, 1990). While this might be a good indication of privacy and obfuscation, questions remain as to the viability of DNA data utility. The dot matrix in Figure 33.11 shows regions of similarity between the original and obfuscated protein sequences. The *x*-axis represents the obfuscated protein sequence, while the *y*-axis shows the original protein sequence. A diagonal line in the matrix would represent an ideal perfect match for similarity. The nonaligned lines represent the mismatch between the two protein sequences.

unnamed protein product

Sequence ID: lcl|10113 Length: 165 Number of Matches: 1

Range 1: 1 to 165 <u>Graphics</u>   ▼ Next Match ▲ Previous Match

NW Score	Identities	Positives	Gaps
-51	32/178(18%)	61/178(34%)	24/178(13%)

```
Query   1    QDSSGLEVAPAKEDAWYSR-TMKFVQRQHPHLGEPKRGIKVIFWIPETN-PMVVLRLGSL   58
Sbjct   1    R.AQSVPGSSTV.RVLGTHD.ADD.IYRTS..ASLG.RDQYSTNE.NSSR.RSLP.T.AA   60

Query   59   SPLGPISGNRRQVQSVFRRTMEQCG*DVLHLYPTQAGPRSARRGGAQAIDN*PPCIHYGT   118
Sbjct   61   E..--LG.--L.PRHYS.HPLR-------.GAWRK..RNYK.NAQVV.FNQLSLSVR-SS   108

Query   119  RDFKPSQWSSQYRVYRILP*LTNCDPPQV-----KPLPLRHAV----RVIM*TLRGLT    167
Sbjct   109  QP..L.RH.T*-QLFASGTG.SD*WQ.H.LL*LP**..GP.*LGSRY.HGPCFNNQIF   165
```

FIGURE 33.10

The pairwise alignment between original and obfuscated protein sequences.

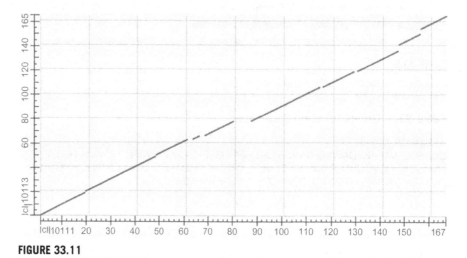

FIGURE 33.11

The original and obfuscated protein sequence dot matrix.

We then used the protein sequence of the original DNA sequence to act as a key and reverse-engineered the obfuscated DNA sequence to obtain the original DNA sequence by reverse translation.

We used the codon frequency table of the obfuscated DNA sequence to generate the original DNA sequence, using the protein sequence of the original DNA sequence as the key. The dot matrix in Figure 33.12 shows regions of similarity between the original and obfuscated DNA sequences after the reverse-engineering process. The x-axis represents the obfuscated DNA sequence, while the y-axis shows the original DNA sequence. A diagonal line in the matrix represents an ideal perfect match or similarity. The nonaligned lines represent the mismatch between the two DNA sequences. As shown in Figures 33.12 and 33.13, there was a 78% similarity between the original and obfuscated DNA sequences after the reverse-engineering process.

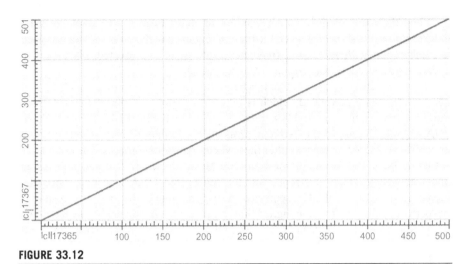

FIGURE 33.12

The original and obfuscated DNA sequence dot matrix, after reverse translation.

Sequence ID: lcl|17367 Length: 501 Number of Matches: 1

Range 1: 1 to 501 Graphics   ▼ Next Match ▲ Previous Match

NW Score	Identities	Gaps	Strand
442	392/502(78%)	3/502(0%)	Plus/Plus

```
Query   1    CAAGACAGTTCCGGGCTGGAAGTAGCGCCGGCTAAGGAAGACGCCTGGTACAGCAGGACT   60
Sbjct   1    .....T...AGT.....T..............G........T..G........T......   60

Query   61   ATGAAACCGGTACAAAGGCAACATCCTCA-CTTGGGTGAACCGAAACGCGGTATCAAGGT   119
Sbjct   61   .....G..................G..T......-.........GA.G..G..T.....   119

Query   120  TACTTTTTGGATACCTGAAACAAATCCCATGGTAGTCCTTAGACTTGGGAGTCTATCACC   179
Sbjct   120  A...........T..G.....T.....G........A.....G...........TAGT..   179

Query   180  CCTAGGGCCCATATCTGGAAATAGACGCCAAGTTCAATCCGTATTCCGACGTACGATGGA   239
Sbjct   180  G..T.....G..TAG...G......GA.G.....A...AGT.....TA.GA.G..T.....   239

Query   240  ACAGTGTGGGTGAGACGTGCTTCATTTATACCCTACGCAGGCTGGACCGAGGTCCGCAAG   299
Sbjct   240  ...A.......A...T..A......C.T.....G..T..A..G..G.....AGT..G..   299

Query   300  GCGCGGCGGTGCACAAGCAATTGACAACTAACCACCGTGTATTCATTATGGTACCAGGGA   359
Sbjct   300  .A.G..G..G..G.....G.....T..T.....G..............C..G..T.....   359

Query   360  CTTTAAGCCGAGTCAATGGGAGCTCGCAATACAGAGTTTACCGCATCTTGCCGTAACTGAC   419
Sbjct   360  T.....................TAGT........G..A....A.G..TC.T.......T..   419

Query   420  AAACTGTGATCCACCACAAGTCAAGCCATTGCCTCTTAGACACGCCGTTAGAGTAATTAT   479
Sbjct   420  T..T........G..G.....A.....GC.T..G.....G..T..G..A..G........   479

Query   480  GTAAACT-TTGCGCGGCTTGAC    500
Sbjct   480  .......C..AG.G.....ACT   501
```

FIGURE 33.13

The dissimilarities between the original and obfuscated DNA sequences after reverse translation.

While the focus of this chapter was not to study various reverse-engineering attacks, our results show that when the protein sequence of the original data was used in combination with the codon frequency table of the obfuscated DNA data to reserve-translate, there was only a 78% success rate.

The results also could mean that this heuristic was good for privacy, with 22% of the data remaining concealed, which is related to the obfuscation done on codons with high frequencies and highly expressed genes. In Figure 33.13, the obfuscated DNA sequence highlighted in red represents the dissimilarities between the original and obfuscated DNA sequences after the reverse-translation process. The dot matrix in Figure 33.14 shows regions of similarity between the original and obfuscated DNA sequences. The x-axis represents the obfuscated DNA sequence, while the y-axis shows the original DNA sequence. A diagonal line in the matrix corresponds to a perfect similarity. The nonaligned lines represent the mismatch between the two DNA sequences. The results in Figures 33.14 and 33.15 show the pairwise alignment between the original DNA sequence and the obfuscated DNA sequence generated from the perturbed codon frequency table without the reverse-engineering process. The results show that there was a 50% similarity, indicating that privacy might be achieved by the concealment provided by the other 50% dissimilarity; yet again, the issue of privacy versus utility resurfaces.

6 CONCLUSION

In this chapter, we have presented a codon frequency obfuscation heuristic for genomic data privacy. DNA data privacy generally remains a challenge. However, data utility remains a challenge with DNA obfuscation—there are more mutations

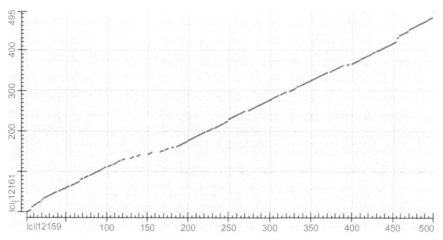

FIGURE 33.14

The original and obfuscated DNA sequence dot matrix.

Sequence ID: lcl|12161 Length: 495 Number of Matches: 1

Range 1: 1 to 495 Graphics   ▼ Next Match ▲ Previous Match

NW Score	Identities	Gaps	Strand
-392	276/557(50%)	119/557(21%)	Plus/Plus

```
Query  1    CAAGAC------AGT-TCCG-GGCTGG--AA--GTAGCGCCGGCTAAGGAAGACGCCTGG  48
Sbjct  1    .G....GCACAA...G...CT..A.C.TC..CG..G.A..GT.T.TT..GC-....A..A  59

Query  49   TACAGCAGGACTATGAAA----CCGGTACAAAGGCAACATCCTCACTTGGGT-GAACCGA  103
Sbjct  60   .......-...TG...T..TCTA....-...TC.-..C.TGG..AG...A...C.G.--..  114

Query  104  AACGCGGTA-TCAAGGTTACTTTTTGGATACCTGAAACAAATCCCATGGTAGTCCTTAGA  162
Sbjct  115  G..-.A...C.....C-.A..------..GC.---....--------...C.------  148

Query  163  CTTGGGAGTCTATCACCCCTAGGGCCCATATCTGGAA-ATAGACGCCAAGTTCAATCCGT  221
Sbjct  149  ---..CC.-.G...---...--.....G.A.G...GC.GC.GAA..GCT..TGGGGG..  198

Query  222  ATTCCGACGTACGATGGAACAGT-GTGGG----TGAGACGTGCTTCATTTATACCCTACG  276
Sbjct  199  -..A.A..C.-...CACT.....C..CATCCTC......A..GGG.T.GG.G.A---.A.  253

Query  277  CAGGCTGGACCGAGGTCCGCAAGGCGC-GGCGGTGCACAAGCAATTGACAACTAACC--A  333
Sbjct  254  ....GC.T.A.T.CAAG.....T..T.A..TA...G-.TTT....---.......G.TT.  309

Query  334  CCGTGTATTCATTATGGTACCAGGGACTTTAAGCCGAGTCAATGGAGCTCGCAATACAGA  393
Sbjct  310  T.-....GAGA.GCTC.CAG...TTT.AA...TC...G--..T.C..CG.A.....T----  362

Query  394  GTTTACCGCATCTTGC-CGTAACTGACAAACT-GTGATCCACCACAAGTCAAGCCATTGC  451
Sbjct  363  ...---...C..AG..A..GGGT..T.GG.T.A...G-.A......T..ATTA.TC.A..  418

Query  452  CTC--------TTA---GACACGCCGTTA---GAGTAATTATGTAAACTTTGCGCG-GCT  496
Sbjct  419  T..CATAATGA...CCT.G.C.A.AC.A.CTG.G..C.CG..A.CGT.ACG...C.CT...  478

Query  497  TGA-------------C  500
Sbjct  479  .C.ATAACCAGATTTT.  495
```

FIGURE 33.15

The dissimilarities between the original and obfuscated DNA sequences.

in obfuscated data. Our proposed model shows that it might be possible to perturb the codon frequency table by redistributing codon frequencies of highly expressed genes within the same amino acid group for confidentiality purposes. Our preliminary results show that even with reverse engineering using the obfuscated DNA codon frequency table in combination with the protein sequence of the original DNA sequence, only 78% was recoverable, indicating that it might be possible to conceal certain sections of information within the DNA sequence. In this proposed heuristic, we envision a well-informed patient with full rights and authorization as to what information within the DNA sequence he or she might want to remain concealed. While the focus in this chapter was to present preliminary results from the testing of the hypothesis, future works will include testing the model against various reverse-engineering attacks. Future research includes running the same tests using real DNA data from living organisms with large base pairs (Big Data). We plan on employing other data privacy algorithms not covered here and developing a prototype of the obfuscation architecture to automate the proposed heuristic.

REFERENCES

Altschul, S.F., Gish, W., Miller, W., Myers, E.W., Lipman, D.J., 1990. Basic Local Alignment Search Tool. J. Mol. Biol. 215, 403–410.

Ayday, E., Raisaro, J.L., Hubaux, J.-P., 2013. Privacy-enhancing technologies for medical tests using genomic data. In: 20th Annual Network and Distributed System Security Symposium (NDSS).

Ayday, E., Raisaro, J.L., Hengartner, U., Molyneaux, A., Hubaux, J., 2014. Privacy-preserving processing of raw genomic data. In: Data Privacy Management and Autonomous Spontaneous Security, pp. 133–147.

Dalenius, T., Reiss, S.P., 1978. Data-Swapping: A Technique for Disclosure Control (extended Abstract). In: American Statistical Association, Proceedings of the Section on Survey Research Methods. Washington, DC, pp. 191–194.

Dnaftb.org, 2011. Concept 19, The DNA Molecule Is Shaped like a Twisted Ladder. DNA From The Beginning - DNA Learning Center, Cold Spring Harbor Laboratory. Online at: http://www.dnaftb.org/19/ (accessed 19.05.14.).

Encyclopedia Britannica Online, DNA sequencing. Encyclopedia Britannica. [Online]. Available: http://www.britannica.com/EBchecked/topic/422006/DNA-sequencing. (accessed 14.05.14.).

El Emam, K., 2011. Methods for the de-identification of electronic health records for genomic research. Genome Med. 3 (4), 25.

Fienberg, S.E., McIntyre, J., 2004. Data swapping: variations on a theme by Dalenius and Reiss. In: Privacy in Statistical Databases. Springer, Berlin Heidelberg, pp. 14–29.

Genome.gov, 2014. A Brief Guide to Genomics - DNA, Genes and Genomes. Genome.gov. Online at: http://www.genome.gov/18016863 (accessed 19.05.14.).

Genomic.org.uk, 2012. Genomics in Theory and Practice - What Is Genomics. Genomic.org.uk. Online at: http://www.genomic.org.uk/ (accessed 19.05.14.).

Google, 2014. Google Scholar Search Results, Search Terms: "DNA Privacy", "Data Privacy". [Online]. Available: http://scholar.google.com/ (accessed 16.05.14.).

Guo, C., Chang, C., Wang, Z., 2012. A new data hiding scheme based on dna sequence. Int. J. Innov. Comput. Inf. Control 8 (1), 139–149.

Heider, D., Barnekow, A., 2007. DNA-based watermarks using the DNA-Crypt algorithm. BMC Bioinformatics 8 (Jan), 176.

Kantarcioglu, M., Jiang, W., Liu, Y., Malin, B., 2008. A cryptographic approach to securely share and query genomic sequences. IEEE Trans. Inf. Technol. Biomed. 12 (5), 606–617.

Malin, B.A., 2005a. An evaluation of the current state of genomic data privacy protection technology and a roadmap for the future. J. Am. Med. Inform. Assoc. 12 (1), 28–34.

Malin, B.A., 2005b. Protecting genomic sequence anonymity with generalization lattices. Meth. Inform. Med. 44 (5), 687–692.

Malin, B., Sweeney, L., 2004. How (not) to protect genomic data privacy in a distributed network: using trail re-identification to evaluate and design anonymity protection systems. J. Biomed. Inform. 37 (3), 179–192.

Muralidhar, K., Sarathy, R., 2003. A theoretical basis for perturbation methods. Stat. Comput. 13 (4), 329–335.

Muralidhar, K., Sarathy, R., Dandekar, R., 2006. Why swap when you can shuffle? a comparison of the proximity swap and data shuffle for numeric data. In: Privacy in Statistical Databases. Springer, Berlin Heidelberg, pp. 164–176.

NIH.gov, Codon. Genetics Home Reference. [Online]. Available: http://ghr.nlm.nih.gov/glossary=codon (accessed 14.05.14.).

OpenWetWare.org, Codon usage optimization OpenWetWare.org/wiki. [Online]. Available: http://openwetware.org/wiki/Codon_usage_optimization (accessed 14.05.14.).

Parameswaran, R., Blough, D., 2005. A robust data obfuscation approach for privacy preservation of clustered data. In: Workshop Proceedings of the 2005 IEEE International Conference on Data Mining, pp. 18–25.

Index

Note: Page numbers followed by *f* indicate figures and *t* indicate tables.

Printed in the United States
By Bookmasters